MW00639275

THE KOREAN WAR

The Korean War

Handbook of the Literature and Research

Edited by Lester H. Brune
Robin Higham, Advisory Editor

Greenwood Press
WESTPORT, CONNECTICUT • LONDON

Library of Congress Cataloging-in-Publication Data

The Korean war : handbook of the literature and research / edited by
  Lester H. Brune.
      p.   cm.
    Includes bibliographical references and index.
    ISBN 0–313–28969–7 (alk. paper)
    1. Korean War, 1950–1953.   I. Brune, Lester H.
  DS918.A1K7   1996
  951.904'2—dc20   95–35710

British Library Cataloguing in Publication Data is available.

Library of Congress Catalog Card Number: 95–35710
ISBN: 0–313–28969–7

First published in 1996

Greenwood Press, 88 Post Road West, Westport, CT 06881
An imprint of Greenwood Publishing Group, Inc.

Printed in the United States of America

The paper used in this book complies with the
Permanent Paper Standard issued by the National
Information Standards Organization (Z39.48–1984).

10 9 8 7 6 5 4 3 2 1

Contents

Part III.   China, the Soviet Union, and the Korean War

Part IV.   Military Aspects of the Korean War

Part V.   The Unification Struggle after the Korean War

Part VI.   The U.S. Home Front and the Korean War

Preface

Research since 1975 has revealed significant new information about the origins and conduct of the Korean War. Details disclosed with the declassification of records about the U.S. involvement in Korean affairs between September 1945 and the outbreak of war in June 1950, information about the evolution of a Korean civil war, and study of the military and the lengthy truce talks have significantly changed the official versions of the war and its origins. Moreover, the gradual opening of archives in London, as well as some archives in Moscow, Beijing, and Seoul, has given scholars previously classified information to add to that gathered after the opening of the U.S. archives in 1975.

Because the definitive history of the Korean War, using these international sources, awaits future, arduous research, this book is designed to give scholars, librarians, and the general public the best information available as of 1994 on questions surrounding the developments in the two Koreas since 1945 and international activities affecting various countries due to the intensification of the cold war. The chapter authors have been asked to provide information regarding the literature that has appeared on the war and its international aspects, as well as on the status of archival sources that influence these studies. A bibliography of references is at the end of each essay.

This book does not provide detailed factual information about each topic. Rather, the chapters acquaint readers with the major works on each topic, describe how recent research has altered the traditional interpretations or raised historical issues about the subject, and take advantage of the availability of archival materials.

To achieve this end, specialists in separate areas have prepared essays on their topics, which I have augmented with data on U.S. national security and diplomatic history. The work of these authors was critical to this project, and although each is listed in the Contributors section, their expertise deserves special thanks and mention. Professor Jian Chen is a prominent researcher on Chinese affairs during the Korean War era and has contributed working papers to the important Cold War International History Project. Jack Gifford has been a long-time student of the Korean War, a subject he has taught at the U.S. Army's Command and General Staff College. Jeffrey Grey has been a historian at Australia's Department of Foreign Affairs and studied the commonwealth armies during the Korean War. In Kim Hwang is a leading expert on Korea's reunification problems, about which he has written three books. Edward Keefer edited the U.S. State Department's *Foreign Relations* volume on Korea and has written articles about U.S. strategy for Korea. Kim Chull Baum is a professor at Seoul's Defense College and has written articles on the Korean War. Callum MacDonald is Great Britain's leading scholar on the Korean War and has published the important work, *Korea: The War before Vietnam.* Warren Trest is senior historian at the U.S. Air Force's Historical Research Agency and specializes on the air force's missions in national defense.

This handbook's part on the home front during the Korean War breaks new ground because this has not been written about previously. The chapters provide vital data for reevaluating U.S. culture during and after the Korean War and the war's positive and negative influences on a nation that had expected World War II to usher in an era of peace. Gary Huey, who specializes in U.S. domestic policy, examines public opinion during the war, an issue that gained greater attention after the Vietnam era.

Chapter 19, on Congress and the war, which I prepared with Mark Leach, covers a topic often sidelined by historians. Researched with assistance by a grant from the Everett Dirksen Congressional Center and Caterpillar Foundation, this material seeks to encourage more historical study about the congressional branch of government and its influence on policy. As we note, much information about Congress and its members is based on contemporary accounts because historians and biographers have neglected the investigation of this branch of government.

Several people deserve special thanks for their assistance with this book. Mark Leach not only assisted with the chapter on Congress but typed the original drafts of much of this work so that I could revise it as needed. Many of the staff at Bradley's Cullom Davis Library, as well as Nial Johnson and Gail Reynolds of Bradley's Audio-Visual Services, provided timely assistance in various ways. The Dirksen Center provided a grant and advice about the study of Congress. Dr. Robin Higham, the advisory editor for this Greenwood series, made excellent suggestions and read much of my material to offer suggestions or approval. Dr. Graham A. Cosmas willingly accepted my request to read and comment on the chapter on the U.S. Navy and Marines. And, as always, my wife, Joan, gave patient and loyal support to all my efforts.

AN IMPORTANT NOTE: Chinese, Japanese, and Korean names follow the Western style, which places the family name last, except for the chapters by Chen Jian on China and Kim Chull Baum on Korean scholars. This system intends to provide better access to bibliographic entries at the end of each chapter.

Lester H. Brune

PART I

Historical Background and General References

1   Introduction and General References on the Korean War

Lester H. Brune

During the Second Gulf War of 1990–1991, President George Bush and many media commentators compared the conflict to Vietnam, World War II, and Hitler's blitzkrieg during the 1930s. Actually, however, the events during and after Desert Shield–Desert Storm resembled the war many Americans have preferred to forget: the Korean War. The United States' little-publicized involvement with Iraq before August 1990 matched the nation's even deeper and less recognized role in dividing Korea and protecting the South Korean regime before June 1950. Before August 1990, inadequate U.S. intelligence and diplomatic data on Iraq were much like the intelligence failure in Korea during early 1950. President Harry Truman's surprise about North Korea's June 25 attack duplicated President Bush's surprise about learning of Iraq's aggression on August 2, 1990, and just as Truman obtained control of an international force to expel North Korea from South Korea, the Bush administration quickly sought and gained United Nations resolutions condemning Iraq's aggression and approving a U.S.-led international UN force to drive Iraq out of Kuwait. Finally, both the intensive U.S. air warfare against North Korea beginning in 1951 and the UN truce that left Kim Il-sung in power corresponded to the intensive aerial bombing of Iraq and the UN cease-fire, which left Saddam Hussein in power.

These startlingly similar elements contrast completely with the Vietnam War and World War II, despite some differences between Korea in 1950 and Iraq in 1990. The three-year war in Korea was not like the 100-day war against Iraq. But the most notable difference is that the Truman administration attempted to overthrow Kim Il-sung, an effort leading to the massive Chinese communist entry into the conflict. These events had no counterpart in Iraq, where Bush called for a cease-fire after liberating Kuwait, and Iraq had no powerful neighbor willing to help because its prewar ally, the Soviet Union, was crumbling and had joined the UN in condemning Iraq.

Although some commentators may have made the Korean analogy in 1990, detailed information about the Korean War is probably still unknown to most people. The problem is that the declassification of official records takes one generation; then another generation of students is necessary before history teachers and textbooks find the proper balance about what should be known regarding critical events in history.

This book explores both the traditional interpretations of the Korean War and recent scholarly findings and trends. This research process has been aided by information from Soviet and Chinese documents that are now being added to the declassified Western documents about the decade after World War II. As readers will see, much work on the issues regarding the origins and conduct of the Korean War still remains; I hope this book will stimulate the process.

Each chapter in this book contains citations on primary sources and references relevant to their topics, as well as general materials covering broad areas of the Korean War period. These materials will be described in terms of general reference material, official government records, papers of Presidents Harry Truman and Dwight Eisenhower, and a variety of special reference works.

GENERAL REFERENCE WORKS

Although dated, Keith D. McFarland's (1986) annotated bibliography on the Korean War remains valuable. For general materials on U.S. history from 1945 to 1955, Frank Friedel's *Harvard Guide* (1974) is valuable but dated. More recent is Francis Paul Prucha's (1994) *Handbook,* a guide to bibliographies and reference books on American history. Mary Beth Norton's *Guide to Historical Literature,* was published for the American Historical Association in 1995. Because the Korean War took place at a time when anticommunism became prevalent in the United States, Peter Buckingham's (1988) bibliography on that phenomenon in America is relevant. Warren Kuehl (1972) edited an index to doctoral dissertations on American history that were written at American and Canadian universities and coedited with Nancy Ferguson (1981) a bibliography on the United States and the United Nations.

Research on diplomatic aspects of the Korean War era must begin with Richard Burns's (1983) *Guide,* a book that the Society for Historians of American Foreign Relations is expected to update in the near future. The quarterly issues of *Foreign Affairs* include source materials and books on international affairs that update Henry L. Roberts's (1955, 1964) and Janis A. Kreslins's (1976) *Foreign Affairs Bibliography;* volumes 3 to 5 cover 1942 to 1972.

For the international aspects of the war, some general reference materials supplement those cited in specific chapters of this book. Patricia Kennedy Grimsted (1993) has edited a directory of the Russian archives in Moscow and St. Petersburg, which includes an essay on Russian archives in transition, a valuable guide to scholars working in Russia or reading about studies based on those archives. William Moss (1993) has prepared a guide to the archives in the People's Republic of China, with interesting information on these documents. The *CCP Research Newsletter* of the Chinese Communist Research Group has frequent articles about Chinese archives and bibliographies, such as those by Odd Arne Westad (1992) and Michael Schonhals (1991). A historical bibliography, the *United States in East Asia* (1985), was published by ABC-Clio press. An annotated bibliography on Japan's period of occupation, compiled by Robert E. Ward and Frank Shulman (1974), covers English-language sources on the topic and includes information on documentary materials in the United States. The *Cumulative Bibliography of Asian Studies* (1972–1973), which is updated annually by the Association for Asian Studies, includes topics on Korea. Han-Kyo Kim (1980) is a scholar's guide to Korea, and George Ginsburgs (1973) edited *Soviet Works on Korea, 1945–1970.*

In military history, the best guide to U.S. sources is edited by Robin Higham (1975) and with Donald J. Mrozek three supplements published in 1981, 1986, and 1993. Higham's volumes have chapters written by various authorities who provide data on each of the armed forces as well as on science and technology, disarmament, museums, and defense policy and diplomacy. Susan Kinnel (1986) has an annotated, selected military bibliography; William M. Arkin (1981), a guide to current military affairs; and John Jessup and Robert Coakley (1979), a guide to the study of military history. John Greenwood and associates have compiled a bibliography, *American Defense Policy since 1945* (1973); Richard Burt and Geoffrey Kent (1974) edited a bibliography on congressional hearings on defense policy; and Herbert Tillema (1991), a bibliography on armed forces conflicts since 1945.

For the U.S. armed forces, an index to periodical articles has been published at regular intervals since 1949 by the U.S. Air Force, Air University. Samuel Miller (1978) has an "aerospace" bibliography and Paola Coletta (1988) an annotated bibliography of naval history. For the U.S. Army, the works of Jessup and Coakley (1979) and Kinnel (1986) should be consulted. Eugene L. Rasor (1994) compiled a bibliography on General Douglas MacArthur. Paul Edwards (1993) has a special bibliography on the war in the Pusan perimeter, where the initial UN Command action became necessary to save South Korea. Arthur Larson (1973) has a guide to national security sources, and Morton Halperin's (1962) bibliography on limited war is valuable because the Korean War appeared to be the first U.S. limited war in contrast to total victory.

Military history about the U.S. allies' role in the Korean War should also be examined. Robin Higham and Jacob Kipp (1978) have jointly edited volumes on various foreign nations; two of them relevant to Korea are by Shinji Kondo on Japanese military history and Gerald Jordan on the British. Higham's (1971) volume on British history covers the early post–World War II period.

Oral history can be an important source, although these memoirs must be checked against documents. Columbia University's Oral History Collections include a variety of material on the Korean War, including special collections on Dwight Eisenhower and Adlai Stevenson. A guide to Columbia's collection was written by Elizabeth Mason and Louis M. Starr (1973), but for recent information, write to the Columbia Oral History Collection at Columbia University or to Microfilming Corporation of America, 1620 Hawkins Avenue, P.O. Box 10, Sanford, NC 27330.

Allen Meckler and Ruth McMullin (1975) list various oral history collections. The U.S. Eighth Army Historical Office (1988) has a Korean War oral history project. Interviews of foreign service personnel have become a major project of the Association for Diplomatic Studies. For a finder's guide and information about these oral histories, write to the Association for Diplomatic Studies, Foreign Affairs Oral History Project, Lauinger Library, Georgetown University, Washington, D.C. 20057. Dennis Kux (1993) has written an article about the status of this program.

OFFICIAL RECORDS

Most official records of the U.S. government have been declassified for the early 1950s. The original documents are located largely in the Washington, D.C., area at the National Archives, the Library of Congress, the Center for Military History, and the Naval Historical Center.

The U.S. National Archives is located on Pennsylvania Avenue in downtown Washington, D.C., but portions of its collections are being moved to the Archives II building in College Park, Maryland, a move expected to be completed in October 1996. For the latest information regarding the status of the record groups being moved, scholars should ask to be placed on the mailing list for the *Record*, the newsletter of the National Archives and Records Administration, by writing to the National Archives Public Affairs (N-PA), Washington, D.C. 20408. If you know the particular record group you wish to locate, you may get information by calling 202-501-5400.

In addition to visiting Washington to do research, scholars have four sources for obtaining documents on microfilm or microfiche. First, the National Archives publishes a catalog, *Microfilm Resources for Research*, which is regularly updated; the latest issue is from 1992. Three other publishers make available a wide variety of official National Archives documents and other archival material. For the latest information on these materials write to Scholarly Resources, 104 Greenhill Avenue, Wilmington, DE, 19805-1897; University Publications of America, 4520 East-West Highway, Bethesda, MD, 20814-3389; or the National Security Archive, Chadwyck-Healy, 1101 King Street, Alexandria, VA, 22314.

Korean researchers using the National Archives should note that the captured North Korean documents are located in Record Group 242, in the U.S. Far East Command's files. The Central Intelligence Agency (CIA) recently began publishing the CIA Cold War Records Series. The two books on the Korean era as of this writing are Scott Koch's (1993), on intelligence estimates of the Soviet Union from 1950 to 1959, and Michael Warner's (1994), on the Truman era. Scholars should read Zachary Karabell and Timothy Naftali's (1994) suggestion about the use of CIA documents and the commentary following their article by the CIA's chief historian, J. Kenneth McDonald. In addition, for historical perspective on using intelligence data, see John Lewis Gaddis (1989) and D. Cameron Watt (1990). Neil H. Peterson (1992) has a bibliography on American intelligence and Gerald K. Haines and David Langbart (1993) a guide to Federal Bureau of Investigation files.

Researchers may benefit from special information about the Library of Congress and the National Archives and other sources in the Washington, D.C., area. For practical suggestions regarding research at the Library of Congress, see the article by Nicholas E. Sarantakes (1994). The Library of Congress has no published information about its microfilm programs, but information on its procedures and materials is available by writing to the Library of Congress, Washington, D.C. 20540, or through the library's e-mail to the Library of Congress Information System (LOCIS) whose computer catalog access is "telnet locus.loc.gov."

Selected U.S. foreign policy documents are available in print. Most notable are the State Department's *Foreign Relations of the United States* series, which began publications for the Korean War era in 1974; there are now forty-nine volumes for the period 1949 to 1954. Although the *FRUS* has recently been plagued with declassification and selection problems, most questions arose after the books on the Korean War era appeared. For information on these issues see Peter L. Hahn's (1992) essay on the ongoing developments. The State Department has also published an annual series of public documents, and a collection for the period 1950 through 1955 appeared in 1957. In 1976, the U.S. Senate Committee on Foreign Relations began publication of the executive sessions of that committee, beginning with the Eightieth Congress (1946–1947).

Official data on the U.S. military services are cited in this book's chapters on each service. In addition, James Schnabel and Robert Watson (1979) have a valuable study on the Joint Chiefs of Staff and Korea.

Three guides offer assistance to researchers using official archives. Jack Saunders's (1983) essay describes National Archives records relating to

Korea. Gerald Haines (1985) has a guide to State Department files. And Jerrold Zwirn (1983) provides a guide to congressional publications on legislation, budgets, and treaties. Steven A. Grant (1977) has a guide to the sources of study on the Soviet Union in the Washington, D.C., area.

Official United Nations documents are held at Lake Success, New York. The UN Office of Conference Services (1963) listed documents for the period 1948 to 1962. Brenda Brimmer and associates (1962) have a guide to UN documents. Peter I. Hajnal (1978) prepared a guide to the UN's documents. UN Secretary-General Trygve Lie has published his memoirs (1954), and his papers are in the first volume of *Public Papers of the Secretaries General of the United Nations, Official Records,* edited by Andrew W. Cordier and Wilder Foote (1969). The UN's Office of Conference Services issues a UN publications catalog; the UN's Dag Hammarskjold Library issues regular indexes of its holdings; and the UN Office of Public Information publishes *Monthly Chronicle* and the annual *Yearbook.* Other libraries with research collections related to the Korean War are the Seely G. Mudd Library, Princeton University; the George C. Marshall Library, Virginia Military Institute, Lexington, Virgina; and the Hoover Institution Library, Palo Alto, California. Data about these and other documentary sources in the United States may be found in *The National Inventory of Documentary Sources in the United States,* which began the publication of microfiche materials in 1983. For a review of this large-scale project, see Linda Matthews's article in the *Journal of American History* (1987). Finally, for manuscript materials not cited in this chapter, scholars should check the *Directory* of the National Archival Publications and Records Commission (1988)

SOURCES FOR PRESIDENTS TRUMAN AND EISENHOWER

Two recently published presidential bibliographies are Richard Dean Burns's (1984) on Truman and R. Alton Lee's (1991) on Eisenhower. The official *Public Papers of the Presidents* series begins with Herbert Hoover. Truman's volumes, published over 1961–1966, and Eisenhower's over 1960–1961. Each president published his memoirs, Truman's in 1955–1956 and Eisenhower's in 1963–1965. Louis Galambos and associates (1989) edited volumes 12 and 13 of Eisenhower's papers on *NATO and the Campaign of 1952,* the two most relevant to the Korean War era.

Researchers who know the particular government agencies and subjects whose manuscripts they are looking for will find the guide to presidential libraries by Dennis Burton and associates (1985) most valuable. Those who are uncertain about the staff personnel involved with the White House should contact the Truman and Eisenhower libraries. The Truman Library in Independence, Missouri, has a *Guide to Historical Materials* (1991). Published material from the Truman Papers includes Robert Ferrell's two books, *Off the Record* (1980) and *The Autobiography of Harry S. Truman* (1980); and Monte Poen's (1982) letters that Truman never mailed.

The director of the Eisenhower Library in Abilene, Kansas, John E. Wickman, has a *Historical Materials* (1984) guide, but scholars should contact the library for recent publications. Robert Griffith (1984) has edited Eisenhower's "letters to a friend," and Robert Ferrell (1981) edited the *Eisenhower Diaries,* the recollections the president wrote down irregularly between 1935 and 1967.

MISCELLANEOUS REFERENCE WORKS

Three reference works that deal specifically with Korea are James I. Matray's (1991) historical dictionary, Harry G. Summers, Jr.'s (1990) almanac, and Stanley Sandler's (1994) encyclopedia on the Korean War. A. M. Prokhorov (1973) is editor of the *Great Soviet Encyclopedia;* Joseph L. Wieczynski (1976–) is editing the *Modern Encyclopedia of Russian and Soviet History.* Donald C. Bacon and associates (1994) have edited the *Encyclopedia of the United States Congress,* Ann O'Connor (1993) has a reference encyclopedia on the U.S. Congress, and John Jessup edits the *Encyclopedia of the American Military* (1994).

Works that provide broader reference data on diplomatic and military affairs include John F. Findling's (1980) *Dictionary of American Diplomatic History;* Roger Spiller's (1984) *Dictionary of American Military History;* and Lester H. Brune's (1985) *Chronological History of United States Foreign Relations.* Donald Bacon and associates (1994) have an encyclopedia on the U.S. Congress, while Joel Silbey (1994) more broadly covers the state legislatures as well as the Congress.

REFERENCES

Arkin, William M. *Research Guide to Current Military and Strategic Affairs.* Washington, DC: Institute for Policy Studies, 1981.

Bacon, Donald C., Roger H. Davidson, and Morton Keller. *The Encyclopedia of the United States Congress.* 4 vols. New York: Simon and Schuster, 1994.

Bohanan, Robert D., comp. *Dwight D. Eisenhower: A Selected Bibliography of Periodical and Dissertation Literature.* Abilene, KS: Eisenhower Library, 1981.

Brimmer, Brenda, et al. *A Guide to the Uses of United Nations' Documents (Including References to Specialized Agencies and Special UN Bodies).* Rev. ed. Dobbs Ferry, NY: Oceana, 1962.

Brune, Lester H. *Chronological History of United States Foreign Relations.* 2 vols. New York: Garland, 1985.

Buckingham, Peter. *America Sees Red: Anticommunism in America, 1870 to the 1980s.* Claremont, CA: Regina Books, 1988.

Burns, Richard Dean, ed. *Guide to American Foreign Relations since 1700.* Santa Barbara, CA: ABC-Clio, 1983.

————. *Harry S. Truman: A Bibliography of His Times and Presidency.* Wilmington, DE: Scholarly Resources, 1984.

Burt, Richard, and Geoffrey Kent, eds. *Congressional Hearings on American Defense Policy, 1947–1971: An Annotated Bibliography.* Lawrence, KS: University of Kansas Press, 1974.

Burton, Dennis A., James B. Rhoads, and Raymond W. Smock, eds. *A Guide to Manuscripts in the Presidential Libraries.* College Park, MD: Research Materials Corporation, 1985.

Chiro, Susan. "America's Battle over How to Remember Its Forgotten War." *New York Times,* November 18, 1990, IV:18.

Coletta, Paolo. *A Selected and Annotated Bibliography of American Naval History.* Frederick, MD: University Press of America, 1988.

Cordier, Andrew W., and Wilder Foote, eds. *Trygve Lie.* Vol. 1 of *Public Papers of the Secretaries General of the United Nations.* New York: Columbia University Press, 1969.

Cumulative Bibliography of Asian Studies. 4 vols. Boston: G. K. Hall, 1972–1973.

Edwards, Paul M., comp. *The Pusan Perimeter, Korea: 1950.* Westport, CT: Greenwood Press, 1993.

Eisenhower, Dwight D. *Public Papers of the Presidents: Dwight D. Eisenhower.* Washington, DC: GPO, 1960–1961.

————. *The White House Years.* 2 vols. Garden City, NY: Doubleday, 1963–1965.

Ferrell, Robert H., ed. *The Autobiography of Harry S. Truman.* Boulder, CO: Colorado Associated University Press, 1980.

————. *The Eisenhower Diaries.* New York: Norton, 1981.

————. *Off the Record: The Private Papers of Harry S. Truman.* New York: Harper & Row, 1980.

Findling, John E. *Dictionary of American Diplomatic History.* Westport, CT: Greenwood Press, 1980.

Freidel, Frank, ed. *Harvard Guide to American History.* 2 vols. Cambridge: Harvard University Press, 1974.

Gaddis, John Lewis. "Intelligence, Espionage, and the Cold War's Origins." *Diplomatic History* 13 (Spring 1989): 191–202

Galambos, Louis, et al., eds. *The Papers of Dwight David Eisenhower.* Vols. 12 and 13: *NATO and the Campaign of 1952.* Baltimore: Johns Hopkins University Press, 1989.

Ginsburgs, George, ed. *Soviet Works on Korea, 1945–1970.* Los Angeles: University of Southern California Press, 1973.

Grant, Steven A. *Scholar's Guide to Washington, DC for Russian/Soviet Studies.* Washington, DC: Smithsonian Institution Press, 1977.

Greenwood, John, et al., eds. *American Defense Policy since 1945: A Preliminary Bibliography.* Lawrence, KS: University of Kansas Press, 1973.

Griffith, Robert, ed. *Ike's Letters to a Friend, 1941–1958.* Lawrence, KS: University of Kansas Press, 1984.

Grimsted, Patricia Kennedy. *Archives in Russia, 1993, A Brief Directory, Part I: Moscow and St. Petersburg.* Moscow and Washington, DC: International Research and Exchange Board (IREX), 1993.

Guide to Historical Materials in the Harry S. Truman Library. 10th ed. Independence, MO: Harry Truman Library, December 1991.

Hahn, Peter L. "Glasnost in America." *Diplomatic History* 16 (Fall 1992): 631–642.

Haines, Gerald K. *A Reference Guide to United States Department of State Files*. Westport, CT: Greenwood Press, 1985.

Haines, Gerald K., and David Langbart. *Unlocking the Files of the FBI: A Guide to Its Records and Classification System*. Wilmington, DE: Scholarly Resources, 1993.

Hajnal, Peter I. *Guide to United Nations Organization, Documentation and Publishing*. Dobbs Ferry, NY: Oceana Publications, 1978.

Halperin, Morton H. *Limited War: An Essay on the Development of the Theory and an Annotated Bibliography*. Cambridge, MA: Harvard University Press, 1962.

Higham, Robin, ed. *A Guide to the Sources of British Military History*. Berkeley: University of California, 1971.

Higham, Robin, and Jacob W. Kipp, eds. *Military History Bibliographies*. New York: Garland, 1978–1992.

Higham, Robin, and Donald J. Mrozek, eds. *Guide to the Sources of United States Military History*. Hamden, CT: Shoe String Press, 1975: Supplement I; II; III. Hamden, CT: Archon Books, 1981, 1986, 1993.

Historical Materials in the Dwight D. Eisenhower Library. Abilene, KS: Eisenhower Library, 1984.

Jentleson, Bruce W., and Gaddis Smith, eds. *The Encyclopedia of U.S. Foreign Relations*. Detroit, MI: Gale Research, 1995.

Jessup, John, ed. *Encyclopedia of the American Military*. New York: Maxwell International, 1994.

Jessup, John E., Jr., and Robert W. Coakley, eds. *A Guide to the Study and Use of Military History*. Washington, DC: Center of Military History, 1979.

Karabell, Zachary, and Timothy Naftali. "History Declassified: The Perils and the Promise of CIA Documents." *Diplomatic History* 18:4 (Fall 1994): 615–626.

Kim, Han-Kyo, ed. *Studies on Korea: A Scholar's Guide*. Honolulu: University of Hawaii Press, 1980.

Kinnel, Susan K., ed. *Military History of the United States: An Annotated Bibliography*. Santa Barbara, CA: ABC-Clio, 1986.

Koch, Scott, ed. *Selected [CIA] Estimates on the Soviet Union, 1950–1959*. Washington: GPO, 1993.

Kirkendall, Richard S., ed. *The Harry S. Truman Encyclopedia*. Boston: G. K. Hall, 1989.

———. *The Truman Period as a Research Field*. Columbia, MO: University of Missouri Press, 1967.

———. *The Truman Period as a Research Field: A Reappraisal, 1972*. Columbia, MO: University of Missouri Press, 1974.

Knox, Donald. *The Korean War: An Oral History from Pusan to Chosin*. New York: Harcourt Brace Jovanovich, 1985.

Kreslins, Janis A., ed. *Foreign Affairs Bibliography: 1962–1972*. Vol. 5. New York: Bowker, 1976.

Kuehl, Warren, ed. *Dissertations in History: An Index to Dissertations Completed in History Departments of United States and Canadian Universities*. Lexington, KY: University of Kentucky Press, 1972.

Kuehl, Warren, and Nancy Ferguson, eds. *The United States and the United Nations: A Bibliography*. Los Angeles: California State University, 1981.

Kux, Dennis. "The Association for Diplomatic Studies: Status Report on Foreign

Affairs Oral History Program." *Newsletter, Society for Historians of United States Foreign Relations* 24:3 (September 1993): 8–13.

Larson, Arthur D. *National Security Affairs: A Guide to Information Sources.* Detroit: Gale, 1973.

Lee, R. Alton, ed. *Dwight David Eisenhower: A Bibliography of His Life and Times.* Wilmington, DE: Scholarly Resources, 1991.

Lie, Trygve. *In the Cause of Peace: Seven Years with the United Nations.* New York: Macmillan, 1954.

McFarland, Keith D. *The Korean War: An Annotated Bibliography.* New York: Garland, 1986.

Mason, Elizabeth, and Louis M. Starr. *The Oral History Collection of Columbia University.* New York: Columbia University Press, 1973.

Matray, James I., ed. *Historical Dictionary of the Korean War.* Westport, CT: Greenwood Press, 1991.

Matthews, Linda. "Review: National Inventory of Documentary Sources in the United States." *Journal of American History* 73 (March 1987): 1087–1089.

Meckler, Alan M., and Ruth McMullin. *Oral History Collections.* New York: Bowker, 1975.

Miller, Samuel D., comp. *An Aerospace Bibliography.* Rev. ed. Washington, DC: GPO, 1978.

Moss, William. *Archives in the People's Republic of China: A Brief Introduction for American Scholars and Archivists.* Washington, DC: Smithsonian Institution, 1993

National Archival Publications and Records Commission. *Directory of Archives and Manuscript Repositories.* Phoenix, AZ: Oryx Press, 1988.

National Archives. *Microfilm Resources for Research.* Washington, DC: National Archives and Records Administration, n.d.

The National Inventory of Documentary Sources in the United States. 4 parts on microfiche. Alexandria, VA: Chadwyck-Healey, 1983.

New York Times. "Exhibit Plans on Hiroshima Stir a Debate." August 28, 1994, A:12.

Norton, Mary Beth. *Guide to Historical Literature.* 3d ed. 2 vols. New York: Oxford University Press, 1995.

O'Connor, Ann, ed. *Congress A to Z: A Ready Reference Encyclopedia.* 2d ed. Washington, DC: Congressional Quarterly, 1993.

Page, Donald M., ed. *A Bibliography of Works on Canadian Foreign Relations, 1945–1970.* Toronto: Canadian Institute of International Affairs, 1973.

Petersen, Neal H. *American Intelligence, 1775–1990: A Bibliographical Guide.* Claremont, CA: Regina Books, 1992.

Poen, Monte M., ed. *Strictly Personal and Confidential: The Letters Harry Truman Never Mailed.* Boston: Little, Brown, 1982.

Prokhorov, A. M., ed. *Great Soviet Encyclopedia.* New York: Macmillan, 1973

Prucha, Francis Paul. *Handbook for Research in American History: A Guide to Bibliographies and Other Reference Works.* 2d ed. Lincoln: University of Nebraska Press, 1994.

Rasor, Eugene L., ed. *General Douglas MacArthur, 1888–1964: Historiography and Annotated Bibliography.* Westport, CT: Greenwood Press, 1994.

Roberts, Henry L., ed. *Foreign Affairs Bibliography: A Selected and Annotated List of*

Books on International Relations. Vols. 3 and 4, 1942–1962. New York: R. R. Bowker for the Council on Foreign Relations, 1955, 1964.

Sandler, Stanley, ed. *The Korean War: An Encyclopedia.* New York: Garland, 1994.

Sarantakes, Nicholas E. "Research Strategy at the Library of Congress." *Newsletter, Society for Historians of American Foreign Relations* 25:2 (June 1994): 34–37.

Saunders, Jack. "Records in the National Archives Relating to Korea." In Bruce Cumings, ed., *Child of Conflict,* pp. 309–326. Seattle: University of Washington Press, 1983.

Schnabel, James F., and Robert J. Watson. *The History of the Joint Chiefs of Staff.* Vol. 3: *The Korean War.* Wilmington, DE: Scholarly Resources, 1979.

Schoenhals, Michael. "Original Red Guard Publications in the Far Eastern Library, Stockholm." *CCP Research Newsletter* 8 (Spring 1991): 58–65.

Silbey, Joel H., et al. *Encyclopedia of the American Legislative System.* New York: Macmillan, 1994.

Spiller, Roger J., ed. *Dictionary of American Military History.* Westport, CT: Greenwood Press, 1984.

Summers, Harry G., Jr. *Korean War Almanac.* New York: Facts on File, 1990.

Tillema, Herbert K. *International Armed Conflict since 1945: A Bibliographic Handbook of Wars and Military Interventions.* Boulder, CO: Westview, 1991.

Truman, Harry S. *Memoirs.* 2 vols. Garden City, NY: Doubleday, 1955–1956.

———. *Public Papers of the Presidents: Harry S. Truman, 1945–1953.* 8 vols. Washington, DC: GPO, 1961–1966.

United Nations. Dag Hammarskjold Library. *The United Nations Documentation System.* New York: United Nations, 1949–.

———. Office of Conference Services. *United Nations Official Records, 1948–1962.* New York: United Nations, 1963.

———. Office of Conference Services. *United Nations Publications Catalogue 1945–.* New York: United Nations, 1964–.

———. Office of Public Information. *United Nations Monthly Chronicle.* New York: UN Office of Public Information, 1964–.

———. Office of Public Information. *Yearbook of the United Nations.* Lake Success, NY: UN Office of Public Information, 1947–48 to present.

U.S. Air Force. Air University. *Air University Library Index to Military Periodicals.* Maxwell Air Force Base, AL: Air University Library, 1949–.

U.S. Army. Eighth Army Historical Office. *Korean War Oral History Project.* Seoul, Korea: Eighth Army Historical Office, 1988.

United States in East Asia: A Historical Bibliography. Santa Barbara, CA: ABC-Clio, 1985.

U.S. Senate. Committee on Foreign Relations. *Executive Sessions of the Senate Foreign Relations Committee.* Historical Series begins with vol. 1 for 1946–47 (80th Congress). Washington, DC: GPO, 1970–.

U.S. State Department. *Foreign Relations of the United States.* 49 vols. for 1949–1954. Washington, DC: GPO, 1974–1989.

———. *American Foreign Policy, 1950–1955: Basic Documents.* 2 vols. Pub. 6446. Washington, DC: GPO, 1957.

Ward, Robert E., and Frank Shulman. *The Allied Occupation of Japan, 1945–1952: An Annotated Bibliography of Western Language Materials.* Chicago: American Library Association, 1974.

Warner, Michael, ed. *The CIA under Harry Truman.* Washington: GPO, 1994.

Watt, D. Cameron. "Intelligence and the Historian." *Diplomatic History* 14 (Spring 1990): 199–204.

Westad, Odd Arne. "Materials on CCP History in Russian Archives." *CCP Research Newsletter* 10–11 (Spring and Fall 1992): 52–53.

Wickman, John E., ed. *Historical Materials in the Dwight D. Eisenhower Library.* Abilene, KS: Eisenhower Library, 1984. For the most recent updated information write to the Eisenhower Library, Abilene, KS 67410.

Wieczynski, Joseph L., ed. *The Modern Encyclopedia of Russian and Soviet History.* Gulf Breeze, FL: Academic International Press, 1976–.

Zwirn, Jerrold. *Congressional Publications: A Research Guide to Legislation, Budgets, and Treaties.* Littleton, CO: Libraries Unlimited, 1983.

2 The Origins of the Cold War, 1945–1950: Historical Interpretations

Lester H. Brune

Almost immediately after learning that North Korea invaded South Korea on June 25, 1950, President Harry S. Truman ordered U.S. military forces mobilized to help South Korea combat "communist aggression." In doing so, Truman extended the containment policy that originated for Europe in 1947 to include East Asia as well, beginning the first "hot war" of the cold war. By the 1980s, however, scholars had uncovered more information about American involvement in Korea, learning that as early as September 1945, U.S. military officers had backed a noncommunist Korean faction against Soviet-supported "rebels." From this perspective, the cold war between the United States and the Union of Soviet Socialist Republics began soon after Japan surrendered to end World War II.

This chapter focuses not on U.S.-Korean relations but on U.S. policy in the European theater, where traditional accounts of the cold war begin. Following Germany's surrender in May 1945, the wartime alliance of the Big Three powers had broken apart due to diplomatic tensions and perceived military threats, a period that became known as the cold war. The Truman Doctrine of 1947 had inaugurated a U.S. containment policy that pitted the "free world" against communist tyranny. Truman's policy resulted in commitments of U.S. economic and military aid to Western Europe in the Marshall Plan (European Recovery Program), the North Atlantic Treaty Organization in 1949, and the establishment of the West German Federal Republic in May 1949.

During the half-century since World War II, the reasons for the origins of the cold war have become a central issue among American and Western European scholars. Divergent schools of interpretation developed, and although each scholarly study of the issue may rise or fall on its own merits, convenience has led to grouping related viewpoints into certain categories. Truman's official explanation for the containment policy soon generated critics who opposed his program based on divergent basic assumptions about U.S. relations with the Soviet Union. After Truman called for a clear national commitment to aid Greece, Turkey, and later Western Europe in 1947, his policy was praised by those who became the official or orthodox school but was objected to by others. Three basic groups of critics appeared between 1945 and 1953: left liberals who wanted to continue cooperation with the USSR, realistic analysts who disliked Truman's moralistic-idealistic rhetoric because it risked unlimited commitments, and a conservative right-wing group, generally comprising those who moved from preference for U.S. isolationism to accept a hard-line anti-communist international stance by 1952.

From the seeds of these liberal, realist, and conservative assumptions, three additional schools of interpretation evolved to qualify or challenge the orthodox explanations for the cold war. During the 1960s while the realists continued to protest the misunderstandings between Washington and Moscow, and conservatives advanced reasons that the communist evil needed to be eradicated, left revisionists expanded on the left-liberal concepts. By the mid-1970s, however, postrevisionist scholars rejected these new left revisionist views and turned to many newly declassified documents to seek a broader, noneconomic perspective on events about the cold war's origins; this middle-way explanation concluded that Harry Truman and Joseph Stalin shared responsibility for the cold war. Most recently, since 1985, new horizons have opened for Western scholars. Mikhail Gorbachev's *glasnost* (openness) policy and the fall of the Soviet empire in 1991 began to make some communist documents available and fostered a post–cold war era during which scholars are expecting to find better answers to questions about the cold war's origins by using these archives.

After citing some of the historiographic materials on the cold war, this chapter briefly examines these six perspectives on the origins of the cold war: orthodox, left liberal, realist, right-wing conservative, left revisionists, postrevisionists, and the post–cold war developments. Although Bruce Cumings (1993) questions grouping authors in this way, these categories have value as a means for guiding scholars to understand the issues reflected by the literature of the cold war and making persons aware of the perspectives that have influenced historical writing.

HISTORIOGRAPHIC LITERATURE ON THE COLD WAR

The best place to begin any study of the cold war is by consulting *The Guide to American Foreign Relations* edited in 1983 by Richard Dean Burns. Second, for a detailed analysis of major cold war interpretation, one should consult Richard Melanson's *Writing History and Making Policy* (1983) and Jerald A. Combs' *American Diplomatic History* (1983). Third are works that deal with particular aspects of these historiographic issues. Robert James Maddox's *The New Left and the Origins of the Cold War* (1973) is a harsh critique of the left revisionists but should be read with Melanson's (1977) analysis of Maddox. An often overlooked article by Irwin Unger (1967) describes how the left revisionists influenced various studies of American history, including the cold war. J. Samuel Walker's essay (1980) describes the variety of studies by the revisionists during the 1970s. Finally, as a comparison to Western historiography on the cold war, Karl Drechsler's 1985 essay represents the view of a historian from the former East Germany (German Democratic Republic).

The journal *Diplomatic History* has frequent historiographic articles on the cold war. John Lewis Gaddis' articles (1983, 1986, 1993) provide updates on recent studies. Lawrence Kaplan (1987) considers European writing on the cold war. Robert McMahon (1988) examines writings on the cold war in Asia. Howard Jones and Randall B. Woods (1993) describe writings during the 1980s. Geir Lundestad (1989) sees constant moralism in U.S. writing. Cumings (1994), critical of those who categorize cold war writings, nevertheless provides significant insights into scholarly interpretations of international affairs.

References and Documents

Although the government files of most Western nations are accessible to scholars for the period from 1941 to 1953, documents from the communist side of the cold war did not begin to open for research until 1985. In using Western documents for research, an indispensable source is Burns's *Guide to American Foreign Relations* (1983). The first chapter has essential information on diplomatic archives and finding aids for those sources.

The most important Western documents for the early cold war are held by the National Archives of the United States and the Public Records Office of the United Kingdom. Many of the U.S. National Archives documents are available on microfilm from the National Archives, Scholarly Resources, and the University Press of America. In addition, the State Department's series, *Foreign Relations of the United States,* is completed for the period to 1953. Jack Saunders's (1983) article describing the National Archives records on the Korean War is also helpful for research on other cold war subjects. Gerald K. Haines has published *A Reference Guide to the United States Department of State Files* (1985). Other important reference materials are listed in the Introduction to this book.

With regard to communist documents on the cold war, the researcher's principal problem is to be aware of the availability of new documents. Although the release of documents from communist archives is uncertain, Western scholars are trying to speed up the release of all cold war documents. Making data widely available is the purpose of a special project newsletter, the *Cold War International History Project Bulletin.* To receive this bulletin, write to the project at the Woodrow Wilson International Center for Scholars, 1000 Jefferson Drive, S.W., Washington, D.C. 20560. Another source for released communist information is the International Research and Exchange Board (IREX), whose *News in Brief* often cites archival data from East European and former Soviet archives.

THE MAJOR INTERPRETATIONS

Official or Orthodox Views

As the Truman administration moved from negotiation toward confrontation with the Soviet Union after 1945, White House decisions made news headlines, which helped Truman to obtain both congressional and public support in forming a U.S. public consensus in favor of the cold war against Stalin. Truman justified his policies by blaming the communists' desire to promote world revolution by disrupting the prospects for international peace after the Axis powers were defeated. Stalin, he said, refused to carry out the promises he had made during wartime conferences such as those at Yalta in February 1945. Stalin had exceeded his reparations requests from Germany and failed to conduct "free" elections in Eastern Europe in order to give communist leaders control of these "captive nations." Stalin also tried to keep his troops in Iran in 1946, aided communist rebels in Greece, and threatened Turkey. All of these efforts, said the president, were designed to subvert free government and to advance communist control of the world.

To counter Soviet subversions, Truman stood firm by assisting Iran; granting economic and military aid to Greece, Turkey, and Western Europe; and airlifting supplies to West Berlin to keep that city free in 1948–1949. Finally, Truman reversed all previous U.S. policies by making a political and military commitment to form the North Atlantic Treaty Organization (NATO) and, later, appointing General Dwight D. Eisenhower as Supreme Commander of NATO's forces in Europe. According to this treaty, the United States would militarily defend its European allies if they were invaded.

The Truman administration's official explanations for U.S. policy formed the basic orthodox version for the origins of the cold war. In addition to Truman's speeches and those of his cabinet members, the official perspective on the Soviet Union's threat to democracy was prepared by George Kennan, whose "long telegram" to the State Department in 1946 and "Mr. X" article in the July 1947 issue of *Foreign Affairs* provided the rationale for containing Soviet power to prevent its expansion. Although his realistic perspective led him to deplore the rhetorical "excesses" derived from his analysis by Truman and Secretary of State Dean

Acheson, Kennan's estimates helped the president gain bipartisan support in obtaining congressional approval for his European program.

As James Aronson (1970) has shown, the American news media generally condemned Soviet actions and applauded Truman's firm stance against communism. In addition, the backing of Democratic New Deal liberals and internationalist Republicans, such as Senator Arthur Vandenberg, enabled Truman to persuade the Republican-dominated Eightieth Congress to approve his requests for aid to Greece and Turkey and the European Recovery Program (Marshall Plan). Truman's containment policies were also approved by prominent diplomatic historians. The textbooks of Samuel F. Bemis (1955), Thomas Bailey (1958), Foster Rhea Dulles (1955), Julius Pratt (1955), and John Spanier (1960) confirmed the validity of Truman's program.

The classic orthodox studies of the cold war's origins were written by Herbert Feis. A former bureaucrat who had served in the State, War, and Treasury departments between 1937 and 1947, Feis knew many of the officials who worked for Roosevelt and Truman. He also had access to official documents before other scholars did and interviewed those who had formulated the official policies of the 1940s. Among Feis's books on the origins of the Cold War are *The Road to Pearl Harbor* (1950), *Churchill, Roosevelt, Stalin* (1957), *Between Peace and War* (1960), and *From Trust to Terror* (1970). Although later scholarship might question, qualify, or refute Feis's conclusions, no serious student of the cold war can ignore them.

In addition to Feis's work, the speeches, diaries, and memoirs of participants in the events of 1945 to 1950 are excellent sources for the orthodox version of the cold war's beginning. Both Truman's and Eisenhower's public addresses and memoirs are easily accessible. Their official statements are in *Public Papers of the Presidents:* Truman's published in 1961–1963 and Eisenhower's in 1960–1961. Truman's *Memoirs* were published in 1955–1956 and Eisenhower's *The White House Years* in 1963–1965. Valuable personal accounts of these years include those by Secretary of State Acheson (1968); James Forrestal (his Diaries, edited by Millis in 1951) and the memoirs of four presidential advisers: James Byrnes (1947), W. Averill Harriman (1975), Lewis Strauss (1962), Paul Nitze (1989), and Clark Clifford (1991). There are also biographies of various leaders: Robert Donovan's (1977, 1982) David McCullough's (1992) and Robert Ferrell's (1994) works on Harry Truman; David McLellan's (1976) on Acheson; volume 4 of Forrest C. Pogue's *George C. Marshall* (1987); David Callahan's (1990) biography of Paul Nitze; and Stephen Ambrose's second volume (1984) on Eisenhower. Robert Ferrell has edited *The Eisenhower Diaries* (1981), and John Foster Dulles's ideas are found in his *War or Peace* (1950). Dulles served Truman by negotiating the 1951 Peace Treaty with Japan and became Eisenhower's secretary of state.

Left-Liberal Critics of Truman's Policies

Between 1946 and 1950, left-wing liberals who disagreed with Truman joined other leftists who believed Truman had abandoned cooperation and compromise with Soviet leaders and enticed Stalin into making uncooperative responses. The leader of this group was Henry A. Wallace, who had been Roosevelt's vice president from 1941 to 1945 but was dropped from the Democratic ticket in favor of Truman during the 1944 campaign. Truman had appointed Wallace as secretary of commerce but fired him on September 20, 1946, after Wallace made a public speech denouncing Truman's "hard-line" attitude toward the Soviet Union. Similar opposition to Truman's policy toward the Soviet Union would be expressed by I. F. Stone, who argued that opportunities for a peaceful world were being foreclosed. A newspaper columnist, Stone became a persistent critic of U.S. policy. His selected articles are available in *The Truman Years* (1973). Robert Cottrell describes Stone's career in *Izzy* (1992).

In 1948, Wallace and his Democratic liberal supporters split with Truman. Wallace's decision to form the Progressive party rather than campaign as an independent Democrat candidate, as some moderate liberals preferred, radicalized the new party by opening it to communists and other opponents of Truman's "Hitlerite methods." As a result, Wallace lost the backing of moderate liberals, many of whom joined the anticommunist Americans for Democratic Action (ADA). Wallace's 1948 campaign is described by Curtis MacDougall (1965), whose work should be read in conjunction with Wallace's book: *Toward World Peace* (1948). The Progressive party's and Wallace's papers are held by the University of Iowa. Progressive opinions of other Wallace supporters may be found in Thomas Paterson's *Cold War Critics* (1971). Significantly, as Richard Griffith (1979) indicates, some "old Progressives" such as Senator Glen Taylor (D, Idaho) accepted Wallace; others took diverse positions in opposing Truman's cold war policies.

Generally Wallace accused Truman of being too harsh toward Stalin. Truman, he said, expected the U.S.S.R. to give up its security zone in Eastern Europe while the United States stopped German reparations and backed undemocratic regimes in Greece and Iran. Wallace urged friendly peace talks with Stalin, a proposition Truman rejected.

Realist Critics of Truman's Moralistic Role

While the left liberals blamed Truman for avoiding peace possibilities, realist scholars of international relations feared that Truman's idealist-moralist rhetoric conflicted with the actual power political relationships that every nation pursues in its own national interests. Truman's universalist appeals, which divided the world between "free" and "tyrannical," exaggerated America's self-righteous vision of unlimited world leadership. This idealistic rhetoric misled the American public, ignored the Soviet Union's security needs, and would overextend America's capability by trying to fulfill globalized aspirations. Even if some U.S. leaders acted pragmatically in particular instances, the realists believed Truman's raising of public expectations and fears would eventually damage the nation's military, political, and economic interests.

One of Truman's realist critics was George Kennan, who left the Policy Planning Office of the State Department in 1949 and took a leave of absence to work at Princeton's Institute for Advanced Studies. As Kennan's *Memoirs* (1967, 1972) explain, he had a growing "difference in outlook" with his State Department colleagues by 1949. Subsequently, Kennan's studies expressed his realistic approach, which cautioned against America's moralist-idealist tendencies. He published *American Diplomacy, 1900–1950* (1951) in order to describe the realist-idealist dichotomy and to warn about the tendencies of Truman's policies. In other articles, lectures, and essays over the next forty-five years, Kennan frequently befuddled analysts, who tried to systematize his thoughts. These critics had difficulty largely because Kennan used the paradoxical views of theologian Reinhold Niebuhr, whose *Irony of American History* (1952) influenced the realist perspective. Niebuhr's realist perspective contended that good human intentions are intermixed paradoxically with evil actions, both good and evil being active in human behavior, rather than the either-or propositions of logical decision making. Thus, critics of Kennan, such as Walter Hixson (1989) and Barton Gellman (1984), must be supplemented with Kennan's essays, *Around the Cragged Hill* (1993). David Mayer's (1988) study seems to understand Kennan better.

Even before Kennan took leave from the State Department, Truman's containment was being questioned by two realists who raised difficult questions about his program: Walter Lippmann and Hans Morgenthau. Lippmann, whose career as an influential journalist is described by Ronald Steel (1980), made balance-of-power assessments of Truman's rhetoric and foreign commitments in his newspaper column "Today and Tomorrow." A selection of these articles were later compiled in two books: *The Cold War* (1947) and *Isolation and Alliances* (1952). Beginning in 1946, he criticized Truman's handling of diplomacy with the Soviet Union because Lippmann did not perceive Stalin as aggressively expanding communist power. Stalin reacted to Anglo-American proposals in a fearful and defensive way, he said, because his goal was to protect the Soviet Union from Western invasions such as Russia had experienced in 1914 and 1941. Thus, Truman's firm stance gave Stalin a rationale for persuading the Soviet people to fear the Western imperial destruction of Russia unless they accepted Stalin's iron rule to defend their homeland.

Lippmann especially disliked the sweeping rhetoric of Truman's March

1947 speech to Congress, in which Truman requested aid for Greece and Turkey but also proclaimed the need for the free world to combat communism anywhere in the world. Such rhetoric, Lippmann thought, would eventually dissipate the nation's strength by trying to fill every power vacuum in Europe and Asia. Truman should recognize Russia's legitimate sphere of influence and define exactly what America's primary national interests were.

Lippmann's basic ideas were given a more systematic form by a political scientist at the University of Chicago, Hans Morgenthau. Like Lippmann, Morgenthau urged the United States to design practical and limited responses to any real Soviet threat, responses based on areas most important to the nation's political, military, or economic interests. All nations had vital concerns that must be accepted, but this required the United States to prepare and define its own interests clearly. Morgenthau's two basic works were *Politics among Nations* (1948), and *In Defense of the National Interest* (1951).

While Morgenthau offered broad, long-term perspectives regarding a power balance situation, William Hardy McNeill wrote a realistic description of the early post–World War II years, *America, Britain, and Russia* (1953). A fellow at Great Britain's Royal Institute of International Affairs and later a historian at the University of Chicago, McNeill saw the origins of the cold war as an inevitable great power conflict because the three principal victors in World War II had divergent security interests. He also viewed the globalist international ideals of Woodrow Wilson and Franklin D. Roosevelt as being subversive of the existing national state system, a tactic that Truman had adopted.

The realist perspective on U.S. power politics was expressed by critics throughout the cold war years. In addition to Morgenthau's analysis, Norman Graebner became a prominent proponent of realistic diplomacy; his 1962 volume, *Cold War Diplomacy*, described U.S.-Soviet relations from the realist perspective. Two political scientists, Henry Kissinger and Zbigniew Brzezinski, also advocated balance-of-power ideas, and, after 1969, they directly affected U.S. policies: Kissinger as an adviser and secretary of state to Presidents Richard Nixon and Gerald Ford, Brzezinski as national security adviser to President Jimmy Carter. Greg Russell (1990) examines Morgenthau's concepts while Joel H. Rosenthal (1991) describes five realists, and Michael J. Smith (1986) has a valuable critique of realist thought from the 1920s to the 1970s.

Conservative Right-Wing Critics

Possibly the conservative critics of Truman's policies had the most, albeit negative, influence on U.S. policy evolution during the cold war. Developing from the group of conservative isolationists who opposed

Roosevelt's internationalism before the Pearl Harbor attack in 1941, these critics accused Roosevelt of permitting Japan's successful raid and appeasing Joseph Stalin during the war, especially at the February 1945 Yalta Conference. While writers such as William Chamberlain (1953, 1962) led the anti-Roosevelt barrage, Senator Robert A. Taft (R, Ohio) became the conservatives' postwar political leader who opposed bipartisanship and Truman's decision to aid Europe while he was decreasing assistance to Jiang Jieshi (Chiang Kai-shek), the Chinese leader who lost to the Chinese communists and retreated to Taiwan in 1949.

Taft's *A Foreign Policy for Americans* (1951) argued that the United States could best protect its liberties by avoiding foreign alliances or interference in other nations. Communist ideas should be fought, but this did not require America to dominate the world or to damage the U.S. economy by large military expenditures. Between 1949 and 1952, Taft and other conservatives became ardent advocates of anticommunism and embraced General Douglas MacArthur's desire to unlease Jiang's military so that nationalist forces on Taiwan could attack the People's Republic of China and enable U.S. forces to liberate North Korea. The final result, Taft expected, would restore "capitalism" to China and allow American forces to withdraw from the Pacific area. Taft's views are sympathetically described by James Patterson (1972), while Ross Koen's *The China Lobby in American Politics* (1974) explains the influence of that lobby and Madame Jiang in convincing Taft and other Republicans that Truman had "lost" China. Justus Doenecke (1972, 1979) has studied the old isolationists and has a guide for their literature.

By 1952, most of Taft's followers had been persuaded to become hardline anticommunists due to the influences of the China Lobby, the "Yalta myth," and Senator Joseph McCarthy (R, Wisconsin), who attacked communist influences in the presidential administrations of Roosevelt and Truman. The China Lobby's and the conservatives' version of how the Democrats lost China is told in Anthony Kubeck's *How the Far East Was Lost* (1963). The earliest description of the China Lobby was in the April 1952 issue of *Reporter* magazine in an essay by Charles Wertenbaker and Philip Horton.

After 1949, the conservatives also adopted what Athan Theoharis (1970) calls the "myth," which asserted that President Roosevelt and other liberals in his administration sanctioned communist aggression to usurp foreign territory through secret agreements made during wartime conferences, such as those at Yalta and Potsdam in 1945. To rectify these injustices, the conservatives wanted to retract the wartime agreements and "roll back" communist aggression by liberating the "captive nations" using any means.

Last, but certainly not least, many conservatives supported McCarthy's accusations against the Democrats for harboring "communists" who helped the Soviet Union make their territorial gains between 1945 and 1950. The campaign known as McCarthyism began in February 1950 and is described in Fred Cook's (1971) journalistic-style biography of McCarthy, *The Nightmare Decade.* Allen J. Matusow has edited a volume of McCarthy's writings (1970), and Susan Hutson has compiled a bibliography on McCarthyism (1979). Also note that Chapter 20 in this book deals with the loyalty issue and McCarthyism.

Following McCarthy's demise in 1954, the conservative right wing included radical anticommunist groups such as the John Birch Society and more moderate groups such as those who rallied around William F. Buckley (1952). While ardent McCarthyites continued to find conspiracies in America, published the news magazine *Human Events,* and nourished both Robert Welch's (1966) John Birch Society and Fred Schwarz's Christian Anti-Communist Crusade, Buckley founded the *National Review* journal and encouraged strong anticommunist writers. The leading conservative critic of U.S. foreign policy was James Burnham, whose books *The Struggle for the World* (1947) and *Containment or Liberation* (1953) described why containment policies were wrong. Burnham wanted the United States to attack communism and liberate people who lived under communist rule. Total victory, not limited war, must be pursued, he advised, a concept that 1964 Republican presidential nominee Barry Goldwater advocated in *Why Not Victory?* (1962).

In addition to Burnham, a group of scholars formed the Foreign Policy Research Institute at the University of Pennsylvania to contribute anti-Soviet studies to the conservative perspective. That institute's most prominent work was *Protracted Conflict* (1959), written by Robert Strauz-Hupe, William R. Kinter, James E. Dougherty, and Alvin Cottrell. Assuming that the Soviet Union followed the Marxist-Leninist desire to promote a worldwide communist victory, *Protracted Conflict* contended that the communists engaged in an endless struggle, using deception, subversion, lies, proxies, or any other means, to defeat capitalism. It envisioned monolithic communist power, with the Kremlin planning ways to provoke troubles around the world in order to destroy freedom and capitalism.

Supporting the conservative views of *Protracted Conflict* were other studies about the aggressive character of Soviet policy. Elliot Goodman published *The Soviet Design for a World State* (1960), and Bertram D. Wolfe described *Communist Totalitarianism* (1961) as a means to keep people under its control while rebellions were fomented elsewhere.

Left Revisionists on Cold War Policy

In contrast to the conservative critics of Truman's cold war containment policies, new left revisionist scholars of the 1960s elaborated on Henry Wallace's complaints that Truman, not Stalin, was primarily to blame for the breakdown of World War II's Grand Alliance. Using official U.S. documents of the 1940s and emphasizing an economic analysis of international policy, these revisionists found that the U.S. cold war program was designed to promote the nation's economic dominance of world resources and trade. One of the early proponents of this interpretation was U.S. diplomatic historian William Appleman Williams, who described the history of American foreign policy as persistently following an imperialist model by using the U.S. government to enlarge the prosperity of its capitalists.

In *The Tragedy of American Diplomacy* (1959), Williams laid out this course of U.S. policy from the republic's inception in 1776 through the 1950s. Published just before John F. Kennedy and Lyndon B. Johnson escalated the Vietnam War, Williams' study nourished the new left dissent against the Indochina conflict, which seemed to derive from the same capitalistic fears of the Soviet threat that began the cold war after 1945. Truman's forceful U.S. response opposed the Third World's wars of liberation from Western colonialism in order to prevent colonial independence rebellions that Moscow supported. Thus, Truman involved the United States in the Indochina problem in 1950 when he recognized the French-backed ruler, Bao Dai. France approved Bao Dai as a collaborator who would prevent a victory by Vietnamese nationalists whose leaders were aided by the Soviet Union.

A host of new left revisionist studies followed Williams' lead, providing details about the economic aspects of U.S. motives in challenging Stalin after 1945. Gabriel Kolko became the foremost exponent of revisionist work on the origins of the cold war, sometimes writing jointly with Joyce Kolko. In *The Politics of War* (1968) and *The Limits of Power* (1972), Kolko unequivocally concluded that American policy in the 1940s was planned to protect and advance the nation's economic prosperity and the needs of Western capitalists for war materials, world trade, and foreign investments. Using documents made available in the printed volumes of *The Foreign Relations of the United States* series as well as memoirs of cold war participants, Kolko rejected the orthodox position that Stalin's aggressive plans caused the cold war. Both Roosevelt and Truman, Kolko claimed, tried to force Stalin to accept American terms regarding a world order. When Stalin resisted, the United States stopped lend-lease aid and loans to Russia and halted German reparations early in 1946. Winston Churchill joined Truman by denouncing Stalin's Iron Curtain and having Great Britain cooperate with the United States in creating military alliances to encircle and contain the Soviet Union.

To encourage more revisionist studies, Richard Barnet and Marcus Raskin established the Institute for Policy Studies in Washington, D.C., to promote liberal studies about the nation's economic, social, and political affairs. Barnet's *Intervention and Revolution* (1968) described the counterrevolutionary role the United States played in the Third World. In addition, Barnet (1972) indicated how American society caused a "permanent war" atmosphere that generated hostility to outsiders.

Two general revisionist works on the cold war are especially valuable: Walter LaFeber's *America, Russia, and the Cold War* (1967) and Thomas McCormick's *America's Half-Century* (1989). LaFeber's account emphasized that the United States was chiefly responsible for the breakdown in Russian relations in order to expand the American empire. McCormick's book used the world systems analysis of hegemonic relations originated by Immanuel Wallerstein (1974) in order to explain Washington's search for global influence before and after 1945. This analysis posited that modern empires seek global hegemony over core industrial nations, less-developed semiperipheral regions, and underdeveloped peripheral areas. The United States, McCormick said, had gradually evolved its world hegemony between 1870 and 1945. Subsequently it assumed world power in 1945, although this hegemony began to decline after 1968 because the nation overextended itself during the Vietnam War and in building global military weapons and alliances against communism.

Most revisionists' studies deal with particular aspects of the origins of the cold war, each emphasizing the American responsibility for certain phases of it with the Soviet Union. Gar Alperovitz's *Atomic Diplomacy* (1967) concluded that Truman used the bomb against Japan in August 1945 in an attempt to keep the Soviet armies out of Manchuria and the Far Eastern sector. Thomas Paterson's *Soviet-American Confrontation* (1972) analyzed Truman's use of economic threats against Stalin after Germany's surrender in 1945, while Bruce Kuklick (1972) deals with the U.S. policy that caused a divided Germany by 1949. Lloyd Gardner's *Architects of Illusion* (1970) examined the motives of individuals who formulated Truman's containment policy.

Postrevisionist Synthesis

Although new left, realist, conservative, and orthodox interpretations of the cold war's origins continue to be found in the historical literature, the mid-1970s brought another interpretation, identified as the postrevisionist school. This group shared an eclectic view of the cold war's origins but borrowed heavily from the orthodox approach. At best, however, these authors emphasized a creative perspective about the period 1941 to 1952 and sought a greater understanding than just the sum of traditional studies. The postrevisionists qualified or rebutted much of the revisionist perspective but also profited from the declassification of most U.S. and British documents dealing with the early cold war period. The postrevisionists claimed to broaden the revisionists' economic insights and the orthodox truths by using multiple historic factors that impinged on both Anglo-American and Soviet decisions from 1945 to 1950.

The postrevisionists' multilevel approach and the availability of greater documentation resulted in more detailed studies on many events after 1941. John L. Gaddis (1972, 1982) explores the early postwar origins of the cold war as well as the broad strategies the United States used in the cold war. Daniel Yergin's *Shattered Peace* (1977) concludes that in contrast to revisionists, the United States and the Soviet Union shared political responsibility for beginning the cold war tensions. Bruce Kuniholm's *The Origins of the Cold War in the Near East* (1980) praised Truman's decisions to protect Iran, Turkey, and Greece but criticized the United States for adopting these relatively easy successes in the Middle East as a pattern for tactics used in Europe and East Asia, where the Soviet Union's national interests were greater. Yergin and Kuniholm adopted less economic and more political realistic views to judge U.S. policy.

Both Vojtech Mastny's *Russia's Road to the Cold War* (1979) and Lynn E. Davis's *The Cold War Begins: Soviet American Conflict over Eastern Europe* (1974) indicate that Soviet ambitions led to cold war confrontation as much as or more so than American goals. Mastny says that Stalin took advantage of the power vacuum in Eastern Europe, using methods that caused disputes with the United States and England. Davis describes America's domestic political factors and Roosevelt's goals in the Atlantic Charter of 1941 as a key to U.S. difficulties in Eastern Europe when the Soviet Union tried to extend its security zones farther west.

Among the many postrevisionist works, several are worth considering because they have influenced studies about the Korean War. Martin J. Sherwin's *A World Destroyed* (1977) seriously qualified Gar Alperovitz's work regarding Truman's decision to use the atomic bomb against Japan by showing that both military and diplomatic considerations throughout World War II influenced his action in August 1945. Alonzo L. Hamby examines the complex domestic American political factors regarding Truman's relations with liberal Democrats in *Beyond the New Deal* (1973). Finally, regarding the impact of U.S. policy on other nations, Norwegian scholar Geir Lundestad describes how Norway and Denmark *invited* the United States to protect them. Lundestad has published his ideas in several articles, as well as in *America, Scandinavia, and the Cold War* (1980).

Post–Cold War Historical Activity

By the mid-1980s, the postrevisionist perspective dominated most Western cold war scholarship, a perspective that became a beneficial take-off point in 1985 for the beginning of the post–cold war era. Soviet chairman Mikhail Gorbachev's program of openness (*glasnost*) inaugurated more contact between Soviet and Western scholars. The early contacts with Russia became an avalance for scholars after the fall of the Berlin Wall and the split-up of the Warsaw Pact alliance in 1989 was followed by Soviet Empire's demise in 1991. When the cold war ended, prospects multiplied for scholars to meet with Soviet scholars and to gain greater access to communist documents about the years since 1917.

John Lewis Gaddis (1993) has suggested that one early activity of post–cold war studies should be to examine the role that the United States played in resisting totalitarianism. Gaddis' article indicates that Soviet scholars stress how terrible Leninist and Stalinist totalitarianism was, citing Dimitri Volkoganov's *Stalin* (1991), and studies on Stalin by Robert Tucker (1990) and Alan Bullock (1992). Generally these accounts conclude that Stalin's decisions may have been rational and sensible, but a psychological dysfunction caused him to "terrorize" Soviet society. These traits of Stalin's character made cold war antagonism inevitable after 1945, forcing Truman to react as he did.

During these years from 1985 to 1992, Melvyn Leffler, who attended several post–cold war conferences with Soviet scholars, prepared a 1992 volume, *A Preponderance of Power,* which concludes that American leaders knew about Soviet strengths and weaknesses but still wanted U.S. power to control the industrial core areas of Japan and Western Europe. Leffler's work is a synthesis of revisionist and postrevisionist work but avoids being tied to any previous categories. Thus, he posits that both political and economic reasons caused the United States to seek world power against communism due to the circumstances of the postwar years and regardless of Stalin's character.

Most recently, Bruce Cumings (1993) questions the entire process of categorizing literature about the cold war. He believes that scholars should ask questions and seek valid explanations of the power exerted by both the United States and the Soviet Union after 1945. Cumings, whose most prominent work is on Korea and shall be referred to frequently in this book, urges scholars to do multiarchival work in searching for truth, being aware that every national government's role is not to search for truth but to find explanations useful for political control.

REFERENCES

Acheson, Dean. *Present at the Creation: My Years in the State Department.* New York: Norton, 1968.
Alperovitz, Gar. *Atomic Diplomacy: Hiroshima and Potsdam.* New York: Vintage, 1967.
Ambrose, Stephen E. *Eisenhower: The President.* New York: Simon & Schuster, 1984.
Aronson, James. *The Press and the Cold War.* Indianapolis: Bobbs-Merrill, 1970.
Bailey, Thomas A. *A Diplomatic History of the American People.* New York: Appleton-Century-Crofts, 1958.
Barnet, Richard. *Intervention and Revolution: The United States in the Third World.* Cleveland: World, 1968.

———. *Roots of War: The Men and Institutions behind U.S. Foreign Policy.* New York: Atheneum, 1972.

———. *The Alliance.* New York: Simon & Schuster, 1983.

Bemis, Samuel F. A. *Diplomatic History of the United States.* 4th ed. New York: Holt, 1955.

Buckley, William F., Jr., "Dean Acheson's Record." *Freeman,* March 10, 1952, pp. 378–380.

Bullock, Alan. *Hitler and Stalin: Parallel Lives.* New York: Knopf, 1992.

Burnham, James. *The Struggle for the World.* London: J. Cape, 1947.

———. *The Coming Defeat of Communism.* New York: John Day, 1950.

———. *Containment or Liberation.* New York: John Day, 1953.

———, ed. *What Europe Thinks of America.* New York: John Day, 1953.

———. *The Web of Subversion: Underground Networks in the U.S. Government.* New York: John Day, 1954; rev. ed. 1959.

Burns, Richard Dean, ed. *Guide to American Foreign Relations since 1700.* Santa Barbara, CA: ABC-Clio, 1983.

Byrnes, James F. *Speaking Frankly.* New York: Harper & Brothers, 1947.

Callahan, David. *Dangerous Capabilities: Paul Nitze and the Cold War.* New York: Harper/Collins, 1990.

Chamberlain, William Henry. *Beyond Containment.* Chicago: Regnery, 1953.

———. *America's Second Crusade.* Chicago: Regnery, 1962.

Clifford, Clark. *Counsel to the President.* New York: Random House, 1991.

Combs, Jerold A. *American Diplomatic History.* Berkeley: University of California Press, 1983.

Cook, Fred. *The Nightmare Decade: The Life and Times of Joe McCarthy.* New York: Random House, 1971.

Cottrell, Robert. *Izzy: A Biography of I. F. Stone.* New Brunswick, NJ: Rutgers University Press, 1992.

Cumings, Bruce. " 'Revising Postrevisionism,' or the Poverty of Theory in Diplomatic History." *Diplomatic History* 17:4 (Fall 1993): 539–571.

Davis, Lynn E. *The Cold War Begins: Soviet-American Conflict over Eastern Europe.* Princeton, NJ: Princeton University Press, 1974.

Doenecke, Justus D. *The Literature of Isolationism: A Guide to Non-Interventionist Scholarship, 1930–1972.* Colorado Springs, CO: R. Myles, 1972.

———. *Not to the Swift: The Old Isolationists in the Cold War Era.* Lewisburg, PA: Bucknell University, 1979.

Donovan, Robert. *The Presidency of Harry S. Truman.* Vol. 1: *Conflict and Crisis.* Vol. 2: *The Tumultuous Years.* New York: Norton, 1977, 1982.

Drechsler, Karl. "Ursachen, Entstehung und Wesen des Kalten Krieges in der Historiographie der USA (Causes, origins and nature of the cold war in U.S. historiography)." In Drechsler, *Die USA: Zwischen Antihitlerkoalition und Kalten Krieg* (The USA: Between the anti-Hitler coalition and the cold war). Berlin: Akademie Verlag, 1985.

Dulles, Foster Rhea. *America's Rise to World Power.* New York: Harper, 1955.

Dulles, John Foster. *War or Peace.* New York: Macmillan Company, 1950.

Eisenhower, Dwight D. *The White House Years.* 2 vols. Garden City, NY: Doubleday, 1963–1965.

Feis, Herbert. *The Road to Pearl Harbor.* Princeton: Princeton University Press, 1950.

————. *The China Tangle: The American Effort in China from Pearl Harbor to the Marshall Mission.* Princeton, NJ: Princeton University Press, 1953.

————. *Churchill, Roosevelt, Stalin: The War They Waged and the Peace They Sought.* Princeton: Princeton University Press, 1957.

————. *Between Peace and War: The Potsdam Conference.* Princeton, NJ: Princeton University Press, 1960.

————. *Japan Subdued: The Atomic Bomb and the End of the War in the Pacific.* Princeton: Princeton University, 1961.

————. *Foreign Aid and Foreign Policy.* New York: St. Martin's, 1964.

————. *Contest over Japan.* New York: Norton, 1967.

————. *From Trust to Terror: The Onset of the Cold War, 1945–1950.* New York: Norton, 1970.

Ferrell, Robert H., ed. *The Eisenhower Diaries.* New York: Norton, 1981.

————. *Harry S. Truman: A Life.* Columbia: University of Missouri, 1994.

Gaddis, John Lewis. *The United States and the Origins of the Cold War, 1941–1947.* New York: Columbia University, 1972.

————. *Strategies of Containment: A Critical Appraisal of Post American National Security Policy.* New York: Oxford University, 1982.

————. "The Emerging Post-Revisionist Synthesis on the Origins of the Cold War" and "Responses." *Diplomatic History* 7 (Summer 1983): 171–204.

————. *The Long Peace: Inquiries into the History of the Cold War.* New York: Oxford University Press, 1987.

————. "The Tragedy of Cold War History." *Diplomatic History* 17:1 (Winter 1993): 1–16.

Gaddis, John Lewis, and Michael J. Hogan. "The New School of American Diplomatic History: An Exchange on the Corporatist Synthesis." *Diplomatic History* 10 (Fall 1986): 357–372.

Gardner, Lloyd C. *Architects of Illusion: Men and Ideas in American Foreign Policy, 1941–1949.* Chicago: Quadrangle, 1970.

Gellman, Barton. *Contending with Kennan: Toward a Philosophy of American Power.* New York: Praeger, 1984.

Goldwater, Barry. *Why Not Victory?* New York: McGraw-Hill, 1962.

Goodman, Elliot. *The Soviet Design for a World State.* New York: Columbia University Press, 1960.

Graebner, Norman A. *Cold War Diplomacy, 1945–1960.* New York: Van Nostrand, 1962.

Griffith, Robert. "The Old Progressives and the Cold War." *Journal of American History* 66:1 (September 1979): 334–347.

Haines, Gerald K. *A Reference Guide to United States Department of State Files.* Westport, CT: Greenwood Press, 1985.

Hamby, Alonzo. "Henry A. Wallace, Liberals, and Soviet-American Relations." *Review of Politics* 30:2 (1968): 153–169.

————. *Beyond the New Deal: Harry S. Truman and American Liberalism.* New York: Columbia University Press, 1973.

Harriman, W. Averill. *Special Envoy, 1941–1946.* New York: Random House, 1975.

Hixson, Walter H. *George F. Kennan: Cold War Iconoclast.* New York: Columbia University Press, 1989.

Hogan, Michael J. "Revival and Reform: America's Twentieth-Century Search for a New Economic Order." *Diplomatic History* 8 (Fall 1984): 287–310.

———. *The Marshall Plan: America, Britain, and the Reconstruction of Western Europe, 1947–1952.* New York: Cambridge University Press, 1987.

Hoopes, Townshend, and Douglas Brinkley. *The Life and Times of James Forrestal.* New York: Alfred Knopf, 1992.

Hutson, Susan Hoffman. *McCarthy and the Anti-Communist Crusade: A Selected Bibliography.* Political Issues Series 5:2. Los Angeles: California State University Press, 1979.

Jones, Howard, and Randall B. Woods. "Origins of the Cold War in Europe and the Near East." *Diplomatic History* 17:2 (Spring 1993): 251–276.

Kaplan, Lawrence. "The Cold War and European Revisionism." *Diplomatic History* 11 (Spring 1987): 143–156.

Kennan, George F. ("X"). "The Sources of Soviet Conduct." *Foreign Affairs* 25 (July 1947): 566–582.

———. *American Diplomacy, 1900–1950.* Chicago: University of Chicago Press, 1951.

———. *Realities of American Foreign Policy.* Princeton, NJ: Princeton University Press, 1954.

———. *Memoirs: 1925–1950 and 1950–1963.* Boston: Atlantic, Little, Brown, 1967, 1972.

———. *Around the Cragged Hill: A Personal and Political Philosophy.* New York: W. W. Norton, 1993.

Koen, Ross Y. *The China Lobby in American Politics.* New York: Harper & Row, 1974.

Kolko, Gabriel. *The Politics of Power: The World and United States Foreign Policy, 1943–1945.* New York: Random House, 1968.

Kolko, Joyce, and Gabriel. *The Limits of Power: The World and United States Foreign Policy, 1945–1954.* New York: Harper & Row, 1972.

Kozicki, Henry. *Western and Russian Historiography: Recent Views.* New York: St. Martin's Press, 1993.

Kubeck, Anthony. *How the Far East Was Lost: American Policy and the Creation of Communist China, 1941–1949.* Chicago: Regnery, 1963.

Kuklick, Bruce. *American Policy and the Division of Germany: The Clash with Russia over Reparations.* Ithaca, NY: Cornell University, 1972.

Kuniholm, Bruce. *The Origins of the Cold War in the Near East: Great Power Conflict and the Diplomacy in Iran, Turkey, and Greece.* Princeton: Princeton University Press, 1980.

LaFeber, Walter F. *America, Russia, and the Cold War, 1945–1975.* New York: Wiley, 1967.

Leffler, Melvyn P. *A Preponderance of Power: National Security, the Truman Administration, and the Cold War.* Stanford: Stanford University Press, 1992.

Lippmann, Walter. *U.S. Foreign Policy: Shield of the Republic.* Boston: Little, Brown, 1943.

———. *The Cold War.* Boston: Little, Brown, 1947.

———. *Isolation and Alliances.* Boston: Little, Brown, 1952.

Lundestad, Geir. *America, Scandinavia, and the Cold War, 1945–1949.* New York: Columbia University Press, 1980.

———. "Empire by Invitation? The United States and Western Europe, 1945–1952." *Journal of Peace Research* 23 (1986): 263–277.

————. "Moralism, Presentism, Exceptionalism, Provincialism, and Other Extravagances in American Writers on the Early Cold War." *Diplomatic History* 13 (Fall 1989): 527–546.

MacArthur, Douglas. *Reminiscences*. New York: McGraw-Hill, 1965.

McCormick, Thomas. *America's Half-Century*. Baltimore, MD: Johns Hopkins University Press, 1989.

————. "World Systems." *Journal of American History* 77:1 (June 1990): 125–132.

MacDougall, Curtis. *Gideon's Army*. New York: Marzani & Munsell, 1965.

McCullough, David. *Truman*. New York: Simon & Schuster, 1992.

McLellan, David S. *Dean Acheson: The State Department Years*. New York: Dodd, Mead, 1976.

McMahon, Robert J. "The Cold War in Asia: Toward a New Synthesis." *Diplomatic History* 12 (Summer 1988): 307–328.

McNeill, William Hardy. *America, Britain, and Russia: Their Cooperation and Conflict*. London: Oxford, 1953.

Maddox, Robert. *The New Left and the Origins of the Cold War*. Princeton, NJ: Princeton University Press, 1973.

————. "The Rise and Fall of Cold War Revisionism." *Historian* 46:3 (May 1984): 416–428.

Markowitz, Norman D. *The Rise and Fall of the People's Century: Henry A. Wallace and American Liberalism, 1941–1948*. New York: Free Press, 1973.

Mastny, Vojtech. *Russia's Road to the Cold War: Diplomacy, Warfare, and the Politics of Communism, 1941–1945*. New York: Columbia University Press, 1979.

Matusow, Allen J., ed. *Joseph R. McCarthy*. Englewood Cliffs, NJ: Prentice-Hall, 1970.

Mayer, David. *George Kennan and the Dilemmas of U.S. Foreign Policy*. New York: Oxford, 1988.

Melanson, Richard. "Revisionism Subdued? Robert James Maddox and the Origins of the Cold War." *Political Science Review* 7 (1977): 229–271.

————. *Writing History and Making Policy: The Cold War, Vietnam and Revisionism*. Lanham, MD: University Press of America, 1983.

Messer, Robert L. *The End of an Alliance: James F. Byrnes, Roosevelt, Truman and the Origins of the Cold War*. Chapel Hill: University of North Carolina Press, 1982.

Millis, Walter, ed. *The Forrestal Diaries*. New York: Viking, 1951.

Morganthau, Hans J. *Politics among Nations: The Struggle for Power and Peace*. New York: Knopf, 1948.

————. *In the Defense of the National Interest*. New York: Knopf, 1951.

Nash, George. *The Conservative Intellectuals in America since 1945*. New York: Basic Books, 1976.

Niebuhr, Reinhold. *The Irony of American History*. New York: Scribner's, 1952.

Nitze, Paul. *From Hiroshima to Glasnost: At the Center of Decision, a Memoir*. New York: Grove Weidenfeld, 1989.

Paterson, Thomas G., ed. *Cold War Critics: Alternatives to American Foreign Policy in the Truman Years*. Chicago: Quadrangle, 1971.

————. *Soviet-American Confrontation*. Baltimore: Johns Hopkins University Press, 1972.

Patterson, James T. *Mr. Republican: A Biography of Robert A. Taft*. Boston: Houghton Mifflin, 1972.

Peterson, F. Ross. *Prophet without Honor: Glen Taylor and the Fight for American Liberalism.* Lexington: University of Kentucky Press, 1974.

Pogue, Forrest C. *George C. Marshall.* Vol. 4: *Statesman, 1945–1959.* New York: Viking-Penguin, 1987.

Pratt, Julius. *A History of United States Foreign Policy.* Englewood Cliffs, NJ: Prentice-Hall, 1955, 2d ed. 1965.

Radosh, Ronald. *Prophets on the Right: Profiles of Conservative Critics of American Globalism.* New York: Simon & Schuster, 1975.

"Revelations from the Russian Archives." *IREX News in Brief* 3 (July–August 1992): 1, 4.

Rosenthal, Joel H. *Righteous Realists: Political Realism, Responsible Power, and American Culture in the Nuclear Age.* Baton Rouge: Louisana State University Press, 1991.

Russell, Greg. *Hans J. Morgenthau and the Ethics of American Statecraft.* Baton Rouge: Louisiana State University Press, 1990.

Saunders, Jack. "Records in the National Archives Relating to Korea, 1945–1950." In Bruce Cumings, ed., *Child of Conflict.* Seattle: WA: University of Washington Press, 1983.

Sherwin, Martin. *A World Destroyed: The Atomic Bomb and the Grand Alliance.* New York: Vintage, 1977.

Smith, Michael J. *Realist Thought from Weber to Kissinger.* Baton Rouge, LA: Lousiana State University Press, 1986.

Spanier, John. *American Foreign Policy since World War II.* New York: Praeger, 1960.

Steel, Ronald. *Walter Lippmann and the American Century.* Boston: Little, Brown, 1980.

Stone, Isadore F. *The Truman Years.* New York: Monthly Review Press, 1953.

Strauss, Lewis. *Men and Decisions.* Garden City, NY: Doubleday, 1962.

Strausz-Hupe, Robert, et al. *Protracted Conflict.* New York: Harper, 1959.

Taft, Robert A. *A Foreign Policy for Americans.* Garden City, NY: Doubleday, 1951.

Theoharis, Athan G. *The Yalta Myths.* Columbia: University of Missouri Press, 1970.

Truman, Harry S. *Memoirs.* 2 vols. New York: Putnam's, 1955–1956.

Tucker, Robert C. *Stalin in Power: The Revolution from Above, 1924–1941.* New York: Norton, 1990.

Unger, Irwin. "The 'New Left' and American History: Some Recent Trends in United States Historiography." *American Historical Review* 72 (July 1967): 1237–1263.

Vandenberg, Arthur H. Jr., ed. *The Private Papers of Senator Vandenberg.* Boston: Houghton Mifflin, 1952.

Volkogonov, Dimitri. *Stalin: Triumph and Tragedy.* Ed. and trans. Harold Shukman. New York: Grove Weidenfeld, 1991.

Walker, J. Samuel. *Henry A. Wallace and American Foreign Policy.* Westport, CT: Greenwood, 1972.

———. "Historians and Cold War Origins: The New Consensus." In *American Foreign Relations: A Historiographical Review.* Ed. Gerald K. Haines and J. Samuel Walker. Westport, CT: Greenwood, 1980.

Wallace, Henry A. *Toward World Peace.* New York: Reynal and Hitchcock, 1948.

———. *The Price of Vision: The Diary of Henry A. Wallace, 1942–1946.* Ed. John Morton Blum. Boston: Houghton Mifflin, 1973.

Wallerstein, Immanuel. *The Modern World-System: Capitalist Agriculture and the Origins of the European World Economy in the Sixteenth Century.* New York: Academic Press, 1974.

Walton, Richard J. *Henry Wallace, Harry Truman, and the Cold War.* New York: Viking, 1976.

Welch, Robert. *The New Americanism and Other Speeches and Essays.* Boston: Western Islands Publishers, 1966.

Wertenbaker, Charles, and Philip Horton. "The China Lobby." *Reporter,* April 15, 26, 1952, pp. 2–24, 5–24.

Williams, William Appleman. *The Tragedy of American Diplomacy.* Cleveland: World, 1959.

Wolfe, Bertram. *Communist Totalitarianism.* Boston: Beacon Press, 1961.

Yergin, Daniel. *Shattered Peace: The Origins of the Cold War and the National Security State.* Boston: MA: Houghton Mifflin, 1977.

3   United States Policy in Asia and Korea

Lester H. Brune

The cold war in Asia differed significantly from that in Europe. Although the rhetoric of American leaders often overlooked or blurred these differences, the confrontation between the Soviet Union and the United States in Europe differed from the start in 1945 because Germany surrendered in May while the Japanese held out until August. Furthermore, nothing in Europe matched the Chinese renewal of its civil war following the evacuation of Japanese troops, nor did Europe experience the anticolonial upsurge that Asian nationalists precipitated after 1945. Finally, the Korean War brought direct conflict between U.S. and communist forces, a situation avoided in Europe throughout the cold war. As Akira Iriye explains in "Was There a Cold War in Asia?" (1977) the gap between American policy perceptions of Asian circumstances and European conditions not only adversely influenced U.S. policy in Asia but is essential for understanding Asian developments.

Generally the literature about U.S. policy in Asia and Korea did not reflect Asia's differences from Europe until the Sino-Soviet conflict became apparent due to the Chinese-Soviet border conflicts of the late 1960s. In addition, the release of classified U.S. documents on the period from 1945 to 1950 clarified that the two communist powers never operated as a Soviet monolith against Washington and its allies. After 1970, therefore, historical literature on Asia shows two important differences between Asia and Europe. First, U.S. policy before and after World War II assumed that Europe was the most vital interest of the United States, with Asia and the Pacific having a secondary role, at best. The lesser role assigned to Asia by U.S. policymakers was a corollary of the fact that underdeveloped colonial areas were less critical than industrialized regions, a perception that led Washington usually to ignore the opposition of Asian nationalists to colonialism. Second, U.S. plans for postwar Asia became uncertain between 1945 and 1950, partly because President Franklin Roosevelt's trusteeship proposals for colonies had been abandoned at Yalta in February 1945 and partly because U.S. hopes for a resurgent, friendly China failed due to the dismal performance of China's nationalist government. This indefinite U.S. policy toward China and Japan also affected Washington's Korean policies after 1945.

Following a review of reference guides on U.S. policy in Asia and Korea, this chapter discusses the literature on U.S. policy as it evolved for Asia and the Pacific rim, regarding China and Japan, and as it developed for Korea from 1945 to 1950.

REFERENCES TO U.S. POLICY IN ASIA

All students of Asia should become familiar with the classic works written by A. Whitney Griswold, John K. Fairbank, and Edwin Reischauer, who pioneered the study of U.S.-Asian relations. An introduction to Griswold's work is Dorothy Borg's (1966) compilation of essays about his perspectives. A place to begin learning more about Fairbank and Reischauer is Akira Iriye's review (1988) of a Fairbank biography by Paul Evans (1988) and memoirs by Fairbank (1982) and Reischauer (1986).

Four general historiographic essays evaluating the traditional versions of America's postwar Asian policy are in Ernest May and James C. Thomson's volume (1972): Peter W. Stanley on the Philippines, Jim Peck on "America and the Chinese Revolution," Robert Dalleck on "The Truman Era," and Morton Halperin on "The Eisenhower Era." The article by D. C. Watt in Yonosuke Nagai and Akira Iriye's *The Origins of the Cold War in Asia* (1977) provides a British scholar's view on U.S. policy. G. Raymond Nunn (1980) has a select guide to Asian reference works, and Nunn and associates (1985) have a selected, annotated guide to studies about Asia and Oceania. Robert McMahon's "Toward a Post-colonial Order" (1989) has valuable footnotes on Asia's colonial issues. Mac Marshall and James Nelson (1975) have a bibliography of source materials on Micronesia; and *The United States in East Asia* (1984) abstracts over 1,000 articles published between 1973 and 1984.

Chinese bibliographies of value to scholars are Tsien Tsuen-hsuin and James Cheng's bibliography of bibliographies (1978) and University Microfilms' regular editions of doctoral dissertations on Asia, which Frank Shulman (1975) edited originally. Articles by Michael Hunt (1992) and Steven Goldstein and He Di (1992) identify Chinese sources for research. An article by Mingde Tsou and Li Jun (1991) explains the attitudes of Chinese scholars regarding American relations. Charles Lilley (1994) reviews five recent books on U.S.-Chinese relations. For literature on U.S. policy in the 1940s see the bibliographies in William Stueck's (1984) book on Albert Wedemeyer and the article by Kenneth Young (1975).

Four notable articles give broad coverage of U.S. relations in the Pacific rim. Akira Iriye's essay (1984) deals with American expansion after 1945. One of Robert J. McMahon's articles (1988) seeks a possible synthesis of recent studies about U.S. policy in Asia; a second article (1986) argues that President Eisenhower's Third World policies were unsatisfactory. Fourth, Judith Munro-Leighton's essay (1992) explains the "postrevisionist" interpretations of U.S.-Asian diplomacy.

Although Japan's role in the Korean War may have been slight, the U.S. occupation of Japan was a critical part of its East Asian program. Delmer Brown's (1949) article appeared before the Korean War but describes documents the Japanese submitted to occupation authorities that were later deposited in the U.S. National Archives. In 1974, Robert Ward and Frank Schulman published a valuable, annotated bibliography on the Allied occupation of Japan. Sadao Asada has two worthwhile publications: an article (1981) on the U.S. occupation and a lengthy bibliography (1989), which is translated from a 1979 Japanese-language work and expanded to include studies not in the original. Asada's latter work (1989) includes an article on the occupation by Iokibe Makoto and associates. Important articles about the United States as Japan's occupation authority include two by Ray Moore (1979, 1981), and those of Carol Gluck (1983) and Akira Iriye (1988). John Dower (1975) emphasizes Japanese and American records available for scholars; Benedict Zobrist (1978) describes sources in U.S. presidential libraries.

Regarding the study of U.S. policy in Korea, the changes in the literature since 1970 are evident by contrasting Richard Leopold's article in Francis Heller's *The Korean War—A 25 Year Perspective* (1977) with John Wiltz's essay in William J. Williams's *A Revolutionary War* (1993). Based on a 1975 conference, Leopold indicates that the Vietnam War led historians to neglect the Korean War and urges greater research on it. For a 1992 conference, Wiltz's traditionalist memories of the Korean War cause him to dispute the revisionist studies of the Korean War since 1975, although he acknowledges the significant changes reflected in such works as those by Bruce Cumings (1981, 1990). Robert Swarthout (1979) compares traditional views about the outbreak of the war with several "revised" versions of the war's beginning. An excellent analysis of recent studies on U.S.-Korean relations is given by Rosemary Foot (1991).

Three important essays describe diverse aspects of U.S.-Korean research. Jack Saunder's description of the U.S. National Archives records on Korea appears in Bruce Cumings' *Child of Conflict* (1983) and is indispensable to research scholars. William Stueck's essay (1986) discusses the international aspects of the Korean War. Finally, Hak-joon Kim's essay in James Cotton and Ian Neary's volume (1989) describes both traditional and revisionist accounts of China's role in the origins of the Korean War. Keith

D. McFarland (1986) has an excellent annotated bibliography on the Korean War. An older but useful bibliography is by Carroll Blanchard (1964).

America's Asian-Pacific Policies to 1950

Although U.S. policy sometimes looked toward Asia at the beginning of the twentieth century, the nation's historic ties with Europe overwhelmed the desires of U.S. leaders who considered giving Asia priority in foreign affairs. During the 1890s, Alfred Thayer Mahan's seapower theories influenced U.S. Navy leaders and some U.S. business interests to envision U.S. control of the Pacific Ocean as the best means to consolidate American power. Mahan's ideas were spelled out in *The Influence of Seapower upon History* (1890), and in other works, such as *Lessons of the War with Spain* (1899) he issued propaganda to stimulate the myth of the China market described by Thomas McCormick's (1963) study.

As president from 1901 to 1909, Theodore Roosevelt advocated a larger navy, but as Raymond Esthus (1967) indicates, he wanted better relations with Great Britain and Japan to counteract the Russia czar's eastward expansion. Subsequently, although Outten Clinard's (1947) and William Braisted's (1958) studies of naval policy show the U.S. Navy's General Board considered Japan as the nation's "most probable enemy" as early as 1907, neither U.S. presidents nor the State Department supported the board's Orange (Japanese) War Plans either before or after World War I.

Details about the clash between the Joint Board of the Army and Navy's Orange Plans and the State Department's "Europe First" policies are given in Lester H. Brune's *The Origins of American National Security Policy, 1900 to 1941* (1981). Particular aspects of the president's and State Department's preference for a Europe First strategy are explained in Harold and Margaret Sprout's (1943, 1946) books on the Washington Naval Treaties of 1922 and Martin Weil's study of the State Department's Europeanists' perspective in *A Pretty Good Club* (1978). Two books that cover the 1922 Washington treaties from different perspectives are by Thomas H. Buckley (1970), who blames U.S. diplomats for the treaties' inadequacies, and Roger Dingman (1976), who concludes that domestic politics determined the Washington Conference's outcome. Chapter 3 of Robert D. Schulzinger's *The Making of the Diplomatic Mind* (1975) also describes the Europeanists.

Eventually, after 1937, President Franklin Roosevelt nudged the Joint Board of the Army and Navy to adopt five, flexible Rainbow War Plans, a tactic leading the board to adopt a Germany First strategy in late 1940. These developments are detailed in Brune's study (1981) and in Louis Morton's "Germany First" (1960). Roosevelt's insistence on this strategy during World War II is illustrated in Mark Stoler's essay, "The Pacific First Alternative in American World War II Strategy" (1980). Edward Miller provides many details in *War Plan Orange* (1991), indicating it remained the basis of the navy's Pacific war strategy after 1941.

Both Iriye's essay, "Was There a Cold War in Asia?" (1977), and Fred Harrington's article, " 'Europe First' and Its Consequences for the Far Eastern Policy of the United States" (1986), find that the Eurocentric primacy of U.S. policy made Franklin Roosevelt reluctant to impose anticolonial policies on Britain and France and influenced him to want a strong, friendly China to replace Japan as the principal Asian power after World War II.

According to Michael Schaller's study (1979), however, the failure of the Chinese nationalist government to act effectively against Japanese forces caused a dispute among Roosevelt's advisers about the wisdom of supporting the nationalists in 1944. These Chinese problems are explained later, but from 1944 until the Korean War began, U.S. plans for a proper Asian policy were never decisive. As Thomas Paterson (1981) explains, when President Truman advocated aid to Europe against communists in 1947, the Asia First interests who favored Jiang Jieshi (Chiang Kai-shek) asked, "If Europe, why not China?" The candid answer, which neither Truman nor Secretary of State George Marshall could publicly state, was that Truman's advisers differed about what to do in China, a controversy in which members of Congress also engaged. This controversy is described in Robert McGlothen's essay (1989) and book (1993) on Acheson's problems in forming a Korean policy and in Robert Blum's *Drawing the Line* (1982), as well as in later chapter references on China and the U.S. Congress.

Asia-Pacific Region: Colonialism and Nationalism

Unlike Europe, where World War I established national boundaries following the defeat of the German, Austrian, and Ottoman empires and the communist victory over the Russian czar's empire, Asia remained under Western European and American imperial control from 1919 through 1945. Japan's attempt to create an Asian empire was thwarted by World War II, but British, French, Dutch, and American imperial ambitions played a critical role in the origins of Asia's "cold war."

Although American leaders gave Asia less importance than Europe, there were American interests in the Pacific area before and after 1941. As Gary Hess' essay in Akira Iriye and Warren Cohen (1992) indicates, the United States had valuable trade in Southeast Asia before 1941. Following World War II, Washington's problem was to define exactly what those U.S. interests required. Lester Foltos (1989) shows that the Joint Chiefs of Staff agreed with the U.S. Navy that the United States should take over Japan's mandated islands in the Pacific, and according to Leonard Gordon (1968), Washington strategists also wanted Taiwan as a strategically important island.

During World War II's summit conferences, Roosevelt persuaded Britain and the Soviet Union to give the United States control of the Japanese mandates, but he could not convince Winston Churchill to accept the demise of European colonies in Asia. As Christopher Thorne (1978) explains, British and U.S. delegates often neared a breaking point over the colonial issue. Subsequently, Walter LaFeber (1975) says, Roosevelt agreed that the Asian colonies would become trusteeships only if their European owners volunteered.

Several general works on the Pacific Islands are worth studying. C. Hartley Grattan (1963) has a historical overview of the islands, while Douglas L. Oliver (1951) provides an anthropological perspective. Julius Pratt (1950) gives a traditional version of U.S. idealism in its "colonial experiment," but Whitney Perkins (1962) questions American motives in claiming to have no imperial ambitions.

Actually, European friends of the United States were often befuddled by the inconsistent stand of American politicians on colonies. Matthew Kust (1958) demonstrates that Americans used moralistic or idealistic sentiments to hide their realistic political and strategic desires. Robert Good (1959) asserts more bluntly that Washington's deceptive rhetoric about imperialism greatly irritated European allies who knew that U.S. leaders sought virtual colonial control over the Asian-Pacific region. The difference was that Americans tended to define imperialism only as political control, while Europeans, and some American scholars, claimed that economic dominance was also a form of colonialism. Favoring the latter perspective, Gabriel Kolko (1988) concludes that the U.S. leaders feared communism and favored the business interests so much that they never made the right choices about the Third World.

Most research on World War II diplomacy indicates that neither Roosevelt nor Churchill prepared policies to fit the strong Asian nationalism that opposed both colonialism and foreign economic imperialism. The significant studies dealing with Asian nationalism are by Hugh Tinker (1964), Selig Harrison (1978), and the essays in *Remaking Asia* edited by Mark Selden (1974). The Selden essays are especially valuable because the authors raise questions about such U.S. interests as "oil imperialism" in Southeast Asia, the use of the International Monetary Fund to create U.S. dependencies, and the connection between American financial interests and the Central Intelligence Agency.

For U.S. policymakers, the issue of Asian nationalism became even more complicated because of its relationship to communism. Although Frank Traeger (1959) gives a traditional view of the Marxian threat in Asia, Neil MacFarlane's study (1985) examines the complex mix of ideas contained in Third World radicalism, concluding that although it resembled com munist theory, it was strongly nationalistic because Asia's national leaders wanted to preserve their region's distinctive cultures. These Asian desires often clashed with Moscow's interests, a factor that Washington usually neglected. Rather, President Truman, Senator Joseph McCarthy, and others in the United States used simplistic but popular rhetoric about defending "freedom from communist tyranny," a situation Athan Theoharis (1971) explores. Other studies referring to the U.S. notion that Asian nationalism was a communist conspiracy are by Gary Hess (1987) and Robert McMahon (1989), who both emphasize U.S. misperceptions about Asian reality.

One particular issue influencing research on Asian nationalism was the "Great Asian Conspiracy." During the 1950s, some U.S. scholars contended that Moscow's monolithic control over Asia's communist rebellions had been accepted during two left-wing conferences held in Calcutta during 1948. According to writers such as Walt W. Rostow (1954), A. Doak Barnett (1961), and Frank Traeger (1959), the Calcutta sessions were directed by Moscow's newly created Cominform (Communist Information Bureau), which ordered Asian delegates to begin rebellions. Subsequently, when uprisings began in Malaya, Burma, Indochina, Indonesia, the Philippine Islands, and eventually Korea, the conspiracy theory appeared to be validated.

These monolithic, Moscow-directed conspiracy plans blended with the simplified rhetoric of freedom versus communism as a popular notion in the United States despite the fact that other Asian experts refuted the conspiracy concept. The opponents of the conspiracy theory included Ruth T. McVey (1958), who wrote a detailed work on the Calcutta conference; Charles McLane (1966); Isaac Deutscher (1966); and John H. Kautsky (1956). Two later essays that reviewed the literature and rejected the "great conspiracy" theory are by John Gittings in Edward Friedman and Mark Selden's *America's Asia* (1969) and Tangawa Yoshihiko in Nagai and Iriye's volume (1977). Nevertheless, from 1948 to the 1970s, the conspiracy theory was widely accepted in the United States to justify the domino theory that Presidents Eisenhower, Kennedy, and Johnson used to explain their Vietnam intervention. Against this broad background of these U.S. views about Asian nationalism and communist influence, Washington's growing interests in specific regions of the Asia–Pacific rim can be better understood.

The Central Pacific Islands: Micronesia Trusteeship. The United States' acquisition of the Micronesia Trusteeship has been the least questioned and least studied aspect of American imperialism since 1945. The United States had acquired the Pacific islands of Midway, Guam, Samoa, Hawaii, and the Philippines before 1914 but after World War I accepted Japan's control of the Marshall, Solomon, and Caroline Island groups under a League of Nations mandate (Yanihara 1940, 1977).

After 1945, American military planners wanted and the United States received control of these former Japanese mandates as well as Okinawa, whose strategic value is explained by Hyman Kublin (1954). Robert Robbins (1947) describes the U.S. view of the trusteeship in 1945. The U.S. Joint Chiefs also sought control of Taiwan, as Joseph Ballantine (1952) and Leonard Gordon (1968) explain, but this island became the headquarters of the Chinese nationalist government when it fled from the Chinese communists in 1949. Ralph Braibanti (1954) indicates that Okinawa was occupied by U.S. forces in April 1945; in 1969, the United States agreed to return it to Japan while retaining U.S. bases under terms of the U.S.-Japan Treaty of 1951.

Micronesia became a U.S. trusteeship in 1947, but research literature on these central Pacific islands is relatively scarce. Early accounts of the U.S. takeover include Earl Pomeroy's study (1951) of the strategic value of the islands and Walter Karig's more romantic view, *The Fortunate Islands* (1948). There are interesting general studies of the islands by John W. Coulter (1957), who sees native culture as impeding progress, and Herold J. Wiens (1962), as well as David Nevin's critical account of U.S. policy in *The American Touch in Micronesia* (1977). Earl Ellis (1992) describes Micronesia as a U.S. Marine Corps base of operations.

As seen in the hearings of a U.S. Congress, House of Representatives subcommittee in 1971, the islanders questioned U.S. control of the islands, and native independence movements sought to change their relationship with America. By the end of 1986, the Marshall Islands and the Federated States of Micronesia had formed their own governments, although the people on the islands of Palua and the Northern Marianas voted for a commonwealth status, similar to Puerto Rico. Nevertheless, all of these islands remained dependent on U.S. economic aid, for which they sanctioned U.S. military bases on their soil.

Information on these developments, which aid in understanding the post-1945 events in Asia, may be found in the following studies: Felix Moos et al. (1981) on the United States and Japan in the Pacific; James H. Webb (1974) on U.S. strategies and Micronesia; and Sue R. Roff (1991) on U.S. policy since 1945.

The Philippines and Southeast Asia. Studies that deal with the dilemma of U.S. colonial policy in this region are by Robert McMahon (1981), who emphasizes Indonesia; Russell Buhite's *Soviet-American Relations in Asia* (1981); and Gary Hess (1987) on Southeast Asia. The problems between the United States and Great Britain in Asia are described by John Sbrega (1983b) and by historians writing in *Imperialism at Bay*, edited by William R. Louis (1978). In addition to McMahon's study on Indonesia (1981), Stanley Hornbeck (1948) has a contemporary account of the Netherlands' problems in these islands, which may be compared with the study by Gerlof Homan (1984).

Regarding the Philippine Islands since 1945, the United States retained much indirect control until the late 1980s. The islands obtained independence in 1946, but as William Pomeroy's essay in Selden's *Remaking Asia* (1971) indicates, the Philippines exemplified a new type of colonial control because they depended on U.S. aid and accepted U.S. military bases. Notable studies on the U.S.-Philippine history are by Stanley Karnow (1989), David Wurfel (1988), Stephen Shalom (1981), and H. W. Brands (1992). Douglas MacDonald (1992) includes a case study of U.S. intervention during the communist uprising in the Philippines from 1950 to 1953. Nick Cullather's article (1993a) and book (1993b) argue that U.S. business interests in the Philippines did not play the dominant role that other authors assume. The U.S. strategic interest was vital.

Details regarding the American role in fighting the communist threat in the Philippines during the Korean War era may be found in serveral sources. Claude Buss (1977) gives a general background of the American role after the Philippines gained independence in 1946. David Wurfel (1966) describes the talks between U.S. and Philippine representatives when Washington sought to keep order in this islands. Richard E. Welch, Jr. (1984), and Dennis Merrill (1993) explain the Philippines' dependency relationship with the United States that was devised between 1946 and 1953. And Roger Dingman (1986) relates Philippine problems to the 1951 peace treaty negotiations with Japan.

Because of the extensive literature on U.S. policy in Southeast Asia, the selected few works cited are those that relate to the Korean War. From the perspective of new interpretations of the 1980s, two important books are Lloyd Gardner's *Approaching Vietnam* (1988) and Gabriel Kolko's *Anatomy of a War* (1985). Gardner gives a broad overview of U.S. policymaking from 1945 to 1954, while Kolko develops insight into the Vietnam conflict from the perspective of the Asian people. A third study, by Ralph B. Smith (1984), gives an international view of the Indochina events.

French relations influenced U.S. policy in Asia because France hoped to retain its Indochina colony. Two valuable studies on U.S.-French relations from 1945 to 1954 are those of Ronald E. Irving (1975) and Irwin M. Wall (1991). Specific articles that should be consulted are George Herring's (1977) account of Truman's policy in restoring French sovereignty in Indochina and Gary Hess' (1978) study of why the United States recognized the French-appointed regime of Bao Dai early in 1950.

UNITED STATES–CHINESE RELATIONS

During World War II, President Roosevelt's decolonization plans for Asia had been thwarted by Winston Churchill, and his hopes for a strong, friendly Chinese ally had disintegrated. Throughout 1944, Roosevelt faced critical decisions on China because his advisers disagreed about the Chinese nationalist government's competence in fighting the Japanese. Roosevelt finally decided to support Jiang Jieshi, the nationalist leader, without demanding that he make government reforms, a choice that started U.S. policy down the slippery slope that later led Jiang's friends to claim that the United States had "lost China" to the communists in 1949.

The 1944 dispute placed Jiang Jieshi's apologists on one side and both General Joseph W. Stilwell and U.S. State Department experts in China on the side that demanded changes in the nationalist government. Stilwell, who represented the U.S. Army in China, had become increasingly upset by Jiang's refusal to replace the elite landlord groups controlling the Guomindang (GMD for Kuomintang) with anticommunist moderates who could clean up the GMD's corruption, fight the Japanese more effectively, and carry out land reform that would attract the support of peasants who had been rallying to Mao Zedong's (Mao Tse-tung) communist party. Stilwell's reform proposals had been stymied because pro-Jiang groups in America, led by Alfred Kohlberg and Henry Luce's *Time-Life* publications, had persuaded many U.S. congressmen and the U.S. public to give heroic stature to Jiang and his "valiant" government officials. Consequently, Roosevelt supported Jiang by recalling Stilwell and appointing Patrick J. Hurley as his special representative to China.

Hurley became an ardent admirer of Jiang. During Hurley's year in China, World War II ended and the Japanese were expelled; Joseph Stalin signed a treaty with Jiang; the United States turned over many Japanese weapons to Jiang's army and continued to send lend-lease assistance to the nationalists; and the U.S. Navy carried Jiang's troops to reoccupy northern China before the communists could get there. When Hurley returned to United States in September 1946, he believed Jiang was in charge and that all was calm in China.

Hurley was mistaken. By November, the State Department learned that Stalin had broken his promises to Jiang by helping the Chinese communists to take over Manchuria and that the truce arrangements Hurley negotiated between Jiang and Mao Zedong had not worked. Most mysterious, however, Hurley resigned his position rather than return to China, and he issued statements that blamed China's problems on U.S. State Department and foreign service officials. Hurley's biographer, Russell Buhite (1973), cannot explain why Hurley acted as he did in the fall of 1946, but his actions corresponded to the China Lobby's claims that American diplomats, not Jiang, were to be blamed for the Chinese nationalists' problems.

President Harry S. Truman dispatched General George Marshall to China in December 1946 and in July 1947 sent General Albert Wedemeyer. Neither of these representatives secured Jiang's full cooperation in trying to obtain a compromise solution to the Chinese civil war. Marshall thought he had nearly achieved peace negotiations when Jiang ordered a new offensive against the communists that spoiled Marshall's plans. Next, Wedemeyer spent six weeks in China, where he became an ardent admirer of Jiang, who convinced Wedemeyer that the Soviet Union wanted to control all of Asia. Wedemeyer also said that Jiang would make "sweeping reforms" if the United States gave him the huge amounts of military and economic aid he wanted.

U.S. State Department officials had heard Jiang's promises of reform many times since 1927, promises Jiang had never fulfilled. In 1947, however, the United States could no longer afford misused funds because they were needed to rebuild Europe's economy. Consequently, Truman rejected Wedemeyer's request for extensive aid to China, a decision that the China Lobby roundly criticized. Unfortunately, perhaps, the State Department waited until August 1949 to explain this decision in a White Paper that provided details about past U.S. relations with Jiang.

The Hurley, Marshall, and Wedemeyer missions to China complicated the situation. After the United States persuaded the Soviet Union to sign the Friendship Treaty with Jiang and Japanese forces withdrew in 1945, the Chinese nationalist government had every chance to succeed. But Jiang refused to reform his government or to broaden his elite base of power by adopting policies to enlist peasant approval. Consequently, Mao's peasant backing grew stronger, the civil war began again in 1946, and the Chinese nationalist fortunes steadily disintegrated.

From 1946 to 1949, Mao Zedong became popular with more Chinese, while Jiang's forces could defend only large city strongholds. Often using arms purchased from Jiang's corrupt officials, the communist armies extended their control over more and more parts of China. Although the United States gave Jiang another $400 million in 1948, the nationalist forces surrendered more quickly than anyone expected. By July 1949, Jiang was withdrawing to the offshore island of Formosa (Taiwan), where he continued the Chinese nationalist regime. On October 1, 1949, Mao Zedong established the People's Republic of China (PRC). Although there were some indications that the United States and the PRC might establish diplomatic relations in 1949, this possibility never materialized, and, with the outbreak of the Korean War in 1950, the two nations began a twenty-year period of nonrecognition while Jiang's nationalist government gained U.S. support in retaining his regime's permanent seat on the United Nations Security Council. (Also see Chapter 10.)

Literature on U.S.-China Relations

The literature on U.S.-Chinese relations written between 1949 and 1970 usually accepted the premise that the Soviet Union sought to expand its control over all of Asia after 1945. From this assumption, the principal difference of interpretative writing focused on why the United States and

Jiang's nationalist government did not prevent the communist victory in China. The most prominent group of early writers expressed the pro-Jiang views of the China Lobby, which blamed Truman and "communists" in the Democratic administration for "losing China." The second group opposed Jiang's regime and contended that the United States should have accommodated Mao as the leader of nationalistic Chinese who might work with the United States to benefit all Chinese. Finally, a group of moderate authors rejected the notion that disloyal Washington officials caused the China debacle but blamed the State Department's misperceptions of Asia and its well-intended but mistaken policies for allowing Mao to succeed.

The events of 1949 in China raised controversy about all aspects of U.S. relations with China from 1941 to 1949, beginning especially with the Stilwell-Jiang dispute of 1944. Stilwell's side of this issue is found in material published by Stilwell (1948, 1976) and in Barbara Tuchman's (1972) sympathetic analysis. The military aspects of Stilwell's concerns are described in the official U.S. Army histories by Charles Romanus and Riley Sunderland (1953, 1956). Jiang's wartime methods of preserving his own forces while sacrificing those of rival commanders are described by Riley Sunderland (1960) and Warren I. Cohen (1967). The tactics that *Time* publisher Henry Luce used to alter correspondent Theodore White's first-hand accounts of Jiang's corrupt government are described by Theodore White (1946, 1978) and illustrated by Harold Isaacs in *Images of Asia* (1962). Additional information on Luce's influence in America are described by Patricia Neils (1990) and T. Christopher Jespersen (1992).

The viewpoints of Jiang's proponents against Stilwell's reformers are presented by one of Jiang's officials, Chin-tung Liang (1972). In addition, there was extensive pro-Jiang literature published in the United States. The most prominent works were by Freda Utley (1952); Claire Chennault (1949), who was the leader of the Flying Tigers aviation unit in China; and John T. Flynn (1951). Anthony Kubeck's book, *How the Far East Was Lost* (1963), became the standard work that blamed "incompetent" Democratic party leaders and "treasonous" State Department bureaucrats for "losing" China. Jiang Jieshi's memoir (1957) claims the Americans caused his demise because they believed the communists' propaganda. Liang's (1977) essay blames the United States for its inept formulation of Stalin's 1946 Treaty, which Jiang signed.

The activity of Hurley, Marshall, and Wedemeyer became as controversial as Stilwell's wartime efforts. Don Lohbeck's (1956) authorized biography describes Hurley's strong antagonism toward Stilwell, while Russell Buhite (1973) has a balanced account of Hurley's strengths and weaknesses. John R. Beal (1970) gives a journalistic account of Marshall's mission, Forrest C. Pogue's fourth volume of Marshall's biography (1987) has a valuable balanced account of the mission, and John F. Melby (1968) offers the interesting diary of a foreign service officer who accompanied both Marshall and Wedemeyer. Ernest R. May (1975) describes Truman's China policy down to the end of the Marshall mission. General Wedemeyer's memoirs (1958) reveal his strong anticommunist position about U.S. policy. William Stueck's *The Wedemeyer Mission* (1984) is critical of the general for becoming strongly partisan in criticizing the Truman administration's policy.

In contrast to the pro-Jiang views of the China Lobby, early literature condemning the nationalist regime expressed the attitudes of those who, like Stilwell, wanted to stop backing Jiang in 1944 if he did not reform his regime. The perspective of this group of traditional authors is emphasized in Robert Dalleck's essay in Ernest May and James Thomson (1972). This group believed that U.S. policymakers should have realized that the Chinese Communist party was, in fact, not dependent on Moscow but representative of the real future of China's economic and political order. They thought that the Chinese did not want to be dominated by either Moscow or Washington but required help to improve their society. Authors in this group include Owen Lattimore (1949), Derk Bodde (1950), John K. Fairbank (1946), and Edwin Reischauer (1950b). Warren I. Cohen's two articles on the Chinese communists (1967) describe the divergent interest between the Chinese and Russian communists. Before 1970, however, this anti-Jiang group was no match for the influential China Lobby described by Roos Koen (1974), Stanley Bachrach (1976), and Joseph Keeley (1969). In fact, the pro-Jiang faction in America delayed the publication of Koen's book, *The China Lobby*, for ten years, a situation Koen describes (1969).

The China Lobby was especially effective in attacking U.S., officials and observers in China whose wartime reports to Washington described the peasant uprisings against their Chinese landlords who either lived abroad or were the Chinese elite. Among the journalists who reported about the peasants' plight and who knew China first-hand were Jack Belden (1949), Edgar Snow (1939, 1957), Graham Peck (1950), and Theodore White (1946). State Department representatives to China who made similar reports on China's indigenous problems included John Carter Vincent, whose career Gary May (1979) describes, O. Edmund Clubb (1974), Owen Lattimore (1949, 1950), John Melby (1968), John Leighton Stuart (1954, 1981), and John S. Service (1971). These reports influenced some members of the Truman administration because their stories disclosed the reality that challenged the romanticized picture of China spread by missionaries, Henry Luce's publications, and U.S. businessmen in China.

These reporters and officials were denounced by the China Lobby as "pro-communist" or as misrepresenting the communists as "agrarian reformers." Their fate was to be branded by the China Lobby and Joseph McCarthy as un-American or communist "spies," a charge that ruined the careers and lives of many Chinese experts in the State Department. Ely J.

Kahn (1975) describes the fate of these "old China hands." For information about particular members of this group, see Robert Newman's article (1983) and book (1992) on Lattimore; Gary May's book on Vincent (1979); and Jerry Israel's article on Snow (1978). Views of the State Department experts are contained in the State Department's *China White Paper* (1949), which sought to explain U.S. policy. Robert Newman (1982) indicates, however, that the American public's reaction to the *White Paper* boomeranged because few people read the lengthy report, but many believed the China Lobby's pedestrian criticism of Secretary of State Acheson as the "Red Dean."

Third, the moderate version of U.S. policy is expressed in the works of Walter Lippmann (1950), Tang Tsou (1963), and Herbert Feis (1953). Tang Tsou agrees with Stilwell's desire for reform but argues that the United States did not do enough to promote these reforms either on or off the Chinese civil war battlefield. His interpretation also complements Feis' belief that the United States should have instituted fundamental economic and social reforms but did not apply its power to do so. Both of these moderate works reflect the idealistic concept that the United States could change the world by taking proper actions, a notion that Jonathan Spence (1969) describes as an arrogant idea shared by Stilwell and others who believed the U.S. mission was to democratize the world. David McLean (1986) describes this concept as one of the myths Americans had regarding Asia and other underdeveloped regions of the world.

Revisionist Studies of U.S.-China Relations

Since the 1960s, revisionist literature has largely rejected the China Lobby's interpretation but found some validity in the work of moderate scholars who criticized U.S. errors and misperceptions regarding China. The anti-Jiang group of earlier writers fared best with the revisionists because the U.S. State Department's declassified documents disclosed the complexities of the China situation faced by the Truman administration, as well as the full reports of the U.S. diplomats in China and their reception in Washington. Approached from an affirmative perspective, research during the years since 1970 emphasizes that the Soviet Union did not control Mao's policies, that the U.S. State Department gave greater consideration to the possibility of recognizing Mao's government than realized, and that events in the Far East demonstrated America's cold war disputes with the Soviet Union as early in Asia as in Europe.

Sino-Soviet Relations: The "Lost Chance". The traditionalist authors' accepted premise that the Soviet Union dominated Chinese communist activity was first disputed by research scholars during the 1960s, about the same time that Sino-Soviet relations clearly became antagonistic. Works by Adam Ulam (1968) and Charles B. McLane (1966) indicate that the

U.S.S.R.'s principal East Asian objectives in 1945 were to gain influence in Manchuria and to have a weak Chinese nationalist government along its southern border. This seemed to be confirmed in Raymond Garthoff's (1966) article, "Soviet Intervention in Manchuria," and in Edmund Clubb's essay (1957). The Chinese Communist Party's independence from Russia is definitely shown in the studies of James Reardon-Anderson (1980) and the Chinese scholar Jun Niu (1992). For a summary review of Niu's work, see Qiang Zhai (1992).

Mao's independence from Moscow's control led scholars to ask whether Mao might have accommodated U.S. interests in 1949 rather than the Soviets'. Both U.S. documents and recent memoirs of Chinese communist officials indicate there was some chance for Sino-U.S. rapprochement, and State Department materials revealed that U.S. officials pursued this possibility more than previous scholars expected. The State Department documents for 1949–1950 indicate that Washington not only realized Mao's capacity for independent action but gave serious consideration to dividing Moscow and Beijing by recognizing and possibly giving economic aid to the PRC.

By 1980, U.S. Sinologists discussed the concept of the "lost chance" in China to dramatize the possible opening to China sought by Secretary of State Acheson and other U.S. officials between late 1948 and the beginning of the Korean War. The chance for better U.S.-Chinese communist relations between 1941 and 1946 is examined in Okabe Taksumi's essay in Nagai and Iriye's volume (1977). Taksumi indicates that during World War II, the Chinese Communist party (CCP) joined "democratic forces" in fighting the fascist states, making the Japanese a common enemy and creating an opening for improved CCP-U.S. relations. Details of this view are given in Warren Cohen's two articles (1967) on the CCP before and during World War II, as well as in an essay by Donald Zagoria (1974). The wartime reports of John S. Service edited by Joseph W. Esherick (1974) also indicate that accommodation was a possibility. Kenneth Chern's (1980) study describes the U.S. policy debate of 1945, which considered a deal with the CCP that was rejected because of America's anticommunist attitudes. Barbara Tuchman (1972) has an interesting article regarding Mao Zedong's possible visit to Washington in 1945. Jun Niu (1992) writes that Mao was impressed with General Marshall's willingness to compromise in 1946 until Jiang launched his new offensive. At the same time, Odd Arne Westad (1993) finds U.S.-Soviet rivalry in China beginning in 1946 with the renewal of the Chinese civil war.

The possibility of improved U.S.-CCP relations after 1945 led to further research on the "lost chance" for a Chinese communist recognition agreement in 1949. In Dorothy Borg and Waldo Heinrichs's *Uncertain Years* (1980), Warren I. Cohen, Michael Hunt, Steven Goldstein, and Steven Levine each adopt different perspectives to examine the evidence for the 1949 "chance" that the United States would recognize Mao's government. They believe Secretary of State Acheson seriously sought some means for agreement before the Korean War closed all channels. To the contrary, however, Cohen's (1978, 1981, 1987) reports of his interviews with officials concluded that there was "little chance" for a U.S.-PRC accord in 1949–1950. He talked with two American officials from the 1949 era and with Chinese associates of Zhou Enlai (Chou Enlai), the foreign minister of the PRC in 1949, who revealed there was hardly any chance for a Sino-American détente before the Korean War.

Other scholars also deny there was any real possibility for the "lost chance" theory to be valid. Robert Blum (1982) indicates Acheson had no consistent policy that favored recognition, and William Stueck (1981) concludes that neither Acheson nor China's representative, Huang Hua, wanted to establish better relations. Nancy Tucker (1983) blames the China Lobby for making it impossible for the Truman administration to seek good relations with Mao. David McLean (1986) argues that American myths about its special relationship with China's "democratic" people caused many Americans to believe that a Soviet conspiracy, assisted by bureaucrats in Washington, enabled Mao to win China. Significantly, whatever the chance was for Washington to recognize the PRC in 1949–1950, researchers such as David Mayer (1986) substantiate that the U.S. State Department's China experts acknowledged Beijing's independence from Moscow in 1949 and secretly pursued policies during the 1950s to encourage a complete Sino-Soviet split.

Recent research based on Chinese materials appears to confirm that the CCP was not likely to accept any offer Acheson may have made to gain better relations with the PRC. Jian Chen (1993) finds U.S.-Chinese confrontation beginning late in 1948 when the Chinese communists captured Angus Ward, the U.S. consul at Mukden. Kuisong Yang (1992) reports that the relations between Moscow and Beijing were not harsh enough to commit Mao to America. Moreover, two memoirs written by Chinese officials from the 1940s confirm Mao's distrust of American leaders: Hua Huang (1992) and Yibo Bo (1992). Similar Chinese opinions were reported in Warren I. Cohen's 1987 article. From a Soviet perspective, historian Sergei N. Goncharov (1991) tells of an interview with Ivan V. Kovalev, who was Stalin's personal representative to China and accompanied Shaoqi Liu to Moscow during the summer of 1949. Liu's visit paved the way for Mao Zedong's December 1949 meetings with Stalin, which resulted in the Sino-Soviet Friendship Treaty of 1950.

U.S. Errors and Misconceptions, 1945–1950. The second finding of most recent scholarship on U.S.-China relations is agreement with moderate traditionalist literature that Washington policymakers made mistakes and often misperceived events in China, but unlike the moderates, revisionists emphasize Jiang Jieshi's responsibility for the loss of China. Thus, although cold war revisionists such as Gabriel Kolko (1968) and Joyce and Gabriel Kolko (1972) speculated that the United States knowingly expanded its economic power in Asia and generated Soviet fears of U.S. control in Asia, U.S. revisionist scholars specializing in China find that uncertainties and human errors characterized Washington's decisions on East Asia. For example, whereas the Kolkos found that Marshall's mission strongly favored Jiang's attempts to control the communists, revisionist Stephen Levine (1977) concludes that Marshall was unsuccessful because he tried to form a nationalist-communist coalition; and Lisle Rose (1976) contends that Marshall conducted an idealistic-type "goodwill" mission intended to benefit China, not to control the Chinese.

Other recent China studies emphasize Truman's attempts to make the Chinese nationalist regime effective, a problem that had plagued Washington for many years. On this problem, as Nancy Tucker (1983) describes, the deterioration of Jiang's GMD made it impossible for the United States to reverse its downfall. Russell Buhite (1978) indicates that Truman had difficulty in dealing with China as a peripheral interest compared to America's vital interest in Europe. Buhite argues that China should have qualified for an interest somewhere in between—that is, as a "major" but not a "vital" interest. These semantics did not help Truman, Marshall, or Acheson, who thought that Europe was an unquestionably vital interest to America. John Feaver's (1981) article on the China aid bill suggests that Truman used a middle way on China because his $400 million aid in 1948 was less than the China Lobby desired, The pro-Jiang group wanted China to be treated with equal or greater value than Europe. From another perspective, William Stueck (1981) indicates that by 1948 the U.S. interest in China was simply to demonstrate credibility by not dropping all its support for Jiang's regime

Relative to Truman's problems and mistakes, some authors imply that cold war friction began in China as early as in Europe. Stueck's study of General Wedemeyer (1984) and Steven Levine's essays on the Marshall mission (1977, 1979) indicate that Washington's leaders were concerned with Soviet threats in China in 1945–1946, at the same time that Europe was threatened. Just as in Europe, the U.S. fears of Soviet communism in Asia were exaggerated, as indicated in the research of Gary May (1979), Russell Buhite (1981), Thomas G. Paterson (1981), Adam Ulam (1968), and Charles McLane (1966).

In the context of the perceived Soviet threat and Jiang Jieshi's ineffective government, Washington had difficult choices to make. The U.S. government could not afford the costs of assisting China with the same vigor that it aided Europe even if a suitable Chinese government had existed. Subsequently, Truman gave limited aid to the Chinese nationalists after 1948 for a variety of reasons. Michael Schaller (1979) indicates the China Lobby's publicity made some aid politically necessary, but Feaver (1981) concludes this aid was a U.S. tactic to obstruct Chinese communists as long as possible.

In addition to previously cited studies, four volumes of essays deal with various topics about U.S.-Chinese relations: by Warren I. Cohen (1983), Harry Harding et al. (1989), Akira Iriye (1990), and Priscilla Roberts (1991).

UNITED STATES–JAPANESE RELATIONS

Whatever the difficulties or defects of the Truman administration's China policy, Japan's future in East Asian strategy concerned Washington after 1945. Because Jiang Jieshi refused to adopt reforms and his regime deteriorated during the Chinese civil war, Japan's status in future years became a critical matter for U.S. policy. Subsequently U.S. policy during its postwar occupation of Japan reflected these changed circumstances by adopting methods to make Japan its most vital friend in Asia.

The literature about U.S.-Japan relations from 1945 to 1953 has been transformed since declassified documents began to appear in the late 1960s. From the end of World War II until the 1960s, the traditional literature described General Douglas MacArthur's success in taking punitive action toward Japan, including the war crimes trials and in forcing changes that democratized Japanese society. MacArthur's punitive program ended after 1948 because the communist threat in Asia required the United States to create a strong, stable Japanese ally.

Since 1970, however, revisionist scholars have found that U.S. occupation policies never used harsh punitive measures against Japan, and the United States had abandoned its democratizing program by permitting Japan's prewar political and industrial elite and the imperial bureaucracy to retain control as the best way to revive Japan as a reliable U.S. ally. In brief, the U.S. occupation enacted few changes in Japan. These changes "reversed" Washington's stated democratization policy by retaining strong, conservative political control in Japan.

Early Literature on Japan's Occupation

During the first twenty years after 1945, the literature of U.S.-Japan relations depicted an American program that transformed the authoritarian prewar Japan into a democratic, politically stable, and economically reconstructed ally by 1953. Friendly U.S. reporters, official U.S. government news reports, and the memoirs of American and Japanese officials during the occupation indicated that the Japanese had accommodated U.S. demands and brought democracy to Japan's society. The Supreme Commander of the Allied Powers (SCAP), General Douglas MacArthur, enacted democratic reforms that redistributed landownership, abolished

Japan's *zaibatsu* economic cartels, established labor unions, approved Japan's democratic constitution in 1947, negotiated the 1951 peace treaty, and created a treaty of alliance between the United States and Japan. In return, Japan became both a material and operational base for U.S. military activity during the Korean War and cold war, helping to protect Asia from communist expansion.

The traditional reports of MacArthur's reform policies in Japan appeared in the memoirs of U.S. officials as early as 1948, when Edwin Martin described his two years in Tokyo as a State Department officer. Soon after, best-selling American author John Gunther (1950) published a laudatory story of MacArthur's work, and Robert Fearey (1950) explained the excellent work he and others on John Foster Dulles' staff did in creating a sound security structure for the United States, a view echoed in Bernard Cohen's (1957) account of the peace settlement. Robert Ward (1968) reported on the benefits of Japan's 1947 constitution, while Robert Dore (1959) wrote a classic account of MacArthur's land reform.

Other early literature praised various aspects of U.S. policy in Japan. Herbert Feis (1967) explained that the United States successfully prevented the Soviet Union from gaining a significant role in postwar Japan. George Kennan's (1967) memoir displayed his pride in making Japan a stable ally after 1949. And Herbert Passin (1966) edited essays that gave a positive analysis of the entire occupation period. Three other memoirs described SCAP favorably: by Eleanor Hadley (1970), Justin Williams (1968, 1979), and William Sebald (1965). The most widely known general description of these eight years was by Edwin Reischauer (1950). Scholars must note, however, that Reischauer significantly altered his initial comments in revised editions of his book in 1957 and 1965.

Some dissenting literature before 1970 criticized U.S. policy during the occupation of Japan. Mark Gayn (1948) argued that MacArthur's alleged democratic revolution in Japan had failed. Interestingly, Gayn's book became a popular best-seller in Japan, although it was hardly noticed in America. Robert Textor (1951) also criticized SCAP policies but gained little attention. Perhaps the most significant early critique of SCAP was Thomas Bisson's *The Zaibatsu Dissolved* (1954), in which the author added research to his SCAP staff experience to note that this dissolution was partly reversed in 1949–1950.

Revisionist Literature on the United States and Japan

After 1970, the release of declassified government documents, the realization that there was a genuine Sino-Soviet split in the communist ranks, and more frequent contact between American and Japanese scholars led to revisions of the traditional interpretations about occupation-era U.S.-Japan relations. Generally the new literature agrees that the United

States had not altruistic but political, economic, and strategic motives for the conduct of its occupation policy. Substantial data indicate that as early as 1944, U.S. postwar planners intended to change Japan by creating a democratic society and a friendly U.S. partner in Asia. Although a U.S.-Japan alliance resulted in 1951, most of Washington's liberal democratizing proposals had been seriously qualified between 1945 and 1952 by a "reverse course," which revived the power of Japan's prewar elite political and economic groups in order to ensure that Japan would became a reliable U.S. ally in containing Asian communism. In October 1948, National Security Council Paper 13/2 identified Japan as the first line of U.S. defense in Asia. In April 1949 when the Chinese nationalist defeat was imminent, the State Department's Policy Planning Staff under Kennan concluded that Japan's economic security required the United States to protect a trading area for Japan at the crossroads of global trade in Southeast Asia as an alternative to Japan's revival of trade with communist China.

Washington's initial postwar plans for Japan are explained in Akira Iriye's article published in his volume edited with Yōnosuke Nagai (1977). Despite the opinions of a few postwar planners, such as Owen Lattimore (1949), who advocated that drastic punishment should be meted out to Japan's prewar leaders, this minority was unable to get its punitive program accepted. As Iriye notes, the approved State Department plans were influenced by former U.S. ambassador to Japan Joseph Grew and by two State Department advisers who have published their memoirs: Hugh Borton (1967) and George Blakeslee (1953). These plans for Japan differed from those for Europe because the United States assumed it would have a unilateral role in Japan, with the Soviets occupying Manchuria and North Korea and the British taking charge in Southeast Asia. As Herbert Feis (1967) explained, the Truman administration successfully assumed this unilateral responsibility for Japan.

Research regarding America's postwar plans for Japan raised controversy regarding the exact proposals of liberal State Department experts as compared to the harsher treatment of Japan advocated by a minority of U.S. officials in 1945. Looking backward from the 1970s, revisionists who criticized the retention of Japan's elite leaders argued that the liberal democratic planners had been soft on Japan. Revisionists such as Howard B. Schonberger (1989), Marlene Mayo (1984), and Susan Deborah Chira (1982) argued that the "soft peace boys" in the State Department such as Joseph Grew had prepared policies that prevented significant land reforms and retained the *zaibatsu*. Steven Schwartzberg (1993) disagrees with these critics, contending that Grew and his colleagues favored both land reform and the *zaibatsu* abolition. Schwartzberg claims that Grew and the "soft peace boys" must be compared with the extreme "hard-line" proponents in 1944 who wanted to destroy Japan's industrial plants permanently and stop all future Japanese trade. Their drastic proposals re-sembled Secretary of the Treasury Henry Morgenthau's plans to return Germany to an agricultural society, a Carthagenian-type policy that Roo-sevelt and Churchill rejected. Grew opposed the hard-liners and advo-cated a peace designed to give Japan a sufficient living standard to satisfy its citizens, not anger them.

Nevertheless, both economic and strategic reasons motivated America's policy in Japan. The strategic character of the U.S. decisions are described by Roger Dingman (1979, 1981). The economic and trade aspects are found in the studies of William Borden (1984) and Andrew Rotter (1984, 1987). In addition, Nancy Tucker (1984) discusses U.S. policy toward Ja-pan's trade with China. In broader strategic terms, Thomas J. McCormick (1989) applies the world systems analysis to U.S. policy in Asia and Eu-rope. McCormick emphasizes the duality of economic and political-military power through which the United States obtained hegemony in Asia's core and peripheral regions, including Japan.

Revisionist research on U.S.-Japan relations indicates that SCAP was bet-ter at making Japan an ally in 1951 than at democratizing Japan's political and economic society because of the reverse course in U.S. policy between 1947 and 1953. These revisionists claimed the reverse course began be-cause the United States wanted to speed up Japan's economic reconstruc-tion in order to make Japan an ally in the cold war. This meant reasserting the position of Japan's old elite leaders and stopping liberal democratic economic and political reforms. For a contrast of traditional views and the revisionist concepts, see the article by Justin Williams (1988), which is followed by John Dower's and Howard Schonberger's revisionist re-sponses.

A central focus of the reverse course literature is the dissolving of the *zaibatsu,* the symbol of the dominance of Japan's prewar economic elite. Officially, the 1951 report of the Holding Company Liquidation Commis-sion (HCLC) stated that SCAP's Deconcentration Law of 1947 had suc-cessfully ended the *zaibatsu.* In contrast, however, the memoirs of the HCLC's later chairman, Iwajirō Noda (1983), and the antimonopoly study by Ryōichi Miwa (1979) both indicate that *zaibatsu* leaders successfully resisted the implementation of the 1947 law and the United States altered its policy from "democratization" to "economic recovery." One major consequence of this U.S. action was that Japan's Ministry of International Trade and Industry (MITI) obtained control of Japan's domestic and for-eign trade relations.

Details about the U.S. reverse course are found in a variety of studies. John Dower (1969) published one of the first articles on the reverse course. John Roberts (1979) describes the role of the American Council on Japan, led by Harry Kern of *Newsweek* magazine in promoting U.S. policy change. Howard Schonberger (1977, 1989) describes the "Japan

Lobby'' in Washington and has a lengthy study about Joseph Dodge, the Detroit banker who promoted the reverse course. The connection between the reverse policy and MacArthur's proposal for an earlier Japanese peace treaty is explained by Takeshi Igarashi (1981). Richard Finn (1992) explains the skills of Japanese conservatives in adjusting to American programs. This is a central theme of Japanese research, as noted in Chapter 8 in this book.

Other studies substantiate that by 1952 Japan's elite political-economic groups had "prevented" democracy from limiting their control of industry and trade. Leon Hollerman (1979) and Yasuhara Yoko (1986) both conclude that American policy helped Japan's bureaucracy devise regulations that governed Japan's domestic and export trade markets. These regulations corresponded to U.S. policies that provided secure Japanese markets in Southeast Asia, a situation explained by Andrew Rotter (1984) and Seigen Miyasato (1981). Michael Schaller (1982, 1985) describes the Japanese industrial boom created by these policies, especially after the Korean War made Japan the major procurement place for the U.S. war effort. Finally, MacArthur's purge of Japan's labor unions, which weakened Japan's trade unions and made workers dependent on industrial policy, is examined by Howard Schonberger (1979) and Eiji Takemoe (1982).

At the same time that the reverse course of U.S. policy reestablished Japan's powerful political and economic elite, John Foster Dulles directed negotiations for treaties of peace and the U.S. alliance with Japan. Kumao Nishimura (1971), the head of Japan's Treaty Bureau in the Foreign Ministry, provides an official Japanese view of the treaty process, while the account by Frederick Dunn (1963) sees the treaties as the means for the United States to pursue the cold war. Ronald Pruessen (1982) examines Dulles' role in the negotiations, while Michael Yoshitsu (1983) has a general account of the talks. John Dower (1979) describes Japanese prime minister Yoshida's important role in these talks.

Criticisms of the treaty negotiations have been raised by Howard Schonberger (1983), who describes their results as giving Japan a "fraudulent independence" and by Roger Dingman (1979) who refers to them as "unequal treaties," a term that recalls earlier treaties through which Western economic imperialists gained dominance over Asian countries. Schonberger (1986) also connects the 1951 peace treaty to the U.S. decision to "force" Japan to recognize nationalist China.

General MacArthur's leadership in the occupation has been praised by some recent scholars and criticized by others. William Manchester's biography (1978) portrays MacArthur favorably, but it must be used carefully because, as John E. Wiltz (1979) shows, the author used data carelessly. A moderate, balanced account of MacArthur's role has been written by Japanese scholar Rinjirō Sodei (1975, 1991). Michael Schaller's

(1989) critical discussion of MacArthur concludes that the general "distorted information and manipulated events to serve selfish, often political, ends." Other works about MacArthur are cited in Chapters 13 through 16 in this book.

As exceptions to the revisionist writing, two works resemble traditional literature on the U.S. occupation of Japan. Theodore Cohen's *Remaking Japan* (1987) is basically a memoir of an SCAP official. John Perry's *Beneath the Eagle's Wing* (1980) refers primarily to the first two years of occupation but must be used carefully because it seems to be poorly researched.

Finally, there are several valuable books of essays by a variety of American and Japanese scholars. These include Ray Moore's *The Day When the Emperor Read the Bible* (1982), Robert E. Ward and Sakamoto Yoshikazu's *Democratizing Japan* (1987), and E. Patricia Tsurumi's *The Other Japan* (1988).

AMERICAN-KOREAN RELATIONS, 1945–1950

During the waning months of World War II, the United States and the Soviet Union agreed to occupy Korea jointly prior to the establishment of a trusteeship under United Nations auspices. Although Korean nationalists expected to gain an independent, unified nation after Japan's defeat in 1945, the two superpowers decided to divide Korea at the 38th parallel, a decision that has left Korea divided until the present day.

Because two years of U.S.-Soviet negotiations failed to reach agreement on methods to unite Korea, the United States referred the problem to the United Nations. In November 1947, the UN General Assembly recognized Korea's right to independence and established a commission to supervise elections, which would create a constitutent assembly to unify the nation as a prelude to the withdrawal of foreign forces. The 1948 elections divided Korea further because the North Korean communists refused to cooperate. Nevertheless, in August 1948, the elected assembly organized the Republic of Korea (ROK) with Syngman Rhee as its president. In September, the Democratic People's Republic of Korea (DPRK) was proclaimed in North Korea, led by Kim Il-sung.

Following the withdrawal of most American and Soviet troops during 1949, an already-festering civil war intensified in Korea, leading to full-scale war on June 25, 1950. North Korea's invasion of the south as a means to attain unity transformed the civil, revolutionary war into a large-scale international conflict when the United States sent air and naval units to aid the ROK on June 27 and urged the United Nations Security Council (UNSC) to authorize a Korean command to evict the North Korean communists from the south. The Korean War lasted until July 1953, when a cease-fire and truce led to peace negotiations intended to unite the country, talks that are officially still ongoing.

As is the case of much cold war literature, the two basic classifications for United States–Korean relations are the early traditional versions based principally on official revelations by the various participants, followed by revisionist studies based on declassified government documents and research data that enabled scholars to find new answers to questions regarding the origins of the Korean War.

Early Literature on U.S.-Korea Relations

Most Americans knew little or nothing about Korea when the war broke out on June 25, 1950. The Truman administration and the United Nations denounced the aggression of North Korea, and most reports blamed the Soviet Union for trying aggressively to expand communism in Asia. Generally spokesmen for the U.S. government and President Truman in his *Memoirs* (1955–1956) claimed that the communists were testing the will of UN members to uphold collective security, just as Adolf Hitler had tested the League of Nations during the 1930s when Britain and France tried to appease the Nazis. In 1950, however, Truman never considered appeasing the communists, whom he believed were testing America.

From 1950 to the 1970s, writers about U.S.-Korea relations looked for reasons why U.S. policy failed to avoid the Korean War. Moderate authors who appeared as apologists for Truman emphasized the complex issues the United States faced in Korea and the "technical" bureaucratic errors made by the Truman administration. A more critical group of U.S. conservatives asserted that Truman's advisers were "soft on communism" and virtually treasonous for placing Korea outside the zone of "vital interests" for U.S. protection. Third, a small, largely unnoticed number of U.S. writers hazarded the idea that the Korean War was not a Soviet plot but that the United States and South Korean president Syngman Rhee shared responsibility for the war because Rhee's talk about attacking North Korea provoked Kim Il-sung. Most significant, however, almost no early U.S. literature on the conflict provided details about the Korean civil war that preceded the 1950 invasion.

The moderates' early interpretation of U.S. relations with Korea displays all or parts of Truman's claim that the Soviets' global plans precipitated the conflict. David Rees' (1964) study is considered the best traditional account of the war and its origins; Robert Leckie's (1963) book is a less scholarly, popular version. Three South Korean authors wrote competent general studies of a traditional character: Soon-sung Cho (1967), Chong-sik Lee (1961), and Chung-kon Kim (1973). As a close friend of South Korea's President Rhee, Robert Oliver (1952, 1978) offers an answer to later authors who claimed Rhee did not represent the best interests of the Korean people.

An important traditionalist assumption was that either the Soviets or a

Sino-Soviet conspiracy ordered North Korea's 1950 invasion. Truman's claim that Stalin's control over Kim Il-sung caused the conflict appeared to be confirmed by many U.S. scholars of Soviet policy, including David Dallin (1948, 1961), A. Doak Barnett (1961), and Marshall Shulman (1963). Soviet experts who differed in defining Stalin's motives but blamed Moscow for the invasion included Raymond Garthoff (1965) and Edgar Snow (1957).

These moderate authors agreed that Soviet expansionism was the cause of the war, but they differed regarding why the Truman administration was unsuccessful in Korea from 1945 to 1950. As noted above, the moderate critics emphasized the complex problems in Korea that caused difficulties and errors in U.S. policy. In addition to Secretary of State Acheson's (1958) description of these problems, both Edwin Reischauer (1950) and Kenneth Scott Latourette (1952) deal with the mixture of Soviet, Chinese, and Korean political issues from 1945 to 1950 as being difficult to handle. Probably the best early description of the Korean difficulties was by George McCune and Arthur Grey (1950), who wrote frequent but seldom-noticed reports about Korea between 1945 and 1953, reports that Keith D. McFarland's (1986) bibliography lists.

More publicized than the moderate writings on Truman's errors in Korea were the books and articles by Asia Firsters, who disliked Truman's Europe First policy and blamed the Truman administration for not strongly opposing the communist threat in Asia. These authors include Robert Oliver (1950, 1952, 1978), John Caldwell and Lesley Frost (1952), Clyde Mitchell (1951), and Walter Judd (1950). Judd, a prominent "China lobbyist" and congressman, published his article in *Reader's Digest,* a popular middle-class journal that, like Henry Luce's *Time* and *Life* publications, was strongly opinionated against Truman as well as alleged communists and "communist sympathizers" in federal government agencies. Also in this conservative group was General Albert Wedemeyer, whose reports on China and Korea (1951, 1958) had allegedly "been suppressed" by Truman until 1951. Finally, both John Gayl (1951) and Thomas Fehrenbach (1963) criticized Truman's defense cuts for leaving U.S. and South Korean forces unprepared in 1950.

Three contemporary reports of the 1950s resulted from journalistic investigations of Truman's decision making during the week of June 25–30, 1950. Two reporters who used White House leaks to describe this crucial week were Albert L. Warner (1951) and Beverly Smith (1951). A later version of this week by Alexander George (1955) provides a good analysis of official thinking about the reasons for Moscow's aggression.

Some early authors questioned Truman's version of the origins of the Korean War. Wilbur Hitchcock's (1951) article in *Current History* suggested that North Korea may have acted alone in initiating the war, while I. F. Stone's (1952) writings about Truman's errors contended that South Korea played a role in precipitating the conflict. Later, Glenn Paige (1968) researched many news accounts and official government releases to describe this crucial week in June 1950. Harold Noble (1975) published his version of events as seen by a U.S. embassy officer in Seoul in June 1950.

Finally, North Korea's version of the war's origins should be considered, although they present polemical claims that the United States and South Korea caused the war. The initial North Korean version was published in 1950 by the Democratic People's Republic of Korea, which claimed to have captured documents from President Rhee's archives to verify that the ROK and the United States started the war. A later similar DPRK story was *Facts Tell* (1960). The contents of these publications are described by Alfred Crofts (1979). The North Korean version of the war's origins continues to be argued in a 1992 report published in *Vantage Point* (1992).

Revisionists on U.S.-Korea Relations

After 1970, the opening of classified U.S. government files combined with researchers who asked new questions resulted in revised interpretations of the traditional explanations for the origins of the Korean War. These revised perspectives rejected previous interpretations that Joseph Stalin or Mao Zedong ordered North Korea to attack South Korea. More important, however, these scholars fully examined the events in Korea from 1945 to 1950, and the role of the United States and the Soviet Union during the occupation. Subsequently, most of today's scholars in the United States, Great Britain, South Korea, and Japan emphasize the revolutionary and civil war actions of various Korean political groups in addition to Moscow's, Beijing's, and Washington's activity in Korea.

Among the revisionist studies, the most important and detailed work is Bruce Cumings' two-volume *The Origins of the Korean War* (1981, 1990). Cumings' bibliographies and detailed notes include both English- and Korean-language sources, as well as documents available in U.S. and British archives. Thus, the revisionist literature on the origins of the Korean War may be briefly described by emphasizing Cumings' interpretation, which other revisionist scholars would challenge or qualify only in details or emphasis. Beginning with data on the formation of the Korean Communist party during the 1920s and the political groups active in Korea or, as in the case of Syngman Rhee, in exile in the United States, revisionists emphasize the expectation of Korean nationalists that Japan's defeat would lead to an independent Korean nation. This hope was thwarted when both Soviet and American military forces entered Korea in September 1945, intending to form a United Nations trusteeship but deciding initially to divide Korea at the 38th parallel as a compromise method of occupation.

For two years, during which U.S.-Soviet negotiations failed to unite Korea, the two superpowers installed regimes that suited their respective preferences. In the South, U.S. military leaders backed an authoritarian, anticommunist group representing Korea's elite landlords and property owners. In the North, the Soviet Union's military general installed a communist and anticaptialist regime. Among historians, a major issue concerning this two-year period is whether either or both superpowers planned to impose the competing regimes that resulted or simply stumbled into the division because both Washington and Moscow had more vital concerns in Europe. Revisionists also examine China's role in the origins of the war, for which recent data are found in articles by Hong-kyu Park (1989) and Xiaoyoan Liu (1992). Chapter 11 in this book gives the most recent research data on China's role in Korea.

Possibly neither superpower saw Korea as "most vital" because in 1948, they agreed to withdraw their forces after the UN special commission on Korea held elections, which the communists boycotted. According to the revisionists, the United States manipulated the UN General Assembly, the UN's secretary-general, and the UN Special Commission on Korea in order to gain international sanctions for containing Soviet expansion in Asia. As a result, the U.S. control of the UN observers in Seoul gave North Korea ample justification for boycotting the 1948 election. Cumings quotes U.S. general John Hodge, the commander in South Korea, as predicting to the secretary of state in 1947 that the communists would boycott the election, leading to the establishment of a "reactionary fascist government" in the South with which the United States might find it "very difficult if not impossible to deal." Hodge was correct. Rhee won the election and afterward was often difficult for the United States to deal with.

Following the election, the U.S.-Soviet troop withdrawal took place in 1949, except for some "advisers." At the same time, the United Nations recognized Rhee's Republic of Korea but not Kim Il-sung's Democratic People's Republic of Korea because it did not participate in the UN elections.

The superpowers' troop withdrawal increased the North-South conflicts in Korea, which had been waged intermittently since 1945. Prior to the arrival of U.S. and Soviet forces in 1945, Koreans set up committees throughout their country in order to prepare for their liberation from Japan. These committees were largely ignored by the leaders of both superpowers' occupation forces, who chose to favor the regimes they had organized—those of Syngman Rhee and Kim Il-sung. While both Rhee and Kim tried to repress their opponents, each side engaged in frequent strikes and violent uprisings. After the U.S. and Soviet troops left, fighting escalated between these conflicting groups in the North and South, as well as across the border at the 38th parallel.

Thus, Korea's civil war persistently verged on large-scale conflict after

1948. The northern communists claimed that southern Koreans preferred communism, and President Rhee frequently asserted that the ROK would eventually attack the North and unite Korea. Rhee's possible attacks appeared to be delayed only by U.S. policy, which provided limited aid to South Korea but made no commitment to help Rhee unite the nation.

By early 1950, U.S. military intelligence reported that a North-South war was a question of when, not if. The war finally began on June 25, 1950 (U.S. time). The Truman administration and the UN delayed their reaction to determine if the UN's initial condemnation of North Korea's attack would bring a withdrawal of Kim Il-sung's forces. On June 27, Truman committed U.S. air and naval units to help the ROK, and the UN Security Council asked member nations to assist South Korea. On June 30, as the communist forces moved farther south, Truman committed U.S. ground troops to protect the ROK.

This brief summary of the revisionist literature does not do justice to the detailed research scholars performed in archives and other sources to investigate the particular activity that took place inside Korea that traditional studies generally avoided. Their recent studies used declassified U.S., Korean, and Japanese records to examine American activity and proposals between 1945 and 1950. Records of the Soviet Union and China have also become gradually available in the 1990s.

The broad terms of these revisionist explanations are the importance of Korean events after 1945; the negotiations between the superpowers from 1945 to 1947 when the occupation forces made history on the ground by forming the governments of the two Korean states; the failure of superpower agreement combined with the U.S. role in having the United Nations supervise Korea's problems although the UN was neither well equipped nor trained to act independently of U.S. support; the growing civil war in Korea from 1946 to 1950; and the complex international questions that developed during these same years in Europe, the Middle East, China, Japan, and Southeast Asia.

Although Cumings' two volumes impinged on all of these issues, revisionist works entailed a variety of specific studies that supported or qualified his findings. In general, other revisionists accepted his basic approach and broad, suggestive concepts but believed he exaggerated some conclusions because of his enthusiasm in presenting the perspective of native Koreans toward superpower intervention. More particularly, Cumings and other revisionists have had great difficulty in persuading the tradition-oriented American public, including television producers, to accept new ideas about the Korean War. During the late 1980s, Cumings and Jon Halliday acted as consultants for Thames Television, a British company that produced the BBC documentary titled *Korea: The Unknown War*, a film accompanied by the Cumings-Halliday book of the same title (1988). The difficulties Cumings and Halliday had with the producers in

England and later, with WGBH of Boston, the major U.S. public television channel, are described in Cumings' *War and Television* (1992). For reviews of the documentary, which was shown in the United States in November 1990, see Lloyd Gardner (1991), Walter Goodman (1990), and Ray Loynd (1990). London and Washington officials censored the production to such an extent that videos of the TV film are not available from either the BBC or WGBH.

An important revisionist conclusion is that communism's origins in Korea were indigenous, not depending on either Chinese or Soviet influence prior to the arrival of Soviet occupation troops in 1945. China's slight concern for Korea between 1940 and 1950 is found in the work of Robert A. Scalapino and Chong-sik Lee (1972) and in Harold Hinton's (1970) volume, which significantly revised his traditional 1966 interpretation. Recent articles by Xiaoyoan Liu (1992) and Hong-kyu Park (1989) examine World War II discussions about Korea's future that settled nothing. Similarly, from the Soviet side, the studies of Allen Whiting (1960) and John Gitting's essay in Edward Friedman and Mark Selden (1971) agree that there was no 1945 Moscow conspiracy to control all of East Asia.

Nor have scholars found evidence that Beijing or Moscow dictated North Korea's attack on South Korea in June 1950. Robert Simmons (1975) indicates there were no direct orders from Stalin or Mao regarding the 1950 invasion. Yufan Hao and Zhihai Zhai (1990) indicate China had no strong security concerns in Korea until the UN forces approached and crossed the 38th parallel in 1951. Because some authors use Nikita Khrushchev's *Memoirs* (1970) to verify the Soviet role in June 1950, scholars should consider John Merrill's (1981) comments about these *Memoirs* before reaching conclusions. Finally, the essays of both Gye-dong Kim and Hak-joon Kim in James Cotton and Ian Neary (1989) confirm that North Korea initiated the 1950 conflict, although Syngman Rhee's talk about a "northern invasion" helped precipitate the attack by creating fear among North Korea's leaders. Most recently John Lewis, Sergei Gorcharev, and Litai Xue (1994) have collaborated on a study of Sino-Soviet relations before 1950. For the latest about this issue, consult Chapters 10 through 12 in this book.

The literature on the relative lack of Soviet or Chinese influence on Kim Il-sung's June 1950 decision is buttressed by studies that demonstrate the independence of various Korean nationalist parties. The independent character of Korea's communist party is described by Ilpyong J. Kim (1975) and Dae-sook Suh (1967). T'ae-su Han (1961) reports on Korea's various political parties during this era. Okonogi Masao's essay in Yonosuke Nagai and Akira Iriye (1977) concludes that domestic forces in both North and South Korea were deterred by Moscow and Washington from more serious armed conflict prior to June 1950. John Merrill has an article (1982) and a book (1989) giving details about Korea's civil war before

1950. Merrill also has an essay on the civil war in Bruce Cumings' *Child of Conflict* (1983). Three works are critical of Syngman Rhee's repressive activity in South Korea: Richard Allen (1960), John Kie-chiang Oh (1968), and James Palais's essay in Frank Baldwin (1973).

Although revisionist literature on Korea's relation to the cold war may emphasize either economic or strategic issues, these categories are less relevant to Korea because economic factors played a lesser role in U.S.-Korean relations than they did with Japan, China, or Southeast Asia. Nevertheless, revisionist authors differ regarding U.S. motivations for its Korean decisions between 1945 and 1950. James Matray (1985) finds that Washington was generally indifferent toward Korea until 1947, when it made limited commitments to assist South Korea and "reluctantly" gave broad military protection to South Korea after June 1950. William Stueck (1981) and Burton Kaufmann (1986) conclude that Washington's international strategic containment policies motivated American decisions and became fixed because of the Korean War. John L. Gaddis' essays in Borg and Heinrichs (1980) and in Nagai and Iriye (1977) discuss Dean Acheson's 1950 speech, which left Korea out of the U.S. defense perimeter, but Bruce Cumings (1991) has a different interpretation of Acheson's speech. Charles Dobbs (1981) contends that the U.S. motive for assisting South Korea was symbolically to show its will to resist the communist challenge in East Asia. Barton J. Bernstein (1977) emphasizes the role of Truman and Acheson in making decisions on Korea, while Robert Jervis (1980) examines the war's connections to U.S. cold war developments. Finally, Rosemary Foot (1985) concludes that the Truman administration's exaggerated perception of communist motives in Asia caused the United States to fight the wrong war in a place of little significance to the nation. She also indicates that the beneficial influence of British advice prevented Truman from blundering into a large-scale war with China in 1950–1951.

Revisionist scholars have come to predominate research on U.S.-Korean relations, but some authors continued to follow the moderate traditional interpretations. Lisle Rose's study (1976) is fairly traditional, claiming the principal U.S. fault during the occupation was the inability of Americans to act with sensitivity toward Korean interests. A moderate version, which critiques revisionist attacks on Truman's policy in Asia, is by John E. Wiltz in William J. Williams's *A Revolutionary War* (1993). Similarly, Erik van Rees (1989) emphasizes the Soviet role in bringing socialism to North Korea, although he deals primarily with the period from 1945 to 1947.

Four volumes of essays on the Korean War are valuable. Of these, three emphasize revisionist studies from 1945 to 1950: Frank Baldwin's *Without Parallel* (1973) Bruce Cumings' *Child of Conflict* (1983), and James Cotton and Ian Neary's *The Korean War in History* (1989). A fourth volume, edited by William J. Williams (1993), covers military aspects of the war except for John Wiltz's essay and Roger Dingman's article on Japan and the war.

REFERENCES

Acheson, Dean. *Power and Diplomacy*. Cambridge, MA: Harvard University Press, 1958.

Allen, Richard C. *Korea's Syngman Rhee: An Unauthorized Portrait*. Tokyo and Rutland, VT: Charles E. Tuttle Co., 1960.

Asada, Sadao. "Recent Works on the American Occupation of Japan." *Japanese Journal of American Studies* 1 (1981): 175–191.

———, ed. *Japan and the World, 1853–1952: A Bibliographic Guide to Japanese Scholarship in Foreign Relations*. New York: Columbia University Press, 1989.

Auer, James E. *The Postwar Rearmament of Japanese Maritime Forces, 1945–1971*. New York: Praeger, 1973.

Bachrach, Stanley. *The Committee of One Million: China Lobby Politics, 1953–1971*. New York: Columbia University Press, 1976.

Baldwin, Frank, ed. *Without Parallel: The American-Korean Relationship since 1945*. New York: Random House, 1973.

Ballantine, Joseph. *Formosa, A Problem for United States Foreign Policy*. Washington, DC: Brookings Institution, 1952.

Barnett, A. Doak. *Communist China and Asia: Challenge to American Policy*. New York: Vintage Books, 1961.

Beal, John. *Marshall in China*. Garden City, NY: Doubleday, 1970.

Belden, John. *China Shakes the World*. New York: Harper and Brothers, 1949.

Bernstein, Barton J. "The Week We Went to War: American Intervention in the Korean War," *Foreign Service Journal* 54 (January 1977): 6–9, 33–35; and 54 (February 1977): 8–16, 33–34.

Bisson, Thomas A. *Zaibatsu Dissolution*. Berkeley: University of California Press, 1954.

Blakeslee, George H. *The Far Eastern Commission: A Study in International Cooperation: 1945 to 1952*. Washington: GPO, 1953.

Blanchard, Carroll H. *Korean War Bibliography and Maps of Korea*. Albany, NY: Korean Conflict Research Foundation, 1964.

Blum, Robert. *The United States and China in World Affairs*. New York: Council on Foreign Relations, 1966.

Blum, Robert M. *Drawing the Line: The Origins of American Containment Policy in East Asia*. New York: W. W. Norton, 1982.

Bo, Yibo. "The Making of the 'Lean-to-One-Side' Decision." Trans. Zhai Qiang. *Chinese Historians* 5 (Spring 1992): 57–63.

Bodde, Derk. *Peking: A Year of Revolution*. Boston: Henry Schuman, 1950.

Borden, William S. *The Pacific Alliance: U.S. Economic Policy and Japanese Trade Recovery, 1945–1955*. Madison, WI: University of Wisconsin Press, 1984.

Borg, Dorothy, comp. *Historian and American Far Eastern Policy*. Occasional Papers of the East Asian Institute. New York: Columbia University, 1966.

Borg, Dorothy, and Waldo Heinrichs, eds. *Uncertain Years, Chinese-American Relations, 1947–1950*. New York: Columbia University Press, 1980.

Borton, Hugh. *American Presurrender Planning for Postwar Japan.* New York: Columbia University East Asian Institute, 1967.

Braibante, Ralph. "The Ryuku Islands: Pawns of the Pacific." *American Political Science Review* 48 (1954): 972–998.

Braisted, William. *The United States Navy in the Pacific, 1897–1909.* Austin: University of Texas Press, 1958.

Brands, H. W. *Bound to Empire: The United States and the Philippines.* New York: Oxford University Press, 1992.

Brown, Delmer M. "Recent Japanese Political and Historical Materials." *American Political Science Review* 43:5 (1949): 1010–1017.

Brune, Lester H. *The Origins of American National Security Policy 1900–1941: Airpower, Seapower, and Foreign Policy.* Manhattan, KS: MA/AH Press, 1981.

Buckley, Thomas H. *The United States and the Washington Conference, 1921–1922.* Knoxville: University of Tennessee Press, 1970.

———. *US-Japan Alliance Diplomacy, 1945–1990.* New York: Cambridge University Press, 1992.

Buhite, Russell. *Patrick J. Hurley and American Foreign Policy.* Ithaca, NY: Cornell University Press, 1973.

———. "Major Interests: American Policy toward China, Taiwan, and Korea, 1945–1960." *Pacific Historical Review* 47:3 (August 1978): 425–452.

Buhite, Russell D. *Soviet-American Relations in Asia, 1945–1954.* Norman: University of Oklahoma Press, 1981.

Buss, Claude A. *The United States and the Philippines: Background for Policy.* Washington, DC: American Enterprise Institute, 1977.

Caldwell, John C., and Lesley Frost. *The Korean Story.* Chicago: Regnery, 1952.

Chen, Jian. "The Ward Case and the Emergence of Sino-American Confrontation, 1948–1950." *Australian Journal of Chinese Affairs* 30 (July 1993): 149–170.

Chennault, Claire Lee. *Way of a Fighter: The Memoirs of Claire Lee Chennault.* New York: G. P. Putnam's Sons, 1949.

Chern, Kenneth S. *Dilemma in China: America's Policy Debate, 1945.* Hamden, CT: Archon Books, 1980.

Chiang Kai-shek (Jiang Jieshi). *Soviet Russia in China: A Summing Up at Seventy.* New York: Farrar, Straus, and Giroux, 1957.

Chira, Susan Deborah. *Cautious Revolutionaries: Occupation Planners and Japan's Post-War Land Reform.* Tokyo: Agricultural Policy Research Center, 1982.

Cho, Soon-sung. *Korea in World Politics, 1940–1950: An Evaluation of American Responsibility.* Berkeley: University of California Press, 1967.

Clinard, Outten. *Japan's Influence on American Naval Power, 1897–1917.* Berkeley: University of California Press, 1947.

Clubb, O. Edmund. "Manchuria in the Balance, 1945–1946." *Pacific Historical Review* 26:4 (November 1957): 377–391.

———. *The Witness and I.* New York: Columbia University Press, 1974.

Cohen, Bernard C. *The Political Process and Foreign Policy: The Making of the Japanese Peace Settlement.* Princeton, NJ: Princeton University Press, 1957.

Cohen, Theodore. *Remaking Japan: The American As New Deal.* New York: Free Press, 1987.

Cohen, Warren I. "The Development of Chinese Communist Policy toward the United States, 1922–1933." *Orbis* 11:1 (1967a): 219–237.

———. "The Development of Chinese Communist Policy toward the United States, 1933–1945." *Orbis* 11:2 (1967b): 551–569.

———. "Who Fought the Japanese in Hunan? Some Views of China's War Effort." *Journal of Asian Studies* 27 (November 1967c): 111–115.

———. "Ambassador Philip D. Sprouse on the Question of Recognition." *Diplomatic History* 2 (1978): 213–217.

———. "Consul General O. Edmund Clubb on the 'Inevitability' of Conflict." *Diplomatic History* 5 (1981): 165–168.

———, ed. *New Frontiers in American–East Asian Relations.* New York: Columbia University Press, 1983.

———. "Conversations with Chinese Friends: Zhou Enlai's Associates Reflect on Chinese-American Relations in the 1940s and the Korean War." *Diplomatic History* 11 (Summer 1987): 283–289.

Cotton, James, and Ian Neary. *The Korean War in History.* Atlantic Highlands, NJ: Humanities International, 1989.

Coulter, John W. *The Pacific Dependencies of the United States.* New York: Macmillan, 1957.

Crofts, Alfred. "The State of the Korean War Reconsidered." *Rocky Mountain Social Science Journal* (April 1974): 109–117.

Cullather, Nick. "America's Boy? Ramon Magsaysay and the Illusion of Influence." *Pacific Historical Review* 62 (August 1993a): 305–358.

———. *Illusions of Influence: The Political Economy of United States–Philippines Relations, 1942–1960.* Stanford, CA: Stanford University Press, 1993b.

Cumings, Bruce, ed. *Child of Conflict: The Korean-American Relationships, 1943–1953.* Seattle: Washington University, 1983.

———. *The Origins of the Korean War.* 2 vols. Princeton, NJ: Princeton University Press, 1981, 1990.

———. *War and Television.* New York: Verso, 1992.

Cumings, Bruce, and Jon Halliday. *Korea: The Unknown War.* New York: Pantheon Books, 1988.

Dallin, David. *Soviet Russia and the Far East.* New Haven, CT: Yale University Press, 1948.

———. *Soviet Foreign Policy after Stalin.* Philadelphia: J. P. Lippincott, 1961.

Democratic People's Republic of Korea. *Documents and Materials Exposing the Instigators of the Civil War in Korea: Documents from the Archives of the Rhee Syngman Government.* Pyongyang: Foreign Languages Publishing House, 1950.

———. *Facts Tell.* Pyongyang: Foreign Language Publishing House, 1960.

Deutscher, Isaac. *Stalin.* London: Penguin Books, 1966.

Dingman, Roger. *Power in the Pacific: The Origins of Naval Arms Limitations, 1914–1922.* Chicago: University of Chicago Press, 1976a.

———. "Reconsiderations: The U.S.-Japan Security Treaty." *Pacific Community* 7:4 (1976b): 471–493.

———. "Theories of, and Approaches to, Alliance Politics." In Paul G. Gordon, ed., *Diplomacy: New Approaches in History, Theory, and Politics,* pp. 246–266. New York: Free Press, 1979.

———. "The U.S. Navy and the Cold War: The Japan Case." In Craig Symonds, ed., *New Aspects of Naval History,* pp. 291–312. Annapolis, MD: United States Naval Institute, 1981.

————. "The Diplomacy of Dependency: The Philippines and Peacemaking with Japan, 1945–1952." *Journal of Southeast Asian Studies* 17 (September 1986): 307–321.

Dobbs, Charles M. *The Unwanted Symbol: American Foreign Policy, the Cold War, and Korea, 1945–1950.* Kent, OH: Kent State University Press, 1981.

————. "Limiting Room to Maneuver: The Korea Assistance Act of 1949." *Historian* 48 (August 1986): 525–538.

Dore, Ronald. *Land Reform in Japan.* London: Oxford University Press, 1959.

Dower, John. *Empire and Aftermath: Yoshida Shigeru and the Japanese Experience, 1878–1954.* Cambridge, MA: Harvard University Press, 1979.

Dower, John W. "Occupied Japan and the American Lake, 1945–1950." In Edward Friedman and Mark Selden, eds., *America's Asia.* New York: Random House, 1969.

————. "Occupied Japan as History and Occupation History as Politics." *Journal of Asian Studies* 34 (February 1975): 485–504.

Dunn, Frederick. *Peace-making and the Settlement with Japan.* Princeton, NJ: Princeton University Press, 1963.

Ellis, Earl H. *Advanced Base Operations in Micronesia.* Washington, DC: U.S. Marine Corps, 1992.

Esherick, Joseph W., ed. *Lost Chance in China, The World War II Despatches of John S. Service.* New York: Random House, 1974.

Esthus, Raymond. *Theodore Roosevelt and Japan.* Seattle: University of Washington Press, 1967.

Evans, Paul. *John Fairbank and the American Understanding of Modern China.* New York: Basil Blackwell, 1988.

Fairbank, John K. "Our Chances in China." *Atlantic* 178:3 (September 1946): 37–42.

————. *Chinabound: A Fifty-Year Memoir.* New York: Harper, 1982.

Feary, Robert, and Edwin M. Martin. *The Occupation of Japan, Second Phase: 1948–50.* New York: NY: Macmillan, 1950; reprint, Westport, CT: Greenwood, 1972.

Feaver, John H. "The China Aid Bill of 1948: Limited Assistance as a Cold War Strategy." *Diplomatic History* 5 (Spring 1981): 107–120.

Fehrenbach, Thomas R. *This Kind of War: A Study in Unpreparedness.* New York: Macmillan, 1963.

Feis, Herbert. *The China Tangle: The American Effort in China from Pearl Harbor to the Marshall Mission.* Princeton, NJ: Princeton University Press, 1953.

————. *Contest over Japan.* New York: Norton, 1967.

Finn, Richard. *Winners in Peace: MacArthur, Yoshida, and Postwar Japan.* Berkeley: University of California Press, 1992.

Flynn, John. *While You Slept; Our Tragedy in Asia and Who Made It.* New York: Devin-Adair Co., 1951.

Flynn, John T. *The Lattimore Story.* New York: 1953.

Foltos, Lester J. "The New Pacific Barrier: America's Search for Security in the Pacific." *Diplomatic History* 13:3 (Summer 1989): 317–342.

Foot, Rosemary. *The Wrong War: American Policy and the Dimensions of the Korean Conflict, 1950–1953.* Ithaca, NY: Cornell University Press, 1985.

————. "Making Known the Unknown War: Policy Analysis of the Korean Conflict in the Last Decade." *Diplomatic History* 15 (Summer 1991): 411–431.

Friedman, Edward, and Mark Selden, eds. *America's Asia: Dissenting Essays on Asian-American Relations.* New York: Random House, 1969.

Gardner, Lloyd C. *Approaching Vietnam: From World War II through Dienbienphu, 1941–1954.* New York: NY: Norton, 1988.

Gardner, Lloyd. "Review: Korea: The Unknown War." *Journal of American History* 78:3 (December 1991): 1176–1178.

Garthoff, Raymond. *Soviet Strategy in the Nuclear Age.* New York: Praeger, 1965.

———. "Soviet Intervention in Manchuria, 1945–46." In R. Garthoff, ed., *Sino-Soviet Military Relations.* New York: Praeger, 1966.

Gayle, John S. "Korea, Honor without War." *Military Review* 30:10 (1951): 55–62.

Gayn, Mark. *Japan Diary.* Rutland, VT: Tuttle, 1948.

George, Alexander L. "American Policy-making and the North Korean Aggression." *World Politics* 7 (January 1955): 209–232.

Gittings, John. *The World and China, 1922–1972.* New York: Harper & Row, 1974.

Gluck, Carol. "Entangling Illusions—Japanese and American Works in the American Occupation of Japan." In Warren I. Cohen, ed., *New Frontiers in American–East Asian Relations,* pp. 169–236. New York: Columbia University Press, 1983.

Goldstein, Steven M., and He Di. "New Chinese Sources on the History of the Cold War." *Cold War International History Project Bulletin* 1 (Spring 1992): 4–6.

Gorcharov, Sergei N. "Stalin's Dialogue with Mao Zedong." Interview with I. V. Kovalev. Trans. Craig Serbert. *Journal of Northeast Asia Studies* 10:4 (Winter 1991–92): 45–76.

Good, Robert C. "The United States and the Atomic Debate." In Arnold Wolfers, ed., *Alliance Policy in the Cold War,* pp. 224–270. Baltimore, MD: Johns Hopkins Press, 1959.

Goodman, Walter, "Review of Television Progress: *Korea: The Unknown War.*" *New York Times,* November 12, 1990, p. C-18.

Gordon, Leonard. "American Planning for Taiwan, 1942–1945." *Pacific Historical Review* 37 (May 1968): 201–228.

Grasso, June. *Truman's Two-China Policy: 1948–1950.* Armonk, NY: M. E. Sharpe, 1987.

Grattan, C. Hartley. *The Southwest Pacific since 1990: A Modern History: Australia, New Zealand, the Islands, Antarctica.* Ann Arbor: University of Michigan Press, 1963.

Grey, Arthur L., Jr. "The Thirty-Eighth Parallel." *Foreign Affairs* 29 (April 1951): 482–487.

Gunther, John. *The Riddle of MacArthur: Japan, Korea and the Far East.* New York: Harper, 1950; reprint, Westport, CT: Greenwood Press, 1974.

Hadley, Eleanor. *Antitrust in Japan.* Princeton, NJ: Princeton University Press, 1970.

Hao, Yufan, and Zhai Zhihai. "China's Decision to Enter the Korean War: History Revisited." *China Quarterly* 121 (March 1990): 94–115.

Han, T'aes-su. *Han'guk chongdang-sa* (A history of Korean political parties). Seoul: Sin t'aeyang-sa, 1961.

Harding, Harry, Yuan Ming, and Pei-ching Ta Hsueh, eds. *Sino-American Relations, 1945–1955: A Joint Reassessment of a Critical Decade.* Wilmington, DE: Scholarly Resources, 1989.

Harrington, Fred Harvey. " 'Europe First' and Its Consequences for the Far Eastern Policy of the United States." In Lloyd Gardner, ed., *Redefining the Past.* Corvallis: Oregon State University Press, 1986.

Harrison, Selig S. *The Widening Gulf: Asian Nationalism and American Policy.* New York: Free Press, 1978.

Heller, Francis H., ed. *The Korean War: A 25-Year Perspective.* Lawrence: Regents Press of Kansas, 1977.

Herring, George. "Truman and the Restoration of French Sovereignty in Indochina." *Diplomatic History* 1 (Spring 1977): 99–117.

Hess, Gary. "The First American Commitment in Indochina: The Acceptance of the Bao Dai Solution." *Diplomatic History* 2 (Fall 1978): 331–350.

———. "Global Expansion and Regional Balances: The Emerging Scholarship on United States Relations with India and Pakistan." *Pacific Historical Review* 56 (May 1987a): 259–295.

———. *The United States Emergence As a Southeast Asian Power 1940–1950.* New York: Columbia University, 1987b.

Hinton, Harold. *Communist China in World Politics.* Boston: Houghton Mifflin, 1966.

Hitchcock, Wilbur. "North Korea Jumps the Gun." *Current History* 20 (March 1951): 136–144.

Holding Company Liquidation Commission (HCLC). *Final Report on Zaibatsu Dissolution.* Tokyo: HCLC, 1951. English version of Mochikabu Kaisha Jinkai, ed. *Mochikabu Kaisha Seiri Jinkai Srakusho: Zaibatsu Isaitai wakaku okonowareta.* HCLC, 1951.

Hollerman, Leon. "International Economic Controls in Occupied Japan." *Journal of Asian Studies* 38:4 (1979): 707–719.

Hinton, Harold. *Communist China in World Politics.* Boston: Houghton Mifflin, 1966.

———. *China's Turbulent Quest: An Analysis of China's Foreign Policy since 1945.* New York: Macmillan 1970.

Homan, Gerlof D. "The U.S. and the Netherlands East Indies: The Evolution of American Anti-Colonialism." *Pacific Historical Review* 53 (November 1984): 436–447.

Hornbeck, Stanley K. "The United States and the Netherlands East Indies." *Annals of the American Academy of Political and Social Science* 255 (January 1948): 124–135.

Huang, Hua. "My Contacts with Stuart after Nanjing's Liberation." Trans. Li Xiaobing. *Chinese Historians* 5:1 (Spring 1992): 47–56.

Hunt, Michael. "Beijing and the Korean Crisis, June 1950–June 1951." *Political Science Quarterly* 107:3 (Fall 1992): 453–478.

Hunt, Michael H., and Odd Arne Westad. "The Chinese Communist Party and International Affairs: A Field Report on New Historical Sources and Odd Research Problems." *China Quarterly* 122 (June 1990): 258–272.

Igarashi Takeshi. "MacArthur's Proposal for an Early Peace with Japan and the Redirection of Occupation Policy toward Japan." *Japanese Journal of American Studies* 1 (1981): 55–86.

Iriye, Akira. "Continuities in U.S.-Japanese Relations, 1941–49." In Yonosuke Nagai and Akira Iriye, eds., *The Origins of the Cold War in Asia.* New York: Columbia University Press, 1977a.

———. "Was There a Cold War in Asia?" in John Chay, ed., *The Problems and Prospects of American–East Asian Relations.* Boulder, CO: Westview Press, 1977b.

———. "Contemporary History as History: American Expansion into the Pacific since 1941." *Pacific Historical Review* 53 (May 1984): 191–212.

———. "Reischauer, Fairbank, and American-Asian Relations." *Diplomatic History* 12 (Summer 1988): 329–341.

Iriye, Akira, and Warren Cohen, eds. *American, Chinese and Japanese Perspectives on Wartime, 1931–49.* Wilmington, DE: Scholarly Resources, 1992.

Irving, Ronald E. *The First Indochina War: French and American Policy, 1945–1954.* London: C. Helm, 1975.

Isaacs, Harold. *Images of Asia: American Views of China and India.* New York: Capricorn, 1962.

Israel, Jerry. "'Mao's Mr. America.' Edgar Snow's Images of China." *Pacific Historical Review* 47 (February 1978): 107–122.

Jervis, Robert. "The Impact of the Korean War on the Cold War." *Journal of Conflict Resolution* 24 (December 1980): 563–592.

Jespersen, T. Christopher. " 'Spreading the American Dream' of China: United China Relief; The Luce Family, and the Creation of American Conceptions of China before Pearl Harbor." *Journal of American–East Asian Relations* 1:3 (Fall 1992): 269–294.

Judd, Walter H. "The Mistakes That Led to Korea." *Reader's Digest* 57:343 (1950): 51–57.

Kahn, E. J. *The China Hands: America's Foreign Service Officers and What Befell Them.* New York: Viking, 1975.

Karig, Walter. *The Fortunate Islands, A Pacific Interlude; An Account of the Pleasant Lands and People in the United States' Trust Territory of the Pacific.* New York: Rinehart, 1948.

Karnow, Stanley. *In Our Image: America's Empire in the Philippines.* New York: Random House, 1989.

Kaufman, Burton Ira. *The Korean War: Challenges in Crisis, Credibility, and Command.* Philadelphia: Temple University, 1986.

Kautsky, John H. *Moscow and the Communist Party of India.* New York: John Wiley and Sons, 1956.

Kawai, Kazuo. *Japan's American Interlude.* Chicago: University of Chicago Press, 1960.

Keeley, Joseph C. *The China Lobby Man; The Story of Alfred Kohlberg.* New Rochelle, NY: Arlington House, 1969.

Kennan, George F. *Memoirs, 1925–1963.* 2 vols. Boston: Little, Brown, 1967, 1972.

Khrushchev, Nikita. *Khrushchev Remembers.* Trans. Strobe Talbott. Boston: Little, Brown, 1970.

Kim, Chum-kon. *The U.S. Imperialists Started the Korean War.* Pyongyang: Foreign Languages Publishing House, 1972.

———. *The Korean War.* Seoul: Kwangmyong Publishing Co., 1973.

Kim, Gye-dong. "Who Initiated the Korean War?" In James Cotton and Ian Neary, pp. 33–50. *The Korean War in History.* Atlantic Highlands, NJ: Humanities Press International, 1989.

Kim, Ilpyong J. *Communist Politics in North Korea.* New York: Praeger, 1975.

Koen, Ross. "McCarthyism and Our Asian Policy." *Bulletin of Concerned Asian Scholars* 1:4 (May 1969): 27–31.

Koen, Ross Y. *The China Lobby in American Politics.* New York: Harper & Row, 1974.

Kolko, Gabriel. *The Politics of War: The World and United States Foreign Policy, 1943–1945.* New York: Random House, 1968.

———. *Anatomy of a War: Vietnam, The United States, and the Modern Historical Experience.* New York: Pantheon, 1985.

———. *Confronting the Third World: United States Foreign Policy, 1945–1980.* New York: Pantheon, 1988.

Kolko, Joyce, and Gabriel. *The Limits of Power: The World and United States Foreign Policy, 1945–1954.* New York: Harper & Row, 1972.

Kubek, Anthony. *How the Far East Was Lost: American Policy and the Creation of Communist China, 1941–1949.* Chicago: Regnery, 1963.

Kublin, Hyman. "Okinawa: A Key to the Western Pacific." *U.S. Naval Institute Proceedings* 80 (1954): 1359–1365.

Kust, Matthew. "The Great Dilemma of American Policy." *Virginia Quarterly Review* 34 (Spring 1958): 224–239.

LaFeber, Walter. "Roosevelt, Churchill and Indochina: 1942–1945." *American Historical Review* 80 (December 1975): 1277–1295.

Latourette, Kenneth S. *The American Record in the Far East, 1945–1951.* New York: Macmillan, 1952.

Lattimore, Owen. *The Situation in Asia.* Boston: Little, Brown, 1949.

———. *Ordeal by Slander.* Boston: Little, Brown, 1950.

Leckie, Robert. *The War in Korea, 1950–1953.* New York: Putnam, 1963.

Lee, Chong-sik. *The Politics of Korean Nationalism.* Berkeley: University of California Press, 1961.

Leopold, Richard W. "The Korean War: The Historian's Task." In Francis H. Heller, ed., pp. 209–224. *The Korean War: A 25-Year Perspective.* Lawrence, KS: Regents Press of Kansas, 1977.

Levine, Steven I. "Soviet-American Rivalry in Manchuria and the Cold War." In Hsüeh Chün-tu, ed., *Dimensions of China's Foreign Relations,* pp. 10–43. New York: Praeger, 1977.

———. "A New Look at American Mediation in the Chinese Civil War: The Marshall Mission and Manchuria." *Diplomatic History* 3 (Fall 1979): 349–375.

Lewis, John W., Sergei N. Goncharov, and Litai Xue. *Uncertain Partners: Stalin, Mao, and the Korean War.* Stanford, CA: Stanford University Press, 1993.

Li, Haiwen. "A Distortion of History: An Interview with Shi Ze about Kovalev's Recollections." Trans. Wang Xi. *Chinese Historians* 5:2 (Fall 1992): 59–64.

Liang, Chin-tung. *General Stilwell in China, 1942–1944: The Full Story.* New York: St. John's University Press, 1972.

———. "The Sino-Soviet Treaty of Friendship and Alliance of 1945." In Paul K. T. Sih, ed., *Nationalist China during the Sino-Japanese War, 1937–1945,* pp. 373–397, 405–408. Hicksville, NY: Exposition, 1977.

Lilley, Charles R. "American–East Asian Relations in the Heroic and Whig Modes." *Diplomatic History* 18 (Winter 1994): 135–141.

Lippmann, Walter. *Commentaries on American Far Eastern Policy.* New York: Institute of Pacific Relations, 1950.

Liu, Xiaoyuan. "Sino-American Diplomacy over Korea during World War II." *Journal of American–East Asian Relations* 1 (Summer 1992): 223–264.

Lohbeck, Don. *Patrick J. Hurley.* Chicago: Regnery, 1956.

Louis, William Roger. *Imperialism at Bay: The United States and the Decolonialization of the British Empire, 1941–1945.* New York: Oxford University Press, 1978.

Loynd, Ray. "Review, TV Program Korea, The Unknown War." *Los Angeles Times,* November 12, 1990, p. F-12.

MacArthur, Douglas. *Reminiscences.* New York: McGraw-Hill, 1964.

McCormick, Thomas. *America's Half-Century.* Baltimore: Johns Hopkins University Press, 1989.

McCormick, Thomas J. "Insular Imperialism and the Open Door: The China Market and the Spanish-American War." *Pacific Historical Review* 32 (1963): 155–169.

McCune, George M., and Arthur L. Grey, Jr. *Korea Today.* Cambridge: Harvard University Press, 1950.

MacDonald, Douglas J. *Adventures in Chaos: American Intervention for Reform in the Third World.* Cambridge: Harvard University Press, 1992.

McFarland, Keith, ed. *The Korean War: An Annotated Bibliography.* New York: NY: Garland, 1986.

MacFarlane, S. Neil. *Superpower Rivalry and Third World Radicalism: The Idea of National Liberation.* Baltimore, MD: Johns Hopkins University Press, 1985.

McGlothlen, Ronald L. "Acheson, Economics, and the American Commitment in Korea, 1947–1950." *Pacific Historical Review* 58:1 (February 1989): 23–54.

———. *Controlling the Waves: Dean Acheson and the U.S. in Asia.* New York: Norton, 1993.

McLane, Charles B. *Soviet Strategies in Southeast Asia: An Exploration of Eastern Policy under Lenin and Stalin.* Princeton, NJ: Princeton University Press, 1966.

McLean, David. "American Nationalism, the China Myth, and the Truman Doctrine: The Question of Accommodation with Peking, 1949–50." *Diplomatic History* 10 (Winter 1986): 25–42.

McMahon, Robert J. *Colonialism and Cold War: The United States and the Struggle for Indonesian Independence, 1945–1949.* Ithaca, NY: Cornell, 1981.

———. "Eisenhower and Third World Nationalism: A Critique of the Revisionist." *Political Science Quarterly* 101 (1986): 453–473.

———. "The Cold War in Asia: Toward a New Synthesis." *Diplomatic History* 12 (Spring 1988): 307–327.

———. "Toward a Post-Colonial Order: Truman Administration Policies toward South and Southeast Asia." In Michael J. Lacy, ed., *The Truman Presidency,* pp. 339–365. New York: University Press, 1989.

McVey, Ruth T. *The Calcutta Conference and the Southeast Asian Uprisings.* Ithaca, NY: Cornell University's Southeast Asia Program, 1958.

Mahan, Alfred Thayer. *Lessons of the War with Spain and Other Articles.* Boston: Little, Brown, 1899.

———. *The Influence of Seapower upon History.* Boston: Little, Brown, 1890; reprint 1928.

Manchester, William. *American Caesar: Douglas MacArthur, 1880–1964.* Boston: Little, Brown, 1978.

Marshall, Mac, and James D. Nelson. *Micronesia, 1944–1974: A Bibliography of Anthropological and Related Source Materials.* New Haven, CT: HRAF Press, 1975.

Matray, James. *The Reluctant Crusade: American Foreign Policy in Korea, 1941–1950.* Honolulu: University of Hawaii Press, 1985.

May, Ernest R. *The Truman Administration and China, 1945–1949.* Philadelphia: Lippincott, 1975.

May, Ernest R., and James C. Thomson, Jr., eds. *American–East Asian Relations: A Survey.* Cambridge: Harvard University Press, 1972.

May, Gary A. *China Scapegoat: The Diplomatic Ordeal of John Carter Vincent.* Prospect Heights, IL: Waveland Press, 1979.

Mayer, David. *Cracking the Monolith: U.S. Policy against the Sino-Soviet Alliance, 1949–1955.* Baton Rouge: Louisiana State, 1986.

Mayo, Marlene. "American Wartime Planning for Occupied Japan: The Role of the Experts." In Robert Wolfe, ed., *Americans as Proconsuls: United States Military Governments in Germany and Japan, 1944–1952,* pp. 29–30. Carbondale, IL: Southern Illinois University Press, 1984.

Melby, John. *The Mandate of Heaven: Record of a Civil War; China 1945–1949.* Garden City, NY: Anchor Books, 1971; original, Toronto: University of Toronto Press, 1968.

Merrill, John. "Review of Khrushchev Remembers." *Journal of Korean Studies* 3 (1981): 181–190.

———. "The Cheju-do Rebellion." *Journal of Korean Studies* 2 (1982): 139–198.

———. *Korea: The Peninsular Origins of the War.* Newark, DL: University of Delaware Press, 1988.

———. *Peninsular Origins of the Korean War.* Newark, DL: University of Delaware Press, 1989.

Merrill, Dennis. "Shaping Third World Development: U.S. Foreign Aid and Supervision in the Philippines, 1948–1953." *Journal of American–East Asian Relations* 2:2 (Summer 1993): 137–160.

Miller, Edward. *War Plan Orange: The U.S. Strategy to Defeat Japan: 1897–1945.* Annapolis, MD: Naval Institute Press, 1991.

Mitchell, C. Clyde. *Korea's Second Failure in Asia.* Washington, DC: Public Affairs Institute, 1951.

Miwa, Ryoiche. "1949-men no dokusen knshiko kaisei" (The revision of the antimonopoly law in 1949). In Nakamura Takafusa, ed., *Senryoki Nikon no Keizai to Seiji* (Japanese economy and politics during the occupation). Tokyo: Daigaku Shuppankai, 1979.

———. *Showa Zaiseishi.* Vol. 2: *Dokusen knishi* (The economic and financial history of the Showa period; vol. 2: Antimonopoly policy). Tokyo: Toyo Keizai Shinposha, 1981.

Miyasato, Seigen. "The Truman Administration and Indochina: Case Studies in Decision Making." *Japanese Journal of American Studies* 1 (1981): 125–134.

Moore, Ray A. "New Japanese Government Materials on the American Occupation of Japan." In Lawrence Redman, ed., *The Occupation of Japan: Impact of Legal Reforms,* pp. 201–207. Norfolk, VA: MacArthur Memorial, 1978.

———. "Reflections on the Occupation of Japan." *Journal of Asian Studies* 38:4 (1979): 721–734.

———. "The Occupation of Japan as History." *Monumenta Nipponica* 36 (1981): 317–328.

———., ed. *Tenno ga Baiburu o yonda Li* (The days when the emperor read the Bible). Kodansha, 1982.

Moos, Felix, et al. *The United States and Japan in the Western Pacific: Micronesia and Papua New Guinea.* Boulder, CO: Westview Press, 1981.

Morton, Louis. "Germany First: The Basic Concept of Allied Strategy in World War II." In Kent Roberts Greenfield, ed., *Command Decisions,* pp. 11–47 Washington: GPO, 1960.

Munro-Leighton, Judith. "A Postrevisionist Scrutiny of America's Role in the Cold War in Asia, 1945–1950." *Journal of American–East Asian Relations* 1 (Spring 1992): 73–98.

Nagai, Yonosuke, and Akira Iriye, eds. *The Origins of the Cold War in Asia.* New York: Columbia University Press, 1977.

Neils, Patricia. *China Images in the Life and Times of Henry Luce.* Savage, MD: Rowman & Littlefield, 1990.

Nevin, David. *The American Touch in Micronesia: A Story of Power, Money and the Corruption of a Pacific Paradise.* New York: Norton, 1977.

Newman, Robert P. "The Self-Inflicted Wound: The China White Paper of 1949." *Prologue* 14 (1982): 151–156.

———. "Clandestine Chinese Nationalist Efforts to Punish Their American Detractors." *Diplomatic History* 7 (1983): 205–222.

———. *Owen Lattimore and the "Loss" of China.* Berkeley: University of California Press, 1992.

Nishimura, Kumao. *San Furanshisuko Heiwa Joyaku* (The San Francisco peace treaty). Vol. 40 in *Nihon Gaiko Shi* (Diplomatic history of Japan). Tokyo: Kajima Kenkyu jo Shuppan Kai, 1971.

Niu, Jun. *Cong Yanan zouxiang. Shijie: Zhongguo gongchandang duiwai guanxi de qiyuan* (From Yinan to the world: The origins of Chinese communist foreign relations). Guzhow: Fujian renmin chubanshe, 1992.

Noble, Harold J. *Embassy at War: An Account of the Early Weeks of the Korean War.* Ed. Frank Baldwin. Seattle: University of Washington Press, 1975.

Noda, Iwajiro. *Zaibatsu kaitai shiki* (Reminiscences on *zaibatsu* dissolution). Tokyo: Nihon Keizai Shinposha, 1983.

Nunn, G. Raymond. *Asia, Reference Works: A Select Annotated Guide.* London: Mansell, 1980.

———. *Asia and Oceania: A Guide to Archival and Manuscript Sources in the United States.* New York: Mansell, 1985.

Oh, John Kie-chiang. *Korea: Democracy on Trial.* Ithaca, NY: Cornell University Press, 1968.

Oliver, Douglas L. *The Pacific Islands.* Honolulu: University Press of Hawaii, 1975; also 1981 and 1951 editions.

Oliver, Robert T. *Why War Came in Korea.* New York: Fordham University, 1950.

———. *Korean Report, 1948–1952; A Review of Governmental Procedures during the Two Years of Peace and Two of War.* Washington, DC: Korean Pacific Press, 1952.

———. *Syngman Rhee and American Involvement in Korea, 1942–60: A Personal Narrative.* Seoul: Panmun, 1978.

Paige, Glenn. *The Korea Decisions (June 24–30, 1950).* New York: Free Press, 1968.

Park, Hong-Kyu. "From Pearl Harbor to Cairo: American Korean Diplomacy." *Diplomatic History* 13:3 (Summer 1989): 343–358.

Passin, Herbert, ed. *The United States and Japan.* Englewood Cliffs, NJ: Prentice-Hall, 1966.

Paterson, Thomas G. "If Europe, Why Not China? The Containment Doctrine, 1947–49." *Prologue* 13 (Spring 1981): 18–38. A revised version appears in Paterson, *Meeting the Communist Threat,* pp. 54–75. New York: Oxford University Press, 1988.

Peck, Braham. *Two Kinds of Time.* Boston: Houghton Mifflin, 1950.

Perkins, Whitney. *Denial of Empire: The United States and Its Dependencies.* Leyden: A. W. Sythoff, 1962.

Perry, John Curtis. *Beneath the Eagle's Wings: Americans in Occupied Japan.* New York: Dodd, Mead, 1980.

Pogue, Forrest C. *George C. Marshall: Statesman, 1945–1959.* Vol. 4 of *George C. Marshall.* New York: Viking Press, 1987.

Pomeroy, Earl E. *Pacific Outpost: American Strategy in Guam and Micronesia.* Stanford, CA: Stanford University Press, 1951; reprint, New York: Russell and Russell, 1970.

Pratt, Julius. *America's Colonial Experiment: How the United States Gained, Governed, and in Part Gave Away a Colonial Empire.* New York: Prentice Hall, 1950; reprint Gloucester, MA: P. Smith, 1964.

Pruessen, Ronald. *John Foster Dulles: The Road to Power.* New York: Free Press, 1982.

Reardon-Anderson, James. *Yenan and the Great Powers: The Origins of Chinese Communist Foreign Policy, 1944–1946.* New York: Columbia University Press, 1980.

Ree, Erik van. *Socialism in One Zone: Stalin's Policy in Korea, 1945–1947.* New York: St. Martin's Oxford, 1989.

Rees, David. *Korea: The Limited War.* New York: St. Martin's, 1964.

Reischauer, Edwin O. *Toward a New Far Eastern Policy.* Headline Series 84. New York: Foreign Policy Association, 1950a.

———. *The United States and Japan.* Cambridge: Harvard University Press, 1950b. Later revised editions, 1957, 1965.

———. *My Life between Japan and America.* New York: Harper & Row, 1986.

Robbins, Robert R. "United States Trusteeship for the Territory of the Pacific Islands." *Department of State Bulletin,* May 4, 1947, pp. 783–792.

Roberts, John G. "The 'Japan Crowd' and the Zaibatsu Restoration." *Japan Interpreter* 12:3/4 (1979): 383–415.

Roberts, Priscilla, ed. *Sino-American Relations since 1900.* Hong Kong: Centre of Asian Studies, University of Hong Kong, 1991.

Roff, Sue Rabbitt. *Overreaching in Paradise: United States Policy in Palau since 1945.* Juneau, AK: Denali Press, 1991.

Romanus, Charles F., and Riley Sunderland. *Stilwell's Mission to China; Stilwell's Command Problems;* and *Time Runs Out.* Washington, DC: Department of the Army, Historical Division, 1953, 1956, 1959.

Rose, Lisle A. *Roots of Tragedy: The United States and the Struggle for Asia, 1945–1954.* Westport, CT: Greenwood Press, 1976.

Rostow, Walter W. *The Prospects for Communist China.* Cambridge, MA: MIT Press, 1954.

Rotter, Andrew J. "The Triangular Route to Vietnam: The United States, Great

Britain and Southeast Asia, 1945–1950.'' *International History Review* 6 (August 1984): 404–423.

———. *The Path to Vietnam: The Origins of the American Commitment to Southeast Asia.* Ithaca, NY: Cornell University Press, 1987.

Sbrega, John J. ''Anglo-American Perspectives on Indochina during the Second World War.'' *Journal of Southeast Asian Studies* 14:1 (March. 1983a): 63–78.

———. *Anglo-American Relations and Colonialism in East Asia, 1941–1945.* New York: Garland, 1983b.

Scalapino, Robert A., and Chong-sik Lee. *Communism in Korea.* Berkeley: University of California, 1972.

Schaller, Michael. *The United States and China in the Twentieth Century.* New York: Oxford University Press, 1979a.

———. *The U.S. Crusade in China, 1938–1945.* New York: Columbia University Press, 1979b.

———. ''Securing the Great Crescent: Occupied Japan and the Origins of Containment in Southeast Asia.'' *Journal of American History* 69 (September 1982): 392–414.

———. *The American Occupation of Japan: The Origins of the Cold War in Asia.* New York: Oxford University Press, 1985.

———. *Douglas MacArthur: The Far East General.* New York: Oxford University Press, 1989.

Schonberger, Howard. ''The Japan Lobby in American Diplomacy, 1947–1952.'' *Pacific Historical Review* 46 (August 1977): 327–359.

———. ''American Labor's Cold War in Occupied Japan.'' *Diplomatic History* 3:3 (1979): 249–272.

———. ''Peacemaking in Asia: The United States, Great Britain, and the Japanese Decision to Recognize Nationalist China, 1951–52.'' *Diplomatic History* 10:1 (Winter 1986): 59–74.

———. *Aftermath of War: Americans and the Remaking of Japan, 1945–1952.* Kent, OH: Kent State University, 1989.

Schulzinger, Robert. *The Making of the Diplomatic Mind: The Training, Outlook and Style of United States Foreign Service Officers, 1908–1931.* Middletown, CT: Wesleyan University Press, 1975.

Schwartzberg, Steven. ''The 'Soft Peace Boys': Presurrender Planning and Japanese Land Reform.'' *Journal of American–East Asian Relations* 2:2 (Summer 1993): 185–216.

Sebald, William. *With MacArthur in Japan: A Personal History of the Occupation.* New York: W. W. Norton, 1965.

Selden, Mark, ed. *Remaking Asia: Essays on the American Uses of Power.* New York: Pantheon, 1974.

Service, John S. *The Amerasia Papers: Some Problems in the History of U.S.-China Relations.* China Research Monograph. Berkeley: CA: University of California, 1971.

Shalom, Stephen R. *The United States and the Philippines: A Study of Neocolonialism.* Philadelphia: Institute for the Study of Human Issues, 1981.

Shulman, Frank J., comp. *Doctoral Dissertations on Asia: An Annotated Bibliographical Journal of Current International Research.* Ann Arbor, MI: University Microfilms, 1975.

Shulman, Marshall. *Stalin's Foreign Policy Reappraised*. Cambridge: Harvard University Press, 1963.

Simmons, Robert. *The Strained Alliance: Peking, Pyongyang, Moscow and the Politics of the Korean Civil War*. New York: Free Press, 1975.

Smith, Beverly. "The White House Story: Why We Went to War in Korea." *Saturday Evening Post*, November 10, 1951, pp. 22–23ff.

Smith, Ralph B. *An International History of the Vietnam War*. Vol. 1: *Revolution Versus Containment*. New York: St. Martin's, 1984.

Snow, Edgar. *Red Star over China*. New York: Garden City Publishing Co., 1939.

———. *Random Notes on China, 1936–1945*. Cambridge: Harvard University Press, 1957.

Sodei, Rinjiro. *Makkasa no 2000-mihi* (MacArthur's two thousand days). Chuo Koron-sha, 1975.

———. "Janus-faced MacArthur." *Diplomatic History* 15:4 (Fall 1991): 621–629.

Spence, Jonathan. *To Change China: Western Advisers in China, 1620–1960*. Boston: Little, Brown, 1969.

Sprout, Harold and Margaret Sprout. *Toward a New Order of Sea Power: American Naval Policy and the World Scene, 1918–1922*. Princeton, NJ: Princeton University Press, 1943.

———. *The Rise of American Naval Power: 1776–1918*. Princeton, NJ: Princeton University Press, 1946.

Stilwell, Joseph W. *The Stilwell Papers*. Ed. Theodore H. White. New York: Sloan, 1948.

———. *Stilwell's Personal File, China, Burma, India, 1942–1944*. Ed. Riley Sunderland and Charles F. Romanus. 5 vols. Wilmington, DE: Scholarly Resources, 1976.

Stoler, Mark. "The Pacific First Alternative in American World War II Strategy." *International History Review* 2:3 (1980): 432–452.

Stone, Isidore F. *Hidden History of the Korean War*. New York: Monthly Review Press, 1952.

Stuart, John Leighton. *Fifty Years in China*. New York: Random House, 1954.

———. *The Forgotten Ambassador: The Reports of John Leighton Stuart, 1946–1949*. Boulder, CO: Westview Press, 1981.

Stueck, William Whitney, Jr. *The Road to Confrontation: American Policy toward China and Korea, 1947–1950*. Chapel Hill: University of North Carolina, 1981.

———. "The Chennault Plan to Save China: U.S. Containment in Asia and the Origins of the CIA's Aerial Empire, 1949–1950." *Diplomatic History* 3 (Fall 1984a): 349–364.

———. *The Wedemeyer Mission: American Politics and Foreign Policy during the Cold War*. Athens, GA: University of Georgia Press, 1984b.

———. "The Korean War as International History." *Diplomatic History* 10 (Fall 1986): 291–310.

Suh, Dae-Sook. *The Korean Communist Movement, 1918–1948*. Princeton, NJ: Princeton University Press, 1967.

Sunderland, Riley. "The Secret Embargo." *Pacific Historical Review* 29:1 (1960): 75–80.

Swartout, Robert, Jr. "American Historians and the Outbreak of the Korean War: An Historiographical Essay." *Asia Quarterly* [Belgium] no. 1 (1979): 65–77.

Takemae, Eiji. *Sengo Rodo Kaikaku: GHQ rodo seisakushi* (Postwar labor reform: A history of GHQ's labor policy). Tokyo Daigaku Shuppankai, 1982.

Textor, Robert. *Failure in Japan, with Keystones for a Positive Policy.* New York: John Day Co., 1951; reprint, Westport, CT: Greenwood Press, 1972.

Theoharis, Athan. *Seeds of Repression: Harry S. Truman and the Origins of McCarthyism.* Chicago: Quadrangle, 1971.

Thorne, Christopher. *Allies of a Kind: The United States, Britain and the War against Japan, 1941–1945.* New York: Oxford University Press, 1978.

Tinker, Hugh. *Ballot Box and Bayonet: People and Government in Emergent Asian Countries.* New York: Oxford University Press, 1964.

———. *Men Who Overturned Empires: Fighters, Dreamers, and Schemers.* Madison: University of Wisconsin Press, 1987.

Truman, Harry S. *Memoirs: Years of Trial and Hope.* Vol. 2. Garden City, NY: Doubleday, 1956.

Traeger, Frank N. "The Impact of Marxism." In Frank Traeger, ed., *Marxism in Southern Asia.* Stanford, CA: Stanford University Press, 1959.

Tsien Tsuen-hsuin, and James K. M. Cheng, comps. *China: An Annotated Bibliography of Bibliographies.* Boston: Hall, 1978.

Tsou, Mingde, and Li Jun. "Introduction to the General Situation Regarding Research in Chinese-American Relations." Trans. Warren I. Cohen and Athena Chou Warmer from the Shanghai *Jiefang Ribao* (Liberation daily), February 11, 1981 *Diplomatic History* 5 (Summer 1981): 273–275.

Tsou, Tang. *America's Failure in China, 1941–1950.* Chicago: University of Chicago Press, 1963.

Tsurumi, E. Patricia, ed. *The Other Japan: Postwar Realities.* Armonk, NY: M. E. Sharpe, 1988.

Tuchman, Barbara W. "If Mao Had Come to Washington: America and China: An Essay in Alternatives." *Foreign Affairs* 51:1 (October 1972a): 44–64.

———. *Stilwell and the American Experience in China 1911–1945.* New York: Macmillan, 1972b.

Tucker, Nancy B. "American Policy toward Sino-Japanese Trade in the Postwar Years: Politics and Prosperity." *Diplomatic History* 3 (Summer 1984): 183–208.

Tucker, Nancy Bernkopf. *Patterns in the Dust: Chinese-American Relations and the Recognition Controversy, 1949–1950.* New York: Columbia University Press, 1983.

Ulam, Adam. *Expansion and Coexistence: The History of Soviet Foreign Policy, 1917–1967.* New York: Praeger, 1968.

U.S. Congress. House. *Micronesian Claims.* Hearings, Ninety-first Congress, Second Session, on H.J. Res. 1161, H.J. Res. 1258, and H.J. Res. 1265. June 16, 23, and September 16, 1970. Washington, DC: GPO, 1971.

U.S. Department of State. *Relations with China, with Special Reference to the Period 1944–49.* Washington, DC: GPO, 1949; Reissued as *The China White Paper, August 1949.* 2 vols. Stanford, CA: Stanford University Press, 1967.

The United States in East Asia: A Historical Bibliography. Santa Barbara, CA: ABC-Clio, 1985.

Utley, Freda. *The China Story.* Chicago: Regnery, 1952.

Vinacke, Harold. *Far Eastern Politics in the Postwar Period.* New York: Appleton-Century-Crofts, 1956.

Wall, Irwin M. *The United States and the Making of Postwar France, 1945–1954.* New York: Cambridge University Press, 1991.

Ward, Robert E. "Reflections on the Allied Occupation and Planned Political Change in Japan." In Robert E. Ward, ed., *Political Development in Modern Japan.* Princeton, NJ: Princeton University Press, 1968.

Ward, Robert E., and Sakamoto Yoshikazu, eds. *Democratizing Japan: The Allied Occupation.* Honolulu: University of Hawaii Press, 1987.

Ward, Robert E., and Frank J. Shulman, comps. *The Allied Occupation of Japan, 1945–1952: An Annotated Bibliography of Western Language Materials.* Chicago: American Library Association, 1974.

Warner, Albert L. "How the Korean Decision Was Made." *Harper's* 202 (June 1951): 99–106.

Webb, James H. *Micronesia and U.S. Pacific Strategy: A Blueprint for the 1980's.* New York: Praeger, 1974.

Wedemeyer, Albert C. "1947 Wedemeyer Report on Korea." *Current History* 20:118 (1951): 863–865.

———. *Wedemeyer Reports.* New York: Holt, 1958.

Weil, Martin. *A Pretty Good Club: The Founding Fathers of the U.S. Foreign Service.* New York: Norton, 1978.

Welch, Richard E., Jr. "America's Philippine Policy in the Quirino Years (1948–1953): A Study in Patron-Client Relations." In Peter W. Stanley, ed., *Reappraising an Empire: New Perspectives in Philippine-American History.* Cambridge: Harvard University Press, 1984.

Westad, Odd Arne. *Cold War and Revolution: Soviet-American Rivalry and the Origins of the Chinese Civil War.* New York: Columbia University Press, 1993.

White, Theodore H. *In Search of History.* New York: Harper & Row, 1978.

White, Theodore, and Annalee Jacoby. *Thunder Out of China.* New York: Harper, 1946.

Whiting, Allen S. *China Crosses the Yalu: The Decision to Enter the Korean War.* New York: Macmillan, 1960.

Wiens, Herold J. *Pacific Island Bastions of the United States.* Princeton, NJ: Princeton University Press, 1962.

Williams, Justin. "Completing Japan's Political Reorientation, 1947–1952: Crucial Phase of the Allied Occupation." *American Historical Review* 73 (1968): 1454–1469.

———. *Japan's Political Revolution under MacArthur: A Participant's Account.* Athens: University of Georgia Press, 1979.

———. "American Occupation Policy for Occupied Japan: Correcting the Revisionist Version," and "Rejoinders" by John Dower and Howard Schonberger. *Pacific Historical Review* 57:2 (May 1988): 179–218.

Williams, William J., ed. *A Revolutionary War: Korea and the Transformation of the Postwar World.* Chicago: Imprint Publications, 1993.

Wiltz, John E. "William Manchester's *American Caesar:* Some Observations." *Military Affairs* (October 1979): 156–157.

Wurfel, David. "Problems of Decolonization." In Frank H. Golay, ed., *The United States and the Philippines,* pp. 149–173. Englewood Cliffs, NJ: Prentice-Hall, 1966.

————. *Filipino Politics: Development and Decay.* Ithaca, NY: Cornell University Press, 1988.

Yamamura, Kozo. "Zaibatsu Prewar and Zaibatsu Postwar." *Journal of Asian Studies* 23 (August 1964): 539–554.

————. *Economic Policy in Postwar Japan: Growth Versus Economic Democracy.* Berkeley, CA: University of California Press, 1967.

Yang, Kuisong. "The Soviet Factor and the CCP's Policy toward the United States in the 1940's." *Chinese Historians* 5:1 (Spring 1992): 17–34.

Yanihara, Tadao. *Pacific Islands under Japanese Mandate.* New York: AMS Press, 1977, reprint of a 1940 book.

Yoko, Yasuhara. "Japan, Communist China, and Export Controls in Asia, 1948–52." *Diplomatic History* 10:1 (Winter 1986): 75–90.

Yoshida, Shigeru. *The Yoshida Memoirs: The Story of Japan in Crisis.* Trans. Yoshida Kenichi. Boston: Houghton Mifflin, 1962.

Yoshitsu, Michael. *Japan and the San Francisco Peace Settlement.* New York: Columbia University Press, 1983.

Young, Kenneth R. "The Stilwell controversy: A Bibliographical Review." *Military Affairs* 39:2 (1975): 66–68.

Zagoria, Donald S. "Mao's Role in the Sino-Soviet Conflict." *Pacific Affairs* (Summer 1974): 139–153.

————. ed. *Soviet Policy in East Asia.* New Haven, CT: Yale University Press, 1981.

Zhai, Qiang. "The Making of Chinese Communist Foreign Relations, 1935–1949: A New Study from China." (A review of Niu Jun, *Cong Yanam shiyie* [From Yanan to the World, 1992]). *Journal of American-East Asian Relations* 1:4 (Winter 1992): 471–477.

Zobrist, Benedict. "Resources of Presidential Libraries for the History of Post–World War II American Military Government in Germany and Japan." *Military Affairs* 42 (1978): 17–19.

PART II

International Aspects of the Korean War

4   The United Nations and Korea

Lester H. Brune

The 1947 United Nations vote to supervise elections to unify Korea was hardly noticed amid the swirl of more prominent issues: the UN's partition plan to resolve the Jewish-Palestine Arab dispute, an investigation into the presence of foreign forces entering the Greek civil war, and the international control of atomic energy. Nevertheless, UN action on Korea in November 1947 became the first in a series of resolutions involving the organization, a series that finally made front-page headlines when war broke out on June 25, 1950.

Between 1947 and 1954, the General Assembly and Security Council played important roles in helping the United States to rally world opinion against communist aggression in Korea. UN activity regarding Korea began in 1947 when the General Assembly agreed to a U.S. proposal to sponsor national elections for an assembly to unify Korea. Over the next six years, the General Assembly agreed to recognize the South's Republic of Korea (ROK) in 1948, the Security Council acted to stop North Korea's aggression in June 1950, and the General Assembly approved the truce to end the war in July 1953. In most of these UN actions, the United States originated proposals that the Security Council or the General Assembly approved despite objections from the Union of Soviet Socialist Republics and its allies.

Although the formation of the United Nations in 1945 had been heralded as a method to maintain global peace, the persistent differences between the United States and the U.S.S.R. after World War II made it impossible to obtain agreement on most UN activity, including specific methods to unite Korea, which the two superpowers had jointly occupied in September 1945. After the Soviet Union rejected several U.S. proposals for Korea's future during 1947, Washington decided to ask the UN to resolve the question. On the basis of a special UN committee report, the

UN General Assembly approved a resolution on November 14, 1947, creating the UN Temporary Commission on Korea (UNTCOK) to supervise elections to unify Korea within the next six months. Both the United States and the Soviet Union indicated they were ready to withdraw their troops from Korea.

After success in obtaining a UN role, Secretary of State Dean Acheson used adroit diplomacy by calling on the General Assembly for support whenever the Security Council might be stymied by the Soviet Union's right to veto measures. Throughout the years of the Korean crisis, this method enabled the United States to determine UN policy on Korea, limited only by the desire of Canada, Great Britain, or India to restrain U.S. proposals that threatened to increase tensions or to expand the war into China or Western Europe. During 1948–1949, two General Assembly resolutions strengthened the UN's commitment to protect the ROK. Following elections in Korea in which the communists refused to participate and North Korea boycotted, the General Assembly approved a U.S. proposal on December 12, 1948, to recognize the ROK as the only legitimate government on the Korean peninsula. In this instance, Britain and Canada persuaded Acheson to alter his resolution's original intent to name the ROK as Korea's "national government," a term implying no rights for North Korea's Democratic People's Republic (DRPK), which the Soviets set up in Pyongyang. Even with the changed wording, the Soviet Union objected to the resolution.

The second resolution committing the UN to the ROK was obtained by the United States on October 21, 1949. Because the UN Temporary Commission's work officially ended after the South Korea election, the 1949 resolution maintained the group as the UN Commission in Korea (UNCOK), asking it to observe and report on developments in Korea. As a result the UNCOK returned to Korea in February 1950. After UN secretary-general Trygve Lie added military experts to its membership, this commission had qualifications to determine that North Korea was the aggressor when it attacked across the 38th parallel on June 25, 1950. On the two resolutions committing the UN to protect South Korea and for details of how the UN followed the lead of the United States in these and other Korean matters, see Jon Halliday's (1973) article, "The United Nations and Korea."

The outbreak of war in Korea came at an opportune moment for the United States to have the Security Council pass resolutions supporting the U.S. decision to assist South Korea with military measures. In January 1950, Jacob Malik, the Soviet delegate to the UN, began a boycott of UN action because the UN refused to seat the delegates of the People's Republic of China, which had gained control of mainland China in 1949. Consequently, in June and July 1950 with the Soviet delegate absent, the only voice and vote of a communist nation on the Security Council was Yugoslavia's delegate, Ales Bebler.

Under these circumstances, the Security Council voted to denounce North Korea's aggression and to assist South Korea in resolutions of June 25 and 27, 1950. The first resolution asked North Korea to stop its hostile action and to withdraw north of the 38th parallel. This resolution was requested by the United States but also urged by the UNCOK, which reported from Korea. Again, although the United States had to accept advice from its allies, Britain and Canada, to eliminate the phrase claiming that the DPRK committed "an unprovoked action of aggression," the Security Council approved the resolution by a 9–0 vote. Bebler of Yugoslavia abstained because he wanted to hear first from a North Korean delegate, a suggestion the council refused.

On June 27, the second resolution called on all UN members to assist in repelling North Korea's aggression. This resolution followed reports from General Douglas MacArthur and the UN Commission on Korea that North Korea had ignored the June 25 resolution by continuing its offensive against South Korea. The resolution followed President Harry Truman's announcement the same day that U.S. naval and air forces had been ordered to assist the ROK. U.S. ground forces were not committed until June 30. Edwin C. Hoyt (1961) examines these early decisions from the perspective of Washington's relating the action to principles contained in the 1945 UN Charter. The most crucial Security Council decision was the interpretation that the Soviet absence was not tantamount to a veto of the council's action.

After Jacob Malik ended the Soviet boycott on August 1, 1950, Secretary Acheson decided to use the General Assembly in order to bypass the Security Council regarding Korean affairs. This tactic was possible because the United States and its allies had a clear majority in the assembly. Not until 1960, when new member nations created from the former European colonies joined the UN, was the U.S. ability to command a majority threatened. Between 1950 and 1953, however, the United States and its Western allies easily gained a majority of General Assembly votes because Acheson's proposals needed only to satisfy friendly allies such as Canada and Great Britain.

Acheson's most important device to legitimatize the UN General Assembly's action was the "Uniting for Peace" resolution, passed on November 3, 1950. Since July 1950, Warren R. Austin, the U.S. delegate to the United Nations, had sought some method permitting the UN to monitor trouble spots around the world so that the UN could act. Acheson agreed with Austin but delayed going to the UN Assembly until finding a resolution that Britain, Canada, France, and other U.S. allies could cosponsor. Finally, on September 19, the United States submitted a proposal that empowered the UN General Assembly to act in the interests of peace. The resolution created the UN Peace Observation Commission to collect data about threats to international peace and asked UN members to designate special forces for a UN unit to keep peace when the Security Council or General Assembly requested. The resolution passed the assembly on November 3, 1950, by a vote of 52 to 5, with two abstentions.

During the remainder of the Korean War, the United States asked the General Assembly for approval of a variety of resolutions that seemed to necessitate broad support. The resolutions are described in James Matray's *Historical Dictionary of the Korean War* (1991). Two important resolutions regarded the prisoner-of-war (POW) issue and proposals leading to the truce of July 1953. During the negotiations for a Korean cease-fire in 1952, the U.S. proposal that POWs should be repatriated on a "voluntary basis" became controversial because it differed from the Geneva Convention of 1949, which provided for the automatic repatriation of all prisoners, a convention that neither the United States, North Korea, nor the People's Republic of China had ratified. Although Acheson first proposed a hard-line position to require voluntary repatriation, he eventually accepted a compromise plan presented by India's UN delegate, Krishna Menon. This resolution, which the UN General Assembly approved on December 3, 1952, became the basis for agreement by the communist Chinese and North Koreans in June 1953. Menon's plan called for a cease-fire, followed by an exchange of willing POWs, and the creation of a Neutral Nations Repatriation Commission to supervise the remaining prisoners of war until a final political agreement was made. Barton Bernstein describes the POW issue in an essay on the Korean armistice for the volume edited by Bruce Cumings (1983).

EVALUATIONS OF U.S.-UN RELATIONS

The methods the Truman administration used to obtain UN support during the war were later criticized by U.S. conservatives and revisionist scholars. For the conservatives, who sought "total victory" over communism and who had usually opposed the UN's role, the compromises that Acheson accepted to maintain UN support were to blame for the failure to win a military victory in Korea. As late as 1970, U.S. senator Thomas J. Dodd argued that the UN had prevented a victory over the communists in Korea. Citing such incidents as opposition to bombing Chinese troops on the Yalu River and accepting the 1953 cease-fire when the United States had a military advantage, Dodd claimed the UN enabled the communist negotiators, to emerge from the Panmunjom negotiations in 1953 and shout: "We have won. We have won."

To the contrary, revisionist scholars interpreted Acheson's policies with the UN as limiting liberal support for the UN as the primary peacekeeping body and for causing tensions with the Soviet Union by making UN interests synonomous with the interests of the United States and the rest of the world. Rober D. Accinelli's (1985) article describes the problems the American Association for the United Nations had with Acheson's Korean policy. Although the association generally backed U.S. efforts against North Korea's aggression, many members of the group believed it was dangerous for Washington to use the UN as a cold war instrument.

From a different perspective, Lynn Miller's (1974) essay on the UN and the cold war contends that Acheson's policy in Korea manipulated the UN to act on problems the United States favored while acting passively on the UN human rights proposals that were politically hazardous within the United States. Thus, Miller finds that the Korean episode was part of the U.S. responsibility in causing the cold war breakdown with Moscow.

LITERATURE ON THE UN AND KOREA

Almost all literature about the Korean War refers of necessity to the UN role in greater or lesser detail, but little scholarly work focuses particularly on the UN. Three scholars have studied the Korean War from a UN perspective. Leland M. Goodrich has a book (1956) that details UN activity as well as an article (1960) that evaluates the results of the UN collective action. Leon Gordenker (1959) covers the same basic data as Goodrich but is less well known. Gordenker also has an article (1958) about U.S. influence on the UN's conduct of Korea's 1948 elections. Taele Yoo's (1965) book gives an Asian view on the UN role during the war. Several studies about the United Nations include material about the Korean War. John Stoessinger's *The United Nations and the Superpowers* (1970) perceives the war in the context of various big-power attempts to use the UN. Robert Riggs (1958) studies U.S. influences on the UN General Assembly, while Tae Jin Kahng (1969) emphasizes the work of the Security Council. The first volume of Evan Luard's (1982) history of the UN describes the first decade as being dominated by the United States and the other Western powers. And the Canadian historian Denis Stairs (1970) explains how other UN members influenced Washington's decisions regarding Korea.

The UN's secretary-general during the war, Trygve Lie (1954), has published his memoirs about these years at the UN, and Stephen Schwebel (1953) wrote a contemporary account of Lie's work that praises his Korean policy for strongly backing collective action. George T. Mazuzan has an article (1978) on the U.S. commitment to the UN, but more important is his (1977) account of Warren Austin, the U.S. delegate to the United Nations. Austin's chief deputy at the UN, Philip Jessup (1974), has a memoir that particularly describes his work on the Korean problem between 1947 and 1950.

SMALL NATIONS' CONTRIBUTIONS TO UN FORCES

Following approval of the UN Security Council resolution of June 27, 1950, the secretary-general made the first of several appeals to UN member nations for military assistance to defend South Korea. The United States wanted aid from many nations, but several factors limited the participation of some nations. Initially, UN commander Douglas MacArthur asked for military units of 1,000 men with equipment and artillery support as well as some prior training.

Eventually twenty-one nations sent some personnel to Korea. Other than the United States, Canada, Great Britain, Australia, and New Zealand, whose roles are described in separate sections of this volume, eleven nations sent military units and five sent medical detachments. During the war, the United States provided approximately 50.3 percent of the ground forces, 85.9 percent of naval forces, and 93.4 percent of air forces used between July 1950 and 1953. South Korea had 40.1 percent of the UN army forces, 7.4 percent of the naval, and 5.6 percent of the air forces.

The nations sending combat forces were Belgium (whose battalion included personnel from Luxembourg), Colombia, Ethiopia, France, Greece, the Netherlands, South Africa, Turkey, Thailand, and the Philippines. Medical detachments were sent by Denmark, India, Italy, Norway, and Sweden. (Some accounts report twenty nations in Korea because they combine Belgium and Luxembourg.) Because the military units of these nations were attached to either U.S. or British combat groups, information on their participation is found in the various military accounts of the war described in the army, navy, and air force sections of this book. Nevertheless, there is some specific literature available about the small units' contributions to the war and to the unique international character of the UN command in Korea.

The interaction between the troops of varied nations is described in Eli Jacques Kahn, Jr.'s, study, *The Peculiar War* (1952), and in Carl N. DeVaney's article (1953). An *Army Information Digest* report (1953) lists the varied national forces, while Benjamin F. Cooling (1983) cites World War II experience to show weapons and language standardization would improve combat operations.

Among the minimal literature on the contributions of smaller nations are the following: Russell W. Ramsey (1967) on Colombia's dispatch of an infantry battalion and a naval frigate to Korea; Harold H. Martin's two articles (1951a, 1951b) describing the French and Greek contingents; P. M. J. McGregor's (1978) article on South Africa's air force squadron; Musrat Ozselcuk's (1980) account of Turkey's 5,000-man brigade; Komon Skordiles' (1954) reports on Ethiopia's battalion of 1,271 soldiers; and Juan F. Villasanta's (1954) description of the Philippines' 10th Infantry Battalion.

Although India sent only a medical detachment to Korea, its neutral stance during the war resulted in more literature than that for the other small contributors. India's UN role in promoting negotiations to end the war are explained by Shiv Dayal (1959) and Ram P. Kaushik's (1972) studies. Initially India was committed to stopping North Korea's aggression, but soon after, it played the role of a neutral nation seeking peace between East and West. India's role as a neutral is also examined by Blema S. Steinberg (1965). Dennis Kux (1992) gives a broad perspective on U.S.-India relations between 1941 and 1990.

Although the contribution of other nations to the Korean War was minimal compared to the U.S. effort, the symbolic need to make the war a collective security action required the cooperation of other UN members, including the role of some of those nations to restrain more extreme actions sometimes proposed by the United States.

REFERENCES

Accinelli, Robert D. "Pro-U.N. Internationalists and the Early Cold War: The American Association for the United Nations and U.S. Foreign Policy, 1947–52." *Diplomatic History* 9:4 (Fall 1985): 347–362.

Army Information Digest. "United Nations Allies in the Korean War." 8:9 (1953): 57.

Bernstein, Barton J. "The Struggle over the Korean Armistice: Prisoners of Repatriation." In Bruce Cumings, ed., *Child of Conflict*, pp. 261–308. Seattle, WA: University of Washington Press, 1983.

Cooling, Benjamin Franklin. "Allied Interoperability in the Korean War." *Military Review* 63:6 (1983): 26–52.

Dayal, Shiv. *India's Role in the Korean Question.* New Delhi, India: Chand, 1959.

DeVaney, Carl N. "Know Your Allies." *Military Review* 32:12 (1953): 11–19.

Dodd, Thomas J. "Is the United Nations Worth Saving?" In Raymond A. Moore, Jr., ed., *The United Nations Reconsidered.* Columbia, SC: University of South Carolina Press, 1970.

Goodrich, Leland M. *Korea: A Study of United States Policy in the United Nations.* New York: Council on Foreign Relations, 1956.

———. "Collective Action in Korea: Evaluating the Results of the UN Collective Action." *Current History* 38:226 (1960): 332–336.

Gordenker, Leon. "The United Nations, the United States Occupation, and the 1948 Election in Korea." *Political Science Review* 73 (1958): 426–450.

———. *The United Nations and the Peaceful Unification of Korea: The Politics of Field Operations, 1947–1950.* The Hague: Nijhoff, 1959.

Halliday, Jon. "The United Nations and Korea." In Frank Baldwin, ed., *Without Parallel*, pp. 109–142. New York: Pantheon Books, 1973.

Hoyt, Edwin C. "The United States Reaction to the Korean Attack: A Study of the Principle of the UN Charter as a Factor in American Policy-Making." *American Political Science Review* 55:1 (January 1961): 45–76.

Jessup, Philip. *The Birth of Nations.* New York: Columbia University Press, 1974.

Kahn, Eli Jacques, Jr. *The Peculiar War.* New York: Random House, 1952.

Kahng, Tae Jin. *Law, Politics, and the Security Council.* 2d ed. The Hague: Nijhoff, 1969.

Kaushik, Ram P. *The Crucial Years of Non-Alignment: USA, the Korean War, and India.* New Delhi, India: Kumar, 1972.

Kux, Dennis. *Estranged Democracies: India and the United States, 1941–1991.* New Delhi, India, and Thousand Oaks, CA: Sage Publications, 1994; originally published at Washington, DC: National Defense University Press, 1992.

Lie, Trygve. *In the Cause of Peace: Seven Years with the United Nations.* New York: Macmillan, 1954.

Luard, Evan. *A History of the United Nations.* Vol. 1: *The Years of Western Dominance, 1945–1955.* New York: St. Martin's, 1982.

McGregor, P. M. J. "History of No. 2 Squadron, SAAF in the Korean War." *Military History Journal* (June 1978): 82–89.

Martin, Harold H. "The Greeks Know How to Die." *Saturday Evening Post* 224:1 (1951a): 26–27, 83–84.

———. "Who Said the French Won't Fight." *Saturday Evening Post* 223:45 (1951b): 19–21, 107–108.

Matray, James. *Historical Dictionary of the Korean War.* Westport, CT: Greenwood Press, 1991.

Mazuzan, George T. *Warren R. Austin at the UN, 1946–1953.* Kent, OH: Kent State University Press, 1977.

———. "America's UN Commitment, 1945–1953." *Historian* 49:2 (1978): 309–330.

Miller, Lynn H. "The United States, the United Nations, and the Cold War." In Lynn H. Miller and Ronald W. Prussen, eds., *Reflections on the Cold War,* pp. 160–182. Philadelphia: Temple University Press, 1974.

Ozselcuk, Musret. "The Turkish Brigade in the Korean War." *International Review of Military History* 46 (1980): 253–272.

Ramsey, Russell W. "The Colombian Battalion in Korea and Suez." *Journal of Inter-American Studies* 9 (October 1967): 541–560.

Riggs, Robert E. *Politics in the United Nations: A Study of United States Influence in the General Assembly.* Urbana: University of Illinois Press, 1958; reprint by Westport, CT: Greenwood Press, 1984.

Schwebel, Stephen M. *The Secretary-General of the United Nations.* Cambridge: Harvard University, 1953.

Skordiles, Komon. *Kagnew, The Story of the Ethiopian Fighters in Korea.* Tokyo: Radio Press, 1954.

Stairs, Denis. "The United Nations and the Politics of the Korean War." *International Journal* (Canada) 25:2 (1970): 302–320.

Steinberg, Blema S. "The Korean War: A Case Study in Indian Neutralism." *Orbis* 8 (Winter 1965): 937–954.

Stoessinger, John G. *The United Nations and the Superpowers.* 2d ed. New York: Random House, 1970.

Villasanta, Juan F. *Dateline Korea: Stories of the Philippine Battalion.* Bacolod City, Philippines: Naleo, 1954.

Yoo, Tae-Le. *The Korean War and the United Nations: A Legal and Diplomatic Historical Study.* Louvain: Librairie Desbarox, 1965.

5   Canada and the Korean War

Lester H. Brune

Sometimes referred to as a middle power during the cold war era of superpowers, Canada aligned with the United States and the North Atlantic Treaty Organization while endeavoring to maintain some independence from many unilateral acts of its neighboring superpower, the United States. This generalization about Canada's international policy applied particularly during the Korean War; although Canadians willingly aided the UN Command in Korea, its government sought to restrain U.S. policy by emphasizing the United Nations' roles and interests and by urging the United States to avoid expansion of the conflict to China or Western Europe. At the same time, Canada sent army, navy, and air force units to the Far East to operate either with the British Commonwealth forces or under the command for the United Nations.

GENERAL STUDIES OF CANADIAN POLICY

Most historical studies about Canada's international relations begin with that nation's primary concern: its relations with its southern superpower neighbor. Although Canada deemed its connections to the British Commonwealth to be essential, its geographic location requires it to accommodate to U.S. activities by trying to avoid strong antagonisms and acting to constrain Washington whenever possible. Denis Stairs (1972, 1974) thoroughly examines Canada's policy during the Korean War, indicating that its leaders emphasized the UN's role as a collective security operation and encouraging the United States to accept limited objectives in Korea. Recently Robert S. Prince (1992–1993) reexamined Stairs' analysis, concluding that there were limitations on the ''constraining'' role Canada followed.

While Canada's policies during the Korean War probably followed

Stairs' constraining structure, Charles P. Stacey (1963) contends that the war significantly redirected Canada's pre-1950 international role, which had emphasized an independent course of action between 1945 and 1948 but moved toward closer cooperation with Washington due to international developments in 1949–1950. Not only did Canada cooperate with the United States in defending South Korea, but the perceived threat of the Soviet Union's aggressive policies resulted in close U.S.-Canadian programs to defend their Arctic frontiers from possible Soviet attack. Yet Stacey also indicates that these cooperative ventures took place within Canada's pattern of avoiding too great a dependence on Washington.

Canada's shift in 1949–1950 corresponded to a victory in national elections for the Liberal party on June 27, 1949. The Liberals were led by Louis S. St. Laurent after William Lyon Mackenzie King resigned the party leadership in 1948. Under Prime Minister St. Laurent, the minister for external affairs, Lester B. Pearson, played a leading role during the Korean War era. Pearson was a strong advocate of the United Nations as an important instrument in maintaining world peace. His memoirs (1972–1975) and his *Foreign Affairs* article in 1951 provide insights into his role during the war years. Rajeshwar Dayal (1973–1974) lauds Pearson's Korean diplomatic efforts, and R. A. MacKay (1971) edits speeches and documents on Canadian foreign policy from 1945 to 1954. Pearson's papers are available at Canada's Public Archives in Ottawa.

Two books deal with Canadian policy in Asia after World War II. Henry F. Angus (1953) has a contemporary account on Canada and the Far East, 1940–1953; and Paul Evans and B. Michael Frolic (1991) examine Canada's policy toward communist China from 1949 to 1970. U.S.-Canadian cooperation in building an Arctic defense system during the 1950s is described in books by Melvin Conant (1962) and Joel Sokolsky (1989). After the Soviet Union successfully tested an atomic bomb in 1949, U.S. intelligence reported that by 1954 the Soviets would have long-range bombers capable of carrying atomic weapons across the North Pole to attack North America. In the context of these predictions, the United States and Canada constructed the Pinetree radar system to detect incoming enemy aircraft. This system was operative by 1954, as preparations began for a more elaborate warning system, which became known as the Mid-Canada Line, operated by Canadians and the U.S. Distant Early Warning System. These two systems were operative by the late 1950s.

Finally, in order to place Canada's Korean War role in a broader historical perspective, three recent accounts of Canada-U.S. relations should be consulted: by Gordon T. Stewart (1992), Robert Bothwell (1992), and J. L. Granatstein and Norman Hillmer (1990). Carl Berger (1986) describes literature on Canadian history during the twentieth century. Berger also has edited a historiographic essay (1972) on U.S.-Canada relations. Additional insight into the neighborly problems of these two

North American nations may be found in essays by Canada's General Charles Foulkes and by former U.S. Secretary of State Dean Acheson in the book edited by Livingston Merchant (1966).

CANADA'S MILITARY ROLE IN KOREA

Between July 1950 and 1953, Canada supplied army, navy, and air force personnel and equipment to assist the UN military forces in Korea. Canada's army units served primarily as part of the 27th (later 28th) Commonwealth Division, although C. C. McDougall's (1951) article describes an all-volunteer brigade, the Canadian Army Special Force, which trained in Fort Lewis, Washington, and operated in Korea under the UN Command. Canada's ground units that operated with the Commonwealth Division reached Korea in February 1951. The first battalion sent was Princess Patricia's Light Infantry. Later, on an annual rotation, this battalion was replaced by the Vandoos and the Royal Canadian Regiments.

The earliest book on Canada's army in Korea was by Canada's Army Headquarters in two volumes (1956). A later official account of Canada's army operations is by Herbert F. Wood (1966). O. A. Cooke (1984) has a bibliography on Canada's military to 1983. Two other studies of Canada's army in Korea are John Melady's *Canada's Forgotten War* (1983) and a five-part study in the *Canadian Army Journal* (1955). Jeffrey Grey's (1988) book on the commonwealth armies notes Canada initially opposed this joint army because it wanted all nations under the UN Command.

Air Force

The Royal Canadian Air Force (RCAF) supplied transport and combat planes for the UN Command in Korea. The transport planes helped to airlift troops across the Pacific to Korea. In this operation, the Thunderbird Transport Squadron was used. In addition, twenty-two RCAF pilots were attached to the U.S. 5th Air Force in Korea. These combat pilots shot down twenty enemy jet fighters. Information on the air force role may be found in the accounts of Herbert Wood (1966) and John Melady (1983) as well as U.S. Air Force histories described in Chapter 14 of this book.

Navy

The first Canadian naval units to go to the Korean War theater were three Canadian ships that served with the UN Command. Charles T. McNair (1951) describes how these ships, the *Cayuga, Sioux,* and *Athabaskon,* were sent in July 1950 and served in September with U.S. naval groups during the Inchon landing. Principally, however, Canada sent destroyers to Korean waters, where they served with the U.S. Navy's Task Force 95 in blockading and escort actions. The Royal Canadian Navy's *Nootka* became the only UN ship to capture an enemy vessel, a North Korean minesweeper.

The fullest story of Canada's navy during the Korean War is by Thor Grimsson and E. C. Russell (1965). Peter Newman (1954) has a brief article on Canada's navy, which includes its role in Korea. John D. Harbron (1966) describes the controversy in Canada's postwar navy regarding the continued use of British traditions.

REFERENCES

Angus, Henry F. *Canada and the Far East, 1940–1953.* Toronto: University of Toronto Press, 1953.

Berger, Carl C. "Internationalism, Continentalism, and the Writing of History: Comments on the Carnegie Series on the Relations of Canada and the United States." In R. A. Preston, pp. 32–54. *The Influence of the United States on Canadian Development.* Durham, NC: Duke University Press, 1972.

———. *The Writing of Canadian History: Aspects of English-Canadian Historical Writing since 1900.* 2d ed. Toronto: University of Toronto Press, 1986.

Bothwell, Robert. *Canada and the United States: The Politics of Partnership.* New York: Twayne, 1992.

Canada. Army Headquarters. General Staff Historical Section. *Canada's Army in Korea: A Short Official History.* Ottawa: Queen's Printers, 1956a.

———. *Canada's Army in Korea: The United Nations Operations, 1950–1953, and Their Aftermath.* Ottawa: Queen's Printers, 1956b.

Canada's Army Journal. "Canada's Army in Korea." 9 (1955) (1):5–29; (2):20–42; (3):20–42; (4):16–34; (5):21–34.

Conant, Melvin. *The Long Polar Watch: Canada and the Defense of North America.* New York: Harper's, 1962.

Cooke, O. A. *The Canadian Military Experience, 1867–1983: A Bibliography.* Ottawa: Department of National Defense, 1984.

Dayal, Rajeshwar. "The Power of Wisdom." *International Journal* 29:1 (1973–1974): 110–121.

Evans, Paul, and B. Michael Frolic, eds. *Reluctant Adversaries: Canada and the People's Republic of China, 1949–1970.* Toronto: University of Toronto Press, 1991.

Grey, Jeffrey. *The Commonwealth Armies and the Korean War.* Manchester, England: Manchester University Press, 1988.

Granatstein, J. L., and Norman Hillmer. *For Better or for Worse: Canada and the United States to the 1990's.* Toronto: Copp Clark Pitman, 1990.

Grimsson, Thor, and E. C. Russell. *Canadian Naval Operations in the Korean War, 1950–1953.* Ottawa: Queen's Printers, 1965.

Harbron, John D. "Royal Canadian Navy at Peace 1945–1955: The Uncertain Heritage." *Queen's Quarterly* 73 (1966): 311–334.

McDougall, C. C. "Canadian Volunteers Prepare for Combat." *Army Informational Digest* 6:6 (1951): 54–57.

MacKay, R. A., ed. *Canadian Foreign Policy, 1945–1954: Selected Speeches and Documents.* Toronto: McClelland & Stewart, 1971.

McNair, Charles T. "The Royal Canadian Navy in Korea." *Army Informational Digest* 6:11 (1951): 50–53.

Melady, John. *Canada's Forgotten War.* Toronto: Macmillan, 1983.

Merchant, Livingston T., ed. *Neighbors Taken for Granted: Canada and the United States.* New York: Praeger, 1966.

Newman, Peter. "The Royal Canadian Navy." *United States Naval Institute Proceedings* 80 (1954): 295–299.

Pearson, Lester B. "The Development of Canadian Foreign Policy." *Foreign Affairs* 30:1 (1951): 17–30.

———. *Mike: The Memoirs of the Right Honourable Lester B. Pearson.* 3 vols. Toronto: University of Toronto Press, 1972–1975.

Prince, Robert S. "The Limits of Constraint: Canadian-American Relations and the Korean War, 1950–1951." *Journal of Canadian Studies/Revue d'études Canadiennes* (Petersborough) (Winter 1992–1993): 129–152.

Smith, Denis. *Diplomacy of Fear: Canada and the Cold War, 1941–1948.* Toronto: University of Toronto Press, 1988.

Sokolsky, Joel. *Defending Canada: U.S.-Canadian Defense Policies.* New York: Priority Press Publications, 1989.

Stacey, Charles P. "Twenty-one Years of Canadian-American Military Cooperation." In David R. Denner, *Canadian–United States Treaty Relations.* Durham, NC: Duke University Press, 1963.

Stairs, Denis. "Canada and the Korean War: The Boundaries of Diplomacy." *International Perspective* 6 (1972): 25–32.

———. *The Diplomacy of Constraint: Canada, the Korean War and the United States.* Toronto: University of Toronto Press, 1974.

Stewart, Gordon. *The American Response to Canada since 1776.* East Lansing: Michigan State University Press, 1992.

Stuart, Reginald C. "Continentalism Revisited: Recent Narratives on the History of Canadian-American Relations." *Diplomatic History* 18:3 (Summer 1994): 405–414.

Wood, Herbert F. *Strange Battleground: The Operations in Korea and Their Effect on the Defense Policy of Canada.* Ottawa: Canada: Queen's Printers, R. Duhamel, 1966.

6   Great Britain and the Korean War

Callum MacDonald

After the United States and the Republic of Korea (ROK), Britain made the largest military contribution to the Unified Command during the Korean War. In 1950 two infantry brigades with armored support were committed to the fighting, which later joined Australian, Canadian, New Zealand, and Indian contingents to form the Commonwealth Division. The bulk of the Far Eastern fleet, consisting of an aircraft carrier, two cruisers, two destroyers, and three frigates, was immediately sent into action. The RAF contributed some Sunderland flying boats and liaison aircraft. A few pilots were rotated through U.S. Air Force and Australian fighter squadrons in the later stages of the war. As the official history by Sir Anthony Farrar-Hockley, *The British Part in the Korean War* (1990), emphasizes, this commitment stretched Britain's already-extended military resources to the limit and deployed forces to an area of the world never before considered vital to British interests.

At the Moscow conference in December 1945, Britain was reluctant to assume any responsibilities in the four-power trusteeship for Korea proposed by the United States. When this scheme collapsed and the ROK was created in 1948, the Foreign Office thought that sooner or later, the new state would fall victim to its communist rival in the North. Nobody believed that Washington would intervene to prevent this outcome; the ROK, like nationalist China, had been written off by the Americans, it was thought. At the highest levels of policymaking, few had much time to spare for Korea. British interests were concentrated in Western Europe, the Middle East, and Southeast Asia. When the Clement Attlee cabinet first met to discuss the crisis, some ministers did not even know where Korea was.

An article by Jong-yil Ra (1989) shows that neglect of Korean issues persisted after June 1950. On the basis of Foreign Office material, Ra concludes that British officials regarded the Rhee regime as hopelessly corrupt and had a low opinion of Koreans' capacity for self-government. In the autumn of 1950, as UN forces swept triumphantly toward the Chinese border, British diplomats predicted that even with the North defeated, a united Korea would fall victim to communist subversion sooner or later. Koreans had been better off under the Japanese. Ra concludes that British thinking on Korea reflected a pervasive racism. Articles by Peter Lowe (1989) and Michael. L. Dockrill (1989) indicate the continuity between the Labour government of Clement Attlee and its Conservative successor under Winston Churchill where Korea was concerned. During the crisis of June 1953, sparked by Rhee's opposition to an armistice, Churchill was quite prepared to contemplate abandoning Korea, arguing that the war had now served its purpose for Britain and the United States. So if Korea was never considered a vital interest in itself, why did two successive British governments commit scarce military resources there? In 1938 Prime Minister Neville Chamberlain had refused to fight for Czechoslovakia, which he described as a far-away country of which Britain knew nothing. Why was the ROK in 1950 treated so differently from Czechoslovakia in 1938?

OFFICIAL VIEWS: COLLECTIVE SECURITY AND THE LESSONS OF HISTORY

Truman's decision to take the Korean case to the UN Security Council and to intervene under the blue banner of the United Nations took British officials by surprise. *The Memoirs of Lord Gladwyn* (1972) reflect this aspect of the crisis. Gladwyn Jebb, the British UN representative, was astonished to find the Americans gearing up for war. He had expected at most a ritual condemnation of the North Korean attack. The British, however, quickly supported the Americans, for the attack was regarded as a case of unprovoked aggression. As Elisabeth Barker (1983) and Sir Anthony Farrar-Hockley (1954) point out, nobody believed the North Korean claim that the South had fired the first shots. The Attlee government, like the Truman administration, viewed the crisis in the global context of the cold war. Pyongyang was regarded as a puppet of Moscow without the capacity for independent action. Thus, greater issues were at stake in Korea than the future of Korea itself. The crisis was the product of world communist expansion directed from Moscow. In responding, the Attlee government applied the lessons of the 1930s, which proved the dangers of appeasing dictators. Each surrender to Hitler had produced only new and more far-reaching demands, leading to world war. The received wisdom was that by risking war earlier, the democracies could have stopped the Nazis without fighting. Totalitarian systems understood only force. Britain should have renounced appeasement and pursued a policy of collective security through the League of Nations, upholding democratic values and international law.

Attlee emphasized these lessons of history to justify British intervention in Korea, paying particular attention to the role of the United Nations. According to Attlee's memoirs, *As It Happened* (1954), Britain had a duty to support the UN. Kenneth Harris' biography, *Attlee* (1982), shows how the prime minister developed this theme in the summer of 1950, when he spoke out in favor of the war. According to Attlee, an act of aggression had been committed, and the UN faced its first serious test since its foundation in 1945. If the UN was not to go the way of the League of Nations, its authority must be upheld. The ROK government might not be a very good one, but that was not the issue. Aggression bred aggression. The fire started in distant Korea could easily spread and swallow up the rest of the world. This emphasis on the lessons of history and the moral imperative of collective security remains the official justification for British intervention. Farrar-Hockley (1990) criticizes interpretations that emphasize British dependence on the United States. He acknowledges that the "special relationship" was a powerful factor but argues that there were worthier reasons for the decision to support the United States, not least Attlee's determination never to use appeasement to buy off aggression. In taking this line Farrar-Hockley admits his personal involvement, for he had fought in Korea as a captain in the Gloucester Regiment and spent over two years as a prisoner of war.

Although Farrar-Hockley refers to the recent revisionist work by Bruce Cumings, whose *The Origins of the Korean War* (1981, 1990) emphasizes the domestic origins of the conflict, he still views Korea not as a civil war but as an attack by one state upon another, largely instigated by the Soviet Union. A similar view is adopted by Max Hastings, the military historian and editor of the right-wing *Daily Telegraph,* in his popular best-seller, *The Korean War* (1987). Hastings follows the example of the first British historian of the war, David Rees, *Korea: The Limited War* (1964), who by connecting Korea with Vietnam hoped that South Vietnam, like South Korea, could be saved from communism. Rees praised Truman's decision to intervene in 1950 as the noblest act of his administration. Hastings laments the lack of will and vision that lost South Vietnam to communism. Rees, Hastings, and Farrar-Hockley see the Korean War, like World War II, as a "good war," upholding international law and drawing the line against communist aggression. For Hastings, the ultimate justification for UN intervention is the transformation of the ROK into a vibrant capitalist society.

Despite the official emphasis on the UN angle, a detailed study of British policy at the United Nations has yet to appear. The memoirs of Sir Gladwyn Jebb (1972) cover his experiences as British representative. There is material on the UN General Assembly debate of November 1952 in the last volume of the earl of Avon's (Sir Anthony Eden) memoirs, *Full Circle* (1965), which he attended as foreign secretary in Churchill's government. The published diary of his principal private secretary, Sir Evelyn Shuckburgh, *Descent to Suez* (1986), contains a useful eyewitness account of events behind the scenes at this session and the abrasive relationship between Eden and Dean Acheson, who clashed over U.S. resistance to an Indian-sponsored resolution on the repatriation of communist prisoners of war. The quarrel is also covered by Sidney Bailey, *The Korean Armistice* (1993), who was a Quaker observer at the UN. Evan Luard includes a chapter on Korea in *A History of the United Nations* (1982). British diplomacy at the UN is also discussed in the general histories by Farrar-Hockley (1990); Callum MacDonald, *Korea* (1986); and Rosemary Foot, *A Substitute for Victory* (1990). These can be supplemented by articles on various key votes. William Stueck (1986) looks at the British role in drafting the UN resolution on a united Korea of October 1950. Michael Dockrill (1986) and Peter Lowe (1989) examine the cabinet crisis over condemning China as an aggressor in January 1951 in which some ministers resisted what they regarded as subservience to Washington. Roger Bullen (1984) discusses the General Assembly debate on the prisoner-of-war issue in October 1952. The lack of specialized studies, however, means that this work must be augmented by reference to other commonwealth countries. Of particular importance are the official history by Robert O'Neill, *Australia in the Korean War* (1981); Ian McGibbon, *New Zealand and the Korean War* (1993); and Denis Stairs on Canadian policy, *The Diplomacy of Constraint* (1974).

If collective security was one safeguard against totalitarian aggression, a second was rearmament. In his memoirs (1954), Attlee claimed that communism was on the march, and the West must not be caught off-guard. In the 1930s, Neville Chamberlain had done too little too late to match the Nazi buildup, encouraging Hitler to take the risks that led to war. The Labour government, determined to avoid the same mistake, increased the arms budget under the impact of the Korean fighting. The prime minister warned that this would mean sacrifices but called on the British people to undergo economic hardship in the cause of national security. These appeals proved remarkably effective despite the later divisive impact of war and rearmament on the Labour party. As Michael Foot's *Aneurin Bevan, 1945–1960* (1973) and John Campbell's *Nye Bevan and the Mirage of British Socialism* (1987) reveal, the only minister critical of increased defense spending was Nye Bevan, who initially swallowed his dissent. Kenneth Morgan, *Labour in Power* (1985), notes that only two Labour members voted against the government when Parliament debated the Korean crisis in early July 1950, and at the Labour party conference in October, a motion critical of British participation was defeated by an overwhelming margin. Martin Gilbert, *Never Despair* (1988), and David Carlton, *Anthony Eden* (1986), show that support for the war and rearmament was bipartisan.

The Conservative opposition leaders had been antiappeasers in the 1930s. Although there were no public opinion polls on the decision to intervene, an article by Jim Hoare (1992), using meager data from the last days of *Mass Observation,* suggests widespread acceptance of the government case. Gallup did poll on the rearmament issue. Robert S. Wybrow's history of polling, *Britain Speaks Out* (1989), shows 78 percent in favor of increased defense spending in August 1950.

CONTEMPORARY CRITICS: ATROCITY, CONSPIRACY, AND CIVIL WAR

The most consistent Korean War criticism came from the British Communist party and its fellow travelers. Although membership had slumped since 1945 and the only two Communist members of Parliament had lost their seats in the general election of February 1950, communists were still influential in some branches of the trade union movement. The party newspaper, the *Daily Worker,* mounted a "peace campaign," which opposed both the war and rearmament, condemning Attlee as an American stooge. The communists echoed the line taken by the Soviet Union when it returned to the United Nations in August 1950, claiming the Korean conflict was a civil war and North Korea was the only legitimate representative of the Korean people. The South had attacked the North as part of an American plot to dominate the Far East. Collective security was a fig leaf for American imperialism. The UN vote was illegal and morally invalid since it had been taken in the absence of the Soviet representative. Alan Winnington of the *Daily Worker,* who defined himself as a professional communist, was the only Western journalist with the Korean People's Army in the summer of 1950. He sent back a series of reports on South Korean atrocities and the American air war that compared the U.S.-UN intervention with Nazi war crimes. Winnington implied that the Korean War was like the Spanish civil war, with Truman and Attlee in the roles of Hitler and Mussolini supporting the forces of reaction. He called on the British people to stop the killing by supporting the World Peace Council, a communist front.

In the autumn of 1950, Winnington's *Daily Worker* articles appeared as a pamphlet, entitled *I Saw the Truth in Korea.* He later put forward the same arguments in *Breakfast with Mao* (1986), the story of his life in the world communist movement. Other pamphlet literature included D. N. Pritt, *Light on Korea* (1950) and *New Light on Korea* (1951), published by Labour Monthly, a communist front. Pritt exploited documents captured by the Korean People's Army in Seoul to prove that South Korea had invaded the north at the instigation of the American imperialists. This material, edited by the North Korean foreign minister, Hon Yon Pak, appeared under the title *Documents and Materials Exposing the Instigators of*

Civil War in Korea (1950). Pritt was no stranger to political controversy, having defended the Soviet invasion of Finland during the "winter war" of 1939–1940. More annoying to the government was Sir John Pratt, a former diplomat and vice chairman of the board of governors of the prestigious School of Oriental and African Studies at the University of London, whose *Korea: The Lie That Led to War* (1951), published by the Britain China Friendship Association, supported claims of South Korean aggression and defended Chinese military intervention. The British edition of I. F. Stone's *The Hidden History of the Korean War* (1952) had little impact on British opinion but alarmed the Foreign Office because of its large sales in India, the leading Asian member of the commonwealth.

The communist peace campaign continued until 1953. American terror bombing remained a consistent theme, but other issues were also exploited, including the controversy over the repatriation of communist prisoners of war and Chinese germ warfare allegations. Monica Felton visited North Korea as part of a delegation from the Women's Peace Council in 1952 and published two pamphlets on her experiences there, *What I Saw in Korea* (1952) and *Korea: Bring the Boys Home* (1952). She accused the Americans of exploiting the prisoner-of-war issue to prolong the conflict and claimed that British captives were being well treated by the Chinese. Their families were urged to lobby members of Parliament, trade unions, and workmates in favor of peace. These arguments were also incorporated in her book, *That's Why I Went* (1953). The Koje prisoner riots of 1952 received wide coverage in the *Daily Worker*. The following year Alan Winnington and Wilfred Burchett's *Koje Unscreened* (1953) compared the Koje compounds with the Nazi concentration camp at Belsen, echoing a familiar theme linking the United States with Hitler's Germany.

Germ warfare claims were also exploited, and the confessions of captured American airmen were published by the World Peace Council in 1952 as *Statements by Two Captured US Air Force Officers on Their Participation in Germ Warfare in Korea*. The subject was taken up by an Anglican clergyman, Hewlett Johnson, the "red" dean of Canterbury, who visited Manchuria in 1952 and wrote about his experiences in *I Appeal* (1952), published by the Britain-China Friendship Association. Johnson, an outspoken opponent of atomic weapons and a supporter of the World Peace Council, had been awarded the Stalin Peace Prize in 1951. His conclusion that the United States had indeed waged germ warfare was widely condemned by the press and led to demands for his expulsion from the Church of England. Further information on Johnson's career can be found in his memoir, *Searching for Light* (1968). He was particularly irritating to the government because foreigners often confused him with the archbishop of Canterbury. Also embarrassing were the activities of the prominent Cambridge biochemist Joseph Needham, a Sinophile who had produced a widely acclaimed study of Chinese science. Needham served on the international scientific commission established by the World Peace Council in 1952, which endorsed communist charges that the United States had waged germ warfare in Korea and northeast China.

Besides communists and figures associated with communist fronts like the World Peace Council, there were those who questioned the noble purposes of the war when they experienced it at first hand. The most prominent was the journalist James Cameron, who was appalled by what he saw around Pusan as a correspondent for *Picture Post* in the summer of 1950. He was particularly critical of the atrocities committed by Syngman Rhee's police under the United Nations flag. In *Point of Departure* (1978), he recalled the scandal in November 1950 when the proprietor spiked his report, illustrated with photographs by Bert Hardy, just as the magazine went to press. A pirated copy was subsequently published by the *Daily Worker*. A brief account of the affair and the controversial pictures can be found in Robert Kee's *The Picture Post Album* (1989). Other reporters who wrote books critical of both the U.S. Army and the ROK police included Reginald Thompson, *Cry Korea* (1951), and René Cutforth, *Korean Reporter* (1955). Hastings (1987) takes issue with such critics, particularly Cameron, whom he accuses of missing the point. The issue was not the nature of the Rhee regime but communist aggression. Moreover, the North Korean regime of Kim Il-sung was much worse and committed its crimes far from the prying eyes of Western journalists, which was the line taken by the Foreign Office at the time.

THE HOME FRONT IN BRITAIN

There is no proper history of the British home front during the Korean War, and the impact of dissent is difficult to judge. Biographies, private papers, and the published parliamentary debates, however, suggest public disillusion with the war following Chinese intervention in November 1950. Polling data produced by Robert J. Wybrow (1989) show support plunging to its lowest point in January 1951 when one in two polled thought that Britain should stop fighting in Korea and three in five believed that there was a real danger of global war. The majority thought that this conflict would be started by the Russians rather than the Americans but also believed that the British people would be less willing to fight than in 1939. Anxiety about the implications of the Korean War was partly calmed by the truce talks that began in July 1951. Wybrow's poll data show steady support for a negotiated settlement from then until the armistice, along with an underlying dissatisfaction about the way the Americans were handling the negotiations. In January 1953, three out of four polled thought that other nations should be represented at Panmunjom rather than leaving the United States to represent the UN position. Callum MacDonald, in *Britain and the Korean War* (1990), suggests that this mood was broadly supportive of government policy with both the outgoing Labour and the new Conservative governments pressing Washington to conclude a Korean armistice.

It is unclear how far the government manipulated public opinion to maintain support for the war. The Labour government was plainly alarmed by the flood of stories about South Korean atrocities, which began in November 1950, just when Chinese intervention was undermining the consensus of the summer, and it did what it could to play down the issue. News management, however, remains a murky area, although behind the scenes, the Foreign Office News Department and the government briefers were active from the very beginning. There was also censorship and self-censorship. Adam Sisman's study of the controversial historian A. J. P Taylor (1994) found that the BBC discontinued a series of six talks on the overseas service after Taylor's first broadcast in July 1950. His offense had been to praise appeasement and criticize the League of Nations/UN principle of collective security as perpetual war for perpetual peace.

The general subject of press censorship is covered by Phillip Knightley, *The First Casualty* (1975), and Trevor Royle, *War Report* (1987), which concentrates on the case of Cameron and *Picture Post*. An article by Howard Smith (1988) on early BBC television newsreels finds that they were more analytical than cinema newsreels, which bought most of their material from the United States. The BBC had its own reporters in Korea who produced a series of short documentaries on various aspects of the war. Television, however, was still in its infancy, with an audience of only 2.1 million by 1953, and probably made little difference to public perceptions. There is no detailed study of the British press and Korea. The cabinet was concerned enough by Winnington's reports and his pamphlet, *I Saw the Truth in Korea* (1951), to consider prosecuting both him and his editor, Johnny Campbell, for treason. They also contemplated a draconian press law banning journalism that brought aid and comfort to North Korea, a move that would have put the *Daily Worker* out of business. The issue is discussed in Winnington (1986) and Peter Hennessy's *Never Again* (1992).

In the end, ministers backed away from this drastic step, which would have given the communists two martyrs and led to accusations of political persecution. The government did, however, refuse to issue visas to Eastern bloc delegates to the Peace Congress, which the World Peace Council planned to hold at Sheffield in November 1950, forcing a last-minute switch to Warsaw. An account of this event can be found in the autobiography by Hewlett Johnson (1968). Morgan (1984) argues that although the government was suspicious of communist influence in labor disputes and prosecuted some strikers under the Conspiracy Act of 1875, it avoided an officially sanctioned anticommunist campaign. Nor did it conduct a witch hunt against communists and fellow travelers in the public service.

"Positive vetting," the screening of officials with access to sensitive information, was delayed until 1951 when the Burgess-MacLean spy scandal and pressure from the Americans led to tougher security procedures. Peter Hennessy (1992) demonstrates a tacit cross-party agreement to keep the communist issue out of electoral politics and to avoid the type of red baiting typical of Senator Joseph McCarthy in the United States. A Conservative politician who demanded the establishment of a Commons committee on "un-English activities" received short shrift from the leaders of both major parties.

NEW APPROACHES: "THE SPECIAL RELATIONSHIP"

As new documentary evidence became available under the thirty-year rule, historians concentrated on the role of the Anglo-American "special relationship" in shaping the foreign policy of the Attlee and Churchill governments. They did not dismiss the importance of collective security and the lessons of the past but suggested that the central factor for Britain in the Korean War was less the United Nations than American participation. These studies were not concerned with the question of who had fired first in June 1950 and avoided moral judgments about aggression inherent in the older historiography. Alan Bullock's biography, *Ernest Bevin as Foreign Secretary* (1983), emphasizes Bevin's commitment to the Atlantic alliance as the central element in British foreign policy. A series of studies by Roger Dingman (1982), Jong-yil Ra (1984), Michael Dockrill (1986), Rosemary Foot (1986), William Stueck (1986), Peter Lowe (1989), and Callum MacDonald (1990) discuss the Korean War in the context of the special relationship. The key role in Anglo-American relations played by Sir Oliver Franks, the influential ambassador in Washington, is analyzed by Peter Boyle (1990) and in Alex Danchev's biography, *Oliver Franks, Founding Father* (1993). Franks believed that by sending troops to Korea, Britain would prove that it was still a world power with a claim to equality within the Atlantic alliance. Ritchie Ovendale, *The English-Speaking Alliance* (1985), places the special relationship in the context of an attempt to create a new security system, including both the United States and the commonwealth, which would sustain Britain's claim to great power status.

These historians broadly agree that the Attlee government welcomed American intervention in Korea as proof of Truman's determination to resist communism and avoid the specter of isolationism. Attlee wanted to demonstrate to the Americans that Britain could still play a global role and was their most valuable ally. At the same time it did not want Washington to be distracted from the vital NATO front or bogged down in a wider war with the People's Republic of China, which Britain, unlike the United States, had recognized. In this connection, Britain was concerned about the influence of the Republican right on U.S. policy, fearing that an inflamed public opinion might drive the Truman administration over the edge in the Far East. Britain therefore pursued a policy of constraint, supporting the United States in the hope of reaping benefits elsewhere while applying quiet pressure at the UN and directly in Washington to limit the war in Korea. This work largely relates to the Attlee government. A major study of Churchill and the Korean War has yet to appear, as has the second volume of Farrar-Hockley's official history covering the period after 1950. MacDonald (1990) and Dockrill (1989) suggest that Churchill was equally anxious to restrain the United States and was concerned that the Eisenhower administration might be too deferential to right-wing Republicans. After the death of Stalin in March 1953, the prime minister was anxious to secure an armistice that would clear the way for détente with the new leadership in Moscow.

Judgments differ on the effectiveness of British policy. MacDonald (1986, 1990) doubts if British diplomacy, most notably Attlee's visit to Washington in December 1950, was a major factor in American decisions. He argues that events on the battlefield rather than British pressure prevented the extension of the war to China after December 1950. In this respect the hero was not Attlee but General Matthew Ridgway. Foot (1986) and Stueck (1986) take a more positive view, arguing that concern for the alliance system was a significant factor in American decisions at the height of the crisis. Dockrill (1986) points out that whatever their other differences, both governments essentially agreed that the war should remain limited. Few would now endorse Attlee's claim in a Grenada Historical Records Interview (1967) that he had prevented Truman from using the atomic bomb. All agree that Britain hoped for more from the Anglo-American special relationship than Washington was willing to concede. In the end Britain had to defer to the United States over key issues like China rather than risk a breach in the alliance on which British security depended.

The special relationship and the related issue of rearmament split the Labour party in April 1951 with the resignation of Nye Bevan as minister of labour. While the immediate trigger was the imposition of health charges on false teeth and spectacles in Hugh Gaitskell's budget, the wider issue was what Bevan regarded as excessive British deference to the United States. He argued that the principle of a free health service was being sacrificed on the altar of an inflated rearmament program designed to please the Americans, a program that was beyond the economic capacity of Britain to sustain. The budget row had been prefigured by the government split over American demands for the condemnation of China as an aggressor at the United Nations in January 1951 (Dockrill 1986; Lowe 1989; MacDonald 1990). On January 25, 1951, the cabinet recommended voting against the United States on this issue as a demonstration of independence, a decision reversed the following day. The political maneuvers over condemning China and the later row over rearmament, which ended with Bevan's resignation, are covered in the biographies of the main protagonists. Of particular importance as a primary source is *The Diary of Hugh Gaitskell* (1983), edited by Phillip Williams, which discusses the crisis through the eyes of the most outspoken pro-American member of the cabinet. Gaitskell feared that any hesitation over China or rearmament would wreck the special relationship on which British security depended.

There is a general consensus that Bevan's resignation fatally weakened the government and poisoned relationships within the Labour party for a decade. It is also usually argued that Korea and rearmament damaged the British economy, which had just recovered from the strains of World War II and had embarked on a promising export drive. Sir Alec Cairncross, *Years of Recovery* (1985), notes that the war and rearmament subjected the economy to strains that precipitated an acute balance-of-payments crisis in 1951 but does not believe that developments after 1950 undermined a budding British economic miracle. He blames other factors for Britain's declining competiveness in world markets. Peter Burnham, *The Political Economy of Postwar Reconstruction* (1990), emphasizes the political motives behind the British rearmament program, which were intended to impress the Americans with Britain's status as a world power and an equal partner in the cold war. Burnham agrees that the rearmament strain created an economic crisis in 1951 but argues that the most serious consequence for Britain's future was to confirm its traditional trade patterns by giving export priority to the dollar areas and the commonwealth at the expense of Western Europe. In this respect, the pursuit of great power status blinded British politicians to their ultimate destiny as part of Europe, a destiny they had consistently rejected since 1945.

A particularly sensitive element in the special relationship was the atomic bomb. This issue more than any other involved considerations of Britain's status as a great power and its role within the Atlantic alliance. The threat of global war that followed Chinese intervention led Britain to demand the right of consultation before the bomb was used, a right that lost after 1945 when the U.S. Congress created an American monopoly.

The issue of control over U.S. air bases in Britain from which any attack on Russia would begin also became acute. At the height of the Berlin crisis in 1948, the government had turned over airfields in East Anglia to the Strategic Air Command without retaining formal rights over how and when they would be used. As John Baylis, *Anglo-American Defence Relations 1939–1984* (1984), points out, this generous deal stemmed from Foreign Secretary Bevin's anxiety to lay the ghost of isolationism to rest and commit the United States to the defense of Western Europe. When Attlee visited Washington in December 1950, he obtained a verbal commitment from Truman on consultation before using the atomic bomb, but this was contrary to the Atomic Energy Act and did not appear in the final communiqué. A formula on the use of British bases did not emerge until the closing weeks of the Labour government, and Churchill was no more successful in regaining a British veto. The atomic issue is covered in the official history by Margaret Gowing, *Independence and Deterrence* (1974). This should be supplemented by Timothy Botti, *The Long Wait* (1987), which incorporates significant U.S. material.

MILITARY ASPECTS: CAMPAIGN STUDIES AND SOLDIERS' TALES

A history of the Commonwealth Division by C. N. Barclay appeared in 1954. Now outdated, it has been displaced by Jeffrey Grey, *The Commonwealth Armies and the Korean War* (1988), which makes extensive use of original archival material. Grey is concerned with organization and bureaucratic politics as much as with operations. H. B. Eaton, *Something Extra* (1993), focuses on small unit actions and the ordinary soldier. Military operations and grand strategy are covered by Farrar-Hockley (1990) and, in the absence of his second volume, must be supplemented with Robert O'Neill, *Australia in the Korean War,* volume 2, *Operations* (1985). Individual unit histories include the British government's *The Royal Ulster Rifles in Korea* (Great Britain 1953), Peter Thomas' *41 Independent Commando Royal Marines* (1990), and J. N. Shipster's *The Die Hards in Korea* (1983) on the Middlesex Regiment. Hastings (1986) also covers battles involving British troops. Eric Linklater's officially approved *Our Men in Korea* (1954) was meant to reassure the home front. A very different picture emerges from Julian Tunstall's book, *I Fought in Korea* (1953). A former public schoolboy who served as a private in the Middlesex Regiment during the first year of the war, Tunstall emphasizes ROK atrocities and the casual destruction British and American troops alike visited on the population. Tunstall's heroes are the ordinary peasants, and although sometimes polemical, it is one of the few soldiers' accounts that shows any real attempt to understand the experience of ordinary Koreans.

There is no definitive study of the battle of the Imjin in which the Gloucester Regiment made its famous last stand against Chinese forces. This awaits the second volume of Farrar-Hockley's official history. U.S. material presented by MacDonald (1986) suggests that General Matthew Ridgway believed the sacrifice was unnecessary and criticized the corps commander for failing to order a timely withdrawal. The later battles of the Hook in 1952 and 1953 are covered by A. I. Barker, *Fortune Favours the Brave* (1974). A rare account of special partisan operations behind the communist lines is provided by Ellery Anderson, *Banner over Pusan* (1960), who was seconded to U.S. special forces in Korea. Naval and fleet air arm operations are discussed by John Landsdown, *With the Carriers in Korea* (1992). An article by Stephen Prince on the Royal Navy (1994), suggests that a British destroyer sank a Russian submarine during operations in the West Korea Sea in 1952, an incident hushed up for political reasons.

There are numerous accounts by ordinary soldiers, many of them Gloucesters who fell into Chinese hands at the Imjin. The most famous is *The Edge of the Sword* (1954) by Farrar-Hockley, an account of his part in the battle as an infantry captain and his later attempts to escape from prisoner-of-war camps. Other books by POWs include Denis Lankford, *I Defy* (1954), and E. S. Jones, *No Rice for Rebels* (1956). S. J. Davies, *In Spite of Dungeons* (1954), recounts the particular difficulties of an army chaplain in Chinese hands. *The Experience of British Prisoners of War in Korea* (Great Britain 1953a) was produced to counter Chinese propaganda claims about the good life in the communist camps. There is no independent study of British POWs like Albert Biderman's *March to Calumny* (1979) on the conduct of U.S. prisoners.

The bitter debate about collaboration that produced several American POW studies never occurred in Britain, although a Scottish Royal Marine, Andrew Condron, was one of the twenty-two UN soldiers who opted for the communists in 1953 and who contributed to *Thinking Soldiers* (1952), a pro-communist propaganda pamphlet. There is a brief essay on Condron in Virginia Pasley's study of the nonrepatriates, *22 Stayed* (1955). Alan Winnington (1986) gives details of Condron's later career in China. There is no account of the British soldier's experience to compare with Donald Knox's study of ordinary GIs, *The Korean War—Pusan to Chosin* (1985). Eric Linklater (1954) presented the officially authorized version. An interesting chapter on life at the front in the second half of the war appears in the actor Michael Caine's autobiography, *What's It All About* (1992). Caine, then Private Micklewhite, served in Korea with the Royal Fusiliers and hated every minute of his time there.

MISSING LINKS: SPOOKS, SPIES, AND OFFICIAL SECRETS

The most obvious gap in the British record is material relating to intelligence, particularly signals intelligence. Revelations about the role of British project ULTRA, which broke the German secret code, transformed historical understanding of World War II. While signals intelligence probably never played a central part in Korea, it must have influenced both diplomatic and military decisions. There was a British signals intercept station at Hong Kong that the Americans considered important enough to plan evacuating to Guam if the Chinese seized the colony. The Secret Intelligence Service (SIS) presumably ran agent networks on the Chinese mainland, both from the colony and from nearby Macao, but nothing is known about these operations. In the light of the close cooperation conducted during and after World War II, intelligence relating to the communist bloc was undoubtedly shared with the United States. The general background on these sensitive topics is covered by James Bamford, *The Puzzle Palace* (1983), and John Baylis (1984).

In 1948 SIS established a station under embassy cover in Seoul, run by Vice-Consul George Blake, who had escaped from Holland in 1940 to join British intelligence. Blake was captured by the North Koreans and at some stage agreed to work for Moscow. By his own account, this conversion was the result of what he had seen in Korea and the reading of Marxist books while a prisoner. Arrested in 1961, he later made a spectacular escape from Wormwood Scrubs prison. His self-serving memoir, *No Other Choice* (1990), throws little light on his activities in Seoul, although his low opinion of the South Korean regime accurately reflects the feelings of most British officials. According to Blake, he was ordered to penetrate the Soviet base at Vladivostock but was unsuccessful. He was also to establish a wide circle of informants that could be activated when the South fell to communism. No official materials have been released to verify these claims, although known British pessimism about the prospects of the ROK provides circumstantial support for the second. A book by E. H. Cookridge, *George Blake: Double Agent* (1970), suggests on the basis of an interview with Blake's former boss in Seoul, Sir Vyvyan Holt, that Blake was well informed about the North through South Korean dissidents with contacts in Pyongyang. According to this account, Blake also warned London about the unpopularity of the Rhee regime.

The Russians ran a damaging intelligence operation in Britain during the Korean War, involving the "Cambridge spies," "Kim" Philby, Donald MacLean, and Guy Burgess. MacLean and Burgess defected in May 1951. Philby, suspected of complicity in their escape, finally fled to Moscow in 1963. The official British report on the Burgess/MacLean affair, *Report Concerning the Disappearance of Two Former Foreign Office Officials* (1955), attempted to minimize the impact of Burgess and MacLean on Anglo-American relations, playing down their access to sensitive material. The relevance of the case to the Korean War rests on the claim that the spy ring had supplied Moscow with complete details of the limitations on MacArthur's military operations in the autumn of 1950, allowing China to intervene, safe in the knowledge that the United States would not retaliate. MacArthur blamed an intelligence leak for the military reverses of late 1950 in *Reminiscences* (1965). William Manchester held the British traitors to blame in *MacArthur: American Caesar* (1978). His charges are based on speculation rather than proof. Better documented is Verne Newton, *The Butcher's Embrace: The Philby Conspirators in Washington* (1991), the product of extensive research in the British and U.S. archives.

While Newton shows that the Cambridge spies had extensive access to U.S. military and diplomatic secrets, conclusive proof is still lacking about Moscow's use of this intelligence and the extent to which it was shared with the Chinese. MacDonald (1986) casts doubt on the importance of

British spies in the Chinese decision to cross the Yalu but suggests that the defection of Burgess and MacLean made Washington reluctant to share sensitive military information thereafter. A definitive judgment about the importance of the Cambridge spies must await revelations from the Soviet archives and more open access by the Chinese. But Beijing is not the only capital determined to guard old secrets. The reluctance of successive British governments to release anything relating to cold war intelligence, despite a recent commitment to greater freedom of information, is notorious, and it is unlikely that historians will gain access to such reports in the near future, if ever.

ARCHIVES AND SOURCES

The official British archive is at the Public Records Office, Kew Gardens, London. The main classes dealing with the Korean War are the records of the cabinet office (CAB), the Defence Departments (DEFE), the Prime Minister's Office (PREM), and the Foreign Office, FO 371 and FO 800. Naval and land operations are covered by the ADM and WO series. For a short essay on the official records and a complete list of the relevant subgroups within each class, readers should consult the official history by Farrar-Hockley (1990). A selection of materials relating to the first year of the war has been published in *Documents on British Policy Overseas,* Series 11, volume 4: *Korea 1950–1951* (1991), edited by H. J. Yasamee and K. A. Hamilton. The British documents must be used in conjunction with the U.S. records at the National Archives and the Truman and Eisenhower presidential libraries. *Documents on British Policy Overseas* should be compared with materials on Anglo-American relations during the same period in the *Foreign Relations of the United States* series. The *Foreign Relations* volumes are particularly valuable as a source on British policy after 1950 because they have far outpaced the publication of the British documents.

A complete run of British newspapers for the period can be found at the British Museum Newspaper Library, Colindale, London. Transcripts of BBC radio broadcasts and documents on news policy are available at the BBC Written Archives Centre, Cavesham Park, Reading, near London. Newsreel material is held by the BBC Film and Video Library, Brentford, Middlesex. Private collections include the Clement Attlee Papers at the Bodleian Library, Oxford, and the Hugh Dalton Papers at the London School of Economics and Political Science. The Ernest Bevin Papers are at Churchill College, Cambridge. Churchill's papers, also at Churchill College, remain closed for the period of the Korean War. Many of his minutes on the subject, however, can be found in the PREM series at the Public Records Office (PRO). The earl of Avon's Papers (Sir Anthony Eden) are at Birmingham University Library. The published record of the House of Commons, *Parliamentary Debates,* is a useful source on political attitudes toward the war. The Imperial War Museum, London, has a sound archive that includes recordings of Attlee's speeches and interviews with British servicemen. It also holds a collection of letters from the front that provide insight into the experiences of ordinary soldiers. The journal of the British Korean Veterans Association, *Morning Calm,* also contains material of this nature. As Farrar-Hockley emphasizes, however, the British archives and sources are not sufficient on their own. The international character of the Korean War makes it necessary to supplement this British material with documents from the Australian, Canadian, New Zealand, and U.S. archives on most diplomatic, military, and economic topics.

REFERENCES

Anderson, Ellery. *Banner over Pusan.* London: Evans Brothers, 1960.

Attlee, C. R. *As It Happened.* London: William Heinemann, 1954.

———. *Clem Attlee: The Grenada Historical Records Interview.* London: Panther Record, 1967.

Avon, Earl of (Sir Anthony Eden). *Full Circle.* London: Cassel, 1965.

Bailey, Sidney. *The Korean Armistice,* London: Macmillan, 1993.

Bamford, James. *The Puzzle Palace,* London: Sidgwick and Jackson, 1983.

Barclay, C. N. *The First Commonwealth Division,* Aldershot: Gale and Polden, 1954.

Barker, A. J. *Fortune Favours the Brave.* London: Leo Cooper, 1974.

Barker, Elisabeth. *The British between the Superpowers, 1945–1950.* London: Macmillan, 1983.

Baylis, John. *Anglo-American Defence Relations, 1939–1984.* London: Macmillan, 1984.

Biderman, Albert D. *March to Calumny.* London: Macmillan, 1979.

Blake, George. *No Other Choice.* London: Jonathan Cape, 1990.

Botti, Timothy. *The Long Wait: The Forging of the Anglo-American Nuclear Alliance, 1945–1968.* Westport, CT: Greenwood Press, 1987.

Boyle, Peter. "Oliver Franks and the Washington Embassy, 1948–1952." In John Zametica, *British Officials and British Foreign Policy, 1945–51,* pp. 189–211. Leicester: Leicester University Press, 1990.

Bullen, Roger. "Great Britain, the United States and the Indian Armistice Resolution on the Korean War, November 1952." In *Aspects of Anglo-Korean Relations, International Studies,* pp. 27–44. London: International Centre for Economics and Related Disciplines, London School of Economics, 1984/1.

Bullock, Alan. *Ernest Bevin as Foreign Secretary.* London: Heinemann, 1983.

Burnham, Peter. *The Political Economy of Postwar Reconstruction.* London: Macmillan, 1990.

Caine, Michael. *What's It All About.* London: Arrow, 1992.

Cairncross, Sir Alec. *Years of Recovery: British Economic Policy, 1945–1951.* London: Methuen, 1985.

Cameron, James. *Point of Departure.* London: Grafton Books, 1978.

Campbell, John. *Nye Bevan and the Mirage of British Socialism.* London: Weidenfeld and Nicholson, 1987.

Carlton, David. *Anthony Eden: A Biography.* London: Allen and Unwin, 1986.

Condron, Andrew. *Thinking Soldiers.* Beijing: New World Press, 1953.

Cookridge, E. H. *George Blake: Double Agent.* London: Hodder, 1970.

Cumings, Bruce. *The Origins of the Korean War.* 2 vols. Princeton: Princeton University Press, 1981, 1990.

Cutforth, René. *Korean Reporter.* London: Heinemann, 1955.

Danchev, Alex. *Oliver Franks, Founding Father.* Oxford: Clarendon Press, 1993.

Davies, S. J. *In Spite of Dungeons.* London: Hodder and Stoughton, 1955.

Dingman, Roger. "Truman, Attlee and the Korean War Crisis." In *The East Asian Crisis, 1945–1951, International Studies,* pp. 1–42. London: International Centre for Economics and Related Disciplines, London School of Economics, 1982/1.

Dockrill, Michael. L. "The Foreign Office, Anglo-American Relations and the Korean War June 1950–June 1951." *International Affairs* (1986): 459–476.

———. "The Foreign Office, Anglo-American Relations and the Korean Truce Negotiations, July 1951–July 1953." In James Cotton and Ian Neary, eds., *The Korean War in History,* pp. 100–119. Manchester: University of Manchester Press, 1989.

Eaton, H. B. *Something Extra: 28 Commonwealth Brigade, 1951–1974.* Edinburgh: Pentland Press, 1993.

Farrar, Peter N. "A Pause for Peace Negotiations: The British Buffer Zone Plan of November 1950." In James Cotton and Ian Neary, eds., *The Korean War in History,* pp. 66–79. Manchester: University of Manchester Press, 1989.

Farrar-Hockley, Sir Anthony. *The Edge of the Sword.* London: Frederick Muller, 1954.

———. *The British Part in the Korean War.* Vol. 1: *A Distant Obligation.* London: HMSO, 1990.

Felton, Monica. *Korea: How to Bring the Boys Home.* London: Britain-China Friendship Association, 1952a.

———. *What I Saw in Korea.* Watford: Farleigh Press, 1952b.

———. *That's Why I Went.* London: Lawrence and Wishart, 1953.

Foot, Michael. *Aneurin Bevan, 1945–1960.* London: Granada, 1982.

Foot, Rosemary. "Anglo-American Relations in the Korean Crisis: The British Effort to Avert an Expanded War, December 1950–January 1951." *Diplomatic History* 10 (Winter 1986): 43–58.

———. *A Substitute for Victory: The Politics of Peacemaking at the Korean Armistice Talks.* Ithaca: Cornell University Press, 1990.

Gilbert, Martin. *Never Despair: Winston S. Churchill, 1945–1965.* London: Heinemann, 1988.

Gowing, Margaret. *Independence and Deterrence: Britain and Atomic Energy, 1945–1952.* London: Macmillan, 1974.

Great Britain. *The Experience of British Prisoners of War in Korea.* London: HMSO, 1953a.

———. *The Royal Ulster Rifles in Korea.* Belfast: Wishart, 1953b.

———. *Report Concerning the Disappearance of Two Former Foreign Office Officials.* London: HMSO, 1955.

Grey, Jeffrey. *The Commonwealth Armies and the Korean War.* Manchester: Manchester University Press, 1988.

Harris, Kenneth. *Attlee.* London: Weidenfeld and Nicholson, 1982.

Hastings, Max. *The Korean War.* London: Michael Joseph, 1987.

Hennessy, Peter. *Never Again: Britain, 1945–1951*. London: Jonathan Cape, 1992.

Hoare, J. H. "British Public Opinion and the Korean War." *BAKS (British Association on Korean Studies) Papers* 2 (1992): 7–28.

Jebb, Sir Gladwyn. *The Memoirs of Lord Gladwyn*. London: Weidenfeld and Nicholson, 1972.

Johnson, Hewlett. *I Appeal*. London: Britain-China Friendship Association, 1952.

———. *Searching for Light*. London: Michael Joseph, 1968.

Jones, Frances S. *No Rice for Rebels*. London: Bodley Head, 1956.

Kee, Robert, ed. *The Picture Post Album*. London: Barrie and Jenkins, 1989.

Knightley, Phillip. *The First Casualty*. New York: Harcourt Brace Jovanovich, 1975.

Knox, Donald. *The Korean War—An Oral History: Pusan to Chosin*. New York: Harcourt Brace Jovanovich, 1985.

Lankford, Denis. *I Defy*. London: Alan Wingate, 1954.

Lansdown, John R. P. *With the Carriers in Korea, 1950–1953*. Worcester: Square One Publications, 1992.

Linklater, Eric. *Our Men in Korea*. London: HMSO, 1954.

Lowe, Peter. "The Significance of the Korean War in Anglo-American Relations." In Michael Dockrill and John W. Young, eds., *British Foreign Policy, 1945–1956*, pp. 126–148. London: Macmillan, 1989a.

———. "The Frustrations of Alliance, the United States and the Korean War, 1950–51." In James Cotton and Ian Neary, eds., *The Korean War in History*, pp. 80–99. Manchester: University of Manchester Press, 1989b.

Luard, Evan. *A History of the United Nations*. Vol. 1: *The Years of Western Domination*. London: Macmillan, 1982.

MacArthur, Douglas. *Reminiscences*. New York: McGraw-Hill, 1964.

MacDonald, Callum. *Korea: The War before Vietnam*. London: Macmillan, 1986.

———. *Britain and the Korean War*. Oxford: Basil Blackwell, 1990.

McGibbon, Ian. *New Zealand and the Korean War*. Vol. 1: *Politics and Diplomacy*. Wellington: Oxford University Press, 1993.

Manchester, William. *MacArthur: American Caesar*. London: Hutchinson, 1978.

Morgan, Kenneth. *Labour in Power*. Oxford: Oxford University Press, 1984.

Newton, Verne. *The Butcher's Embrace: The Philby Conspirators in Washington*. London: Macdonald, 1991.

O'Neill, Robert J. *Australia in the Korean War, 1950–1953*. Vol. 1: *Strategy and Diplomacy*. Vol. 2: *Combat Operations*. Canberra: Australian War Memorial, 1981, 1985.

Ovendale, Ritchie. *The English-Speaking Alliance: Britain, the United States, the Dominions and the Cold War, 1945–51*. London: Allen and Unwin, 1985.

Pasley, Virginia. *22 Stayed*. London: W. H. Allen, 1955.

Pak, Hon Yon. *Documents and Materials Exposing the Instigators of the Civil War in Korea*. Pyongyang: Ministry of Foreign Affairs, 1950.

Pimlott, Ben. *Hugh Dalton*. London: Macmillan, 1985.

———. *The Political Diary of Hugh Dalton, 1918–40, 1945–60*. London: Jonathan Cape, 1986.

Pratt, Sir John. *Korea: The Lie That Led to War*. London: Britain China Friendship Association, 1951.

Prince, Stephen. "The Royal Navy's Contribution to the Korean War." *Journal of Strategic Studies* 17 (June 1994): 94–120.

Pritt, D. N. *Light on Korea*. London: Trinity Trust, 1950.

———. *New Light on Korea*. London: Trinity Trust, 1951.

Ra, Jong-yil. "Special Relationship at War: The Anglo-American Relationship during the Korean War." *Journal of Strategic Studies* 7 (September 1984): 301–317.

———. "Political Settlement in Korea: British Views and Policies, Autumn 1950." In James Cotton and Ian Neary, eds., *The Korean War in History*, pp. 51–65. Manchester: Manchester University Press, 1989.

Rees, David. *Korea: The Limited War*. London: Macmillan, 1964.

Royle, Trevor. *War Report*. Worcester: Mainstream Publishing, 1987.

Sisman, Adam. *A. J. P. Taylor: A Biography*. London: Sinclair-Stevenson, 1994.

Shipster, Colonel J. N. *The Die Hards in Korea*. London: Austin Reed, 1983.

Shuckburgh, Sir Evelyn. *Descent to Suez: Diaries, 1951–56*. London: Weidenfeld and Nicholson, 1986.

Smith, Howard. "The BBC Television Newsreel and the Korean War." *Historical Journal of Film, Radio and Television* 8 (1988): 227–252.

Stairs, Denis. *The Diplomacy of Constraint: Canada, the Korean War and the United States*. Toronto: University of Toronto Press, 1974.

Stone, I. F. *The Hidden History of the Korean War*. London: Turnstile Press, 1952.

Stueck, William. "The Limits of Influence: British Policy and American Expansion of the War in Korea." *Pacific Historical Review* 55 (1986): 65–95.

Thomas, Lieutenant Colonel Peter. *41 Independent Commando Royal Marines, Korea—1950 to 1952*. Portsmouth: Royal Marines Historical Society, 1990

Thompson, Reginald. *Cry Korea*. London: Macdonald, 1951.

Tunstall, Julian. *I Fought in Korea*. London: Lawrence and Wishart, 1953.

Williams, Philip M. *Hugh Gaitskell*. Oxford: Oxford University Press, 1982.

———, ed. *The Diary of Hugh Gaitskell, 1945–1956*. London: Jonathan Cape, 1983.

Winnington, Alan. *I Saw the Truth in Korea*. London: People's Press, 1951.

———. *Breakfast with Mao: Memoirs of a Foreign Correspondent*. London: Lawrence and Wishart, 1986.

Winnington, Alan, and Wilfred Burchett. *Koje Unscreened*. Beijing: Foreign Languages Publishing House, 1953.

World Council of Peace. *Statements by Two Captured US Air Force Officers on Their Participation in Germ Warfare in Korea*. Beijing, 1952(?)

Wybrow, Robert J. *Britain Speaks Out*. London: Macmillan, 1989.

Yasamee, H. J., and K. A. Hamilton. *Documents on British Policy Overseas*. Series 11. Vol. 4: *Korea, 1950–1951*. London: HMSO, 1991.

7   Australia, New Zealand, and the Korean War

Jeffrey Grey

Australia and New Zealand participated in the Korean War as members of the United Nations, partners in the emerging Western alliance, and dominions of the British Commonwealth. Both countries committed forces to the United Nations Command (UNC) from their tiny peacetime military establishments and acted in concert with the United States diplomatically and in the UN. In both countries, involvement in the Korean War provoked some domestic dissent on the left, but in neither case did it become a major issue in domestic politics, and its impact at home was minimal. By contrast, participation in the Korean War and the changed strategic and international political circumstances it generated had a profound impact on the national security affairs of both countries.

The Korean War has not featured in the historical writing of either country to any great extent. The minor scale of the involvement and the lack of a domestic political dimension, together with a tendency in the universities to ignore or downplay military history, has meant that few monographic studies have appeared outside the official histories. Korea remains a largely unknown conflict, sandwiched between the great national drama of World War II, especially in the Pacific, and the long and traumatic involvement in Vietnam. Recent government-driven initiatives to orient Australians more directly toward the Asia and Pacific regions have in fact been selective in their emphases, focusing heavily on Southeast Asia, and although the Republic of Korea is Australia's fourth-largest trading partner, most Australians know little or nothing about it; the same applies to New Zealand, only more so.

This chapter deals with the official histories, considers other writings dealing with Australian and New Zealand participation, and touches on strategic and policy studies as well. There are divergent interpretations of some issues, but the small number of writers in the field belies any sense of contending schools of thought, nor have all issues attracted equal attention.

OFFICIAL HISTORIES

The Australian and New Zealand official histories of the Korean War form part of a tradition of writing that goes back to World War I and the first Australian official historian, C. E. W. Bean. Unlike the United States, where official history programs sponsored by the armed services and the organizations responsible for their writing have enjoyed a continuing institutional identity since World War II, the antipodean Australian–New Zealand histories have been the property of no single agency or service, and an official historian has been appointed specifically to write them, with the organization in support of the effort raised and then disbanded on each occasion. The histories dealing with the activities of each service have also covered domestic politics, economics, and home front issues, where appropriate, and have included sustained treatment of medical issues also.

Australia's official histories of the two world wars ran to twelve and twenty-two volumes, respectively, and these historians have always boasted that their work has been free of government censorship or interference except for the preservation of security concerning some intelligence matters. In New Zealand World War I was treated inadequately by five semi-official volumes published in the 1920s; World War II was covered by a series that ran to more than fifty detailed volumes; the last volumes, dealing with the home front, only appeared in 1986.

Robert O'Neill was appointed Australia's official historian for the Korean War in 1970. He had served as a junior officer with an infantry battalion in Vietnam in 1966–1967 and then moved into academic life, one of the few university-based historians at that time to take much interest in military affairs. O'Neill's first volume, *Strategy and Diplomacy* (1981), deals with the higher-level decision making and political and strategic context in which Australia's deployment to Korea was made. The second, *Combat Operations* (1985), examines the experiences of the three services on an individual basis since "with rare exceptions, they did not fight together," while senior command and staff positions on the UNC Headquarters were closed to non-Americans. This volume concludes with relatively brief sections by other authors dealing with the medical problems encountered and the experiences of the small number of Australians taken prisoner by the Chinese and North Koreans.

O'Neill's first volume provides the fullest and most sophisticated account yet published of the genesis of the Australia–New Zealand–United States (ANZUS) Treaty, which linked the three and played a large part in the defense and foreign policy of the Pacific dominions for more than thirty years. With "a belief that the personalities of politicians, their advisers and the chief external actors have a major impact on the formation of national policy," O'Neill hoped to give this notion some treatment in his history but was mostly frustrated, since the private as opposed to public record proved disappointing. However, the origins of ANZUS owed much to the single-mindedness of the minister for external affairs between 1950 and 1951, Percy Spender, whose skillful diplomacy persuaded the Americans to enter into a multilateral treaty in an area of the world of little inherent strategic or diplomatic interest to them at that time. Spender had been equally tenacious in sponsoring Australia's decision to commit ground combat forces in September 1950 while Prime Minister Robert Menzies was in the mid-Atlantic, effectively unable to influence the decision-making process. "Spender," notes O'Neill, "was able to justify vigorous tactics by spectacular results." In doing so, "he established a foundation for Australia's foreign policy which served the government well, both externally and domestically, for the next twenty years."

Significant though ANZUS is to the story of Australian diplomacy in this period, it was not the only dimension of Australian strategic policy, or of Australian diplomatic involvement in Korea, and O'Neill ranges widely. Australia's role within the United Nations was generally a supporting one, and the minor UN member nations had no active role at Panmunjom. On the question of forced versus voluntary repatriation of prisoners of war, the Australian government decided in February 1952 to support the U.S. position of voluntary return and did not change this stance for the rest of the war despite British doubts and contrary inclinations. In the various UN commissions on Korea, Australia played an active part, which had its origins in prewar conditions. The UN Temporary Commission on Korea (UNTCOK) and its successors, the UN Commission on Korea (UNCOK), had been created in 1947 to oversee elections in Korea, ultimately held in the South only, and Australia had sent representatives to both. Although Australia extended diplomatic recognition to the Republic of Korea in August 1949, its diplomatic officials protested Rhee's authoritarian behavior and brutal repression of opponents, and the Australian delegate on UNTCOK absented himself from South Korea's inaugural celebrations in August 1948. James Plimsoll, the Australian delegate to the UN Commission for the Unification and Rehabilitation of Korea (UNCURK), exercised an ameliorating influence on Rhee and his policies, and when he was to return to another post in Australia at the end of 1951, U.S. ambassador John J. Muccio pressed successfully for his reappointment. O'Neill shows that through Plimsoll's activities, the Australian government retained a level of influence on affairs inside Korea that it could not have achieved otherwise and that was not enjoyed by any UN member government other than the United States.

Australian policy also reflected longer-standing and traditional engagement within the empire-commonwealth, and this was complicated by the changing role of the dominions. Australia had asserted a leading role for itself as the commonwealth representative in the Pacific after 1945. This leadership had taken concrete form in the British Commonwealth Occupation Force in Japan, which had been commanded and largely administered by Australia, in consultation with Britain, India, and New Zealand. After the South Koreans, the British were America's main ally in the war and attempted to assert their influence over decision making and policymaking in Washington and Tokyo, with mixed results. In doing so, Britain made little allowance for the competing interests of the dominions and, in fact, excluded them from such arrangements as they were able to extract from Washington. London resented Britain's exclusion from ANZUS and did not help in forging a commonwealth, as opposed to purely British, position on Korean War issues, although by this stage this was generally impossible in any case.

Thus, O'Neill's first volume marked something of a departure in the structure and organization of Australian official histories. In contrast to two volumes in the World War II series on political and social issues whose focus was largely domestic and failed to produce a volume on national strategy, O'Neill's decision to devote a volume to foreign policy reflected the changing nature of Australia's participation in international affairs.

O'Neill's second volume was more in the traditional style of official history writing. Beginning with Bean, operational history had treated in great detail, often down to platoon and section level, the experiences and actions of Australian soldiers and, in the air and naval dimensions, of individual ships and aircraft. The result in O'Neill's case is 800 pages of detailed narrative, which, while it attempts to place the Australian actions into their broader operational context, spends much of its time at slit-trench level. There are few controversies, for in the Australian experience, there was little from which to generate them. An exception is the treatment of the Australian-born journalist Wilfred Burchett, who covered the war from the North Korean side for a French newspaper and whose activities will be discussed here.

The New Zealand tradition of official history is more variegated than its Australian counterpart, not least because since World War II, the New Zealand government has maintained a small cell within the Ministry of Internal Affairs to supervise the production of official histories. The first of a projected two-volume series, *New Zealand and the Korean War*, Ian McGibbon's *Politics and Diplomacy* appeared in 1992. Like O'Neill's work, this official history is divided between statecraft and operations, and for many of the same reasons. New Zealand's contribution to the UNC was smaller than Australia's, from an equally unprepared peacetime defense force, and New Zealand could hope to exercise even less influence in the decision-making process than its larger neighbor. McGibbon's history places ANZUS much less at center stage than does O'Neill, reflecting New Zealand's relatively lesser part in its initiation and the differing motivations behind New Zealand's commitment of forces. Where Spender was motivated consciously by his longer-term plan to conclude a strategic alliance with the United States, support for UN principles was uppermost in Wellington, along with support for a British Commonwealth position. Negotiating a security arrangement with the United States was not unimportant and, once secured, quickly became "basic to our whole foreign policy," in the words of Prime Minister Sidney Holland. But the original motivation for involvement was less bound to considerations of meshing New Zealand and U.S. foreign policy, however much that had become the case by the time the armistice was signed. The Korean War, concludes the official historian, had a major impact on the way New Zealand approached the conduct of international affairs.

Domestically the Korean War's impact in New Zealand was minor. There was opposition from the Communist party, as in Australia, and a serious waterfront dispute in February 1951 that was broken through drafting troops to load ships and handle cargo. Economically the Korean War brought a commodities boom to a number of countries, and in New Zealand this is remembered for the tremendous filip given to the wool industry, despite later inflationary pressures. Increasing intolerance of political dissent characterized New Zealand as in other countries, a function of the cold war climate that the fighting in Korea accentuated.

The official histories represent the only major, sustained historical writing on Australian and New Zealand involvement in the Korean War. Although the foreign ministries of both countries publish collections of diplomatic documents, neither has treated Korea, although the second volume in the series *Documents on New Zealand External Relations, the Surrender and Occupation of Japan* (1982), edited by Robin Kay, impinges on it slightly. There is occasional discussion of Australian and New Zealand involvement in the official histories produced by the U.S. Army and by the British government, but the observation of an earlier Australian official historian, Gavin Long, holds generally true: the smaller partners in an alliance must write their own histories if they wish their stories to be told in any detail.

SECONDARY WORKS

Other writings on the Korean War are similarly few in number, and although most develop our understanding of Australian involvement at various levels, they do not deviate much from the broad outline provided by O'Neill. There is almost no other New Zealand writing of any consequence other than by the official historian, and the neglect of the subject is exemplified by the complete failure to mention the Korean War even in passing in the *Oxford History of New Zealand* (1981).

Early descriptions of Australian involvement in the fighting, very much in the style of the Christmas annuals produced for the forces in the two world wars, appeared soon after the armistice. Norman Bartlett's *With the Australians in Korea* (1954), liberally illustrated, provided a racy, journalistic narrative of action on land, sea, and in the air, followed by first-hand accounts of the fighting by men actually engaged in it and by journalists covering the war. Although similarly dated, of more historical interest is George Odgers' *Across the Parallel* (1952). Odgers, who wrote about the air war in the southwest Pacific area for the official history of World War II, had a long career in defense journalism. His account of the experiences of the Australian No. 77 fighter squadron in the first two years of the war describes the fight for air superiority and the problems of close air support. Odgers is knowledgeable in discussing the problems of adapting to the jet age in aerial combat, a particular problem for the Royal Australian Air Force (RAAF), which was equipped with piston-engine aircraft in 1950. The RAAF's adaptation to jets in this period has been touched on by Alan Stephens in *Power Plus Attitude* (1992), especially in its implications for doctrinal evolution. Stephens demonstrates that the RAAF's roles and mission in Australia's defense system came to be driven not by doctrinal necessity but by the inadequacy of the aircraft chosen as the first generation of front-line jet fighter. These issues and others of a narrowly operational nature are also the subject of David Wilson's *Lion over Korea* (1994).

Australian naval activity in Korean waters has received some treatment, although it tends to be episodic. The Korean War provided the first test of Australia's newly acquired fleet air arm and naval aviation capability, and the personal experiences and observations of air crew flying missions from the HMAS *Sydney* are featured in three chapters of *Reflections on the Royal Australian Navy* (1991), the collected proceedings of a naval history workshop sponsored by the RAN. In this collection, British naval historian Eric Grove provided a paper on British and Australian naval policy in the Korean War era. Alastair Cooper (1994) has examined the background to Anglo-Australian naval relations in the decade after World War II, while Tom Frame's *Pacific Partners* (1992) looks briefly at the Korean War as a basis for building naval cooperation with the emerging partner in Australia's maritime security planning, the U.S. Navy.

Recent writing on the ground war has concentrated on the battle of Kapyong in April 1951 during the Chinese Fifth Phase Offensive, with two books treating the battle from broadly similar perspectives and one that dissents mildly from the version offered in the official history. Bob Breen's *The Battle of Kapyong* (1992) attempts to clarify the conflicting accounts of the battle offered by participants, especially the sequence of events that led to the withdrawal of the forward companies of the Australian battalion engaged in the early hours of April 24. His account suggests that break-downs in radio communications late on April 23 between battalion head-quarters and the forward positions led to added confusion in the midst of strong Chinese attacks and forced responsibility for the conduct of the latter stages of the battle onto the forward company commander. Jack Gallaway's *The Last Call of the Bugle* (1994), a sentimental participant's history, which argues, in a manner familiar in Australian historiography, for the superiority of the citizen soldier over the regular, goes further in its indictment of Australian unit command at the battle, while setting the engagement in the context of the first nine months of the Australian commitment to the ground fighting. Although offering much useful personal detail, Gallaway's conclusions should be treated with some caution. Much better is Breen's *The Battle of Maryang San* (1991), which deals with the Australian part in Operation COMMANDO in October 1951, described by the official history as "probably the greatest single feat of the Australian Army during the Korean War." The work's distinguishing feature is its focus on unit and battalion-level operations. The "democratic" style of these histories gives detailed accounts of the deeds of low-ranking individuals, a feature familiar in Australian historiography pioneered by the official historian of World War I, C. E. W. Bean.

Higher-level concerns have been treated by Jeffrey Grey in *The Commonwealth Armies and the Korean War* (1988), which looks at command, logistics, administration, and interoperability in both a commonwealth and UNC context. Grey argues that although the commonwealth military contribution worked well on the ground because of common procedures, equipment, and outlook, the Korean War marked the final occasion on which such military cooperation could be sustained, given the increasingly divergent aims and interests of the contending parties. The experience of working within an American command was not altogether happy and contributed in part to the decision in 1964 to extend the standardization agreements between Britain, the United States, and Canada to include Australia and New Zealand. Yet American commanders generally granted their commonwealth subordinates a degree of independence, which helped to smooth command relations.

The commonly accepted versions of Australia's Korean involvement have been seriously questioned only in academic historical writing by Gavan McCormack. His *Cold War Hot War* (1983) argues from a left revisionist position encountered in similar U.S. writings, and his notes make clear his dependence on such work. McCormack rehearses many arguments familiar to readers of the cold war's revisionist literature and applies a level of scrutiny to events in South Korea that events in North Korea never receive. He accepts as evidence the germ warfare "confessions" of captured American pilots without understanding the context of, for example, the Schwable case, which he cites in support but which explodes the validity of such evidence. Despite its subtitle, little of the book deals with Australian policy or activity during the Korean War; that which does is generally an indictment of it because McCormack is severely critical of O'Neill's official history. McCormack's second, and more sustained, dissent centers on the activities and treatment of the journalist Wilfred Burchett, accused of involvement in the interrogation of UN prisoners of the Chinese while covering the war for the Paris evening paper, *Ce Soir*. His defense of Burchett, considered a traitor by some Australians for his Korean activities, exposes some weaknesses and flaws in the prosecution case, while ignoring the fact that a journalist involved in the activities of a prison camp administration, no matter how benign, cannot claim impartial status. McCormack's case also ignores Burchett's stated support for left-wing revolutionary causes in the Third World. Although it may be true that Burchett's coverage of the Panmunjom truce talks made up nothing, he did not tell the whole truth in his articles about conditions in Chinese prison compounds along the Yalu and about other events on the North Korean side. In the phrase of French writer Jacques Marcuse, Burchett was at the very least a "Vested Interest Person," one whose career depended on access and whose access depended on writing in a certain way. While McCormack rightly identifies cold war concerns as lying at the heart of the indictment against Burchett, his defense of this curious figure is not entirely convincing.

More recently, scholars have turned to the dominions' role in the early cold war, which provides a context for understanding the background to Australian and New Zealand commitment to Korea. At present, this remains confined largely to journal literature and recent graduate theses. However, the works of David Lee (1992, 1993), Chris Waters (1990), and David Lowe (1991) point in fruitful directions for further scholarship on Australia's role in containment in the Far East. Ian McGibbon (1977, 1991) and Rob Eaddy (1983) have done much the same for New Zealand. In Britain, Ritchie Ovendale's *The Foreign Policy of the British Labour Governments* (1984) examines the ways in which the empire's approach to the cold war differed between empire governments of the same political stripe.

ARCHIVAL SOURCES

Archival access to records of the commonwealth government and its agencies is governed by legislation and conforms broadly to a thirty-year rule; the same is true in New Zealand. Material relating to the Korean War in both countries is therefore generally available to academic and private (as opposed to official) researchers. In Australia, relevant material is divided basically among three repositories. Files generated by the Departments of Defense, the Treasury, External Affairs, and the Prime Minister are held in the Canberra repository of the Australian Archives. Because the individual departments responsible for the armed forces did not move from Melbourne to the seat of federal government, Canberra, until 1959, some material relating to army and navy administration and policy may also be found in the Melbourne office of Australian Archives, although air force files are in Canberra. The operational records of all units (unit war diaries, ships' reports of proceedings, headquarters files) together with personal papers (such as diaries, letters, and photographs) are held by the Australian War Memorial, Canberra. There are as well some relevant sets of personal papers of politicians and officials in the National Library of Australia, Canberra. As is the case for most of Australia's other wars, the fact that Australian units fought as part of larger, British formations means that some records relevant to Australian participation are held in Britain. For the Korean War the headquarters diaries of the 27th and 28th Commonwealth Brigades and the 1st Commonwealth Division are at the Public Record Office, Kew, as are Admiralty records for Task Group 95.1.

Much the same may be said for New Zealand records. The National Archives in Wellington contain ministry files and operational records and some private papers. There are more private papers in the Alexander Turnbull Library, Wellington. Some records are still retained by the New Zealand Ministry of Defence.

In general, the only difficulties experienced with access to Korean War–era material occur with documents that originated with another government, in which case the permission of that government must be obtained before access is granted. If this material is still restricted there, permission to release it in Australia is generally refused. For example, files relating to the postrelease interrogations and debriefing of commonwealth prisoners of war, conducted in 1953 after the cease-fire, are closed in the Public Record Office for seventy-five years, as is material relating to the committee set up to report on prisoner conduct while in captivity. This material, although held also in Australia, is restricted there as well. On the other hand, because so much was copied from London to the capitals of the participating dominions, material that may not have been retained for archival preservation in one country may well still be extant in another. This involves research costs, however, which are increasingly difficult to sustain.

FUTURE DIRECTIONS IN RESEARCH

The historiography of Australian and New Zealand involvement in the Korean War offers a number of opportunities for further work. The second volume of the New Zealand official history will deal with New Zealand's ground and naval contributions to the UNC, on which nothing else has been written. There is scope for analysis of operations in Korea during the static phase of the war in 1952–1953, in which Australian soldiers participated in quite large battles, at the Hook and Point 355 on the Jamestown Line, for example, while the impact of the Korean War on the postwar army, itself in the process of transformation, has received no attention at all. As with many other areas of Australian naval history, the Royal Australian Navy's deployment awaits its student, although there seems little more to be said about the Royal Australian Air Force in this context. Nothing has been written on the veterans of this war. Although ANZUS is now a well-worked field, the broader issues of cold war containment and strategy in the Far East and the role of the Pacific dominions in both empire and American strategy still have something to offer. Cold war issues in the domestic sphere have hardly been touched. Although the oppositional movements to involvement in Korea were both tiny and confined to the fringes of politics, they merit study as intellectual and political antecedents of the much larger and more active movements against the Vietnam War in the 1960s. More generally, writing on the Korean War as a whole will benefit from examining and comparing the experiences of the smaller UN forces and the policies and attitudes of their governments as a means of breaking down the relentlessly Amerocentric nature of most of the writing in the field.

REFERENCES

Bartlett, Norman. *With the Australians in Korea.* Canberra: Australian War Memorial, 1954.

Breen, Bob. *The Battle of Maryang San.* Sydney: Australian Army (Training Command), 1991.

———. *The Battle of Kapyong.* Sydney: Australian Army (Training Command), 1992.

Cooper, Alastair. "At the Crossroads: Anglo-Australian Naval Relations, 1945–1960." *Journal of Military History* 58:4 (October 1994).

Eaddy, R. R. "New Zealand in the Korean War: The First Year: A Study in Official Government Policy." Master's thesis, University of Otago, 1983.

Frame, T. R., ed. *Reflections on the Royal Australian Navy.* Sydney: Kangaroo Press, 1991.

———. *Pacific Partners: A History of Australian-American Naval Relations.* Sydney: Hodder & Stoughton, 1992.

Gallaway, Jack. *The Last Call of the Bugle: The Long Road to Kapyong.* St. Lucia: University of Queensland Press, 1994.

Grey, Jeffrey. *The Commonwealth Armies and the Korean War: An Alliance Study.* Manchester: Manchester University Press, 1988.

Kay, Robin, ed. *Documents on New Zealand External Relations.* Vol. 2: *The Surrender and Occupation of Japan.* Wellington: Government Publisher, 1982.

Lee, David. "The National Security Planning and Defence Preparations of the Menzies Government, 1950–1953." *War and Society* 10:2 (October 1992): 119–138.

————. "Australia and Allied Strategy in the Far East, 1952–1957." *Journal of Strategic Studies* 16:4 (December 1993): 511–538.

Lowe, David. "Australia, Southeast Asia and the Cold War, 1948–1954." Ph.D. thesis, University of Cambridge, 1991.

McCormack, Gavan. *Cold War Hot War: An Australian Perspective on the Korean War.* Sydney: Hale and Iremonger, 1983.

————. "Korea: Wilfred Burchett's Thiry Years War." In Ben Kiernan, ed., *Burchett: Reporting the Other Side of the World*, pp. 162–211. London: Quartet, 1986.

McGibbon, Ian. "The Defence of New Zealand, 1945–1957." In A. D. McIntosh, ed., *New Zealand in World Affairs*, pp. 143–176. Wellington: Price Milburn, 1977.

————. *New Zealand and the Korean War.* Vol. 1: *Politics and Diplomacy.* Wellington: Oxford University Press, 1992.

————. "Forward Defence: The Southeast Asian Commitment." In Malcolm McKinnon, ed., *New Zealand in World Affairs, 1957–1972*, pp. 9–39. Wellington: New Zealand Institute of International Affairs, 1991.

Odgers, George. *Across the Parallel: The Australian 77th Squadron with the United States Air Force in the Korean War.* London: William Heinemann, 1952.

O'Neill, Robert. *Australia in the Korean War, 1950–1953.* Vol. 1: *Strategy and Diplomacy.* Canberra: Australian War Memorial, 1981.

————. *Australia in the Korean War, 1950–1953.* Vol. 2: *Combat Operations.* Canberra: Australian War Memorial, 1985.

Ovendale, Ritchie, ed. *The Foreign Policy of the British Labour Governments, 1945–1951.* Leicester: Leicester University Press, 1984.

Stephens, Alan. *Power Plus Attitude: Ideas, Strategy and Doctrine in the Royal Australian Air Force, 1921–1991.* Canberra: Australian Government Publishing Service, 1992.

Waters, C. W. P. "Anglo-Australian Diplomacy 1945–1949: Labour Governments in Conflict." Ph.D. thesis, University College, University of New South Wales, 1990.

Wilson, David. *Lion over Korea: 77 Fighter Squadron RAAF, 1950–1953.* Canberra: Banner Books, 1994.

8   Japan and the Korean War

Lester H. Brune and In K. Hwang

Japanese and American scholars disagree when evaluating the Korean War's impact on Japan. Americans view the war as the catalyst that melded the United States' uncertain East Asian policies by producing definite containment programs for the western Pacific to match policies devised earlier for Europe. The Japanese, however, perceive the years from 1950 to 1952 as finalizing negotiations that ended the U.S. occupation of Japan and revived its economy, protected by the U.S.-Japan Mutual Security agreement that exempted Japan from any necessity to rearm. Japan's disastrous World War II episode had ended, and a new era began.

Because Japanese perceptions focused on the results of World War II, few Japanese writers, as Roger Dingman notes (1993), give primary attention to the Korean War's influence. Whether Japanese historians accept the "continuities" or "reverse course" of U.S. occupation policy, they agree in emphasizing that U.S. policy was pragmatic, adapting its decisions to shifts reflecting international circumstances and ending by benefiting Japan's recovery. For the Japanese, the important factor between 1945 and 1952 was that U.S. decisions helped to reconstruct Japan as a reliable U.S. ally, which recognized U.S. primacy in the western Pacific. The new Japan would be a stable, peaceful, and reformist nation, becoming part of a liberal international order.

Within this general pattern of occupation history, postwar Japanese historiography finds Japanese scholarship shifting from early criticism of General Douglas MacArthur's regime for not making radical reforms to a 1970s reevaluation that emphasized the political skills of Japanese leaders who worked pragmatically with Americans to benefit Japan. The essay by Iokibe Makoto, Asada Sadao, and Hosoya Masahiro in Asada's *Japan and the World* (1989) indicates that during the 1950s and 1960s, Japanese writing about the occupation was dominated by left-of-center scholars whose positions in the universities resulted from the postwar reaction to Japan's fascist wartime leadership. These scholars criticized U.S. policy for not fully "demilitarizing and democratizing" Japan because it "reversed course" and allowed Japanese conservatives and bureaucrats to regain power. By the 1970s, however, many Japanese writers had reevaluated these early accounts. Assisted by recently opened documents in Washington and Tokyo, the reevaluation described the continuity by which MacArthur's officials in the Supreme Command for the Allied Powers (SCAP) interacted with Japanese political and economic leaders who cooperated in creating Japan's new regime.

Although both U.S. and Japanese scholars often diverge in interpretations of the occupation's original intentions and the desired results after six years of occupation, both groups generally agree that the results of democratization and demilitarization were not radical but centrist in terms of Japan's historical development. Washington's 1945 plans for the occupation had been influenced by prewar U.S. ambassador to Japan Joseph Grew and others who believed Japan had a liberal heritage before being subverted by fascists in 1931 and who wanted to revive Japan's liberal propensities rather than have the United States adopt the policies of hard-liners in Washington who advocated strong punitive measures. Although U.S. policy was publicized as designed to democratize and demilitarize Japan, this terminology was interpreted in varied ways by SCAP officials and by later scholarship. Moreover, advocates of the continuity of U.S. policy, such as Akira Iriye in the book he edited with Yonosuke Nagai (1977), find evidence that U.S. planners anticipated friction with the Soviet Union after World War II and believed Japan would play a crucial role as a U.S. ally in Asia.

In implementing U.S. policy, SCAP officials had to work within the existing Japanese political and bureaucratic framework in order to enact any lasting changes. Not suprisingly, postwar developments raised basic questions regarding industrial management versus labor unions, the relation of antitrust prosecution to Japan's history of *zaibatsu* cartels, and Japan's future armaments policy. These issues were as controversial in the United States as they were in Japan's occupation era; yet SCAP personnel had to work with Japanese officials to achieve what was deemed best at any given moment.

Before North Korea attacked South Korea, SCAP activity with Japanese officials had gone far toward agreement on Japan's future political and economic situation. Prior to June 1950, many basic U.S. plans for Japan's future had been finalized or neared completion. SCAP devised a constitution that Japan's Diet approved in 1947. SCAP's limits on dissolving Japan's *zaibatsu* had largely resulted in the retention of the large industrial groups. And preliminary discussions had begun on peace and security treaties with Japan. In fact, John Foster Dulles visited Seoul June 18–20,

1950, and was in Tokyo when North Korea attacked on June 25. Dulles was discussing U.S.-Japanese security problems and urging Japan to raise an army of 300,000 men as a defense force, a proposal Japan's prime minister, Shigeru Yoshida, did not accept.

In the context of such decisions, the events of 1949–1950 simply finalized U.S. occupation goals by signing a peace treaty and alliance with Japan. During 1949, the Chinese communist victory and the Soviet Union's successful testing of an atomic bomb resulted in Washington's clarification of its Asian containment policy. Thus, despite Soviet objections, the United States quickly obtained a peace treaty and alliance with Japan and made Japan a base of operations during the Korean War. These events solidified the U.S. expectation that Japan possessed Asia's best industrial infrastructure for contributing to the U.S. cold war in the Pacific region.

During the Korean War, Japan became the base for U.S. offshore military procurement, adding to the military equipment that General MacArthur had brought to Japan under Operation Roll-up after 1947. While serving the UN forces during the Korean conflict, Japan's military industries rapidly increased the nation's economy. Although the Korean War was primary to U.S. activity, Japan focused on the growth of its domestic economy and the achievement of peace and security treaties. The U.S. treaties became the salutary consequence of World War II, and the role of Japanese leaders in adjusting to U.S. demands was more significant to Japanese history than the Korean War.

This chapter describes the research literature regarding the Japanese perspective on the occupation and its relation to the Korean War.

REFERENCE MATERIAL ON JAPAN AND THE KOREAN WAR

The two indispensable bibliographical volumes regarding the occupation of Japan are Robert Ward and Frank Shulman's (1974) work on Western-language materials on the Japanese occupation and the companion Japanese-language work edited by Sakamoto Yoshikazu and others (1972). Ward and Shulman also describe SCAP's archives, which are available in Washington or on microfiche from University Press of America. Frank Shulman (1970) also compiled a list of doctoral dissertations on Japan and Korea published between 1877 and 1969. Cecil H. Uyehara (1959) describes studies on the communist and noncommunist left wing in Japan since 1945. Thaddeus Ohata (1981) has a bibliography of Japanese materials at the Library of Congress, Washington D.C., and John Dower (1986) describes post-1945 literature as part of his seven basic bibliographies.

Five works provide occupation-era data based on interviews with SCAP and Japanese personnel or documents from the period. Eugene Dooman and Gordon Beate (1970) describe Columbia University's oral history project on Japan's occupation era. A compilation of interviews with occupation officials from Japan's weekly journal, *Shukan Shincho* (1970), has been published. Jun Eto (1978) edited a volume of twelve interviews with Japanese leaders and (1981–1982) joined others in editing four volumes of documents from Japan's Foreign Ministry during the occupation period. Finally, Tokyo University's Law Faculty edited four volumes of studies based on SCAP directives, which are described in Ward and Shulman's (1974) bibliography. Ward and Shulman also give details on the documentary materials about the U.S. Far East Command in Tokyo.

For literature since 1974 on Japan's occupation, Sadao Asada's edited volume, *Japan and the World* (1989), contains a valuable overall introduction by Chihiro Hosoya, as well as a guide to documents, archives, and reference works by Tokushiro Ohata, Sadao Asada, and Sumio Hatano; and an essay on the occupation period by Makota Iokibe, Sadao Asada, and Masahiro Hosoya. Richard Perren (1992) provides annotations for over 700 studies about the Japanese occupation. Harry Wray and Hilary Conroy (1983) edited interpretive essays about modern Japanese history written by prominent scholars such as Edwin O. Reischauer and Eiji Takamae. The National Committee of Japanese Historians (1985) published a bibliography of studies that appeared between 1979 and 1982 for an international meeting at Stuttgart, Germany.

Two more specialized bibliographies may serve scholars studying Japanese industry and women: Karl Boger's (1988) annotated bibliography on Japan's postwar industry and Hesung Chong Koh's (1982) guide for studying a variety of issues on Korean and Japanese women, including society and culture, history, family, language, and English translations of Japanese fiction written by women.

Several historiographic articles are worth checking. Sadao Asada (1981) evaluated works of the 1970s on the occupation. John Dower (1989) described the vast variety of literature on the occupation era. Carol Gluck (1983) evaluates both Japanese and U.S. writers on the occupation. Researchers on Japan should know about the Japanese Foreign Ministry's indexes of the ministry's postwar records available from 1971 to 1987. Gaiko Shiryokan (Diplomatic Records Office) will send a copy on request to its office at Azabudai 1-5-3, Minatoku, Tokyo 108. Scholars may also profit by using the *Nihon Gaikoshi Jiten* (Encyclopedia of Japanese diplomatic history) published in 1979. The U.S. archives on Japan are covered in Chapter 1 of this book.

LITERATURE ON JAPAN AND THE KOREAN WAR

Impact of the Korean War on Japan

As Roger Dingman (1993) indicates, few studies by Japanese scholars on the Korean War directly show Japan's role during the war. The single monograph that does this is by Masao Oknogi (1986). Japan's official ten-volume history about the Korean War, edited by Rikusen Kenkyu Fukyu Kai (1966), does not mention Japan's involvement in the war. The other notable Japanese study on Korea during the period 1945 to 1952 is by Yoshio Morita (1964), whose account ends when Japan's troops evacuated Korea in 1945–1946. Morita and Osada Kaneko (1979–1980) edited a collection of documents on Korea covering the period of Morita's book.

Some articles contemporary with the Korean War noted the war's effect on Japan's future security. Examples from essays in the journal *Contemporary Japan* of 1950 and 1951 include those of Kichisaburo Nomura and Hitoshi Ashida, both of whom discuss the Korean War's significance in defining U.S. protection for Japan; and by Shigeru Yoshida, who indicates that U.S. action in Korea demonstrated that the United States would defend Japan against communism.

Later Japanese studies that mentioned the Korean War usually associated it with the cold war, the 1951 peace treaty, and the U.S.-Japan security agreement. Yui Daisaburo (1985) describes the Korean War's influence on the negotiating of the peace treaty. Takeshi Igarashi (1986) gives little attention to the Korean War, only relating it to the cold war's influence in the formulation of the U.S.-Japan security alliance.

Although Japanese scholars give primary attention to the U.S. occupation as the concluding phase of World War II's consequences, some Western scholars have used Japanese documents to describe the Korean War's relation to Japanese history. Two important articles by Reinhold Drifte (1989) and Roger Dingman (1993) as well as the volume of essays edited by William Nimmo (1990) deal with the Korean War's impact on Japan.

Drifte combines informative details from varied sources to explain Japan's direct involvement in Korea to assist UN forces. Japan was not only the logistical base for American forces but also for other UN forces under the UN-Japan Status of Forces agreement of 1950. In June 1950, the United States had fewer than 100,000 troops in Japan; by 1953 the United States had 263,350 personnel in Japan, including Okinawa. The United States also hired many Japanese to perform nonmilitary duties at these bases and recruited Japanese technicians to go to Korea, where they operated dredges in Korean harbors, as well as power plants and other factories that Japan had built during its occupation of Korea. During negotiations regarding the 1951 peace treaty, Japan rejected John Foster

Dulles's request that they raise a 300,000-man army, but they agreed to organize a 75,000-man national police reserve (Keisatsuyobotai), which received military, not police, training.

Most significant, perhaps, the United States hired Japanese mercenaries, naval personnel, and some Korean residents in Japan to assist in South Korea. When MacArthur made his famous landing at Inchon, Korea, Drifte estimates that nearly 2,600 seamen and dockers who were involved had been recruited in Japan. Japanese personnel operated forty-six minesweepers and thirty-five LST landing craft at Inchon. Drifte indicates, however, that he could not ascertain the precise number of Japanese casualties during this invasion.

Both Drifte and Dingman agree that the Korean War provided the economic boost for Japan that revitalized Japan's industry. Before the Korean War began, U.S. officials had sought methods to revive Japan's economic status. During the war, Japanese sales under the U.S. offshore procurement program stimulated orders for military equipment that totaled nearly $3.4 billion by 1954. Many Japanese companies, including Toyota, were revived by filling American defense orders, which generated investments that served Japan's long-term economic growth.

Roger Dingman's article and William Nimmo's volume cover broader aspects of the Korean War's influence on Japan's society, culture, military security, and the economy. Dingman accepts the Japanese view that the Korean War was only a secondary event in Japan's history. Nevertheless, he shows the war resulted in U.S. decisions that affected many aspects of Japan's society. For example, he contends that the war internationalized Japan's outlook, making Japanese more open to strangers than previously. In 1994, Dingman was preparing a book to elaborate on his article's findings.

Early Literature on the Occupation

Japanese literature on the Allied occupation was initially dominated by left-wing academic critics who believed SCAP's reverse course had not reformed Japanese society in the manner they expected. These views predominated in accounts of the occupation until a reevaluation began during the late 1960s and featured studies that described benefits Japan received from the occupation.

This general pattern of early writing was not universal because some Japanese writers perceived the reverse course as SCAP's realistic continuation of its democratization in adapting to Japan's problems. Three examples of favorable literature about the occupation were Kazuo Kawai's (1960) emphasis on positive gains for Japan; Kozo Yamamura's (1964, 1967) information on the dissolution of the *zaibatsu*, which was only partly accurate in claiming success for the dissolution; and Prime Minister Shig-

eru Yoshida's (1962) memoirs, which explained how his relations with
U.S. authorities assisted Japan's recovery.

More representative of Japanese scholarship through the 1960s are two
multivolume studies about the occupation era. One is Seizaburo Shinobu's (1965–1967) four-volume study emphasizing Japan's political history
from 1945 to 1952. The second is the five-volume history of the Pacific
war in which the last volume covers the Allied occupation. These volumes
were edited by Rekishigaku Kenkyukai (Historical Science Society) and
published in 1953–1954. A third early study in this group, a joint venture
of diplomatic historians and international law specialists, was edited by
Hogakkai Kokusai (1952).

Each of these early studies gave details of SCAP policy based on its many
directives that went beyond military policies. These scholars were not communists but liberal-left advocates who condemned ultranationalism and
believed MacArthur's policy yielded too much in retaining the old bureaucracy and political-military leadership. They termed the San Francisco
peace treaty one-sided because it did not permit leftist wartime delegates
from Great Britain and Australia to play a role in the negotiations. Thus,
they believed SCAP failed to democratize or demilitarize Japan sufficiently, a theme that U.S. historical revisionists described in great detail
during the 1970s, when Japanese scholars reevaluated the early literature
in a more conservative fashion.

Reevaluation of the Occupation

Using memoirs such as Yoshida's (1962) and obtaining newly declassified documents in Washington and Tokyo, Japanese researchers who lived
in the late 1960s when Japan's "economic miracle" brought prosperity,
looked back more favorably in studying the Allied occupation. Their reevaluations either recognized the reverse course or followed Akira Iriye's
continuities approach to U.S. occupation policy as seen in his essay in
Yonosuke Nagai and Akira Iriye (1977). The reverse course is emphasized
by Takeshi Igarashi (1981, 1986), indicating that MacArthur's call for an
early peace was related to broad changes in U.S. policy toward Japan.
Whether Japanese scholars find continuities or a reverse course in U.S.
policy, their reevaluation no longer charged a failure of SCAP policy but
perceived Japan's political and economic leaders as gaining advantages
for Japan by resisting or manipulating SCAP orders to obtain what was
best for Japan. Not surprisingly, one of the first reevaluations was Masataka
Kosaka's (1968) biography of Yoshida. A study that reevaluated the entire
occupation era was Kosaka's *One Hundred Million Japanese* (1972). Kosaka
used "realistic" international theory perspectives as enabling Yoshida and
other Japanese leaders to act pragmatically in dealing with the American
authorities.

Other Japanese studies that reevaluated specific parts of occupation history followed this pattern; that is, the early literature was largely critical of U.S. policy for reversing course and not reforming Japan's basic leadership structure; later literature disclosed that the United States may never have intended a radical democratization of Japan but preferred to work with conservative and cooperative Japanese leaders to strengthen Japan as a valuable U.S. ally in the western Pacific. From this perspective, Japan became a valuable ally during the Korean War even though this American requirement was secondary to Japan's desire to recover from World War II and reestablish a leading role in world affairs.

SCAP's Punitive Policies

The punitive aspects of SCAP's demilitarization program received more attention in contemporary comments on the occupation than they have received in later research. For the early literature on punitive and other SCAP policies, Robert Ward and Frank Shulman's (1974) bibliography gives details for each year of the occupation. In the case of punitive policies, SCAP activity involved reparations, war crime trials and purges, and demilitarization. Scholars should note that SCAP's frequent unilateral action in these areas caused complaints from the two groups MacArthur should have consulted because they represented the eleven Allied nations that fought against Japan: the Far East Commission (FEC) and the Allied Council on Japan. Generally the complaints from these two groups were overridden or ignored by SCAP as the United States often avoided hardline policies and either acted pragmatically or reversed course with regard to Washington's 1945 plans.

Regarding reparations, the smaller Asian nations, which had suffered most from Japan's aggressive warfare, had expected large Japanese reparations to reconstruct their societies and revive their economy. After 1947, however, SCAP minimized and finally stopped all reparations because they handicapped Japan's recovery. This decision ignored the benefits from reparations expected by Japan's wartime victims, especially Burma, Vietnam, the Philippine Islands, Indonesia, and nationalist China.

Washington's official explanations for ending the reparations are found in two *U.S. State Department Bulletins,* for May 26 and June 26, 1949, the latter article explaining the U.S. repudiation of complaints by delegations from the Philippines and nationalist China. Later, Bruce M. Brenn's (1967) article explained the U.S. justification for cutting back reparations. In contrast, the Australian writer W. F. Petrie (1950) argues that the United States ignored the views of Asian delegates on the FEC and Allied Council. These SCAP changes aided Japan, and articles by Takeo Ozawa (1956) and the Ajia Kyokai (Asia Society) list of achievements (1960) indicate Japan's benefits even though some problems developed.

War Crime Trials

During World War II, American officials, in particular, called for war crime trials of Germans and Japanese even though such action was unprecedented. At the July 1945 Potsdam Conference of U.S., British, and Soviet leaders, the "Big Three" agreed to establish war crime tribunals, and the surrender terms Japan signed on September 2, 1945, included such trials. In January 1946, General MacArthur established the International Military Tribunal for the Far East (IMTFE) in order to prosecute Japan's war criminals. Similar to the Nuremberg Tribunal for Germany, the IMTFE held hundreds of trials for little-known Japanese defendants as well as the highly publicized Tokyo trials of twenty-eight eminent Japanese leaders. In addition, Richard Lael (1982) describes the trial of General Tomoyuki Yamashita in Manila before the tribunal's work ended in November 1948. In addition, separate British and Australian tribunals were established in Southeast Asia and the South Pacific. The Tokyo tribunal sentenced General Tojo Hideki and six others to death for major war crimes and committed sixteen others to life in prison.

Records of the IMTFE, including the final judgment (1958), are available for research in Washington or by purchase of microfilm from the National Archives. Ward and Shulman (1974) describe the archives in detail and list contemporary articles arguing for and against the trials. Of interest are the publication of the tribunal's report by chief prosecutor Joseph Keenan and Brendan Brown (1950) which indicated the value of the trials. Also, students should note a report from the Soviet Union, *Materials on the Trial of Former Servicemen* (1950), which claimed the tribunal rejected its accusations that the Japanese army in Asia used bacteriological weapons for experiments on prisoners during World War II. For a discussion of later evidence on the Soviet Union's claims, see John W. Powell's (1980, 1981a, 1981b) articles on Japan's experiments on prisoners of war during World War II.

In 1970, Richard H. Minear (1971) published *Victors' Justice*, which cited international law to condemn the IMTFE for conducting "political trials." Three Japanese publications examine the trials. Chihiro Hosoya, Ando Nisuke, and Onuma Yasuaki (1984) edited papers from an international symposium on war crime trials. Two Japanese scholars linked data on the trials to the need for the Japanese people to consider their responsibility for the vast death and destruction caused by Japanese support of the "fifteen years of war" in Asia: Yosuaki Onuma (1985) and Saburo Ienaga (1985).

Purges

Closely related to the war crime trials was SCAP's policy of purging Japanese extreme nationalist and militaristic organizations and leaders.

The purges' intent was to democratize Japan by abolishing right-wing fascist groups, which subverted democracy. Eventually SCAP removed over 200,000 people from public offices or managerial postitions because they were connected with aggressive groups or war activity. SCAP's description of these actions is in *The History of the Non-military Activities of the Occupation of Japan,* monograph number 7, *The Purge, 1945 to December 1951* (1952).

The purge was, however, diverted from its original fascist target to include left-wing groups, union leaders, and mass media personnel who went too far in complaints against SCAP or the continued use of Japan's old bureaucratic leadership. Hans Herman Baerwold (1959) worked for SCAP, giving an inside view of how its purpose was undermined because domestic and international factors affecting Japan and the United States caused the liberal left to be seen as more dangerous than the fascist right. Two Western scholars who have studied these purges are Ivan Morris (1960) and John K. Emmerson (1978). In William Nimmo's edited essays (1990), Steve Y. Rhee examines the purges in terms of the postwar activity of Japan's Communist party. The purges are also mentioned in other parts of this essay on SCAP policy.

Demilitarization and Japan's Constitution

SCAP's original demilitarization program in September 1945 involved both the demobilization of Japan's armed forces and the destruction of Japan's military manufacturing facilities so that Japan would never again threaten Asia's peace. Japan's demobilization was readily completed by 1947, the same year that SCAP persuaded the Japanese to adopt a no-war constitution.

The Constitution of 1947 was adopted by Japan from a model constitution prepared by SCAP officials. Following Japan's surrender, General MacArthur asked Japanese leaders to form a constitutional commission to revise its Meiji-era Constitution of 1889–1890. The commission failed to do this to SCAP's satisfaction, and early in 1947, SCAP's government section drew up a constitution for Japan's government to accept. Aided by Emperor Hirohito's proclamation telling the Japanese people he was not divine, Japan's Diet (Assembly) approved the constitution in November 1946, to become effective on May 3, 1947. Because of SCAP's involvement in drafting the document, the constitution was not totally acceptable to the Japanese. The most controversial clause was Article 9, which renounced war as a means of settling international disputes and forbade the creation of Japanese armed forces.

SCAP's drafting of the constitution as a benefit to Japan is described by Justin Williams, Sr. (1979), who served in the office of MacArthur's staff that prepared the document. During the 1960s, the Japanese government created a special commission to study the 1947 Constitution and recommend amendments. This report was translated by John M. Maki (1964), but Japan's government took no action on the report. The linguistic problems SCAP had in preparing Japan's constitution by defining words and their meanings are explained in Kyoko Inoue's (1991) study.

As Reinhard Drifte (1982, 1989) indicates, Article 9 of the constitution caused questions in August 1950, after Prime Minister Yoshida announced that Japan would cooperate with UN forces in Korea. Opposition parties in the Diet argued that Yoshida violated Article 9's ban on Japan's waging war. Yoshida responded that the Potsdam Declaration and the 1945 surrender terms required Japan to cooperate with the occupation authorities. In addition, he said, Japan's aid was "spiritual cooperation" with UN directives.

Significant studies on the no-war provision are by Theodore Hart McNelly (1962), who says Article 9 was not intended to disarm Japan permanently, and Ikuhiro Hata (1976) who indicates Article 9 resulted from a compromise in 1947 between MacArthur and Japan's prime minister, Shidehara Kijuro, who agreed to the no-war clause so that Japan could retain its emperor. Hata believes Japan's new arms industry was valid.

Japan's arms industry was revived as a military procurement base for the use of UN forces in Korea after June 1950. Japan's rearming because of Korea is explained by Herbert Bix (1974). An American scholar, Bix argues that the U.S. procurement program became the basis for Japan's industrial recovery. Similarly, two Japanese scholars, Kato Yozo (1979) and Nitta Shunzo (1971), describe the militarization of Japan's industry, although neither scholar relates this directly to an impact of the Korean War.

There are five other important studies about Japan's rearmament. Mike Mochizuki (1993) describes the U.S. policy of first disarming and then rearming Japan. James Auer (1973) provides a broad survey of Japan's armaments history from 1945 to 1971. Frank Kowalski (1969) explains the development of Japan's 75,000-man National Police Reserve after the Korean War began. And John Dower (1969) connects the armaments revival in Japan to the treaties of peace and security the United States signed with Japan in 1951. Meirion and Susie Harries (1972) have written a general study of Japan's militarization.

Although the peace treaty with Japan ending the occupation was separate from the U.S.-Japan Mutual Security Agreement, both were negotiated at the same time and signed on September 8, 1951. The U.S. Senate ratified the peace treaty and approved the security agreement on March 20, 1952. The two treaties had been discussed in Washington and Tokyo since 1947, but the outbreak of the Korean War hastened the completion of the documents. The war also ensured that the United States would sign the treaty even though the Soviet Union and communist China refused to accept it following meetings in San Francisco.

Appointed by President Harry Truman, John Foster Dulles had charge of the negotiations with Japan, opening direct peace discussions with Japan's prime minister, Yoshida, in January 1951. By March 1951, the United States and Great Britain had agreed on a draft peace treaty, which would be discussed with delegates from all of Japan's World War II enemies at San Francisco in September. Following four days of discussion, the United States, Japan, and delegates of forty-eight other nations signed the peace treaty. The Soviet Union, the People's Republic of China, and other communist delegations opposed Dulles' tactics of permitting no amendments to the draft. They boycotted the final session and refused to sign the treaty.

Despite this "one-sided" peace with the United States and its allies, Japan's Diet approved the treaty in November 1951, and the U.S. Senate ratified it the next spring. The treaty's most significant parts stated that Japan would lose its overseas possessions, no further reparations would be levied against Japan, and Japan would be allowed to rearm for defensive purposes.

Following the San Francisco conference, Dulles remained concerned about problems with Great Britain and nationalist China regarding Japan. Having recognized the People's Republic of China, the British disliked the fact that communist China could not represent mainland China. At San Francisco, Dulles argued that after Japan made a peace treaty with others, Tokyo could decide to accept nationalist or communist China. Initially, Japan preferred to recognize communist China because the nationalist Chinese argued with the Japanese. Dulles eventually pressed Japan to recognize nationalist China. In 1956, Japan and the Soviet Union made a mutual declaration to end their state of war without resolving their disputes over rights to the Kuril Islands, which Russian forces occupied in 1945.

Because the Joint Chiefs of Staff and the U.S. Defense Department linked a peace treaty to retaining American bases in Japan, Dulles and his staff negotiated a separate U.S.-Japan alliance treaty along with the peace treaty. The Korean War made it obvious to most Washington planners that potential communist aggression in Asia required advanced U.S. military bases in Japan. As a result, the conclusion of a security alliance with Japan paralleled U.S. discussion of the peace treaty. The U.S.-Japan security agreement of 1951 permitted American garrison forces to remain in Japan following the peace treaty. Japan would only have self-defense forces, and the United States would protect Japan from outside aggressors. Because other Pacific nations expressed concern about a revived Japanese nation, the United States also signed security pacts with the Philippines, New Zealand, and Australia.

The Japanese peace treaty and security agreements are described by John M. Allison (1952), one of the U.S. officials who prepared these agreements. Other accounts by U.S. officials during the occupation era are

Bernard C. Cohen's (1957) on the peace process and John Foster Dulles' (1952) article justifying these arrangements with Japan. Two U.S. scholars whose essays should be considered are John Dower's (1969) article on the security treaty and Japan's police reserve and Roger Dingman's (1979) discussion of the effects of Japan's domestic politics on the 1951 treaties. An article by Howard Schonberger (1984) examines Dulles' problem in persuading Japan to recognize nationalist China rather than communist China.

Japanese literature on the peace and security treaties often includes information on various delegations at the 1951 San Francisco conference. The volume by Kumao Nishimura (1971) gives an insider's view of the treaty process because the author was involved for Japan's Foreign Ministry. An early critical work that opposed the treaty is by Yuichi Takano (1963) who claims the U.S.-Japan security treaty violated the United Nations Charter. Chihiro Hosoya (1984) examines U.S. and British documents and describes the differences between the Pentagon and the State Department regarding the treaties, as well as differences between the United States and Great Britain. Interesting essays from the perspective of such Pacific nations as Australia, the Philippines, New Zealand, India, and the Republic of China and one by Kimura Hiroshi on the Soviet Union have been edited by Akio Watanabe and Seigen Miyazato (1986). Miyazato (1990) also has an essay that favors the diplomacy of Secretary Dulles.

SCAP and Japan's Economic Reforms

The Korean War may have been the most crucial factor in solidifying U.S. policy to assist the economic recovery of Japan. Although the dispute among scholars concerning the reverse course or continuity of U.S. occupation policy involves the question of exactly when Washington decided to help Japan strengthen its economy, both groups generally agree that the United States did assist Japan's economic recovery and that the Korean War gave an impetus to economic developments by making Japan the major U.S. procurement base for armaments. Although Japan's overall economic rebuilding had far to go after the Korean truce in 1953, the sales and investments derived from its economic role during the Korean War provided the necessary foundation for the growth in Japan's economy over the next thirty years.

One critical area of Japan's economy that SCAP policy hardly touched was banking. As William M. Tsutsui (1988) explains, SCAP officials did not plan well regarding Japan's banking industry. Moreover, when banking questions arose, bureaucratic conflicts between SCAP's divisions of finance and antitrust could not resolve the daily issues involved in bank operations. SCAP tried some cosmetic changes, but Japanese conservatives in the banking area did not follow SCAP prescriptions. By 1948, the United States ended any attempts to change Japan's banking structure. Similar conclusions are found in the research of Takafusa Nakamura (1979).

SCAP's New Deal–like antitrust division ultimately performed little better than the finance division in breaking up the financial-industrial cartels known as the *zaibatsu*. This hierarchy of wealthy Japanese families controlled Japan's industrial and business activities, and SCAP slated them for destruction in accordance with U.S. antitrust legislation at home. Nevertheless, whether by the original design of U.S. planners ("continuities") or by a "reverse course" of Washington policymakers, the *zaibatsu's* interlocking business organization generally survived the occupation; first, by Japanese economic leaders' ability to manipulate SCAP orders; later, because U.S. policy consciously agreed to retain the *zaibatsu* as the best quick method of promoting Japan's economic recovery.

Although SCAP officials publicized the claim that Japan's *zaibatsu* were abolished, most Japanese and American scholars who reevaluated these claims concluded that most *zaibatsu* survived the occupation. An example of the extensive economic power of Japan's *zaibatsu* is given by Eleanor Hadley (1948), who compares the market shares of Mitsubishi to that of nineteen large U.S. corporations ranging from General Motors, Westinghouse, and Grace Shipping Lines to Woolworth stores and the Statler Hotel chain. Although a later book by Hadley (1970) rationalizes SCAP's general success with antitrust activity, Thomas Bisson (1954) contends that MacArthur's dissolution program was largely unsuccessful. Noboru Shirota and others (1971) demonstrate that the Mitsubishi cartel's survival and later success was related to the military procurement begun in 1950. A well-balanced early account of SCAP's antitrust program is Martin Bronfentrenner's essay in Grant K. Goodman's (1968) volume on the occupation.

Various Japanese studies about the U.S. dissolution policy provide details about the Japanese leaders' evasion of SCAP decrees. Although the Holding Company Liquidation Commission's (HCLC) final report (1951) describes the *zaibatsu* dissolution, Masuhiro Honoya (1983, 1984) explains how the reverse course prevented the abolition of more *zaibatsu*. Iwajiro Noda (1983), who was chairman of HCLC, describes the problems that occurred when the commission dealt with SCAP officials, the Japanese government bureaucracy, and representatives of Japanese companies in trying to dissolve or reorganize the *zaibatsu*. Ryoichi Miwa (1981) has a detailed account of U.S. anti-*zaibatsu* policy. The American revisionist scholar Howard Schonberger (1973) also has an important article about SCAP's failure to abolish the *zaibatsu*.

In addition to reviving Japan's big business enterprises, U.S. policy resulted in a centralized government trade bureaucracy, the Ministry of International Trade and Industry (MITI), which regulated Japan's export market and enhanced Japan's peacetime prosperity through international trade. The creation of MITI and its great success in managing Japan's foreign trade surplus and limiting foreign imports is described by Chalmers Johnson (1977, 1982) and by Takashi Shiraishi (1989). Leon Hollerman (1979) emphasizes that U.S. economic reforms gave Japan's government concentrated control of the economy and prevented free trade principles from operating.

Labor Unions

At the same time that the *zaibatsu*'s survival enhanced the position of Japan's wealthy elite, SCAP labor policies obstructed the development of labor unions. Following Japan's surrender in 1945, reaction against Japan's "fascist" leaders stimulated the rise of left-wing labor unions and parties, most of which were not communist but left-of-center social democratic groups. In 1946, these unions attempted to obtain industrial contracts that would pay better wages. Strikes resulted, however, because old-time industrial managers wanted to preserve their dominant role in labor-management relations. Siding with the business executives, MacArthur ordered all strikes to stop and began a purge of the left-wing labor groups. Together with the *zaibatsu*'s revival, the labor purge weakened Japan's union movement. During the 1950s, Japan's industrial leaders obtained a cooperative, hard-working, and docile manufacturing force whose job security was guaranteed as long as Japan's prosperity continued. Yet as Ronald Dore (1973) and Oyama Yoichi's (1985) studies show, Japan's corporations instituted welfare programs that bound workers to depend on the factories' performance as essential to their well-being.

An early account of Japan's postwar labor problems and the SCAP purge is Iwao Frederick Ayusawa's (1962, 1966) two-volume study and his later general study, *A History of Labor in Modern Japan*. Toshio Kurokawa (1964) describes Japan's low-wage policy that resulted from SCAP methods. SCAP official Miriam E. Farley (1950) wrote an early account of the occupation's labor problem, which must be compared with Joe Moore's (1983) later research on events during the occupation and MacArthur's crackdown on labor unions. There are three studies on particular aspects of SCAP's labor policies. Sheldon M. Garon (1984) sees continuity in SCAP policy because it used Japan's old bureaucracy regarding labor decisions. Andrew Gordon (1985) gives attention to labor's status in Japan's heavy industry, and Gail M. Nomura (1978) discusses the effect of occupation reform on the work by women.

Among the survey studies of the occupation's economic policies, four are especially notable. Yumi Hiwarti (1990) explains how postwar politics influenced SCAP's policies. Takafusa Nakamura, in the volume edited by Haruhiro Fukui et al. (1993), gives an excellent summary of the occupation's overall effect on Japan. Jon Halliday (1975) has a survey of Japanese capitalism emphasizing the reverse course influence, which was urged by American businessmen such as Ford Motor Company's Roy Morgan. Finally, Chitashi Yanaga (1979) surveys the status of Japanese businessmen in political issues.

Land Reform

One of the earliest economic attempts by SCAP officials was land reform. The intention of Washington planners was to democratize Japan by dividing up the large estates of Japan's old nobility for the use of many small farmers. Eventually, however, the relative success of land reform became dubious because the creation of many small farms cut Japan's food production by hindering the use of agricultural mechanization, essential to modern farming.

Although Robert Dore's *Land Reform* (1959) is considered a classic work on SCAP's success, students must consult Minoru Shimazai's (1966) essay, which argues that Dore ignored the historical context of Japan's agricultural economy. Shiro Tohata's (1963, 1964) articles admit that the land reform was an important first step in reform, but Japanese agriculture had to be further modernized. Tuvia Blumenthal (1970) explains Japan's problem in having small farmers trying to increase agricultural production on a competitive world basis.

Important works by Japanese include the memoir of Keiki Owada (1986), an agricultural official during the occupation, and Japan's Ministry of Agriculture and Forestry's (Nippon Norinsho) general account of SCAP's land efforts (1950). For a Marxist perspective on land reform, see Kushito Sakamoto's (1955) work. And for valuable Japanese documents on land reform, see the compilation between 1979 and 1982 by Nochi Kaikaku Shiryo Hensen Iankai (Committee on Complete Documentation of Land Reform).

JAPAN'S CULTURE AND THE KOREAN WAR

There has been limited research and literature regarding the cultural impact on Japan resulting from the U.S. occupation and the Korean War. From 1945 to 1970, Japanese education received the greatest attention, with fewer accounts covering the cultural areas of the mass media, literature, religion, and cinema. None of these, however, has had much attention in recent years, and apparently no significant research covers the occupation's impact on Japan's fine arts, architecture and music.

General Works on Culture during the Occupation

An early general explanation of the U.S. occupation's influence on the Japanese was a 1951 article by Henry C. Bush. More recently, Robert C. Christopher's essay in Paul Gordon Lauren and Raymond Wylie's (1989) book provides an overview of the occupation. More detailed surveys have been published by two Japanese scholars: Rinjiro Sodei (1985) and a history written by Eiji Takemae and Akira Amakawa (1977). In addition, Shiso no Kagaku Kenkyukai (Research Group on the Science of Thought) has two volumes (1972, 1978) of essays by authors who specialize in diverse aspects of Japanese life during the occupation.

The available studies about Japanese cultural developments from 1945 to 1953 have interpretive controversies similar to issues regarding political and economic affairs: questions about U.S. policy as being one that reversed course or maintained continuity, as well as the issue about whether the occupation drastically suppressed Japan's cultural development or benefited Japan's cultural trends begun before the militaristic factions gained control in 1931.

The question of reverse course in U.S. policy toward cultural life is challenged by Peter Frost's essay for the volume edited by Ray Moore (1992). Frost believes U.S. policy change was slight and accepts the continuity ideas described by Akira Iriye in the book edited with Nosuka (1977). Ray Moore's book of conference essays (1982) also includes articles by Howard Schonberger and Takeshi Igarashi that emphasize the validity of the reverse course. The reverse course in cultural affairs is also justified in Kyoko Hirano's *Mr. Smith Goes to Tokyo* (1992) and in her article "The Japanese Tragedy" (1988).

The controversy over whether the occupation suppressed or benefited Japanese cultural life tends to divide scholars along conservative or liberal lines of analysis. In an essay for Ray Moore's book (1982) and in two other studies (1978, 1989), Jun Eto argues the conservative view that SCAP's censorship of Japan's militaristic-nationalistic tradition had a negative influence on Japanese cultural traditions. Eto's complaints against SCAP's censorship are rejected by Gordon Daniels (1982), who describes the right-wing Japanese government's censorship of cultural activities during the era from 1931 to 1945. Kyoko Hirano (1992) indicates that Eto's analysis is a by-product of right-wing Japanese ideas, which U.S. occupation policy tried to defuse in order to turn Japanese culture back to the "democratic" developments of the 1920s.

Education and the Occupation Era

The area that America's idealistic reformers especially sought to "democratize" was the system of education. In 1945, the U.S. occupation policy to "democratize" Japan adopted guidelines to regulate and censor Japan's educational and cultural institutions and practices away from militaristic aggression and emperor worship toward the liberal Japanese ideas of the 1920s.

SCAP's educational programs hoped to alter the Japanese school system by introducing a "democratic" curriculum and instructional system and by decentralizing the national government's control over local schools. Ben C. Duke (1964) summarizes the type of educational reforms U.S. occupation authorities desired, including the creation of local school boards and making education available to all Japanese children. For a variety of articles indicating the objectives of SCAP's educational policies and SCAP's critics see the extensive listing of materials in the bibliography by Robert Ward and Frank Schulman (1974).

With one notable exception, most recent literature on the U.S. influence in education finds beneficial results for Japan. The exception is the thirty-year struggle that Saburo Ienaga has had with Japan's government because U.S. policy gave the Japan's Ministry of Education (MOE) the ability to censor Japanese textbooks. For details see his article, "The Glorification of War in Japanese Education" (1993–1994). Evidently Ienega's position represents the opposite extreme from Jun Eto's preference for Japan's militarist tradition.

Two authors who emphasize SCAP's positive results are Toshio Nishi (1982) and Herbert Passin (1982). Although finding the U.S. policy salutary, Yoshizo Kubo (1984) emphasizes that these policies also assisted the United States in gaining a strong anticommunist ally for the cold war.

Two other books on education are noteworthy. Eiichi Suzuki (1983) analyzes SCAP documents on education, which, he finds, tended to follow a policy of continuity for the period from 1945 to 1953. He also shows that SCAP succeeded in education because the Japanese educators were willing to "democratize" their schools. Second, Thomas Burkman (1982) has edited a volume of essays that discuss various educational and social aspects of U.S. occupation policy.

Mass Communication, Literature, and Cinema

Research about Japan's mass communications media, as well as Japanese literature and the movie industry, deal principally with SCAP measures to regulate or censor Japanese activity in these areas. Thomas Burkman (1988) has essays on the censorship policy of SCAP, including Carol Gluck's excellent essay on the relationship between political power and censorship. In Burkman's volume, opposing views about the censorship policy are given by Robert M. Spaulding and Harubara Akihiko.

Western scholars evaluating Japanese culture should read Masao Miyoshi's *Off Center: Power and Culture* (1991). Miyoshi provides a perspective similar to that which Edward Said's *Orientalism* provides for Western scholars whose "colonialist" attitudes on the Middle East and Islam result in misunderstanding.

SCAP's regulations of the mass media are chronicled in the 1987 publication of Nippon Hoso Kyokai (NHK), the Broadcasting Corporation of Japan. William Coughlan (1952) describes SCAP's censorship policy, which governed journalists from America and other Allied nations as well as the Japanese. Jun Eto's article in Roy Moore's (1989) volume, as well as Eto's book (1989), are critical of SCAP for suppressing Japan's traditions. Sozo Matsuura (1975) has a general account of SCAP's censorship, which is more balanced than Eto's book. Finally, Monica Braw (1991) focuses on the specific case of MacArthur's censoring stories about the atomic bomb's consequences.

Literature about different cultural fields under SCAP's control indicates the direction such studies have taken in recent years. Japanese fiction in the postwar years has been the subject of articles by Jun Eto (1980) and Jay Rubin (1985), while a volume of essays resulting from a conference on fiction in Japan and West Germany has been edited by Ernestine Schlart and J. Thomas Rime (1991). Marlene Mayo wrote an essay about SCAP's regulations of Japan's radio broadcasting in Thomas Burkman's (1988) volume.

SCAP control over Japan's film industry is described in the excellent study by Kyoko Hirano (1992), which also has a useful bibliography of relevant materials and interviews by the author. David Conde's (1965) account of SCAP policy gives the perspective of a "radical New Dealer" who was dismissed from his job with SCAP in 1947 because he moved too far to the left in promoting Japan's films. A general survey of Japanese films since 1945 can be found in Joseph L. Anderson and Donald Richie (1982). Tadao Sato (1983) describes MacArthur's effort to purge "communists" in Japan's film industry, a move that paralleled the post-1945 attempts of the U.S. House Committee on Un-American activities to end "communist" influence in Hollywood.

Possibly the Korean War's greatest impact on Japan's culture was due to the numerous American soldiers and sailors who passed through Japan on the way to Korea's battlefronts and returned to Japan for rest and recreation between 1950 and 1954. These servicemen brought America's popular culture to Japan, with items ranging from Coca-Cola to country music and more. These influences are described by Shumsuke Kamei (1976) and in David W. Plath's essay in Carol Gluck and Stephen R. Graubard's *Showa* (1992), about the occupation era.

Religion and the Occupation

SCAP's democratization program involved religion because of the connection between Japan's Shinto religion and the emperor's divine character. To counteract their perception of divine right, MacArthur's regime wanted to abolish the idea of the emperor's divinity and to separate church and state in Japan. William P. Woodward (1972), who served in the religious division of SCAP's Department of Civil Information and Education (CIE), gives a well-balanced account of these U.S. programs. As Woodward notes, General MacArthur frequently mentioned that Christianity was Japan's best defense against communism, a view emphasized by Lawrence S. Wittner (1971), whose article also notes that SCAP's promotion of Christianity achieved little in Japan.

There are four notable studies regarding the occupation and Japanese religion. Kujiro Takeda (1988) explains the historical development of Japan's concept of the divine emperor. Nakahira Masanori (1989, 1992) examines the role of former U.S. ambassador Joseph Grew in ending this idea. David Reid (1991) gives a reverse twist to SCAP's religious influence religion, showing how Japan's culture changed the ideas of Christianity.

Korean Minority in Japan

Immediately after Japan surrendered in 1945, many Koreans living in Japan returned to Korea. Nevertheless, when the Korean War began in 1950, an estimated 700,000 Koreans still resided in the Japanese islands. Although Roger Dingman's essay (1993) indicates that one impact of the Korean War was the internationalization of Japanese perspectives on the world, the situation in 1950 was that Japan classified resident Koreans as aliens and discriminated against them in jobs and other areas of life.

The best short essay on the Korean minority in Japan from 1950 to 1953 is Lee Kwang-Kyu's article in the volume edited by William Nimmo (1990). This fascinating article indicates that Koreans living in Japan were divided between those who favored North Korea (the Cho-ryon) and those who preferred South Korea (the Min-dan). During the Korean War, the Cho-ryon had dominant influence, largely because, as described by Sung-hwa Cheong (1991), South Korea's president, Syngman Rhee, adopted strong anti-Japanese policies and harassed Tokyo's leaders regarding fishing rights and other disputes. Both Richard Banks Mitchell (1967) and the coauthored book by Lee Changsoo and George DeVos (1981) indicate that 700 to 750 Koreans in Japan volunteered to fight with the UN forces in South Korea. This small number was probably due to the split between the Koreans described by Lee Kwang-kyu's article. The Korean War also led Japan to deport about 8,000 Koreans, principally because they were accused of being "communists."

REFERENCES

Ajia Kyokai (Asia Society). "Japan's War Reparations—Achievements and Problems." *Asian Affairs* 4 (March 1960): 99–111.

Allison, John M. "The Japanese Peace Treaty and Related Security Pacts." *Proceedings of the American Society of International Law,* April 24–26, 1952, pp. 35–43.

Anderson, Joseph L., and Donald Richie. *The Japanese Film: Art and Industry.* Exp. ed. Princeton, NJ: Princeton University Press, 1982.

Asada, Sadao. "Recent Works on the American Occupation of Japan: The State of the Art." *Japanese Journal of American Studies* 1 (1981): 175–191.

———, ed. *Japan and the World, 1853–1952: A Bibliographic Guide to Japanese Scholarship in Foreign Relations.* New York: Columbia University Press, 1989.

Ashida, Hitoshi. "Japan: Communists' Temptation." *Contemporary Japan* 20 (January–March, 1951): 15–24.

Auer, James. *The Postwar Rearmament of Japanese Maritime Forces, 1945–1971.* New York: Praeger, 1973.

Ayusawa, Iwao Frederick. *Organized Labor in Japan.* 2 vols. Tokyo: Foreign Affairs Association of Japan, 1962.

———. *A History of Labor in Modern Japan.* Honolulu: East-West Center Press, 1966.

Baerwald, Hans. *The Purge of Japanese Leaders under the Occupation.* Berkeley: University of California Press, 1959.

Berger, Thomas U. "From Sword to Chrysanthemum: Japan's Culture of Anti-Militarism." *International Security* 17:4 (Spring 1993): 119–150.

Bisson, Thomas. *Zaibatsu Dissolution.* Berkeley: University of California Press, 1954.

Bix, Herbert P. "Japan: The Roots of Militarism." In Mark Selden, ed., *Remaking Asia,* pp. 319–327. New York: Pantheon Books, 1974.

Blumenthal, Tuvia. "Agricultural Development in Postwar Japan." *Asian and African Studies* (Jerusalem) 6 (1970): 113–125.

Boger, Karl, ed. *Postwar Industrial Policy in Japan: An Annotated Bibliography.* Metuchen, NJ: Scarecrow Press, 1988.

Braw, Monica. *The Atomic Bomb Suppressed: American Censorship in Occupied Japan.* Armonk, NY: M. E. Sharpe, 1991.

Brenn, Bruce M. "United States Reparations Policy toward Japan, September, 1945 to May, 1949." In Richard Beardsley, ed., *Studies on Japanese History and Politics.* Ann Arbor, MI: University of Michigan Press, 1967.

Burkman, Thomas W., ed. *The Occupation of Japan: Educational and Social Reform.* Norfolk, VA: Douglas MacArthur Foundation, 1982.

———, ed. *The Occupation of Japan: Arts and Culture.* Norfolk, VA: Douglas MacArthur Foundation, 1988.

Bush, Henry C. "Impact of American Culture." *Contemporary Japan* 20 (July–September 1951): 331–340.

Changsoo, Lee, and George DeVos. *Koreans in Japan: Ethnic Conflict and Accommodation.* Berkeley: University of California, 1981.

Cheong, Sung-hwa. *The Politics of Anti-Japanese Sentiment in Korea.* Westport, CT: Greenwood Press, 1991.

Cohen, Bernard C. *The Political Process and Foreign Policy: The Making of the Japanese Peace Settlement.* Princeton, NJ: Princeton University Press, 1957.

Cohen, Jerome Bernard. "Japan: Reform versus Recovery." *Far Eastern Survey,* June 23, 1948, pp. 137–142.

Conde, David. "Nikon Eiga no senryo-shi" (The history of Japanese cinema under the occupation). *Sekai* (August 1965): 248–255.

Coughlan, William J. *Conquered Press: The MacArthur Era in Japanese Journalism.* Palo Alto, CA: Pacific Books, 1952.

Daniels, Gordon. "Japanese Domestic Radio and Cinema Propaganda, 1937–1945: An Overview." *Historical Journal of Film, Radio, and Television* 2:2 (1982): 115–132.

Dingman, Roger. "Theories of, and Approaches to, Alliance Politics." In Paul G. Lauren, ed., *Diplomacy: New Approaches in History, Theory, and Policy.* New York: Free Press, 1979.

———. "The Dagger and the Gift: The Impact of the Korean War on Japan." In William J. Williams, ed., *A Revolutionary War: Korea and the Transformation of the Postwar World.* Chicago: Imprint Publications, 1993.

Dooman, Eugene, and Gordon Beate. *Occupation of Japan Project.* New York: Oral History Research Office, Columbia University, 1970.

Dore, Ronald. *Land Reform in Japan.* London: Oxford University Press, 1959.

———. *British Factory, Japanese Factory.* Berkeley: University of California Press, 1973.

Dower, John. *Japanese History and Culture from Ancient to Modern Times: Seven Basic Bibliographies.* New York: M. Weiner, 1986.

Dower, John W. "The Eye of the Beholder: Background Notes on the U.S.-Japan Military Relationship." *Bulletin of Concerned Asian Scholars* 11 (October 1969): 21–25.

———. *Empire and Aftermath: Yoshida Shigeru and the Japanese Experience, 1878–1954.* Cambridge: Harvard University Press, 1979.

———. "Occupied Japan and the Cold War in Asia." In Michael J. Lacey, *The Truman Presidency,* pp. 366–409. Cambridge: Cambridge University Press, 1989.

Drifte, Reinhard. "Some New Aspects on the Genesis of Article 9 of the Japanese Constitution." *Proceedings of the British Association for Japanese Studies* 6 (1982): p. 2.

———. "Japan's Involvement in the Korean War." In James Cotton and Ian Neary, eds., *The Korean War in History.* Atlantic Highlands, NJ: Humanities Press International, 1989.

Duke, Ben C. "American Education Reforms in Japan Twelve Years Later." *Harvard Educational Review* 34 (1964): 525–536.

Dulles, John Foster. "Security in the Pacific." *Foreign Affairs* 30:2 (January 1952): 175–187.

Emmerson, John K. *The Japanese Thread.* New York: Holt, Rinehart and Winston, 1978.

Eto, Jun. *Mo hitotsu no sengo-shi* (Another history of the postwar period). Tokyo: Kodansha, 1978.

———. "The American Occupation and Post-War Japanese Literature." *Studies of Comparative Literature* 38 (September 1980): 1–18 and in *Hikaku Bungaku Kenkyu* (September 1980): 1–18.

———. *Tozareta gengo kukan: Senryo-gun no ken'etsu to sengo Nippon* (The closed space: The occupation forces censorship and postwar Japan). Tokyo: Bunges shunju-sha, 1989.

Eto, Jun, et al. *Senryo Shiroku* (Historical documents on the Allied occupation of Japan). 4 vols. Tokyo: Kodansha, 1981–1982.

Farley, Miriam S. *Aspects of Japan's Labor Problems.* New York: John Day, 1950.

Frost, Peter. "General MacArthur's Vision of Reform." *Journal of Japanese Studies* 10:2 (Summer 1984): 539–540.

Fukui, Haruhiro, Peter H. Merkle, and Hubertus Müller-Groeling, eds. *The Politics of Economic Change in Japan and West Germany.* Vol. 1: *Macroeconomic Conditions and Policy Responses.* London: Macmillan, 1993.

Gaiko Shiryokan, comp. *Gaimusho kiroku maikurofiumae kensakubo* (Indexes to the [postwar] records of the Japanese Foreign Ministry). Mimeo. 9 vols. 1971–1987.

Garon, Sheldon M. "The Imperial Bureaucracy and Labor Policy in Postwar Japan." *Journal of Asian History* 43 (May 1984): 441–457.

Gluck, Carol "Entangling Illusions—Japanese and American Views of the Occupation." In Warren Cohen, ed., *New Frontiers in American–East Asian Relations,* pp. 169–236. New York: Columbia University Press, 1983.

Gluck, Carol, and Stephen A. Graubard, eds. *Showa: The Japan of Hirohito.* New York: Norton, 1992.

Goodman, Grant K., comp. *The American Occupation of Japan: A Retrospective View.* Lawrence, KS: University of Kansas, 1968.

Gordon, Andrew. *The Evolution of Labor Relations in Japan: Heavy Industry, 1853–1955.* Cambridge: Council on East Asian Studies, Harvard University, 1985.

Hadley, Eleanor. "Trust Busting in Japan." *Harvard Business Review* 26:4 (July 1948): 425–440.

———. *Antitrust in Japan.* Princeton, NJ: Princeton University Press, 1970.

Halliday, Jon. *A Political History of Japanese Capitalism.* New York: Pantheon, 1975.

Harries, Meirion, and Susie. *Sheathing the Sword: The Demilitarization of Postwar Japan.* New York: Macmillan, 1972.

Hata, Ikuhiko. *Shiroku: Nihon Nihon Saigunei* (The historical record: Japan's rearmament). Tokyo: Bungei shunju, 1976.

Hata, Ikuhiko, and Sodei Rinjiro. *Nihon senryo hishi* (A secret history of the occupation of Japan). Vol. 2. Ashai Shimbunsha, 1977.

Hidaka, Rokuro. "Impact of the Occupation on Japanese Life." *United Asia* 8 (September 1956): 235–238.

Hirano, Kyoko. "The Japanese Tragedy: Film Censorship and the American Occupation." *Radical History Review* 41 (May 1988): 67–92.

———. *Mr. Smith Goes to Tokyo: Japanese Cinema under the American Occupation, 1945–1952.* Washington, DC: Smithsonian Institution, 1992.

Hiwarti, Yumi. *Sengo seiji to NichiBei kankei.* (Postwar politics and Japanese-American relations). Tokyo: Tokyo daigaku shuppan kai, 1990.

Hollerman, Leon. "International Economic Controls in Occupied Japan." *Journal of Asian Studies* 38 (1979): 707–719.

Hosoya, Chihiro. *San Furanshisuko e no michi* (The road to San Francisco). Tokyo: Chuo koron sha, 1984.

Hosoya, Chihiro, Ando Nisuke, and Onuma Yasuaki, eds. *Kokusai shenpojiumu: Tokyo saiban o tou* (The Tokyo war crimes trials questioned: The proceedings of an international symposium). Tokyo: Kodansha, 1984.

Hosoya, Masahiro. "Economic Democratization and the 'Reverse Course' during the Allied Occupation of Japan, 1945–1952." *Kokusaigaku ronshu* (July 1983): 59–104.

Ienaga, Saburo. *Senso sekinin* (War responsibility). Tokyo: Iwanami Shoten, 1985.

———. "The Glorification of War in Japanese Education." *International Security* 18:3 (Winter 1993–1994): 113–133.

Igarashi, Takeshi. "Tai-Nichi kowa no teisho seisaku no tenkan" (MacArthur's proposal for an early peace with Japan and the redirection of occupation policy toward Japan). *Shiso,* no. 628 (October 1976): 21–43, reprinted in *Japanese Journal of American Studies* 1 (1981): 55–86.

———. *Tai-Nichi kowa to reisen: Sengo Nichi-Bei kankei no keisei* (The peace with Japan and the cold war: The formation of postwar Japanese-American relations). Tokyo: Tokyo Doigaku Shuppaokai, 1986a.

———. *Tai-Nichi kowa to reisen* (The Japanese peace settlement and the cold war). Tokyo: Tokyo daigaku shuppan sha, 1986b.

Inoue, Kyoko. *MacArthur's Japanese Constitution: A Linguistic and Cultural Study of Its Making.* Chicago: University of Chicago Press, 1991.

International Military Tribunal for the Far East. *Judgment of the International Military Tribunal for the Far East.* Tokyo: Tribunal, November 12, 1948.

Japan, Norinsho. (Ministry of Agriculture and Forestry) editorial supervisors. *Nochi kaikaku tenmatsu gaiyo* (Land reform: A general account). Tokyo: Nosei Chosakai, 1951; reprint, Ochanomizo Shobo, 1977.

Johnson, Chalmers. "MITI and Japanese International Economic Policy." In Robert A. Scalapino, ed., *The Foreign Policy of Modern Japan,* pp. 227–279. Berkeley: University of California Press, 1977.

———. *MITI and the Japanese Miracle.* Stanford, CA: Stanford University Press, 1982.

Kamei, Shunsuke: *Saakasu ga kita: Amerika taishu tanka oboegaki* (Here comes the circus: A note on American popular culture). Tokyo: Tokyo Daigaku Shippan, 1976.

Katzenstein, Peter J., and Nobuo Okowara. "Japan's National Security Policy: Structures, Norms, and Policies." *International Security* 17:4 (Spring 1993): 84–118.

Kawai, Kazuo. *Japan's American Interlude.* Chicago: University of Chicago Press, 1960.

Keenan, Joseph, and Brendan F. Brown. *Crimes against International Law.* Washington, D.C.: Public Affairs Press, 1950.

Koh, Hesung Chong, ed. *Korean and Japanese Women: An Analytical Bibliographical Guide.* Westport, CT: Greenwood Press, 1982.

Kokusai, Hogakkai, ed. *Heiwa joyaku no Sogo Kenkyu* (A comprehensive study of the peace treaty). 2 vols. Tokyo: Yuhikaku, 1952.

Kosaka, Masataka. *Saisho Yoshido Shigeru* (Prime Minister Yoshida Shigeru). Tokyo: Shuo Koronsha, 1968.

———. *100 Million Japanese: The Postwar Experience.* Tokyo and Palo Alto, CA: Kodansha, 1972.

Kowalski, Frank. *Nihon saisunbi* (Japan's rearmament). Trans. Katsuyama Kijiro. Tokyo: Saimul shuppamkai, 1969.

Kubo, Yoshizo. *Tai-Nichi senryo seisaku to senge kyoiku kaikaku* (Allied occupation policy toward Japan and postwar educational reforms). Tokyo: Sanseido, 1984.

Kurokawa, Toshio. *Nihon no terchingin kozo* (Japan's low wage structure). Tokyo: Otsuki Shoten, 1964.

Lael, Richard L. *The Yamashita Precedent: War Crimes and Command Responsibility.* Wilmington, DE: Scholarly Resources, 1982.

Lauren, Paul Gordon, and Raymond Wylie, eds. *Destinies Shared.* Boulder, CO: Westview Press, 1989.

McNelly, Theodore Hart. "The Renunciation of War in the Japanese Constitution." *Political Science Quarterly* 77:2 (September 1962): 350–378.

Maki, John M., trans. *Japan's Commission on the Constitution: The Final Report (Kenpo chosakai hokokusho).* Seattle, WA: University of Washington, 1964.

Masanori, Nakahira. *The Japanese Monarchy, 1931–1991: Ambassador Grew and the Making of the "Symbol Emperor System."* Armonk, NY: M. E. Sharpe, 1992. Original in Japanese, *Shocho Tennosei e no michi.* Tokyo: Iwanami, 1989.

Materials on the Trial of Former Servicemen of the Japanese Army Charged with Manufacturing and Employing Bacteriological Weapons. Moscow: Foreign Languages Publishing House, 1950.

Matsuura, Sozo. "Senryo-ka no genron dan'atsu (Media oppression under the occupation). In Ryusuke Sagara, ed., *Dokumento: Showa-shi* (Document: Showa era history), pp. 258–266. Tokyo: Heibon-sha, 1975.

Minear, Richard H. *Victors' Justice: The Tokyo War Crimes Trials.* Princeton, NJ: Princeton University Press, 1971.

Mitchell, Richard Banks. *The Korean Minority in Japan.* Berkeley, CA: University of California Press, 1967.

Miwa, Ryoichi. "1949- nen no dokusen kinshiho kaisei" (The revision of the Anti-Monopoly Law in 1949). In Nakamura Takafusa, ed., *Senryoki Nihon no keizai to seyi.* (Japanese economy and politics during the occupation). Tokyo: Tokyo Kaizai Shinposha, 1981a.

———. *Showa zaiseishi.* Vol. 2: *Dokusen kinshi* (The economic and financial history of the Showa period. Vol. 2: Antimonopoly policy). Tokyo: Toyo Keizai Shinposha, 1981b.

Miyasato, Seigen. "John Foster Dulles and the Peace Settlement with Japan." In Richard Immerman, ed., *John Foster Dulles and the Diplomacy of the Cold War*, pp. 189–212. Princeton, NJ: Princeton University Press, 1990.

Miyoshi, Masao. *Off Center: Power and Culture: Relations between Japan and the United States.* Cambridge, MA: Harvard University Press, 1991.

Mochizuki, Mike M. "The Disarming and Rearming of Japan." In Richard Dean Burns, ed., *Encyclopedia of Arms Control and Disarmament.* 3 vols. New York: Charles Scribner's Sons, 1993.

Moore, Joe. *Japanese Workers and the Struggle for Power, 1945–1947.* Madison: University of Wisconsin Press, 1983.

Moore, Ray, ed. *Tenno ga baiburu yonda hi* (The day when the emperor read the Bible). Tokyo: Kodansha, 1992.

Morita, Yoshio. *Chosen shusen no kiroku* (Korea at the end of the war: Collected documents). Tokyo: Gannado, 1964.

Morita, Yoshio, and Osada Kaneko, eds. *Chosen shusen no kiroku: Shiryohen* (Korea at the end of the war: Collected documents). 3 vols. Tokyo: Gannado, 1979–1980.

Morris, Ivan. *Nationalism and the Right Wing in Japan: A Study of Postwar Trends.* New York: Oxford University Press, 1960.

Nagai, Yonosuke, and Akira Iriye, eds. *The Origins of the Cold War in Asia.* New York: Columbia University Press, 1977.

Nakamura, Takafusa, ed. *Senryoki Nihon no keizai to seiji* (Japanese economy and politics during the occupation). Tokyo: Daigaku Shuppankai, 1979a.

Nakamura, Takafusa. *Showa zaiseishi.* Vol. 12: *Kin'yu* (Economic and financial history of the Showa period. Vol. 12: Money and banking, pt. 1). Tokyo: Toyo Keizai Shinposha, 1979b.

National Committee of Japanese Historians. *Historical Studies in Japan, 1979–1982: A Bibliography of Japan at the XVIth International Congress of Historical Science at Stuttgart.* Tokyo: Yankawa Shuppansha, 1985.

Nihon Gaikoshi Jiten. [The Encyclopedia of Japanese Diplomatic History]. Edited by Gaimusho Gaiko Shiryokan Nihon Gaikoshi Jiten Hensan Iinkai [Committee for Japanese Diplomatic History Encyclopedia Data Section of Ministry of Foreign Affairs]. Tokyo: Okurasho Insatsukyoku, 1979.

Nihon Kanri Horei Kenkyukai, ed. *Nihon kanri horei kinkyukai.* (Studies on SCAP directives to Japan), nos. 1–35 by the Faculty of Law, Tokyo University. Tokyo: Yuhikaku, 1946–1953.

Nimmo, William, ed. *The Occupation of Japan: The Impact of the Korean War.* Norfolk, VA: General Douglas MacArthur Foundation, 1990.

Nippon Hoso Kyokai (NHK) Hoso Bunka Chosa Kenkyu-jo. *GHQ hunsho ni yoru senryo-ki hoso-shi nenpyo* (Chronicle of the broadcast history under the occupation according to GHQ documents). Tokyo: Nippon Hoso Kyokai (Broadcasting Corporation of Japan), 1987.

Nishi, Toshio. *Unconditional Democracy: Education and Politics in Occupied Japan, 1945–1952.* Stanford, CA: Hoover Institution Press, 1982.

Nishimura, Kumao. *San Furanshisuko heiwa joyaku* (The San Francisco Peace Treaty). Vol. 27 of Kajima heiwa kenkyu jo, ed. *Nihon gaiko shi* (A Diplomatic history of Japan). Tokyo: Kajima kenkyu jo shuppan kai, 1971.

Nochi Kaikaku Shiryo Hensen Iinkai (Committee to Compile Documents on Land Reform), ed. *Nochi kaikaku Kaikaku shiryo shusei* (Collected documents on the land reform). 16 vols. Tokyo: Nosei Chosakai Shobo, 1974–1982.

Noda, Iwajiro. *Zaibatsu kaitai shiki.* (Reminiscences on *zaibatsu* dissolution). Tokyo: Nihon Keizai Shinposha, 1983.

Nomura, Gail M. "The Allied Occupation of Japan: Reform of Japanese Government Labor Policy on Women." Ph.D. dissertation, University of Hawaii, 1978.

Nomura, Kichisaburo. "A Peace Treaty and Japan's Security." *Contemporary Japan* 19 (July–September 1950): 350–357.

Ohata, Thaddeus. *Japanese National Government Publications in the Library of Congress.* Washington: Library of Congress, GPO, 1981.

Okonogi, Masao. *Chosen senso* (The Korean War). Tokyo: Chuo Koron sha, 1986.

Onuma, Yasuaki. *Tokyo saiban kara sengo sekinin mo shiso e* (From the Tokyo trials to the idea of postwar responsibility). Yushindo, 1985.

Ota, Takashi, ed. *Sengo Nihon Kyoikushi* (A history of education in postwar Japan). Tokyo: Iwanami Shoten, 1978.

Overseas Consultants, Inc. *Report on Industrial Reparations: Survey of Japan to the United States of America.* New York: Overseas Consultants, February 1948.

Owada, Keiki. *Hishi Nihon no nochi kaikaku: Ichi nosei tantosha no kaiso* (The secret

history of Japan's land reform: Reminiscences of an agricultural adminis-
trator). Tokyo: Nihon Keizai Shinbunsha, 1986.

Ozawa, Takeo. "Japanese Foreign Debts and Reparations Problems." *Asian Affairs* 1 (September 1956): 274–289.

Passin, Herbert. *Japanese Education: A Bibliography of Materials in the English Literature.* New York: Teachers College, Columbia University, 1970.

———. *Society and Education in Japan.* Tokyo: Kodansha International, 1982.

Perren, Richard, comp. *Japanese Studies from Pre-History to 1990: A Bibliographic Guide.* New York: St. Martin's, 1992.

Petrie, W. F. "Reparations since the Surrender: Changes in the Attitude towards Japanese." *Australian Outlook* 4:1 (March 1950): 51–61.

Piccigallo, Philip R. *The Japanese on Trial: Allied War Crimes Operations in the East, 1945–1951.* Austin: University of Texas Press, 1980.

Powell, John W. "Japan's Germ Warfare: The U.S. Cover-up of a War Crime." *Bulletin of Concerned Asian Scholars* 12 (October–December 1981a): 2–17.

———. "Japan's Biological Weapons, 1930–1945." *Bulletin of the Atomic Scientists* 37 (October 1981b): 43–53.

Reid, David. *New West: The Cultural Shaping of Japanese Christianity.* Berkeley: Asian Humanities Press, 1991.

Rekishigaku Kenkyukai (Historical Science Society), ed. *Tai-Heiyo Sensoshi* (A history of the Pacific war). 5 vols. Tokyo: Toyo Keizai Shinposha, 1953–1954 (revised edition in 6 vols. by Aoki Shoten, 1971–1973).

Rikusen Kenkyu Fukyu Kai (Institute to Study Land Warfare), ed. *Chosen senso* (The Korean War). 10 vols. Tokyo: Hara Shobo, 1966.

Rubin, Jay. "From Wholesomeness to Decadence: The Censorship of Literature under the Allied Occupation." *Journal of Japanese Studies* 11:1 (Winter 1985): 71–103.

Said, Edward. *Orientalism.* New York: Random House, 1978.

Sakamoto, Kushito. "Marxian Studies of Agricultural Problems of Post-war Japan." *Japan Science Review: Economic Sciences* 2 (1955): 71–83.

Sato, Tadao. *Tsuihosha-Tahi: Eiga no reddo paaji* (The expelled: The red purge in film). Tokyo: Iwanami Shoten, 1983.

Schlart, Ernestine, and J. Thomas Rime, eds. *Legacies and Ambiguities: Postwar Fiction and Culture in West Germany and Japan.* Washington, DC: Woodrow Wilson Center Press, 1991.

Schonberger, Howard. "Zaibatsu Dissolution and the American Restoration of Japan." *Bulletin of Concerned Asian Scholars* 5 (1973): 16–31.

———. "John Foster Dulles and the China Question in the Making of the Japanese Peace Treaty." In Thomas W. Burkman, ed., *The Occupation of Japan: The International Context.* Norfolk, VA: Douglas MacArthur Foundation, 1984.

Shimazai, Minoru. "Some Comments on R. P. Dore's *Land Reform in Japan.*" *Developing Economies* 4 (June 1966): 256–263.

Shinobu, Seizaburo. *Sengo Nihon seijishi, 1945–1952* (A political history of postwar Japan, 1945–1952). 4 vols. Tokyo: Keiso Shobo, 1965–1967.

Shiraishi, Takashi. *Japan's Trade Policies, 1945 to the Present Day.* London: Athlone Press, 1989.

Shirota, Noboru, et al. *Mitsubishi gungusho-Nihon no sangum fukugotai to shihon shin-*

shutsu (The Mitsubishi arsenal—Japan's military-industrial complex and capital expansion). Tokyo: Gendai Hyoronsha, 1971.

Shiso no Kagaku Kenkyukai (Research Group on Science of Thought), ed. *Kyodo Kenkyu: Nihon Senryo* (Joint research on the occupation of Japan). Tokyo: Tokuma Shoten, 1972.

———. *Kyodo Kenkyu: Nihon senryo kenkyu jiten* (Encyclopedia of the Allied occupation of Japan). Tokyo: Tokuma Shoten, 1978a.

———. *Kyodo Kenkyu: Nihon Senryogun-sono hikari to kage* (Joint research on the occupation forces in Japan: Their light and shadow). 2 vols. Tokyo: Tokuma Shoten, 1978.

Shukan Shincho (weekly journal), ed. *Makkasa no Nihon* (MacArthur's Japan). Tokyo: Shinchosha, 1970.

Shulman, Frank J. *Japan and Korea: An Annotated Bibliography of Doctoral Dissertations in Western Languages, 1877–1969.* Chicago: American Library Association, 1970.

Shunzo, Nitta. "Shin sangyo seisaku to sangun fukugo" (The new industrial policy and the military-industrial complex). *Keizai hyoron* (November 1971): 41–42.

Sodei, Rinjiro, ed. *Sekaishi no naka no Nihon senryo* (The Allied occupation of Japan in world history). Tokyo: Nihon Hyoronsha, 1985.

Suzuki, Eiichi. *Nihon senryo to kyoiku kaikaku* (Educational reform in occupied Japan). Tokyo: Keiso Shobo, 1983.

Takano, Yuichi. "International Law and the Japan-U.S. Security Agreement." *Journal of Social and Political Ideas in Japan* [Japan] 1 (1963): 67–70.

Takeda, Kujiro. *The Dual Image of the Japanese Emperor.* London: Macmillan Education, 1988.

Takemae, Eiji, and Amakawa Akira. *Nihon senryo hishi* (A secret history of the occupation of Japan). Vol. 1. Tokyo: Asaki Shimbunsha, 1977.

Tohata, Shiro. "Land Reform: Results and Problems." *Contemporary Japan* 27 (October 1963): 673–684; 28 (September 1964): 83–97.

Tsutsui, William M. *Banking Policy in Japan: American Efforts at Reform during the Occupation.* New York: Routledge, 1988.

U.S. State Department. "Draft Treaty on the Disarmament and Demilitarization of Japan." *Department of State Bulletin,* June 30, 1946, pp. 1113–1114.

———. "Reductions of Japanese Industrial War Potential." *Department of State Bulletin,* September 14, 1947, pp. 513–516.

———. "Japanese Reparations and Level of Industry." *Department of State Bulletin,* May 26, 1949, pp. 667–670.

———. "U.S. Repudiates Philippine and Chinese Complaints on Japanese Reparations Removals." *Department of State Bulletin,* June 26, 1949, pp. 831–833.

Uyehara, Cecil H. *Leftwing Social Movements in Japan: An Annotated Bibliography.* Tokyo: Tuttle, 1959.

Ward, Robert E., and Yoshikazu Sakamoto, eds. *Democratizing Japan: The Allied Occupation.* Honolulu: University of Hawaii Press, 1987.

Ward, Robert E., and Frank J. Shulman, eds. *The Allied Occupation of Japan.* Chicago: American Library Association, 1974.

Watanabe Akio, and Seigen Miyazato, eds. *San Furanshisuko kowa* (The San Francisco peace settlement). Tokyo: Tokyo daigaku shuppan sha, 1986.

Watanabe, Takeshi. *Senryoka no Nihon Zaisei Oboegaki* (Notes on the financial history of occupied Japan). Tokyo: Nihon Keizai Shinbunsha, 1966.

———. *Tai-senryogun kosho hiroku: Watanabe Takeshi nikki* (A secret account of negotiations with the occupation forces: Watanabe Takeshi diary). Ed. Japan, Okurasho (Finance Ministry). Tokyo: Toyo Keizai Shinposha, 1983.

Williams, Justin, Sr. *Japan's Political Revolution under MacArthur: A Participant's Account.* Athens, GA: University of Georgia Press, 1979.

Wittner, Lawrence S. "MacArthur and the Missionaries: God and Man in Occupied Japan." *Pacific Historical Review* 40 (1971): 77–98.

Woodard, William P. *Tenno to Shinto* (The Allied occupation of Japan and Japanese religion). Trans. Yoshiya Abe. Leiden, Netherlands: Bull 1972.

Wray, Harry, and Hilary Conroy, eds. *Japan Examined: Perspectives on Modern Japanese History.* Honolulu: University of Hawaii, 1983.

Yamamura, Kozo. "Zaibatsu Prewar and Zaibatsu Postwar." *Journal of Asian Studies* 23 (August) 1964: 539–544.

———. *Economic Policy in Postwar Japan—Growth versus Economic Democracy.* Berkeley: University of California, 1967.

Yanaga, Chitoshi. *Big Business in Japanese Politics.* New Haven, CT: Yale University Press, 1979.

Yoichi, Oyama, ed. *Kyodai Kigyo to Rodosha: Toyota no Jirei* (A study of the Toyota Motor Corporation). Tokyo: Ochanomizushobo, 1985.

Yoshida, Shigeru. "Japan and the Crisis in Asia." *Foreign Affairs* 29 (January 1951): 171–181.

———. *The Yoshida Memoirs: The Story of Japan in Crisis.* Trans. Kenichi Yoshida. Boston: Houghton Mifflin, 1962.

Yoshikazu, Sakamoto, et al., comps. *Nihon Senryo bunken mokuroku* (A bibliography on the Allied occupation of Japan). Tokyo-Nihon Gakujutsu Shinokokai (Japan Society for the Promotion of Science), 1972.

Yozo, Kato. *Shiroku- Jieitai- shi* (The personal history of the self-defense force). Tokyo: Seiji Geppou Sha. 1979.

Yui Daisaburo. "Chosen senso to katamen kowa" (The Korean War and the one-sided peace). In Rekishigaku kenkyukai, ed. *Koza Nihon Rekishi II Gendai I* (Lectures on Japanese history). Tokyo: Toko Nihon rekishi shuppan kai, 1985.

9 The Korean Scholars on the Korean War

Kim Chull Baum

The Korean War, which started on June 25, 1950, and came to a truce on July 27, 1953, was one of the biggest in the history of the world. The number of servicemen killed in the war ranked sixth following those in World War II, World War I, the Napoleonic wars, the Spanish Civil War, and the Thirty Years War. Moreover, most of the big powers of the world were involved in the war under the United Nations flag.

Nevertheless, the Korean War has been defined as a limited war, which ended with neither side's emerging as a victor or a loser. The characteristics and origins of the war have yet to be fully clarified, and the North Korean aggressor is still denying its responsibility. Under these conditions, divergent views have confronted scholars, particularly regarding the origins of the war.

The Korean War has been an attractive subject of study for many scholars around the world because it brought about significant changes not only in the political, economic, and social status of the Korean peninsula but also in the cold war structure of the world. Carroll Blanchard's (1964) Korean War bibliography points out that over 10,000 articles had been written as essays, books, or newspaper articles by 1960. Since then, scholarship devoted to the study of the Korean War has continued to expand, in both quantity and quality. A turning point in the study of the war came in the 1990s when the Soviet Union began to release some war-related documents, which it had held secret in its archives. The release of these and other documents provided new information for the debate among various scholars by favoring an orthodox interpretation of the war, especially regarding the origins of the war.

THE EARLY STAGE OF RESEARCH BY KOREAN SCHOLARS

Although most literature about the war has been contributed by foreign scholars, Korean scholars played a meager role in its study prior to the 1960s. Only since the 1970s have domestic scholars become engaged in intensive study of the conflict. The first bibliographic work by a Korean scholar describing available materials is Park Hong-kyu's *The Korean War: An Annotated Bibliography* (1971). Another bibliographic work is the "Selected Bibliography of the Korean War," prepared by Rhee Sang-woo, Paik Chong-Chun, and Ohn Chang-Il (1984).

Kim Hak-joon's *Korean Affairs and International Politics* (1975) was the first work in the Korean language that made an inquiry using Korean War–related documents. The work was outstanding because it dealt with different assumptions regarding the Korean War despite the fact that South Korean society at that time was dominated by the official government views. Kim Hak-joon's *Dictionary of Korean Politics* (1990) contains a collection of useful materials about the Korean War. Both of these works are important guidebooks for students of the Korean War.

Other reference works by Korean scholars include Park Myung-rim's "The Point of Argument Regarding Korean War History" (1989); Lee Wan-bum's "Domestic Trends Regarding the Korean War Study," (1990); Lee Choon-kun's "Bibliographic Essay on Korean War" (1990); and a recent essay by Kim Hak-joon (1993). Clearly the analytic study of the Korean War by Korean scholars has lagged behind foreign scholars. One reason is that as victims of the war, Koreans view the North with hostility. To them, the war was an invasion triggered by North Korea and the Soviet communists and resulted in further aggravating their national division, thus imposing great damage on the whole nation. Another reason is that Korean scholarship remained undeveloped due to the unstable social conditions after World War II, followed by the Korean War and then by post-war rehabilitation struggles.

Korean scholars embarked on the study of the Korean War only after the 1960s, and these studies did not begin to be systematized until the 1970s when some Korean students obtained doctoral degrees from universities in the United States and other countries. These were mainly students of international politics who tended to believe that the Korean War was a national disaster caused by foreign forces. Thus, in the Korean case, investigation of the war by Korean political scientists preceded that study done by Korean historians.

There are many different theories regarding the Korean War's origins. Even the traditional theoreticians who share the opinion that the war was the product of Soviet hegemonistic policies reach different conclusions in answering the question, Why did the Soviet Union under Joseph Stalin attack South Korea? Diverse arguments about this issue started soon after the end of the war, although most Korean scholars were initially indifferent to them. In 1963, however, Soh Jin-chul's (1963) doctoral thesis, "Some Causes of the Korean War of 1950," made an intensive inquiry into Stalin's initiation of the war. In 1964, Lee Jong-hak's *History of the Korean War* also supported the theory that Stalin had played a leading role in the war. From a different perspective, Lee Chong-sik (1966) presented the view that a North Korean power struggle between Kim Il-sung and Park Hon-young caused the war, an interpretation that Kim Roy E.'s (Kim Ung-taek) doctoral thesis (1967) also supported.

The doctoral thesis (1958) of the former South Korean ambassador to Singapore, Yoon Young-kyo, represents the typical view of Korean scholars in the 1960s that UN forces intervened in the conflict to uphold the cause of justice by repelling North Korean aggression. Regarding prisoner-of-war issues during the conflict, Kim Myong-whai's (1960) doctoral thesis insists that the treatment of prisoners should be consistent with the principles of individual rights rather than state policy.

Other Korean scholars' doctoral theses from foreign countries included studies about the UN role: by Kim Jong-myong (Shomei Ichikawa) completed in 1965 at Japan's Meiji University, by Yoo Tae-ho in 1965 at Belgium's Louvin University, and by Kim Taek-hwan in 1968 at Germany's Munich University.

South Korean government organizations such as the Republic of Korea's Training, Information and Education Bureau in the Defense Ministry began issuing chronological accounts of the Korean War as early as 1951, and the five volumes of the *Book of the Korean War* were published yearly from 1951 to 1955. Also, the War History Editing Committee of the Republic of Korea's Defense Ministry began in 1966 to issue research materials by publishing two volumes of *A Study of the Korean War History*. These books represented the official view of the Korean government that the war was a southward invasion concocted jointly by the Soviet Union and China and triggered by North Korea. The books focused on depicting the war from the point of view of both military tactics and strategy.

After 1967, the War History Editing Committee began publishing books that gave greater depth of information from both the historical and political perspectives. These volumes include *Liberation and the Building of Armed Forces* (1967), *The Invasion of the North Korean Puppet Forces* (1967), *The Account of Defensive Operations Along the Nak Dong River* (1970), *All-Out Counter-Attack Operations* (1971), *The Invasion by Chinese Forces* (1972), and *The Participation of U.N. Forces* (1980). These works represented the government perspective of the war, which most Korean scholars supported at this early stage of war studies.

As early as the 1950s, some left revisionists in the United States presented views that seemed to agree with a Marxist perspective regarding the war. They cited the war as an internal conflict and depicted its origins as derived from U.S. imperialist policy or by South Korean aggression in its role as a tool of U.S. imperialism. One of these early U.S. accounts was Wilbur Hitchcock's (1951) article. Of course, South Korean scholars opposed these assertions, while North Korea was encouraged to see such opinions emerging. North Korea's Foreign Language Publishing House published such works as *Documents and Materials Exposing the Instigators of the Civil War in Korea* (1958) and *History of the Just Fatherland War of the Korean People* (1961). This publisher in Pyongyang also printed representative documents showing its official stance, which supported the left revisionist views. In the 1970s, revisionist concepts would be introduced into South Korean schools, and since the 1980s, they have been used in the studies by many South Korean scholars.

Revisionist-oriented works supporting Pyongyang's stance of labeling the war as a "fatherland liberation war" also began to be published by Korean scholars residing in Japan. These include Kim Sam Kyu's *Korea Today* (1956) and *History of the Korean War* (1967). These publications resembled Japanese scholarship at that time, which inclined toward leftist theory in its analysis of the Korean War.

WORKS BY KOREAN SCHOLARS, 1970s AND 1980s

The 1970s

During the 1970s, various documents, particularly U.S. documents in the *Foreign Relations of the United States* series and British documents, began to be opened and encouraged Korean scholars to use them to inquire into both the domestic and the international causes of the war. With the help of captured North Korean documents held by the United States, they also directed attention to the possibility that power struggles within North Korea might have been one of the reasons for the origins of the war, in addition to the Soviet or Chinese role in instigating the North's attack.

Research papers focusing on North Korea's responsibility for the war also appeared in South Korea during the early 1970s. Kim Jom-kon, a retired general who once served as the deputy chief of intelligence of the Korean Army headquarters, wrote a 1972 doctoral thesis, "The Study of the Communist Struggle Pattern in Korea, 1945–1950." He also published *The Korean War and Workers' Party Strategy* (1973a) and *The Korean War* (1973b) whose English translation was published in 1973 by Seoul's Kwang-myong Publishing. This volume has been cited by foreign scholars as the best work representing a Korean scholar's view.

In the mid-1970s, some U.S. scholars began to interpret the Korean War as the product of power struggles on the Korean peninsula and claimed that the Soviet Union was rather surprised to learn of the outbreak of the war. The principal writing that expressed this view was Robert

Simmons's *The Strained Alliance* (1975). Simmons' assertions provoked heated critics even in United States, where William Stueck's (1976) critical review appeared in *World Politics*. A South Korean scholar, Koh Byong-chul, also refuted Simmons's ideas in a review for the *American Political Science Review* (1977).

Several South Korean scholars, however, accepted Simmons's perspective and investigated relations between North Korea, China, the Soviet Union, and Western powers. In his doctoral thesis Ra Jong-yil (1971) wrote about U.S.-British relations during the Korean War. Park Doo Bok (1975) studied China's participation in the war, presenting the conclusion that China sent troops to the Korean peninsula in an effort to assure Stalin of Mao's support and thus guarantee China's secure future. Suh Jae-man (1973) examined Turkey's influence on the Korean war, while both Perrin Kwan Sok (1971) and Lee Kwang Ho (1974) studied the relationship of the United Nations to Korea's unification problems. Many of these Korean students returned home to advance the study of the Korean War.

The 1980s

The volume of Korean War studies increased during the 1980s, although the political atmosphere in South Korea was not yet mature enough to accommodate the divergent views regarding the war. For example, in November 1980, a quarterly magazine, *Hyondaesa* (Modern History), was issued by the Seoul Press Culture Club, but it was banned as soon as the first issue was published. The journal was a collection of Korean War–related essays written by comparatively moderate scholars not belonging to any group. The government's ban implied that the war remained too sensitive a subject to be dealt with by civilians.

Despite this atmosphere, leftist revisionist scholars continued to expand their influence and introduced various views, including those favoring North Korea's stance on the war's origins. This provoked ideological disputes between South Korean traditionalists and the emerging revisionists. But in the long term, such disputes helped to develop systematic research activities by Korean War students.

In this respect, the 1980s was a period during which new horizons were opened for Korean War studies by South Koreans. An increasing number of students dealt with the issue of the war as they did research for doctoral studies at home and abroad. At the same time, essays written by foreign revisionists were translated, forcing domestic traditionalist scholars to cope with these trends.

Consequently, Korean scholars in the 1980s wrote some interesting doctoral dissertations, among them Lee Se-ki's (1980) study of the Sino-Soviet confrontation in relation to the war, which found that Stalin probably played a leading role in 1950. Kim Chull Baum's (1984) study argued that the U.S. decision to withdraw in 1949 became a direct cause of the war by referring to factors involved in Washington's decision-making process. Among other dissertations were Yang Dae-hyun's (1982) study of the truce talks ending the war and Kim Gye-dong's (1988) analysis of the war as foreign intervention.

Scholars also embarked on the study of the war's results. A volume of essays prepared by the Sung Sin Women's University Press, *The Impact of the Korean War on the People and Society of Korea* (1986), was a typical collection of such works. Kim Hak-joon contributed greatly to the enhancement of such studies in *The Korean War* (1989).

Among the first translations of U.S. revisionist influence was I. F. Stone's *The Hidden History of the Korean War*, which Paik Woe-kyung (1987) translated to make available to scholars in South Korea. The translation of Stone's and other revisionists' essays was mainly done by nonscholarly leftists or college students rather than by academicians. Nevertheless, the translations brought a change in South Korea's academic sector because many publications that were critical of the government's position on the Korean War were introduced into the country.

Stone's book drew the attention of North Korean specialists because its allegations supported the Pyongyang regime's official position regarding the war. Next, Ki Kwang Shu (1988) translated Robert R. Simmons's book *The Strained Alliance* (1975), referred to previously. The translation, titled *The Internal War of Korea: The Internal War Aspect and the Northern Alliance*, spread revisionists' conclusions that the war was a civil war, through an allegation that the Soviet Union had been totally uninformed of even the date of the attack. Of course, as Soviet post–cold war documents showed, these claims were false. At the time, however, neither Koh's (1977) nor Stueck's (1976) reviews of Simmons had been translated.

Kim Ja-dong (1986) published one of two translations (Kim Ju-hwan also has a translation) of Bruce Cumings's *Origins of the Korean War*. Cumings's revisionist study attracted many leftist students in Korea but lost its popularity after 1989 when Soviet documents appeared, with the result that Cumings' second volume, *The Roaring of the Cataract, 1947–1950* (1990), has not been translated yet.

Other translated works of importance are Chung Dae-hwa's (1988) publication of Karunakar Gupta's "How Did the Korean War Begin?" (1972), a revisionist essay concluding that the war was triggered by South Korea; Cha Sung-su and Yang Dong-ju (1989) translated *Korea*, by Jon Halliday and Bruce Cumings, which was now titled *The Process of the Korean War*. John Merrill's doctoral thesis, "Internal Warfare in Korea, 1948–1950," was translated by Sin Sung-hwan as *The Domestic Background of the Korean War* (1988). The new title placed emphasis on favoring North Korea by branding the conflict as a "liberation war."

Leftist revisionist essays were also published by domestic writers. One typical study was Choi Tae-hwan and Park Hye-kang's *A Portrait of a Young Revolutionary* (1989).

Because revisionist views prevailed in much of South Korean society, the Institute for International Study of Seoul National University attempted to promote an understanding of the war by publishing *The Reevaluation of the Korea War: A Critique of Communist Theory* (1990). This collection criticized revisionist views, especially those of foreign revisionists, and contained Roh Jae-bong's "Reevaluation of the Korean War Study," Kim Yong-ku's "Russian Interpretation of the Korean War," Chung Jong-wook's "Chinese Interpretation of the Korean War in the Context of China's Intervention," and Ha Young-son's "North Korean Interpretations of the Korean War."

Nevertheless, foreign revisionist essays made a great impact on the domestic scene. Encouraged by foreign revisionist views, some leftist scholars in South Korea encouraged pro-Pyongyang sentiments by blaming the Korean War on South Korea or U.S. imperialist policy. For example, Choi Jang-jip and others wrote *A Study of the Korean War* (1990), which expressed revisionist views of the origins, process, and characteristics of the Korean War and their perspectives on North Korean socialism. Other ideological revisionist essays that attracted many readers among young South Korean students were Noh Min-young's (1991) *Reevaluation of the Korean War* and Lee Sun-kyo's *The Korean War Must Be Rewritten* (1990).

In an effort to cope with the new interpretations, the Ministry of Information of South Korea published *The Origins and Truth of the Korean War* (1990). In addition, traditional scholars engaged in intensive efforts to criticize the revisionist views. Scholars devoted to the study of the Korean War met in May 1987 to found the Korean War Study Association and hosted a two-day seminar on June 15–16 in Seoul. During the seminar, thirteen research papers were presented by scholars from South Korea, the United States, Japan, and Germany. Kim Chull Baum edited these studies in *The Korean War* (1989). The association has since hosted several seminars and continues to publish seminar papers in book form.

The Korean Society of Diplomatic History also promoted Korean War studies by publishing essays in *The Korean War Seen from the Context of Diplomatic History* (1989). Also, Japanese scholar Masao Okonoki's doctoral thesis was translated into Korean and published in Seoul in 1986 as *The Korean War: The Process of U.S. Intervention.*

RECENT KOREAN SCHOLARLY LITERATURE

The 1980s trend of heated ideological arguments between traditionalists and revisionists initially appeared to extend into the 1990s. Revisionists engaged in vigorous activities to spread their views in works such as the Korean Political Science Research Association's *A Collection of Treaties, the*

40th Anniversary of the Korean War (1990). These essays were written mostly by young students with master's degrees and contained diverse topics on the war. For example, the author of "The Domestic and External Background and Origins of the Korean War" insisted that due to the Korean War, the South could only rely on the United States and adopt capitalism while the North had no choice but to adopt socialism.

But 1990 was a turning point in Korean War study, especially for the traditionalist scholars who were able to use new evidence from post–cold war sources from the Soviet Union to prove their interpretations of the war, especially its origins. In June 1990, the Korean Association of International Studies, as part of its commemoration of the fortieth anniversary of the Korean War, published *Historical Reevaluation of the Korean War*. This collection of research papers, which had been presented at a summer seminar, has eight articles dealing with the roles played by South Korea and other nations and seven articles dealing with the results of the war. The Institute for Social Science's quarterly, *Sasang* (Thoughts), in June 1990 had a special issue, "War and Revolution, the Korean War and April Student Revolution." In *Sasang,* Kim Chull Baum's contribution, "Current Status of Studies on the Origins of the Korean War," gave a criticism of revisionist views. Other articles were by James Matray, Jonathan Pollack, Ko Byong-chul, and Lee Jae-chun. The June 1990 issue of the Institute for International Affairs's *Kukje Jongse* (International Situation) also marked the war anniversary.

Ha Yong Sun's *New Approaches to the Study of the Korean War* (1990) introduced a new attitude regarding the arguments between the two competing interpretations of the war by suggesting that the traditionalists must abandon their concentration on international aspects of the war while the revisionists must not focus attention only on the domestic situation. Instead, both groups should examine all related factors, including the South-North division and the international and domestic structures in combination with all other historic factors.

Principally, the 1990s has been characterized by the influx of documentary materials into South Korea regarding the Korean War from the former communist bloc nations. The normalization of relations between Seoul and Moscow and between Seoul and Beijing has prompted academic exchanges. The documents released from the Soviet archives and testimony by both Soviet and Chinese scholars have provided evidence to counter the distorted allegations by the revisionists. Based on this new evidence, South Korean scholars have published new research works. Ra Jong-yil's *The Korean War Seen through Testimonies* (1991) is based on interviews given by seventeen persons, including former North Koreans Choe Tae-hwan, Han Marcos, and Ju Young-bok, and a Russian, Smolchekov, among others. Kim Chull Baum's *The Truth and Testimonies* (1990) deals with evidence showing Soviet responsibility and its support of North Korea as well as the process of Chinese intervention in the war. Kim introduces Li Sang-jo's testimony that "Stalin approved Kim Il-sung's invasion plan," Ju Young-bok's testimony that "I translated the Russian version of the attack order," and similar testimonies by a number of former North Koreans now living in exile in Russia. Among these exiles, Choo Young-bok's memoir is *The Korean War I Had Experienced* (1990). In addition, a former leading official of the South Korean Workers' Party, Park Gap-dong published his memoir, *The Korean War and Kim Il-sung* (1990), which revealed evidence depicting Pyongyang's responsibility for starting the war.

Kim Chull Baum, chairman of the Korean War Study Association, published *The Korean War and the United States* (1990), which was based on his doctoral thesis at New York University. He supplemented this volume with new materials and issued a revised edition in 1995 using the same title and adding a subtitle, *U.S. Policy toward South Korea*.

Kim Chull Baum's War Study Association continued to host international seminars during the early 1990s and published its seminar papers. Papers presented at the June 1990 seminar were edited by Kim Chull Baum and James Matray (1991, 1993) and published in both Korea and the United States. The volume is titled *Korea and the Cold War*. One essay in this book by Kim Hak-joon describes "International Trends Regarding the Korean War Study," and refers to all existing research to conclude that the war apparently was the product of a well-prepared attack plan of the North and was prepared at the initiative of the North Korean leadership. The volume also has articles on the international origins of the war, General Douglas MacArthur's role in the war, the truce talks, the Chinese and Russians' roles, and security questions in the Korean peninsula.

In 1990, Kim Chull Baum edited *Perspectives of the Korean War,* with twelve parts, some of which deal with North Korea. The essays represent typical views maintained by traditional scholars in South Korea and contain recent findings on the war.

Since the 1990s, sociological concepts have been introduced into Korean War studies. For example, the Korean Sociological Association published *The Korean War and Changes in Korean Society* (1992) and *The Korean War and the Construction of a Socialist System in North Korea* (1992). The first book deals with the effect of the Korean War on the birth rate, changes in the population structure in the South and the North, the motives of North Koreans who deserted to the South, prevailing ideology and anticommunist ideology, religion in connection with the war, and other topics. The latter book has data dealing with North Korea's penal code, its foreign relations, the process of carrying out socialist projects, and changes in life patterns after the war.

For the Han Kuk Jon Jang Sa Editorial Board (1990–1992), South Korean scholars exerted joint efforts to produce *The Korean War History,* a monumental five-volume work examining all aspects of the war years.

Since 1993, however, more documents have been released by the Russian archives, providing South Korean scholars with new opportunities to advance their studies. Kim Chull Baum, in a contribution to *Chosun Ilbo* (1993), a Seoul-based daily, has given a systematic analysis of all important evidence available hitherto. These new documents unmasked various decisive facts, including evidence that Kim Il-sung had planned to occupy the Ongjin peninsula ten months prior to the start of the Korean War; had attempted on four occasions to induce enormous military aid from the Soviet Union by providing Moscow with false information that the South Korean Army had commenced offensive actions; and that Kim Il-sung had once to be stopped by Stalin from stepping into an adventurous action. Through his investigation, Kim Chull Baum concluded that Kim Il-sung was the chief instigator of the Korean War. Russian documents conveyed to South Korean president Kim Young-sam as gifts from Russian president Boris Yeltsin during the former's visit to Moscow contained similar evidence. Professor Kim wrote an essay about these new findings for the *East Asian Review* (1994). Park Mun-su also wrote an article on the papers received from Yeltsin in the *Korea Observer* (Autumn 1994).

The works published after the revelation of the Russian documents reinforced the traditionalist views on the war's origins. For example, Shin Hwa-bong's *The Day of Opening the Truce Line* (1993) presents the traditionalist view. Another interesting work published in 1993 was Ahn Chon's *The Study on the Day of the Outbreak of War.* The author focused on disproving revisionist theory based on extensive interviews with the people who lived near the South-North border areas at the time of the war's outbreak.

Yang Dae-hyun's *Testimony of History* presents an interesting analysis of the process by which the United States took over command of the South Korean Army and the impact of South Korean president Syngman Rhee's unilateral action of releasing prisoners of war in 1953. Kim Young Hoon's *Secret Records* is one of great works on this topic because it is based on a vast volume of materials the author collected for ten years, focusing on presenting evidence that North Korea was the chief instigator of the war.

Ra Jong-yil's *The Unfinished War* (1994) is an extensive analysis of the British position on the war. Ra points out that London's perspective of Korea following the termination of World War II was that it would be difficult to prevent the Korean peninsula from being communized. Concerning U.S. policy during the period after 1945, Kim Chull Baum's essay is contained in Phillip Williamson's *Security in Korea* (1994).

In November 1994, the Korean War Study Institute and the Korean Affairs Study Institute of California University at Berkeley cohosted in Seoul a seminar, "Reflections on Korean Conflict." During the seminar,

Kim Chull Baum's yet unpublished paper, "The Role of USSR and China in the Outbreak of the Korean War," emphasized that both the Soviet Union and China, though they shared different roles, had been deeply involved in the war, even during the preparatory stages. The Soviet Union rendered operational and logistic support, while China prepared manpower.

OTHER WORKS ON THE KOREAN WAR

The works already listed focused mostly on international political aspects of the war. Some Korean scholars have approached the war from the military point of view. Among these are *History of the Korean War* by Kim Yang-myong (1976) and the Joint Chief of Staff Headquarters' *The Korean War History* (1984).

A number of memoirs of the war have also been published. Among them are *A Secret Record,* by Chung Il-kwon (1986), a retired general and former army chief of staff, and *Reflections on the Korean War,* by Paik Sun-yup (1989), who also is a retired general and former army chief of staff. A series of war accounts carried by the Seoul-based *Joongang Daily News* (Joongang Ilbo) were published in eight volumes in 1983. These books collected various testimonies providing valuable evidence regarding the origins and process of the war. Korean versions of American veterans' memoirs were also published in Korea. Among them are General Mark Clark's *From the Danube to the Yalu* (1954) and Ambassador Harold Noble's *Embassy at War* (1975). Noble was ambassador to Seoul at the time of the Korean War. Kang Chang-ku translated into Korean the book by Japanese writer Harukata Sasaki, *The Korean War* (1976–1977).

Television documentaries on the Korean War that have been shown in Korea are a Japanese production by NHK in 1991 and a production by Donga Press and South Korea's KBS-TV, which was broadcast in 1992.

To summarize, Russian and other recently released documents have served to terminate the long-lasting dispute over who originated the Korean War. However, questions regarding the war's progress, its effects, and its strategic evaluation remain only partially answered. Similarly, the Korean War remains an unfinished war because genuine peace on the Korean peninsula has yet to be attained.

REFERENCES

Ahn, Chon. *The Study on the Day of the Outbreak of War: A Critique on the Inducement Theory of the War.* Seoul: KwaHak Kyo Yuk Sa, 1993.

Blanchard, Carroll H., Jr. *Korean War Bibliography and Maps of Korea.* Albany, NY: Korean Conflict Research Foundation, 1964.

Cha, Sung-Su, and Yang Dong-Ju, trans. *Process of the Korean War.* Original work by

Bruce Cumings and Jon Halliday, *Korea: The Unknown War*. Seoul: Tae Am Publishing, 1989.

Choi, Jang-Jip, et al. *A Study on the Korean War: Understanding Korean Modern History*. Seoul: Tae Am Publishing, 1990.

Choi, Tae-hwan, and Park Hye-kang. *A Portrait of a Young Revolutionary: A War Account by a North Korean Army Lt. Col. Choi Tae Hwan*. Seoul: Kong Dong Che Publication, 1989.

Choo, Young-bok. *The Korean War I Had Experienced*. Seoul: Koryo Won, 1990.

Chung, Dae-Hwa, trans. *How the Korean War Began*. Original work is by K. Gupta in *China Quarterly* 52 (October 1972): 699–712. Seoul: Sin Hak Mun Sa, 1988.

Chung, Il-Kwon. *A Secret Record: War and Truce*. Seoul: Donga Daily, 1986.

Clark, Mark. *From the Danube to the Yalu*. New York: Harper & Row, 1954.

Foreign Language Publishing House. *Documents and Materials Exposing the Instigators of the Civil War in Korea: Documents from the Archives of the Rhee Syngman Government*. Pyongyang, 1950.

———. *Panmunjom*. Pyongyang, 1958.

———. *History of the Just Fatherland War of the Korean People*. Pyongyang, 1961.

Gupta, Karunakar. "How Did the Korean War Begin?" *China Quarterly* 52 (1972): 699–716.

Ha, Yong Sun, ed. *New Approaches to the Study of Korean War: Beyond Traditionalism and Revisionism*. Seoul: NaNam, 1990.

HanKuk Jon Jang Sa (History of the Korean War) Editorial Board. *History of the Korean War*. 5 vols. Seoul: HangRim Publishing, 1990–1992.

Hitchcock, Wilbur. "North Korea Jumps the Gun." *Current History* 20 (March 1951): 136–144.

Huh, Man Ho. "La Constance de l'Unité Nationale Coreenne: essai d'une novelle interpretation de la guerre de Coree." Ph.D. dissertation, Ecole des Hautes Etudes en Science Sociales, 1988.

Institute for International Affairs. *Kukje Jongse* (International situation). Special Edition Commemorating the Korean War (June 1990a).

———. *Reevaluation of the Korean War: A Critique of Communist Theory*. Seoul: Seoul National University, 1990b.

Institute for Social Sciences. *Sasang* (Thought). Special Issue: *War and Revolution: Korean War and April Student Revolution*. (June 1990).

Institute of Far Eastern Studies. *Korean War and the Construction of the Socialist System in North Korea*. Seoul: IFES, Kyung Nam University, 1992.

Joint Chiefs of Staff. *The Korean War History*. Seoul: JCS, 1984. *Joongang Daily News*, ed. *Testimonies of the Nation*. 8 vols. Seoul: Joongang Daily, 1983.

Kang, Chang Koo, trans. *Korean War*. Original is in Japanese by Harukata Sasaki. Seoul: Byong Hak Sa, 1976–1977.

Ki, Kwang Suh, trans. of Robert Simmons, *The Strained Alliance: Peking, Pyongyang, and Moscow and the Politics of the Korean Civil War*. Seoul: Yul Sa Ram Chull Pan Sa 1988.

Kim, Chull Baum. "U.S. Withdrawal Decision from South Korea, 1945–1949." Ph.D. dissertation, State University of New York at Buffalo, 1984.

———, ed. *The Korean War: Great Power Politics and South-North Discord*. Seoul: Pyong Min Sa, 1989.

————. *Truth and Testimonies: The True Picture of the Korean War Unmasked 40 Years After.* Seoul: Eul Yoo Publishing, 1990.

————. *Korean War and the United States.* Seoul: Pyong Min Sa, 1990; 2d ed. Seoul: Pyong Min Sa, 1995.

————, ed. *Perspectives of the Korean War.* Seoul: Eul Yoo, 1990.

————. "U.S. Policy on the Eve of the Korean War: Abandonment or Safeguard?" In Phillip Williamson, ed., *Security in Korea: War Stalemate and Negotiation.* Boulder, CO: Westview Press, 1994.

————. "An Inquiry into the Origins of the Korean War: A Critique of the Revisionist View." *East Asia Review* 6:3 (Summer 1994): 3.

————. "The Role of USSR and China in the Outbreak of the Korean War." Presented at the Seminar of the University of California at Berkeley, November 1994.

Kim, Chull Baum, and James Matray, eds. *Korean and the Cold War: Division, Destruction and Disarmament.* Seoul: Ptong Min Sa, 1991; U.S. edition is by Claremont, CA: Regina Books, 1993.

Kim, Gye-dong. "Foreign Intervention in Korea 1950–1954." Ph.D. dissertation, Oxford University, 1988.

Kim, Hak-Joon. *Korean Affairs and International Politics.* Seoul: Park Yong Sa Publishing, 1975.

————. *The Korean War: Origins, Process, Truce and Influence.* Seoul: Park Yong Sa 1989.

————. *Dictionary of Korean Politics.* Seoul: Han Kil Sa, 1990.

————. "Trends in Korean War Studies: A Review of the Literature." In Kim Chull Baum and James Matray, eds., *Korea and the Cold War.* Claremont, CA: Regina Books, 1993.

Kim, Ja Dong, trans. of Bruce Cumings, *Origins of the Korean War: Liberation and the Emergence of Separate Regimes, 1945–1947.* Seoul: Il Wol Su Gak, 1986.

Kim, Jom-Kon. "The Study of Communist Struggle Pattern in Korea 1945–1950: With Emphasis on Armed Struggle." Ph.D. dissertation, Kyong Hee University, 1972.

————. *The Korean War and Workers' Party Strategy.* Seoul: Park Yong Sal, 1973a.

————. *The Korean War.* Seoul: Kwangmyong Publishing, 1973b.

Kim, Jong-myong (Shomei Ichikawa). "A Study of the Korean War and the United Nations." Ph.D. dissertation, Meiji University, 1965.

Kim, Myong-whai. "Prisoners of War as a Major Problem of the Korean Armistice, 1953." Ph.D. dissertation, New York University, 1960.

Kim, Roy E. (Kim Ung-taek). "Sino-Soviet Dispute and North Korea." Ph.D. dissertation, University of Pennsylvania, 1967.

Kim, Sam Kyu. *Korea Today.* Tokyo: Kwaedo, 1956.

————. *History of the Korean War: Reevaluation of Modern History.* Tokyo: Korea Hyoronsha, 1967.

Kim, Taek-hwan. "Die Vereinten Nationen und ihre kollektiven Sicherheitsmassnahme: Studie uber die UN-Aktion gegen die Intervention der VR China inm Koreakrieg" (The United Nations and collective security: A study of UN action against the intervention of the People's Republic of China in the Korean War). Ph.D. dissertation, Munich University, 1968.

Kim, Yang Myong. *History of the Korean War*. Seoul: Ilsin Sa, 1976.

Kim, Young Hoon. *Secret Records: Division and War*. Seoul: Dana Publishing, 1994.

Koh, Byoung-chul. Review of Robert Simmons, *The Strained Alliance*. *American Political Science Review* 71 (September 1977): 1328–1330.

Korean Association of International Studies. *Historical Reevaluation of the Korean War*. Seoul: KAIS, 1990.

Korean Political Science Research Association. *A Collection of Treaties: The 40th Anniversary of the Korean War*. Seoul: YokSa Bi Pyong Sa, 1990.

Korean Society of Diplomatic History. *The Korean War Seen from the Context of Diplomatic History*. Seoul: Pyong Min Sa, 1989.

Korean Sociological Association. *The Korean War and the Changes in Korean Society*. Seoul: Pulbit Publishing, 1992.

———. *The Korean War and the Construction of a Socialist System in North Korea*. Seoul: Pulbit Publishing, 1992.

Korean War Studies Institute. *Bibliogaphies Related with the Korean War*. Seoul, Korean War Studies Institute, 1985.

Lee, Chong-sik. "Communist Satellite Politics: The Case Study of the Korean War" Unpublished, 1966.

Lee, Choon-kun. "Bibliographic Essay on Korean War." In *Tong Il Mun Je Yon Ku* (A study of unification affairs) 2: (Summer 1990).

Lee, Jong Hak. *History of the Korean War*. Seoul: Jong Eum Sa, 1969.

Lee, Kwang Ho. "A Study of the United Nations Commission for the Unification and the Rehabilitation of Korea: The Cold War and the United Nations Subsidiary Organ." Ph.D. dissertation, University of Pittsburgh, 1974.

Lee, Se Ki. "A Study on the Origins of the Korean War in Connection with Sino-Soviet Confrontation." Ph.D. dissertation, Korea University, 1980.

Lee, Sun-kyo. *The Korean War Must Be Rewritten*. Seoul: KaRam Mun Hak Sa, 1990.

Lee, Wan Bum. "Domestic Trends Regarding the Korean War Study." *Korea and International Politics* 6:2 (Autumn 1990). Seoul: Chung Nam University Institute of Far Eastern Studies, 1990.

Masao, Okonoki. *The Korean War: The Process of U.S. Intervention*. Seoul: Chung Gye Yon Ku So, 1986.

Ministry of Information. *The Origins and Truth of the Korean War: An Analysis of False Perspective by Revisionists*. Seoul: 1990.

Noble, Harold. *Embassy at War*. Edited by Frank Baldwin. Seattle: University of Washington Press, 1975.

Noh, Min-young. *Reevaluation of the Korean War: Unfinished War*. Seoul: Hanul, 1991.

Paik, Woe-kyung, trans. of I. F. Stone, *The Hidden History of the Korean War*. Seoul: Sin Hak Mun Sa, 1987.

Paik, Sun-yup. *Reflections on the Korean War: The Army and I*. Seoul: DaeRyuk Yon Ku So, 1989.

Park, Doo Bok. "A Study of Chinese Participation in the Korean War." Ph.D. dissertation, Mun Hwa University, 1975.

Park, Gap-dong. *The Korean War and Kim Il Sung*. Seoul: Baram gwa Mulgyol Publishing, 1990.

Park, Hong-kyu. *The Korean War: An Annotated Bibliography*. New York: Marshall Demmer, 1971.

Park, Mun-su. "Stalin's Foreign Policy and the Korean War: History Revisited." *Korea Observer* 25:3 (Autumn 1994).

Park, Myung Rim. "The Point of Argument Regarding Korean War History." In *The View of Korean History before and after Liberation.* Seoul: Han Kil Sa, 1989.

Perrin, Kwan Sok. "The Problem of Korean Unification and the United Nations, 1945–1955." Ph.D. disseration, University of Utah, 1971.

Ra, Jong-yil. "British-American Relations During the Korean War." Ph.D. dissertation, Cambridge University, 1971.

———. *The Korean War Seen through Testimonies.* Seoul: Yejin Publishing, 1991.

———. *The Unfinished War: Korea and Great Power Politics, 1950–1990.* Seoul: Jonyewon, 1994.

Republic of Korea. Ministry of Defense. *The Korean War.* Seoul: Information and Education Bureau, 1951–1955.

Rhee, Sang-Woo, Paik Chong-Chun, and Ohn Chang-Il, eds. "Selected Bibliography of the Korean War." *Korea and World Affairs* 8:2 (Summer 1984): 442–473.

Shin, Hwa-bong. *The Day of Opening the Truce Line.* Seoul: Han Kuk Non Dan, 1993.

Simmons, Robert R. *The Strained Alliance: Peking, Pyongyang, Moscow and the Politics of the Korean Civil War.* New York: Free Press, 1975.

Sin, Sung-hwan, trans. *The Domestic Background of the Korean War, 1948–1950: An Invasion or Liberation War?* Original work by John Merrill, *Internal Warfare in Korea, 1948–1950: The Local Settings of the Korean War.* Seoul: Kwa Hak Kwa Sa Sang, 1988.

Social Science Institute of North Korea. *History of the Just Fatherland War of the Korean People.* Pyongyang: Social Science Institute, 1961.

Soh, Jin Chul. "Some Causes of the Korean War of 1950: A Case Study of Soviet Foreign Policy in Korea (1945–1950) with Emphasis on Sino-Soviet Collaboration." Ph.D. dissertation, University of Oklahoma, 1963.

Stueck, William W. "The Soviet Union and the Origins of the Korean War." *World Politics* 28 (July 1976): 622–635.

Suh, Jae-man. "The Influence of the Korean War on Turkish Foreign Policy." Ph.D. dissertation, Ankara University, 1973.

Sung Sin Women's University Press. *The Impact of the Korean War on the People and Society of Korea.* Seoul: Sung Sin Women's University Press, 1986.

War History Editing Committee. *History of the United Nations Forces in Korea.* 5 vols. Seoul: South Korean Defense Ministry, 1967–1970. For more detailed data in the Korean Language see: Chon-sa p'yonch'an wiwonhoe. *Han'guk Chonjaengsa.* 9 vols. Seoul: Kukpang-bu, 1967–1970.

———. Seoul: Ministry of Defense's series of studies on the Korean War:
Liberation and the Building of Armed Forces (1967).
The Invasion of the North Korean Puppet Forces (1967).
The Account of Defensive Operations along the Nak Dong River (1970).
All Out Counter Attack Operations (1971).
The Invasion by Chinese Forces (1972).
The Participation of UN Forces (1980).

Yang, Dae-hyun. "Korean Truce Talks: Multi-dimensional Situational Analysis" Ph.D. dissertation, Munich University, 1982.

————. *Testimony of History: Secret History of the Armistice Talks.* Seoul: Hyung Sol
    Publishing, 1993.
Yoo, Tae-ho. "The Korean War and the United Nations: A Legal and Diplomatic
    Historical Study." Ph.D. dissertation, University of Louvin, 1965.
Yoon, Young Kyo. "United Nations Participation in Korean Affairs 1945–1954."
    Ph.D. dissertation, American University, 1958.

PART III

China, the Soviet Union, and the Korean War

10 Sino-Soviet Historiography and Research Materials

Lester H. Brune

Sergei N. Goncharov, John W. Lewis, and Xue Litai's *Uncertain Partners: Stalin, Mao, and the Korean War* (1993) is a seminal work in the historiography of relations between the People's Republic of China and the former Soviet Union. The three authors admit that their work is not the final, definitive study, which only future declassified documents can reveal, and already Michael Sheng (1994) offers an alternative to their interpretation. Nevertheless, their data and the collegiality of this joint venture are a milestone in the study of the origins of the Korean War and Sino-Soviet interaction. As the book's preface indicates, the Soviet, Chinese, and Korean sources they found throw new light on the topic, with new materials including manuscripts of Mao Zedong, some of which are translated in their appendix; the personal archive of I. V. Kovalev, Joseph Stalin's representative to Beijing; and interviews with officials and scholars of the three nations.

Undoubtedly the value of *Uncertain Partners* heralds a new era of historical study about the cold war, but future study depends on access to documentary evidence that is still classified or withheld and on the coordination of the new evidence with the previous work of Western Sinologists and Sovietologists, as John W. Lewis' presence in the above study illustrates. Much is being gleaned from archives and new publications in Moscow and Beijing, but the enthusiasm of researchers using these resources has already disclosed pitfalls to avoid by using the new information within the context of past study to yield properly balanced literature that is checked carefully with other sources.

CHINESE HISTORIOGRAPHY

As Chen Jian indicates in Chapter 11 of this book, documents have become available to provide new knowledge about China's role in the

Korean War. Looking at the past, Qiang Zhai (1989) describes how previous Chinese writing about the United States and East Asia had hewed to the Chinese Communist party's ideological views until the late 1970s, before real change appeared in literature that acknowledged other non-ideological factors of history. Both the reality of the Chinese disputes with Moscow in the late 1960s and President Richard Nixon's visit to Beijing in 1972 opened the way to conferences between U.S. and People's Republic of China (PRC) scholars and the accessibility of memoirs and interviews with officials of the PRC going back to the civil war of the 1940s. This process was assisted after the mid-1980s by *glasnost* in the Soviet Union, which gradually disclosed Moscow's perspective on the relations between Stalin and Mao.

Between 1945 and the 1970s, Western literature on the PRC was dominated by U.S. Sinologists, as indicated in the essays by D. W. Watts and Allen S. Whiting in the volume edited by Yonosuke Nagai and Akira Iriye (1977). Even before Nixon's visit to Beijing, however, U.S. scholars had begun to question the traditional studies about China and its foreign relations. The Sino-Soviet split and U.S. problems in Vietnam led students to doubt previous studies that had championed the nationalist government of Jiang Jieshi (Chiang Kai-shek) or described the inability of the United States to support the modernization of Chinese society as it had intended.

By the 1970s, revisionist interpretations of Chinese history and the communist victory in 1949 may be discerned among the Sinologists. Briefly, those who favored Jiang's nationalists and blamed Washington for the "loss" of China were represented by the works of Freda Utley (1951), Anthony Kubek (1963), and Chin-tung Liang (1972). Second, an "old school" of American scholars of Chinese history viewed the communist victory as an unfortunate attempt by communists to modernize China by violence, a group represented in the works of John Fairbank (1968); A. Doak Barnett and Edwin Reischauer (1970); A. Doak Barnett (1985); and Tang Tsou (1963). These authors were respected scholars of Chinese history, but the revisionists who challenged their concepts argued that they were wrong in perceiving U.S. intentions as having been designed to lift up and modernize the Chinese people. Rather, as Jim Peck and Edward Friedman's essays in Friedman and Mark Selden's (1969) volume indicates, the revisionists believed that the U.S. interest in China corresponded with nineteenth-century European imperialism in seeking "unequal treaties," which gave advantages to U.S. merchants and investors in China.

More particularly regarding the literature of the PRC foreign policy, Yu Bin (1994) explains how a "new generation of scholarship" developed during the 1980s. Surveying the literature from the 1940s to the present, he finds five genres of literature, each having some value for understanding the historians' problems before greater documentation became available after 1980. Briefly stated, Yu Bin first identifies three traditional schools of interpretation immediately after 1945: an "old China" group, represented by such works as C. P. Fitzergerald (1964) and the essays compiled by John K. Fairbank (1968), which found continuity between past Chinese history and the events bringing Mao Zedong to power and still influence such scholars as Chih-yu Shih (1990); a Maoist ideological group represented by such scholars as Benjamin Schwartz (1968) and Harold Hinton (1972), who emphasize that China's post-1949 policies followed communist principles; and the "realists" such as Allen Whiting (1960) and Michael Yahuda (1978), who applied Hans Morgenthau's Western-style analysis to Chinese foreign policies.

Yu Bin indicates that scholarship on China's foreign affairs adjusted in two ways during the late 1960s. First, to perceive the Sino-Soviet-Western relationship evident in the Sino-Soviet split and President Nixon's visit to China, researchers such as Gerald Segal (1982) and the authors of essays edited by Ilpyong Kim (1987) described the evolution of this triangular relationship. Second, the "factionalist" school represented by Thomas Gottlieb (1977) and Peter Van Ness (1984) investigated the internal political factions within the CCP that influenced both the domestic and foreign policies of China.

Yu Bin finally examines the recent studies of the 1980s in which are found new approaches to the study of China's foreign policy, which he calls the "institutional" and the "perceptional." These two perspectives are represented by Doak Barnett's (1985) study of the institutional processes involved in Chinese decision making and in David Shambaugh's (1991) "perceptional" work that investigates how China looked at the United States. Yu Bin believes Western scholarship has become more specialized than in the past because of new information coming from mainland China, arguing that narrower approaches limit the fuller understanding of Chinese policy. He prefers the recent studies of Lowell Dittmer (1992) and Chih-yu Shih (1990), who search for broad interrelationships among political institutions, individuals, and society.

Historians studying China's foreign policies can profit by reading books of essays on China and Sino-American relations, which offer a variety of interpretations of U.S.-Chinese relations. Three valuable books of essays are edited by Ernest A. May and James W. Thomson (1972), Waldo Heinrichs and Dorothy Borg (1980), and Warren I. Cohen and Dorothy Borg (1983). Some helpful general works for gaining familiarity with different perspectives are Warren I. Cohen's (1971) interpretive survey of U.S.-China relations, which has had various editions; Gordon Chang's (1990) broad study of U.S.-China-Soviet relations after 1945; Qingzhao Hua's (1993) study of Truman's diplomacy; He Di's (1994) research on Mao's perceptions of the United States, which uses the memoirs of Mao's body-guard Zhe Shi (1991); and Charles R. Shrader's (1995) work on the lo-gistics of the communist ground forces in the war.

RESEARCH MATERIALS ON CHINA

Between 1970 and 1994, the domination of Sinology by U.S. scholars gradually broadened to reach the level exemplified by the 1993 study of Goncharov, Lewis, and Xue. As Allen S. Whiting's essay in Nagai and Iriye (1977) shows, the initial new material for scholars had been some of Mao Zedong's writings for the period 1949 to 1968 translated by the Joint Pub-lication's Research Service (1974) and analyzed by Stuart Schram (1974a, 1974b), a specialist on Mao's writing.

From this beginning, as Qiang Zhai (1989) explains, conferences be-tween Western and Chinese scholars led to interviews with Chinese offi-cials and the accessing of some Chinese documents and publications. William Moss (1993) has perhaps the best introduction to PRC archives for Western scholars. Jungquo Luo and Xiangze Jiang's essay in Cohen and Borg (1983) is slightly out of date regarding Chinese materials but can be supplemented by the excellent article on both central and provin-cial government sources by Michael H. Hunt and Odd Arne Westad (1990) and the Chinese Communism Research Group's *CCP Research News-letter* report (1993) on China's Central Archives. The *CCP Newsletter* has frequent articles of special interest, such as Odd Arne Westad's (1992b) on Russian archival holdings about CCP history, and Frederick C. Teiwes (1992) on a scholar's problems in using interviews of officials. The *Cold War International History Project Bulletin (CWIHP Bulletin)* often has infor-mation of value to Chinese scholars, including an article on new sources by Steven G. Goldstein and He Di (1992). Among the items about China that the *CWIHP Bulletin* has recently mentioned are a catalog of PRC publications and journals available from China Publication Services, P.O. Box 49614, Chicago, Illinois 60649; and the forming of the Society for Scholars of Sino-U.S. Relations, with information available from that so-ciety, Attention of Tao Wenzhao, 1 Dongchang Hutong, Wangfujing Dajie, Beijing 100006 China, Fax (86-1) 513-3228. The journal *Chinese Historians* has Yan Xu's (1993) article on Chinese casualties in Korea and also cites literature about the navy and air forces of the People's Liberation Army when the Korean War began. This journal has frequent articles about Chinese foreign policy and may be subscribed to by writing to Li Xiaobing, History Department, University of Central Oklahoma, 100 North Univer-sity Drive, Edmond, OK 73034.

SOVIET HISTORIOGRAPHY

The breakup of the Union of Soviet Socialist Republics between 1989 and 1992 forced Western Sovietologists to reconsider their cold war assumptions about totalitarianism within and outside the Soviet empire. Not only did the breakup surprise most scholars, but more documentary evidence became available from Soviet files, from published memoirs of former officials, and from interviews and meetings with former Soviet individuals. Subsequently, Western Sovietologists who had disagreed about Soviet and Russian history and foreign policy had to reexamine their perspectives on the years from 1917 to 1992. With more Chinese communist information also becoming available on the cold war and the Korean War, scholars of these subjects became anxious to determine how communist documents would affirm or alter their previous understanding of Soviet history. More than in China as of 1994, documents on the history of the Soviet Union since 1917 have gradually become available since 1989, and although the status of some of these records is still uncertain, scholarship on the origins of the cold war and the Korean War is now in an important stage.

Between 1945 and the 1990s, Western scholarship on the Soviet Union and the cold war had developed divergences on two levels of interpretations. On one level, the earliest post-1945 studies of the Soviet Union usually validated the U.S. containment policy in the cold war by emphasizing the totalitarian nature of the Soviet regime, which since 1917 had sought to achieve global communist control by using whatever methods were necessary. During the 1960s, however, a revisionist group of scholars challenged the monolithic-totalitarian model of Soviet power, claiming that the Soviet system had shown flexibility in trying to improve its society and caution in its foreign relations so that positive changes had taken place, especially after Stalin's death in 1953.

On the second level of analysis, scholars disputed whether the communist revolution had been an aberration of Russian cultural history due to the Leninist-Stalinist cult's break with the past or had been derived naturally from a Russian culture that had always possessed one or another form of autocracy, czarist or bolshevik, and therefore could only move toward the socialist ideal. The first of these levels of difference was the more significant regarding the Soviets' international activity, although, generally, those who saw communism as a Russian aberration more readily accepted the totalitarian nature of communist rule. Eduard Mark's (1989) essay extensively examines the historiography on the historical role of Lenin and Stalin. Seeking to remain neutral, he studied most previous books on the Soviet Union from 1917 to 1950, as well as almost all articles and forty newspapers that wrote about Soviet history.

In 1993, the *National Interest,* a neoconservative journal, devoted an entire issue edited by Charles H. Fairbanks, Jr. to articles discussing the Soviet breakup and the "Sins of the Scholars," that is, the mistaken belief of those who thought the Soviet Union could reform itself. In this issue, Richard Pipes, Robert Conquest, and Martin Malia in particular held to their hard-line views of Soviet totalitarianism and defended their position by blaming the "Sins of the Scholars" on the revisionists, claiming that the *glasnost* literature of former Soviet officials, such as Dmitrii A. Volkogonov (1991, 1994), revealed how bad Lenin and Stalin had been. A more balanced article in the *National Interest* was by Peter Rutland (1993), who explained various reasons that the Sovietologists' "conventional wisdom" had failed to anticipate the events of 1991–1992. His possible reasons included the divergent political bias of the hard-line and revisionist views, the isolation of Soviet area studies from the social sciences, the scholars' lack of background in the languages and history of non-Russian peoples, rivalry between émigré and native American authors, the readiness of leading scholars to become media pundits, and scholars' dependence on funds from the Pentagon/CIA, which may have influenced their conclusions. As an example, Rutland notes that the revisionists Frederick J. Fleron, Jr., and Erik P. Hoffman (1991) stress the importance of the social sciences research whose analysis concluded that the Bolsheviks took complete control because the Russian people were too hungry to desire the political freedom they could later seek, a view the hard-liners reject.

In contrast to most of the *National Interest* articles, Stephen Cohen had previously made the revisionists' case in *Rethinking the Soviet Experience* (1985). Cohen first criticized the hard-line Sovietologists whose positions had not changed since the 1950s. These hard-line authors included not only Conquest (1968, 1990) and Pipes (1954, 1980, 1989) but also David Dallin (1964, 1971), Max Beloff (1971), and Carl Friedrich and Zbigniew K. Brzezinski (1956), whose work had solidified the hard-line totalitarian model. In *Dilemmas of Change in Soviet Politics,* Brzezinski (1969) wrote that after Stalin's death, the actions of Nikita Khrushchev and Leonid Brezhnev were not reforms but the degeneration of the dictatorship so that the bureaucracy could maintain power. The only good thing the communist leaders could do would be to let their rule wither away. Brzezinski's (1989) recent book describes communism's failure to help Russia.

In opposition to these hard-line attitudes, Cohen advocated the revisionists' position described in his own work (1973, 1980) and in selected essays he edited with Alexander Rabinowitz and Robert Sharlett (1980). The revisionist perception that the Soviet system was flexible and reform was possible is also described by authors such as Robert Tucker (1963, 1971, 1990) and William McCagg (1978). Other revisionists were J. Arch Getty (1985), who played down Stalin's purges, and Jerry Hough, who retained Merle Fainsod's name from his previous text, *How Russia Is Ruled* (1953), but changed the title to *How Russia Is Governed* (1979). In another study, Hough (1988) discussed the Soviet Union's transition toward a Western-style system, which appeared possible during the mid-1980s.

The intensity of the debate between the hard-line and revisionist Sovietologists in the United States appears again in an article by Jane

Burbank (1991) and the response by Robert W. Thurston (1993). Burbank is especially critical of the revisionists for not fully accepting the views of those who lived under and fled the Soviet experience, although she appears to want to settle the dispute. Thurston sees her article as an emotional charge against revisionists. He especially has details about the disagreement over Stalin's purges as led, respectively, by Conquest and Getty.

To some degree, this hard-line and revisionist dispute about whether the *glasnost* and *perestroika* of Mikhail Gorbachev were evidence of Russian reform or indicative of the disintegration of the entire communist system may hinge on what remnants of the Soviet system finally remain in the future. Unlike the revisionists, who at this date have the old communist Boris Yeltsin and many *nomenklatura* in place, the hard-liners have the empire's breakup to verify that the communist system will completely disintegrate, a perspective given by Brzezinski (1967) and expressed by "Z" (Martin Malia) in a *Daedalus* article (1990). However, as Dimitri K. Simes (1995) indicates, both Yeltsin and his critics in Russia still retain the visions of empire, whether under the czars or the communists. More troubling in this respect is Yevgenia Albats' (1994) contention that the Soviet KGB still has a hold on Russian society.

Recent writing by Soviet historians is described in the essays by N. N. Bolkhovitinov and A. N. Sukhov in Henry Kozicki's (1993) volume. Bolkhovitinov regrets the way that Soviet historians contributed to international confrontations during the cold war, citing the "distressing list" of Soviet literature compiled by L. Okinshevich (1976). Sakharov cites recent efforts to correct past Soviet historical literature, including I. D. Kovalchenko's plea for factual research (1989) and Roy A. Medvedev's articles on Stalinism (1979). Medvedev's (1989) revision of his 1971 book argued that, despite Stalinism, the U.S.S.R. could become a social democracy. All scholars should also read the historiographic essay by Soviet historians Vladislav Zubok and Constantine Pleshakov (1994), which examines the continued problems in assessing Stalinism.

RESEARCH MATERIALS ON THE FORMER SOVIET UNION

The two best methods for keeping abreast of the status of archives in the former Soviet Union are the publications of the International Research and Exchange Board (IREX), such as that of Patricia Kennedy Grimstead (1993), and the *CWIHP Bulletin,* whose issues have included James G. Hershberg's "Report from Moscow" (1992) and Mark Kramer's "Archival Research in Moscow: Progress and Pitfalls" (1993). Hershberg (1994) also edited the most recent *Bulletin,* which is devoted almost entirely to research in the former Soviet Union. It includes an article by David Holloway on the sources used in his recent book (1994); Hershberg's own "Russian Archives Review"; a translation of two documents on the origins of the Korean War, which Boris Yeltsin gave to South Korea in June 1994; and other topics mentioned elsewhere in this book. All its *Bulletin* issues update materials about communist and former communist archives, including Korea and China, and the History Project publishes irregularly dated working papers.

Other articles about Soviet archives and some warnings about evaluating them are by Grimstead (1992) on recent developments in the Soviet archives; Odd Arne Westad (1992a), a Norwegian who is a member of the Russian Foreign Ministry's International Advisory Group; Gerry Gendlin (1994), a visiting professor at the Moscow State Institute of International Relations; and German scholar Johannes Kuppes (1992). Dmitrii A. Volkogonov's (1992) comments were given when he opened an exhibit of Soviet documents at the National Archives in Washington, D.C.

Researchers should be aware of several incidents regarding the release of some Soviet memoirs and documents without the benefit of careful scholarly analysis. Two of these instances involved Jerrold Schecter—the first when he edited and translated *Khrushchev Remembers: The Glasnost Tapes* (1990), tapes not used in Nikita Khrushchev's earlier *Khrushchev Remembers* (1970, 1974). The sensational part regarded Julius and Ethel Rosenberg as spies, which *Time* magazine (1990) highlighted in publishing excerpts of the book. Although other reviewers noted the book's harsher treatment of Stalin and data on the 1962 Cuban missile crisis, the Rosenberg comments led Walter Schneir (1990) to raise questions about the authenticity of the tapes, for which he received no satisfactory answers.

More recently, Pavel Sudoplatov's (1994) memoir, which Schecter was also involved in, resulted in extensive questioning of accuracy because it claimed to implicate Robert Oppenheimer, Neils Bohr, Leo Szliard, and others as spies regarding atomic secrets. Criticisms that seem to have demolished Sudoplatov's claims were made not only by Walter Schneir (1994) but by Thomas Powers (1994), Priscilla Johnson McMillan (1994), an *Izvestia* reporter, Sergei Leskov (1994), and Vladislav Zubok and Yuri Smirnov in Hershberg (1994). Significantly, Sudoplatov's (1995) reply to his critics discloses the ongoing dispute in Moscow by which the KGB claims Soviet spies in the 1940s and not Soviet scientists were responsible for the success of their atomic program in 1949.

Grimsted's essay, "Russian Archives in Transition," in *Archives in Russia* (1993), describes problems such as the purchase of rights to reproduce archives that Russian agencies signed with the Hoover Institute, Crown Publishing, and Yale University Press, which will publish the first books in the *Annals of Communism* series in 1995.

In addition to the compilation of L. Okinshevich (1976), available bibliographies on the Soviet Union include Thomas Hammond's (1966) annotated list of works in thirty languages, which Roger E. Kanet (1974) updates; Stephan M. Horak's (1978) annotated guide; Anthony Thompson's (1979) general volume; and George Ginsburgs' (1973) volume about Soviet writings on Korea. A new bibliography on the past fifteen years is much needed.

REFERENCES

Albats, Yevgenia. *The State within a State: The KGB and Its Hold on Russia: Past, Present, and Future.* New York: Farrar, Straus & Giroux, 1994.

Barnett, A. Doak. *The Making of Foreign Policy in China.* Boulder, CO: Westview Press, 1985.

Barnett, A. Doak and Edwin O. Reischauer, eds. *The United States and China: The Next Decade.* New York: Praeger, 1970.

Beloff, Max. *Soviet Policy in the Far East, 1944–1951.* Freeport, NY: Books for Libraries Press, 1971.

Bin, Yu. "The Study of Chinese Foreign Policy: Problems and Prospects." *World Politics* 46 (January 1994): 235–261.

Brzezinski, Zbigniew K. *Ideology and Power in Soviet Politics.* New York: Praeger, 1967.

———. comp. *Dilemmas of Change in Soviet Politics.* New York: Columbia University Press, 1969.

———. *The Grand Failure: The Birth and Death of Communism in the Twentieth Century.* New York: Scribner's, 1989.

Burbank, Jane. "Controversies over Stalinism: Searching for a Soviet Society." *Politics and Society* 19:3 (September 1991): 325–340.

Chang, Gordon H. *Friends and Enemies: The United States, China and the Soviet Union, 1948–1972.* Stanford, CA: Stanford University Press, 1990.

Charlton, Michael. *The Eagle and the Small Birds: Crisis in the Soviet Empire from Yalta to Solidarity.* Chicago: University of Chicago Press, 1985.

Chinese Communism Research Group, ed. "Introduction to the Central Archives." *CCP Research Newsletter* 88 (Spring 1993): 29–47.

Cohen, Stephen. *Bukharin and the Bolshevik Revolution: A Political Biography, 1888–1938.* New York: A. A. Knopf, 1973.

———. *An End to Silence: Uncensored Opinion in the Soviet Union from Roy Medvedev's Underground Magazine Political Diary.* New York: Norton, 1982.

———. *Rethinking the Soviet Experience.* New York: Oxford University Press, 1985.

Cohen, Stephen, Alexander Rabinowitz, and Robert Sharlett, eds. *The Soviet Union since Stalin.* Bloomington: Indiana University Press, 1980.

Cohen, Warren I. *America's Response to China.* New York: Wiley, 1971.

Cohen, Warren I., and Dorothy Borg, eds. *New Frontiers in American–East Asian Relations.* New York: Columbia University Press, 1983.

Conquest, Robert. *The Great Terror: Stalin's Purge of the Thirties.* New York: Macmillan, 1968.

———. *The Great Terror: A Reassessment.* New York: Oxford University Press, 1990.

Cumings, Bruce. *The Origins of the Korean War.* 2 vols. Princeton, NJ: Princeton University Press, 1981, 1990.

Dallin, David. *From Purge to Coexistence: Essays on Stalin's and Khrushchev's Russia.* Chicago: Henry Regnery, 1964.

———. *Soviet Russia and the Far East.* Hamden, CT: Archon Books, 1971.

Di, He. "The Most Respected Enemy: Mao Zedong's Perception of the United States." *China Quarterly* 137 (March 1994): 144–158.

Dittmer, Lowell. *Sino-Soviet Normalization and Its International Implications, 1945–1990.* Seattle: University of Washington Press, 1992.

Fainsod, Merle. *How Russia Is Ruled.* Cambridge: Harvard University Press, 1954.

Fairbank, John K., ed. *The Chinese World Order.* Cambridge: Harvard University Press, 1968.

Fitzgerald, C. P. *The Chinese View of Their Place in the World.* London: Oxford University Press, 1964.

Fleron, Frederick J., Jr., and Erik P. Hoffman. "Sovietology and Perestroika: Methodology and Lessons from the Past." *Harriman Institute Forum* (September 1991).

Frankel, Charles H., Jr., ed. "Sins of the Scholars." *National Interest* no. 31 (Spring 1993): 67–122.

Friedman, Edward, and Mark Selden, eds. *America's Asia: Dissenting Essays on Asian-American Relations.* New York: Random House, Vintage, 1969.

Friedrich, Carl, and Zbigniew Brzezinski. *Totalitarian Dictatorship and Autocracy.* New York: Praeger, 1956.

Gendlin, Gerry. "Accessing the Archives of the Former Soviet Union." *Perspectives* (American Historical Association Newsletter) 32:3 (March 1994): 7–8.

Getty, J. Arch. *Origins of the Great Purges: The Soviet Communist Party Reconsidered, 1933–1938.* New York: Cambridge University Press, 1985.

Ginsburgs, George. *Soviet Works on Korea, 1945–1970.* Los Angeles: University of Southern California Press, 1973.

Goldstein, Steven M., and Di He. "New Chinese Sources on the History of the Cold War." *Cold War International History Project Bulletin* 1 (Spring 1992): 4–6.

Goncharov, Sergei N., John W. Lewis, and Litai Xue. *Uncertain Partners: Stalin, Mao, and the Korean War.* Stanford, CA: Stanford University Press, 1993.

Gottlieb, Thomas. *Chinese Foreign Policy Factionalism and the Origins of the Strategic Triangle.* Report R-1902-NA. Santa Monica, CA: Rand, 1977.

Grimsted, Patricia K. *A Handbook for Archival Research in the USSR.* Washington and Princeton, NJ: International Research and Exchange Board (IREX), 1989, and Supplement I, *Major Archives and Manuscript Depositories in Moscow and Leningrad,* 1991.

———. "Beyond Perestroika: Soviet Area Archives after the August Coup." *American Archivist* 55:1 (December 1992): 94–122.

———. *Archives in Russia: 1993, A Brief Directory.* Moscow and Washington: International Research and Exchange Board (IREX), 1993.

Hammond, Thomas T., comp. and ed. *Soviet Foreign Relations and World Communism: Annotated Bibliography of 7,000 Books in 30 Languages.* Princeton, NJ: Princeton University Press, 1966.

Heinrichs, Waldo, and Dorothy Borg, eds. *Uncertain Years: Chinese American Relations, 1947–1950.* New York: Columbia University Press, 1980.

Hershberg, James D. "Soviet Nuclear History" and other articles. *Cold War International History Project Bulletin,* no. 4 (Fall 1994): most of the entire issue.

Hershberg, James D., et al. "Report from Moscow." *Cold War International History Project Bulletin* 1 (Spring 1992): 1, 16–29.

Hinton, Harold C. *China's Turbulent Quest.* Bloomington: Indiana University Press, 1972.

Holloway, David. *Stalin and the Bomb: The Soviet Union and Atomic Energy, 1939–1956.* New Haven, CT: Yale University Press, 1994.

Horak, Stephen M., ed. *Russia, the USSR and Eastern Europe: A Bibliographic Guide to English Language Publications, 1964–1974.* Littleton, CO: Libraries Unlimited, 1978.

Hough, Jerry F. *Russia and the West.* New York: Simon and Schuster, 1988.

Hough, Jerry F., and Merle Fainsod. *How Russia Is Governed.* Cambridge: Harvard University Press, 1979.

Hua, Qingzhao. *From Yalta to Panmunjom: Truman's Diplomacy and the Four Powers, 1945–1953.* Ithaca, NY: Cornell University Press, 1993.

Hunt, Michael H., and Odd Arne Westad. "The Chinese Communist and International Affairs: A Field Report on New Historical Sources and Old Research Problems." *China Quarterly* 122 (June 1990): 258–272.

Kanet, Roger E. *Soviet and East European Foreign Policy: A Bibliography of English and Russian Language Publications, 1967–1971.* Santa Barbara, CA: ABC-Clio, 1974.

Kim, Ilpyong, ed. *The Strategic Triangle: China, the United States and the Soviet Union.* New York: Paragon House, 1987.

Kramer, Mark. "Archival Research in Moscow: Progress and Pitfalls." *Cold War International History Project Bulletin* 3 (Fall 1993): 1, 18–39.

Khrushchev, Nikita. *Khrushchev Remembers.* 2 vols. Trans. Strobe Talbott. Boston: Little, Brown, 1970, 1974.

Kovalchenko, I. D. *Issledovanie istiny samo dolzhno byt' stinno* (Factual research should itself be factual). *Kommunist* (Communist), no. 2 (1989).

Kozicki, Henry, ed. *Western and Russian Historiography.* New York: St. Martin's Press, 1993.

Kubek, Anthony. *How the Far East Was Lost.* Chicago: Regnery, 1963.

Kuppes, Johannes. "Die Pandores-Buchse Sowjetisher Archive Offnentsich" (The Soviet archives' Pandora's box is opened). *Deutschland Archiv* (German archive) 6 (June 1992): 639–643.

Leskov, Sergei. "An Unreliable Witness [Pavel Sudoplatov]." *Bulletin of the Atomic Scientists* 50:4 (July–August 1994): 33–36.

Liang, Chin-tung. *General Stillwell in China: The Full Story, 1942–44.* New York: St. Johns University Press, 1972.

Li, Zhisui, with Anne Thurston. *The Private Life of Chairman Mao.* New York: Random House, 1994.

Luo, Jungqu, and Xiangze Jiang. "Research in Sino-American Relations in the People's Republic of China." In Warren Cohen and Dorothy Borg, eds., *New Frontiers in American–East Asian Relations.* New York: Columbia University Press, 1983.

McCagg, William O., Jr. *Stalin Embattled, 1945–1948.* Detroit, MI: Wayne State University Press, 1978.

McMillan, Priscilla Johnson. "Flimsy Memoirs [Pavel Sudoplatov]." *Bulletin of the Atomic Scientists* 50:4 (July–August 1994): 30–33.

Malia, Martin. *The Soviet Tragedy: A History of Socialism in Russia, 1917–1991.* New York: Free Press, 1994.

Mao Zedong. *Jianguo Yilai Mao Zedong Wengao Diyi Ce, 1949.9–1950.12* (Mao Zedong's manuscripts since the founding of the republic, volume 1, September 1949–December 1950): Beijing: Central Press of Historical Documents, 1987.

Mark, Eduard. "October or Thermidor? Interpretations of Stalinism and the Perceptions of Soviet Foreign Policy in the United States, 1927–1947." *American Historical Review* 94 (October 1989): 937–962.

May, Ernest A., and James C. Thomson, Jr., eds. *American–East Asian Relations, A Survey.* Cambridge: Harvard University Press, 1972.

Medvedev, Roy A. *On Stalin and Stalinism.* New York: Oxford University Press, 1979.
———. *Let History Judge: The Origins and Consequences of Stalinism.* Rev. New York: Columbia University Press, 1989; orig. ed., 1971.

Moss William. *Archives in the People's Republic of China.* Washington, DC: Smithsonian Archives, 1993.

Nagai, Yonosuke, and Akira Iriye. *The Origins of the Cold War in Asia.* New York: Columbia University Press, 1977.

Okinshevich, Leo, comp. *United States History and Historiography in Postwar Soviet Writing, 1945–1970: A Bibliography.* Santa Barbara, CA: ABC-Clio, 1976.

Peck, James. "America and the Chinese Revolution." In Ernest R. May and James C. Thomson, Jr., eds., *American–East Asian Relations: A Survey.* Cambridge: Harvard University Press, 1972.

Pipes, Richard. *The Formation of the Soviet Union, Communism and Nationalism, 1917–1923.* Cambridge: Harvard University Press, 1954.
———. "Militarism and the Soviet State." *Daedalus* 109 (Fall 1980): 1–12.
———. *Russia Observed: Collected Essays on Russian and Soviet History.* Boulder, CO: Westview Press, 1989.

Powers, Thomas. "Were the Atomic Scientists Spies?" *New York Review of Books,* June 9, 1994, pp. 10–18.

Rutland, Peter. "Sovietology: Notes for a Post Mortem." *National Interest,* no. 31 (Spring 1993): 109–123.

Schecter, Jerrold L., with Vyocheslav V. Luchkov, trans. and ed. *Khrushchev Remembers: The Glasnost Tapes.* Boston: Little, Brown, 1990.

Schneir, Walter. "Time Bomb." *Nation,* December 3, 1990, pp. 682–688.
———. "Sudo-History." *Nation,* June 6, 1994, pp. 804–808.

Schram, Stuart, ed., *Chairman Mao Talks to the People: Talks and Letters, 1956–1971.* New York: Pantheon, 1974a.
———. "Mao Tse-Tung: A Self Portrait." *China Quarterly* 57 (January–March 1974b): 156–165.

Schwartz, Benjamin I. *Communism and China: Ideology in Flux.* Cambridge: Harvard University Press, 1968.

Segal, Gerald. *The Great Power Triangle.* London: Macmillan, 1982.

Shambaugh, David. *Beautiful Imperialist: China Perceives America, 1972–1990.* Princeton, NJ: Princeton University Press, 1991.

Sheng, Michael. "The United States, the Chinese Communist Party, and the Soviet Union, 1948–1950: A Reappraisal." *Pacific Historical Review* 63:4 (November 1994): 521–536.

Shi, Zhe. *Zai lishi Jjen shenbian* (Together with historical giants: Shi Zhe's memoirs). Beijing: Central Press of Historical Documents, 1991.

Shih, Chih-yu. *The Spirt of Chinese Foreign Policy: A Psychocultural View.* New York: St. Martin's Press, 1990.

Shrader, Charles R. *Communist Logistics in the Korean War.* Westport, CT: Greenwood Press, 1995.

Simes, Dimitri K. "Russia's Imperial Consensus." *Washington Post National Weekly,* January 2–8, 1995 pp. 23–24.

Southerland, Daniel. "The Horrors of Mao." *Washington Post National Weekly,* August 1–7, 1994, p. 6.

Sudoplatov, Pavel A. "Letter to appear in paperback edition of *Special Tasks.*" *Cold War International History Project Bulletin,* no. 5 (Spring 1995): 156–158.

Sudoplatov, Pavel, and Anatoli Sudoplatov, with Jerrold L. and Leona P. Schecter. *Special Tasks: The Memoirs of an Unwanted Witness—a Soviet Spymaster.* Boston: Little, Brown, 1994.

Teiwes, Frederick C. "Interviews on Party History." *CCP Research Newsletter* 10/11 (Spring–Fall 1992): 1–15.

Thompson, Anthony, ed. *Russia/U.S.S.R.* World Bibliography Series 6. Santa Barbara, CA: ABC-Clio, 1979.

Thurston, Robert W. "Stalinism and Professionalism: A Reply to Jane Burbank" and "Burbank Responds." *Politics and Society* 20:3 (September 1993): 367–377.

Time, ed. "Thanks to Them," October 1, 1990, p. 75.

Tsou, Tang. *America's Failure in China, 1941–1950.* 2 vols. Chicago: University of Chicago Press, 1963.

Tucker, Robert C. *Forces for Change in Soviet Society.* Santa Monica, CA: Rand, 1956.

———. *The Soviet Political Mind: Stalinism and Post-Stalin Change.* New York: Praeger, 1963.

———. *The Soviet Political Mind: Stalinism and Post-Stalin Change.* New York: Norton, 1971.

———. *Stalin in Power: The Revolution from Above, 1928–1941.* New York: W. W. Norton, 1990.

Utley, Freda. *The China Story.* Chicago: Regnery, 1951.

Van Ness, Peter. "Three Lines in Chinese Foreign Relations." In Dorothy Solinger, ed., *Three Visions of Chinese Socialism.* Boulder, CO: Westview Press. 1984.

Volkogonov, Dimitrii A. *Stalin: Triumph and Tragedy.* London: Weidenfeld and Nicholson, 1991.

———. "Unlocking Russia's Unknown History." *Prologue* 24:4 (Winter 1992): 353–360.

———. *Lenin: A New Biography.* Trans. Harold Shukman. New York: Free Press, 1994.

Ward, Chris. *Stalin's Russia.* New York: Routledge, 1993.

Westad, Odd Arne. "The Foreign Policy Archives of Russia: New Regulations for Declassifications and Access." *Newsletter Society for Historians of American Foreign Relations.* 23:2 (June 1992a): 1–9.

———. "Materials on CCP History in Russian Archives." *CCP Research Newsletter* 10–11 (Spring–Fall 1992b): 52–53.

Whiting, Allen. *China Crosses the Yalu: The Decision to Enter the Korean War.* Stanford, CA: Stanford University Press, 1960.

Xu, Yan. "The Chinese Forces and Their Casualties in the Korean War: Facts and Statistics." Trans. Li Xiaobing. *Chinese Historians* 6:2 (Fall 1993): 45–58.

Yahuda, Michael. *China's Role in World Affairs.* New York: St. Martin's Press, 1978.

"Z" (Martin Malia). "To the Stalin Mausoleum." *Daedalus* (Winter 1990): 295–344.

Zhu, Yuanshi. "Liu Shaoqi 1949 Nian Mimi Fangsu" (Liu Shaoqi's secret visit to the Soviet Union in 1949). *Dangde Wenxian* (Party documents) 3 (1991).

Zhai, Qiang. "Recent Chinese Writings on 1945–1955: Sino-U.S. Relations." *Newsletter of Society for Historians of American Foreign Relations* 20:4 (December 1989): 75–84.

———. "The Making of Chinese Communist Foreign Relations, 1935–1949: A New Study from China." *Journal of American–East Asian Relations* 1:4 (Winter 1992): 471–477.

Zhongguo renmin Zhiyuanjum knagMei yuanChao (A battle history of resistance to America and aid to Korea by the Chinese people's Volunteer Army). Beijing: Junohi Kexue, 1988.

Zubok, Vladislav, and Constantine Pleshakov. "The Soviet Union." In David Reynolds, ed., *The Origins of the Cold War in Europe: An International Perspective.* New Haven and London: Yale University Press and St. Edmundsbury, 1994.

11   Chinese Policy and the Korean War

Chen Jian

When Mao Zedong's government sent the "Chinese People's Volunteers" to fight in the Korean War in October 1950, the newly established Chinese communist regime had just celebrated its first anniversary. Mao Zedong's revolutionary regime faced enormous challenges on the home front, among them, achieving political consolidation, rebuilding a war-shattered economy, and finishing reunification of the country. Why, then, did the Beijing leadership decide to send troops to Korea? What was the Chinese experience during the Korean War? What role did China play in the beginning, continuation, and conclusion of the war?

The pursuit of scholarly answers to these questions has long been hindered by the absence of access to reliable Chinese sources. Before the mid-1980s, most studies about China's involvement in the war had to rely on information gleaned from contemporary Chinese newspapers and official statements, and it was difficult for scholars to draw a comprehensive picture about the scope and changing process of Chinese involvement in Korea, let alone provide an accurate account of Beijing's decision making. As a result, scholars had to speculate on Beijing's motives and intentions during various stages of the war.

The end of the cold war, echoed by the continuous flourishing of China's reform and opening policy, changed the situation. Since the mid-1980s, many fresh and meaningful materials concerning China's involvement in the Korean War have been released, offering the opportunity to reexamine China's experiences during the war. This chapter reviews the literature on China and the Korean War in both Chinese and English. Although it covers all important issues related to Chinese policy toward the Korean War, its emphasis is China's entry into the war.

UNDER THE INFLUENCE OF THE COLD WAR:
THE EARLY SCHOLARSHIP

The Korean War erupted as the cold war was escalating. Accordingly, the study of China's relations with the war, in both the West and in China, was strongly influenced by the intensifying cold war atmosphere. Although Western and Chinese scholars differed dramatically in their interpretations of the war's origins, process, and consequences, they seemingly shared one common feature in their studies: consciously or unconsciously they tried to use the study of the war to prove that the other side had been the guilty party.

Throughout the 1950s, scholars in the West generally viewed China's involvement in the war as a reflection of a well-coordinated communist plot of worldwide expansion. They argued that the entire international communist movement obeyed Moscow's monolithic leadership, that neither Beijing nor Pyongyang had the freedom to make its own foreign policy decisions, and that the Korean conflict was in essence part of a life-and-death confrontation between the communists and the "free world." The North Korean invasion of the South, as viewed by President Harry Truman, as well as many later students of the Korean War, represented the first step in a general communist plot to "pass from subversion" to "armed invasion and war" in their scheme of world conquest. Correspondingly, Beijing's involvement in the Korean War was regarded as an action subordinate to Moscow's overall cold war strategy. Scholars in the West widely believed that Beijing's policy behavior was aggressive, violent, and irrational.

Chinese scholars angrily challenged these interpretations by demanding that it was the "U.S. imperialists" and their "lackeys" who should be held responsible for starting and then expanding the war. They argued that Washington, as the head of the declining yet still aggressive international capitalist camp, had been eager to establish a reactionary American hegemony in the Asian-Pacific region after World War II, which inevitably led to American aggression in Korea and Taiwan. In face of the American threat to vital interests of revolutionary China, China had no other choice but to fight to beat the threats from the U.S. imperialists. China's involvement in the Korean War, according to the standard interpretation by Chinese scholars in the 1950s and 1960s, was an action necessary for serving China's national security interests, promoting the country's socialist revolution and construction, and defending the safety of the "east gate" of the socialist camp. They thus called China's Korean War experience the "Great War to Resist America and Assist Korea."

Neither Chinese nor Western scholars had been able to use first-hand Chinese source materials to support their studies during the 1950s and 1960s. Almost all Western studies about Chinese policy toward Korea were based on information obtained from Chinese newspapers, journal articles, and broadcasts. The studies by Chinese scholars used only what had been provided by the government in Beijing, and few of them bothered to supply footnotes to support their arguments. These "studies," not surprising at all, are of little scholarly value.

THE EMERGENCE OF THE "CHINA UNDER THREAT" THESIS

A real breakthrough in the study of China's involvement in the Korean War came in 1960, when Allen S. Whiting published his highly acclaimed study, *China Crosses the Yalu: The Decision to Enter the Korean War.* Using both Western intelligence sources (which Whiting, an American diplomat, was in a privileged position to access) and Chinese journal and newspaper information, Whiting challenged many of the prevailing interpretations of the dynamics of Beijing's decision to enter the Korean War, arguing that the decision was the result of a series of highly rational considerations. He pointed out that unlike the Soviet Union, the People's Republic of China (PRC) did not directly participate in the planning for the North Korean invasion of the South. After the outbreak of the war, he believed, Beijing tried to terminate the conflict through political settlement, and only after the attempts for a political solution failed in late August 1950 did Beijing begin necessary military preparations, in early September. He emphasized that after the Inchon landing, Beijing tried both public and private channels to prevent UN forces from crossing the 38th parallel. Beijing entered the war only after all warnings had been ignored by Washington and, therefore, in the Beijing leadership's judgment, the safety of the Chinese-Korean border was severely menaced. Whiting thus concluded that Beijing's management of the Korean crisis was based primarily on a perception that the United States threatened China's national security interests. Although Whiting lacked access to Chinese archival materials and as a result had to focus on the analysis of the environment in which the Beijing leadership made its decision to go to war than on a close examination of the decision-making process, his study was a landmark in the field. His "China under threat" thesis, which emphasized a need to understand Beijing's security concerns, would strongly influence an entire generation of scholars in the West.

In the late 1960s and early 1970s, when China was experiencing the Cultural Revolution, which made any meaningful historical study impossible, a more critical perspective on the cold war in general and the Sino-American confrontation in Korea in particular emerged in the West. In the wake of the American debacle in Vietnam, the beginning of the normalization of the relations between Beijing and Washington, and the declassification of new archival documentation in Western countries, especially the United States, many Western scholars became more critical toward the U.S. presence in East Asia than their predecessors had been. In regard to China's involvement in the Korean War, several scholars, such as Melvin Gurtov and Robert Simmons, followed Allen Whiting's footsteps, paying more attention to Chinese communist leaders' concerns for China's national security as a decisive factor in Beijing's decision making. They generally argued that Beijing did not welcome the Korean War because Mao Zedong and his comrades faced difficult tasks of economic reconstruction and political consolidation at home and gave priority to liberating nationalist-controlled Taiwan. Many of these scholars stressed that Beijing's decision to enter the Korean War was simply a reluctant reaction to the imminent threats to the physical security of Chinese territory. While most scholars believed that the American decision to cross the 38th parallel triggered China's intervention, some speculated that if UN forces had stopped at the parallel, China would not have intervened.

Two books published in the 1970s are particularly important. In *China under Threat* (1980) Melvin Gurtov and Byong-moo Hwang devoted a chapter to China's involvement in Korea. Although the book had taken a domestic-primacy approach in reconstructing the objectives and motives of Beijing's foreign policy, arguing that "the chief purpose of foreign policy in China is to protect and promote the radical socialist revolution at home," its main thesis echoed Whiting's findings. Gurtov and Hwang believed that Beijing's entrance into the Korean War has to be understood in the context of the imminent threat posed to China's physical security by UN forces' marching toward the Yalu. They argued that "China's central concern [in sending troops to Korea] was to stop invading UN forces at the doorstep of the northeast region, to prevent the spread of the war into Chinese territory."

Robert R. Simmons, in *The Strained Alliance* (1975), focused on the relationship among Pyongyang, Beijing, and Moscow. He argued that the origin of the Korean War was a peninsular phenomenon. The outbreak of the war was a logical outgrowth of the tensions accumulated in Korea's political development in the years after the end of World War II. By stressing that the relationship of the Chinese, Soviet, and Korean communists had been rigid prior to the Korean War, Simmons suggested that neither China nor the Soviet Union should be viewed as responsible for the war.

This interpretation, regarding the Korean War as a revolutionary civil war (which was later turned into a international war by Washington's decision to intervene), gained full strength in Bruce Cumings' highly influential, and controversial, two-volume study, *The Origins of the Korean War*, published, respectively, in 1981 and 1990. Focusing on the indigenous roots of the war, Cumings closely examined the emerging confrontations between the revolutionary and counterrevolutionary forces in the peninsula prior to the war's outbreak, arguing that Moscow played no significant role in bringing about a military conflict in Korea. His study of China's connection with the war was compatible with his thesis. By carefully reading the inner-party documents and propaganda materials of the Korean communists captured during the war, he pointed out that the strategies and practices of the Chinese revolution had more profound impacts on the Korean revolutionaries than did those of the Soviet Union. He also argued that as the North Korean communists had provided their Chinese comrades with substantial support during China's civil war from 1946 to 1949 and as the ties between the Chinese and North Korean communists had been very close, "in retrospect, what a historian would have trouble explaining is why the Chinese did not intervene in the Korean War." Although the new flood of Chinese and Russian sources has undermined the circumstantial evidence that Cumings used to build his arguments, such as that Moscow played no significant role in North Korea's invasion of the South, his thesis that the Korean War was in essence a revolutionary civil war still deserves scholarly attention.

The 1980s also witnessed the efforts of several Western scholars to study the Chinese experience during the Korean War by gaining new information through interviews with Chinese. Warren I. Cohen (1987), after conversing with Zhou Enlai's former associates in Beijing, wrote that Mao and his comrades had been shocked by the outbreak of the war and that Beijing made the decision to dispatch troops to Korea at a time when the U.S.-led UN forces, ignoring all of Beijing's warnings, marched toward the Yalu. Anthony Farrar-Hockley (1984), after extensive interviews with former Chinese POWs, reported the Beijing leaders had transferred large numbers of troops into Manchuria months before deciding to enter the war. British author Russell Spurr's (1988) book on China's decision to enter the war used a database of allegedly "extensive interviews" with the Chinese participants in the war. However, the book's overall strength was diminished by the author's inability to distinguish fact from hearsay and imagination. These studies (especially that of Cohen) have enriched our knowledge of certain aspects of China's involvement with the Korean War. In terms of the interpretations they have offered, however, Whiting's "China under threat" thesis has continued to dominate the field.

RECENT SCHOLARSHIP ON THE ORIGINS OF CHINESE INTERVENTION

A more fundamental change in the 1980s was the emergence of a variety of new Chinese sources: personal memoirs of those who were involved in Beijing's intervention in Korea, scholarly articles and monographs by Chinese researchers with archival access, official academic publications using classified documents, openly or internally published collections of the Chinese Communist Party's (CCP) Central Committee and regional bureau documents, and the internally published collections of Mao Zedong's papers. Although it is clear that these new sources were released on a selective basis and sometimes for purposes other than a desire to make the truth known, they nevertheless have created new opportunities for study.

Since the late 1980s and early 1990s, the prospect for new studies has been reinforced by the end of the cold war and the collapse of the former Soviet Union; scholars now have access to the documents that had been locked in the party's archives. Even with the tremendous difficulties created by the legacies of a bureaucratic system that had long been the symbol of the communist state and the chaos characterized by an unprecedented process of transition from socialism to market-oriented capitalism, scholars can now support their studies with evidence rather than educated guesses.

All of this became the background of a flood of publications on China's involvement in the Korean War in the 1990s. Because the origins of the war have long been a question of international attention and because most of the recently available materials are related in one way or another as to how the war started, a large portion of the new studies about China's involvement in Korea focus on Beijing's decision to enter the war.

Jonathan Pollack's "The Korean War and Sino-American Relations" (1989) was the first major effort by a Western scholar to use recently available Chinese sources for exploring China's involvement in the war. In his discussion of Beijing's motives for entering the conflict, Pollack reconfirmed Whiting's "China under threat" thesis, arguing that "Mao's paramount calculations concerned security." In 1990, Hao Yufan and Zhai Zhihai published an article in the *China Quarterly* on China's entry into the war with the support of information from interviews and documentary sources. They pointed out that Stalin and Kim Il-sung were the main designers of the attack on the South; Beijing, although having been informed of "Kim's plans," did not play an active role in the coming of the war. They also pointed out that the relationship between the Chinese and Soviet communists in the early 1950s was close but not harmonious. Not until Beijing's leaders sent Chinese troops into Korea would Stalin begin to believe Mao Zedong was not another Josip Tito. In regard to Beijing's motives for entering the war, although claiming that they attempted to offer an alternative to Whiting's interpretations, Hao and Zhai virtually followed Whiting's thesis, arguing that it was a deep-rooted security concern related to the defense of China's border safety that drove Mao and his fellow leaders to enter the Korean conflict.

Michael Hunt's (1992) article indicates that Beijing's motives underlying its decision to enter the Korean war were more complicated. Although concerns for defending China's northeast border certainly played a decisive role in bringing Mao Zedong and his comrades in Beijing to a decision to dispatch troops to Korea, Hunt calls scholars' attention to other factors that influenced the decision-making process, such as Mao's sense of "an international duty to rescue the beleaguered Korean revolution and to help maintain revolutionary morale around the world" and the concerns over the "revival of reactionary sentiment in China and elsewhere in Asia." Hunt particularly points out that top CCP leaders had been divided on whether to send troops to Korea, and he warned that "any effort to pin down the exact motive behind Mao's decision to intervene must enter a mind as complicated as the crisis it wrestled with."

Zhang Shuguang's (1992) and Thomas J. Christensen's (1992) work on China during the war concern the deterrence approach but have widely different perspectives. Zhang's work, *Deterrence and Strategic Culture,* finds that the strategic considerations of Beijing's leaders around 1949–1950 were defensive by nature. While Mao and his comrades perceived the "American threats" presented to the "new China," they used every means available to deter further American menace to China's vital national security interests. During the early stage of the war, Beijing's every movement sought to deter the perceived American attempt to bring the war to China. When Chinese troops finally entered the war in October 1950, their military operational plans were still designed for deterrence. Zhang also argued that American policies in East Asia and Korea were designed for deterrence. Thus, Zhang draws a picture of a confrontation between two actors (China and the United States) who had adopted a defensive and deterrent policy against each other but perceived the other side as the attacker. Zhang therefore calls for the need to study the interactions between the misperceptions and differences caused by different strategic cultures.

Christensen, in his article "Threats, Assurances, and the Last Chance for Peace," uses new Chinese sources to challenge the traditional deterrence interpretation of China's decision to enter the Korean War. He argues that the origins of Beijing's intervention in Korea had been a complicated process and that Mao reached the decision to enter the war with reluctance. In choosing intervention, Mao considered not only what would follow if China were to enter the war but also, and more fundamentally, calculated what would occur if China failed to do so. He found that the financial and domestic political prices were too high for him not to intervene. Christensen thus suggests that the standard deterrence theory was too simplistic in describing the interactions of Beijing's and Washington's policies, especially because that theory has failed to take the highly complicated background of Beijing's decision for intervention into its consideration.

An international team composed of three top scholars, Sergei N. Goncharov, John W. Lewis, and Xue Litai, coming respectively from Russian, American, and Chinese backgrounds, published in late 1993, *Uncertain Partners: Stalin, Mao and the Korean War,* a comprehensive new study of the making of the Sino-Soviet alliance and its relationship to the origins of the Korean War. Basing their study on an impressive use of new Chinese and Russian sources, the three authors demonstrated that the relationship of Beijing, Moscow, and Pyongyang had long been complex. Although both Mao and Stalin were communists, their policymaking was nevertheless determined primarily by their perceptions of China's and the Soviet Union's national security interests, which differed sharply in terms of goals, means, and emphases in 1949 and 1950. When Mao visited the Soviet Union from December 1949 to February 1950, he had to overcome the barriers presented to him by a highly suspicious Stalin, who neither trusted Mao nor was willing to grant Mao with the freedom of action in East Asia. Kim Il-sung sensed the divergences between Beijing and Moscow and used them to win the backing of both Moscow and Beijing for his plans to invade the South. Consequently, a "reckless war-making of the worst kind" came into being.

In interpreting Beijing's motives to enter the war, the three authors, like Whiting and many others, emphasized Mao's concerns for China's national security interests, defined mainly as the concern over the need to defend China's physical safety (including the defense of the Chinese-Korean borders and the maintenance of Beijing's influences over traditional Chinese spheres of suzerainty). They argued that after the outbreak of the Korean War, the Beijing leadership reluctantly turned its main attention from Taiwan to Korea, a major contribution of the book being to link Beijing's Korean policy with the Taiwan question. Throughout the process the Beijing leaders used in deciding to enter the war, Mao and his comrades had to deal with not only the pressure caused by the intensifying crisis in Korea but also the problems brought about by their Soviet ally. The most serious challenge the Beijing leadership had to face came on the eve of China's entry into the Korean War, when Stalin reneged on his promise that the Soviet Union would provide the Chinese land forces with an air umbrella in Korea. Still Mao decided to enter the war; in the long run, however, a Chinese-Soviet split became inevitable.

In 1994, Columbia University Press published Chen Jian's *China's Road to the Korean War: The Making of the Sino-American Confrontation,* a comprehensive study based on a critical use of recently available Chinese sources. Challenging the widely accepted notion that Beijing's decision to enter the Korean War had been a response to the American mistake of crossing the 38th parallel, Chen argues that China's entry was determined by more complicated factors. Chen points out that while it is true that Mao and his comrades as China's leaders had to base their foreign policymaking in general and their management of the Korean crisis in particular on concerns over China's national security interests, it should be noted that their definition of such interests had been penetrated by a revolutionary agenda. Domestically, Mao and the CCP leadership were eager to strengthen the inner dynamics of the revolution, so that it would continue to advance after nationwide victory. Internationally, they were willing to pursue China's central position in the international community. Communist China thus emerged as a revolutionary power, which had its own language and behaved according to its own code of norms in international affairs. All of this made Beijing collide with Washington even before the outbreak of the Korean War. In addition to safeguarding China's physical security, Beijing's management of the Korean crisis had to be understood in the context of the escalating confrontation between communist China and the United States in East Asia in 1949 and 1950. Moreover, in pinning down Beijing's motives, one has to take into consideration the CCP's need to turn the outside pressure into the dynamics for mobilizing the Chinese population under its terms, and one should never forget that Mao and his comrades were eager to revitalize China's great power status through the promotion of revolutions following the Chinese model. Chen thus calls scholars' attention to the need to redefine the rationale underlying China's foreign policy in general and Beijing's management of the Korean crisis in particular.

In contrast, the interpretations offered by Chinese writers on the Great War to Resist America and Assist Korea that appeared in the late 1980s and early 1990s have hardly changed their previous orientations. Almost all Chinese authors continued to argue that the Beijing leadership did not welcome the Korean War because China faced difficult tasks of economic reconstruction and political consolidation at home and had to give priority to liberating nationalist-controlled Taiwan. They stress that the Chinese decision to enter the war was simply a reaction to the threats to China's security interests created by the UN forces' march toward the Yalu. While most scholars believe that the American decision to cross the 38th parallel triggered China's intervention, some scholars assume that if the UN forces had stopped at the parallel, China would not have intervened. Accordingly, they argue that China's aims in participating in the Korean War were solely to defend the Chinese-Korean border.

These interpretations have been challenged by new Chinese writing. For example, Beijing's active preparations for entering the war started as early as mid-July 1950, almost two months before the Inchon landing. In defining Beijing's war aims while making the decision to send troops to Korea in early October 1950, Mao Zedong made it clear that he aimed to drive the American forces out of the Korean peninsula so that not only China's security interests but also the interests of the "Eastern revolution" would be served. He would not give up the goal of pursuing total victory in Korea until mid-1951, when Chinese troops in Korea suffered a major setback in their fifth offensive campaign. All of this points out that Beijing's management of the Korean War had a nature more complicated than a simple response to the American mistake of crossing the 38th parallel and more aggressive than the mere defense of China's physical safety.

In an overall sense, compared with the situation of five years, or even two or three years, earlier, our knowledge of China's entry into the Korean War and the causes underlying it has been improved dramatically as the result of the availability of new Chinese materials and the new scholarship based on these sources. In my opinion, new interpretations in five areas are the most important:

1. The Chinese and North Korean communists had a close relationship prior to the outbreak of the Korean War. During China's civil war from 1946 to 1949, the Korean communists offered their comrades in Manchuria substantial support, which allowed the Chinese communists to occupy a favorable position in their life-and-death confrontation with the Chinese nationalist forces. From summer 1949 to spring 1950, as many as 50,000 to 70,000 Korean-nationality Chinese People's Liberation Army soldiers returned from China to Korea, where they would play a crucial role in North Korea's invasion of the South. However, problems did exist between the Chinese and North Korean Communists. Kim Il-sung would not visit Beijing to inform Mao Zedong and the CCP leadership of his plans to attack the South until mid-May 1950, and possibly he did not inform Beijing of the exact schedule of the invasion.

2. The relationship between Beijing and Moscow was close yet not always harmonious. The Sino-Soviet alliance treaty signed in February 1950 during Mao Zedong's visit to the Soviet Union symbolized a high level of cooperation between China and the Soviet Union, resulting in a major Soviet commitment to the supply of military equipment to China and the defense of China's territorial security if threatened by hostile imperialist forces. Further, during Mao's stay at Moscow, he and Stalin discussed the Korean issue, giving Kim Il-sung a de facto green light for the latter's plan to attack the South. The outbreak of the war, however, made it clear to the Beijing leadership that the reliability of the Sino-Soviet alliance was by no means unlimited. Mao and his comrades would learn with great disappointment in October 1950, on the eve of their dispatch of Chinese troops to Korea, that the Soviet Union would not provide the Chinese forces in Korea with an air umbrella until at least two months later and that Stalin would ask his Chinese comrades to pay for the military equipment they were to obtain from the Soviet Union.

3. The Beijing leadership started its preparations to enter the war early in July 1950, when Mao Zedong ordered the formation of the Northeast Border Defense Army. On August 5 and 18, Mao twice set up deadlines for Chinese troops to complete preparations for entering operations in Korea, respectively for the end of August and the end of September. On the eve of the Inchon landing, during which the UN forces recaptured Seoul in September 1950, Mao pushed the Chinese military to accelerate

preparations to enter the war. In the meantime, Beijing started mobilizing all of China by introducing the nationwide "Great Movement to Resist America and Assist Korea."

4. Mao Zedong played a crucial role at every juncture of the Beijing leadership's making of a decision to send troops to Korea. Although top Chinese communist leaders had differing views on whether China should enter the conflict, Mao used both his wisdom and authority to convince his colleagues at the party's Politburo that to enter the war was China's only choice. Chen Jian (1994) thus claims that "without Mao's leadership role, Beijing's response to the Korean crisis could have been dramatically different."

5. When Mao Zedong and his fellow leaders made the decision to send Chinese troops to Korea, they hoped to win a glorious victory by driving the American and "puppet" forces out of the Korean peninsula. They thought the war would be regional, conventional, short, and limited (as opposed to a total war); they neither anticipated that China's intervention would lead to a world war involving the two superpowers, nor believed it would evolve into a nuclear holocaust.

Nevertheless, we still do not fully understand the causes underlying and the process leading to China's entry into the war. For example: How solid was the Sino-Soviet alliance signed in February 1950, and in what ways was it related to the outbreak of the Korean War? What was the relation of the Taiwan question and the Korean question in the Beijing leadership's strategic thinking? When and in what way did Moscow promise Beijing that it would provide the Chinese ground forces in Korea with an air umbrella? To what extent and in what nature did the Beijing leadership have pre-knowledge of Kim Il-sung's schedule to attack the South? Our knowledge of these (and many other) questions is far from adequate.

RECENT SCHOLARSHIP ON CHINA'S WARTIME EXPERIENCES

In recent years, scholars have also made dramatic efforts to explore other issues related to China's involvement in the Korean War. Due to the continuous unavailability of key Chinese sources, however, the progress achieved is much less impressive than that it is in the study on China's entry into the war. Still there are several things to report.

Regarding China's attitude toward nuclear weapons during the Korean War, Mark A. Ryan (1989) has written a highly valuable monograph, *Chinese Attitudes toward Nuclear Weapons*. Basing his study on an extensive reading of available Chinese sources, Ryan carefully examines the changing Chinese perceptions of nuclear weapons and their impact on the Beijing leadership's management of the Korean crisis, as well as its command of Chinese military operations in Korea. He finds that Chinese treatment of nuclear weapons had been realistic in that it was based on the assessment of "the likelihood of American nuclear weapons use and the political preconditions underlying the U.S. consideration of such a decision." He further argues that China's Korean War experience had great impact on the future development of the country's strategic policy-making.

Although in Ryan's study one will not find how top Beijing leaders perceived the role of nuclear weapons while making important decisions, his excellent study of the general Chinese perception of nuclear weapons makes the information offered by new Chinese sources in this regard more understandable. In the practical formulation of its war strategy, according to new Chinese sources, top leaders in Beijing paid little attention to whether Americans would use nuclear weapons in Korea. The Beijing leadership's basic conviction was that the Korean conflict would be determined by ground operations, not by the use of the atomic bomb. If this is the case, one may now assume that, following Ryan's logic, Beijing's leaders understood the nature of the nuclear weapon and were convinced the weapon could not be used.

Ryan's study also touches on the Chinese claim that Americans conducted biological warfare and chemical warfare in Korea and in China's Northeast. According to new Chinese sources, in early 1952 both Chinese People's Volunteers' commanders in Korea and top Chinese leaders in Beijing truly believed that Americans had used biological weapons against the Chinese and North Koreans. On February 18, 1952, for example, Nie Rongzhen sent to Mao and Zhou a report pointing out that there was clear evidence that the Americans had been engaged in biological warfare in Korea. The next day, Mao read the report and instructed Zhou Enlai to "pay attention to this matter and take due measures to deal with it." Because no evidence has ever been produced on the American side to confirm this Chinese version of the story, what really happened in Korea in the winter of 1951–1952 must be regarded as one of the most mysterious aspects of the Korean War. In any case, though, there is no doubt that the Beijing leadership did find in this matter an effective weapon to confront Washington's use of the POW issue to gain a politically superior position.

Xu Yan (1990) and other military scholars in Beijing summarize China's changing military strategies during the war. Before China's entry into the war, Mao and Beijing's military planners believed that by outnumbering the enemy forces and possessing a higher morale, the Chinese troops, with the assistance of the North Koreans, would be able to fight an offensive war and drive Americans out of the peninsula. As the result of Stalin's reneging on providing the Chinese ground forces in Korea with an air umbrella, Mao had to change strategy by ordering his troops to maintain a defensive status for six months and then mount an offensive if the situation allowed. General MacArthur's careless march toward the Yalu offered the Chinese a golden opportunity to start successful sudden attacks, and from late October to early December 1950, the Chinese troops drove the American-headed UN forces back to the 38th parallel. Mao then insisted that the Chinese troops cross the 38th parallel and continue their offensive operations until the Americans had been kicked out of the peninsula. However, the overextension of Chinese supply lines and the lack of air support combined to make the Chinese offensive fruitless. Gradually realizing that the Chinese troops, lacking stable logistical supply and being poorly equipped, did not have the strength to win a total victory in Korea, Mao had to order a dramatic strategic change from one stressing offense to one of "positive defense" in summer 1951. In the meantime, Beijing had adopted a strategy of rotating Chinese troops in Korea in order to maintain combat effectiveness. From summer 1951 to summer 1953, the Chinese high command had focused on how to supply the troops in Korea, to prevent the Americans from landing in the rear of the Chinese–North Korean lines, and to hold every inch of land gained in the military confrontation along the 38th parallel.

In English literature, the Chinese military experience during the Korean War remains a weak linkage. Most authors treat China's changing military strategies as an element of the background of U.S.-UN military activities during the war. In order to establish a more comprehensive picture of China's military operations in Korea, it is of fundamental importance to pursue a scholarly dialogue between Chinese and Western scholars, as well as between the source materials on which they have conducted the study. We have seen some successful efforts in this regard, especially through Zhang Shuguang's forthcoming comprehensive study on how China fought the Korean War and John Toland's (1991) readable account of the Chinese experience during the war, yet the path ahead is long.

How did the war end? Almost all Chinese scholars, such as Chai Chengwen and Zhao Yongtian (1989), agree that China's initiative finally ended the war. New Chinese sources indicate that when armistice negotiations began in 1951, Chinese leaders and negotiators thought the war would end soon. Xu Yan (1990), Qi Dexue (1991), and Shen Zonghong and associates (1988), all leading scholars on the war, argue that the United States was unwilling to walk out of the war without claiming a victory, thus prolonging the fighting for another two years. Xu Yan and Qi Dexue particularly point out that in November 1951, Mao Zedong and Zhou Enlai believed that an armistice in Korea could be reached by the end of the year, and they failed to anticipate that the POW issue would become the single remaining obstacle to an armistice agreement. When the POW issue emerged, the Beijing leadership understood that this was a serious political struggle they could ill afford to lose. Both Xu Yan and Qi Dexue point out that Beijing viewed the military conflict in Korea as of a clear political nature. These interpretations need to be examined against other sources and the existing Western scholarship on the Korean War.

What were Chinese expenditures and casualties during the war? Xu Yan (1993) used archival sources for the facts and statistics about China's forces and casualties and points out that in spring 1953, Chinese forces in Korea reached a record high: 1.35 million. During the war, the total number of Chinese deaths reached 152,000, and the number of combat-related wounded soldiers was around 230,000. China's direct military expenditures during the war were about 10 billion yuan (equal to U.S. $2.7 billion), with 3 billion yuan of it spent on weapons and other military equipment purchased from the Soviet Union. A critical use of these figures, the most authoritative among all available statistics as of now, will offer a new basis on which new studies can be pursued.

In terms of the impact of the Korean War on China's domestic and foreign policies, many have argued that it was largely adverse. In addition to the loss of hundreds of thousands of soldiers on the battlefield and spending of billions of dollars for military purposes (at the expense of China's economic reconstruction), China's participation in the war prevented Beijing from recovering Taiwan, made Beijing more dependent on Moscow than before, and excluded Beijing from the UN until the early 1970s. Chen Jian, in the conclusion to *China's Road to the Korean War,* argues that, from Mao's perspective, China's gain through the Korean War was considerable: it stimulated a series of political and social revolutions in China that would otherwise have been inconceivable during the early stage of the PRC; it symbolized China's rise to prominence in the international arena; it helped strengthen Mao's leadership position within the Chinese Communist party; and it offered the Beijing leadership invaluable opportunities to test and redefine China's security strategy. In any case, the legacies of China's involvement in the Korean War have been felt in China and in other parts of the world long after the conclusion of the war.

CONCLUSION

The study of China's experience in the Korean War has achieved great progress in the past several years, but how to dig deeper into the origins, process, and consequences of China's involvement in the war remains a challenge to scholars. Scholars must now get access to Chinese sources. In actuality, most of the Chinese information that became available over the past decade was released on a highly selective basis and frequently for purposes other than having the truth known. Unless scholars, both Chinese and non-Chinese, are offered free and equal access to the original documents, there is always the possibility that a study might be misled by incomplete data.

It is equally important to pursue extensive and effective dialogues between scholars from different backgrounds and holding different views. The Korean War was simultaneously a civil war (especially as far as the origins of the war is concerned) and an international war. The study of it thus needs to reflect an international perspective while not ignoring the importance of the interplays of local, regional, and international developments. In this sense, we should regard the progress that has been achieved in the study of the Korean War as no more than a new point of departure.

REFERENCES

Chai Chengwen and Zhao Yongtian. *Banmendian tanpan* (The Panmunjom negotiations). Beijing: People's Liberation Army Press, 1989.

Chang, Gordon H. *Friends and Enemies: The United States, China, and the Soviet Union.* Stanford: Stanford University Press, 1990.

Chen Jian. "The Sino-Soviet Alliance and China's Entry into the Korean War." Working Paper 1, Cold War History Project. Washington, DC: Woodrow Wilson Center, December 1991.

———. "China's Changing Aims during the Korean War, 1950–1951." *Journal of American–East Asian Relations.* 1:1 (Spring 1992): 8–41.

———. *China's Road to the Korean War: The Making of Sino-American Confrontation.* New York: Columbia University Press, 1994.

Christensen, Thomas J. "Threats, Assurances, and the Last Chance for Peace: The Lessons of Mao's Korean War Telegrams." *International Security* 17:1 (Summer 1992): 122–154.

Cohen, Warren I. "Conversations with Chinese Friends: Zhou Enlai's Associates Reflect on Chinese American Relations in the 1940s and the Korean War." *Diplomatic History* 11:2 (1987): 283–289.

Cumings, Bruce. *The Origins of the Korean War.* 2 vols. Princeton: Princeton University Press, 1981, 1990.

Ding Xuesong, et al. "Recalling the Northeast Bureau's Special Office in North Korea during the War of Liberation in the Northeast." *Zhonggong dangshi ziliao* (Materials of CCP history), no. 17 (March 1986).

Du Ping. *Zai zhiyuanjun zongbu: Du Ping huiyilu* (My days at the headquarters of the Chinese People's Volunteers: Du Ping's memoirs). Beijing: People's Liberation Army Press, 1988.

Farrar-Hockley, Anthony. "A Reminiscence of the Chinese People's Volunteers in the Korean War." *China Quarterly,* no. 98 (June 1984): 287–304.

Foot, Rosemary. *The Wrong War: American Policy and the Dimensions of the Korean Conflict, 1950–1953.* Ithaca, NY: Cornell University Press, 1985.

———. *A Substitute for Victory: The Politics of Peacemaking at the Korean Armistice Talks.* Ithaca, NY: Cornell University Press, 1990.

———. "Make the Unknown War Known: Policy Analysis of the Korean Conflict in the Last Decade." *Diplomatic History* 15:3 (Summer 1991): 411–431.

Goncharov, Sergei N., John W. Lewis, and Xue Litai. *Uncertain Partners: Stalin, Mao and the Korean War.* Stanford, CA: Stanford University Press, 1993.

Gurtov, Melvin, and Byong-moo Hwang. *China under Threat: The Politics of Strategy and Diplomacy.* Baltimore: Johns Hopkins University Press, 1980.

Han Huaizhi, et al. *Dangdai zhongguo jundui de junshi gongzuo* (The military affairs of the contemporary Chinese Army). Beijing: Press of Chinese Social Sciences Press, 1989.

Han Nianlong, et al. *Dangdai zhongguo waijiao* (Contemporary Chinese diplomacy). Beijing: Chinese Social Sciences Press, 1987.

Hao Yufan, and Zhai Zhihai. "China's Decision to Enter the Korean War: History Revisited." *China Quarterly* 121 (March 1990): 94–115.

Hong Xuezhi. *Kangmei yuanchao zhanzheng huiyi* (Recollections of the War to Resist America and Assist Korea). Beijing: People's Liberation Army Literature Press, 1990.

Hoyt, Edwin P. *The Day the Chinese Attacked: Korea, 1950.* New York: McGraw-Hill, 1990.

Hunt, Michael H. "Beijing and the Korean Crisis, June 1950–June 1951." *Political Science Quarterly* 107:3 (Fall 1992): 453–478.

Jianguo yilai Mao Zedong wengao (Mao Zedong's manuscripts since the founding of the People's Republic). Vols. 1–4. Beijing: Central Press of Historical Documents, 1987–1991.

Kim Chull Baum. "An Inquiry into the Origins of the Korean War—A Critique of the Revisionist View." *East Asian Review* 6:2 (Summer 1994).

Li Xiaobing, and Glenn Trancy, trans. "Mao's Telegrams during the Korean War, October–December 1950." *Chinese Historians* 5:2 (Fall 1992).

Li Xiaobing, Wang Xi, and Chen Jian, trans. "Mao's Dispatch of Chinese Troops to Korea: Forty-six Telegrams, July–October 1950." *Chinese Historians* 5:1 (Spring 1992): 47–56.

Mao Zedong Junshi Wenxuan (Selected military works of Mao Zedong). Beijing: Soldiers' Press.

Nie Rongzhen. *Nie Rongzhen huiyilu* (Nie Rongzhen's memoirs). Beijing: People's Liberation Army Press, 1986.

Peng Dehuai. *Peng Dehuai zhisu* (Peng Dehuai's self-account). Beijing: People's Press, 1981.

Pollack, Jonathan. "The Korean War and Sino-American Relations." In Harry Harding and Yuan Ming, eds., *Sino-American Relations, 1945–1955: A Joint Reassessment of a Critical Decade.* Wilmington, DE: Scholarly Resources, 1989.

Qi Dexue. *Chaoxian zhanzheng juece neimu* (The inside story of the decision making during the Korean War). Liaoning: Liaoning University Press, 1991.

Ryan, Mark A. *Chinese Attitudes toward Nuclear Weapons: China and the United States during the Korean War.* Armonk, NY: M. E. Sharpe, 1989.

Shen Zonghong, et al. *Zhongguo renmin zhiyuanjun kangmei yuanchao zhanshi* (History of the War to Resist America and Assist Korea by the Chinese People's Volunteers). Beijing: Press of Military Science, 1988.

Shi Zhe. *Zai lishi juren shenbian: Shi Zhe huiyilu* (Together with historical giants: Shi Zhe's memoirs). Beijing: Central Press of Historical Documents, 1991.

Simmons, Robert R. *The Strained Alliance: Peking, Pyongyang, Moscow, and the Politics of the Korean War.* New York: Free Press, 1975.

Spurr, Russell. *Enter the Dragon: China's Undeclared War against the U.S. in Korea.* New York: Newmarket, 1988.

Stueck, William. *The Korean War as International History*. Princeton: Princeton University Press, 1995.

Tan Jingqiao, et al. *Kangmei yuanchao zhanzheng* (The War to Resist America and Assist Korea). Beijing: Chinese Social Sciences Press, 1990.

Toland, John. *In Mortal Combat: Korea, 1950–1953*. New York: William Morrow, 1991.

Weathersby, Kathryn. "The Soviet Role in the Early Phase of the Korean War: New Documentary Evidence." *Journal of American-East Asian Relations* 2:4 (Winter 1993): 425–458.

Weida de kangmei yuanchao yundong (The Great Movement to Resist America and Assist Korea). Beijing: People's Press, 1954.

West, Philip. "Interpreting the Korean War." *American Historical Review* 94:1 (February 1989): 80–96.

Whiting, Allen S. *China Crosses the Yalu: The Decision to Enter the Korean War*. New York: Macmillan, 1960.

Xu Yan. *Diyici jiaoliang: kangmei yuanchao zhanzheng de lishi huigu yu fansi* (The first test of strength: A historical review and evaluation of the War to Resist America and Assist Korea). Beijing: Chinese Broadcasting and Television Press, 1990.

———. "The Chinese Forces and Their Casualties in the Korean War: Facts and Statistics." Trans. Li Xiaobing. *Chinese Historians* 6:2 (Fall 1993).

Yang Chengwu. *Yang Chengwu huiyilu* (Yang Chengwu's memoirs). Beijing: People's Liberation Army Press, 1992.

Yang Dezhi. *Yang Dezhi huiyilu* (Yang Dezhi's memoirs). Beijing: People's Liberation Army Press, 1991.

Yao Xu. *Cong yalujiang dao banmendian* (From the Yalu River to Panmunjom). Beijing: People's Press, 1985.

Zhai Qiang. *The Dragon, the Lion, and the Eagle: Chinese-British-American Relations, 1949–1958*. Kent, OH: Kent State University Press, 1994.

Zhang Shuguang. *Deterrence and Strategic Culture: Chinese-American Confrontations, 1949–1958*. Ithaca, NY: Cornell University Press, 1992.

———. *Military Romanticism: China Fights the Korean War*. Lawrence, KA: University of Kansas Press, 1995.

Zhang Shuguang, and Chen Jian, eds. *Chinese Communist Foreign Policy and the Cold War in East Asia: Documentary Evidence*. Chicago: Imprint Publications, 1994.

Zhang Xi. "Peng Dehuai and China's Entry into the Korean War." Trans. Chen Jian. *Chinese Historians* 6:1 (Spring 1993): 1–30.

12 The Soviet Union and the Korean War

Lester H. Brune

Immediately after learning that North Korea had invaded South Korea on June 25, 1950, President Harry Truman asserted unequivocally that this was Soviet aggression aimed at expanding communist control around the world. No prominent Western leader challenged Truman's claim, and for the next twenty years no one except the "obviously lying" communists in North Korea and Moscow and the little-publicized news columnist I. F. Stone (1952) raised serious questions about Truman's assertions. In the late 1960s, some Western scholars began to challenge Truman's view, but only after better U.S.-Soviet relations developed during the 1970s and 1980s were sufficient Soviet and Chinese documents and memoirs available to confirm what these revisionists often had to surmise in the literature from 1970 to 1990—that is, that North Korea's leader instigated the invasion and Joseph Stalin cautiously and somewhat reluctantly agreed to the risky venture.

Because U.S. and Western official political opinion claimed the Soviets had ordered North Korea to attack in 1950, the literature written before 1970 concurred that Soviet aggression was behind the war. Sovietologists such as Philip Mosely (1960) and Adam Ulam (1968) indicated that Moscow ordered, planned, and supported North Korea as well as China after the Chinese intervened in October and November 1950. Also, the British author David Rees (1964), whose work became the classic reference on the war, indicated that Stalin engineered the attack.

In the late 1960s, however, this orthodox version was more carefully examined by revisionist scholars. Asking questions about the Soviet Union's relationships with the Korean communist party, the career of Kim Il-sung, the political factions in Korea from 1945 to 1950, the United States in dividing Korea in 1945, the UN activity in Korea before June 25, 1950, the Chinese, and the civil war in Korea before large-scale fighting took place, these scholars uncovered information about Korea that had been ignored, forgotten, or deliberately kept secret. Moreover, their data were supplemented not only by declassified documents in Washington and London but also by improved U.S. relations with China after 1972 and with the Soviet Union during the détente of the 1970s and, more so after Mikhail Gorbachev initiated policies of reform (*perestroika*) and openness (*glasnost*) after 1984. These developments gave historians new opportunities for learning about the cold war generally, and the Korean War in particular. Although these scholarly ventures are still in the transition stage regarding the full use of Soviet documents, this chapter reviews the literature of the past twenty-five years in three areas of Soviet policy related to the Korean War: the war's relation to Soviet and Western policy in Europe, the Soviet role in the origins of the Korean War, and the Soviet Union's military role during the Korean War.

THE SOVIET UNION, KOREA, AND EUROPE

When the Korean War broke out in June 1950, the Truman administration and Western European leaders in the North Atlantic Treaty Organization feared that Kim Il-sung's attack was part of Moscow's plan to divert NATO's attention to the Far East and give Moscow an advantage in Europe. Shortly after rallying the UN to support U.S. actions in Korea, Truman's advisers began talking with NATO members about the war's potential difficulties in Europe, where localized Soviet attacks on Yugoslavia or a broader Soviet thrust across West Germany seemed possible. NATO had been organized as a political group in 1949, but its role as a military group was not completed and had raised important questions about the role of the Federal Republic of Germany and the permanence of U.S. troops stationed in Europe. The idea of a European defense community (EDC) had been projected, but because the future of Germany and the Federal Republic's sovereignty had not been resolved, and France, in particular, was troubled about its role in NATO and the EDC, the issues had been slighted. The outbreak of the Korean War, however, prompted Truman and NATO leaders to hasten their military preparations against the Soviet Union and its Eastern European allies. As noted in Chapter 19 in this book, the U.S. status in NATO caused a great debate in the United States, while Europeans were both cheered by Truman's willingness to defend South Korea and fearful of what Moscow intended. For an interesting description of the situation in the United States and Europe, see Kai Bird's (1992) study about John S. McCloy, who was the U.S. high commissioner to Germany in 1950, and James Hershberg's (1993) study on the life and times of James Conant, who organized a "Europe First" group during the summer of 1950 before becoming the U.S. high commissioner to Germany.

While Walter LaFeber (1989) indicates that Truman's military plans for NATO began in the fall of 1950, both Ernest R. May (1989, 1992) and William Stueck (1991, 1993) examine the crucial question about the Soviet Union's capabilities and intentions in Europe during the summer of 1950. May and Stueck conclude that U.S. intelligence estimates of a Soviet arms buildup in 1949–1950 were probably accurate and that the Soviets may have been preparing for at least a local attack if the communists had succeeded in Korea and if NATO forces had not rapidly increased. Both May and Stueck disagree with Matthew Evangelista's (1982–1983) estimate that Western intelligence had exaggerated the Soviet buildup in 1950, citing articles by the Soviet analyst V. N. Donchenko (1970) and Vojtech Mastny (1984–1985).

The estimates about Soviet capabilities and intentions remain unclear, as seen in William Burr's "Soviet Cold War Strategy" in Hershberg's *Cold War International History Project Bulletin* (1994). Burr concludes there was probably a Soviet buildup in 1949–1950 due to Stalin's fear of further defections in Eastern Europe following his break with Tito. To verify this, Burr describes a report partly declassified in 1990 that was prepared for the Department of Defense by Ernest R. May and associates (1981) and cites two recent reports on declassified Central Intelligence Agency documents edited by Scott A. Koch (1994) and Michael Warner (1994), plus an article by John Duffield (1992).

In line with Burr's conclusions about Stalin's concern with Eastern Europe, both Mastny (1984–1985) and Stueck (1991, 1993) use evidence from East European émigrés to confirm the possibility of Soviet plans for war in Europe during 1949–1950. Karel Kaplan (1978), who had been a Communist party member in Czechoslovakia, reported that Stalin told a 1951 meeting of Eastern European defense ministers that they would have a military advantage in seizing control of the continent before 1954. Bela Kiraly (1982), who had been in Hungary's Defense Ministry from 1948 to 1951, claimed that Hungary, Rumania, and Bulgaria had been ordered by Stalin to prepare for an attack on Yugoslavia after Marshal Tito was condemned by Moscow. In addition to V. N. Donchenko's (1970) article on Soviet forces in 1950–1951, May (1989) cites other literature supporting U.S. intelligence estimates in 1950, including William T. Lee and Richard F. Staar's (1986) description of Russia's post-1945 military policy and Alexander Boyd's (1977) explanation of Russian's increased procurement of jet aircraft. On the value of émigré rumors, such as Kaplan's and Kiraly's, see Boris I. Nicolaevsky's *Power and the Soviet Elite* (1965).

Although Stalin wielded totalitarian power, there is evidence he was not spared internal friction in Moscow, which affected his decisions during 1949 and 1950. Not only did Stalin's yielding in the 1948–1949 Berlin crisis contrast with Mao Zedong's 1949 victory in China, but he experienced a host of troubles in the Soviet Empire's East European satraps.

First, the Cominform had to expel Marshal Tito's Yugoslavia for heresy in hostility toward Moscow. Next, Stalin had to eliminate the "deviationists" from communist ranks in Poland, Rumania, Bulgaria, and Hungary, including Bulgaria's deputy premier and Hungary's foreign minister. Although reports in various issues of the *Cold War International History Project's Bulletin* and P. J. Simmons' working paper (1992) indicate these East-Central European countries are slower than Russia in releasing documents to scholars, a symposium on the Stalinistic purges in Eastern Europe is reported in articles by Johannes Kuppes (1992) and Jan Foitzik (1992).

While his Eastern European "allies" troubled him, Stalin also had internal disputes in the Kremlin. In 1949, Stalin had to replace well-known foreign minister Vyacheslav Molotov with Andrei Y. Vishinsky and to purge other party members following the death in 1948 of his heir apparent at the time, Andrei Zhdanov. These internal troubles are described in letters published by Stalin's daughter, Svetlana Alliluyeva (1967), and in studies by Werner G. Hahn (1982) and Gavriel D. Ra'anan (1983). Nikita Khrushchev's (1970, 1974) memoirs also disclose the factional disputes and purges by Stalin during the Korean War era, all of which heightened Stalin's paranoia and made him bellicose, according to Adam Ulam (1973).

Whatever the exact situation was regarding Stalin's policy or potential threat to Europe in 1950, the Truman administration and its NATO allies hastened to protect Europe by naming Dwight D. Eisenhower as commander of NATO forces in December 1950 and by building up U.S. troops and military bases for the evolving European defense community. These decisions were made possible by the perception of the Soviets as having engineered the Korean War.

STALIN'S ROLE IN THE KOREAN WAR ORIGINS

From 1950 to 1970, the views of Philip Mosely (1960), Adam Ulam (1968), and other hard-line Sovietologists mentioned by Stephen Cohen (1985) predominated the literature of Soviet policy, and they complemented President Truman's 1950 condemnation of Soviet aggression. These basic arguments, which justified the belief that Stalin ordered North Korea to attack, were compiled in articles edited in 1972 by Lloyd Gardner. Gardner's introductory essay proposed that in 1950 it made little difference exactly why North Korea launched the war because of the assumption that Kim Il-sung, Mao Zedong, and Stalin shared the communist goal of world conquest, and their aggression reflected the sense of urgency in the Western nations that impelled Truman to fight the communists in June 1950.

In contrast to Gardner's essay the revisionists' concern was to understand why and how Kim Il-sung's forces attacked because the resulting war heightened cold war tensions, which were maintained for nearly forty years. In many respects, the questions revisionists asked, investigated, and answered were not "revised" versions because information about the U.S.-Soviet-Chinese-Korean relations before 1950 had not been thoroughly studied. With few exceptions, such as I. F. Stone (1952), the revisionists were the first to research the record between August 1945, when U.S. and Soviet troops arrived in Korea, and June 1950, when the war began. As declassified official records and other data were researched, the revisionists found an array of information to show that the Korean War originated in the Koreans' desire for unity. Because Chapter 10 in this book describes the Sovietologists' research on Russia's general policies, this section shall summarize specific materials on Soviet policy in Korea that led to North Korea's attack and influenced Moscow's decisions.

Revisionist Studies

During the 1970s the article by Robert Slusser (1977) and the essays and book by Robert Simmons (1973, 1974, 1977) were among the earliest to examine Soviet motives in East Asia and the relations among Kim Il-sung, Mao Zedong, and Stalin, as well as the events in Korea preceding the war. Slusser concluded that Stalin's interests in East Asia matched those of the nineteenth-century czars who sought warm-water seaports and strategic bases for trade and military operations in the Pacific Ocean region. Stalin had moved to fulfill these objectives during the Big Three World War II conferences by gaining permission to occupy the Kurils and the southern part of the Sakhalin islands, which were formerly Japanese, and to make a treaty in 1945 with Jiang Jieshi's (Chiang Kai-shek's) nationalists while Russian troops occupied Manchuria. After declaring war against Japan on August 8, 1945, the Red Army had quickly moved into Manchuria and by August 10 occupied the Korean seaport of Rashin (Nadjin).

Slusser gives little attention to Stalin and Kim Il-sung, but Simmons focuses on Korea's internal politics after 1945 and the relations among Pyongyang, Beijing, and Moscow. His 1977 essay describes the political factions seeking power in Korea, each expecting to lead a united Korea free of Japanese control. These intra-Korean divisions resulted in the U.S. supporting Syngman Rhee's conservative and antireform group while the Soviet Union selected Kim Il-sung as the most forceful leader willing to work with the Russians, with Pak Hon Yong as Kim's deputy. Pak had perhaps the largest popular following in South Korea but was rejected by the U.S. military commander and was forced to flee Seoul in 1948 to avoid execution by the Republic of Korea's purge of Rhee's southern opponents. Without certain evidence, Simmons conjectured that Pak had urged Kim to begin the 1950 war by promising a widespread southern uprising against Rhee. Although Kim made Pak the scapegoat for this after the war, Bruce Cumings' (1973, 1991) study of Korea's internal politics disagrees, arguing that Kim and all other Koreans, including Rhee, wanted their nation united.

Cumings' two volumes (1981, 1990), as discussed in Chapter 3 in this book, provide the most thorough study of the events in Korea, but Cumings emphasized U.S. policy that influenced these events. Because his analysis was completed before *glasnost* opened Soviet archives, he stated that most of his observations on the Soviet role were speculative.

Nevertheless, even before the Soviet archives opened, the revisionists, using Western archives and attending conferences with Chinese and Soviet scholars and officials, had pieced together a version of Stalin's relations with Kim Il-sung that demonstrated that Kim initiated the 1950 attack on South Korea and had to persuade Stalin that North Koreans would win quickly, that the United States would not intervene, and that Mao Zedong supported Kim's decision.

Thus, in James I. Matray's *Historical Dictionary of the Korean War* (1991), the entries by Matray and Walter LeFeber generally substantiate this Soviet role, lacking only the documentary evidence from Soviet archives. Matray's entry, "The North Korean Invasion of South Korea," outlines the historic controversy about the war's origins about which revisionists themselves disagreed, even though they agreed that Truman's version of Soviet aggression was wrong. Although Cumings (1991) argued that the Republic of Korea (ROK) may have attacked first at Ongin on June 25, most revisionists accepted James Merrill's (1988) study, which concluded that Kim had asked for and received Stalin's approval as well as Mao's by March 1950. Merrill primarily used Khrushchev's (1970, 1974) memoirs; the book by Pavel Monat (1960), a Polish embassy official in Pyongyang; and U.S. intelligence data from North Korean defectors. In addition, "Lim Un," a North Korean exile writing under an assumed name, provided data about Kim's war preparations before June 1950. Merrill also indicated that Kim began extensive military preparations with Soviet equipment and relocated North Korean civilians from the 38th parallel border area by June 25, 1950. Thus, Matray concludes that Kim had prepared and wanted to attack because Rhee had destroyed many southern communist guerrillas by early 1950. Moreover, Kim feared that Rhee was gaining greater economic and political strength for the ROK.

Walter LaFeber's *Dictionary* entry, "Joseph Stalin," more particularly indicates that Kim visited Moscow in 1949 when he first sought Soviet approval to unify Korea. Stalin, however, asked Kim to reconsider his plans carefully and to request Mao's opinions before having a second Moscow meeting at which Stalin agreed. Stalin had to be assured that Kim would win and the war would not directly involve the Soviet Union in a conflict with the United States. As LaFeber explains, Stalin wanted to avoid Soviet involvement not only in June 1950 but later, in October 1950, when Kim and Mao requested Stalin's aid after the UN forces crossed the 38th parallel to try to conquer all of North Korea. LaFeber believes Stalin was more concerned about Europe than about East Asia in 1951.

Post-*Glasnost* Studies

The revisionist studies between 1970 and 1990 paved the way for studies about Soviet policy toward Korea by Sergei N. Goncharov, John W. Lewis, and Xue Litai, *Uncertain Partners* (1993), Kathryn Weathersby (1993b, 1993c), and Mun Su Park (1994). "The Decision for War in Korea" in *Uncertain Partners* relies on extensive interviews with or published accounts by North Korean, Soviet, and Chinese officials involved in Korean events in 1950 as well as works such as Merrill's (1988). Unlike Merrill, Goncharov, Lewis, and Xue Litai use the Russian version of Khrushchev's memoirs on Korea (1991). Weathersby's reports are based on intensive research in the Soviet Archives of the Central Committee of the Communist Party of the Soviet Union and the Foreign Ministry. Because her research was largely done under the auspices of the Cold War International History Project, one of her articles is in that project's *Bulletin* (1993a), giving background information for and reprinting a 1966 document, "On the Korean War, 1950–1953, and the Armistice Negotiations," compiled by staff members of the Soviet Foreign Ministry. Her second article, a History Project Working Paper (1993b), analyzes the 1966 document and other documents found in Moscow. Weathersby's article in the *Journal of American–East Asian Relations* (1993c) reprints eleven documents from the Soviet archives, including the 1966 document, and has an explanation for Kim's initiation of the attack on the South. Stalin's role was that of "facilitator rather than initiator," a phrase Weathersby uses in responding to Adam Ulam's letter contending that Stalin could not be pressured to do anything he "had not planned in the first place." Ulam's letter and Weathersby's reply are in Hershberg's 1994 *Cold War International History Project Bulletin*. It should be noted that *Uncertain Partners* has a special footnote about the 1966 document, which the authors find substantiates all of their data.

In contrast to Weathersby, *Uncertain Partners* first provides new details about Kim Il-sung's relations with the Soviet Union from 1939 to 1940 when he went to Siberia for training as a military officer, until 1948 when he had been selected and assisted by the Russians in becoming the North Korean leader. Their account also concludes that in 1948–1949, Stalin wanted Kim to stage frequent border raids and to harass Rhee's government. These raids did not succeed, however, because of Rhee's repressive actions, which caused Kim to prepare for a large-scale invasion and request Stalin's approval for North Korea's attack. Although reluctant to risk involvement with the United States, Stalin approved Kim's plans after getting Mao Zedong's agreement.

In 1994, Russia's president, Boris Yeltsin, visited Seoul and gave the ROK's president, Kim Young Sam, approximately 200 documents covering about 600 pages concerning the Soviet Union's role in the Korean War. A Korean professor, Mun Su Park (1994), has analyzed the papers, which the ROK released to the public, finding that Kim Il-sung had sought Stalin's permission to invade South Korea as early as the spring of 1949. After first refusing Kim's request, Stalin, with Mao Zedong's approval, finally agreed to let Kim prepare for the attack in February 1950. Although Stalin began helping Kim to build up his military forces during 1949, before approving the attack he wanted assurances that the Soviet Union would not be involved and the United States would not intervene. Thus, although the new documents confirm that Stalin was cautious, they also show he gave "overwhelming support" to Kim, who also had Mao's consent for the attack to begin. Park cites other documents indicating that Stalin was surprised that the United States intervened and regretted not having representation in the UN Security Council to cast a veto in June 1950, a topic that requires more documentation to understand fully.

Thus, Park, Weathersby, and the authors of *Uncertain Partners* agree that Soviet aid to Kim was essential in supporting the full-scale invasion Kim desired. Stalin's motives are less clear, but his reasons evidently were not part of a larger communist plot to take over the Pacific region. Rather, Weathersby and the authors of *Uncertain Partners* conjecture that Stalin wanted to tie the Chinese communists more firmly to Moscow and to prevent any possibility of good relations between the United States and Mao Zedong. Weathersby is continuing research in Moscow, and the authors of *Uncertain Partners* agree that more documentary evidence is needed from the former Soviet Union, China, and North Korea.

THE SOVIET UNION'S MILITARY ROLE IN KOREA

The studies by Park, by Goncharov, Lewis, and Xue Litai, and by Weathersby mention Soviet military aid and Soviet forces sent to Korea, but they do not present the extensive material that is found in the article by Jon Halliday (1993). Chapter 11 in this book deals with the Chinese intervention during the fall of 1950, but Park, the authors of *Uncertain Partners,* and Weathersby do not give details beyond mentioning Stalin's reluctance to send Soviet aircraft and pilots as well as antiaircraft units, but finally doing so while disguising his involvement.

Uncertain Partners has a valuable table that lists Stalin's military assistance to North Korea from 1949 to 1951 and shows that Stalin was willing to supply tanks, warplanes, artillery, mortar, and some naval vessels but less willing to send troops while requiring Soviet advisers to use North Korean uniforms and to avoid capture by the enemy. Nevertheless, after UN forces threatened to take over North Korea in October 1950, Stalin gradually agreed to send aircraft support and, later in 1951, antiartillery units to help his "partners."

Halliday (1993) provides details about the Soviet Union's air operations in Korea, based primarily on extensive interviews with Soviet air force officers who had been in Korea or on previously published memoirs of Soviet and Chinese officials and secondary materials from various sources. Many of the Soviet interviews are mentioned by Halliday, Park, Weathersby, and the authors of *Uncertain Partners*. A few of these shall be mentioned as illustrative. One of great interest is the article by Dimitrii Volkogonov (1993), which covers the war's origins as well as developments in 1950. There are two articles by Georgei Lobov (1991a, 1991b), who commanded the Soviet Union's 303 Air Defense Force in Korea, and an interview with a Soviet pilot in Korea, Alexsandr Smorchkov (1990). Finally, Chull Baum Kim (1991) has edited a series of articles, including one by Taoka Jin, about Soviet general Ivan N. Kozhedub, a World War II Soviet ace who commanded an interceptor group in Korea. Steven J. Zaloga (1991) summarizes some of this information about the Soviet air force in Korea.

Using these and other data, Halliday states that because Stalin refused to send ground troops or naval forces to Korea, the one time that U.S. and Soviet personnel had direct combat during the cold war was during the air operations by Soviet pilots and antiaircraft units during the Korean War, a fact that some literature does not yet recognize because both superpowers kept the data secret. Halliday examines some of the controversial details regarding U.S. and Soviet combat deaths and aircraft destroyed during these air operations; this chapter briefly describes Halliday's more certain information about the direct involvement of Soviet personnel in Korea and the Soviet-U.S. decisions to keep this secret.

Halliday finds that Stalin readily offered equipment to North Korea and China but avoided sending Soviet personnel until late October or November 1950 (the precise dates are uncertain). During October, China pressured Stalin to provide air support for the Chinese intervention, but Stalin was reluctant and refused air cover for the Chinese when they initially crossed the Yalu River. By November 1950, Soviet planes, pilots, and support personnel arrived in China, where they established bases at Dandong. From an initial group of 32 MiGs, the Soviets sent 150 planes by April 1951, in addition to aircraft, including bombers, given to China because the North Korean air force had been wiped out by that time.

By April 1951, Stalin also deployed two antiaircraft (AAA) divisions in the Korean theater, with fixed AAA units along the Yalu River, while mobile units went inside North Korea operating south as far as Pyongyang and having control posts along all these routes. Rotating these units by regiment, approximately 72,000 Soviet personnel served in Korea, with the peak at one time being 26,000 in 1952, when the U.S. air war was its most intensive.

Second, Halliday describes how strictly Stalin circumscribed the Soviet air operations, which weakened their potential effectiveness but were part of the Russian design to maintain secrecy about Soviet involvement. The Soviet operations were limited to defensive action against UN bombers and escort aircraft that attacked in North Korea and over China. Although the United States officially claims few U.S. planes crossed into Chinese airspace, the Soviet pilots describe constant U.S. attacks into China, with some U.S. pilots shooting down Soviet planes as they were taking off from Chinese airfields or landing, out of fuel. Perhaps, as Halliday says, the U.S. pilots interpreted "hot pursuit" into China in the broadest possible way. Halliday cites various figures on planes shot down and air-to-air combat deaths but admits these are uncertain, for neither side has fully disclosed this information.

In fact, during and after the war, both sides maintained silence on these activities. Stalin initiated the secrecy not only by curtailing Soviet operations so that Soviet airmen would not be captured beyond battle lines, but by disguising Soviet aircraft and pilots. Soviet pilots were ordered to operate only defensively by attacking UN aircraft when they arrived to hit North Korea. Soviet aircraft could not attack or bomb UN bases and ground units but stayed in defensive regions, especially in what U.S. pilots called "MiG Alley" along the Yalu River's northwest Korean border. Stalin also ordered the air units to disguise their planes and equipment with Chinese or North Korean insignia, to carry forged identification information in case they were captured, and to speak Chinese or Korean over their communication networks. Speaking a foreign language was nearly impossible for Soviet pilots and was the one order they usually violated. The UN air personnel could not, however, tell the Russian language from Chinese or Korean. Halliday cites only one instance in 1952 when a U.S. reporter who knew Russian had a story censored and accepted a U.S. official's order not to disclose his information.

Stalin's secret measures were successful only because U.S. authorities knew but did not publicize Soviet involvement. Halliday cites a memo of Paul Nitze that explains that the Truman administration feared that any disclosure of Soviet combat fighters in Korea would cause the American public to demand war against the Soviet Union, which could precipitate another world war. Later, President Eisenhower agreed with this policy, and the Soviet involvement never become a U.S. media event.

Stalin's limits on the air operations had a U.S. military advantage because the defensive nature of Soviet operations enabled the UN to maintain air control over most of North Korea and to bomb successfully any target selected. The Soviet limitations kept a supply line open from China to North Korea that sustained the communist side until 1953, but Soviet activity could not effectively prevent the destruction of the bridges and the giant dam at Supung/Suiho on the Yalu River. Nor could Soviet aircraft stop the intensive U.S. Air Force bombing attacks in 1952–1953 that destroyed most of North Korea, including in May 1953 the irrigation dams near Pyongyang that watered most of North Korea's rice crop. Halliday's footnote cites an interview in which Dean Rusk stated that nuclear weapons were unnecessary in Korea because "we were bombing with conventional weapons everything that moved in North Korea, every brick standing on top of another." Halliday's book coauthored with Cumings (1988) emphasizes the near-total destruction that the U.S. bombing raids inflicted on all North Koreans.

Halliday does not deal with details about the Soviet antiaircraft units that bothered U.S. Air Force officials because the Soviets' advanced electronic warning system permitted its AAA batteries and MiGs to spot quickly and attack U.S. bombers and their escort aircraft. This information is given by Daniel T. Kuehl (1992), who discusses the effects of electronic warfare on U.S. B-29 bombers after the Soviet equipment began to arrive in late November 1950. Although Kuehl seems unaware that Soviet personnel were directly involved and indicates the Chinese used Soviet equipment, his data conclude that the United States learned more about the newest Soviet radar and realized that these data were vital in contingency planning for cold war nuclear attacks on the Soviet Union by the U.S. Strategic Air Command. Between April and October 1951, the communists' success in destroying or disabling a high percentage of B-29 bombers forced the U.S. Air Force to abandon its daylight bombing raids. Night raids were initially more successful, until the communists adjusted their electronic equipment to the new conditions. Because of these tactics, U.S. personnel searched for better methods to counteract the communist electronic devices. Kuehl concludes, however, that the U.S. Air Force had allowed its "electronic capability to atrophy" between 1945 and 1950 and had to relearn its methods in Korea.

Most interesting for historians is what Stalin's willingness to restrict Soviet air operations reveals about the Soviet Union's policy during the Korean War. Apparently, both before giving Kim Il-sung permission to attack and after Kim's quick victory failed, Stalin's purpose was to keep North Korea as a communist friend but not to try to conquer the entire Korean peninsula unless it could be done without a significant Soviet commitment. This corresponds with other data that showing Stalin was "Europe First" as much as U.S. policy was "Europe First."

REFERENCES

Alliluyeva, Svetlana. *Twenty Letters to a Friend (by) Svetlana Alliluyeva*. Trans. Priscilla Johnson McMillan. New York: Harper & Row, 1967.

Bird, Kai. *The Chairman: John J. McCloy, The Making of the American Establishment.* New York: Simon & Schuster, 1992.

Boyd, Alexander J. *The Soviet Air Force since 1918.* London: Macdonald and Jane's, 1977.

Cohen, Stephen. *Rethinking the Soviet Experience.* New York: Oxford University Press, 1985.

Cumings, Bruce. "American Policy and Korean Liberation." In Frank Baldwin, ed., *Without Parallel: The American-Korean Relationship since 1945,* pp. 39–108. New York: Random House, Pantheon, 1973.

———. *The Origins of the Korean War.* 2 vols. Princeton, NJ: Princeton University Press, 1981, 1990.

Donchenko, V. N. "Demobilizasiya Sovetskoi armii i reshenie problem kadrove v pervye poselevoennye gody" (Demobilization of the Soviet army and decisions on questions of cadres during the postwar years). *Istoriya SSSR,* no. 3 (1970): 94–99.

Duffield, John. "The Soviet Military Threat to Western Europe: US Estimates in the 1950s and 1960s." *Journal of Strategic Studies* 17 (June 1992): 208–227.

Evangelista, Matthew A. "Stalin's Postwar Army Reappraised." *International Security* 7 (Winter 1982–1983): 110–138.

Foitzik, Jan. "Die Stalinistischen Sauberungen in den Ostmitteleuropaeischen Kommunistischen Parteien. Ein Vergleichender Ueberblick" (The Stalinistic purges in the East Central European Communist parties: A comparative overview). *Zietschrift Für Geschichtswissenshaft* (Magazine for history) 8 (1992): 737–749.

Gardner, Lloyd, ed. *The Korean War.* New York: Quadrangle Books, 1972.

Goncharov, Sergei, John W. Lewis, and Xue Litai. *Uncertain Partners: Stalin, Mao and the Korean War.* Stanford, CA: Stanford University Press, 1993.

Hahn, Werner G. *Postwar Soviet Politics: The Fall of Zhdanov and the Defeat of Moderation.* Ithaca, NY: Cornell University Press, 1982.

Halliday, Jon. "Air Operations in Korea: The Soviet Side of the Story." In William J. Williams, ed., *A Revolutionary War.* Chicago: Imprint Publications, 1993.

Halliday, Jon, and Bruce Cumings. *Korea: The Unknown War.* New York: Pantheon, 1988.

Hershberg, James G. *James B. Conant: Harvard to Hiroshima and the Making of the Nuclear Age.* New York: Alfred A. Knopf, 1993.

———. "Soviet Nuclear History" and other articles. *Cold War International History Project Bulletin* 4 (Fall 1994): entire issue.

Holloway, David. *Stalin and the Bomb: The Soviet Union and Atomic Energy, 1939–1956.* New Haven, CT: Yale University Press, 1994.

Kaplan, Karel. *Dans les archives du comité central: trente ans de secrets du bloc sovietique.* (In the archives of the Central Committee: Thirty years of Soviet-bloc secrets). Paris: A. Michel, 1978.

Khrushchev, Nikita. *Khrushchev Remembers* and *Khrushchev Remembers: The Last Testament.* Trans. Strobe Talbott. Boston: Little, Brown, 1970, 1974.

———. "The Korean War." *Ogonek* (Small Flame), no. 1 (January 1991).

Kim, Chull Baum, ed. *The Truth about the Korean War: Testimony 40 Years Later.* Seoul: Eulyoo Publishing, 1991.

Kiraly, Bela. "The Aborted Soviet Military Plans against Tito's Yugoslavia." In

Wayne S. Vucinich, ed., *At the Brink of War and Peace: The Tito-Stalin Split in a Historic Perspective.* New York: Brooklyn College Press, 1982.

Koch, Scott A., ed. *Selected Estimates of the Soviet Union, 1950–1959.* Washington, DC: History Staff, Center for the Study of Intelligence, Central Intelligence Agency, 1994.

Kuehl, Daniel T. "Refighting the Last War: Electronic Warfare and the U.S. Air Force B-29 Operations in the Korean War, 1950–1953." *Journal of Military History* 56 (January 1992): 87–111.

Kuppes, Johannes. "Die Pandora-Buchse Sowjetischer Archive Offnet Sich" (The Soviet Archive's Pandora's box is opened). *Deutschland Archiv* (German archive) 6 (June 1992): 639–643.

LaFeber, Walter. "NATO and the Korean War: A Context." *Diplomatic History* 13: 4 (Fall 1989): 461–478.

Lee, William T., and Richard F. Staar. *Soviet Military Policy since World War II.* Stanford, CA: Hoover Institute Press, Stanford University, 1986.

Lim, Un (pseud.). *The Founding of a Dynasty in North Korea: An Authentic Biography of Kim Il Sung.* Tokyo: Jiyu-Sha, 1982.

Lobov, Georgi. "U.S. Air Actions in Korea Recalled." Moscow Radio Broadcast in Korean, September 2, 1991. FBIS SOV-91-197, October 10, 1991a, pp. 12–14.

———. "V nebe Severnoy Koreiji" (In the sky of North Korea) *Aviatsiya i kosmonavtika* (Aviation and Cosmonautics), October 1990. Translated in JPRS-UAC-91-003, June 18, 1991b, pp. 27ff.

Matray, James I., ed. *Historical Dictionary of the Korean War.* Westport, CT: Greenwood Press, 1991.

Mastny, Vojtech. "Stalin and the Militarization of the Cold War." *International Security* 9 (Winter 1984–1985): 109–129.

May, Ernest R. "The American Commitment to Germany, 1949–1955." *Diplomatic History* 13:4 (Fall 1989): 431–460.

———. "The U.S. Government, a Legacy of the Cold War." *Diplomatic History* 16: 2 (Spring 1992): 269–277.

May, Ernest R., John Steinbruner, and Thomas Wolfe. *History of the Strategic Arms Competition, 1945–1972.* Ed. Alfred Goldberg. Washington, DC: Office of the Secretary of Defense, Historical Office, 1981. Declassified with deletions, December 1990.

Merrill, John. *The Peninsular Origins of the War.* Newark, DE: University of Delaware Press, 1988.

Monat, Pawel. "Russians in Korea: The Hidden Bases." *Life,* June 27, 1960, pp. 76–102.

Mosely, Philip. *The Kremlin and World Politics: Studies in Soviet Policy and Action.* New York: Random House, Vintage, 1960.

Nicolaevsky, Boris I. *Power and the Soviet Elite: "The Letter of an Old Bolshevik" and Other Essays.* New York: Praeger, 1965.

Park, Mun Su. "Stalin's Foreign Policy and the Korean War: History Revisited." *Korea Observer* 25:3 (Autumn 1994): 341–381.

Ra'anan, Gavriel. *International Policy Formation in the USSR: Factional "Debates" during the Zhdanovschina.* Hamden, CT: Archon Books, 1983.

Rees, Davis. *Korea: The Limited War.* New York: St. Martin's Press, 1964.

Simmons, P.J. "Archival Research on the Cold War Era: A Report from Budapest, Prague and Warsaw." Working Paper 2, Cold War International History Project, May 1992.

Simmons, Robert R. "The Korean Civil War." In Frank Baldwin, ed., *Without Parallel: The American-Korean Relationship since 1945*. New York: Random House, Pantheon, 1973.

———. *The Strained Alliance: Peking, Pyongyang, Moscow and the Korean Civil War*. New York: Free Press, 1974.

———. "The Communist Side: An Exploratory Sketch." In Francis Heller, ed., *The Korean War: A 25-Year Perspective*. Lawrence, KS: Regents Press of Kansas, 1977.

Slusser, Robert M. "Soviet Far Eastern Policy, 1945–1950: Stalin's Goals in Korea." In Yonosuke Nagai and Akira Iriye, *The Origins of the Cold War in Asia*. New York: Columbia University Press, 1977.

Smorchkov, Aleksandr. "Heroic Pilot Recalls His Days in Korea." Moscow International Broadcast Service, June 11, 1990. Trans. in FBIS SOV 90-121, June 22, 1990, pp. 9ff.

Stone, I. F. *The Hidden History of the Korean War*. New York: Monthly Review Press, 1971; orig. ed., 1952.

Stueck, William. "The Korean War in Historical Perspective." In Chae-jin Lee, ed., *The Korean War: Forty-Year Perspectives*. Claremont, CA: Keck Center for International and Strategic Studies, 1991.

———. "The Korean War, NATO, and Rearmament." In William J. Williams, ed., *A Revolutionary War*. Chicago: Imprint Publications, 1993.

Ulam, Adam. *Expansion and Coexistence: Soviet Foreign Policy, 1917–67*. 2d ed. New York: Praeger, 1968.

———. *Stalin*. New York: Viking, 1973.

———. *The Communists: The Story of Power and Lost Illusions: 1948–1991*. New York: Charles Scribner's, 1992.

Volkogonov, Dmitrii. "Sleduyet li etogo boyat'sia?" (Should we fear this?). *Ogonek* (Small flame), June 25, 1993.

Warner, Michael, ed. *The CIA under Truman*. Washington, DC: History Staff, Center for the Study of Intelligence, Central Intelligence Agency, 1994.

Weathersby, Kathryn, commentary and trans. "New Findings on the Korean War." *Cold War International History Project Bulletin* 3 (Fall 1993a): 1, 14–18.

———. "Soviet Aims in Korea and the Origins of the Korean War, 1945–1950: New Evidence from the Archives." Working Paper 8, Cold War International History Project, November 1993b.

———. "The Soviet Role in the Early Phase of the Korean War: New Documentary Evidence." *Journal of American–East Asian Relations* 2:4 (Winter 1993c): 425–458.

Zaloga, Steven J. "The Russians in MiG Alley." *Air Force Magazine* 74:2 (February 1991): 74–77.

PART IV

Military Aspects of the Korean War

13   The U.S. Army in the Korean War

Jack J. Gifford

The U.S. Army found the war in Korea hard to deal with, in both the actual fighting and understanding what the army did there. Overall the army disliked the war, and its first postwar reaction was the cry, "No More Koreas." This led to neglect, and Korea soon became the forgotten war. Much the same response to the Korean War marks the military literature on the ground war, with writers finding the war confusing and hard to put into any coherent framework.

For the U.S. Army, as for the nation, Korea was the wrong war in the wrong place. General Omar Bradley, chairman of the Joint Chiefs, and Lieutenant General J. Lawton Collins, army chief of staff, fought primarily in the European theater during World War II and fully supported the Truman administration's Europe First policy. To them, the fighting in Korea drew attention and, more important, resources away from the critical area, Europe. Partly for this reason, most of the early writing about the Korean War became personal narratives or studies of limited scope. Not until the Center of Military History's volumes on the war began to appear were there larger and more comprehensive works on the Korean War.

The first flurry of significant books on the Korean War appeared just after the first official history became available in 1962 and as U.S. involvement in Vietnam grew. A second spate of literature came out as the 1988 Seoul Olympics approached and merged with those reassessing the war in the aftermath of the Soviet Union's collapse. This recent category is not yet complete because the full implications of the cold war's end and the Korean War, the first serious military operation of the U.S.-Soviet confrontation, has not been fully digested.

Little recent documentary material has added to information about the army's participation in the war, although recent studies indicate 25,000

Russians served in Korea. Only when dealing with criticisms of MacArthur, being responsible as the agent of the army for the crossing of the 38th parallel that brought China into the war, has some archival research found new evidence. These works indicate what hard-liners long suspected, such as the Chinese decision to intervene was taken before the United States crossed the 38th parallel and with Stalin's promised support. Until the Inchon landing of September 1950, both the Chinese and the Russians apparently hoped that the North Koreans would drive the enemy into the sea at Pusan without assistance.

There is no orthodox-revisionist-postrevisionist pattern to literature about the army's role in Korea. Of course, the Vietnam War influenced works about Korea written after 1962, but there is no clear revisionist interpretation of army actions. There are, however, certain questions about army operations in Korea that most books deal with, and in answers to these questions divergent interpretations of the army's role appear. The first question concerns responsibility for the U.S. Army's lack of readiness for combat when President Truman committed it to action. Also controversial is the command decision to keep X Corps separate from the 8th Army during the advance toward the Yalu River after the Inchon landing. Three other questions regard the performance of the 8th Army when it was attacked by the Chinese in late November 1950; the relief of MacArthur in 1951; and finally the behavior of American POWs. Other chapters of this book deal with such issues as the disagreement about crossing the 38th parallel and the failure to anticipate the Chinese intervention, but these involve policymaking above army level. Although MacArthur's strong opinions on both subjects had influence on Washington's thinking, the responsibility was not his.

The literature reviewed here is about the army in Korea, but since U.S. Marines also fought as infantry during much of the Korean War, many of the books examined have substantial sections devoted to Marine Corps operations. In addition, a few works are hard to categorize, such as those describing the Inchon landing, which involved marines as part of an army corps and an army division. The books reviewed here are judged to be primarily about the army.

GENERAL HISTORIES OF THE ARMY IN THE KOREAN WAR

Because each of the official U.S. Army histories deals with selected portions of the war, this chapter begins with works that cover the entire length of the war and often feature diplomatic and political aspects of it.

The general history to start with is T. R. Fehrenbach's *This Kind of War: A Study in Unpreparedness* (1963). Published one year after the first official army history and when U.S. involvement in Vietnam increased under President John F. Kennedy, *This Kind of War* is a cautionary tale, but in many respects, it became the orthodox interpretation and remained popular among military officials, which reprinted it as recently as 1993. Fehrenbach explains why the United States fought to a draw in Korea and why the war became unpopular. He holds that American shortcomings in the war stemmed from the fact that liberal democracies like the United States disdain standing armies and object to the use of force to obtain political gains. Fehrenbach writes:

Any kind of war short of jihad was, is, and will be unpopular with the people. Because such wars are fought with legions, and the Americans, even when they are proud of them, do not like their legions. They do not like to serve in them, or even allow them to be what they must. For legions have no ideological or spiritual home in the liberal society. The liberal society has no use or need for legions—as its prophets have long proclaimed. Except that in this world are tigers.

Fehrenbach said the United States fought in Korea with an army composed not of legionnaires but one that reflected civilian desires. As such, it was poorly trained, poorly equipped, and poorly motivated, a situation he blames on American society. The nation's antimilitary tradition made it impossible for the U.S. Army to have a respectable military force in the period after World War II. Fehrenbach's condemnation of the military drawdown after World War II interests military officials, who argue that we must never again be caught unprepared because policymakers see no immediate danger. Yet other military historians fault the military leaders of that time for not keeping what troops they had well trained and battle ready in recognition of the nature of American society.

Fehrenbach comments on other military issues of the war as well. He supports the decision to keep X Corps separate for the drive to the Yalu, holding that Korea's geographic conditions made it impossible for the 8th Army to coordinate the movements of X Corps on the opposite coast and claiming that the separation did not contribute to the defeat of the divided forces when the Chinese attacked. However, he ignores the logistics debacle resulting from MacArthur's decision to transfer X Corps by sea for the invasion of Wonsan and the resulting delay of its advance to the north because Wonsan's harbor had to be cleared of sea mines.

Fehrenbach attributes the relief of General Douglas MacArthur, commander in chief of the Far East, to a fundamental difference in policy between the army's old timers, who were led by MacArthur and believed in total war, and the architects of containment, President Harry S. Truman and Secretary of State Dean Acheson, who accepted a limited war. There was no common ground for an acceptable policy. As long as MacArthur was fighting a defensive war in the South or when, after Inchon, he pushed into North Korea, the split between his views and the Truman administration's was muted. After the Chinese entered the war, however, nothing could conceal the divergence between the theater commander and the commander in chief. When MacArthur proved unwilling to back off, Truman had no option but to relieve him.

Finally, on the behavior of U.S. prisoners of war, Fehrenbach does not underplay the communists' mistreatment of American POWs and responsibility for the deaths of thousands of prisoners. He accepts, however, that the men undergoing captivity did not perform as well as they might have, which upholds the opposition of army leaders to the post-1945 changes in the code of military discipline.

Until recently many people considered David Rees' *Korea: The Limited War* (1964) the best one-volume treatment of the war. Rees, a British journalist, places the war in its international context. In an underplayed manner, Rees notes that Britain had fought limited wars most of the time, and, as a world power, the United States would have to adapt to this necessary practice. Rees comments that British internal politics serves as a reminder that allies of the United States also have domestic problems, which may influence their responses to U.S. initiatives. On the whole, Rees gives U.S. leaders credit for a good job under trying circumstances in responding to unfamiliar and unanticipated military problems. He gives Secretary of State Acheson high marks while hinting that, like most other Americans, Acheson was a little naive about international relations.

Rees covers some political background of the war but devotes most attention to the war's combat actions. Overall he does not seriously question the fighting capacity of the U.S. Army after its slow start. Except for emphasis on the role of British Commonwealth forces, his views closely parallel those of Fehrenbach, adding little that is different. Like most other early writers on the war, Rees argues that, disagreeable as it may have been and despite several mistakes, the U.S. effort in Korea was worthwhile and had positive results.

Rees's tone is repeated in Clay Blair's *The Forgotten War* (1987), the most thorough recent work on the war. Because containing communism was less in vogue during the 1980s, Blair is less certain than Rees that the cost of containment in Korea was worth the sacrifices. Along with many of his contemporaries, he suggests that success in Korea was partly responsible for the willingness of U.S. leaders to get involved in Vietnam a decade later.

Blair's study begins with a diatribe against President Truman, contending that Truman's dislike of and disdain for the regular army and contempt for West Pointers led him to disregard the U.S. Army's proposals to maintain a respectable post-1945 fighting force and brought disastrous results for the men sent to fight in Korea. He attacks Truman for placing budgetary savings ahead of military readiness in an echo of 1980s' cost cutting. His arguments, however, overlook the respect Truman had for

General George Marshall and Marshall's role in Truman's cabinet. This disclaimer aside, Blair makes the point that Truman's grasp of military matters was sketchy at best and caused his poor military decisions in the years before 1950.

Nevertheless, the U.S. Army's high command does not escape criticism. Although Blair aided the preparation of General Omar Bradley's (1951) memoir, he was most critical of the performance of the army staff, including the high command in the Far East. In addition to condemning MacArthur, Blair rakes over almost all high-ranking officers in Korea as being too old, too inexperienced, and, as a group, too incompetent to hold commands in a wartime theater.

MacArthur and Lieutenant General Edward Almond, who was both the Far East Command's chief of staff and commander of X Corps, share the blame for having X Corps remain a separate command and for the landing fiasco at Wonsan. Blair suggests these critical mistakes were responsible for many of the problems that followed. General Walton Walker, commander of the 8th U.S. Army, gets harsh words, although Blair is aware that his death in December 1950 prevented anyone from hearing his side of the story. Thus, he keeps an open mind as to what Walker might have done differently to achieve more. Blair holds Walker and his corps commanders partly to blame for the 8th Army's defeat in November 1950, although real responsibility lay with MacArthur's ill-judged offensive. Blair thinks MacArthur may have deliberately sought to force Truman to relieve him.

Although partially concealed by his method of tracing actions of various commanders throughout their stay in Korea, Blair strongly suggests that those who fought in northwest Europe in 1944–1945 learned the wrong lessons for fighting in Korea and proved unable to adjust to the different methods needed to fight and win in Korea's mountainous terrain. Blair approaches these ideas tangentially because a direct approach would implicate Omar Bradley. Yet he suggests that officers who fought under General Eisenhower in Europe received preferential treatment in the post-1945 army and that few high-ranking officers with experience in the Far Eastern or Italian theaters appeared in Korea. He speculates that officers with experience in these latter two theaters would have had less to unlearn than the northwest European veterans. More explicit is the suggestion that officers with armor experience were particularly unsuited to the Korean situation because many officers who did well in General George S. Patton's 3d U.S. Army's armored sweeps in France and Germany did not do well in Korea. Further, he suggests that some armored officers in Korea who received praise from their superiors deserved court-martials instead. On a positive note, Blair praises General Matthew B. Ridgway for turning the 8th Army into a first-class combat organization.

Ridgway replaced Walker as commander of the 8th Army in December 1950 and MacArthur as Far East commander in April 1951.

Starting with the president and working down, Blair writes primarily about leaders and leadership. The enlisted men who fought and died do not figure prominently, and, in fact, when not in direct contact with an officer they are practically invisible. A discussion of leadership in which the led are indistinguishable chess pieces makes it easier to isolate the leaders' efforts but may seriously distort the results because units differ and the problems leaders encounter depend on the personalities of the men under their command. Blair's failure to consider these possibilities casts doubt on his conclusions, for the fact is that some units fight better than others for reasons having little or nothing to do with leadership.

Whatever its shortcomings, Blair's book is useful. During the war, everyone knew that command mistakes were made, and Blair names names and places, though his strictures and praise may leave out significant factors. He pinpoints times when things went wrong and offers an explanation, even when partial, of why they went wrong. Yet he explains why some operations worked. In the end, Blair offers a fascinating view of American leadership in wartime, although his theoretical grasp of war seems thin and he does not replace Fehrenbach, much less Carl von Clausewitz, as a guide.

Joseph C. Goulden's *Korea: The Untold Story of the War* (1982) represents a journalistic approach to leadership during the Korean War. Goulden does not write about the army but about the senior army officer on duty, Douglas MacArthur. Using some intelligence materials obtained under the Freedom of Information Act, Goulden works that information into an "untold story." He seems to accept these sources uncritically, and some information seems to be war stories without adequate checks for veracity. While highly critical of MacArthur, Goulden does not satisfactorily support his evaluations, and, in fact, his information goes far to justify MacArthur's positions. His largest source for material hostile to MacArthur is the 1951 congressional hearings and files, which often contain unsupported statements by partisan supporters of President Truman.

Generally critical of the command decisions of the Truman administration and the army, Goulden is supportive of the fighting men at the front, even when the actions he describes do not justify his generalizations. For instance, if troops performed poorly, Goulden blames the high command, preferably MacArthur, for not giving the troops sufficient training, equipment, or leadership.

Goulden's book is not only that of an investigative reporter but a product of post-Vietnam disillusionment. There are complaints that in the middle of a desperate war the South Koreans were not democratic or as sensitive to civil rights as Americans. When he mentions North Korean atrocities against American soldiers, he always adds that Americans and South Koreans were equally guilty of misconduct.

Although telling war stories with a flair, Goulden has no real grasp of military affairs, and his discussions of combat are superficial and disjointed. He uses the fashionable interest in movement warfare and largely dismisses the two years of positional warfare after 1951. He also emphasizes the State Department's efforts to drive the military out of any policymaking role. During the occupation of Japan from 1945 to 1950, General MacArthur had operated as Eisenhower did during World War II, without paying much attention to the State Department. But after 1945, the State Department tried to claim credit for the successes in Japan while crowding MacArthur out and replacing him with someone from the State Department. Goulden indicates that after fighting broke out in Korea, the State Department increased its efforts to move MacArthur out of policymaking. Finally, after MacArthur's relief in 1951 and in the subsequent congressional hearings, the State Department won by asserting the need for civilian control of military policy at home and overseas. Framing MacArthur's dismissal in terms of a military threat to civilian control appealed to Truman, although D. Clayton James (1993) shows that MacArthur was grossly insubordinate.

Goulden's treatment highlights the congressional hearings when Secretary of Defense George Marshall, formerly secretary of state, rallied the Joint Chiefs of Staff behind a position that meant a major change in a theater commander's powers and an increased role for the State Department. Later in Vietnam, MacArthur's relief had a chilling effect on military leaders, who became reluctant to question decisions they knew were militarily unsound.

Max Hastings in *The Korean War* (1987) has a very different approach, explaining almost all of the U.S. military problems in terms of the poor quality of American infantrymen, a perspective he used in an earlier book on the Normandy D-Day campaign of World War II. Hastings writes that only the dregs of the U.S. Army served in the infantry, and, with the exception of a few professionals, this was true of the officers as well. Given the poor human material, lack of training, discipline, and initiative is expected. This derogation of the frontline troops puts Hastings at odds with most other writers.

Although Hastings agrees that the U.S. budgetary restrictions before 1950 left the army in bad shape, he suggests the problems of Task Force Smith and the 24th Division, the first to reach Korea in July 1950, stemmed more from lack of will and fighting spirit than lack of training or equipment. The men in these units had not expected to be called to fight and did not fight well when called.

Again disagreeing with most other commentators except Fehrenbach, Hastings supports MacArthur's decision to keep Lieutenant General Edward Almond's X Corps separate from the 8th Army for the drive to the Yalu, citing the low morale, lack of fighting spirit, and disorder of General Walker's staff. He suggests the 8th Army staff was permanently demoralized after fighting for the Pusan Perimeter and lacked aggressiveness. Almond, however, was an aggressive fighter, whom Hastings believes might have gone far had he not been under MacArthur and over Major General Oliver P. Smith, who commanded the 1st Marine Division.

Hastings attributes the intelligence failure on the Chinese intervention to the ineptness of U.S. intelligence at all levels, blaming MacArthur and everyone else. As is often the case with British authors, Hastings attributes this flaw to American society, which accepts a poor intelligence system and faulty analysis.

Hastings also implies that racism was apparent in the insensitive U.S. treatment of the Koreans, and the Americans' prejudice made it impossible for them to appreciate the military virtues and capacities of their Asian friends and foes. He insists the 8th Army was routed by the Chinese assault, which caused a panic-ridden retreat back to South Korea's original border, ending only when General Ridgway reestablished some fighting spirit in the army, which was aided by Chinese supply difficulties as they advanced south.

Hastings supports Britain's position in continuing relations with the People's Republic of China (PRC) during the war and puts Chinese behavior in the best possible light. Repeating the old charge of American "give-up-itis," he not only absolves the Chinese of poor treatment of American POWs but argues the Chinese would not have attacked in November 1950 if MacArthur had not pushed north of the neck of Korea. He also downplays the extent of Russian involvement and support for Chinese intervention.

Hastings presents the relief of MacArthur as a constitutional issue of civilian versus military control, attributing the general's relief to his unwillingness to accept the status quo ante bellum for ending the war. In contrast to Blair, he does not describe the disagreements between MacArthur and the State Department over the control of policy decisions.

James Stokesbury's series of short books on various wars includes *A Short History of the Korean War* (1988). Keeping the study brief leaves little space for analysis, resulting in a conventional military history following standard lines. Nevertheless, this excellent introduction covers all the major operations in easily followed prose.

Stokesbury holds Truman's budget cuts responsible for the lack of military readiness in July 1950. He sees Wonsan as a mistake for which MacArthur and Almond are to blame but has no comment on the 8th Army's defeat in 1950. He favors MacArthur in the quarrel with Truman but claims MacArthur was insubordinate, so that Truman had to relieve him.

Another author with a short study on Korea is Edgar O'Ballance (1969), who presents a strong anticommunist interpretation. He makes a casual comment on the softness of U.S. occupation troops but says nothing about U.S. troops being unprepared to fight in July 1950, the 8th Army's defeat in November 1950, or the separation of X Corps in October 1950. O'Ballance writes extensively about MacArthur's relief and was among the first to claim that China's decision to intervene was taken in conjunction with the Soviets in August, basing his claim on the Russians' release of a telegram stating Stalin had modified his previous promise of air support for the Chinese intervention. The telegram was dated October 10, 1950, whereas the first U.S. troops crossed the 38th parallel on October 9.

Distorting MacArthur's proposals to deal with China's entry into Korea, O'Ballance speculates that MacArthur's full-scale aerial interdiction of Manchuria, combined with an amphibious Chinese nationalist force landing in Korea and an 8th Army attack from the south could have destroyed Chinese forces in Korea. This collapse, he believes, would have made it impossible for the communists to maintain control of China's mainland. To support this counterfactual opinion, he agrees with MacArthur that the Soviets would not have intervened to aid China. Nevertheless, O'Ballance supports Truman's relief of MacArthur. The general pushed publicly against the president's policy and Truman had to relieve him.

John Toland's *In Mortal Combat* (1991) is concerned primarily with combat actions but devotes considerable space to the war's political background. His study lists ill-defined chapter sources and lacks a bibliography and footnotes, so his information is difficult to check, and some of his stories contain material known to be false. Thus, Toland seems prone to accept war stories based on interviews at face value. He tells stories in S. L. A. Marshall's style and shares Marshall's shortcomings, but Toland is the better writer. Toland holds Truman and Secretary of Defense Louis Johnson responsible for the military's sad shape in 1950 and believes MacArthur contributed significantly to X Corps' problems at Wonsan. On other controversies, he has little to say.

D. Clayton James is best known for his multivolume biography of MacArthur (1985) but also has completed *Refighting the Last War* (1993), which is organized topically. James uses interviews and other data gathered while researching his volumes on MacArthur. A conscientious historian, James treats the interview material with care, and his analysis contains enough narrative to support his conclusions. James' essays are on Truman, Admiral C. Turner Joy who negotiated with the communists, and the three generals commanding in Korea: MacArthur, Ridgway, and Clark. His topical essays discuss Truman's decision to aid South Korea, the Inchon landing, the decision to cross the 38th parallel, MacArthur and Truman, and limited war. In his prologue, James discusses the U.S. problems in connecting political objectives with military strategies and the senior U.S. military leaders' failure to study these connections after World War II and the Korean War.

James considers the key decisions of the war but has no in-depth analysis of some of the basic military controversies. This book gives no comment on U.S. military readiness when war broke out, but James thinks MacArthur was responsible for the ill-conceived Wonsan operations and sees the 8th Army's retreat in early December 1950 as a strategic withdrawal, not a panic flight.

Nowhere, however, is James' ability to cut through verbiage and reach solid conclusions more vigorous than in his chapter on the Truman-MacArthur controversy. James finds that the commitment of both to high moral principles led to their dispute, with each doing his duty as he saw it, a situation causing irreconcilable differences and MacArthur's eventual insubordination. James strongly disputes that MacArthur's actions threatened civilian control of the military.

Closely associated with the Truman-MacArthur dispute is James' information indicating the accuracy about MacArthur's suspicions of who in Washington leaked classified data to cast aspersions on the general's fitness. Although the efforts to remove MacArthur failed before 1951, they added to distrust between MacArthur and the State Department.

THE OFFICIAL HISTORIES

Any in-depth study of the Korean War needs to begin with the official histories, the *U.S. Army in the Korean War,* published by the Center of Military History. Heavily based on primary documents and on letters and interviews with the participants, these volumes are as close to original documents as most readers require. Each official U.S. Army historical volume covers selected portions of action in Korea.

The first volume in the Official History series is Roy Appleman's *South to the Naktong, North to the Yalu* (1961), which covers the period from the opening battles at Pusan to mid-November 1950. This book was not well received by army officials because it stepped on many toes. Perhaps because Korea was not an overwhelming victory like World War II, the army was sensitive to criticism, and Appleman was very critical. Despite official displeasure, this is an excellent account of the war, covering its first five months in great detail. Appleman used official records and documents extensively, held hundreds of interviews with participants, and corresponded with survivors. Like others who fought in Korea, he was concerned about seeing the war through the eyes of the men who did the fighting. And although he never used Tennyson's line that "someone had blundered," it must have occurred to him. Those who blundered were not happy with Appleman's work, and other authors wrote the remaining

Official History volumes, none of which matched the quality of Apple-man's.

Describing the early battles in great detail, Appleman indicates the army did not do well in its first engagements, for which he criticizes the train-ing, organization, and equipment of the forces sent to Korea. By impli-cation, he also blames those responsible for the army's status in 1950 and for the decision to commit such troops to combat. Appleman casts doubt on the military leadership in Korea, but other than his unrelieved nega-tives about the all-black 24th Regiment, Appleman does not question the fighting spirit of the troops, though they were badly led, badly trained, out of condition, and very green.

Appleman's criticisms about the 24th Regiment drew heavy ojections from African Americans and others who considered his comments racist. Several books, including that by Clay Blair (1989), have refuted Apple-man, but the official history of the 24th is still being edited. One current study responding to Appleman is by Charles Bussey (1991) and will be discussed. Because both the U.S. ally, South Korea, and its communist enemies were Asiatic, other questions of racism continued to be raised. There were questions about Republic of Korea (ROK) allies' efforts in the war, but of all books in English, Appleman's probably gives the greatest coverage to ROK troops, being unsparing of criticism when it is deserved but offering praise for their hard fighting. Almost alone, he notices that without ROK troops holding the northern front, the UN forces could not have held the Pusan Perimeter. He also refers to the heavy casualties the ROK's forces sustained in their stout defense. Nevertheless, similar to the U.S. troops, the ROK troops were poorly trained, equipped, and led.

Appleman also covers Task Force Smith, the first infantry unit to engage the North Koreans at Osan in July 1950, and uses this battle to examine the army's failings in the early fighting. He describes what happened, allowing the mistakes and problems to appear, so that readers may eval-uate the shortcomings. As Appleman indicates, lacking antitank mines, with only six rounds of antitank ammunition, and with only 2.36-inch rocket launchers (bazookas), the army could not stop North Korea's thirty-three T-34 Soviet-built tanks that drove through their position. The bazooka's failure devastated soldier morale, with repercussions in the weeks after the first fighting. He notes that the army units lacked com-munications with the air force, which precluded close air strikes, and with its own headquarters. Appleman does not indicate who was at fault, but there was plenty of blame for everyone, which embarrassed the army, and Appleman publicized that embarrassment.

The volume continues by discussing the retreat that penned U.S. forces in the Naktong (Pusan) Perimeter, after which the army did better in defending Pusan, with Marine Corps participation. Appleman does not discuss the Chinese intervention in detail but shows that the high command reluctantly accepted that substantial numbers of Chinese troops were in Korea. Without comment, he describes the abandonment of the 3d Battalion, 8th Army at Unsan, which left 600 troops to be captured or killed by the communists, one of the most shameful and little-known incidents in U.S. military history. Appleman's volume is long and packed with names, dates, and details; it is essential reading for anyone who is interested in the army in Korea.

Billy Mossman's *U.S. Army in the Korean War* (1990) takes the official army story from November 1950 to the beginning of the 1951 armistice negotiations. Official history at its worst, it is not well written and almost never critical of the U.S. Army but directs plenty of criticism at almost everyone else. All UN forces come in for a share of Mossman's complaints, but most of these are reserved for ROK troops, whom Mossman finds responsible for almost everything that went wrong. The book's clearest picture is the defeat of the 8th Army on the Chongchon in November 1950. Mossman ignores the chaos of the battlefield and gives the impression that the army was in full control and made an orderly withdrawal under pressure. Other works indicate the engagement was more confused and less creditable to the army.

Although his book was published forty years after the event, Mossman repeats the claim that Lin Piao commanded the Chinese forces in Korea in the opening battles, whereas evidence shows that Peng Teh-huai was the commander. In another instance, Mossman describes General Almond's ridiculous orders to Colonel Don Faith, who led the trapped task force on the east side of Chosin reservoir in November 1950, as an attempt to improve morale. In this episode, Almond ordered Faith to resume the attack to the Yalu against forces that had already savaged the unit and would destroy it as an organized force over the next seventy-two hours. "Don't let a bunch of Chinese laundrymen stop you," Almond told Colonel Faith.

MacArthur's relief is covered in about two pages, and Mossman later mentions, in passing, that MacArthur appeared before Congress to give a speech and later testified before congressional hearings. These events, which changed the way the army conducted operations, deserve attention.

Mossman concludes with the opening of peace talks in 1951, suggesting that everyone in the high command in Korea was satisfied with the decision and the resulting hold on offensive operations. He implies that the truce talks were a good idea that saved American lives, although his own casualty figures indicate that over half of all U.S. casualties occurred after that date. In sum, Mossman carefully treads on no toes by arguing that all decisions were the best possible and glossing over setbacks that are blamed on someone besides the U.S. Army. The book has excellent maps on the battles of the period.

Truce Tent and Fighting Front (1966) by Walter T. Hermes is the official history covering the period in Korea during the stalemate from mid-1951 to the war's end in July 1953. As is customary for writing about this time frame, Hermes emphasizes the truce talks, with little analysis of military events. The fighting of the last two years was almost entirely a "war of posts," that is, heavy fighting with repeated battles over key terrain: Old Baldy, White Horse Hill, the Hook, Pork Chop Hill. In describing these events, Hermes never examines the strategic significance of the battles or their effect on the U.S. Army because a war of posts was contrary to the principles of war taught and believed in by the U.S. Army. Therefore, these actions violated army doctrine and left commander officers confused and often angry. The two principles that have always dominated army thinking are the offensive to seize the initative as the only way to achieve decisive results and the massing of forces at critical times and places. Neither of these concepts fits a war of posts. Thus, most U.S. Army officers agreed with MacArthur's analysis, which said that they were being asked to die for a "tie," a perspective that meant avoiding such conflicts in the future or "no more Koreas." Hermes also omits discussion of the controversial rotation policy in place during this period.

Hermes carefully toes the official line, offering no criticism of the war of posts and ignoring any indication that other approaches were possible. He supports the official Washington position, occasionally disputed by the 8th Army, that enemy positions were so well fortified they could not be broken without excessive casualties and for no strategic purpose. This meant never mentioning or glossing over in a few pages a UN forces attack in October 1951 that punched a ten-mile-wide, ten-mile-deep hole in enemy fortifications, and ended with UN forces completely through the fortified area and in position to cut off substantial Chinese–North Korean elements. Eighth Army commander James Van Fleet considered an amphibious landing to link up with the drive, but the success was not exploited. The official army history plays down the incident, and every official ignored it as much as possible.

Hermes' approach to the peace talks mirrored his discussion of these years, which assumed the official position that negotiators worked hard to bring an inflexible opponent to terms. He overlooks disagreements within the army and between the army and the two presidential administrations over the negotiations. As the talks progressed, Ridgway's communications with Washington came to sound much like MacArthur's, for he constantly protested his instructions for conducting negotiations with the communists until May 1952, when he became the commander of NATO forces and was replaced by General Mark W. Clark. Hermes also pays little attention to the debate over U.S. POWs' behavior or to the State Department's gaining policymaking powers. His appendix cites the disposition of the POWs, which shows that at the war's end in July 1953, the UN Command repatriated 82,493 enemy prisoners and the Chinese and North Koreans

repatriated 13,444. In September, the UN turned over 22,000 nonrepatriates to the Neutral Nations Commission; the communists delivered 350
UN nonrepatriates.

James Schnabel's *U.S. Army in the Korean War* (1972) deals marginally
with the fighting in Korea but focuses on the skirmishes in Washington,
D.C., where Schnabel gives the Joint Chiefs–army chief of staff views about
the quarrel with MacArthur. Writing during the Vietnam War, Schnabel
gives no support to a field commander unhappy with his mission. He
disputes the wilder charges against MacArthur but emphasizes that the
national command authority has the answers and should not be questioned by the man in field, whose job is the actual fighting. This creates
some difficulties when Schnabel chronicles the army's loss of authority to
the State Department. Schnabel does not focus on MacArthur's removal
and the congressional hearings. He offers little explanation about the
army's lack of preparation for combat in 1950 and the decision to send
it to Korea despite its weaknesses. Schnabel is also silent on the controversy regarding the army's poor performance during its first year in Korea.

The fifth volume of official army history is Albert A. Cowdrey's *The
Medics' War* (1987), which gives a detailed analysis of the Medical Department's shortcomings at the outbreak of war. Part of the blame was budget
and personnel cuts, but neither did the Medical Department make the
best use of its assets before 1950. As is often the case, the army's peacetime
needs came first, and little effort was given to the Medical Department's
preparation for possible wartime casualties.

The Medical Department made great strides during the war, as attested
by the increasing percentages of wounded men who survived. The use of
helicopters to evacuate the wounded came into its own because the early-
evacuation pilots used ingenious field expedients to keep passengers alive
during the early days. These methods included running hoses from the
engine through casualty pods to keep men from freezing in the Korean
winter and jury-rigged intravenous lines for patient blood transfusions during flight.

While the medics were proud of their performance in Korea, Cowdrey
sometimes gets carried away. For example, his report on the medic's job
during the prisoner exchange (Operation Big Switch) does not portray
the whole story. Many physical problems of the POWs were not identified
by medics at the time of the exchange, which later required that the U.S.
Congress pass legislation to compensate Korean War POWs because of the
deficiencies of their original physical examinations. Furthermore, the psychological examinations the army used focused on obtaining derogatory
information about POW behavior in the prison camps, not on the mental
condition of the prisoners. After a multiple choice examination, the psy-
chologists noted if the combat soldiers who came out of a prison camp
were aggressive and frustrated about their captors.

SPECIAL STUDIES OF THE ARMY IN KOREA

Prisoners of War

In addition to several personal POW narratives, there are three major works about U.S. prisoners of war and their behavior in Korea. First, William L. White (1955) deals with U.S. and communist POWs, comparing and contrasting UN treatment of POWs with communist treatment of them. This method provides a basis for evaluating the communists' mistreatment of U.S. prisoners, an approach used in the late 1960s to analyze the Vietnamese communists' treatment of U.S. POWs. Moreover, this method enables White to counteract communist claims that the UN had mistreated its prisoners, a claim the communists made in order to argue that the United Nations had forced Chinese and North Korean POWs to repudiate communism and refuse repatriation. During the negotiations leading to the 1953 truce, the POW issue had become a central issue because the United States did not want to force POWs held by the UN to be repatriated.

In contrast to White's comparative method, two other authors, Albert Biderman and Eugene Kinkead, assessed how the U.S. Army and Air Force handled the prison behavior of its men who were held by the enemy. These authors represented the divergent opinions within the U.S. armed forces about how prisoners behaved and how they should have acted, an interservice quarrel that continued throughout the Vietnam experience. Overall, the U.S. Army's hard line is best expressed in Eugene Kinkead's *In Every War But One* (1959), while the air force accepted the soft-line approach found in Albert Biderman's principal work, *March to Calumny* (1963). Kinkead presented the views of U.S. Army officials who had opposed the Doolittle Board's post-1945 reforms that replaced the traditional Articles of War with the Uniform Code of Military Justice. The army felt these changes destroyed army discipline by taking away the powers of noncommissioned officers (NCOs) and company commanders that had enabled its highly disciplined forces to win World War II. Without the traditional articles, they thought the U.S. Army was headed for disaster on the battlefield. Of course, the civilians who were not regular army and had experienced strict discipline in World War II as well as U.S. Air Force officials had not agreed with the army's objections to the Doolittle reforms. After 1950 the hard-line advocates believed the army's poor combat performance in the early days of the Korean War and the alleged disgraceful behavior of U.S. POWs in Korea confirmed their views. Thus, the hard-liners depicted U.S. POW behavior in the darkest colors, even if they had to mute criticism of the communist treatment of POWs.

Therefore, Kinkead (1959, 1960) places the worst possible construction on the U.S. POW actions. In particular, by using the term "give-up-itis," he blamed the POWs for their own deaths, the implication being that if the men had discipline and will, most of them would have survived. By his blaming prisoners for their high death rate, the communists were not seen as inhumane. One hard-line army major insisted the prisoners got enough calories to survive and the Chinese could not be faulted for their treatment, although his analysis left out the effects of cold, dysentery, and injuries.

Kinkead finds that prisoners not only showed a lack of discipline by dying, but also that the survivors' "collaboration" with their captors showed a similar lack of discipline. Kinkead's definition of collaboration was broad enough to catch anyone. If a prisoner said anything other than name, rank, and serial number, he was a collaborator in Kinkead's view. In addition, Kinkead indicates many prisoners signed peace petitions, made propaganda broadcasts, and wrote letters and articles attacking U.S. actions in Korea. He is highly critical of those who yielded by signing germ warfare confessions.

In addition to his book (1963), Biderman has other works (1956, 1957, 1959, 1961) and a book with Herbert Zimmer (1961) containing many articles that refute Kinkead's charges. In particular, Biderman contends that harsh treatment and conditions in the prison camps rather than give-up-itis caused the high death rate. In refuting Kinkead, Biderman fails to give a rounded picture of life in POW compounds, but there are many POW accounts about the harsh prison treatment. Of course, Biderman's studies came out before information about the Korean POWs was developed after the posttraumatic stress disorder (PTSD) syndrome that the Vietnam experience more fully explained.

Among veterans' memoirs and 1950s' accounts of the POWs' experience, a sampling indicates relatively few U.S. POWs acted poorly under extremely harsh treatment in communist prisons. POWs Robert L. Sharpe (1951), John W. Thornton (1981), and Thomas D. Harrison (1953) describe their difficult experiences, with Harrison estimating that 95 percent of the prisoners in his camp resisted communist inducements. Walker M. Mahurin (1962) describes the communist methods causing him to sign a germ warfare statement, and General William F. Dean (1973) explains the psychological trials he endured. Finally, *U.S. News and World Report* (1953, 1955a, 1955b) articles described prisoners' stories about their harsh treatment. These accounts indicate that confessions usually can be obtained by determined interrogators, prisoners cannot totally abstain from communicating with their captors about the necessities of life, and when 300 men are placed in an unheated room with temperatures well below zero and are told no one eats until all sign a peace petition, all sign it. Their articles and confessions with stilted communist jargon really said nothing that partisan U.S. politicians did not say when the Republicans were called the party of the rich exploiting the poor and Democrats were called warmongers. Also, it is true that the communists, especially the North Koreans, treated the POWs poorly. Jeffrey Grey's article on "brainwashing" in James I. Matray's dictionary (1991) is an excellent summary of the POW issue.

Army Logistics

Of two major works on U.S. Army logistics during the Korean War, the most recent is James A. Huston's (1989) description of army logistics from the upper echelon's perspective, which is based on official statements and after-action reports. At this level, the logistics people faced and overcame problems so that the soldiers doing the fighting never lacked anything they needed. In contrast, an earlier study, by John Westover (1955), looked at the logistics picture at the lower levels, where many problems were persistently encountered: radios having short ranges or often not working, decayed ammunition, shortages of shells, the late delivery of winter clothing, and many daily details about which the people at the upper level filtered out complaints and shortage reports so that their official reports gave a picture of a logistics system that met all its challenges. This high optimism is obviously false. Some combat failures were clearly logistical, like the dropping of 40-mm shells to Task Force Faith's tank detachment in the rear, rather than to the main body, which desperately needed shells to fight the Chinese encirclement of the 8th Army east of Chosin. Although the Chinese overran the army on December 1, 1950, the troops might have been saved if the air force had delivered the 40-mm shells to the proper destination.

In accordance with a report for high ranking officials, Huston's book is chronologically organized so that everything flows smoothly, although it is a little dry where statistical tables successfully conceal any problems. Westover's book, however, is filled with reports by men in the field explaining field expedients used to make do when the logistics organization failed to provide needed materials. Only in interviews with higher-ranking officers did Westover report that everything was working well. This striking difference in views about the supply system is symptomatic of the army bureaucracy's diffusion of responsibility and denial of errors. In reality, the army had little difficulty getting materials it needed to Korea, but the system faltered in moving material from supply dumps to the units in combat. Veterans of both the Vietnam and Desert Storm wars report the problem still exists.

Combat Activity

S. L. A. Marshall wrote several books and articles on the Korean War that all had the same theme. For that reason only his *The River and the*

Gauntlet (1953) will be discussed in detail. His more famous *Pork Chop Hill* (1956), the *Military History of the Korean War* (1963), and the recent *Infantry Operations and Weapons in Korea* (1988) all follow the same line. Marshall is an all-out apologist for the U.S. Army and its fighting men. He provides approval of the weapons available to the army, their employment by the troops, and the tactics that accompanied these weapons. At other times the personalized manner of Lieutenant Joe Clemmons delivers the same optimistic message in *Pork Chop Hill* and a movie of the same title.

The River and the Gauntlet best exemplifies Marshall's technique and message. Marshall built his reputation by conducting interviews with men just out of battle during World War II to learn in detail what actually occurred. By cross-checking the stories of men who participated in the same battle, he formed a story of the action and the men. He glides over the fact that men at the center of action who were killed or wounded were not interviewed. Also, he leaves unstated that men just returning from combat are inclined to present themselves and their buddies in the best possible light.

In *The River and the Gauntlet,* Marshall used his World War II method by concentrating on the 8th Army's 2d Infantry Division, which was virtually destroyed after the Chinese attacked in November 1950, but survivors withdrew to the south and after rebuilding in January 1951 again took part in heavy combat. Marshall ignores the fact that one-third of the division did not get to the south and was not present for his review in 1951. Given the events of their retreat in November 1950, the surviving members of the 2d Division supported each other's stories of how well they performed in difficult circumstances. Consequently, Marshall's story is that despite the brave and determined fighting of practically everyone and despite the skillful use of available weapons, the Chinese overwhelmed the 2d Division by sheer numbers.

With little analysis, Marshall finds there was a lack of leadership at the small unit level, which, combined with the poor training, left troops unready for battle in encountering the Chinese. He denies that the 8th Army was routed but offers no explanation of why the army that had an overwhelming firepower advantage fell back to the 38th parallel, abandoning equipment as they went. Intended to refute charges that the U.S. Army did not perform well in the face of the Chinese attack, Marshall carries out this mission admirably. His defense of the 8th Army has remained the orthodox interpretation, stating that General Walker planned a rapid and orderly withdrawal to a defensible line close to his supply base at Inchon. But his story cannot convince anyone familiar with other facts showing something went wrong. Only occasionally does the opposite picture emerge of Walker's flying above the retreating troops, shouting over a loudspeaker for units to turn and fight, but being totally ignored by the panicked, fleeing troops. Donald Knox and Albert Coppel (1988) describe this different view, and Max Hastings (1987) endorses it.

Edwin P. Hoyt's three books on Korea (1984a, 1984b, 1985) give attention to the marines but are primarily about the army. Using secondary sources and official reports, whatever value his books have lie in interpretation and analysis. Having been a news correspondent in the Far East, Hoyt writes sympathetically about China, sometimes seeming to be an apologist for Mao's regime. Unfortunately, his data on the Chinese entry into the war do not have the benefit of recent research from Chinese and Soviet sources. Hoyt is critical of the army's high command, especially MacArthur, is friendly toward the marines, and criticizes most of the Truman administration's decisions. Finally, Hoyt blames MacArthur and other generals for splitting the 8th Army and X Corps in 1950 without indicating that officers who objected by suggesting other plans were overridden by MacArthur.

In 1986, television producer Donald Knox published *Korea: An Oral History,* which creates a mosaic of individual stories, tied together with brief connective comments, which flow like a novel. The contents are derived from interviews, letters written at the time, and official documents, a technique that results in a superb first-hand account from the viewpoint of the men who fought in Korea. Knox offers no analysis but allows facts to speak for themselves, though he explains events when necessary. In summary, his book supports the view of the war developed earlier by Fehrenbach and Appleman: an army with poor leadership and poor training learning to fight the hard way and suffering heavy and perhaps unnecessary losses in the process.

After Knox's death cut short his plans for a second volume, Albert Coppel used his materials to write *Korea: An Oral History, Uncertain Victory.* It has Knox's name (1988) with Coppel's but the final product is unbalanced because some speakers get too much space, and continuity is lacking. There is interesting material, but it fails to hold attention as Knox's own work did.

More recently, Rudy Tomedi's *No Bugles, No Drums* (1993) tries to adopt Knox's style. Tomedi's narrators are mainly persons who became senior officers, which gives an official spin to the work. But Tomedi is no expert on the Korean War, and there are a number of small but irritating errors of fact. He gives a different perspective of the Korean events, seeing them from another angle than do the better-known descriptions of combat. The most impressive account is Harry Summers' report on how Ridgway turned the 8th Army around after taking command from General Walker.

Shelby Stanton's (1989) title indicates his book is about the U.S. X Corps, but it actually is about Lieutenant General Edward (Ned) Almond, who commanded the X Corps in Korea. Stanton shows that Almond was a blatant racist, a conclusion that is hard to fault, but in the case of Korea, Stanton asserts that racism made Almond a poor commander. Although evidence is strong that Almond was not an ideal corps commander, it is harder to prove that racism was the reason. During World War II, some racists were excellent commanders. However, Stanton's case is that Almond misused black soldiers, although there is evidence that he also made poor use of the all-white units he commanded, and his strained relations with the Marine Corps were not because they were black marines. Yet Almond's corps lost an entire regimental combat team to the Chinese in 1950 because he ordered them into strategically impossible positions.

Nevertheless, Stanton writes the first sustained criticism of Almond, for Roy Appleman's (1987) account blames not Almond but MacArthur for events in 1950. Stanton agrees with most other literature that MacArthur was responsible for the decision to separate Almond's X Corps from Walker's 8th Army in October and for the decision to move X Corps to the east coast for the amphibious landing at Wonsan, a disastrous mistake that contributed substantially to the 8th Army's failure when it encountered the Chinese a few weeks later.

In the area of strictly professional criticism, Stanton faults Almond for constant interference with subordinate units, skipping channels and sometimes not informing his division or regimental commanders about moving their units. The chief item linking Almond's racism to incompetence as a corps commander is Stanton's charges that Almond misused the 65th Regiment at Chosin because he felt a Puerto Rican outfit with many blacks was not a reliable combat organization.

Russell A. Gugelar's *Combat Actions in Korea* (1987) was originally published during the war and covers only the early stage of the conflict. Faced with a libel suit, the author issued a revised edition that left out the contested episode. Gugelar describes small unit actions and is in the category of lessons learned. It was intended to show junior officers and noncommissioned officers how to fight in Korea. Being based on comments by those present in the combat described, Gugelar's work has problems similar to S. L. A. Marshall's, for the participants' stories are not always accurate, as the libel suit indicates. Despite these shortcomings, Gugelar offers an excellent view of war at the small unit level, an important view because the geographical compartmentalization caused by Korea's mountains made the war a small unit war.

As Gugelar points out, this compartmentalization meant that one company might be desperately engaged while the other companies in the battalion might be unaware of the fight unless they used wire or radio communications with the company engaged. They usually did not communicate, and Gugelar emphasizes how radios often did not work or were blocked by the mountains while wires remained unstrung and more often were cut by the enemy. Gugelar says little about the operational or strategic context of the battles described, nor does he question the equipment used. He does criticize small unit leadership and the poor training and motivation of some troops.

Roy Appleman has recently written four books on the Korean War: one (1990b) describes Ridgway's role after 1951, and the others are about the Chinese intervention. Appleman's *Escaping the Trap* (1990a) is mainly about Marine Corps operations and, like the Ridgway volume, is not reviewed here. The other two emphasize army activity during the communist attack on the 8th Army and the destruction of Task Force Faith, which began as Task Force MacLean. *East of Chosin* (1987) describes the Chinese defeat of an American regimental combat team during the fall of 1950. In contrast to Stanton's account of X Corps, Appleman is careful about blaming General Almond for the destruction of Torch Force, although Almond's insistence on continuing offensive action after the Chinese had savaged his forces speaks for itself. Appleman accepts the X Corps commander's excuse, a very poor one, that he followed MacArthur's wishes for an all-out offensive. Appleman places a share of the responsibility on the division commander, Major General David Barr, who was absent from the scene either because he wrote the task force off or opposed losing additional men trying to save the task force. Appleman says the assistant divisional commander, General Henry I. Hodes gave orders to withdraw the supporting tank battalion, an act which most investigators believe sealed the fate of Task Force Faith.

In addition, the Marine Corps shares responsibity because it had operational control of Task Force Faith at the time the critical decisions were made. The Marine Corps commanders were too busy extricating their own force to spare time for the army units across the reservoir. Nevertheless, Marine Corps aircraft flew extensive air cover for Task Force Faith until nearly the end.

Appleman's *Disaster in Korea* (1989) explains the 8th Army's defeat in such detail that it is sometimes hard to follow. For example, Appleman asks: Did Colonel Paul Freeman have authority to withdraw by the coast route? This action saved Freeman's regiment from heavy losses, but critics and other students of the fight know the division was not rolled up from the rear but decimated when on the move. If Freeman had followed the rest of the division, he would have achieved only the loss of his regiment.

Appleman extensively covers the fight to keep open the inland flank of the 8th Army's withdrawal. Both ROK and Turkish forces faltered here, but the 1st Cavalry Division did excellent work. Perhaps Appleman gives insufficient coverage and credit to the British forces that covered the retreat. Also, he is critical of the panic-stricken flight from Pyongyang and the abandonment of enormous quantities of supplies but is unclear whether General Walker was at fault or if it was impossible to rally the fleeing troops.

Personal Narratives

Although General Matthew B. Ridgway's memoir appeared in 1956, his later analytical work (1967) should have illuminated the fighting. But when he wrote the second volume, he was thinking as much about about Vietnam as Korea. He did not want to expand the Vietnam War, and this influenced his views about Korea and his concern about national policy.

Ridgway is critical of sending poorly prepared troops into battle in Korea, but he does not assign responsibility. He is critical of MacArthur's decisions, excluding the Inchon landing and his giving Ridgway a free hand with the 8th Army in Korea. Ridgway thinks separating the 8th Army from X Corps for the northern push was a mistake and strongly supports Truman's decision to relieve MacArthur, just as he later supported the commander in chief's control over the war in Vietnam.

As for the fighting ability of the 8th Army at the time of its collision with the Chinese, he is skeptical. When he took command of the 8th Army a month after its defeat by the Chinese, he was critical of the force, which he found to be a road-bound, defeatist organization that did not prepare its positions, did not tie in with adjacent units, and did not train. Because of his criticisms of the army, there are implicit negative views of its fighting capacity under its previous commander. Among other things, Ridgway felt General Walker did not visit the frontline units often enough and did not display proper concern for the well-being and morale of his men.

Ridgway defends his own approach to fighting the war by inflicting heavy casualties on the Chinese to force them to stop the fighting. This was based on his high regard for human lives and the conviction that the Chinese could not afford a constant drain of their most highly trained troops. On the contrary, the Chinese government in the 1950s was engaged in a massive domestic purge of potential enemies within China, with estimates that as many as 25 million perished, making the losses in Korea mere pinpricks. Most observers believe Ridgway erred in thinking that killing Chinese would give peace, but because of his reputation, few have emphasized this point. Moreover, Ridgway's opinion gave credence to the Truman administration's policies in Korea.

In Korea as in Vietnam, Ridgway and the United States faced the classic problem of limited wars: how to bring the enemy to the bargaining table. In both regions, the United States found that body counts were not sufficient. Ridgway says his decision to meet at Kaesong for truce talks was a mistake, but he gives no alternative of what would have been done differently if the meetings had been held elsewhere. He had already rejected the normal method of putting pressure on an enemy by taking territory because Truman, the State Department, and U.S. allies feared any advance into North Korea would reduce chances for a negotiated peace. As a firm believer that theater commanders should adhere to the administration's policy, Ridgway could not call for an offensive advance, and he doubted that the air force could apply enough pressure to bring about a cease-fire.

The memoirs of Ridgway's successor, General Mark W. Clark (1954), describe an unabashed conservative and adherent of MacArthur's view that Truman should have won a total victory in Korea. Clark served when the armistice negotiations got bogged down in the fall of 1952, making his command more political than military in nature, because the principal UN action was the extensive bombing of North Korea. Clark became dismayed when President and former General Dwight D. Eisenhower did not change Truman's policy but accepted a truce in July 1953.

Army Chief of Staff J. Lawton Collins' (1969) memoir appears to be more open and frank than most other accounts. Collins accepts some responsibility for the army's lower budgets before the war but says Congress rather than the president was responsible for the underfunding. Collins criticizes Secretary of Defense Louis Johnson and believes if Johnson had not resigned in 1950, he would have been removed. The low budgets after 1945 left the army unable to meet its missions and with almost no funds for new equipment and training. Collins notes that the demobilization after World War II and the conversion of the U.S. industry back to pre-1941 production levels halted defense production. Until the summer of 1952, insignificant amounts of war material were available, an unpalatable fact behind much of Washington's quarrel with MacArthur, who never accepted that the United States had insufficient supplies to expand the war in the Far East. For similar reasons, Washington hesitated to equip the Chinese nationalists or to arm additional South Korean troops before 1950. The Korean War expended almost all the equipment left from World War II, and, given concerns about possible Soviet actions in Europe, the U.S. government was unwilling to divert any North Atlantic Treaty Organization stocks to the fighting in the Far East. Thus, Truman lacked not only the desire but also the military means to support additional forces in MacArthur's theater. Military historians should study more about the post-1945 demobilization and the army's reaction because the loud public demand to "get the boys home now" was a cry politicians of neither political party could ignore.

Collins criticizes MacArthur for not placing X Corps under General Walker for the advance to the Yalu, but indicates that MacArthur stuck to plans G-3 drew up despite some objections. MacArthur also mistakenly rejected arguments that moving X Corps by sea to Wonsan would cause logistics difficulties. Finally, Collins insists the 8th Army's withdrawal from North Korea in 1950 was orderly, in accordance with high-level planning.

On the relief of MacArthur, Collins is circumspect but leaves room for speculation that he opposed MacArthur's recall. Recent documents show that Truman overstated his case in saying all the chiefs of staff approved MacArthur's dismissal because a special plea from Marshall was needed to persuade the chiefs to present a united front so that public doubters would drop their opposition. Collins believes MacArthur was relieved because he refused to accept the Europe First policy, which the State Department, Secretary of Defense Marshall, and the Joint Chiefs approved.

Charles Bussey's *Firefight at Yechon* (1991) is a personal narrative of the war by a retired lieutenant colonel who believes he was denied a Congressional Medal of Honor because he is black. Bussey's memoir describes what it meant to be a black officer and how racism affected the army before and during the Korean War. He served in the Japanese occupation forces before going to Korea and is much franker about the events than other officers who wrote about their experiences. He indicates that occupation problems involved most of their time and that maintaining combat readiness was not a serious consideration for anyone. His description of the occupation troops in Japan helps to explain why these first troops sent to Korea did not do very well. An engineer, Bussey was part of the group of engineers that gave a good account of themselves in Korea, and his pride in the engineers' work is evident. His book, however, is essential for the flavor of Korean combat it presents. In addition, it is the best first-hand account of the U.S. armed forces' integration problem during the Korean War, an untold aspect of the Korean conflict.

Both Clay Blair (1987) and Clayton James (1993) refer to but give no details about the integration issue. Unlike the air force and navy, U.S. Army officials had resisted the implementation of Truman's 1948 executive order for equal opportunity in the armed forces until January 1950, when it accepted the principle of gradual integration. The implementation of integration in the army had not begun when the Korean War began. During the war, integration began, due especially to the shortages of infantry personnel during the first year. After some formerly white battalions had success in using black replacements, more units integrated, and many all-black regiments disbanded. Despite problems, the Korean War sped the integration of the U.S. Army although this raised bigger issues of equal treatment.

Allen Wilkinson's *Up Front Korea* (1967) is the story of an enlisted man who was in the 2d Infantry Division at Fort Lewis in 1950. When the Korean War began, his unit shipped to Korea and was soon engaged in heavy combat. His memoir shows that few of the riflemen of infantry companies survived the first year of fighting unscathed. Wilkinson has no comments on strategic matters but gives the view from the foxhole, often reading like a posttraumatic syndrome therapy used after the Vietnam War.

RESEARCH INFORMATION ON U.S. ARMY HISTORY

In addition to the National Archives, primary sources are found at various army historical agencies. The principal locations to begin research are the Center of Military History in Washington, D.C, the Military History Institute at Carlisle Barracks, Pensylvania, and the Combat Studies Institute at Fort Leavenworth, Kansas. As B. Franklin Cooling indicates in Robin Higham and Donald Mrozek's *Guide to the Sources of U.S. Military History* (1993), the above centers will help researchers find material at other locations, such as 68 command and subordinate historical offices, 27 National Guard historians, 102 museums, and 26 branch schools. About these, the U.S. Army, Center of Military History (1989), has a directory.

Researchers should also become familiar with the variety of professional journals that may contain worthwhile materials on military history. The most prominent are *Armed Forces and Society, Army Times, Military Review,* the *Journal of Military History* (formerly *Military Affairs*), *Minerva: Quarterly Report on Women and the Military,* and *Parameters, the Journal of the Army War College.*

REFERENCES

Alexander, Bevin. *Korea: The First War We Lost.* New York: Hippocrene, 1986.

Appleman, Roy E. *South to the Nakong, North to the Yalu.* Washington, DC: 1961.

———. *East of Chosin: Entrapment and Breakout in Korea.* College Station, TX: Texas A&M Press, 1987.

———. *Disaster in Korea: The Chinese Confront MacArthur.* College Station, TX: Texas A&M Press, 1989.

———. *Escaping the Trap: The U.S. Army X Corps in Northeast Korea, 1950.* College Station, TX: Texas A&M Press, 1990a.

———. *Ridgway Duels for Korea.* College Station, TX: Texas A&M Press, 1990b.

Biderman, Albert D. *Communist Techniques of Coercive Interrogation.* Lackland Air Force Base, TX: 1956.

———. "Communist Attempts to Elicit False Confessions from Air Force Prisoners of War." *Bulletin, New York Academy of Medicine* 33 (1957): 616–625.

———. "Effects of Communist Indoctrination Attempts: Some Comments Based on Air Force Prisoner of War Study." *Social Problems* 6:4 (1959): 304–313.

———. *March to Calumny: The Story of American POW's in the Korean War.* New York: Macmillan, 1963

Biderman, Albert D., and Herbert Zimmer, eds. *The Manipulation of Human Behavior.* New York: Wiley, 1961.

Black, Robert W. *Rangers in Korea.* New York: Ivy Books, 1989

Blair, Clay. *The Forgotten War: America in Korea, 1950–1953.* New York: Times Books, 1987.

Bradley, Omar N. *A Soldier's Story.* New York: Holt, 1951.

Bussey, Charles M. *Firefight at Yechon: Courage and Racism in the Korean War.* Washington: Brassey's, 1991.

Clark, Mark W. *From the Danube to the Yalu.* New York: Harper & Row, 1954; reprint, Tab Books, 1988.

Collins, J. Lawton. *War in Peacetime: The History and Lessons of Korea.* Boston: Houghton Mifflin, 1969.

Cowdrey, Albert A. *The Medic's War.* Washington, DC: Center of Military History, Department of the Army, 1987.

Dean, William F. *General Dean's Story.* New York: Viking, 1954; reprint Westport, CT: Greenwood Press, 1973.

Fehrenbach, T. R. *This Kind of War: A Study in Unpreparedness.* New York: Macmillan, 1963

Goulden, Joseph C. *Korea: The Untold Story of the War.* New York: Times Books, 1982.

Gugelar, Russell A. *Combat Actions in Korea.* Rev. ed. Washington, DC: Center of Military History, Department of the Army, 1987.

Harrison, Thomas D., with Bill Stapleton. "Why Did Some G.I.'s Turn Communist?" *Collier's* 132:13 (1953): 25–28.

Hastings, Max. *The Korean War.* New York: Simon & Schuster, 1987.

Hermes, Walter G. *Truce Tent and Fighting Front.* Washington, DC: Center of Military History, Department of the Army, 1966.

Higgins, Marguerite. *War in Korea.* Garden City, NY: Doubleday, 1951.

Higham, Robin, and Donald Mrozek. *Guide to the Sources of U.S. Military History: Supplement III.* Hamden, CT: Archon Books, 1993.

Hinshaw, Arned L. *Heartbreak Ridge.* New York: Praeger, 1989.

Hoyt, Edwin P. *The Pusan Perimeter.* New York: Stein & Day, 1984a.

———. *On to the Yalu.* New York: Stein & Day, 1984b.

———. *The Bloody Road to Panmunjom.* New York: Stein & Day, 1985.

Huston, James A. *Guns and Butter, Powder and Rice.* Selinsgrove, PA: Susquehanna University Press, 1989.

James, D. Clayton. *The Years of MacArthur: Triumph and Disaster, 1945–1964.* Boston: Houghton Mifflin, 1985.

———. *Refighting the Last War: Command and Crisis in Korea.* New York: Free Press, 1993.

Kinkead, Eugene. *In Every War But One.* New York: Norton, 1959.

———. *Why They Collaborated.* New York: Longman, 1960.

Knox, Donald. *The Korean War: An Oral History, Pusan to Chosin.* San Diego, CA: Harcourt Brace Jovanovich, 1985.

Knox, Donald, and Albert Coppel. *The Korean War: An Oral History, Uncertain Victory.* San Diego, CA: Harcount Brace Jovanovich, 1988.

Leckie, Robert. *Conflict: The History of the Korean War, 1950–1953.* New York: Putnam, 1962.

Lineer, Thomas A. "Evolution of Cold War Rules of Engagement: The Soviet Combat Role in the Korean War." Master's thesis, Fort Leavenworth, Command and General Staff School, 1993.

Mahurin, Walker M. *Honest John.* New York: Putnam's, 1962.

Marshall, S. L. A. *The River and the Gauntlet.* New York: Morrow, 1953.

———. *Pork Chop Hill.* New York: Morrow, 1956.

———. *Military History of the Korean War.* New York: F. Watts, 1963.

———. *Infantry Operations and Weapons in Korea.* San Francisco, CA: Presidio Press, 1988.

Matray, James I. *Historical Dictionary of the Korean War.* Westport, CT: Greenwood Press, 1991.

Mossman, Billy C. *U.S. Army in the Korean War: Ebb and Flow.* Washington, DC: Center of Military History, Department of the Army, 1990.

O'Ballance, Edgar. *Korea, 1950–1953.* London: Faber & Faber, 1969.

Politello, Dario. *Operation Grasshopper.* Wichita, KS: Robert R. Longo, 1958.

Poole, Walter. *The History of the Joint Chiefs of Staff: The Joint Staff and National Policy.* Vol. 4: *1950–1952.* Washington, DC: History Division, Joint Chiefs of Staff, 1979.

Rees, David. *Korea: The Limited War.* New York: St. Martin's Press, 1964.

———, ed. *The Korean War: History and Tactics.* London: Crescent Books, 1984.

Ridgway, Matthew B. *Soldier: The Memoirs of Matthew B. Ridgway.* New York: Harpers, 1956.

———. *The Korean War: History and Tactics.* New York: Doubleday, 1967.

Schnabel, James F. *U.S. Army in the Korean War: Policy and Direction: The First Year.* Washington, DC: Office of the Chief of Military History, Department of the Army, 1972.

Sharpe, Robert L. "God Saved My Life in Korea." *Saturday Evening Post* 223:29 (1951): 26–27, 95–96.

Stanton, Shelby. *America's Tenth Legion X Corps in Korea.* Novato, CA: Presidio Press, 1989.

Stokesbury, James L. *A Short History of the Korean War.* New York: Morrow, 1988.

Thornton, John W. *Believed to Be Alive.* Middlebury, VT: Ericksson, 1981.

Toland, John. *In Mortal Combat.* New York: Morrow, 1991.

Tomedi, Rudy. *No Bugles, No Drums: An Oral History of the Korean War.* New York: John Wiley, 1993.

U.S. Army, Center of Military History. *U.S. Army Historical Directory, 1989.* Washington, DC: Center of Military History, 1989.

U.S. News and World Report. "Real Story of Returned Prisoners." 34:22 (May 29, 1953): 54–58.

———. "How Reds Tortured U.S. Prisoners." 39:10 (Sept. 2, 1955): 26–27.

———. "Red Torture Broke Few G.I.'s." 39:9 (Aug. 26, 1955): 38–39.

Westover, John G. *Combat Support in Korea.* Washington, DC: Combat Forces Press, 1955.

White, William L. *Captives of Korea.* New York: Scribners, 1955.

Wilkinson, Allen B. *Up Front Korea.* New York: Vantage Press, 1967.

14   Air Force Sources: Rethinking the Air War

Warren A. Trest

Recently published proceedings of the Fifteenth Military History Symposium of the United States Air Force Academy, held October 14–16, 1992, will help to demythologize institutional lore that Korean hostilities were just a horizontal slice of cold war history sandwiched between "the triumphant Allied victory in World War II and the American tragedy in Vietnam." Contributors to this synoptic volume, edited by William J. Williams (1993) and titled *A Revolutionary War: Korea and the Transformation of the Postwar World* (1993), treat the experience as a seminal event whose military and political legacies have been catalysts for the chills and thaws in East-West relations. Two presentations from a session addressing the war's transformation in airpower appear in Williams's book: "Naval Air Operations in Korea" by Richard P. Hallion and "Air Operations in Korea: The Soviet Side of the Story" by Jon Halliday. These insightful discussions add interpretatively to any reconsideration of airpower in Korea. Neither their treatment nor the proceedings as a whole, however, shed new light on the air force's imprint on the war or the war's imprint on the air force.

   While revelations about Russian air force participation in Korea have been forthcoming since *glasnost* and the fall of the Soviet empire, no scholarly, analytical revisionist history of the air war gleaned from the study of communist documents has as yet resulted. Halliday's interpretations are informative but unreliable since they are drawn almost exclusively from interviews with Soviet participants, whose service ribbons have faded and whose memories have dimmed. While the Soviet Union may have kept its full involvement in the air war a state secret, much of Halliday's basic material was known to Western intelligence during hostilities, as documented in Robert F. Futrell's classic official history, *The United States Air Forces in Korea* (1961). The same goes for Steven J. Zaloga's article, "The Russians in MiG Alley" (1991). Halliday and Zaloga provide more detailed accounts of the Soviet air experience, however, and widen our exposure to that aspect of the air war.

Hallion's paper, which observes that the navy and marine pilots flew 41 percent of U.S. sorties in Korea, helps put the total air combat experience in perspective. Hallion reveals that the war drove changes in naval air weaponry, while air force histories such as Futrell's two-volume *Ideas, Concepts, Doctrine* (1989) found no trace of America's first jet air war in the transformation of service doctrine, technology, or force posture during the decade following the cessation of hostilities in Korea. The air force may have dominated the skies over Korea, but what the service gleaned from the war differed institutionally from the navy, the Marine Corps, or the army. The air force's corporate gleanings from the war have been more inferential than experiential.

Futrell explains how the strategic-minded air force was ready-made for the "massive retaliation" strategy of President Dwight D. Eisenhower and his secretary of state, John Foster Dulles. The Eisenhower-Dulles strategy essentially armed Allied nations to fight their own wars if attacked, while the United States provided a regional nuclear umbrella to deter wider aggression. As the linchpin in massive retaliation, the air force rewrote its doctrine and equipped its forces accordingly, building up a lethal global nuclear posture at the expense of conventional air capabilities. Even the tactical air forces shelved the lessons of Korea and joined the so-called nuclear binge. The air force equipped its tactical squadrons at home and abroad with new century-series fighters (F-100s and F-105s), which were designed and built to be nuclear workhorses—neglecting, in the process, to develop modern all-purpose or air-superiority fighters. A decade later, the air force had to discard its predominantly nuclear doctrine and to reconfigure its weapon systems, including the mighty B-52 strategic bombers, to fight another limited air war in Southeast Asia. It also had to rely on a navy-developed fighter (the F-4) to fight for air supremacy in the deadly skies over North Vietnam.

By reawakening interest in the Korean air war and encouraging scholars to invest intellectually and analytically in the total airpower experience, the academy proceedings could produce a bumper crop for air force history. The climate appears favorable for revisionists to take a new look at the air war and its relevance to the postwar transformation in airpower. Nearly all, if not all, relevant air force documents have been declassified, and access to Soviet archives should help round out any new and objective reexamination of the air war.

BEDROCK: OFFICIAL AND UNOFFICIAL SOURCES

When the Office of Air Force History reprinted a revised edition of Futrell's *The United States Air Force in Korea, 1950–1953* in 1983, Richard H. Kohn wrote in the Foreword that since the first printing in 1961, the work had become a "model for official military history." Pulitzer Prize–winning journalist Mark S. Watson had reviewed the first edition for *Saturday Review* in January 1962, describing it as "a faithful record" of Far East air forces in the war and "a useful survey, whose occasional service partisanship is probably inevitable." He contrasts Futrell's conclusion that airpower was "the decisive factor in the outcome of the ground war" with Roy E. Appleman's criticisms of air force support in the first volume of the army's official Korean War history, *South to the Nakong, North to the Yalu* (1961). While institutional memory and utility are the raison d'être of official history, Watson notes the air force's inclination "to regard many of its Korean War experiences not as models but as examples of what not to do next time."

Futrell's history is a scholarly compass for any serious study of the air force's wartime experience in Korea. Beyond the richness of his narrative, copious footnoting and a useful bibliography point the way to an El Dorado of primary and secondary source materials, many of which are now part of the Air Force Historical Research Agency collection at Maxwell Air Force Base, Alabama. Included among the extensive holdings at Maxwell are unit histories and supporting documents, an early U.S. Air Force official evaluation of air operations (1952), the official U.S. Air Force *FEAF Report on the Korean War* (1954), and three formerly classified historical studies that Futrell prepared during and immediately after the war and that served as the foundation for his definitive history. In addition to the vast wartime collection preserved by Futrell and his colleagues, the research agency has added a solid quarry of official and unofficial source documents on the war to its holdings during the intervening years. The agency's extensive collection of personal papers include, for example, those of General Otto P. Weyland, who served successively as vice commander and commander of Far East Air Forces during the war. The agency's oral history collection contains interviews with air force participants.

Complementing Futrell's comprehensive history is an early topical study, *The Greatest Airlift* (1954), by Annis G. Thompson. Futrell described Thompson's work as an "authoritative though popularly written story of USAF air transport in Korea." Another early study that extended into the Korean War period is Frank E. Ransom's official account, *Air-Sea Rescue 1941–1952* (1953). Futrell's summary of air force experience in the war appears in *A History of the United States Air Force, 1907–1957,* edited by Alfred Goldberg (1957). With the exception of periodical literature, little else pertaining to the history of air force operations in Korea appeared in print during the first postwar decade.

Periodical literature of the Korean War era adds to the bedrock of historical information on the air force's role in the conflict. James T. Stewart's *Airpower* (1957) is a compilation of articles from the Air University's professional journal, the *Air University Quarterly Review,* between 1951 and

1954. Stewart's collection features General Weyland's personal account, "The Air Campaign in Korea," in the fall 1953 issue of the *Review*. Other informed articles about the air war are in the wartime pages of *Air Force*, the official journal of the unofficial Air Force Association; *Air Power Historian* (formerly *Aerospace Historian*), the quarterly publication of the Air Force Historical Foundation; and *Airman* magazine. *Aviation Week*'s wartime issues contain additional information, mostly technical in nature. Researchers should also review "The Truth about Our Air Power," by air force chief of staff General Hoyt S. Vandenberg, as told to Stanley Frank, in the *Saturday Evening Post*, February 17, 1951; Laurence C. Craigie's "The Air War in Korea" (1952); William G. Key's "Air Power in Action" (1951a); and various pieces written by General Carl Spaatz as military columnist for *Newsweek* during the Korean War period.

Scholars revisiting the air war will want to mine relevant Air Force and Joint Chiefs of Staff files in the National Archives and to research the holdings at the Air Force Academy Library. The academy holdings comprise a treasure of personal papers and oral history interviews not available at the Historical Research Agency. The Library of Congress has the papers of General Hoyt S. Vandenberg, air force chief of staff during the Korean War; these are essential to any comprehensive study of airpower in the war. Visits to the General Douglas MacArthur Archives in Norfolk, Virginia, and to the U.S. Army Military History Institute at Carlisle Barracks, Pennsylvania, can help fill in the army's views of air force support in Korea. The papers of General Matthew Ridgway and Lieutenant General Edward Almond are particularly relevant to any treatment of army–air force differences over air support for ground troops. The Truman and Eisenhower presidential libraries provide insights into political decisions concerning the uses of airpower in Korea.

A HISTORICAL ECLIPSE: THE FORGOTTEN AIR WAR

Bibliographies on air force history confirm that the explosion in analogous Korean War study one might reasonably have expected from the reverberation of limited aerial warfare in Southeast Asia never occurred. Futrell's bibliographic essay, "The U.S. Army Air Corps and the United States Air Force, 1909–1973," in *A Guide to the Sources of U.S. Military History* (1975), edited by Robin Higham, suggests that the opposite was true. While student theses on some aspects of the air war were completed at Air University and other armed forces schools, no new institutional study of the air force's experience in Korea appeared in print from the start of the airpower buildup in Southeast Asia in 1964 through the withdrawal of American forces in 1973. An annotated bibliography on air force history compiled by Mary Ann Cresswell and Carl Berger (1971) supports this observation. Interestingly, the published proceedings of the U.S. Air

Force Academy's 1968 Military History Symposium, *Command and Commanders in Modern Warfare* (1971), contain only a passing reference to the Korean War.

Two Rand Corporation studies during the Vietnam era were exceptions to the lack of comparative analyses on air force operations in the Korean War. These were *Some Historical Notes on Air Interdiction in Korea* (1966) by Gregory A. Carter and *The Evolution of the Airborne Forward Air Controller* (1967) by James A. Farmer and M. J. Strumwasser. Maurer Maurer's official study, *USAF Credits for Destruction of Enemy Aircraft, Korean War* (1963), however, contains no analysis. It complies the record of official kills of enemy planes by air force pilots in the war.

A literary lapse in the academic and popular genres of Korean War air history is more understandable. When the nobler passion for saving South Vietnam turned to disenchantment on America's campuses in the aftermath of the 1968 Tet Offensive, military history appeared to become an interim casualty of the Vietnam War. Interest in Korean War study had already fallen victim to the nation's preoccupation with Vietnam. Little of real value about the air force's experience in Korea came from university presses or commercial publishers during the roller coaster of soul searching over America's protracted Southeast Asia intervention. Robert Jackson's pedestrian treatment, *Air War over Korea* (1973), did not demand a learned audience. Some good general coverage of the Korean War appeared in print before and amid the slump in military history, however, and these added more holistic fiber and perspective to the body of knowledge on the air force's contribution. David Rees' *Korea: The Limited War* (1964) provides general coverage of the air fighting. Futrell deemed Rees' book to have been "the best overall history of the Korean conflict" published during the Vietnam period. Matthew B. Ridgway's *The Korean War* (1967) contains personal views of a senior ground commander on the effectiveness of airpower. Robert Leckie's *Conflict* (1962) also has useful material on the air campaign.

A slump in coverage of air force actions in the Korean conflict was equally obvious in periodical literature. The *Air University Review,* for example, carried only a single article on the Korean War throughout America's protracted military operations in Vietnam. The exception was Philip D. Caine's "The United States in Korea and Vietnam: A Study in Public Opinion" (November–December 1968). This timely comparative study reflected the growing division between the hawks and the doves over the Vietnam War. Another probable reason for the *Review*'s fading interest in the Korean experience was the journal's orientation toward subjects of current air force professional interest. Other journals showed a similar declining interest in the history of the Korean air war. *Aerospace Historian* interrupted the trend with Donald Cable's "Air Support in the Korean

War'' (1969). James Cole's "Lamplighters and Gypsies" (1973), and James L. Brooks, "That Day over the Yalu" (1975). In 1976, Tim Cline's "Forward Air Control in the Korean War" appeared in the *American Aviation Historical Society Journal,* a publication (unaffiliated with the air force) started in the aftermath of Korean hostilities.

BEYOND VIETNAM: A RENAISSANCE IN THE MAKING

Two decades beyond America's abandonment of the Vietnam War, the national psyche, still scarred by the experience, manifested no leftover estrangements from its warrior heritage. Muted by dissonance over the war, military history regained some of its resonance within academia and suburbia in the 1980s. A renaissance of sorts resulted, and is still in the making, for historical literature about America's past wars and the soldiers, sailors, marines, and airmen who fought them. Any focusing of this renascent interest on Korean War history, however, appeared to be overshadowed in the early 1990s by the Niagara of literature commemorating the fiftieth anniversary of World War II.

Clearly the best new official work about the Korean War period to appear during the 1980s was Doris M. Condit's *The Test of War, 1950–1953* (1988), volume 2 in the Office of the Secretary of Defense history series. Condit's book covers a broad range of national security matters, including the air war in Korea, as viewed from the policymaking locus. Reprinting Futrell's classic history in 1983, the Office of Air Force History also published new topical volumes that addressed elements of airpower in Korea and other wars. Richard H. Kohn and Joseph P. Harahan edited two volumes (1983, 1986) of roundtable interviews with retired air force generals that offer personal insights into the Korean air war. Another official volume, *Case Studies in the Development of Close Air Support,* (1990), has a chapter on air support in the Korean War by Allan R. Millett. Noel F. Parrish's chapter, "Hoyt S. Vandenberg: Building the New Air Force," in *Makers of the United States Air Force* (1987) contains insights into Vandenberg's handling of Korean air war matters while he was air force chief of staff.

The proceedings of the U.S. Air Force Academy's biennial Military History symposia have served as a bellwether for changes in the historical climate both within and outside the air force milieu since the series debuted in 1967. The symposium theme that ushered in the 1980s, *The American Military and the Far East* (1980), pointed toward a rebirth of historical interest in the air force's Asian experience and that of the other military arms. A subsequent revival of institutional interest within the air force about its experiences in the Korean War was matched by a rise in scrutiny by professional journals and by university presses and commercial publishers.

Despite the revival of interest in the Korean War, the bibliographic trail of published works on the air campaign remains uneven. First of the new volumes to appear, Jerry Scutts' *Air War over Korea* (1982), fits into the genre of popular literature about the air war. Also adding to the war's popular culture are Douglas Evans' *Sabre Jets over Korea* (1984) and Chester A. Blunk's *"Every Man a Tiger."* The popularly written *Korea: The Air War, 1950–1953* (1991) was authored by Jack C. Nichols and Warren E. Thompson.

While no new full scholarly treatment of the air war appeared during the mini-renaissance in Korean War history, there was anatomical scrutiny of some facets of the air war presented in recent generic historical volumes. Philip S. Meilinger's biography, *Hoyt S. Vandenberg* (1989), is compelling reading for its coverage of Vandenberg's leadership, inter alia his personal imprint on the Korean air campaign while serving as chief of staff. Other intellectual treatment is contained in Futrell's chapter, "A Case Study: USAF Intelligence in the Korean War," appearing in the published proceedings of the thirteenth academy symposium, *The Intelligence Revolution: A Historical Perspective* (1991). Thomas A. Cardwell's *Command Structure for Theater Warfare* (1984) briefly addresses the Korean air campaign. Other new works, such as Appleman's *Ridgway Duels for Korea* (1990), provide one-dimensional views of air force operations in Korea, researched and written from the perspective of another service.

The prospects for a mini-renaissance were buttressed by a rise in periodical literature about the air force and the Korean War. Lawrence R. Benson's "The USAF's Korean War Recruiting Rush . . . and the great Tent City at Lackland Air Force Base" (1978) led a rush to revisit the air war in the 1980s. Ben Fithian and Francis J. Amody opened the decade with articles on F-94 aerial combat, appearing respectively in the *Navigator* (1981) and in the *American Aviation Historical Society Journal* (1982). Amody followed with another article, "Skynights, Nightmares and MiGs" (1989). Other pieces on aerial combat included Dan Allsup's "Robinson Risner: Korean War Ace" (1989); Skip Holm's "Yalu River Raider" (1984); and David McLaren's "Mustangs in Aerial Combat" (1985). McLaren's discussion, "Air Support in Korea: Mustang Style," appeared in *Aerospace Historian* (1986).

Futrell's "Tactical Employment of Strategic Air Power in Korea" (1988b) provides scholarly treatment of a subject bearing upon airpower application in wars after Korea, and is still relevant today. Theodore Jamison's "Nightmare of the Korean Hills" (1989) treats another side of the air war. Daniel Calingaert's "Nuclear Weapons and the Korean War" (1988) is a vital source for serious students of the air war. In 1989, the *Air Force Journal of Logistics* printed two articles addressing logistics support for the air war: Bryce Poe's "Korean War Combat Support: A Lieutenant's

Journal" and Margarita Rivera's "Airlift of Cargo and Passengers in the Korean War."

During the 1990s, professional journals continued to show an interest in publishing scholarly articles about the air force's role in the Korean War. Daniel Kuehl's "Refighting the Last War: Electronic Warfare and U.S. Air Force B-29 Operations in the Korean War 1950–53" (1990) is an example of the exceptional work now being done on the air war. Others are Roger F. Kropf's "The US Air Force in Korea: Problems That Hindered the Effectiveness of Air Power," (1990); Michael A. Kirtland's "Planning Air Operations: Lessons from Operation Strangle in the Korean War 1950–53" (1992); Roger Launius' "MATS and the Korean Airlift" (1990); and T. R. Milton's "The Equalizer in Korea" (1991), which addresses the 5th Air Force's contribution to the air war.

A little-known aspect of the air war comes to light in Forrest L. Marion's "The Grand Experiment: Detachment F's Helicopter Combat Operations in Korea, 1950–1953" (1993). Charles R. Shrader's "Air Interdiction in Korea" (1992) adds a different perspective on the 5th Air Force's interdiction campaign. Zaloga's "The Russians in MiG Alley" (1991) opens the door to additional revelations about the enemy's uses of airpower in Korea. Finally, Ronald R. Fogleman's thought-provoking "Modernization for Korean War Stopped Post-WWII Reduction, Made US Ready" (1991), is taken from a keynote address the author presented to the U.S. Air Force's Academy's fifteenth Military History Symposium in October 1992. It lays a foundation and a challenge for new generations of scholars to go beyond bedrock history to the search for airpower's holistic imprint on the war and the war's imprint on airpower's transformation.

A TIME FOR RETHINKING THE AIR WAR

Edited by William J. Williams, the symposium proceedings entitled *A Revolutionary War: Korea and the Transformation of the Postwar World* (1993) are nourishment for military historians whose profession asks more from them than thinking in cycles of chronology and commemoration. These scholars might find irony, however, in the volume's appearance in print at a time when the market has been flooded with historical literature celebrating the fiftieth anniversary of World War II. Surviving the surfeit of commemorative literature, the published proceedings could become another effective bellwether for historical awareness and production, leading beyond passive chronology to a new wave of useful scholarship about airpower and the Korean War.

What better time to rethink the Korean air war? The accumulation of four more decades of analogous air warfare experience affords a panoramic view of airpower history that was not available for research and erudition during the Korean War period. The maturing of the air force as an institution over this forty-year span—along with a corresponding maturation in force denominators such as aerospace technology, air doctrine, and weapon systems modernization—opens new vistas for reinterpreting evidence, reconstructing events, and paralleling lessons learned through a wider lens of historical analysis. The end of the cold war and the breaking down of barriers with former enemies should illuminate the search.

A general history analyzing airpower's imprint on the Korean War and the war's imprint on modern airpower would be timely and useful. The academy symposium proceedings conveyed this theme but did not purport to give full, retrospective treatment of the war as a crucible for today's airpower. Air force scholars reluctant to undertake comprehensive retrospection of the air war will find there are still historical bits and pieces worthy of their attention. The failure to reconcile doctrinal differences for the command and control of airpower, for example, has been one leftover problem from the Korean War that still hinders the effective application of joint airpower today. William Momyer's *Air Power in Three Wars* (World War II, Korea, Vietnam) (1978) and Cardwell's *Command Structure for Theater Warfare* (1984) address the problem from the air force point of view, while a new book, *Joint Air Operations: Pursuit of Unity in Command and Control, 1942–1991* (1993), by James A. Winnefeld and Dana J. Johnson provides more objective treatment of the controversy. An updated version of a 1991 Rand study, the Winnefeld-Johnson volume has been expanded and revised to include the joint air experience in Operation Desert Storm. All three volumes enrich the literature on airpower, but a need remains to clarify more precisely how the command and control problems affected the direction and outcome of air campaigns in Korea and thereafter.

A sampling of periodical literature thus far into the 1990s suggests that a new generation of scholars has begun to build upon the foundation of bedrock air force history by critically reexamining the various core mission elements of the air war. The studies cited by Kirtland, Kropf, Kuehl, and Launius, for example, analyze different aspects of the air war from the perspective of today's air force. Their work is an indication that other sides and ramifications of air combat in Korea are worthy of study. Close air support and interdiction are but two core missions that invite retrospective analysis and comparison with analogous uses of airpower. Other suggested topics include air superiority, strategic bombing, aerial reconnaissance, air intelligence, air commando operations, airlift, and air doctrine. Reconsideration of the war as the new air force's baptism of fire under the National Security Act of 1947, as the dawn of jet air warfare introduced by the Luftwaffe at the end of World War II, and as the precursor for limited air warfare in the nuclear age offers more challenges for complete airpower scholars.

Completing this survey of air force sources on the Korean War reveals that Futrell's bedrock history and the Air Force Historical Research Agency's collection at Maxwell Air Force Base in Alabama are still the best places to start for new studies of the air war. Many documents in the Research Agency collection, including unit histories written while the war was being fought, are not available elsewhere. Other useful reservoirs of Korean War literature located at Maxwell are the Air University Library and *Air Power Journal.* Joan Hyatt's *Korean War, 1950–1953: Selected References* (1992) is a helpful guide to the four decades of Korean War literature available at the Air University Library. Michael Kirtland's (1990, 1992) indexes to the *Air Power Journal* and its antecedent, the *Air University Review,* pinpoint all articles on the Korean War that have appeared in those professional journals.

Scholars whose fields of study focus only on the air force's role in the Korean War might well find that the primary and secondary sources available at Maxwell are adequate for their research needs. Those who explore air force operations in the larger context of national policy, joint military application, or analogous air warfare experience should start with Futrell's work and the Air Force Historical Research Agency before expanding their research into the extensive holdings pertaining to the other services, the Joint Chiefs of Staff, the Defense Department, and related agencies. Researchers who limit their study to the Korean War period will likely find that all documents relating to their study are no longer classified. A scholar who seeks to compare the air war to more recent analogous experience, however, probably will need to apply for a temporary clearance, which government agencies may grant conditionally to legitimate scholars. The time it takes to acquire such a clearance might be an inconvenience, but the new worlds of research it opens up make that a small price to pay.

REFERENCES

Albert, Joseph L., and Billy C. Wylie. "Problems of Airfield Construction in Korea." *Air University Quarterly Review* 5 (Winter 1951–1952): 86–92.

Albright, Joseph G. "Two Years of MiG Activity." *Air University Quarterly Review* 6 (Spring 1953): 88–89.

Allsup, Dan. "Robinson Risner: Korean War Ace." *Airmen* 31 (September 1987): 34.

Amody, Francis J. "We Got Ours at Night; The Story of the Lockheed F-94 Starfire in Combat." *American Aviation Historical Society Journal* 27 (1982): 148–150.

———. "Skynights, Nightmares and MiGs." *American Aviation Historical Society Journal* 34 (Winter 1989): 308–313.

Appleman, Roy E. *South to the Nakong, North to the Yalu.* Washington, DC: Government Printing Office, 1961.

———. *Ridgway Duels for Korea.* College Station, TX: Texas A&M University Press, 1990.

Baer, Bud. "Three Years of Air War in Korea." *American Aviation,* July 6, 1953, pp. 20–21.

Barcus, Glenn O. "Tally for TAC." *Flying* 53 (July 1953): 17, 65.

Bauer, Eddy. "Trial of Strength in Korea." *Interavia* 53 (1950): 567–573.

Benson, Lawrence R. "The USAF's Korean War Recruiting Rush . . . and the Great Tent City at Lackland Air Force Base." *Aerospace Historian* 25 (1978): 61–73.

Blair, Clay. *Beyond Courage.* New York: David McKay, 1955.

Blunk, Chester L. *"Every Man a Tiger": The 731st USAF Night Intruders over Korea.* Manhattan, KS: Sunflower University Press, 1987.

Bowers, Ray. "Korea: Proving Ground in Combat Air Transportation, ' *Defense Management Journal* 12 (July 1976): 62–66.

Brooks, James L. "That Day over the Yalu." *Aerospace Historian* 22 (June 1975): 65–69.

Bunker, William B. "Organization for an Airlift." *Military Review* 31 (April 1951): 25–31.

Cable, Donald. "Air Support in the Korean War." *Aerospace History* 16 (Summer 1969): 26–29.

Caine, Philip D. "The United States in Korea and Vietnam: A Study in Public Opinion." *Air University Review* 20 (January, February 1968): 49–55.

Calingaert, Daniel. "Nuclear Weapons and the Korean War." *Journal of Strategic Studies* 11 (June 1988): 177–202.

Cardwell, Thomas A., III. *Command Structure for Theater Warfare: The Quest for Unity of Command.* Maxwell AFB, AL: Air University Press, 1984.

Carter, Gregory A. *Some Historical Notes on Air Interdiction in Korea.* Santa Monica, CA: Rand, 1966.

Cline, Tim. "Forward Air Control in the Korean War." *American Aviation Historical Society Journal* 21 (Fall 1976): 257–262.

Cole, James, Jr. "Lamplighters and Gypsies." *Aerospace Historian* 20 (March 1973): 30–35.

Condit, Doris M. *The Test of War, 1950–1953.* Washington, DC: Historical Office, Office of the Secretary of Defense, 1988.

Craigie, Laurence C. "The Air War in Korea." *Aeronautical Engineering Review* 11 (June 1952): 26–31.

Cresswell, Mary Ann, and Carl Berger. *United States Air Force History, An Annotated Bibliography.* Washington, DC: Office of Air Force History, 1971.

Crews, Thomas. *Thunderbolt Through Ripper: Joint Operations in Korea, 25 January–31 March 1951.* Carlisle Barracks, PA: Army War College, 1991.

Davison, W. P. "Air Force Psychological Warfare in Korea." *University Quarterly Review* 4 (Summer 1951): 40–48.

Degovanni, George. *Air Force Support of Army Ground Operations: Lessons Learned during World War II, Korea, and Vietnam.* Carlisle Barracks, PA: Army War College, 1989.

Dews, Edmund, and Felix Kozaczka. *Air Interdiction: Lessons from Past Campaigns.* Santa Monica, CA: Rand, 1981.

Dixon, Joe C., ed. *The American Military and the Far East: Proceedings of the Ninth Military History Symposium,* United States Air Force Academy, 1–3 October 1980. Washington, DC: Office of Air Force History, 1980.

Dolan, Michael J. "What's Right and Wrong with Close Air Support." *Combat Forces Journal* 1 (July 1951): 24–30.

Dorn, W. J. Bryan, and O. K. Armstrong. "The Great Lessons of Korea." *Air Force* 34 (May 1951): 28–32.

Dupre, Flint O. "Night Fighters in MiG Alley." *Air Force* 36 (November 1953): 29–30, 70.

Evans, Douglas. *Sabre Jets over Korea: A Firsthand Account.* Blue Ridge Summit, PA: TAB, 1984.

Farmer, James A., and M. J. Strumwasser. *The Evolution of the Airborne Forward Air Controller: An Analysis of Mosquito Operations in Korea.* Santa Monica, CA: Rand, 1967.

FEAF Bomber Command. "Heavyweights over Korea." *Air University Quarterly Review* 6 (Fall 1953): 114–119.

Finletter, Thomas K. "Air Power in the Korean Conflict." *Vital Speeches of the Day,* September 15, 1950, pp. 732–735.

Fithian, Ben. "The F-94. First Kill in Korea." *Navigator* 28 (Winter 1981): 15–18.

Fogleman, Ronald R. "Modernization for Korean War Stopped Post-WWII Reduction, Made US Ready." *Officer* 68 (December 1991): 28–30, 41–42.

Futrell, Robert F. "Air War in Korea: II." *Air University Quarterly Review* 4 (Spring 1951): 108–109.

———. "The Korean War." In *A History of the United States Air Force, 1907–1957.* Ed. Alfred Goldberg. Princeton, NJ: Van Nostrand, 1957.

———. *The United States Air Force in Korea, 1950–1953.* New York: Duell, 1961. Reprint, New York: Arno, 1971; Washington, DC: Office of Air Force History, 1983.

———. "A Case Study: USAF Intelligence in the Korean War." In Walter T. Hitchcock, ed., *The Intelligence Revolution, A Historical Perspective, Proceedings of the Thirteenth Military History Symposium, U.S. Air Force Academy,* October 1988a. Washington, DC: Office of Air Force History, 1991.

———. "Tactical Employment of Strategic Air Power in Korea." *Airpower Journal* 2 (Winter 1988b): 29–41.

———. *Ideas, Concepts, Doctrine: Basic Thinking in the United States Air Force, 1907–1960.* Vol. 1. Maxwell AFB, AL: Air University Press, 1989.

Goldberg, Alfred, ed. *History of the United States Air Force, 1907–1957.* Princeton, NJ: Van Nostrand, 1957.

Greenough, Robert B. "Communist Lessons from the Korean War." *Air University Quarterly Review* 5 (Winter 1952–1953): 22–29.

Higham, Robert. *Guide to the Sources of U.S. Military History.* Hamden, CT: Shoe String Press, 1975.

Hightower, Charles D. *The History of the United States Air Force Airborne Forward Air Controller in World War II, the Korean War, and the Vietnam Conflict.* Fort Leavenworth, KS: Army Command and General Staff College, 1984.

Holm, Skip. "Yalu River Raider." *Air Progress* 46 (September 1984): 41–49.

Hyatt, Joan. *Korean War, 1950–1953: Selected References.* Maxwell AFB, AL: Air University Library, 1992.

Jabara, James. "Air War in Korea." *Air Force* 34 (October 1951): 53, 60.

Jackson, Robert. *Air War over Korea.* New York: Scribner, 1973.

Jamison, Theodore. "Nightmare of the Korean Hills: Douglas B-26 Invader Operations in the Korean War, 1950–1953." *American Aviation Historical Society Journal* 34 (Summer 1989): 82–93.

Jessup, Alpheous. "Korean Airpower Lessons: They Will Influence Plans for the Future Planes, Equipment." *Aviation Week,* October 2, 1950, pp. 16–18.

Johnson, Robert S. "Working on the Railroads." *Air Force Magazine* 35 (March 1952): 25–29 ff.

Key, William G. "Air Power in Action: Korea, 1950–51." *Pegasus* 17 (October 1951a): 1–16.

———. "Combat Cargo: Korea, 1950–51." *Pegasus* 17 (November 1951b): 1–15.

Kirtland, Michael A., ed. *Air University Review Index, 1 May 1947 through January–March 1987.* Maxwell AFB, AL: Air University Press, 1990.

———. "Planning Air Operations: Lessons from Operation Strangle in the Korean War." *Airpower Journal* 6 (Summer 1992): 37–46.

———. ed. *Airpower Journal Index, 1987–1991.* Maxwell AFB, AL: Air University Press, 1993.

Knight, Charlotte. "Air War in Korea." *Air Force* 33 (August 1950): 21–25.

———. "The New Air War—Sabres vs MiGs." *Collier's,* April 21, 1951, p. 26.

———. "Korea: A Twenty-fifth Anniversary." *Air Force Magazine* 58 (June 1975): 59–63.

Kohn, Richard H., and Joseph P. Harahan, eds. *Air Superiority in World War II and Korea: An Interview with General James Ferguson, General Robert M. Lee, General William W. Momyer, and General Elwood R. Quesada.* Washington, DC: Office of Air Force History, 1983.

———, eds. *Air Interdiction World War II, Korea, and Vietnam: An Interview with General Earle E. Partridge, General Jacob E. Smart, General John W. Vogt, Jr.* Washington, DC: Office of Air Force History, 1986.

Kropf, Roger F. "The US Air Force in Korea: Problems That Hindered the Effectiveness of Air Power." *Airpower Journal* 4 (Spring 1990): 30–46.

Kuehl, Daniel. "Refighting the Last War: Electronic Warfare and U.S. Air Force B-29 Operations in the Korean War 1950–53." *Journal of Military History* 56 (January 1992): 87–111.

Launius, Roger. "MATS and the Korean Airlift." *Airlift* 12 (Summer 1990): 16–21.

Leckie, Robert. *Conflict: The History of the Korean War, 1950–51.* New York: Putnam's, 1962.

McLaren, David. "Mustangs in Aerial Combat: The Korean War." *American Aviation Historical Society Journal* 30 (Summer 1985): 94–101.

———. "Air Support in Korea: Mustang Style." *Aerospace Historian* 33 (June 1986): 74–86.

McNitt, James R. "Tactical Air Control in Korea." *Air University Quarterly Review* 6 (Summer 1953): 86–92.

Marion, Forrest L. "The Grand Experiment: Detachment F's Helicopter Combat Operations in Korea, 1950–1953." *Air Power History* 40 (Summer 1993): 38–51.

Maurer, Maurer. *USAF Credits for Destruction of Enemy Aircraft, Korean War*. USAF Historical Study No. 81. 1963.

Meilinger, Philip S. *Hoyt S. Vandenberg: The Life of a General*. Bloomington: Indiana University Press, 1989.

Merrill, Frank. *A Study of the Aerial Interdiction of Railways during the Korean War*. Fort Leavenworth, KS: Army Command and General Staff College, 1965.

Millar, Ward M. *Valley of the Shadow*. New York: McKay, 1955.

Millberry, R. I. "Engineer Aviation Forces in Korea." *Air University Quarterly Review* 7 (Spring 1954): 99–115.

Miller, Duncan. *The United States Air Force History: An Aerospace Bibliography*. Washington, DC: Office of Air Force History, 1979.

Millett, Allan R. "Korea, 1950–1953." In *Case Studies in Development of Close Air Support*. Ed. Benjamin Franklin Cooling. Washington, DC: Office of Air Force History, 1990.

Milton, T. R. "The Equalizer in Korea." *Air Force Magazine* 74 (October 1991): 72–76.

Momyer, William. *Air Power in Three Wars: WWII, Korea, Vietnam*. Washington, DC: Department of the Air Force, 1978.

Nichols, Jack C., and Warren E. Thompson. *Korea: The Air War 1950–1953*. London: Osprey, 1991.

Nigro, Edward. "Early Troop Carrier Operations in Korea." *Air University Quarterly Review* 7 (Spring 1954): 86–89.

Office of the Secretary of Defense. "Air War in Korea." *Air University Quarterly Review* 4 (Fall 1950): 19–39.

Owen, Elmer G., and Wallace F. Veaudry. "Control of Tactical Air Power in Korea." *Combat Forces Journal* 1 (April 1951): 19–21.

Parrish, Noel F. "Hoyt S. Vandenberg: Building the New Air Force." In *Makers of the United States Air Force*. Ed. John L. Frisbee. Washington, DC: Office of Air Force History, 1987.

Paszek, Lawrence. *United States Air Force History, A Guide to Documentary Sources*. Washington, DC: Office of Air Force History, 1973.

Poe, Bryce. "Korean War Combat Support: A Lieutenant's Journal." *Air Force Journal of Logistics* 13 (Fall 1989): 3–7.

Ransom, Frank E. *Air-Sea Rescue, 1941–1952*. U.S. Air Force Historical Study #95. Washington, DC: U.S. Air Force, 1953.

Rees, David. *Korea: The Limited War*. New York: St. Martin's, 1964.

Reid, W. M. "Tactical Air in Limited War." *Air University Quarterly Review* 8 (Spring 1956): 40–48.

Ridgway, Matthew. *The Korean War*. Garden City, NY: Doubleday, 1967.

Risedorph, Gene. "Mosquito." *American Aviation Historical Society Journal* 24 (Spring 1979): 45–51.

Rivera, Margarita. "Airlift of Cargo and Passengers in the Korean War." *Air Force Journal of Logistics* 13 (Fall 1989): 8–11.

Roberts, Chris. "Tactical Air Power Lessons from Korea." *Interavia* 9 (1954): 143–146.

Ruestow, Paul. "Air Force Logistics in the Theater of Operations." *Air University Quarterly Review* 6 (Summer 1954): 45–46.

Scholin, Allan R. "On the Graveyard Shift—B-26s Prowl the Korean Skies." *Air Force Magazine* 56 (September 1973): 102–106.

Scutts, Jerry. *Air War over Korea.* London: Arms and Armour, 1982.

Shrader, Charles R. "Air Interdiction in Korea." *Army Logistician* (March–April 1992): 11–13.

Simpson, Albert F. "Tactical Air Doctrine: Tunisia and Korea." *Air University Quarterly Review* 4 (Summer 1951): 5–20.

Sleeper, Raymond S. "Korean Targets for Medium Bombardment." *Air University Quarterly Review* 4 (Spring 1951): 18–31.

Soltys, Andrew T. "Enemy Antiaircraft Defenses in North Korea." *Air University Quarterly Review* 7 (Spring 1954): 75–81.

Stanglin, Douglas, and Peter Craig. "Secrets of the Korean War." *U.S. News and World Report,* August 9, 1993, pp. 45–47.

Sterne, Paul J. "The Build-Up of Enemy Air Potential." *Air University Quarterly Review* 4 (Summer 1951): 84–89.

Stewart, James T. ed. *Airpower: The Decisive Force in Korea.* Princeton, NJ: Van Nostrand, 1957.

Strawbridge, Dennis, and Nannette Kahn. *Fighter Pilot Performance in Korea.* Chicago: University of Chicago Press, 1955.

"Tactical Air Rescue in Korea." *Air University Quarterly Review* 6 (Fall 1953): 120–123.

Teschner, Charles G. "The Fighter-Bomber in Korea." *Air University Quarterly Review* 7 (Summer 1954): 71–80.

Thompson, Annis G. *The Greatest Airlift: The Story of Combat Cargo.* Tokyo: Dai-Nippon Printing Company, 1954.

Thyng, Harrison R. "Air-to-Air Combat in Korea." *Air University Quarterly Review* 6 (Summer 1953): 40–45.

Tormoen, George E. " 'Political Air Superiority' in the Korean Conflict." *Air University Quarterly Review* 6 (Winter 1953–1954): 78–84.

Tyrrell, John V. *Air Power in Korea.* Norfolk, VA: Armed Forces Staff College, 1985.

U.S. Air Force. *Operations in Korea, 1951.* Vol. 71, *U.S. Air Force Studies.* (Originally classified.) Washington, DC: United States Air Force Office, 1952.

———. *Far East Air Force (FEAF) Report on the Korean War.* (Originally classified.) Washington, DC: GPO for U.S. Air Force, March 26, 1954.

Vandenberg, Hoyt. "The Truth about Our Air Power." *Saturday Evening Post,* 17 February 1951, 20–21ff.

Watson, George M., Jr. *The Office of the Secretary of the Air Force.* Washington, DC: Center for Air Force History, 1993.

Watson, Mark. "Tactics for Limited Conflict." *Saturday Review* 45 (January 27, 1962): 19 ff.

Weyland, Otto P. "The Air Campaign in Korea." *Air University Quarterly Review* 6 (Fall 1953): 3–28.

Wikeham-Barnes, P. G. "Air Power Difficulties in the Korean Conflict." *Military Review* 33 (April 1953): 73–81.

Williams, William J., ed. *A Revolutionary War: Korea and the Transformation of the Postwar World.* Chicago: Imprint Publications, 1993.

Winchester, James H. "Report on Korean Air Losses." *Aviation Age* 16 (November 1951): 38–39.

Winnefeld, James A., and Dana J. Johnson. *Joint Air Operations: Pursuit of Unity in Command and Control, 1942–1991.* Annapolis: Naval Institute Press, 1993.

Yool, W. M. "Air Lessons from Korea." In *Brassey's Annual: The Armed Forces Year-Book.* Ed. H. G. Thursfield. New York: Macmillan, 1951.

Zaloga, Steven. "The Russians in MiG Alley." *Air Force Magazine* 74 (February 1991): 74–77.

Zimmerman, Don Z. "FEAF: Mission and Command Relationships." *Air University Quarterly Review* 4 (Summer 1951): 95–96.

15　The U.S. Navy and Marines in the Korean War

Lester H. Brune

The Korean War played an important role in U.S. naval history, helping to revive the navy and marines from their post–World War II doldrums caused by budget cuts in the nation's defense operations and exaggerated claims that atomic weapons made the navy obsolete for future wars. Following the bombing of Hiroshima and Japan's surrender in August 1945, strategic airpower advocates argued that long-range land-based aircraft were the only viable means for delivering atomic weapons on enemy targets and that no significant naval force threatened America. At the same time, President Harry Truman's policies to demobilize the armed forces and cut defense budgets required naval leaders to adjust to an era when pre-1941 seapower concepts might no longer apply. These difficulties faded quickly, however, after North Korean forces crossed the 38th parallel on June 25, 1950. During the ensuing war, it soon became obvious that the navy and marines had a central role in carrying out the cold war containment policies the Truman administration evolved between 1947 and 1953.

Beliefs that the Korean War is the "forgotten war" appear to be well suited regarding literature about the U.S. Navy and Marine Corps during that conflict. Although both Dean Allard (1985) and Richard Hallion (1993) explain that the Korean War was a major turning point for the U.S. Navy in the nation's post-1945 security structure, comparatively few detailed studies examine the naval aspects of the war, except for the official histories. Many U.S. Navy and Marine records are now available on the Korean War, and objective study of these documents could reveal important data about topics such as rapid mobilization, the development of weapons systems, and the navy-marine role in a post–cold war era during which small wars are more likely than the large-scale nuclear conflict that had been planned from 1950 until the Soviet Union's demise in 1991.

Because of the need for greater research on this period of naval history, this chapter concludes with detailed information about available sources for study, after first reviewing the literature that has appeared on the U.S. Navy and Marine Corps during the Korean War.

NAVAL AND MARINE CORPS STUDIES OF THE KOREAN WAR

The Eve of the War

As Dean Allard (1978) indicates, the U.S. Navy experienced five difficult years between the end of World War II and the Korean War. The surrender of Japan, which was attributed to the atomic bomb, precipitated an aura about U.S. Air Force superiority, which increased after the air force was separated from the U.S. Army and given equal status to the other two military services in the national military establishment created in 1947. Because some Washington authorities believed that naval ships would be obsolete sitting ducks in future atomic warfare, U.S. seapower seemed to be nonessential. The low point of respect for the navy's role was reached in 1949 when Secretary of Defense Louis Johnson cancelled the navy's supercarrier plans and caused the "revolt of the admirals," who publicly protested the Defense Department's action. Interservice rivalry, not defense unity, surfaced for public attention during subsequent congressional hearings in which U.S. Air Force officials tried to retain their monopoly of strategic delivery methods for nuclear weapons while the admirals argued that carrier aviation provided more flexible security methods in giving worldwide protection of the U.S. national interests.

In early 1950, the admirals' concepts gained greater attention. Following congressional hearings conducted by the House Armed Services Committee chaired by Representative Carl Vinson (Georgia), a March 1950 report favored the navy's balanced-force concept by which naval carrier aviation complemented the U.S. Air Force's Strategic Air Command in offering a global nuclear force against the Soviet Union and its allies. Also in April 1950, the National Security Council recommended that President Harry Truman adopt NSC-68, a document calling for a large-scale U.S. military buildup of all the nation's armed forces to meet the global threat of communism.

Action on NSC-68 was pending in June 1950, so that without the Korean War, the recommendations of Vinson's committee report and NSC-68 would have been delayed at best, forgotten at worst, because Truman was not yet committed to fulfill them. North Korea's attack promoted these two documents to the forefront of U.S. plans for the rapid increase in defense expenditures to strengthen the armed forces not only in East Asia and Europe but also around the world.

For the U.S. Navy, the results of the Korean War proved to be salutary. Although initial wartime expansion appropriated funds to activate "mothballed" vessels left over from World War II and to call up naval and marine reserve units, between July 1950 and July 1953 the U.S. Navy gained new weapons systems and a huge budgetary expansion. Among these advancements were two new aircraft carriers, a new class of destroyers, and guided missile cruisers. Also by 1952, the *Nautilus* submarine, the world's first nuclear-powered ship, began to be built.

The unification of the armed forces and the creation of the national military establishment are described by Demetrios Caraley (1966) and Paolo Coletta (1975, 1981b). The Marine Corps' relation to unification is explained by Gordon W. Keiser (1982). From the navy's viewpoint, James Forrestal had a crucial role in the unification because he protected the navy's desire to allow each of the three services to retain its separate duties, a decision that would weaken the secretary of defense. Forrestal's *Diaries* (1957) and the biographies by Townsend Hoopes and Douglas Brinkley (1992) and by Robert Albion and Robert Connery (1962) give details about Forrestal's later difficulties as the first secretary of defense. Paul Hammond (1959) assesses defense reorganization and explains in an article (1962) the dispute between advocates of the supercarrier and the B-36 long-range bomber that the air force developed to strike at Moscow. Steve Rearden (1979) and Doris M. Condit (1988) describe the activity of the reorganized Defense Department from 1947 to 1953. For a broader perspective regarding post-1945 security strategy disputes, consult the studies by Warner R. Schilling and associates (1962), David Rosenberg (1979), and Dean Allard (1985).

Navy and Marine Operations in Korea

The outbreak of the Korean War in June 1950 required the U.S. Naval Forces, Far East (NAVFE) to change from a "housekeeping" group under General Douglas MacArthur's Tokyo command headquarters to becoming an organization for combat using the 7th Fleet, naval ships of the British Commonwealth, and naval forces of the Republic of Korea. The NAVFE became the naval component of the UN Command and was led by Vice Admiral C. Turner Joy until June 4, 1952, when, after Joy became a delegate to armistice negotiations, Vice Admiral Robert P. Briscoe took command.

The NAVFE formed four combat commands plus the Military Sea Transport Service (MSTS), which brought U.S. mainland forces to Korea via Japan. The four combat groups were the 7th Fleet Striking Force (Task Force 77), which operated aircraft carriers in the Sea of Japan, off Korea's east coast; the Blockading and Escort Force (TF 95), which operated on both coasts of Korea and included a minesweeping group; the Amphibious Force (TF 90), which operated at the Inchon landing and elsewhere as described below; and the Naval Forces Japan (TF 96), which secured U.S. bases in Japan and provided antisubmarine protection.

The overall aspects of U.S. Navy and Marine Corps operations during the Korean War are described in the U.S. Marine Corps official history (1954–1972) and in Richard Hallion's book (1986) and article (1993), James A. Field's (1962) volume, and in work by Malcolm W. Cagle and Frank Manson (1957). Although Albert Cowdrey's *The Medics' War* (1988) is primarily about the army, it contains information on navy and Marine Corps medical units in Korea. There is a variety of other worthwhile literature about the U.S. Marines during the Korean War. Ernest H. Giusti (1967) explains the mobilization of the marine reserve units. Henry Berry (1988) compiles oral history memoirs of marines who were in Korea. Two other memoirs about the war are Martin Russ' (1957) war journal and Francis Fox Parry's (1987) description of his work with marine artillery units in three wars. Allan Millett (1993) has a biography of General Gerald C. Thomas, who commanded the 1st Marine Division in Korea before becoming the Marine Corps assistant commandant in Washington, D.C., from 1952 to 1954.

Carrier Strike Forces

In the Korean theater from 1950 to 1953, eleven large attack carriers served Task Force 77: the USS *Antietam, Boxer, Bon Homme Richard, Essex, Kearsarge, Lake Champlain, Leyte, Oriskany, Philippine Sea, Princeton,* and *Valley Forge.* These ships had 24 carrier air groups totaling 100 squadrons, including 22 naval reserve squadrons. Their aircraft included 38 F4U Corsairs, 35 F9F Panthers, 23 AD Skyraiders, and 4 F2H Banshee squadrons.

In addition to these TF 77 aviation units, the Blockading and Escort Force (TF 95) employed four escort carriers and one light carrier, which included the light carrier *Bataan* and the escorts *Bairoko, Badoeng Strait, Rendova,* and *Sicily.* These units served U.S. Marine Corps air squadrons and worked with the Australian carrier HMAS *Sydney* and four British carriers: *HMS Glory, Ocean, Theseus,* and *Triumph.*

During the war U.S. Navy and Marine forces flew 275,912 sorties compared to the U.S. Air Force's 392,139. The navy flew 40 percent of the interdiction missions, 53 percent of the close support missions, 36 percent of the counterair sorties, 30 percent of the reconnaissance missions, and 100 percent of the antisubmarine patrols.

As Callum McDonald (1986) explains, the U.S. Navy and U.S. Air Force had several interservice disputes regarding close air support and interdiction operations. During the early part of the war, the two services had difficulty in communicating with the ground forces because of different radio systems and tactical methods. The air force conceived combat support as an adjunct to artillery, operating only beyond 1,000 yards of the frontlines, while the navy and marines operated as close as 50 to 100 yards from friendly forces. The 1st Marine Aircraft Wing also had tactical air control parties (TACP) at the battalion level with airplanes directly overhead for quick reaction to an alert from friendly ground forces, a system enabling the planes to respond quickly to calls for assistance. Although the air force eventually improved its communications methods, the marines' system functioned best, and, as William Momyer (1978) explains, the U.S. Air Force adopted the Marines' system in Vietnam. Richard Hallion (1993) concludes that the air force and navy methods complemented each other but caused problems in Korea because of the intense prewar defense disputes.

The U.S. Navy and Marine aviation units had extensive action during the Korean War, including close air support of UN ground forces and air attacks to interdict supplies or destroy strategic enemy targets. During the war's initial phases at the Pusan Perimeter and in the Inchon landing of September 1950, aircraft of the navy and marines joined with air force planes to support UN troops and to interdict communist troops and supplies. When the war stalemated during the summer of 1951, the UN's aviation forces principally flew interdiction bombing raids, known as Operation Strangle, until June 1952, when aircraft under Vice Admiral J. J. "Jocko" Clark and Air Force Brigadier General Jacob E. Smart cooperated in an "air pressure" bombing campaign designed to force the enemy's surrender. This 1952–1953 air pressure campaign began with raids to destroy North Korea's power generation facilities such as those at Suiho and to demolish both Pyongyang's military facilities and North Korea's extractive mining and oil facilities. In October 1952, the so-called Cherokee Strikes bombed enemy frontline facilities and forces as close as 300 miles from combat zones in order to disrupt the enemy supply lines.

In addition to the accounts of naval air activity in Korea in the general books of Hallion (1986) and Field (1962), there is an article about the marines' air operations by Charles L. Dockery (1985). Literature about close air support include studies by Allan Millett (1990) and John Thach (1975). The problems of close air support experienced by the navy and air force are discussed by Callum McDonald (1986), P. G. Wykeham Barnes (1952), and David Detzer (1977). The essays edited by Richard Kohn and J. P. Harahn (1983) compare air interdiction activity in World War II, Vietnam, and the Korean War. Vice Admiral Clark's (1967) memoirs include insight into the "air pressure" bombings. Barrett Tillman and Joseph Handleman (1984) describe the bombings of Hwachon Dam and Carlson's Canyon, with the latter raids being the subject of James Michener's *The Bridges at Toko-Ri* (1953).

Marine Helicopter Activity

The U.S. Marine Corps pioneered innovations in the use of helicopters during the Korean War. When the marines initially arrived at Pusan in August 1950, the 1st Marine Aircraft Wing had observation Squadron Six (VMO-6) with four Sikorsky H03S-1 helicopters for observation duty. This was the first U.S. helicopter unit sent on overseas duty. Later this unit was joined by a helicopter transport squadron with fifteen Sikorsky HRS-1 ten-seated cargo helicopters. This transport squadron made the first aerial resupply by carrying over 18,000 pounds of gear and 74 marines to the 2d Marine Battalion on Korea's East Front near the Soyang River. In November 1951, the transport squad carried 950 troops to the combat front and brought 950 back to the rear.

The marines' helicopter squadrons activity included airlifting medical casualties from the battlefield, resupplying combat units, moving combat troops to and from the battlefield, observing battlefield activity, and performing air-sea rescues. By the time the Korean truce ended the conflict in July 1953, both the U.S. Army and Air Force had adopted many of the marines' methods. Thomas L. McClellan (1988) describes the marines' airmobile tactics in Korea.

Blockade and Escort Activity

In addition to the U.S. Marines' assigned aviation activity, Task Force 95's mission was to control the seas around Korea in order to prevent the entrance of communist supplies and to protect the efficient flow of UN equipment and supplies. This task force also interdicted enemy road and rail line through the use of fighter and fighter-bomber aircraft and launched commando raids to destroy enemy bridges and tunnels. Task Force 95's battleships, cruisers, and destroyers bombarded enemy shore installations, trucks, and locomotives.

TF 95's most dangerous sea duties were minesweeping operations, especially at North Korea's ports of Wonsan and Chinampo. Enemy mines sank four U.S. minesweepers and one tugboat as well as damaging five other ships. During the war, the minesweepers destroyed 1,535 enemy mines. The antimine operations are described by Arnold Lott (1959) and James A. Meacham (1967). Tamara Melia's (1991) study of mine countermeasures includes the chapter, "The Wonsan Generation: Lessons Relearned." Joseph Karneke's (1959) *Navy Diver* is a personal account of antimine operations.

Amphibious Forces

Task Force 90 not only conducted decoy commando operations to act as a constant threat to communist-controlled regions but also engaged in two significant amphibious projects at Inchon on September 15, 1950, and in Wonsan-Chosin-Hungnam operations from October through December 1950. Called Chromite operation, the Inchon-Seoul landing in September was arguably the most significant offensive UN victory of the Korean War. Preceded by and supported with air strikes and naval gunfire, the 1st, 2d, and 3d Battalions of the 5th Marines hit the beaches at Wolmi-do, and at Inchon's Red, Black, and Blue sectors on September 15, achieving each of their major D-day objectives, including the occupation of Inchon and capturing the railway to Seoul. Following this success, the marines were joined by the U.S. Army's 3d and 7th Infantry divisions to form the X Corps under the command of Lieutenant General Edward Almond. During this period, the 1st Marine Aircraft Wing began operations out of Kimpo Airfield near Seoul. By September 28, Seoul had been captured, and the marines continued to drive northward until October 7, when Operation Chromite ended. During the Inchon offensive, 366 marines were killed in action, 49 died of wounds, 6 were missing in action, and 2,029 suffered wounds.

The Inchon landing is explained in works by Michael Langley (1979), B. F. Halloran (1972), Robert Heinl (1968), and Walter J. Sheldon (1968). Lieutenant General Victor Krulak's (1984) memoirs include data about Inchon. Edwin Simmons (1987) explains Inchon as a war games exercise in postwar naval training, and Bruce Pirnie (1982) assesses the risks involved in MacArthur's plans for Chromite. Maurice Roach (1976) describes the 8,000-mile movement of Marine Corps forces from the Mediterranean Sea to augment the units operating in the Korean theater, and Ann Jensen's "To the Yalu" (1990) examines the offensive north of the 38th parallel following the capture of Seoul.

Prior to Chromite, the 1st Marine Provisional Brigade had been hastily organized in July 1950 in order to reinforce the UN troops at Pusan (Naktong) who fought to keep the communists from taking over the entire Korean peninsula. The first Pusan landing is described in Nicholas Canzona's (1985) article. Lynn Montross and Canzona have details of the Pusan operations in Volume 2 of the official U.S. Marine Corps history of the Korean War (1955). Activities of the 1st Marine Division are described by Tom Bartlett (1980).

Wonsan, Chosin, and Hungnam Operations

Originally scheduled for October 20, 1950, as a landing and invasion above the 38th parallel, the capture of Wonsan by Republic of Korea armies on October 10 would have made the X Corps landing simple except for the fact that the harbor was heavily mined with an estimated 4,000 contact and magnetic mines supplied to North Korea by the Soviet Union. After a major minesweeping operation, the 1st Marine Division landed between October 25 and 27 and moved toward the Chosin Reservoir on the northeast border between North Korea and China. After November 24, however, the X Corps' 1st Division of marines and the army infantry ran into trouble when four Chinese communist armies crossed the Yalu River border and attacked toward the Chosin sector. After overwhelming the U.S. Army's 31st Infantry Regiment and the 41st Commando Battalion of the British Royal Marines, the Chinese trapped the U.S. Marines at Chosin. Under heavy fire, the marines held fast until December 8, when they were ordered to evacuate. The marines withdrew and finally reached Hungnam on December 11.

Between December 10 and 14 from Hungnam, Navy Task Force 95, backed by TF 77's carriers and ships, directed the evacuation and redeployment of five divisions of the X Corps consisting of the 1st Marine Division, the 3d and 7th U.S. Army divisions, and the Republic of Korea's I and II Corps. This included 22,215 marines who were deployed to the Pusan sector to join the U.S. 8th Army, which fought to stop the Chinese offensive in January 1951. From October 26 to December 15, 1950, the Wonsan-Chosin-Hungnam operations resulted in 664 marines killed in action; 114 dying from wounds; 192 missing in action; 3,508 wounded; and 7,313 nonbattle casualties, most of whom suffered frostbite from the severe cold. The U.S. Marines estimated that the Chinese suffered 10,000 deaths and 5,000 wounded and that China's 9th Army Group of 120,000 had been made useless. For their valor, the marines were awarded both an army and a navy Presidential Unit Citation.

The Wonsan-Chosin-Hungnam action of the U.S. Marines is described by Lynn Montross and Nicholas Canzona in volume 3 of the official Marine Corps history of the Korean War (1957), Robert Leckie's *March to Glory* (1960), and William Hopkins's *One Bugle, No Drums: The Marines at Chosin Reservoir* (1986). Eric Hammel (1984) gives details of the Chosin engagement at ''Hill 1282,'' while the articles by Kenneth Condit and Ernest Giusti (1952) are worth reading. James Doyle and Arthur J. Mayer (1979) describe the evacuation at Hungnam. Both Burke Davis' (1962) biography of General Lewis B. Puller and John Gooch's *Military Misfortunes* (1990) have data about the 8th Army's defeat by the Chinese in the fall of 1950, which indicates why the marines did better than the army.

Naval Forces, Japan

Because combat forces that had been in Japan before the war were dispatched to Korea, the security of the Japanese islands had to be maintained by U.S. Army, Air Force, and Navy units. Navy Task Force 96 had the responsibility for protecting the waterways off Japan from any communist threats and for protecting the logistics supply routes from Japan to the UN forces in Korea. Thus, Task Force 96 had essential duty, albeit less glamorous than the other U.S. Navy combat commands. These operations are described in the general naval histories of the war by Hallion (1986), Field (1962), and Cagle and Manson (1957).

GENERAL NAVY AND MARINE HISTORIES

In order to place the role of the Korean War into the broad context of U.S. Navy and Marine history, there are a variety of general histories to consult. The history of U.S. naval power is described in Elmer B. Potter's *Seapower: A Naval History* (1981) and in Edwin B. Hooper's *U.S. Naval Power in a Changing World* (1988), which compares the American navy to other nations. Both Edward Beach (1986) and Paolo Coletta (1978) have brief histories of the navy since 1776. The studies of Michael Isenberg (1993), Norman Friedman (1987), Paul Ryan (1981), and Edward Hooper's (1976), volume 1 of the *United States Navy and the Vietnam Conflict,* explain the navy's adjustment to its cold war role after 1945. Craig M. Cameron (1994) has fascinating data on the 1st Marine Division from 1941 to 1951. John Cable's *Gunboat Diplomacy* (1981) includes the Korean War in studying the use of naval forces in limited wars. Richard Hewlett (1974) describes the beginning of the "nuclear navy" after 1947, while D. S. Fahrney (1982) explains the navy's pioneer role in developing guided missiles.

Basic histories of the U.S. Marine Corps are by Allan Millett (1991), Edwin Simmons (1976), William D. Parker (1970), and Robert Moskin (1977). The evolution of Marine Corps missions for U.S. national security is examined by Thomas Roe and associates (1962).

General studies about naval aviation are important because the aircraft carrier played a larger role in navy operations after 1945. Although the U.S. Navy's plans for carriers were stymied in 1949 when Secretary of Defense Louis Johnson blocked the construction of a supercarrier, the Korean War overturned political opposition to modernizing carriers. David A. Rosenberg and Floyd D. Kennedy (1975) explain the carrier's strategic role during the cold war era, and Desmond Wilson (1965) describes the development of attack carriers. Norman Friedman (1981), Gareth Pawlowski (1971), and Norman Polmar (1969) discuss the broad history of carrier aviation. Peter Mersky (1983) has a history of Marine Corps aviation after 1917, and the marines' innovations in helicopter combat aircraft are described by Eugene Rawlins (1976), William Fails (1978), and Lynn Montross (1954). The official U.S. Navy Department's history of naval aviation from 1910 to 1980 was published in 1981.

RESEARCH AND REFERENCE DATA

Bibliographies

Numerous guides are available to assist research in the history of the U.S. Navy and Marine Corps. Recent bibliographies on the navy include two by Paolo Coletta (1981a, 1988), another by Susan Kinnell and Suzanne Ontiveros (1986), and an updated supplement by Benjamin Labaree (1988) to Robert Albion's (1972) fourth edition.

For data on the 1950s, the U.S. Navy's History Division has a bibliography (1972), and Clark Reynolds has an article about the literature of naval aviation (1974). For periodical articles on both the navy and the marines, the Air University Library's Periodical Index has had regular issues since 1949 that cover all branches of the armed forces. In addition, Charles Schultz has an index of navy articles (1972–), which is issued by the Mystic Seaport Museum, Connecticut.

For literature on the marines, the U.S. Marine Corps Historical Division has published updated bibliographies since 1961. Michael O'Quinlivan and James Santelli (1970) provide an annotated bibliography of the U.S. Marines in the Korean War. Santelli (1968) also edited a bibliography about marine aviation's close air support activity, an important aspect of U.S. Marine operations in Korea. Other bibliographies about U.S. naval history are by J. B. Moran (1973), Charles Dollen (1963), and Jack Hillard and Harold Bivins (1971).

Finally, there are six specialized reference books for historical study. Jack Sweetman (1984) has a chronology for both the navy and marines, while chronologies have been published for the U.S. Marines by the Marine Corps History and Museums Division (1965) and for the navy by David M. Cooney (1965). A dictionary of naval terms has been compiled by John Noel and Edward Beach (1988) and of naval abbreviations by Bill Wedertz (1970). Finally, Robert Heinl (1966) has a volume on noteworthy military and naval quotations.

Oral Histories

Oral history collections have been compiled by the U.S. Navy and U.S. Marines. In addition to those interviewed at the Columbia University Oral History Archives cited elsewhere in this volume, Benis Frank (1973) identifies this material for the marines, and both John Mason (1973) and Paul Stillwell (1983) provide information on the U.S. Naval Institute's oral histories collection. Oral history data regarding the navy's research and development activity are given by Carole Nowicke (1985).

Dissertations

Doctoral dissertations on all aspects of military history are indexed by Allen Millett and B. Franklin Cooling III (1972), and this index continues to be updated in the *Journal of Military History,* formerly *Military Affairs* (1937–).

Documented Papers

Collections of navy and Marine Corps papers and documents are described in three publications, but scholars should contact the document centers below for the latest information. The three valuable guides to documents are the Naval Historical Foundation's (1974) list of manuscripts at the Library of Congress; Charles Wood's (1974) catalog of Marine Corps collections; and Dean Allard and Betty Bern's (1970) informative volume on sources in the Washington, D.C., area.

In addition to the U.S. National Archives, the important manuscript sources to check for U.S. Navy and Marine Corps history are the U.S. Naval History Division at the Washington Navy Yard, Washington, D.C.; the U.S. Marine Corps Historical Center at the Washington Navy Yard, Washington, D.C.; the Naval Historical Collection, U.S. Naval War College, Newport, Rhode Island; and the U.S. Marine History and Museums Division, Arlington, Virginia.

Official Biographical Materials

Both the navy and marines have a variety of biographical literature about their service personnel. Roger Spiller (1983) has a *Dictionary of Military Biography* covering all of the armed forces. Karl Schuon's (1963, 1965) biographical volumes cover both the U.S. Navy and U.S. Marines, and Jane Blakeney (1957) describes famous marines. Regarding high-ranking naval officials, Clark Reynolds (1978) writes about famous admirals; Robert Love (1980) about the chief of naval operations; and Paolo Coletta and coworkers (1980) edited two volumes of essays on the secretaries of the navy.

Official lists of naval and marine personnel are issued regularly by the U.S. Bureau of Naval Personnel (1941–) and the U.S. Marine Corps (1943–). The official annual reports of the secretary of the navy have been issued since 1948 as part of the reports of the secretary of defense.

Ships and Aircraft

Many studies of the navy and marines require knowledge about the ships and aircraft available to these services. The basic source for these data is Jane's *All the World's Fighting Ships* in volumes issued since 1898 and Jane's *All the World's Aircraft* issued since 1909. The U.S. Naval History Division published a dictionary of the navy's ships in five volumes (1959); and the U.S. Marine Corps has a book about its aircraft from 1903 to 1965 (1967). Other works regarding the ships and aircraft are by John Rowe and Samuel Morison (1972), Gordon Swanborough and Peter Bowers (1968), Paul Matt (1962), and William Larkins (1959). Norman Friedman (1982) described the evolution of destroyers in the navy, while Stefan

Terzibaschitsch (1980, 1981, 1988) has studies about the U.S. Navy's aircraft carriers, escort carriers, and cruisers.

Periodicals

Important journals with articles and reviews an U.S. Navy and Marine Corps history are *Naval Aviation News* (1919–), *Naval War College Review* (1948–), *Fortitudine* (1970–); *Proceedings of the United States Naval Institute* (1874–); *Marine Corps Gazette* (1916–); *Naval Aviation News* (1919–); *Leatherneck* (1917–); *Naval Review* (1962); and *Naval History* (1986–). Articles on all U.S. armed forces are included in the *Journal of Military History*, which formerly was *Military Affairs* (1937–).

REFERENCES

Air University Library, Index to Military Periodicals. Maxwell Air Force Base, AL 1949–.

Albion, Robert G. *Naval and Maritime History: An Annotated Bibliography.* 4th ed. Mystic Seaport, CT: Marine Historical Association, 1972.

Albion, Robert G., and Robert H. Connery. *Forrestal and the Navy.* New York: Columbia University Press, 1962.

Allard, Dean. "An Era in Transition, 1945–53." In Kenneth J. Hagan, ed., *In Peace and War: Interpretations of American Naval History, 1775–1978.* Westport, CT: Greenwood Press, 1978.

———. "Recent Perspectives on the Post-1947 Navy." In U.S. Naval Academy, History Department, ed., *New Aspects of Naval History: Selected Papers from the 5th Naval History Symposium.* Baltimore, MD: Nautical and Aviation Publishing Company of America, 1985.

Allard, Dean, and Betty Bern, eds. *U.S. Naval History Sources in the Washington Area and Suggested Research Subjects.* Washington, DC: Government Printing Office, 1970.

Barnes, P. G. Wykeham. "The War in Korea with Special References to the Difficulties of Using Air Power." *Journal of the Royal United Services Institution,* no. 586 (May 1952): 151ff.

Bartlett, Tom. "The Fabulous, Frozen Fighting First." *Leatherneck* 63 (December 1980): 16–21.

Beach, Edward L. *The United States Navy: 200 Years.* New York: Henry Holt and Co., 1986.

Berry, Henry. *Hey, Mac, Where Ya Been? Living Memories of the U.S. Marines in the Korean War.* New York: St. Martin's Press, 1988.

Blakeney, Jane. *Heroes, U.S. Marine Corps, 1861–1955.* Washington, DC: Blakeney Publishers, 1957.

Cable, James. *Gunboat Diplomacy: The Political Application of Limited Naval Forces, 1919–1979.* London: Macmillan, 1981.

Cagle, Malcolm W., and Frank A. Manson. *The Sea War in Korea.* Annapolis, MD: U.S. Naval Institute, 1957.

Cameron, Craig M. *American Samurai: Myth, Imagination, and the Conduct of Battle in the First Marine Division, 1941–1951.* New York: Cambridge University Press, 1994.

Canzona, Nicholas A. "Marines Land at Pusan: August 1950." *Marine Corps Gazette* 69 (August 1985): 42–46.

Caraley, Demetrios. *The Politics of Military Unification.* New York: Columbia University Press, 1966.

Clark, J. J. "Jocko," with C. J. Reynolds. *Carrier Admiral.* New York: David McKay, 1967.

Coletta, Paolo E. "The Defense Unification Battle, 1947–1950: The Navy." *Prologue* 7:1 (1975): 6–17.

———. *The American Naval Heritage in Brief.* Washington, DC: University Press of America, 1978.

———. *A Bibliography of American Naval History.* Annapolis, MD: Naval Institute Press, 1981a.

———. *The United States Navy and Defense Unification. 1947–1953.* East Brunswick, NJ: Associated University Presses, 1981b.

———. *An Annotated Bibliography of U.S. Marine Corps History.* Lanham, MD: University Press of America, 1986.

———. *A Selected and Annotated Bibliography of American Naval History.* Frederick, MD: University Press of America, 1988.

Coletta, Paolo E., Robert G. Albion, and K. Jack Bauer, eds. *American Secretaries of the Navy.* 2 vols. Annapolis, MD: Naval Institute Press, 1980.

Condit, Doris M. *History of the Office of Secretary of Defense.* Vol. 2: *The Test of War, 1950–1953.* Washington, DC: Office of the Secretary of Defense, 1988.

Condit, Kenneth W., and Ernest H. Giusti. "Marine Air at the Chosin Reservoir" and "Marine Air Covers the Breakout." *Marine Corps Gazette* 36 (July–August 1952).

Cooney, David M. *A Chronology of the U.S. Navy: 1775–1965.* New York: Watts, 1965.

Cowdrey, Albert. *The Medics' War.* Washington, DC: U.S. Army Center of Military History, 1988.

Davis, Burke. *Marine! The Life of Lt. Gen. Lewis B. (Chesty) Puller.* Boston: Little, Brown, 1962; New York: Bantam, 1988.

Detzer, David. *Thunder of the Captains: The Short Summer of 1950.* New York: Crowell, 1977.

Dockery, Charles L. "Marine Air over Korea." *Marine Corps Gazette* 69 (December 1985): 38–42.

Dollen, Charles, and the Library Staff of the University of San Diego. *Bibliography of the United States Marine Corps.* New York: Scarecrow Press, 1963.

Doyle, James H., and Arthur J. Mayer. "December 1950 at Hungnam." *Proceedings, U.S. Naval Institute* 105 (April 1979): 44–65.

Fahrney, D. S. "Guided Missiles—U.S. Navy the Pioneer." *Journal of the American Aviation Historical Society* 27 (Spring 1982): 21–26.

Fails, William R. *Marines and Helicopters, 1946–1973.* Ed. William Sanbito. Washington, DC: Headquarters, QMC, 1978.

Field, James A., Jr. *United States Naval Operations: Korea.* Washington, DC: GPO, 1962.

Forrestal, James V. *The Forrestal Diaries.* Ed. Walter Millis. New York: Viking Press, 1951.

Fortitudine. Washington, DC: 1970–.

Frank, Benis M. *Marine Corps Oral History Collection Catalog.* Washington, DC: U.S. Marine History and Museums Division, 1973.

Friedman, Norman. *Carrier Air Power.* Annapolis, MD: Naval Institute Press, 1981.

———. *U.S. Destroyers: An Illustrated Design History.* Annapolis, MD: Naval Institute Press, 1982.

———. *The Postwar Naval Revolution.* Annapolis, MD: Naval Institute Press, 1987.

Giusti, Ernest H. *The Mobilization of the Marine Corps Reserve in the Korean Conflict.* Washington, DC: Historical Branch, G-3 Division Headquarters U.S. Marine Corps, 1967.

Gooch, John. *Military Misfortunes: The Anatomy of Failure in War.* New York: Free Press, 1990.

Hallion, Richard P. *The Naval Air War in Korea.* Baltimore, MD: Nautical and Aviation Publishing Co. of America, 1986.

———. "Naval Air Operations in Korea." In William J. Williams, ed., *A Revolutionary War: Korea and the Transformation of the Postwar World.* Chicago: Imprint Publications, 1993.

Halloran, B. F. "Inchon Landing." *Marine Corps Gazette* 56 (September 1972): 25–32.

Hammond, Paul Y. *Organizing for Defense.* New York: Columbia University Press, 1959.

———. "Super Carriers and B-36 Bombers: Appropriations, Strategy and Politics." In Harold Stein, ed., *American Civil-Military Decisions.* Birmingham: University of Alabama Press, 1962.

Hammel, Eric M. "Hill 1282." *Leatherneck* (December 1984): 26–31.

Heinl, Robert D. *Dictionary of Military and Naval Quotations.* Annapolis, MD: U.S. Naval Institute, 1966.

———. *Victory at High Tide: The Inchon-Seoul Campaign.* Philadelphia: Lippincott, 1968.

Hewlett, Richard. *The Nuclear Navy, 1946–1962.* Chicago: University of Chicago Press, 1974.

Hillard, Jack B., and Harold A. Bivins. *An Annotated Reading List of United States Marine Corps History.* Washington, DC: History and Museums Division, Headquarters U.S. Marine Corps, 1971.

Hooper, Edwin B. *The Navy Department: Evolution and Fragmentation.* Washington, DC: Naval Historical Foundation, 1978.

———. *United States Naval Power in a Changing World.* New York: Praeger, 1988.

Hooper, Edwin B., Dean Allard, and Oscar Fitzgerald. *The United States Navy and the Vietnam Conflict.* Vol. 1: *The Setting of the Stage to 1959.* Washington, DC: GPO, 1976.

Hoopes, Townsend, and Douglas Brinkley. *Driven Patriot: The Life and Times of James Forrestal.* New York: Knopf, 1992.

Hopkins, William B. *One Bugle No Drums: The Marines at Chosin Reservoir.* Chapel Hill, NC: Algonquin Books, 1986.

Isenberg, Michael T. *The United States Navy in an era of Cold War and Violent Peace, 1945–1962.* New York: St. Martin's Press, 1993.

Jane's All the World's Aircraft. New York: Various publishers, 1909–.

Jane's All the World's Fighting Ships. New York: Various publishers, 1898–.

Jensen, Ann. "To the Yalu." *Proceedings, U.S. Naval Institute* 116 (February 1990): 58–64.

Journal of Military History, formerly *Military Affairs* (American Military Institute). 1937–.

Karneke, Joseph S., as told to Victor Boesen. *Navy Diver.* New York: G. P. Putnam's, 1959.

Keiser, Gordon W. *The U.S. Marine Corps and Defense Unification, 1944–1947.* Washington, DC: National Defense University Press, 1982.

Kinnell, Susan K., and Suzanne R. Ontiveros, eds. *American Maritime History: A Bibliography.* Santa Barbara, CA: ABC-Clio, 1986.

Klimp, Jack J. "The Battle for Seoul: Marines and MOUT (Military Operations in Urbanized Territory)." *Marine Corps Gazette* 65 (November 1981): 79–82.

Kohn, Richard H., and J. P. Harahn, eds. *Air Interdiction in World War II, Korea, and Vietnam.* Washington, DC: Office of Air Force History, 1983.

Krulak, Lt. Gen. Victor H., USMC (Ret.). *First to Flight: An Inside View of the U.S. Marine Corps.* Annapolis, MD: Naval Institute Press, 1984.

Labaree, Benjamin W. *A Supplement (1971–1986) to Robert G. Albion's Naval and Maritime History: An Annotated Bibliography.* 4th ed. Mystic, CT: Mystic Seaport Museum, 1988.

Langley, Michael. *Inchon Landing: MacArthur's Last Triumph.* New York: Times Books, 1979.

Larkins, William T. *U.S. Marine Aircraft, 1914–1959.* Concord, CA: Aviation History Publications, 1959.

Leatherneck. Quantico, VA, and Washington, DC: 1917–.

Leckie, Robert. *The March to Glory.* New York: World, 1960.

Lott, Arnold S. *Most Dangerous Sea: A History of Mine Warfare Operations in World War II and Korea.* Annapolis, MD: U.S. Naval Institute, 1959.

Love, Robert. *The Chiefs of Naval Operations.* Annapolis, MD: Naval Institute Press, 1980.

McClellan, Thomas L. "Operation Bumblebee: How the U.S. Marine Corps Developed Airmobile Tactics during the Korean War." *USA Aviation Digest* (June 1988): 38–44.

MacDonald, Callum. *Korea: The War before Vietnam.* New York: Free Press, 1986.

Marine Corps Gazette. Quantico, VA, 1916–.

Mason, John T., Jr. "An Interview with John T. Mason, Jr., Director of Oral History." *Proceedings, U.S. Naval Institute* (July 1973): 42–47.

Matt, Paul R., comp. *United States Navy and Marine Corps Fighters, 1918–1962.* Ed. Bruce Robertson. Los Angeles: Aero Publishers, 1962.

Meachum, James A. "Four Mining Campaigns." *Naval War College Review* (June 1967): 75–129.

Meid, Pat, and James M. Yingling. *Operations in West Korea.* Washington, DC: U.S. Marine Corps Historical Branch, 1972.

Melia, Tamara Moser. *"Damn the Torpedoes": A Short History of the U.S. Naval Mine Countermeasures, 1777–1991.* Washington, DC: Department of the Navy, Naval Historical Center, 1991.

Mersky, Peter B. *U.S. Marine Corps Aviation—1912 to the Present.* Annapolis, MD: Nautical and Aviation Publishing Company of America, 1983.

Michener, James. *The Bridges at Toko-Ri.* New York: Random House, 1953.

Millett, Allan R. "Korea, 1950–1953." In Benjamin F. Cooling, ed., *Case Studies in the Development of Close Air Support.* Washington, DC: Office of Air Force History, 1990.

———. *Semper Fidelis: The United States Marine Corps.* Rev. ed. New York: Free Press, 1991.

———. *In Many a Strife: General Gerald C. Thomas and the U.S. Marine Corps, 1917–1956.* Annapolis, MD: Naval Institute Press, 1993.

Millett, Allan R., and B. Franklin Cooling III. *Doctoral Dissertations in Military Affairs.* Manhattan, KS: Kansas State University Library, 1972. Annually thereafter in *Military Affairs* and its successor publication, *Journal of Military History.*

Momyer, William M. *Airpower in Three Wars.* Washington, DC: GPO, 1978.

Montross, Lynn. *Cavalry of the Sky: The Story of U.S. Marine Combat Helicopters.* New York: Harper and Brothers, 1954.

Montross, Lynn, and Nicholas A. Canzona. *The Pusan Perimeter.* Washington, DC: U.S. Marine Corps Historical Branch, 1954.

———. *The Inchon-Seoul Operations.* Washington, DC: U.S. Marine Corps Historical Branch, 1955.

———. *The Chosin Reservoir Campaign.* Washington, DC: U.S. Marine Corps Historical Branch, 1957.

Montross, Lynn, Hubard D. Kuokka, and Norman W. Hicks. *The East-Central Front.* Washington, DC: U.S. Marine Corps Historical Branch, 1962.

Moran, J. B. *Creating a Legend: The Descriptive Catalog of Writing about the U.S. Marine Corps.* Chicago: Moran Andrews, 1973.

Moskin, J. Robert. *The U.S. Marine Corps Story.* New York: McGraw-Hill, 1977.

Naval Aviation News. (U.S. Office of Naval Operations). Washington, DC, 1919–.

Naval Historical Foundation. *Manuscript Collection: A Catalog.* Washington, DC: Library of Congress, 1974.

Naval History. Annapolis, MD: U.S. Naval Institute, 1986–.

Naval Review. Annapolis, MD: U.S. Naval Institute, 1962–.

Naval War College Review (U.S. Naval War College). Newport, RI: 1948–.

Noel, John V., and Edward L. Beach. *Naval Terms Dictionary.* Annapolis, MD: Naval Institute Press, 1988.

Nowicke, Carole Elizabeth, et al. *Index of Oral Histories Relating to Naval Research and Development.* Bethesda, MD: David W. Taylor Naval Ship Research and Development Center, 1985.

O'Quinlivan, Michael, and James S. Santelli. *An Annotated Bibliography of the United States Marine Corps in the Korean War.* Rev. ed. Washington, DC: Historical Division, Headquarters U.S. Marine Corps, 1970.

Parker, William D. *A Concise History of the United States Marine Corps, 1775–1969.* Washington, DC: Historical Division, Headquarters U.S. Marine Corps, 1970.

Parry, Col. Francis Fox, USMC (Ret.). *Three-War Marine.* Pacifica, CA: Pacifica Press, 1987.

Pawlowski, Gareth L. *Flat-Tops and Fledglings: A History of American Aircraft Carriers.* South Brunswick, NJ: A. S. Barnes, 1971.

Pirnie, Bruce R. "Inchon Landing: How Great Was the Risk?" *Joint Perspectives* (Summer 1982): 86–97.

Polmar, Norman. *Aircraft Carriers: A Graphic History of Carrier Aviation and Its Influence on World Events.* Garden City, NY: Doubleday, 1969.

Potter, Edward B., ed. *Sea Power: A Naval History.* 2d ed. Annapolis, MD: Naval Institute Press, 1981.

Rawlins, Eugene W. *Marines and Helicopters, 1946–1962.* Washington, DC: History and Museums Division, Headquarters U.S. Marine Corps, 1976.

Rearden, Steven L. *History of the Office of the Secretary of Defense.* Vol. 1: *The Formative Years, 1947–1950.* Washington, DC: Office of the Secretary of Defense, 1979.

Reynolds, Clark G. *Command of the Sea.* New York: William Morrow and Co., 1974.

———. *Famous American Admirals.* New York: Van Nostrand, 1978.

———. "Writing on Naval Flying." *Aerospace Historian* 31 (1984): 21–29.

Roach, Maurice E. "First Through the Suez Canal." *Marine Corps Gazette* 60 (August 1976): 46–48.

Roe, Thomas G., et al. *A History of Marine Corps Roles and Missions, 1775–1962.* Washington, DC: Historical Branch, G-3 Division, Headquarters U.S. Marine Corps, 1962.

Rosenberg, David. "American Postwar Air Doctrine and Organization: The Navy Experience." In Alfred F. Hurley and Robert C. Erhart, eds., *Air Power and Warfare: Proceedings of the 8th Military History Symposium, United States Air Force Academy.* Washington, DC: GPO, 1979.

Rosenberg, David A., and Floyd D. Kennedy, Jr. *U.S. Aircraft Carriers in the Strategic Role.* Washington, DC: Lulejian Associates, 1975.

Rowe, John S., and Samuel L. Morison. *The Ships and Aircraft of the U.S. Fleet.* Annapolis, MD: U.S. Naval Institute, 1972.

Russ, Martin. *The Last Parallel: A Marine's War Journal.* New York: Rinehart and Co., 1957.

Ryan, Paul B. *First Line of Defense: The U.S. Navy since 1945.* Stanford, CA: Hoover Institution Press, 1981.

Santelli, James S. *An Annotated Bibliography of the United States Marine Corps' Concept of Close Air Support.* Washington, DC: Historical Branch, G-3 Division, Headquarters U.S. Marine Corps, 1968.

Schilling, Warner R., Paul Y. Hammond, and Glenn H. Snyder. *Strategy, Politics, and Defense Budgets.* New York: Columbia University Press, 1962.

Schultz, Charles R., comp. *Bibliography of Naval and Maritime History: Periodical Articles.* Mystic Seaport, CT: Marine Historical Association, 1971.

Schuon, Karl, ed. *U.S. Marine Corps Biographical Dictionary.* New York: Watts, 1963.

———. *U.S. Navy Biographical Dictionary.* New York: Watts, 1965.

Sheldon, Walter J. *Hell or High Water: MacArthur's Landing at Inchon.* New York: Macmillan, 1968.

Simmons, Edwin H. *The United States Marines, 1775–1975.* New York: Viking Press, 1976.

———. "War-Gaining Inchon." *Fortitudine* (Fall 1987): 3–6.

Spiller, Roger J., ed. *Dictionary of American Military Biography.* 3 vols. Westport, CT: Greenwood Press, 1983.

Stillwell, Paul. *United States Naval Institute Oral History Collection: Catalog of Transcripts.* Annapolis, MD: Naval Institute Press, 1983.

Swanborough, Gordon, and Peter M. Bowers. *United States Navy Aircraft since 1911*. New York: Funk and Wagnalls, 1968.

Sweetman, Jack. *American Naval History: An Illustrated Chronology of the U.S. Navy and Marine Corps, 1775–Present*. Annapolis, MD: Naval Institute Press, 1984.

Terzibaschitsch, Stefan. *Aircraft Carriers of the U.S. Navy*. New York: Mayflower Books, 1980.

————. *Escort Carriers and Aviation Support Ships of the U.S. Navy*. Annapolis, MD: Naval Institute Press, 1981.

————. *Cruisers of the U.S. Navy 1922–1962*. Annapolis, MD: Naval Institute Press, 1988.

Thach, John S. "Right on the Button: Marine Close Air Support in Korea." *Proceedings, U.S. Naval Institute* 101 (November 1975): 54–56.

Tillman, Barrett, and Joseph G. Handleman. "The Hwachon Dam and Carlson's Canyon: Air Group 19's Princeton Deployment of 1950–1951." *Hook* 12 (Spring 1984).

U.S. Bureau of Naval Personnel. *Register of Commissioned and Warrant Officers of the United States Navy*. Washington, DC: GPO, 1941–.

U.S. Deputy Chief of Naval Operations (Air Warfare) and Commander. Naval Air Systems Command. *United States Naval Aviation, 1910–1980*. Washington, DC: GPO, 1981.

U.S. Joint Chiefs of Staff. *The History of the Joint Chiefs of Staff, 1945–1952*. 4 vols. Wilmington, DE: Michael Glazier, 1979–1980.

U.S. Marine Corps. *Combined Lineal List of Officers on Active Duty in the Marine Corps*. Washington, DC: GPO, 1943–.

————. Division of Reserve. *The Marine Corps Reserve: A History*. Washington, DC: U.S. Marine Corps, Division of Reserve, 1966.

————. Historical Branch, G-3 Division, Headquarters U.S. Marine Corps. *Marine Corps Aircraft, 1913–1965*. Rev. ed. Washington, DC: The Branch, 1967.

————. Historical Division. Headquarters U.S. Marine Corps. *Marine Corps Historical Bibliographies*. Washington, DC: The Division, 1961–.

————. History and Museums Division. Headquarters U.S. Marine Corps. *A Chronology of the United States Marine Corps*. 4 vols. Washington, DC: History and Museums Division, Headquarters U.S. Marine Corps, 1965–.

————. *U.S. Marine Operations in Korea, 1950–1953*. 5 vols. Washington, DC: 1954–1972. Also see separate volumes by Lynn Montross and Nicholas A. Canzona; Lynn Montross, Hubard D. Kuokka, and Norman W. Hicks; and Pat Meid and James M. Yingling.

U.S. Navy Department. *Annual Report of the Secretary of the Navy*. In *Annual Report of the Secretary of Defense*. Washington, DC: GPO, 1948–.

U.S. Naval History Division. *Dictionary of American Naval Fighting Ships*. 5 vols. Washington, DC: GPO, 1959–.

————. *United States Naval History: A Bibliography*. 6th ed. Washington, DC: GPO, 1972.

Proceedings of the U.S. Naval Institute. Annapolis, MD: 1874–.

Wedertz, Bill. *Dictionary of Naval Abbreviations*. Annapolis, MD: U.S. Naval Institute, 1970.

Wilson, Desmond P., Jr. *Evolution of the Attack Aircraft Carrier: Case Study in Technology and Strategy.* Washington, DC: Center for Naval Analyses, 1965.

Wood, Charles Anthony. *Marine Corps Personal Papers Collection Catalog.* Washington, DC: U.S. Marine History and Museums Division, 1974.

16 Truman and Eisenhower: Strategic Options for Atomic War and Diplomacy in Korea

Edward C. Keefer

In January 1956, Secretary of State John Foster Dulles claimed in an interview for *Life* magazine that he had passed an "unmistakable warning" to the People's Republic of China (PRC) that unless the negotiations for the armistice to end the war in Korea were concluded, the United States would deploy atomic weapons against China. Dulles suggested that this atomic threat compelled the Chinese and North Koreans to the armistice signing at Panmunjom on July 27, 1953, thus ending the Korean War. Dulles' statement and a later collaborating assertion by President Dwight D. Eisenhower in his memoirs, *Mandate for Change* (1963), sparked a controversy about strategic options and atomic diplomacy during the Korean War that is still debated by historians today. The Dulles-Eisenhower statements raise intriguing historical questions. Did the Eisenhower administration send such a signal to the Chinese? Did the Chinese receive the message and recognize it as a bona-fide threat? Did the Chinese modify their action accordingly? Were Eisenhower and Dulles prepared to use atomic weapons? Was Eisenhower the only American president to use the threat of nuclear weapons in Korea?

President Harry S. Truman had his own very public controversy over the potential use of conventional and atomic weapons in Korea and China. For Truman, it was very much a political crisis rather than a scholarly debate. United Nations commander Douglas MacArthur used his enormous military prestige, greatly reinforced by his successful counterattack in Korea, to press the Truman administration both publicly and through official channels to carry the war to China. When the Chinese entered the war and sent Unified Command forces reeling down the peninsula, MacArthur's calls for attacks on China took on special urgency. Truman's rejection of MacArthur's advice and his eventual firing of the general sparked a crisis that rocked the United States.

The MacArthur-Truman controversy was one of the nation's most serious challenges to civilian control of the U.S. military and a rejection of the concept of limited war in pursuit of containment of communism. The logical conclusion of MacArthur's campaign was to use U.S. atomic power not only to roll back communism in Korean peninsula but to cross the Yalu and continue the process against China. Opponents of Truman in the Senate insisted on hearings, which became the focal point for examination of Truman's strategy in Korea. Ever since these so-called Truman-MacArthur hearings in 1951, historians and biographers have been refighting the arguments raised in those congressional hearings. Through his diplomatic and military advisers, Truman defended his actions by arguing that the United States did not have the military resources to expand the war in Korea. In addition, Truman insisted that his commitment to limited war was complete.

Scholars have suggested more recently that Truman, although not prepared to go as far as MacArthur suggested, was at least prepared to employ hints, feints, and the threat of atomic war as diplomatic tools in Korea. They also maintain that MacArthur's ideas were shared by much of the Truman administration's military establishment. This new scholarship concludes that Eisenhower's "atomic ultimatum" was not unique but was part of a general willingness by both the Eisenhower and Truman administrations to use the atomic threat for diplomatic and political purposes. Truman's hints and feints and Eisenhower's supposed atomic ultimatum threat go to the heart of the broader strategic issue of the usefulness of nuclear weapons in diplomacy and limited war. They raise the question whether the threat of nuclear war could not merely deter an opponent but also compel a nonnuclear nation—such as China in 1950–1953—to agree to take action against which it was opposed.

THE EISENHOWER ADMINISTRATION

Memoirs and Early Accounts

The Eisenhower administration's role in ending the Korean War has recently undergone concentrated historical attention and is perhaps the best place to start. Until the opening of the official U.S. government records on the last years of the Korean War in the early 1980s, historians relied heavily on Eisenhower administration officials' memoirs and Dulles' statements in *Life*. Eisenhower recounts in *Mandate for Change* that he found the continued stalemate in Korea intolerable and felt obligated to consider a major offensive in Korea. To keep the attack from becoming "overly costly," Eisenhower decided it would have to be an atomic one. But before making this decision, Eisenhower recalled that he decided to let the "Communist authorities understand that in the absence of satisfactory progress towards peace, the United States would not be bound by the 'gentleman's agreement' to confine the hostilities to the Korean peninsula." Eisenhower continues, "In India and the Formosa Straits Area, and at the truce negotiations at Panmunjom, we dropped the word, discreetly of our intention. We felt quite sure it would reach Soviet and Chinese Communist ears." Two years after publication of *Mandate for Change,* Eisenhower met with President Lyndon B. Johnson to discuss the Vietnam War. In the course of their conversation—declassified many years later—Eisenhower informed Johnson that the "Chinese were told that they must agree to an armistice quickly, since he [Eisenhower] planned to remove the restrictions of area and weapons if the war had to be continued."

Another collaborating recollection comes from Eisenhower's special assistant and former campaign chief of staff, Sherman Adams, in his *First Hand Report* (1961). Given Adams' general insulation from foreign policy deliberations, his imprecise terminology—"atomic missiles" were moved to Okinawa in spring 1953—and some confusion with chronology, it seems safer to assume that Adams' remembrances are based on his impressions and perhaps White House corridor talk rather than first-hand knowledge. Nevertheless, three key officials, including Eisenhower, stated that the administration had passed an atomic warning to China and that the threat worked. Historians who first studied the Eisenhower administration and the Korean War, as well as others writing considerably later, have relied heavily on these recollections.

Robert J. Donovan, *Eisenhower* (1956); former UN negotiator at Panmunjom C. Turner Joy, *How the Communists Negotiate* (1955); David Rees, *Korea* (1964); Herbert Parmet, *Eisenhower and the American Crusades* (1972); Harold C. Hinton, *China's Turbulent Quest* (1973); Joseph Goulden, *Korea* (1982); and Daniel Calingaert, "Nuclear Weapons and the Korean War" (1988) generally accept the Eisenhower-Dulles-Adams scenario. Although most of these works were hardly critical of Eisenhower, they believed that the president was content to allow John Foster Dulles to take the lead in foreign policy. Since Dulles was so closely associated with the theory of brinkmanship and massive retaliation, it seemed logical that the atomic threat was the initial example, or at least the practical inspiration, for the "New Look," Eisenhower's policy that relied on atomic deterrence to contain communism rather than more expensive conventional weapons and forces.

Soon other scholars began to look more critically at Eisenhower's and Dulles' assertions. Dulles' statement about Korea in *Life* magazine could be interpreted not so much as a historical account of the end of the Korean War but as an after-the-fact justification of the New Look policy or a warning to the Soviet Union and China about future U.S. resolve. Townsend Hoopes, *The Devil and John Foster Dulles* (1973), and Peter Lyon,

Eisenhower, Portrait of a Hero (1974), expressed skepticism about the atomic threat ending the war in Korea. Edward Friedman, "Nuclear Blackmail and the End of the Korea War" (1975), took this skepticism to its ultimate conclusion. Looking from the perspective of Beijing, Friedman saw no evidence that the Eisenhower administration's atomic saber rattling had any effect on China's actions in Korea except perhaps to increase Chinese leaders' commitment of conventional forces and thus to prolong the war. Friedman deemed the whole idea a complete fable.

Eisenhower, Korea, and Revisionists

Such was the main shape of the battle lines until the early 1980s, some thirty years after the end of the Korean War, when the U.S. government systematically declassified the vast majority of records of the Eisenhower administration at the Eisenhower Library in Abilene, Kansas; released most of the records of the major foreign policy agencies, and published a selection of the best of them in the Department of State's *Foreign Relations* series. New scholarly inquiry focused on Eisenhower's National Security Council (NSC) discussions in which the question of the use of atomic weapons in Korea was examined and debated from winter to late spring 1953. These records of NSC sessions were taken by NSC official S. Everett Gleason, a trained diplomatic historian who produced a summary of discussions that captured much of the give and take of debate among Eisenhower and his advisers. These accounts were prepared originally on the understanding that they would not be released, thus allowing the participants to speak freely. Kept at the Eisenhower Library, the records were eventually made public in the 1980s. They are some of the most revealing documents on high-level deliberations of any presidential administration.

In these discussions, the picture of Eisenhower that emerged is one of a president very much in charge, hardly dominated by John Foster Dulles or his brother, director of central intelligence Allen W. Dulles. These NSC records provided inspiration for the Eisenhower revisionists, most notably Robert A. Divine, *Eisenhower and the Cold War* (1981); Fred I. Greenstein, *The Hidden Hand Presidency* (1982); and Stephen E. Ambrose, *Eisenhower* (1984). These proponents of Eisenhower rejected the old critical view of Ike as a genial father figure more interested in his golf swing than affairs of state. They see Eisenhower as a subtle practitioner of statesmanship and international relations who was content to allow John Foster Dulles to shine in the limelight of publicity but determined to play the predominant role in foreign policy formulation. If Eisenhower was such a masterful president, it followed that his plan to end the Korean War was based at least in part on a carefully calibrated atomic threat passed to the Chinese. Ambrose takes the argument one step further, suggesting that it was immaterial whether the messages were passed to Beijing, because the Ei-

senhower administration in its public statements and its private examination of atomic policy—much of which leaked to the press—made it
amply clear that they would, as a last resort, use atomic weapons if no
armistice was forthcoming. Such a conclusion is also shared in part by
Burton I. Kaufman, *The Korean War* (1986). Military historian Max Hastings, *The Korean War* (1987), also accepts that the atomic threat worked
but considers it a bluff by Eisenhower and Dulles. Still, Hastings concedes
that this bluff was successful and swiftly ended armistice negotiations,
which had dragged on for years.

Eisenhower and the atomic threat had come full circle: from acceptance
to rejection to general acceptance again. At this point, a group of historians concentrated their attention on the issue once more. This second
critical look at the Eisenhower administration's record revived much of
the skepticism about the atomic threat.

In an article titled, "President Dwight D. Eisenhower and the End of
the Korean War" (1986), Edward Keefer examined the Eisenhower administration's deliberations on Korea at the NSC and concluded that they
were not as well planned or rational as the revisionists have claimed or
the president implied. The Eisenhower team thrashed around for months
before approving contingency plans that they hoped would end the war
in Korea. In vain Eisenhower sought an atomic quick fix to the Korean
War, but his advisers insisted that atomic weapons could only be used with
a costly conventional campaign on the Korean peninsula. The president
apparently authorized the ultimatum to China as a fallback only after he
realized the hard truth that atomic strategy provided no miracle end to
the war. The ultimatum was obliquely passed after clear signs that the
Chinese and North Koreans were prepared to make concessions at Panmunjom. In effect, Keefer argued that the atomic threat was an encour-
agement to a process that had already begun rather than a take-it-
or-leave-it ultimatum.

Part of the problem with assessing the atomic threat is that only one of
the three messages it apparently comprised has been found. Dulles used
his trip to India to enlist Prime Minister Nehru as a messenger. As published in *Foreign Relations of the United States, 1952–1954*, vol. 15, *Korea*,
Dulles' account of the conversation with Nehru makes the warning sound
rather oblique: "The United States would make a stronger rather than
lesser military exertion and this might well extend the area of conflict" if
the negotiations at Panmunjom failed. Nehru claimed that his notes of
the meeting with Dulles did not contain any reference to an atomic threat
and that he certainly did not pass a message to China, according to Nehru's aide, Escott Reid, *Envoy to Nehru* (1981).

Conceivably Dulles was too oblique with Nehru. Significantly, on the
next day, Nehru asked for clarification of what was meant by "intensified
operation," but Dulles let the matter drop. In the official account of the

Dulles-Nehru meeting, the message is far less definitive than Dulles' description in the *Life* interview, where the secretary of state claimed the message had been made unmistakably clear to avoid miscalculation by Beijing and Pyongyang. Or possibly Dulles is referring to a series of messages sent to the Chinese. Eisenhower's description of the word being passed in the China area and at Panmunjom points to possible clandestine messages to Beijing through its old adversary, the Jiang Jieshi (Chiang Kaishek) government on Taiwan and through lower-level officials at the Panmunjom talks. These two messages have never been found. If they were passed, their clandestine nature would hardly qualify them as clear and unmistakable. There were broader hints at the high levels of the armistice talks and in Moscow that American patience was growing thin, but there was no specific atomic ultimatum included. For these reasons, Richard K. Betts, *Nuclear Blackmail and Nuclear Balance* (1987), characterizes these messages as at best "faint signals which resulted in ambiguous results." John Gaddis, *The Long Peace* (1987), concludes that given available sources, it is impossible to determine how effective Eisenhower's threats were in persuading Beijing and Pyongyang, but he adds that "it seems safe to conclude that they could not be disregarded."

The whole question of the atomic threat was examined in greatest detail in *International Security*'s winter 1988–1989 edition, which published three articles on the question of Truman, Eisenhower, and atomic superiority. The first, Marc Trachtenburg, "A 'Wasting Asset,' " provides an overview of U.S. strategic thinking about atomic warfare during the Truman and Eisenhower administrations. Trachtenburg does not address the question of the Eisenhower atomic threat in any detail, except to suggest that during late 1952 and early 1953, as the result of an extraordinary buildup of American military power, including the production of tactical atomic weapons able to be deployed by fighter aircraft, the United States enjoyed a window of opportunity that would soon become a wasting asset as the Soviet Union moved to produce thermonuclear weapons. Trachtenburg suggests that newly developed American strength led to a willingness to escalate in Korea if the war could not be satisfactorily concluded.

Rosemary Foot, "Nuclear Coercion and the Ending of the Korea War," provides the most detailed discussion and elaborates more fully than in her analytical book, *The Wrong War* (1985). Foot's contention is "that, although nuclear coercion probably had some influence on ending the conflict, it did not play the dominant role that Eisenhower and Dulles ascribe to it." Foot notes that the first Chinese concession came in March 1953 before the threat had been made. Still, Foot acknowledges, as Keefer maintained, that the Chinese made a small but significant concession on June 8, providing support to the idea that the atomic threat had some effect in Beijing, Pyongyang, and Moscow. Foot ultimately believes that Zhou Enlai's concession of March 30, which acknowledged the possibility of nonrepatriation, got the ball rolling. For each concession from the communist side, there were corresponding concessions from the U.S.-UN Command. Foot states that domestic economic pressures, the Kremlin's desire for better relations with the West after Stalin's death, and increased UN Command conventional bombing could as easily explain the end of the Korean War. Nevertheless, Foot acknowledges that Beijing recognized a new belligerence in the Eisenhower administration and realized that the May Panmunjom proposal represented the last best offer, and refusal would mean an expanded and probably nuclear war. Although not prepared to accept Eisenhower's and Dulles' easy assertion that the atomic threats ended the war, Foot concedes that they played a part, a position incorporated into her companion study, *A Substitute for Victory* (1990). Concentrating on the little-studied armistice negotiations, Foot restates her argument that Eisenhower and Dulles used more conventional diplomatic and military signals to force minor concessions by the communists and reiterates even more definitely that the atomic threat, if it was even passed, was greatly oversold by the Eisenhower administration. Foot credits Zhou Enlai with making the real concessions before Dulles' alleged ultimatum and notes that Mao Zedong and the Chinese had little to fear from the U.S. atomic punch.

Former Kennedy and Johnson national security adviser and now a professor of history, McGeorge Bundy in *Danger and Survival* (1988) supports Foot's thesis. He makes a succinct case that Eisenhower and Dulles were of the same mind: they believed that clear evidence of readiness to use atomic weapons would increase the chance of an armistice and that they got their messages across to Beijing and its allies. The problem, Bundy suggests, is that it is not clear that these beliefs were correct. Bundy suggests that when it came to actually using these weapons, the leading Eisenhower figures were not of the same mind. He concludes that "Dulles might well have favored the use of nuclear weapons, that [JCS chairman] Bradley would not have, and that Eisenhower had no intention of deciding before he had to." If Eisenhower had seriously planned to use nuclear weapons, Bundy suggests that he should have begun diplomatic negotiations with the allies to pave the way, a process that was hardly begun. Bundy follows Foot in suggesting that the death of Stalin, Chinese willingness to exchange sick and wounded prisoners, domestic costs of the war to China, and a general awareness of the Eisenhower administration's determination caused the end of the war.

In the last of the *International Security* articles, Roger Dingman, "Atomic Diplomacy during the Korea War," states most definitively that Eisenhower "did not, then [May 22] or later, apply nuclear pressure to speed the armistice talks to conclusion." Dingman believes that "Washington never came close to tactical use of the atomic bomb in Korea," but he suggests that Truman used the threat of nuclear retaliation more effectively than Eisenhower, a bold assertion we will return to later in this chapter. For the time being, let us examine the Eisenhower component of Dingman's thesis. Dingman views the Eisenhower administration's approach to atomic weapons as cautious and based on clear constraints: growing Soviet atomic strength, lack of forward-deployed atomic weapons, lack of a clear policy view, and splits within the Republican party on how atomic war in Korea would affect America's limited atomic stockpile. Dingman interprets the NSC discussions during the spring of 1953 as "discursive" and "more tentative and educational" than "decisive" policy deliberations. The major bureaucratic players—the Pentagon, the Department of State, and the Joint Chiefs of Staff—according to Dingman were all content with discussion rather than action. For these reasons Eisenhower acted "more like an owl than a hawk." The final decision on May 20, after Dulles had left for the Near East and South Asia, was that if the war had to be expanded, it would most likely be with atomic weapons. Dingman suggests this is at best a statement of intention and by no means a decision actually to use weapons. According to Dingman, Eisenhower ended the Korean War not by "coercive atomic policy" but by "non-nuclear persuasive diplomacy" that focused on Moscow's ability to convince Beijing and Pyongyang to accept the principle of nonrepatriation of prisoners of war.

A related approach to Dingman's is taken by British historian Callum A. MacDonald, who in *Korea: The War before Vietnam* (1986), states emphatically that Zhou Enlai, the Chinese foreign minister, rather than Dulles, played his own brand of nonatomic brinkmanship. MacDonald believes both sides were forced to compromise and implies that "Dulles' atomic bluster" was merely a coverup for U.S. concessions. MacDonald suggests that deploying atomic weapons in Korea would have seriously disrupted the Western alliance system, a price the Eisenhower administration was not prepared to pay. Both sides realized the basic fact that bluff could not win the war and "compromised to end a struggle whose costs were out of all proportion to its benefits."

The question of Zhou Enlai's role brings to the fore the question of Chinese perception of the atomic threat. Mark A. Ryan, *Chinese Attitudes toward Nuclear Weapons* (1990), addresses this issue. Ryan's strength is to concentrate on the battlefield realities and Chinese strategic policy rather than the Eisenhower administration's policy deliberations. Ryan makes a number of challenging assertions in arguing that there were very great limitations on Eisenhower's freedom of action to make nuclear war. The small size of the U.S. nuclear stockpile until mid-1955 meant that atomic war against China would have left the U.S. nuclear arsenal dangerously depleted in the face of potential escalation to global war with the Soviet Union. Ryan also reminds us that in 1953, tactical nuclear weapons were extremely low yield and would hardly have been decisive on the battlefield. The atomic weapon most effective against the extensive system of defensive tunnels dug by the Chinese and North Koreans, the MK8—the first weapon capable of penetrating underground before exploding—was never successfully produced in meaningful numbers until after the war. Ryan also notes that the successful development of the MK7, capable of being delivered by F-84 Thunderjet fighter-bombers in winter-spring 1953, marked the point at which the United States had achieved true capability to use atomic weapons in Korea. Looking at the Chinese defenses, he suggests that the Chinese air force would have put up a strong resistance to U.S. tactical nuclear bombing attacks. Chinese tunnel systems in Korea and China would have lessened the impact of such an attack, and Chinese lines of supply were ultimately impervious to either conventional or nuclear bombing. Ryan's overall conclusion is that China would not have been bludgeoned out of the Korean War by means of strategic atomic attacks upon Chinese territory.

The Atomic Bomb Issue

What then remains to be done to resolve the question of the Eisenhower atomic threat? Obvious missing links are the two other messages Eisenhower claims he passed to the Chinese through the Chinese nationalists and at the armistice talks. When the research was undertaken for *Foreign Relations, 1952–1954*, Vol. 15, *Korea,* these messages were not found, nor have they been subsequently discovered at the Eisenhower Library. While it is possible that they will never surface, the Central Intelligence Agency's new policy of openness offers some hope that they might be found in that agency's files. Even if these two other messages were discovered and they were more explicit than the warning Dulles thought he was delivering through Nehru, the question still remains, Did the Chinese receive the message? While the People's Republic of China has not released its official files, Western scholars have begun to interview Chinese participants and comb the Chinese press and memoirs for clues, to good effect. The records of the former Soviet Union offer another potential source, given the Russian government's new commitment to the historical record. Consultations between Soviet and Chinese high-level officials on the question of U.S. intentions in Korea in 1953 might well hold the key to resolving the mystery of if and how Beijing and Moscow responded to the atomic threat.

There are other steps that historians can take before Russia or China releases foreign policy records for this period. Certainly those who examine nuclear options open to Eisenhower in Korea should have a clearer idea about the technical limitations of the U.S. atomic arsenal in 1953. It is a common misunderstanding to assume that Eisenhower's nuclear weapons were the "city-busting" weapons of mass destruction that were dropped on Hiroshima and Nagasaki by the Truman administration, when, in fact, Eisenhower's weapons were low-yield tactical atomic bombs. Military historians and experts on the history of science and technology should cross-pollinate knowledge with historians of diplomatic and political history. Finally, there is one field of U.S. records that probably still needs to be systematically examined, the files of the Atomic Energy Commission and its leading officials, a trail blazed by Roger Dingman's article in *International Security.*

THE TRUMAN ADMINISTRATION

The Truman-MacArthur Controversy

One of the great truisms of the initial historiography on the Korean War is that Eisenhower, the wartime hero and lifelong military man, was far more willing to use atomic weapons in Korea than Harry Truman, the civilian from Independence, who actually authorized the unleashing of atomic weapons on Japan in 1945. This view gained support from the MacArthur hearings, when the Truman administration's leading military-political officials made a conscious effort to downplay their offensive options in Korea in response to savage criticism from MacArthur and conservative Republicans in Congress. The thrust of recent scholarship on the Truman administration, however, emphasizes how easily MacArthur carried the Truman administration across the 38th parallel and stresses the seriousness of the consideration that his administration gave to implementing some of the kinds of action MacArthur espoused.

The starting point for examining the strategic options of the Truman administration in Korea are the MacArthur hearings—more formally, U.S. Senate, *Military Situation in the Far East: Hearings before the Armed Services and Foreign Relations Committee,* 82nd Congress, 1st session (1951). For the decade or so after the war, these massive, often repetitive, but revealing hearings were the basis for much of what was written about the Korean War. These hearings were highly partisan and extremely controversial, and they created a large body of polemic literature that falls into two basic categories: conservative pro-MacArthur rollback anticommunists and liberal pro-Truman containment anticommunists. A few examples should suffice. On the MacArthur side there is Courtney Whitney, *MacArthur: His Rendevous with Destiny* (1956), by a MacArthur confidante who follows the straight pro-MacArthur line. Charles Willoughby and John Chamberlain, *MacArthur, 1941–1951* (1954), is also in the hagiography school of MacArthur writing. In these and similar works now relegated to the backs of library shelves, MacArthur is portrayed as a far-seeing hero, martyred by the Truman administration, which disregarded his call to win the Korean War by taking the fight to "Red China." The most partisan of these books sees a communist conspiracy in the Truman administration; the less partisan views Truman as merely a dunderhead. Douglas A. MacArthur joined the fray with his *Reminiscences* (1964). Political scientists Alvin J. Cotrell and James E. Dougherty, "The Lessons of Korea" (1958), provided perhaps the most scholarly early defense of MacArthur during the 1950s when they argued that "the gravest error in Korea was the failure to respond decisively during the first days of the Chinese communist intervention."

During the early 1950s, however, Truman had powerful supporters, including most of the establishment liberal press. Arthur M. Schlesinger, Jr., and Richard Rovere, *The General and the President* (1951), charged to Truman's defense well before MacArthur began to fade even slightly. Journalist John Dille, *Substitute for Victory* (1954), is another early work in support of the president. Truman provided an extensive defense of his Korean actions in volume 2 of his memoirs, *Years of Trial and Hope* (1956); and Secretary of State Dean Acheson, *Present at the Creation* (1969), provided a justification for his and Truman's actions in Korea. These works see MacArthur's plan to reunify Korea by force as ensuring a general war with China and potentially a global war with the Soviet Union. They argue that Truman made the right decision to forgo the serious risks involved in reunifying Korea under noncommunist leadership and the suicidal risks of attacking China with either conventional or atomic weapons. A book that goes well beyond the liberal defense of Truman is I. F. Stone, *The Hidden History of the Korean War* (1952). Independent journalist and radical gadfly, Stone maintains with more passion than evidence that MacArthur, John Foster Dulles, and Jiang Jieshi (Chiang Kai-shek) masterminded the Korean War as a crusade against the People's Republic of China. Having duped Truman and Acheson into virtual war with China, MacArthur foolishly pushed Truman too far by entering the realm of politics and thus caused his own downfall. In Stone's view, Truman had no options. He was trapped in a war that fueled U.S. prosperity and full employment.

With the passing influence of Joseph McCarthy and the red scare and with the acceptance of the concept of limited war, historians looked more dispassionately at the Truman-MacArthur controversy. A seminal work is John W. Spanier, *The Truman-MacArthur Controversy and the Korean War* (1959), which sees the outcome of the controversy as a vindication of civilian control over the military and views limited war as the only rational response in the face of global atomic war. Another study that strives for an even-handed approach to the controversy is Trumbull Higgins, *Korea and the Fall of MacArthur* (1960). British military historian David Rees, *Korea: The Limited War* (1964), as the title makes clear, is another early study drawing inspiration from the idea of limited war, outlined by Henry Kissinger in *Nuclear Weapons and Foreign Policy* (1957). As the first of many good British historians to study the Korean conflict, Rees dispels the charge put forward by MacArthur partisans that the British Labour gov-

ernment of Clement Atlee had any real part in Truman's decisions not to
carry the fight to China and to fire MacArthur. The publication in 1967
of Allen Guttmann (ed.), *Korea and the Theory of Limited War,* in the series
Problems in American Civilization, was ostensibly meant to shed light on
the issues raised in the controversy, but Guttman sides squarely with the
view that Truman's decision for limited war was the only rational one, a
ringing endorsement of conventional liberal wisdom of the time.

Truman, Korea, and the Revisionists

The revisionism of the late 1960s and 1970s that dominated the history
of U.S. policy toward Vietnam and the cold war in general was not much
applied to the Korean War. There were a few exceptions; the best examples are Joyce and Gabriel Kolko, *The Limits of Power* (1972); Robert
Simmons, *The Strained Alliance* (1975); and Frank Baldwin, ed., *Without
Parallel: The Korean American Relationship since 1945* (1974). These revisionist scholars began to question the orthodox view that the Korean War was
a classic reaction to communist aggression, but they were neither numerous enough nor was the bulk of their argumentation definitive enough to
present a fully compelling case.

Just after these early revisionists began to publish on Korea, U.S. official
historians working for the Joint Chiefs of Staff released a massive declassified two-volume history of the war: James F. Schnabel and Robert J. Watson, *The History of the Joint Chiefs of Staff: The Joint Chiefs of Staff and National
Policy,* Vol. 3, *The Korean War* (1978–1979). What differentiates this work
from the Department of the Army's official histories of the war produced
during the 1960s is that the Joint Chiefs of Staff historians are more interested in strategy and options than the traditional view from the battleground usually used by military historians. Schnabel and Watson provide
important information on atomic options, especially their discussion of
UN Commander Mark Clark's attempts to interest both Truman and President-elect Eisenhower in adding an atomic dimension to 0-plan 8–52,
which was a major air, ground, and naval offensive against North Korea
and China devised in late 1952. Unfortunately, Schnabel and Watson's
work has never been widely available in book form.

With the release of official U.S. and British records in the late 1970s
and early 1980s (roughly thirty years after the fact), historians rushed to
explain the origins of the Korean War. These scholars include Charles M.
Dobbs (1981), James I. Matray (1985), William W. Stueck, Jr. (1981), and
John Merrill (1989). Matray, Dobbs, and Merrill fall within the liberal
revisionist school, seeing the Korean War as having its origins in a combination of local tensions in the Korean peninsula and cold war decisions
made beyond Korea, mostly in Washington. Stueck is the exception in not
accepting the emerging consensus that the Korean War was essentially a

civil one. As good as these books are, they have been overshadowed by radical revisionist Bruce Cumings' two volumes, *The Origins of the Korean War* (1981, 1990), whose massive scholarship and breathtaking knowledge of Korea has come to dominate the literature on the origins of the war. Cumings interprets the outbreak of fighting in Korea in June 1950 as merely a continuation of a civil war that had been ongoing since 1945, a view that is virtually the new orthodoxy. He views U.S. entry into the war not as a response to aggression but as part of a U.S. plan to maintain its world markets and capitalism and as the triumph of Secretary of State Acheson's internationalist view of containment. Although it is a vast simplification of Cumings' work, his revisionism is often cited as proof that the United States was responsible for the Korean War.

This revisionism calls into question the idea that Truman had any choice about whether to intervene in Korea. The revisionists argue that the stage was already set—that the Truman administration by its previous actions had already intervened in South Korea. When the sporadic fighting erupted into full civil war, the United States had no choice but to come to the side of South Korea, which it had nurtured and supported against the wishes of the majority of the Korean people.

The Revised View of Truman and MacArthur

As James Matray pointed out in a review in *Diplomatic History* in 1992, although there has been much reexamination of the origins of the war, there has as yet been no equivalent outburst of revisionism on the Korean War years themselves and the strategic decisions facing Truman. As has been seen, there is considerable discussion and scholarly ferment on the strategic decisions and options of the Eisenhower administration, and there are signs that the process is also beginning for the Truman administration as well. Compared to Eisenhower, who only had to end the war on acceptable terms, Truman faced a series of difficult strategic choices.

Both the traditional and revisionist views hold that Truman had very few options after the war broke out in Korea. The traditionalists see Truman's reacting to North Korea's invasion across the 38th parallel, a clear-cut example of aggression by the communist bloc. Although historians have quibbled whether Stalin gave Kim Il-sung the green light or was taken by surprise by his North Korean protégé, for almost thirty years they have generally accepted that Truman had no choice but to meet North Korean aggression with U.S. military force. For very different reasons, as we have seen, the new revisionists seek to undercut this orthodox view by claiming that the United States had already made its decision to intervene in Korea.

In an ironic twist, revisionists have partly resurrected the reputation of Douglas MacArthur, or at least blurred the differences between him and

Truman. Bruce Cumings' introduction to an edited collection of essays, *Child of Conflict* (1983), tentatively suggests that MacArthur's rollback of communism in Korea was not merely a creation of the vainglorious general and his conservative allies but the logical conclusion to the philosophy espoused in NSC-68, the "smoking gun" in most revisionists' views of the cold war. Cumings writes, "In fact the rollback policy drew together a far more broadly based coalition behind Korea policy than existed before. It healed splits between internationalists, containment advocates, baitcuters, and rollbackers, leaving only some isolated internationalists in its wake." Cumings suggests that the inevitable debacle caused by the Chinese intervention and American retreat down the peninsula has been laid purposely at MacArthur's feet by most liberal historical accounts of the war. These works have characterized MacArthur as a "lone wolf," when in fact the Truman administration was in favor of MacArthur's march north so long as it was succeeding. Cumings admits that this coalition would have been strained if and when MacArthur crossed the Yalu. The Asia Firsters would have cheered the retaking of the mainland (or parts of it) for the Chinese nationalists; the Europe Firsters would have opposed it as an unnecessary risk of World War III. But MacArthur's bold decision to retake Korea was not in Cumings' view an aberration; it was widely supported by Truman and his administration.

This general view of MacArthur has been accepted and amplified by most recent scholarly biographies and monographs. D. Clayton James, *The Years of MacArthur*, Vol. 3, *Triumph and Disaster, 1945–1964* (1985), presents an objective view of the controversial general. An analytical rather than biographic treatment is D. Clayton James with Anne Sharp Wells, *Refighting the Last War* (1993), in which James notes that despite allegations of warmongering, MacArthur never proposed using nuclear weapons while he was commander in chief in the Far East, a conclusion that requires a bit of hair splitting about informal and formal recommendations. James acknowledges that as a private citizen in 1952, MacArthur recommended to President-elect Eisenhower and John Foster Dulles a radioactive barrier across the North Korean border with China and a conventional reinvasion of the North. This was the last Korean War advice Eisenhower ever sought from MacArthur.

James observes that both Truman and Eisenhower considered the use of atomic weapons, but lack of suitable targets, terrain problems, the powerful negative symbolism of deploying nuclear weapons against Asians again, and the fear of Soviet counterstrike all combined to discourage their use. Michael Schaller, *Douglas MacArthur: Far Eastern General* (1989), suggests that Truman's civilian advisers and the Joint Chiefs of Staff were carried along by MacArthur's reputation, force of personality, and the daring but deceptively easy Inchon victory. Schaller reiterates this argument in "Douglas MacArthur: The China Issue, Policy Conflict and the

Korean War," in Chull Baum Kim and James I. Matray (eds.), *Korea and the Cold War* (1993). Rosemary Foot, *The Wrong War* (1985), states that the decision to move north from the 38th parallel was conditioned by powerful U.S. domestic factors, the lack of resistance from U.S. allies or the Soviet Union, or any real challenge from the U.S. government bureaucracy. Thus, if MacArthur carried the Truman administration forward toward disaster, Truman and his advisers made the journey without kicking and screaming, as they would later have us believe.

MacArthur's reaction to the Chinese intervention was to call for an offensive operation against China, another key strategic option for Truman. In the MacArthur hearings, the Truman administration went to great lengths to argue that the United States did not have conventional strength in the air or adequate atomic stockpile to undertake such an offensive. Recent scholarship, based on the now-declassified records of U.S. military planning, paints a different picture and shifts the terms of reference for the Truman administration's consideration of potential use of the atomic option. The idea that Truman was absolutely unwilling to break what Eisenhower called the "gentleman's agreement" to limit the fighting to Korea and not to use atomic weapons has lately come under some doubt.

Truman and Atomic Diplomacy in Korea

One of the most extensive examinations of Truman's use of atomic policy is Roger Dingman's "Atomic Diplomacy during the Korea War" (1988–1989), which was examined earlier for its comments about the Eisenhower administration. Relying on the papers of senior air force and Atomic Energy Commission officials, Dingman discerns a clear pattern that he believes holds true for the entire Korean War: that "atomic diplomacy was an element of American statecraft throughout the conflict." Dingman states that there were four periods when the Truman administration considered the use of atomic weapons: twice in the early war days of July 1950, in November 1950 just after the massive Chinese intervention in the war, and finally in April 1951. He maintains that while neither Truman nor Eisenhower actually came close to deploying the bomb, Truman came closest in April 1951.

Dingman holds that Truman used the threat of atomic weapons for political and diplomatic purposes. He authorized the deployment of nuclear-configured B-29 bombers across the Atlantic to England and across the Pacific to Guam in July 1950 to send signals to the enemy. Truman made his famous public statement about using atomic bombs in November 1950. Finally in April 1951, Truman authorized the deployment of B-29s with atomic weapons on board to Guam, where they would be poised to move to Okinawa for a possible counterattack on communist forces thought to be massing to repel UN forces as they again crossed the 38th parallel. As Dingman notes, Truman was accepting McArthur's strategic concept for Korea while at the same time disapproving of his public vetting of it and making the final decision to relieve him. After the relief of MacArthur, Dingman believes Truman deliberately and subtly used atomic diplomacy to deter Moscow and Beijing and make sure that they did not interpret MacArthur's firing as a sign of weakness or timidity and to quell U.S. domestic criticism as well. Dingman states that this was Truman's last—albeit his most serious—consideration of use of nuclear weapons, the closest point the United States ever came to using tactical nuclear weapons during the Korean War.

Recent military histories of the war have collaborated and even anticipated Dingman's thesis. Callum A. MacDonald, *Korea: The War before Vietnam* (1986), and Bruce Cumings and Jon Halliday, *Korea: the Unknown War* (1988), both cite a trial run for use of nuclear weapons in Korea, code-named Operation Hudson Harbor, in which U.S. Air Force B-29 bombers overflew and dropped dummy or conventional weapons on North Korea as a training exercise for an atomic attack and a means of signaling U.S. resolve at the then-recessed armistice talks. Cumings and Halliday see Truman's public rattling of the atomic bomb in November 1950 not as a *faux pas* but as a "carefully weighed threat based on atomic contingency planning to use the bomb." British military historian and journalist Max Hastings, *The Korean War* (1987), summarizes the new view of the Truman administration's policy toward atomic weapons in Korea. Posing the question of how close Truman came to using atomic weapons against China, he responds: "much closer, the answer must be, than the allies cared to believe at the time." Hastings suggests that "if Truman and his fellow members recoiled from bearing responsibility for so terrible an act, America's leading military men, from the Joint Chiefs downward, were far more equivocal and seemed less disturbed by the prospect."

In *Danger and Survival: Choices about the Bomb in the First Fifty Years* (1988), McGeorge Bundy asks us not to forget that while Truman allowed contingency planning for atomic war and authorized the development of new and more effective weapons, he was determined never to use them. Bundy bases his conclusions on Truman's state of mind as given in part in the private musings of the president, which are collected in Robert H. Ferrell (ed.), *Off The Record* (1980). The problem is that Truman's most definitive private statement that he would not use atomic weapons was on April 24, 1954, after the end of the war and when he was a former president with ample time for reflection. His diary entry of May 1952, during the war and when he was commander in chief, is far more belligerent. He suggests that the negotiators ask their communist counterparts at Panmunjom whether they want an end to the war or "China and Siberia destroyed." While considerable evidence shows that Truman was personally frustrated by his inability to use atomic weapons, the question remains: Is there any reason to believe that this frustration could ever overcome Truman's determination not to use atomic or conventional weapons against China?

Other factors beyond Truman's personal sentiments limited his freedom of action. If nuclear weapons were deployed in a less-than-favorable situation like Korea and they proved inconclusive on the battlefield, it would seriously diminish their psychological deterrent effect. Such was the reasoning behind atomic energy chairman Gordon E. Dean's opposition to U.S. Air Force attempts to gain control of the weapons in spring 1951, as made clear in Robert M. Anders (ed.), *Forging the Atomic Shield* (1989). In addition, the allies in Korea, especially the United Kingdom and the commonwealth nations of Canada and Australia, have been traditionally credited with moderating Truman's supposed inclination to use the bomb. In part, this interpretation stems from Atlee's summit with Truman in December 1950, which some have considered a successful attempt by the British Labour prime minister to stop a decision to use atomic weapons and to begin a campaign to undermine MacArthur. More recent work has generally discredited this idea. Rosemary Foot, "Anglo-American Relations in the Korean Crisis: The British Effort to Avert an Expanded War" (1986); Roger Dingman, "Truman, Atlee, and the Korean War Crisis" (1982); and William Stueck, "The Limits of Influence" (1986), all emphasize that the British influence on Truman has been overrated and accomplished very little beyond allowing breathing and reflection time. Robert O'Neill, *Australia in the Korean War* (1981); Denis Stairs, *The Diplomacy of Constraint* (1974); and Michael L. Dockrill, "The Foreign Office, Anglo-American Relations, and the Korean War, June 1950–June 1951" (1986), write from the perspective of their own countries' respective diplomatic papers and memoirs and therefore naturally stress their own nation's moderating influence on Washington. Certainly the allies' influence was not without effect, but determining just how significant is difficult.

The problem of the use of atomic weapons within a multinational coalition (albeit dominated by the United States) that fought the Korean War was raised when both Truman and Eisenhower planned for the end of the fighting. Both administrations sought a public warning to China, to be released after the armistice was signed, that should the armistice be broken, the allies would apply "greater sanctions" (a hint of atomic weapons) against China. The multilateral negotiations for this warning and its transformation into the far-less-belligerent "Joint Policy Statement" provide a good way to gauge the contraints on U.S. policy because of its allies in Korea.

If a new synthesis is emerging on Truman and atomic war, it holds that Truman was prepared to use atomic contingency planning, deployment of actual weapons near the battlefield, public statements, and even trial nonnuclear bombing runs to influence his opponents in Korea and to quiet his critics in the United States. Because of some very clear limitations, he was not prepared to use atomic weapons again except under the most dire circumstances.

The literature on the Truman administration and the Korean War years is at the take-off point. Much of the research has been done in the form of scholarly articles. Good monographs are appearing; others are in progress. William Stueck is working on a study that will stress the international aspects of the war. As Western and Chinese scholars work through Chinese sources, a clearer picture of how the Chinese perceived the Truman administration and the UN Command will emerge. The kind of in-depth study Bruce Cumings brought to the internal developments within the Korean peninsula from 1945 to 1950 still needs to be done for the war years. The Korean War, initially overshadowed by scholarship on World War II and then the controversy surrounding about the Vietnam War, is finally receiving its due. The intriguing historical question of potential atomic war in Korea, so intensively studied and debated, has and will continue to act as a powerful catalyst for rigorous intellectual examination of the entire war years. The results of this reexamination are already appearing, with the promise of more to come. Korea need no longer be thought of as the "unknown" or the "forgotten" war.

REFERENCES

Acheson, Dean. *Present at the Creation: My Years in the State Department.* New York: Norton, 1969.

Adams, Sherman. *First Hand Report: The Story of the Eisenhower Administration.* New York: Harper and Brothers, 1961.

Ambrose, Stephen E. *Eisenhower: The President.* New York: Simon and Schuster, 1984.

Anders, Robert M., ed. *Forging the Atomic Shield: Excerpts from the Office Diary of Gordon E. Dean.* Chapel Hill, NC: University of North Carolina Press, 1989.

Baldwin, Frank, ed. *Without Parallel: The Korean-American Relationship since 1954.* New York: Pantheon, 1974.

Betts, Richard K. *Nuclear Blackmail and Nuclear Balance.* Washington, DC: Brookings Institution, 1987.

Bundy, McGeorge. *Danger and Survival: Choices about the Bomb in the First Fifty Years.* New York: Random House, 1988.

Calingaert, Daniel. "Nuclear Weapons and the Korean War." *Journal of Strategic Studies* 11:2 (June 1988): 177–202.

Cotrell, Alvin J., and James E. Dougherty. "The Lessons of Korea: War and the Power of Man." *Orbis* 2:1 (Spring 1958): 39–65.

Cumings, Bruce. *The Origins of the Korean War.* 2 vols. Princeton: Princeton University Press, 1981, 1990.

———, ed. *Child of Conflict: The Korean-American Relationship, 1943–1953.* Seattle: University of Washington Press, 1983.

Cumings, Bruce, and Jon Halliday. *Korea: The Unknown War*. New York; Pantheon, 1988.

Dingman, Roger. "Truman, Atlee, and the Korean Crisis." In *East Asian Crisis, 1945–1951, International Studies*. London: International Center for Economics and Related Discipline, London School of Economics, 1982.

———. "Atomic Diplomacy during the Korean War." *International Security* 13:3 (Winter 1988–1989): 50–91.

Dille, John. *Substitute for Victory*. New York: Doubleday, 1954.

Divine, Robert A. *Eisenhower and the Cold War*. New York: Oxford University Press, 1981.

Dobbs, Charles M. *The Unwanted Symbol: American Foreign Policy, the Cold War, and Korea*. Kent, OH: Kent State University Press, 1981.

Dockrill, Michael L. "The Foreign Office, Anglo-American Relations, and the Korean War, June 1950–June 1951." *International Affairs* 62:3 (Summer 1986): 459–476.

Donovan, Robert J. *Eisenhower: The Inside Story*. New York: Harper and Brothers, 1956.

Eisenhower, Dwight D. *The White House Years: Mandate for Change, 1953–1956*. Garden City, NY: Doubleday, 1963.

Ferrell, Robert H., ed. *Off the Record: The Private Papers of Harry S. Truman*. New York; Harper & Row, 1980.

Foot, Rosemary J. *The Wrong War: American Policy and the Dimensions of the Korean Conflict, 1950–1953*. Ithaca, NY: Cornell University Press, 1985.

———. "Anglo-American Relations in the Korean Crisis, December 1950–January 1951." *Diplomatic History* 10:1 (Winter 1986): 43–57.

———. "Nuclear Coercion and the Ending of the Korean Conflict." *International Security* 13:3 (Winter 1988–1989): 92–112.

———. *A Substitute for Victory: The Politics of Peacemaking at the Korean Armistice Talks*. Ithaca, NY: Cornell University Press, 1990.

———. "Making Known the Unknown War: Policy Analysis of the Korean Conflict in the Last Decade." *Diplomatic History* 15:3 (Summer 1991): 411–431.

Friedman, Edward, "Nuclear Blackmail and the End of the Korean War," *Modern China* 1:1 (January 1975): 75–91.

Gaddis, John L. *The Long Peace: Inquiries into the History of the Cold War*. New York; Oxford University Press, 1987.

Goulden, Joseph C. *Korea: The Untold Story of the War*. New York: Times Books, 1982.

Greenstein, Fred I. *The Hidden Hand Presidency: Eisenhower as Leader*. New York: Basic Books, 1982.

Guttmann, Allen, ed. *Korea and the Theory of Limited War*. Boston: Heath, 1967.

Hastings, Max. *The Korean War*. New York: Simon and Schuster, 1987.

Higgins, Trumbell. *Korea and the Fall of MacArthur: A Precis in Limited War*. New York: Oxford University Press, 1960.

Hinton, Harold C. *China's Turbulent Quest: An Analysis of China's Foreign Relations since 1949*. New York: Macmillan, 1973.

Hoopes, Townsend. *The Devil and John Foster Dulles*. Boston: Atlantic–Little, Brown Books, 1973.

James, D. Clayton. *The Years of MacArthur.* Vol. 3: *Triumph and Disaster, 1945–1964.* Boston: Houghton Mifflin, 1985.

James, D. Clayton, with Anne Sharp Wells. *Refighting the Last War: Command and Crisis in Korea, 1950–1953.* New York: Free Press, 1993.

Joy, C. Turner. *How the Communists Negotiate.* New York: Macmillan, 1955.

Kaufman, Burton I. *The Korean War: Challenges in Crisis, Credibility, and Command.* Philadelphia: Temple University Press, 1986.

Keefer, Edward C., ed. *Foreign Relations of the United States, 1952–1954, Korea.* Vol. 15. Washington, D.C.: Government Printing Office, 1984.

———. "President Dwight D. Eisenhower and the End of the Korean War." *Diplomatic History* 10:3 (Summer 1986): 267–289.

Kim, Chull Baum, and James I. Matray, eds. *Korea and the Cold War: Division, Destruction, and Disarmament.* Claremont, CA: Regina Books, 1993.

Kissinger, Henry A. *Nuclear Weapons and Foreign Policy.* New York: Harper and Brothers, 1957.

Kolko, Joyce, and Gabriel. *The Limits of Power: The World and United States Foreign Policy, 1945–1954.* New York: Harper & Row, 1972.

Lyon, Peter. *Eisenhower, Portrait of a Hero.* Boston: Little, Brown, 1974.

MacArthur, Douglas A. *Reminiscences.* New York: McGraw-Hill, 1964.

MacDonald, Callum A. *Korea: The War before Vietnam.* New York: Free Press, 1986.

McMahon, Robert J. "The Cold War in Asia: Towards a New Synthesis?" *Diplomatic History* 12:3 (Summer 1988): 307–327.

Matray, James I. *The Reluctant Crusade: American Foreign Policy in Korea, 1941–1950.* Honolulu: University of Hawaii Press, 1985.

———. "Villain Again: The United States and the Korean Armistice Talks." *Diplomatic History* 16:3 (Summer 1992): 473–480.

Merrill, John. *Korea: The Peninsular Origins of the War.* Newark, DE: University of Delaware Press, 1989.

O'Neill, Robert J. *Australia in the Korean War, 1950–1953.* Vol. 1: *Strategy and Diplomacy.* Canberra: Australian War Memorial/Australian Government Publishing Service, 1981.

Parmet, Herbert S. *Eisenhower and the American Crusades.* New York: Macmillan, 1972.

Rees, David. *Korea: The Limited War.* New York: St. Martin's Press, 1964.

Reid, Escott. *Envoy to Nehru.* New York: Oxford University Press, 1981.

Ryan, Mark A. *Chinese Attitudes towards Nuclear Weapons: China and the United States during the Korean War.* Armonk, NY: M. E. Sharpe, 1990.

Schaller, Michael. *Douglas MacArthur: Far Eastern General.* New York: Oxford University Press, 1989.

Schnabel, James F., and Robert J. Watson. *The History of the Joint Chiefs of Staff: The Joint Chiefs of Staff and National Policy.* Vol. 3, parts I and II: *The Korean War.* Washington, DC: Historical Division, Joint Secretariat, Joint Chiefs of Staff, April 1978, March 1979.

Schlesinger, Arthur M., Jr., and Richard Rovere. *The General and the President.* New York: Farrar, Straus, 1951.

Shepley, James, "How Dulles Averted War." *Life,* January 16, 1956, pp. 70–72.

Simmons, Robert. *The Strained Alliance: Peking, Pyongyang, Moscow and the Politics of the Korean Civil War.* New York: Free Press, 1975.

Spanier, John W. *The Truman-MacArthur Controversy and the Korean War.* Cambridge: Harvard University Press, 1959.

Stairs, Denis. *The Diplomacy of Constraint: Canada, the Korean War and the United States.* Toronto: University of Toronto Press, 1974.

Stone, I. F. *The Hidden History of the Korean War.* New York: Monthly Review Press, 1952.

Stueck, William W., Jr. *The Road to Confrontation: American Policy Towards China and Korea, 1947–1950.* Chapel Hill, NC: North Carolina University Press, 1981.

———. William W., Jr. "The Limits of Influence: British Policy and American Expansion of the War in Korea." *Pacific Historical Review* 55:1 (February 1986): 65–95.

Trachtenburg, Marc. "A 'Wasting Asset': American Strategy and the Shifting Nuclear Balance, 1949–1954." *International Security* 13:3 (Winter 1988–1989): 5–49.

Truman, Harry S. *Memoirs: Years of Trial and Hope.* Garden City, NY: Doubleday, 1956.

U.S. Senate. *Military Situation in the Far East. Hearings before the Armed Services and Foreign Relations Committee.* U.S. Senate, 82d Cong. 1st sess., 1951.

Whitney, Courtney. *MacArthur: His Rendevous with History.* New York: Knopf, 1956.

Willoughby, Charles A., and John Chamberlain. *MacArthur, 1941–1951.* New York: McGraw-Hill, 1954.

PART V

The Unification Struggle after the Korean War

17 Korea's Unification Struggle

In K. Hwang

The Korean War broke out in the midst of a national struggle for unification but ended in a stalemate without one side winning decisively over the other. Korea still remains divided, and the unification struggle continues. Ever since the "temporary" division of the country in 1945, national unification has been a sacred mission for every Korean. Today every aspect of Korean society, both North and South, is affected by the goal of unification. Despite the profound and dramatic changes in recent years in the international and domestic political environments (such as the end of the cold war); the establishment of diplomatic relations between South Korea and Russia, and South Korea and China; simultaneous entry of the two Koreas into the United Nations; and the inter-Korean Basic Agreement (including the nonaggression provision); unremitting mutual distrust and suspicion between the Pyongyang and Seoul governments persist. The basic demands of the two sides remain incompatible.

The fundamental problems of unification in the 1990s are essentially the same as those plaguing the two Korean governments before the Korean War. In the most general terms, they relate to a single, central concern: Which side should rule the unified Korea, the North or the South?

There are two sets of political dynamics at work, each complicating the other: the two Koreas themselves and the major world powers of China, Russia, Japan, and the United States, all with security and economic interests in the Korean peninsula. Before the end of the cold war, the peninsula was held hostage to the overarching conflict between the United States and the Soviet Union. The end of the cold war had some mitigating effects on the peninsula, enabling the entry of both Koreas into the United Nations, but the major powers will continue to have considerable influence, as shown by the recent U.S. involvement in the nuclear negotiation with North Korea, along with the Chinese pressure. Korean unification will have the best chance of success only when there is a double consensus between the two Koreas and between the four powers.

SOURCES

Since the unification policy has been the monopoly of the Korean governments, most unification studies have been undertaken by the government branches. In South Korea, the National Unification Board and the ministries of Foreign Affairs and National Defense are the main sources. In North Korea, more rigid governmental monopoly can be assumed. However, a plethora of books and articles on unification in both Korean and English, as well as in other languages, have been published since the division.

Bibliographies

Despite a wealth of printed materials on unification, there is no single bibliographical volume. However, the major works in the field include extensive notes and bibliographies. Among the more recent noteworthy publications are Young Whan Kihl's *Politics and Policies in Divided Korea* (1984); Hakjoon Kim's *Unification Policies of South and North Korea* (1986); Bong-youn Choy's *A History of the Korean Reunification Movement* (1984); Tae-hwan Kwak et al. (eds.), *Korean Reunification* (1984); and Won-myoung Lee's *Zur Frage der Nation Und der Wiederverinigung im geteilten Korea* (1989).

General Reference Works

There are several useful reference volumes. *Reunification of Korea: 50 Basic Documents* was edited by Han-kyo Kim in 1972. *Korean Unification: Source Materials with an Introduction*, volumes 1 through 3, was edited, respectively, by Se-jin Kim (1976), Chong-shik Chung (1979), and Sang-woo Rhee (1986); it covers, in chronological order, the period from 1943 to 1986 and provides treaties, communiqués, major policy statements, speeches, press interviews, position statements, and proposals by both sides. *Tongil Munje Yongu* (The study of Korean unification) was published by the Ministry of Foreign Affairs (ROK) in 1966; and *The Policy of Republic of Korea for Peaceful Unification* by the same ministry appeared in 1975.

Periodicals

Many periodicals and journals deal with unification issues. The National Unification Board publishes *Tongil Munje Yongu* (Journal of unification affairs) each month. Other periodicals are *Korea and World Affairs, East*

Asian Review, North Korean News, Journal of East Asian Affairs, Asian Survey, and Pacific Affairs.

Research Institutes

Most research institutes dealing with Korean unification have their own publications or conference proceedings. Some are governmental or government affiliated, and others are private and semiprivate. The most important are the Research Center for Peace and Unification of Korea (Seoul); Korean Institute for Defense Analysis (Seoul); Research Institute for National Unification (Seoul); Council on U.S.-Korea Security Studies (Washington, D.C.); Association of National Unification, Council on Korean Reunification (ad hoc); Research Committee on Korean Reunification (Bradley University); Institute for Korean National Reunification (Seoul); and Committee for the Peaceful Reunification of the Fatherland (Pyongyang).

DIVISION OF KOREA: 1945–1950

Geographical Factors

Much of modern Korean history, including the Japanese annexation, the division at the 38th parallel, the ensuing war, and the current impasse between Seoul and Pyongyang, is explained by Korea's geostrategic location and the fact that it is the weakest and smallest state in Northeast Asia surrounded by big powers.

Hakjoon Kim (1986), Bong-youn Choy (1984), Shannon McCune (1956), and Gregory Henderson (1968) all point out Korea's geographic predicament, describing its location variously as a "dagger pointed at the heart of Japan," a "hammer ready to strike at the head of China," a lips-teeth relationship with China, or a vital outlet to the Pacific from the Russian view. The Korean adage, "When the whales fight it is the shrimp in the middle that get crushed," is a poignant reminder. In fact, Korea was divided by the two great powers without the knowledge of the Korean people. The casualness of the division mentioned by Dean Rusk appears in *Foreign Relations of the United States* 1945 (1969).

Gregory Henderson's "Korea: Militarist or Unification Policies" (1976) shows that the Korean division at the 38th parallel was a prime example of Korea's being used as a pawn by the major powers in their international game. A similar view is expressed in James Matray's *The Reluctant Crusade* (1985); although sympathetic to the U.S. position in the light of the American-Soviet cold war rivalry, Matray sees Korea as a captive of the cold war.

Pre-1950 Unification Efforts

After Korea was divided into the Soviet and American zones, twice in early October 1945, General John R. Hodge, the U.S. occupation head in the South, invited Soviet general Ivan M. Chistiakov of the North to Seoul to discuss unification and the removal of the 38th parallel border. On October 9, Chistiakov refused, and each occupation general set up a separate military government in his zone, foreshadowing the perpetuation of Korea's division.

The failure of the Hodge-Chistiakov meeting led to the December 21, 1945, Moscow agreement by the foreign ministers of the United States (James F. Byrnes), the Soviet Union (V. M. Molotov), and the United Kingdom (Anthony Eden). Later, nationalist China also adhered to the agreement; the details are provided in the U.S. Department of State's *Moscow Meeting of Foreign Ministers* (1946). One of the best works available on the initial U.S. efforts toward unification is *The Record on Korean Unification, 1943–1960,* published by the Department of State in 1960, with a narrative and collection of official documents that provide the record on Korean unification as shown by the policies and actions of the United States, the United Nations, the Soviet Union, and the Republic of Korea.

Due to the intense opposition by the Korean nationalists to the Moscow agreement's five-year international trusteeship proposal, no progress was made, and a joint U.S.-U.S.S.R. conference also failed by the summer of 1947. After the frustrating experiences with the Soviet negotiator, the United States dumped the Korean unification question on the United Nations in September.

United Nations Unification Attempts

Despite Soviet opposition, the UN General Assembly on November 14, 1947, adopted a U.S.-proposed resolution providing for a program for Korean unification and independence. A United Nations Temporary Commission on Korea (UNTCOK) was formed to advise on the establishment of a national government. It helped to establish the government of the Republic of Korea (ROK) with Syngman Rhee as president in 1948 in South Korea, but it failed to set up a unified government with North Korea because the Soviets refused to receive UNTCOK. Subsequently the North established a separate government, known as the Democratic People's Republic of Korea (DPRK), with Kim Il-sung as premier.

The details of establishing two rival governments are well documented in George McCune's *Korea Today* (1950). An official in the State Department in 1944–1945, McCune was instrumental in shaping decisions at this critical time. He was born in Pyongyang, lived nearly half his life there, and later was on the faculty of the University of California. *Korea Today* has become one of the classic works on postwar Korea. Kyung Cho Chung published *Korea Tomorrow* (1956) to extend McCune's work. Joungwoon A. Kim's *Divided Korea* (1975) contains newer research material.

Unification Struggle between the Two Koreas

No sooner had the two governments been established than the struggle for national unification began. Each side claimed its sovereignty over the other through their respective constitutional and legal interpretations. The ROK argued that it was the only lawful national government in Korea because it was created by the United Nations following a free election. Moreover, the ROK constitution stipulated that its jurisdiction extended over the entire Korean peninsula and its adjacent islands. To justify and legitimize such a claim, the ROK National Assembly reserved one hundred vacant seats for future North Korean representatives. President Rhee interpreted this to mean that the ROK should "march north" to recover the "lost territory," occupied illegally by the DPRK, even by military means if necessary.

Meanwhile, the DPRK declared itself the only lawfully elected people's government in Korea and designated Seoul, the capital of the ROK, as its own capital, while considering Pyongyang (now the capital of the DPRK) as the revolutionary capital for all Korea. The DPRK also declared national unification as its goal and demanded that the governments of the Soviet Union and the United States withdraw their occupying troops. Data on these North-South claims can be found in Hakjoon Kim (1986).

Parallel with these claims, military skirmishes became commonplace along the border, although by the summer of 1949 all occupying foreign troops withdrew from the peninsula and left Koreans alone on their peninsula for the first time in half a century. But the problem of who would rule all of Korea was unresolved, and a peaceful settlement for national unification was not expected under such hostile conditions. When Kim Il-sung's North Korean regime opted for a military solution on June 25, 1950, the DPRK launched a full-scale military attack against the ROK. Though clearly the Korean War was begun by the North Korean invasion of the South, its origins have been one of the prime topics of international controversy. Bruce Cumings' *The Origins of the Korean War* (1981) expostulates that the war was the extension of the civil strife that had been going on since the Japanese annexation of Korea in 1910. Other chapters in this book provide more details on the outbreak of the war.

UNIFICATION STRUGGLE AFTER THE WAR

When the war broke out in 1950, the Korean question was again placed before the United Nations. On the day of the North Korean invasion,

June 25, 1950, the UN Security Council adopted a U.S.-sponsored resolution denouncing the North Korean breach of peace and calling for a cessation of hostilities and the withdrawal of the North Korean army to the 38th parallel. After North Korea refused to withdraw, war between UN forces led by the United States and North Korea forces, aided by communist China, lasted for three years. On July 27, 1953, the war ended in a truce, not in the imposition of surrender and a peace treaty. Thus, in the 1990s, Korea remains divided as before at the 38th parallel (more or less). The unification struggle has not ended between the two Koreas.

Leland M. Goodrich's *Korea: A Study of U.S. Policy in the United Nations* (1956) is one of the best studies dealing with the Korean problem in the United Nations. Beginning with a brief account of the troubled historical past of Korea, which has long known invasion and the threat of invasion, Goodrich sets the stage for Korea's catastrophic hour resulting from World War II: the division of a once-united nation into two separate countries. He examines the Korean problem in the UN and the armistice negotiations, and he concludes with a thoughtful discourse on the problems facing Korea and the world community.

The U.S. Department of State's *The Korean Problem at the Geneva Conference* (1954) provides the most detailed account of the competing approaches to unification, with lists of participants, schedules of meetings, statements by the participants, proposals from each side, and the final declaration by the sixteen nations that participated in the Korean War. The competing unification proposals made by North Korea, South Korea, and the Soviet Union can also be found in the Department of State's *The Record on Korean Unification* (1960).

The Geneva participants on the Allied side were delegates from the ROK and all the countries (except the Union of South Africa) that had contributed military forces to the UN Command; the communist side was represented by the DPRK, the People's Republic of China, and the Soviet Union. The ROK's unification proposal was the same as one it had advocated in 1948 when Seoul argued that since the ROK had been established by free elections under UN supervision, what remained to be done was a similar election in the DPRK to elect its representatives to fill the vacant seats reserved for North Korea in South Korea's National Assembly. Yet the DPRK refused to accept any UN role in the Korean settlement and demanded that an all-Korean election be held for an all-Korean national assembly to establish a unified government. Pyongyang wanted the Supreme People's Assembly of North Korea and the National Assembly of South Korea to elect their respective representatives to an all-Korean commission that would arrange and ensure free, democratic, general elections. All foreign military forces were to withdraw from Korean territory within six months, and a guarantee of the peaceful development of Korea by those countries most interested in the maintenance of peace in the Far East would be ensured.

In response, the ROK side, realizing that the majority of the sixteen nations favored an all-Korean election and simultaneous withdrawal of all foreign troops, modified its earlier position. On May 22, the ROK presented a comprehensive fourteen-point proposal for the unification of Korea. The principal points of the ROK proposal that remained basic to all subsequent discussions were that there should be free elections under UN supervision and based on a UN census, that UN forces would leave Korea only after a unified government had been achieved, and that the UN would guarantee the territorial integrity of an independent Korea.

The majority of the allied representatives, including the United States, supported the ROK proposal. There was general agreement among the allies that the UN should supervise Korean elections, that UN forces should remain until a new government was active, and that communist Chinese forces should be withdrawn before the elections. The allied delegations repeatedly asserted the UN's authority to deal with the Korean problem and opposed communist efforts to deny the UN role in a unification settlement.

In response, the North Korean and communist Chinese delegates categorically rejected the ROK's proposal, objecting specifically to the UN role in supervising the all-Korean elections. The Soviet delegate restated the communist position and proposed a resolution whose main points the DPRK adopted as its basic terms. The most important parts of this proposal called for "free elections" but required a representative body based on population, a temporary government from the representatives of the existing DPRK and the ROK, and the withdrawal of all foreign forces, including the UN's, prior to an all-Korean election. Particularly, it denied a UN role in this process.

Since the communist proposal excluded the UN from a supervising role in the all-Korean commission and assigned this function to a neutral nations supervising commission, no progress was made at Geneva toward a final settlement on Korean unification. On June 15, 1954, the allied side acknowledged that the Geneva conference had been in vain.

In addition to the two State Department volumes issued in 1954 and 1960 and listed earlier, Hakjoon Kim (1986) and Pyo-Wook Han's *The Problem of Korean Unification* (1987) and his "Divided Korea in a Divided World" (1957) deal with the detailed politics of the Geneva conference. Han was a veteran career diplomat who began his duty with the establishment of the Korean embassy in Washington, D.C.

THE POST-GENEVA UNIFICATION STRUGGLE

After the Geneva failure, North and South Korea reverted to their respective pre-Geneva position: the North's communization or liberation of the ROK being advocated by Kim Il-sung, and the South's "marching north to unify" being the slogan of the Syngman Rhee regime. The

United Nations did not abandon its responsibility for the Korean problem, but because of North Korean and communist Chinese obstruction, UN work since 1954 has concentrated on assisting the ROK to rebuild its war-torn economy. In a resolution of November 29, 1955, the UN General Assembly reaffirmed its intention to search for a Korean solution according to UN objectives.

The DPRK also concentrated on economic recovery and reconstruction through its Three-Year Economic Plan, introduced in January 1954, with the idea of *Juche* (self-reliance or independence) initiated by Kim Il-sung's famous speech, "On Exterminating Dogmatism and Formalism and Establishing *Juche* in Ideological Work" on December 28, 1955. This speech promulgated a unique North Korean way (Kim's way) to achieve the Korean revolution, not the Russian or Chinese way. Kim's *Juche* later developed into the ruling political doctrine for North Korea and was incorporated into the unification strategy. *Kim Il Sung Sonjip* (Selected works of Kim Il-sung) published in 1961 and *On Juche in Our Revolution* (1977) include Kim's major writings, speeches, and reports. Kim Jon Il, his son, elaborated the same *Juche* idea in *On the Juche Idea* (1982). Colin Mackerras's article "The *Juche Idea* and the Thought of Kim Il Sung" (1985), Byung Chul Koh's "Ideology and Political Control in North Korea" (1970), and Han-shik Park's "The Ideology of North Korean Communism" (1979) all provide critical analysis on this pseudo-Marxist nationalism or Kimilsungnism.

Since the 1954 Geneva conference, North Korea has taken more initiatives than South Korea on the unification program and by 1960 emerged as the temporary victor in the unification competition because the Rhee government was overthrown by a student uprising in April 1960, protesting Rhee's failure to build democratic institutions and provide economic reconstruction. The North's unity initiatives included an offer to hold a 1955 joint conference of representatives of North and South Korea to negotiate national unification (October 30, 1954); a proposed nonaggression pact between the two Koreas with simultaneous reductions of both sides' armed forces (March 7, 1955); a request for an international conference of the powers concerned about a solution for the Korean unification question (April 28, 1956); and withdrawal of all foreign troops from Korea and a mutual reduction of armed forces to 100,000 (September 20, 1957, and again on February 5, 1958). In addition, the DPRK stressed economic and cultural exchanges between the two sides and methods for peaceful unification. None of these was fulfilled.

In contrast, the Rhee government kept up the slogan, "March north to unify," and called for a united Korea by driving out Chinese Communist troops and by crushing the North Korean regime (July 14, 1954); through withdrawal of the communist members from the Neutral Nations Supervisory Commission; and through general elections in North Korea alone rather than an all-Korean election (February 21, 1958). Meanwhile, the Chinese communist troops were withdrawn from North Korea by the end of 1958.

Hakjoon Kim (1986) gives a critical review of the unification competition during the years after Geneva; Se-jin Kim (1976) provides a narrative summary with a collection of documents, proposals, official statements, and speeches; and Bong-youn Choy (1984) is more than a dry historical recitation, containing unification viewpoints of other leading scholars and commentators.

Kim Il-sung's Confederation Proposal

While South Korea was going through a tumultuous political reorganization to form the Second Republic after the overthrow of the Rhee regime in 1960, the relatively stable DPRK proposed a comprehensive and composite unification plan: a confederation unification formula. In celebrating the fifteenth anniversary of Korean liberation, Kim Il-sung proposed the formation of a confederal unification under which both the North and South governments would, "as a temporary measure," retain their existing governments, while economic intercourse and other cooperative ventures were begun. Also, each government would reduce its military forces to 100,000 to reduce tensions while representatives of both governments met to consult about the political future.

South Korea's Second Republic, headed by Chang Myon, offered a counterproposal on August 17, 1960, which rejected the confederation. Nevertheless, the Chang government abandoned Rhee's "march north and unify" slogan, signaling the end of ROK's military unification posture. In opposing Kim's confederation, the ROK's foreign minister, Chung Il Hyong, indicated that various UN resolutions required that the UN supervise an election and that the UN recognize ROK as Korea's legitimate government. In addition, he noted that the DPRK had not renounced plans to destroy the ROK.

Nevertheless, the Second Republic continued to have political, economic, and social instability because the rebellious voices of students continued to escalate. The nation's mood was to find a quick solution to unification, and various new unification movements arose. The Council for Independence and National Unification was formed by the socialist parties, the student organizations, the Association for Permanent Neutralization of Korea, and labor unions, all of which came into being soon after the Second Republic was established. Many council members were interested in U.S. senator Michael Mansfield's proposed neutralization based on Austria's neutral pattern. To initiate this process the council requested an opening of trade between North and South and an exchange of cultural missions, sports teams, and newspaper correspondents before holding any formal discussions on the unification issue; it proposed that in due time, a free general election should be held to unify the country. These suggestions coincided with some North Korean unification proposals and on May 5, 1961, the National Student League urged that a North-South Student Conference should be held on May 20 in Panmunjom. This would be the largest Korean unification event since a North-South Korean Political Leaders Coalition Conference in 1948 in Pyongyang.

The North Korean regime announced its support for the student conference and guaranteed the South Korean delegates personal safety and freedom to travel anywhere in the North, a decision that caught the South Korean government in the middle. The ROK feared that suppressing the student unification movement could lead to a recurrence of the 1960 student demonstrations that brought down the Rhee regime, while supporting the student unification movement would allow right-wing political forces to charge it with accepting a "communist-oriented" event. On May 16, 1961, four days before the scheduled conference, an ROK military coup d'état led by army officer Park Chung Hee took care of the issue. The Second Republic ended abruptly, and all unification efforts initiated by the people collapsed because the military junta outlawed all newly formed progressive political and social organizations and arrested most leaders of the National Student League. The prospects for a peaceful unification of Korea became unpredictable.

Yong-soon Yim's *Politics of Korean Unification* (1988) analyzes South Korea's internal political transformation during the period 1960–1961. C. I. Eugene Kim and Ke-soo Kim's article (1964) covers the same events, and Sung Joo Han's *The Failure of Democracy in South Korea* (1974) is pivotal for anyone delving into the collapse of the Chang Myon regime.

The Unification Struggle under Park Chung Hee

Between 1961 and 1971, General Park considered unification secondary to economic reconstruction, political stability, and strong defense to meet any challenge from North Korea. He completely excluded any compromised or negotiated settlement with the DPRK and refused to deal with Kim Il-sung, whom he called a "first-rate war criminal." Park did not change this position until August 1971, when the news of Nixon's visit to China in February 1972 was announced. Park's desire for "victory over communism" was reflected in every aspect of political, social, educational, and cultural life in South Korea. To defeat communism, he wanted the South to strengthen its economic recovery through successive five-year plans starting in 1962.

Park's anticommunist unification ideas were expounded in his three books (1976, 1962a, 1962b), and Park's economic achievement is described by David C. Cole and Princeton Lyman (1971) and in *Economic*

Development in the Republic of Korea edited by Lee-jay Cho and Yoon Hyung Kim (1991).

North Korean Reaction. The emergence of South Korea's strongly anti-communist military dictatorship following the 1961 coup seemed to have alarmed North Korea. With Seoul under totalitarian rule, the DPRK had little room to manipulate, maneuver, or influence South Korean politics. Therefore, the North Korean regime adopted a clandestine, subversive tactic for its unification strategy. It concluded mutual defense treaties with the Soviet Union (July 6, 1961) and China (July 11, 1961) since the ROK had already concluded a treaty with the United States in October 1953. Kim Il-sung advocated waging a war of liberation against the ROK by awakening South Koreans to mobilize for a revolutionary movement to expel American imperialists and by a final violent struggle to destroy the ROK.

Meanwhile in the South, President Park's anticommunist stance never changed despite an assassination attempt on Park's life by a North Korean commando unit on January 21, 1968, and North Korea's seizure of the U.S. naval intelligence vessel *Pueblo* on January 24, 1968. Source materials on these events are in *Anbo Tongil Munje Kibon Jaryo-Jin* (Basic documents on security and unification) published by the Dong-A Ilbo in Seoul (1971). The *Pueblo* incident is described by Byung C. Koh (1969); by Sheldon W. Simon (1970); and in memoirs of *Pueblo* Captain Lloyd Bucher (1970) and his second-in-command, Edward E. Murphy, Jr. (1971).

North Korea's UN Tactics. Since the creation of the ROK under UN supervision, the DPRK had opposed any UN role in the Korean reunification process. By 1960, however, increased African and Asian membership in the UN had altered that group's pro-ROK position. UN members agreed to invite representatives from both Koreas to debate at the UN, insisting that the Korean problem must be solved by Koreans. Taking advantage of the new international mood after 1963, the DPRK not only denied the UN authority on Korea but also proposed its own unification agenda, such as the conclusion of a mutual nonaggressive pact, the reduction of armed forces to 100,000 or fewer on each side, the creation of an all-Korean economic committee, the holding of an international conference to discuss the Korean issue, and North-South direct negotiations. Chonghan Kim (1970) has an insightful article dealing with UN-Korean relationships during this period, as does Chi Young Park in "Korea and the United Nations" (1985).

Between 1971 and 1979. The escalation of the Sino-Soviet conflict during the late 1960s resulted in military clashes along those nations' borders and at the Damansky (Chen Pao) islands in the Ussuri River and persuaded the Chinese leaders to seek better relations with the United States. The "Ping-Pong" diplomacy of April 1971, followed by Secretary of State Henry Kissinger's secret visit to Beijing in July 1971, enabled the People's

Republic of China (PRC) to be admitted to the United Nations in October 1971 and permitted President Richard Nixon to visit the PRC in February 1972. These events had an impact on Korea's scheme of national unification. Immediately following the news that Nixon would go to the PRC, Kim Il-sung declared that the DPRK would discuss the unification issue with all political parties and social organizations in South Korea. In response, the ROK proposed an inter-Korean Red Cross meeting to discuss the problem of locating divided families. Thus, for the first time since the division of the country, Red Cross representatives of the two Koreas began a dialogue on September 20 at Panmunjom, which culminated in the historic North-South Joint Communiqué in 1972. These steps seemed to usher in a new era of hope for national reconciliation and unification. The Joint Communiqué enunciated the principles that unification shall be achieved through peaceful means and by a broad national unity, transcending differences in ideas and systems. This communiqué is described by Se-jin Kim (1976) and the 1973 special issue of *South-North Dialogue in Korea.*

However, nothing concrete resulted from either the Red Cross talks or the North-South Political Coordinating Committee due to the deep mutual distrust between the two groups. In the midst of an impasse of the Red Cross and Coordinating Committee meetings, President Park, on June 23, 1973, announced another seven-point declaration on peace and unification; it said that although unification efforts should continue, the two Koreas should act separately, even allowing North Korea to join the UN. Regarding Park's proposal, *Foreign Policy for Peaceful Unification of the Republic* (1975) was published by the ROK's Ministry of Foreign Affairs. Joon Il Rhee's "Proposals Made by ROK since July 4, 1972" (1979) deals with the same subject.

DPRK's "Confederal Republic of Koryo." Ten hours after Park's seven-point announcement, North Korea's Kim Il-sung countered with a "five-point unification program" that negated the ROK statement on going separate ways by repeating earlier confederal concepts and objecting to ROK items such as two UN memberships. In both 1960 and 1970, the DPRK had suggested a similar confederation for unification, but this third proposal would institute a confederal government within the two existing Korean systems: the designation of a "Confederal Republic of Koryo," harkening back to an ancient unified Koryo kingdom (935–1392). Kim urged that neither state join the UN separately.

Among works drawn on the problems of this North Korean unification proposal are articles by Yong-Soon Yim (1984), Jong-youl Yoo's "Unification Policies of North Korea in the 1970's" (1980), and Dong-book Lee (1980). Mr. Lee was once a spokesman for the South-North Coordinating Committee.

In November 1973, while North-South talks were being discussed, the

UN General Assembly decided to abolish the UN Commission for the Unification and Rehabilitation of Korea (UNCURK) which it had set up in October 1950. The ongoing impasse in the North-South dialogue and the abolition of UNCURK forced the ROK to seek an alternate guarantee of its security. Thus in 1974, Park Chung Hee proposed a nonaggression pact in which the two Koreas would agree to maintain the existing armistice and not wage war against each other or interfere in the other's internal affairs.

On March 2, 1974, North Korea's Fifth Supreme People's Assembly answered that if the outdated armistice agreement were replaced with a peace agreement, the question must be settled with the United States, which signed the armistice and held the real power. But in August, the ROK rejected the North's proposal, replying that unification should be obtained through the North-South dialogue, which together with an agreement not to wage war could establish mutual trust and lead to free general elections throughout Korea.

One new element in President Park's August 1974 response was the call for all-Korean elections without the customary phrase "under United Nations supervision." This deletion, however, was not a real change in ROK policy but reflected South Korea's passive acceptance of recent UN action that made the phrase meaningless.

Before 1974 ended, new North-South tensions arose. In November, the ROK government announced that North Korea had been constructing infiltration tunnels since 1972 at various points along the 155-mile truce line and appealed to the UN, but North Korea ignored the UN Command's request to send a joint observer team to investigate the tunnel. In addition, during the last two weeks of the Vietnam War in 1975, the North Korean high command moved elements of its armored divisions into position near Korea's demilitarized zone to reinforce troops already there and built a new airfield close to the DMZ, bringing North Korean aircraft within a few minutes' flight time of Seoul.

The fall of Indochina to the communists in April 1975 had a serious impact on both Koreas. Clearly the solution of Vietnam's problems had come through civil war, which made South Korea more inclined to suppress the civil war element in the unification of Korea and to stress international arrangements. In contrast, the Vietnam solution emboldened North Korea to move toward a military solution in Korea. Not surprisingly, this situation ended the North-South dialogue inaugurated by the Joint Communiqué of 1972 and led both to disconnecting the hot line for communication between Pyongyang and Seoul in March 1976, and to the last Red Cross meeting in March 1978. No progress had been made toward Korean unification despite the numerous proposals and counterproposals.

The most dynamic influence on Korea during the 1970s was UN-Korean relations. Chonghan Kim's article, "Korean Reunification: UN Perspectives'' (1984), analyzes the shifting UN tactics employed by both North and South Korea every year until 1975.

THE UNIFICATION COMPETITION IN THE 1980s

Maneuvers regarding unification continued during the 1980s because both Korean governments wanted to be seen as advocating one nation. In the ROK, the new military regime of Chun Doo Hwan gained power in December 1979, following the assassination of President Park on October 26. In the DPRK, Kim Chong Il was designated as heir apparent to his father, Kim Il-sung, at the Sixth Congress of the Korean Workers' party (Communist party) held in October 1980. Also at this Congress, Kim Il-sung announced for the fourth time a confederation formula for unification, using a slightly new designation, ''Democratic Confederal Republic of Koryo'' (DCRK). Although most DPRK proposals were repetitions or modifications of ideas long advanced by Kim, two new elements were added in 1980: the DCRK would be transformed into a ''permanent peace and nuclear-free zone'' and should have a neutral, nonaligned foreign policy. In addition, the DCRK was to be constituted with the existing governmental systems of the two Koreas intact by way of setting up a supreme National Confederal Assembly composed of equal representation from both sides and a certain number of representatives of overseas nationals. These ideas were published in Kim Il-sung's ''Let Us Reunify the Country Independently and Peacefully'' (1980) and in volume 3 of Sang-woo Rhee's *Korean Unification* (1986). A critical analysis of the programs is presented by C. I. Eugene Kim and Ke-soo Kim (1982), Sung Chul Yang (1982), Jae Kyu Park (1984), and Tuk-chu Chón (1980) who compares Korea's experience to Germany's since World War II.

In response to Kim's 1981 proposal, President Chun of South Korea proposed an exchange of visits between himself and Kim Il-sung, and on January 22, 1982, he proposed the United Democratic Republic of Korea (UDRK) by outlining seven basic Korean relations and eight programs. The inter-Korean relationships were to be based on equality and reciprocity, mutual nonaggression under the armistice, mutual respect for existing foreign relations, and the establishment of liaison offices in Seoul and Pyongyang. Chun's programs included methods to draft a constitution and hold all-Korean elections to form a government. As a follow-up step on February 1, Seoul's minister of the National Unification Board, Son Chae-sik, proposed cooperative projects for highways, postal exchanges, reuniting families, a joint tourist zone, free trade, access to each other's regular radio programs, and other joint ventures. These proposals represented a dramatic move intended to score propaganda points for Chun. North Korea denounced the package for being divisive and claimed the projects were no more than a fraction of the ideas Pyongyang had already laid down. As a result, there were no major changes toward unification until the end of Chun's presidency.

Articles that discuss Chun's proposals include those of Young Whan Kihl (1982), Yong-soon Yim (1984), Sung Chul Yang (1984), and Oran R. Young (1983).

Roh Tae Woo's Nordpolitik

With the inauguration of the Sixth Republic on February 25, 1988, President Roh Tae Woo introduced *Nordpolitik* (northern policy), which referred to South Korea's new policy toward communist countries such as China, the Soviet Union, and Eastern Europe states, just as *Ospolitik* referred to West Germany's policy toward eastern communist states during the 1970s. In July 1988, Roh proposed gaining unity by first conducting North-South visits of Korean professionals and families, to be followed by trade agreements and ROK aid to the DPRK in improving its relations with Japan and the United States. Further, Roh proposed a summit meeting with Kim Il-sung. A series of offers followed: Kim agreed to a summit to discuss U.S. troop withdrawal and his confederation plan; Roh declared the ROK would never use force first against the DPRK; and Pyongyong offered a comprehensive plan for peaceful reunification, including the phased withdrawal of U.S. troops and tripartite talks with Washington to ease political and military conflict. *Nordpolitik* seemed to be aimed at successfully conducting the Twenty-fourth Summer Olympiad in Seoul from September 17 through October 3, 1988. Seoul wanted to invite as many countries as possible, especially communist countries, including North Korea, but Kim Il-sung rejected Roh's proposals and refused to participate in the Olympics.

Meanwhile, the ROK steadily improved relations with the Soviet Union, China, and the Eastern European nations. The Soviet and Chinese participation in the Seoul Olympics engendered tremendous prestige for the ROK, further isolating the DPRK from the international community. The Seoul government established diplomatic relations with the Soviet Union in September 1990 and with China in August 1992, whereas the Pyongyang regime is trying in the 1990s to establish relations with the United States and Japan.

The pertinent articles dealing with South Korea's *Nordpolitik* are Mane Heo's "Peace Build-up on the Korean Peninsula" (1987); Sang-seek Park's "Northern Diplomacy and Inter-Korean Relations" (1988); Byung-joon Ahn's "South Korea's New Nordpolitik" (1988); and Choung-il Chee's "South Korea's Foreign Policy in Transition" (1988).

Korean National Community Unification Formula

Buoyed with the success of the Olympics and confident in *Nordpolitik's* progress, President Roh introduced another unification policy in September 1989, Korean National Community Unification. It was based on a commonwealth idea as an interim institution by which the two governments would move from joint councils, secretariats, and ministries in both capitals toward a single constitution and elected government. North Korea rejected Roh's plan as a scheme for perpetuating two separate Koreas and for not dealing with the elimination of U.S. troops from South Korea.

On the characteristics of this "community" unification formula, Tae Woo Roh's *Korea: A Nation Transformed: Selected Speeches* (1990) is a primary source. Three articles that analyze this formula are by Hongkoo Lee (1989), Byung Chul Koh (1989), and Sung-joo Han (1989).

UNIFICATION DIALOGUE IN THE 1990s

The 1990s ushered in a new era of international political order when the fall of the Berlin Wall in November 1989 brought German unification and the collapse of the Soviet Union. These changes in the international environment brought a significant shift in inter-Korean relations because both Koreas were admitted to the United Nations in September 1991.

The North-South Basic Agreement, 1991

On September 4, 1990, the prime ministers of North and South Korea met in Seoul for the first time since Korea's division in 1945. Subsequently, after five more rounds of high-level talks between Seoul and Pyongyang, the Agreement on Reconciliation, Non-Aggression, and Exchanges and Cooperation between the North and the South (Basic Agreement) was signed in 1991. The Basic Agreement calls for the removal of political and military confrontation in order to achieve national reconciliation and reduce tension; the realization of multifaceted exchanges and cooperation to advance common national interests and prosperity; and a pledge to exert joint efforts to achieve peaceful unification.

The Basic Agreement obligates the two Koreas to recognize each other, not to interfere with each other's internal affairs, or vilify each other, or attempt any acts of sabotage or subversion against the other. Furthermore, both sides would endeavor to transform the armistice into a solid state of peace between the two by committing to mutual nonaggression, observing the military demarcation line, and building military confidence by installing a telephone hot line between the two military authorities and carrying out cooperative exchanges in various fields.

The full text of the Basic Agreement is found in *Korea and World Affairs* (1991). A critical analysis and assessment is given in the following four articles: Dong Won Lim's "Inter-Korean Relations Oriented toward Reconciliation and Cooperation" (1992); Se-hyun Jeong's "Legal Status and Political Meaning of the Basic Agreement" (1992); Byung Chul Koh's "The Inter-Korean Agreement of 1972 and 1992" (1992); and Tae-hwan Kwak's "Korean Reunification: Problems and Prospects" (1992).

On the same day the Basic Agreement was signed, the two sides issued a joint statement saying that they shared the view that no nuclear weapons should exist on the Korean peninsula and agreed to hold a meeting at Panmunjom on December 31, 1991. An agreement to denuclearize the Korean peninsula was jointly declared and would become effective on February 19, 1992. However, before North Korea accepted this pact, it demanded that South Korea should be the first to denuclearize. As a result, on September 28, 1991, U.S. president George Bush announced the unilateral removal of all U.S. tactical ground and sea-based nuclear weapons throughout the world, followed by President Roh's November 9 Declaration of Denuclearization of the Korean Peninsula and his December 18 Declaration of the Absence of Nuclear Weapons in South Korea. Finally, on January 30, 1992, North Korea signed the Safeguards Accord with the International Atomic Energy Agency (IAEA), more than six years after signing the Nuclear Non-Proliferation Treaty (NPT) in December 1985.

North Korea's nuclear ambitions added another complication to the unification problem after 1992. Among the numerous articles treating this issue are those of Nogwan Chung's (1992) on the North's nuclear status; Michael J. Mazarr's (1992) discussing world opinion of the activity; Andrew Mack's "North Korea and the Bomb" (1991); and Joseph Bermudez (1991), Young-sun Song (1991), and Leonard Spector and Jacqueline Smith (1991), who discuss the DPRK's nuclear threat.

Following the Basic Agreement and the Joint Declaration of Denuclearization of the Korean Peninsula, some guarded optimism evolved, but it was dashed when North Korea announced on March 12, 1993, that it was pulling out of the NPT after balking at a special inspection demand made by the IAEA over two suspect facilities for the North's nuclear program. By withdrawing from the NPT, Pyongyang removed the legal basis for the IAEA's special inspection but complicated its relations with Seoul, the United States, and its neighboring nations. Seoul responded immediately by freezing economic cooperation with North Korea, an action that halted the unification process.

Unification Perspective under Kim Young Sam

Installed on February 25, 1993, as South Korea's first civilian president in thirty-two years, Kim Young Sam became preoccupied with South Korea's internal political reforms. Regarding unification policy, Sam adopted a gradual process, starting with inter-Korean reconciliation and cooperation, which may lead to the second and intermediate phase of a Korean commonwealth (a state association). The third and final stage of unification would be based on the principle of "one people and state" and was to follow sometime after a summit conference between leaders in the North and South. This would probably be a process that takes an indefinite period of time. Furthermore, Sam has repeatedly stated opposition to a German-style "absorptive" unification. Kim Young Sam's comprehensive unification plan appears in *Korea's Unification Policy* published by the National Unification Board in October 1993.

On April 7, 1993, Kim Il-sung announced a program for national unity that urged inter-Korean contacts and the removal of threats of war. Kim offered nothing new, and the ROK did not respond due to the ongoing North Korean nuclear question. The recent North Korean unification dispute with the South is detailed in Young Whan Kihl's "The Politics of Inter-Korean Relations" (1994).

The nuclear issues with the United States arose in 1992–1993 because North Korea appeared to be developing nuclear weapons and did not cooperate with the IAEA, which inspects nuclear facilities under the NPT. Although the DPRK threatened to withdraw from the NPT, it reconsidered. After several high-level talks with U.S. officials in New York, Korea's deputy foreign minister, Kang Sok-ju, announced in June 1993 that the DPRK would "suspend" its withdrawal. Nevertheless, Pyongyang continued to refuse the IAEA's full-scope inspection of its nuclear facilities and though the spring of 1994 refused IAEA inspectors access to a critical laboratory so that the IAEA could not confirm if North Korea's atomic know-how and materials were for peaceful use. The IAEA referred the matter to the UN Security Council, which issued a threat of economic sanctions against North Korea.

During the standoff, former president Jimmy Carter visited Pyongyang on June 15 and negotiated a deal with Kim Il-sung to freeze his nuclear program in return for suspension of threatened economic sanctions. Carter also brokered plans for leaders of the two Koreas to meet, but Kim Il-sung's sudden death on July 8 put everything on hold. Kim will likely be succeeded by his eldest son, Kim Jong Il, whose regime may continue the employment of nuclear weapons to preserve its separate existence. No substantial change in inter-Korean relations is expected soon, even if the nuclear issue is resolved. To the economically poor North, the possession of nuclear weapons can be thought of as a cheaper "ultimate deterrent" and an indispensable lever to enhance its status and power regarding South Korea and the rest of the world. For these reasons, the prospects for Korean unification will probably be "no war, no peace" but "constant struggle" for hegemony.

Useful literature on recent North Korean nuclear issues includes that by Bruce Cumings (1993); Jin-hyun Paik (1993); Kongdan Oh and Ralph Hassig (1994); the Asia Society's *Divided Korea: Part I and Part II* (1992, 1993); and "North Korea—A Potential Time Bomb" (1994) in *Jane's Intelligence Review.* In addition, Byung C. Koh's "The War's Impact on the Korean Peninsula" (1993) assesses the long-term result of the 1950 Korean War on the military, economic, political, and psychological status of the two Koreas. On the unification prospect, Professor Young Whan Kihl of Iowa State University edited a book (1994) of nineteen essays covering various aspects of unification by diverse specialists on Korea. In addition, both Nicholas Eberstadt (1992–1993) and Manwoo Lee's article (1993) assess the future of unification.

AN ALTERNATIVE: NEUTRALIZED REUNIFICATION OF KOREA

The pioneer advocate for the idea of the neutralized reunification of Korea was Sam-kyn Kim, former editor-in-chief of the *Dong-A Ilbo* (Korean daily newspaper) and editor of the *Korea Hyoron* (Korea review). Kim devoted his entire life to the cause of a neutral, reunited Korea until his death in 1989. Soon after, a committee for publishing *Genrojin Kim Sam kyu* (the publicist Kim Sam Kyu) was formed in Japan. For many years Yong Jeung Kim published a bulletin in Washington, D.C., *Voice of Korea* (1943–1961) in which the same idea was often advocated. More recent publications on this subject include In K. Hwang's three books (1980, 1987, 1990); Bong-youn Choy (1984) on the reunification movement; and a Ministry of Public Information's (ROK) volume (1965). The best and most authoritative introduction to the theoretical concept of neutrality for world peace is *Neutralization and World Politics* edited by Princeton scholars Cyril E. Black and others in 1968. Other pertinent articles dealing with the same idea are by Johan Galtung (1989); Ho-jeh Lhee (1987); Yo Han Chu (1964); Donald S. McDonald (1989); Hongkoo Lee (1970); and Sam Kyu Kim (1972).

REFERENCES

Ahn, Byung-Joon. "South Korea's New Nordpolitik." *Korea and World Affairs* 12:4 (Winter 1988): 693–705.
Asia Society. *Divided Korea: Part I and II.* New York, 1992, 1993.

Berger, Carl. *The Korea Knot: A Military-Political History.* Philadelphia: University of Pennsylvania Press, 1957.

Bermudez, Joseph. "North Korea's Nuclear Program." *Jane's Intelligence Review* (September 1991): 404–411.

Black, Cyril E., et al., eds. *Neutralization and World Politics.* Princeton, NJ: Princeton University Press, 1968.

Bucher, Lloyd, with Mark Rascovich. *Bucher: Mystery.* Garden City, NY: Doubleday, 1970.

Chee, Choung-il. "South Korea's Foreign Policy in Transition: North Politics." *Korea and World Affairs* 12:4 (Winter 1988): 737–753.

Cho, Lee-jay and Yoon Hyung Kim, eds. *Economic Development in the Republic of Korea.* Honolulu: University of Hawaii Press, 1991.

Chon, Tuk-chu. "Is the Korean Confederation Practical? A Comparative Analysis on the East German Concept and the North Korean Concept of a Confederation." *Korea and World Affairs* 4:2 (Summer 1980): 349–362.

Choy, Bong-youn. *A History of the Korean Reunification Movement: Its Issues and Prospects.* Peoria, IL: Research Committee on Korean Unification in the Institute of International Studies at Bradley University, 1984.

Chu, Yo Han. "Risks Involved in Korean Unification through Neutralization." *Korean Quarterly* 6:3 (Autumn 1964): 24–32.

Chung, Chong-shik, ed. *Korea Unification Source Materials.* Vol. 2. Seoul: Research Center for Peace and Unification, 1979.

Chung, Kyung Cho. *Korea Tomorrow: Land of Morning Calm.* New York: Macmillan, 1956.

Chung, Nogwan. "Implications of North Korea's Nuclear Development Policy." *East Asian Review* 4:2 (Summer 1992): 32–49.

Cole, David C., and Princeton N. Lyman. *Korean Development: The Interplay of Politics and Economics.* Cambridge: Harvard University Press, 1971.

Committee for Publishing *Genrojin Kim Sam Kyu* (The publicist Kim Sam Kyu). Tokyo: Asahishimbunsha, 1989.

Cumings, Bruce. *The Origins of the Korean War.* 2 vols. Princeton, NJ: Princeton University Press, 1981.

———. "It's Time to End the 40-Year War." *Nation,* August 23–30, 1993, pp. 206–208.

Dallin, David J. *Soviet Foreign Policy after Stalin.* Philadelphia: J. B. Lippincott, 1961.

Democratic People's Republic of Korea. *Documents and Materials Exposing the Instigators of the Civil War in Korea: Documents from the Archives of the Rhee Syngman Government.* Pyongyang: Foreign Language Publishing House, 1950.

Dong-A Ilbo. *Anbo Tongil Munje Kibon Jaryo-Jip* (Basic documents on security and unification). Seoul: Dong-A Ilbo, 1971.

Eberstadt, Nicholas. "Can the Two Koreas Be One." *Foreign Affairs* 71:5 (Winter 1992–1993): 150–165.

Galtung, Johan. "The Neutralization Approach to Korean Unification." In Michal Haas, ed., *Korean Reunification: Alternate Pathways.* New York: Praeger, 1989.

Goodrich, Leland M. *Korea: A Study of U.S. Policy in the United Nations.* New York: Council on Foreign Relations, 1956.

Han, Pyo Wook. "Divided Korea in a Divided World." Korea Embassy Information Bulletin (Washington, DC), April and May 1957.

———. *The Problem of Korean Unification: A Study of the Unification Policy of the Republic of Korea, 1948–1960.* Seoul: Research Center for Peace and Unification of Korea, 1987.

Han, Sung-joo. *The Failure of Democracy in South Korea.* Berkeley: University of California Press, 1974.

———. "The Functions and Limits of a New Unification Formula." *Korea and World Affairs* 13:4 (Winter 1989): 647–655.

Henderson, Gregory. *Korea: The Politics of the Vortex.* Cambridge: Harvard University Press, 1968.

———. "Korea: Militarist or Unification Policies." In William Barnds, ed., *The Two Koreas in East Asian Affairs.* New York: New York University Press, 1976.

Heo, Mane. "Peace Build-up on the Korean Peninsula: With Special Reference to 'North-Diplomacy.'" *Korea and World Affairs* 11:2 (Summer 1987): 286–303.

Heritage Foundation. "The U.S. Response to Possible North Korean Aggression." Washington, DC, December 15, 1993.

Hwang, In K. *The Neutralized Unification of Korea in Perspective.* Cambridge, MA: Schenkman Publishing Co., 1980.

———. *One Korea via Permanent Neutrality: Peaceful Management of Korean Unification.* Cambridge, MA: Schenkman Books, 1987.

———. *The United States and Neutral Reunited Korea: Search for a New Basis of American Strategy.* Lanham, MD: University Press of America, 1990.

Jane's Intelligence Review. "North Korea—A Potential Time Bomb." London, April 1994.

Jeong, Se-hyun. "Legal Status and Political Meaning of the Basic Agreement Between the South and the North." *Korea and World Affairs* 16:1 (Spring 1992): 5–21.

Kihl, Young Whan. "South Korea's Unification Policies in the 1980s: An Assessment." *Korea and World Affairs* 6:1 (Spring 1982): 73–95.

———. *Politics and Policies in a Divided Korea: Regimes in Contest.* Boulder, CO: Westview Press, 1984.

———, ed. *Korea and the World: Beyond the Cold War.* Boulder, CO: Westview Press, 1994.

Kim, Chonghan. "The United Nations and the Dilemma of Korean Reunification." *Journal of Asian Studies* 13:4 (December 1970): 419–431.

———. "Korean Reunification: U.N. Perspective." In Tae Hwan Kwak, Chonghan Kim, and Hong Nack Kim, eds., *Korean Reunification: New Perspective and Approaches.* Seoul: Kyunam University Press, 1987.

Kim, C. I. Eugene, and Ke-soo Kim. "The April Korean Student Movement." *Western Political Quarterly* 17:1 (March 1964): 83–92.

———. "Various Formulae for Korean Unification." *Korea and World Affairs* 6:1 (Spring 1982): 39–56.

Kim, Hakjoon. *Unification Policies of South and North Korea: A Comparative Study.* Seoul: Seoul National University Press, 1986.

Kim, Han-kyo. *Reunification of Korea: 50 Basic Documents.* Washington, DC: Institute for Asian Studies, 1972.

Kim Il-sung. *Kim Il Sung Sonjip* (Selected works of Kim Il-sung). 6 vols. Pyongang: Choson Rodong-clang Chulpansa (North Korean Communist Party's Publisher), 1960.

———. *On Juche in Our Revolution.* New York: Weekly Guardian Associates, 1977.

————. "Let Us Reunify the Country Independently and Peacefully." *Report to the Sixth Congress of the Worker's Party of Korea on the Work of the Central Committee.* Pyongyang: Foreign Language Publishing House, 1980.

Kim, Jong Il. *On the Juche Idea.* Pyongyang: Foreign Language Publishing House, 1982.

Kim, Joungwoon A. *Divided Korea: The Politics of Development, 1945–1972.* Cambridge: Harvard University Press, 1975.

Kim, Sam Kyu. "Peaceful Unification of Korea." *Japan Quarterly* 19:4 (October–December 1972): 415–422.

————. *Korea Hyoron* (Korea review): 1964–1989. Tokyo: Korea Hyoronsha, 1989.

Kim, Se-Jin, ed. *Korean Unification: Source Materials with Introduction.* Vol. 1. Seoul: Research Center for Peace and Unification, 1976.

Kim, Yong Jeung. *Voice of Korea, 1943–1961.* Washington, DC: Korean Affairs Institute, 1961.

Koh, Byung Chul. "Ideology and Political Control in North Korea." *Journal of Politics* 32:3 (August 1970): 655–674.

————. "The Pueblo Incident in Perspective." *Asian Survey* 9:4 (April 1969): 264–280.

————. "Seoul's New Unification Formula: An Assessment." *Korea and World Affairs* 13:4 (Winter 1989): 656–671.

————. "The Inter-Korean Agreement of 1972 and 1992: A Comparative Assessment." *Korea and World Affairs* 16:3 (Fall 1992): 463–482.

————. "The War's Impact on the Korean Peninsula." *Journal of American–East Asian Relations* (Spring 1993): 57–76.

Kwak, Tae-hwan. "Korean Reunification: Problems and Prospects." *Journal of East Asian Affairs* 6:2 (Summer–Fall 1992): 334–363.

Kwak, Tae-hwan, et al., eds. *Korean Unification.* Seoul: Kyungnam University Press, 1984.

Lee, Dong-Book. "South-North Dialogue in Korea." In Chong-shik Chung and Hakjoon Kim, eds., *Korean Unification Problems in the 1970's.* Seoul: Research Center for Peace and Unification, 1980.

Lee, Hongkoo. "Neutralization and Unification of Korea: Polemics or Semantics?" *Journal of Asiatic Studies* 8:4 (December 1970): 311–316.

————. "Unification through a Korean Commonwealth: Blueprint for a National Community." *Korean and World Affairs* 13:4 (Winter 1989): 635–646.

Lee, Manwoo. "The Two Koreas and the Unification Game." *Current History* 92: 578 (December 1993): 421–435.

Lee, Won-Myoung. *Zur Frage der nation Und der Wiedervereinigung im geteilten Korea: Ein Koreanischer Weg Oder die Anwendung der Deutschland-Formel als Modus Vivendi* (Dealing with the question of nationhood and reunification in a divided Korea: A Korean way or the incorporation of the German formula as a modus vivendi). Seoul: Research Center for Peace and Unification of Korea, 1989.

Lhee, Ho-jeh. "The Prospect of Neutralized Unification of Korea." In Sung Joo Han and Robert Meyers, eds., *Korea: The Year 2000.* Lanham, MD: University Press of America, 1987.

Lim, Dong Won. "Inter-Korean Relations Oriented toward Reconciliation and Co-operations: With the Emphasis on the Basic South-North Agreement." *Korea and World Affairs* 16:2 (Summer 1992): 213–223.

McCune, George M. *Korea's Postwar Political Problem*. New York: Institute of Pacific Relations, 1947.

———. *Korea Today*. Cambridge: Harvard University Press, 1950.

McCune, Shannon. *Korea's Heritage: A Regional and Social Geography*. Tokyo: Charles E. Tuttle Co., 1956.

McDonald, Donald S. "Security in Northeast Asia: Two Koreas or One?" *Washington Quarterly* 11 (Autumn 1989): 139–153.

Mack, Andrew. "North Korea and the Bomb." *Foreign Policy* 83 (Summer 1991): 87–104.

Mackerras, Colin. "The Juche Idea and the Thought of Kim Il Sung." In Colin Mackerras and Nick Night, eds., *Marxism in Asia*. New York: St. Martin's Press, 1985.

Matray, James Irving. *The Reluctant Crusade: American Foreign Policy in Korea, 1941–1950*. Honolulu: University of Hawaii Press, 1985.

Mazarr, Michael J. "North Korea's Nuclear Program: The World Responds, 1989–1999." *Korea and World Affairs* 16:2 (Summer 1992): 294–318.

Ministry of Foreign Affairs (ROK). *Tongil Munje Yongu* (The study of Korean unification). Vol. 1. Seoul, 1966.

———. *Foreign Policy for Peaceful Unification of the Republic of Korea: References*. Seoul, 1975.

Ministry of Public Information (ROK). *Thus Neutralized Unification Is Impossible for Korea*. Seoul: Ministry of Public Information, 1965.

Murphy, Edward R., Jr. *Second in Command*. New York: Holt, Rinehart, & Winston, 1971.

National Unification Board (ROK). *Korea's Unification Policy*. Seoul, October 1993.

Oh, Kongdan, and Ralph C. Hassig. "North Korea's Nuclear Program." In Young Whan Kihl, ed., *Korea and the World—Beyond the Cold War*. Boulder, CO: Westview Press, 1994.

Paik, Jin-hyun. "Nuclear Conundrum: Analysis and Assessment of Two Koreas' Policy Regarding the Nuclear Issue." *Korea and World Affairs* 17:4 (Winter 1993): 627–647.

Park, Chi Young. "Korea and the United Nations." In Youngok Koo and Sung-joo Han, eds., *The Foreign Policy of the Republic of Korea*. New York: Columbia University Press, 1985.

Park, Chung Hee. *The Country, the Revolution and I*. Seoul: Hollym Corporation, 1962.

Park, Chung Hue, *Our Nation's Path: Ideology of Social Reconstruction*. Seoul: Dong-A Publishing Co, 1962.

———. *Toward Peaceful Unification: Selected Speeches by President Park Chung Hee*. Seoul: Secretariat for President, 1976.

Park, Han-shik. "The Ideology in North Korean Communism." In Jae Kyn Park and Jung Gun Kim, eds., *The Politics of North Korea*. Seoul: Institute for Far Eastern Studies, Kyungnam University, 1979.

Park, Jae Kyu. "North Korea's Democratic Confederal Republic of Koryo: A Critique." In Tae Hwan Kwak, Chonghan Kim, and Hong Nack Kim, eds.,

Korean Reunification: New Perspectives and Approaches. Seoul: Kyungnam University Press, 1984.

Park, Sang-seek. "Northern Diplomacy and Inter-Korean Relations." *Korea and World Affairs* 12:4 (Winter 1988): 706–736.

Public Relations Association of Korea. *South-North Dialogue in Korea: A Special Issue Marking the First Anniversary of the July 4 South-North Communique no. 001.* Seoul, 1973.

Rhee, Joon Il. "Proposals Made by ROK since July 4, 1972." In Chong-shik Chong and Hakoon Kim, eds., *Korean Unification Problems in the 1970's.* Seoul: Research Center for Peace and Unification, 1979.

Rhee, Sang-woo, ed. *Korean Unification: Source Materials with an Introduction,* Vol. 3. Seoul: Research Center for Peace and Unification of Korea, 1986.

Roh, Tae Woo. *Korea: A Nation Transformed: Selected Speeches.* New York: Pergamon Press, 1990.

Schulman, Marshall. *Stalin's Foreign Policy Reappraised.* Cambridge: MA: Harvard University Press, 1963.

Simon, Sheldon W. "The Pueblo Incident and the South Korean 'Revolution' in North Korea's Foreign Policy: A Propaganda Analysis." *Asian Forum* 5:3 (July–September 1970): 202–203.

Song, Young-sun. "The Korean Nuclear Issue." *Korea and World Affairs* 15:3 (Fall 1991): 471–493.

Spector, Leonard, and Jacqueline Smith. "North Korea: The Next Nuclear Nightmare?" *Arms Control Today* 21:2 (March 1991): 8–13.

U.S. Department of State. *Moscow Meeting of Foreign Ministers.* (Publication 2448.) Washington, DC: GPO, 1946.

———. *The Korean Problem at the Geneva Conference April 26–June 15, 1954.* Washington, DC: GPO, 1954.

———. *The Record on Korean Unification, 1943–1960.* Washington, DC: GPO, 1960.

———. *Foreign Relations of the United States, 1945: The British Commonwealth and the Far East.* Vol. 14. Washington, DC: GPO, 1969.

Yang, Sung Chul. "Korean Unification: Autism and Realism." *Korea and World Affairs* 6:1 (Spring 1982): 57–72.

———. "Twins: Is One Korea Possible?" In Tae Hwan Kwak Chonghan Kim, and Hong Nack Kim, eds., *Korean Reunification: New Perspectives and Approaches.* Seoul: Kyungnam University Press, 1984.

Yim, Yong-soon. "Issues and Problems of Korean Unification." In Tae Hwan Kwak, Chonghan Kim, and Hong Nack Kim, eds., *Korean Reunification: New Perspectives and Approaches.* Seoul: Kyungnam University Press, 1984.

Yim, Yong-soon. *Politics of Korean Unification: A Comparative Study of Systemic Outputs.* Seoul: Research Center for Peace and Unification of Korea, 1988.

Yoo, Jong-youl. "Unification Policies of North Korea in the 1970's." In Chong-shik Chung and Hakjoon Kim, eds., *Korean Unification Problems in the 1970's.* Seoul: Research Center for Peace and Unification, 1980.

Young, Oran R. "Korean Unification: Alternative Theoretical Perspective." *Korean and World Affairs* 7:1 (Spring 1983): 57–69.

PART VI

The U.S. Home Front and the
Korean War

18 Introduction and General Culture during the Korean War

Lester H. Brune

When President Harry S. Truman decided to send forces to defend South Korea following the communist attack on June 25, the American public and Congress generally supported his action. But the euphoria of late June 1950 lasted only five months. In November, Chinese forces intervened, ending General Douglas MacArthur's proclamation of a "home-by-Christmas" offensive, and recapturing Seoul on January 4, 1951. Although Truman issued a Declaration of National Emergency and the UN forces prepared for a counterattack by late January, Truman's political opponents launched an attack on his national security policies. The Chinese attack and the dissent against Truman's policies perplexed many Americans and divided members of both major political parties. The nation's post–World War II anticipation of global cooperation had already become depressed by the cold war antagonism between the United States and the Soviet Union. Now the United Nations forces' failure to score a quick victory in Korea caused controversy regarding the limitations of national power, a difficulty for Americans who, as Denis Brogan (1952) observed, believed their nation was omnipotent.

The dismay expressed toward Truman's security policies added to the pre–Korean War opposition to Truman's domestic reform program. Basic to these arguments was concern about the communist challenge abroad and the proper methods for adjusting twentieth-century industrialization to the earlier agricultural-based U.S. traditions. Domestic differences about devising democratic solutions to the problems of labor and management in manufacturing establishments, of the divergence between metropolitan and rural needs, and of the aspirations of minority groups had reached crisis proportions before 1941 and were exacerbated by World War II.

The New Deal reforms of President Franklin D. Roosevelt had resolved the worst effects of the Great Depression of 1929 to 1933, but Roosevelt's attempt to expand these reforms encountered obstacles after 1938 because conservative Democrats and Republicans wanted to restrict or end reforms, a position they resumed following the end of World War II. In contrast, progressive liberals in each party contended that the only way to combat the extremes of communism and fascism was to create a broadbased, prosperous consumer population, a solution proposed by the British economist John Maynard Keynes but which conservative Americans believed was "socialistic."

The United States had in fact emerged from World War II as the most productive nation in the world, and Truman's policies for converting the nation's economy from wartime to peace had avoided an expected depression. The comparative prosperity of the 1940s produced a postwar babyboom but also encouraged advocates of women's and minority rights to expect a brighter future. African Americans who had served in the armed forces anticipated the recognition of their equal voting and economic rights. Women who were in the armed forces or undertook wartime manufacturing jobs sought to retain the advantages they had gained. In sum, a widening spectrum of economic, political, and social rights was accepted by liberal and progressive American leaders but rejected by conservatives and reactionaries, who benefited from the good old days of the past.

Political leaders who advocated going beyond Roosevelt's New Deal reforms were stymied by the Republican victory in the 1946 congressional elections, but Truman's surprising victory over opposing groups of Republicans, Dixiecrats, and Progressives in 1948 enabled the president to propose a list of Fair Deal reforms in January 1949. Truman's program included civil rights legislation, national medical insurance, federal aid to education, maximum agricultural subsidies, and other reforms to advance economic and social democracy. This liberal vision faced immediate opposition in Congress, solidifying the supporters of Senator Robert A. Taft's Republican conservatives and southern Democrats who would have made the Fair Deal difficult to obtain even if the Korean War had not diverted Truman's attention to East Asia.

This combination of internal and foreign policy conflicts between 1950 and 1953 has led historians to question the reality of the so-called age of consensus and conformity by the "silent generation" with which some observers first categorized the postwar era of the 1950s. Although Truman and Eisenhower consolidated and extended basic New Deal legislation and a prosperous middle class evolved in suburbia, these developments coexisted with growing antagonisms between those who wanted to obstruct or retract recent changes in domestic and foreign policy and those who moved steadily ahead to transform American society.

The chapters in this part on the home front describe the literature on

the U.S. domestic front during the Korean War. After citing historiographic data about the home front, there are separate chapters on general
studies about the culture, Congress and the elections of 1950 and 1952,
disloyalty charges and McCarthyism, public opinion, women and minorities, and cinema and television.

HISTORIOGRAPHIC DATA ON THE HOME FRONT

Because political, economic, social, and cultural developments occur
over a span of years, historical materials about the Korean War's effects
on society are part of a broader analysis of changes before and after 1950.
Consequently, historiography about the war era covers the presidential
years of both Truman and Eisenhower. As it happens, historical literature
about both presidents has gone through a transition from early orthodox
accounts to revisionism and synthesis regarding the value of their role in
history. Finally, during the 1980s, studies of the era became what William
O'Neill (1986) describes as a "functional rather than a moralistic or ideological interpretation," using terms of what was attained compared to
what was possible at that time.

Historiographical essays about Truman must begin with the four volumes edited by Richard Kirkendall (1967, 1974) and Francis Heller (1977,
1981). Kirkendall's 1967 volume describes the early literature about the
Truman presidency, and his 1974 volume reflects the early outpouring of
revisionist studies, which found fault with Truman's failures in domestic
legislation. As an advocate of the orthodox interpretation that praised
Truman's achievements, Alonzo Hamby's essay in the 1974 study divided
studies into his own "liberal" version and studies by "radical liberals"
who blamed the president for not moving strongly toward reaching his
Fair Deal objectives. This second group is represented in Kirkendall's 1974
essays by Harvard Sitkoff and Barton Bernstein, who give details about
revisionist studies on the domestic front.

Francis Heller's edited essays are more specialized. The 1975 volume
has John Wilz's detailed account of U.S. society during the war but also
includes Richard Leopold's article, "The Historian's Task," regarding research on the period. Heller's 1981 book contains essays about various
economic topics, as well as a historiographic essay by Darrel Cody regarding research on economic developments.

Four other historiographic articles deal with U.S. society during the
Korean era: Robert Griffith's articles in Michael Lacey's volume (1989)
and in the *Wisconsin Magazine of History* (1975); Geoffrey Smith's (1976)
excellent analysis of the literature; the essay by Robert J. Williams (1979);
and Charles Full's article in William Levantrosser's (1986) volume.

For an excellent list of the early literature about Eisenhower, Vincent
DeSantis (1976) excels. Gary W. Reichard (1978) examines the changing

views of scholars who study the Eisenhower era; while Mary McAuliffe (1981) and Anthony Joes (1987) describe revisionist literature. Recent essays on Eisenhower historiography are by Robert F. Burke (1988), and Stephen G. Rabe (1993).

In addition, bibliographic data on all aspects of the Truman and Eisenhower years are contained in the works by Richard D. Burns (1984) and R. Alton Lee (1991). These two volumes also include graduate school dissertations about topics pertaining to the life and times of each president.

GENERAL STUDIES ABOUT U.S. CULTURE, 1945–1960

Eric Goldman's (1956) study, *The Crucial Decade,* continues to be a valuable starting point for studying U.S. society during the postwar era. The atmosphere of this period is also recreated by contemporary articles, including Archibald MacLeish's in the *Atlantic Monthly* (1949), which expresses liberals' fear that the United States was adopting totalitarian methods to fight Soviet totalitarianism; Senator Robert A. Taft's (1948) article, which illustrates the conservatives' fear of New Deal reforms as "socialistic"; Denis Brogan's (1952) commentary on the U.S. public's belief in their nation's omnipotence, a claim Reinhold Neibuhr (1952) also warned against; and *Time* magazine's (1951) description of the "silent generation," an appellation that may have described only part of society, as David Halberstam's (1993) study concludes. The rise of the middle class after 1933, which C. Wright Mills (1951) describes, influenced the growth of popular culture, a phenomenon seen best in Bernard Rosenberg and David White's (1957) edition of essays on a vast array of popular culture topics that began to challenge the elitist canon of artistic endeavors more than previously. These popular artifacts are depicted in *Time-Life* (1969–1970) books in *The Fabulous Century* series covering 1940 to 1960 and in the essays on U.S. culture during this period edited by Dale Carter (1992), Larry May (1989), and Bernard Rosenberg and David White (1957).

John Brooks (1966) describes the years from 1939 to 1960 as transforming American society, not only in terms of international commitments but the growing prosperity of the nation, which altered traditional rural-urban-suburban patterns of life. Some of the perplexity of these changes is described by Les Adler and Thomas J. Paterson (1970), who indicated that popular concepts shifted from extreme anti-Nazism in 1945 to extreme anticommunism by 1950, in an article that elicited controversy in the *American Historical Review.* Barton J. Bernstein and Allen Matusow (1966) edited a collection of documents about the Truman administration, and Bernstein edited a volume of essays (1970), *Politics and Policies of the Truman Administration.* This latter volume laid the groundwork for revisionist accounts of Truman's domestic policies. One of the best general revisionist accounts of the home front is the study by Douglas Miller and Marion Novak (1977), who find the 1950s were not "happy days" but a decade of racism, sexism, poverty, and corporate exploitation. Paul Carter (1983) is less polemic in revising the 1950s, and his account should be read.

Balanced descriptions of the era are the most common among historians. These include William Chafe's essay in Michael Lacey (1989), which finds limited reform during the Truman and Eisenhower era with no "full commitment" from either president. In varying degrees of praise and blame, other works that focus on this era are Stephen Whitfield's article (1975) and book (1991) about the culture of the cold war; William Graebner's (1991) description of the doubts about the nation erected in the 1940s; Richard Pells' (1985) analysis of liberal perspectives during the 1950s; and John Diggins' *Proud Decades* (1988). A variety of viewpoints about all aspects of the culture of the cold war in the 1950s are expressed in the essays edited by Larry May (1989) and by Dale Carter (1992). William L. O'Neill (1986) writes an antirevisionist account of the period, attacking those who would not renounce Stalin's Russia, especially those who tried to explain the dilemma of left-wing liberals such as Lillian Hellman (1976).

Special attention is usually given to the influence of nuclear weapons on America's postwar society, especially after the Soviet Union successfully tested an atomic bomb in 1949. As early as December 1945, *Life* magazine's article, "30-hour War," reached a large audience and startled American's into considering the bomb's possible effect on their lives. JoAnne Brown (1988) explains how American school children were instructed about the bomb and civil defense measures. More broadly, both Paul Boyer (1985) and Alan Winkler (1984, 1993) examine the effect of nuclear weapons on U.S. culture after 1945. Lawrence Wittner (1993) explains the peace movement's attempt to control nuclear arms at this time, while H. W. Brands (1993) emphasizes how U.S. officials exaggerated Soviet power in order to create a "devil" for Americans to combat. Learning how to live with the bomb's threat was especially problematic during the Korean War. The use of the bomb was often discussed, especially after President Truman raised the question of its possible use following the Chinese intervention in the war during November 1950.

REFERENCES

Adler, Les, and Thomas G. Paterson. "Red Fascism: The Merger of Nazi Germany and Soviet Russia in the American Image of Totalitarianism, 1930s–1950s." *American Historical Review* 75 (April 1970): 1046–1064. Also see follow-up criticisms and commentary on this article in *American Historical Review* 75 (December 1970): 2155–2164, and 76 (April 1971): 575–580.

Bernstein, Barton J., ed. *Politics and Policies of the Truman Administration.* Chicago: Quadrangle, 1970.

Bernstein, Barton, and Allen J. Matusow, eds. *The Truman Administration: A Documentary History.* New York: Harper & Row, 1966.

Boyer, Paul. *By the Bomb's Early Light: American Thought and Culture at the Dawn of the Atomic Age.* New York: Pantheon, 1985.

Brands, H. W. *The Devil We Knew: Americans and the Cold War.* New York: Oxford University Press, 1993.

Brogan, Denis W. "Illusions of American Omnipotence." *Harper's* 205 (December 1952): 21–28.

Brooks, John. *The Great Leap: The Past Twenty-five Years in America.* New York: Harper & Row, 1966.

Brown, JoAnne. " 'A Is for Atom, B Is for Bomb': Civil Defense in American Public Education 1948–1963." *Journal of American History* 75 (June 1988): 68–90.

Burke, Robert F. "Eisenhower Revisionism Revisited: Reflections on Eisenhower Scholarship." *Historian* 59 (1988): 196–209.

Burns, Richard Dean, ed., *Harry S. Truman: A Bibliography of His Times and Presidency.* Wilmington, DE: Scholarly Resources, 1984.

Carter, Dale, ed. *Cracking the Ike Age: Aspects of Fifties America.* Aarhus, Denmark: Aarhus University Press, 1992.

Carter, Paul A. *Another Part of the Fifties.* New York: Columbia University Press, 1983.

DeSantis, Vincent P. "Eisenhower Revisionism." *Review of Politics* 38 (1976): 190–207.

Diggins, John R. *The Proud Decades: America in War and in Peace, 1941–1960.* New York: Norton, 1988.

Goldman, Eric. *The Crucial Decade, 1945–1955.* New York: Knopf, 1956.

Graebner, William. *The Age of Doubt: American Thought and Culture in the 1940s.* Boston: Twayne, 1991.

Griffith, Robert. "Truman and the Historians: The Reconstruction of Postwar American History." *Wisconsin Magazine of History* 59 (1975): 20–50.

Halberstam, David. *The Fifties.* New York: Villard Books, 1993.

Heller, Francis, ed. *The Korean War: A 25-Year Perspective.* Lawrence: Regents Press of Kansas, 1977.

———, ed. *Economics of the Truman Administration.* Lawrence: Regents Press of Kansas, 1981.

Hellman, Lillian. *Scoundrel Time.* Boston: Little, Brown, 1976.

Joes, Anthony James. "Eisenhower Revisionism and the American Politics." In Joann P. Kreig, ed., *Dwight D. Eisenhower,* pp. 283–296. Westport, CT: Greenwood Press, 1987.

Kirkendall, Richard, ed. *The Truman Period as a Research Field.* Columbia, MO: University of Missouri Press, 1967.

———, ed. *The Truman Period as a Research Field: A Reappraisal, 1972.* Columbia, MO: University of Missouri Press, 1974.

Lacey, Michael, ed. *The Truman Presidency.* New York: Cambridge University Press, 1989.

Lee, R. Alton, ed. *Dwight D. Eisenhower: A Bibliography of His Life and Times.* Wilmington, DE: Scholarly Resources, 1991.

Levantrosser, William F., ed. *Harry S. Truman: The Man from Independence*. Westport, CT: Greenwood Press, 1986.

Life Editors. "The 36-Hour War: Arnold Hints at the Catastrophe of the Next Great Conflict." *Life*, November 19, 1945, pp. 27–35.

McAuliffe, Mary. "Eisenhower the President." *Journal of American History* 68 (1981): 625–632.

MacLeish, Archibald. "The Conquest of America." *Atlantic Monthly* 184 (August 1949): 17–22.

May, Larry, ed. *Recasting America: Culture and Politics in the Age of Cold War*. Chicago: University of Chicago Press, 1989.

Miller, Douglas, and Marion Novak. *The Fifties: The Way We Really Were*. Garden City, NY: Doubleday, 1977.

Mills, C. Wright. *White Collar: The American Middle Classes*. New York: Oxford University Press, 1951.

Niebuhr, Reinhold. *The Irony of American History*. New York: Scribner, 1952.

O'Neill, William L. *American High: The Years of Confidence, 1945–1960*. New York: Free Press, 1986.

Pells, Richard H. *The Liberal Mind in a Conservative Age: American Intellectuals in the 1940s and 1950s*. New York: Harper & Row, 1985.

Rabe, Stephen G. "Eisenhower, Revisionism: A Decade of Scholarship." *Diplomatic History* 17:1 (Winter 1993): 97–116.

Reichard, Gary W. "Eisenhower as President: The Changing View." *South Atlantic Quarterly* 77 (1978): 265–281.

Rosenberg, Bernard, and David White, eds. *Mass Culture: The Popular Arts in America*. Glencoe, IL: Free Press, 1957.

Smith, Geoffrey S. " 'Harry, We Hardly Know You': Revisionism, Politics and Diplomacy, 1945–1954: A Review Essay." *American Political Science Review* 70 (1976): 560–582.

Taft, Robert A. "The Case against President Truman." *Saturday Evening Post*, September 25, 1948, pp. 18–19.

Time Editors. "The Younger Generation." *Time*, November 5, 1951, pp. 46ff.

Time-Life Editors. *The Fabulous Century*. Vols. 5 and 6: *1940–1950, 1950–1960*. New York: Time-Life Books, 1969, 1970.

Whitfield, Stephen. "The 1950s: The Era of No Hard Feelings." *South Atlantic Quarterly* 74 (Summer, 1975): 289–307.

———. *The Culture of the Cold War*. Baltimore: Johns Hopkins University Press, 1991.

Williams, Robert J. "Harry S. Truman and the American Presidency." *Journal of American Studies* 13 (1979): 393–408.

Winkler, Allan M. "A Forty-year History of Civil Defense." *Bulletin of the Atomic Scientists* 40 (June–July 1984): 16–23.

———. *Life under a Cloud: American Anxiety about the Atom*. New York: Oxford University Press, 1993.

Wittner, Lawrence. *The Struggle against the Bomb: A History of the Nuclear Disarmament Movement through 1953*. Stanford, CA: Stanford University Press, 1993.

19 Congress during the Korean War

Lester H. Brune and Mark Leach

Historical studies usually focus on the White House rather than Capitol Hill despite the fact that the U.S. Constitution gave Congress a central role in the nation's government. The president's role is readily described because the executive makes daily decisions and appears to speak for the nation. In contrast, the multimember Congress has to argue, debate, and compromise before enacting legislation. Nevertheless, the final action or inaction of Congress may restrict, qualify, or prevent the president from acting on particular matters. Congress may be the ultimate determinant of what the nation does. Thus, even when the president became leader of the world's greatest power in 1945, the chief executive was influenced in varying degrees by Congress, making historical accounts that ignore Congress incomplete.

The Korean War occurred during a particularly crucial era for questions about the division of political powers between the president and Congress. Since 1938, a bloc of conservative Democratic and Republican party members had limited President Franklin D. Roosevelt's domestic program, and after 1945 they wanted to restrict President Truman's powers. After the Republicans gained control of Congress in the off-year elections of 1946, Truman had to fend off conservative attempts to reverse Roosevelt's New Deal measures while obtaining bipartisan support from some Republicans to gain congressional approval for his international programs for Europe between 1946 and 1948. Yet, Truman's unexpected victory in 1948 made the conservative bloc led by Republican Senator Robert A. Taft and southern Democratic Senator Richard Russell more determined to limit the president's power in foreign affairs and to prevent liberal reforms from being enacted to advance concepts of social and economic democracy.

An Everett Dirksen Congressional Center and Caterpillar Foundation grant assisted in the preparation of this chapter.

Political developments on the eve of the war's outbreak favored the conservatives' attempts to obstruct Truman's Fair Deal program and re-direct his Cold War containment policies. President Truman announced his Fair Deal agenda to Congress in January 1949, but by early 1950, do-mestic and foreign events had adversely influenced Truman's relations with Congress.

First, in March 1949, Vice-President Alben Barkley and other "friends" of Truman in Congress tried but failed to change the Senate rules on cloture, which permitted one-third of the Senate to thwart the preferences of a majority by filibustering. Consequently, under existing rules, the Taft-Russell minority could continue using the filibuster unless Truman weak-ened his legislative proposals sufficiently to satisfy the conservatives.

Second, during the summer of 1949, Republican Senator Arthur Van-denberg, the leader of the bipartisan foreign policy bloc in Congress, dismayed Secretary of State Dean Acheson by joining the Taft-Russell group in passing foreign aid legislation that significantly restricted the Truman administration's plans. As a result, the Senate revised Truman's foreign aid request by cutting the appropriation by nearly one-third and by eliminating the president's discretionary power in allocating funds to U.S. allies. Rather than allow the president to decide the amount various allied nations received, Congress specifically listed what funds each nation or region would receive. As Acheson indicates in *Present at the Creation* (1969), the approved legislation severely limited negotiations with allied powers and decreased foreign aid just when the nation's relations with NATO and other allies became critical to Truman's containment policy.

These two forebodings regarding congressional relations with the White House were as crucial as two highly publicized international events in September and October 1949 for which conservatives in Congress blamed the Truman administration, regardless of how irrational the accusations were. On September 23, 1949, the Truman administration announced that the Soviet Union had successfully tested an atomic bomb. Although, as Gregg Herken (1981) indicates, scientists had warned since 1945 that there were no real atomic secrets and the Soviet Union would soon have an atomic bomb, members of the Truman administration and the Amer-ican public generally assumed that the bomb's technology was evidence of U.S. superiority and that the communists could not develop a bomb for ten or twenty years. Subsequently, after the Soviets' successful test, Truman's opponents searched for, and claimed to find, spies and disloyal Americans in the Democratic administration who had helped Russia ac-quire atomic power. Between 1948 and 1952, the three most celebrated cases of spies were those of Alger Hiss, who was convicted on January 21, 1950, of perjury for denying to a congressional committee that he had been a Communist party member; Julius and Ethel Rosenberg, who were convicted of espionage in 1950 and executed in 1952; and Klaus Fuchs, a

British physicist arrested for espionage in February 1950. As Herken indicates, although scientists' warnings were reprinted in *Bulletin of Atomic Scientists* (1949), members of Congress continued to emphasize the role of spies, as seen in the House of Representatives Committee on Military Affairs published reports of the special Joint Committee on Atomic Energy between 1945 and 1952, including the report *Soviet Atomic Energy* (1951).

The second event in the fall of 1949 that startled many Americans took place less than a month after the news of Russia's atomic bomb when communists proclaimed the formation of the People's Republic of China (PRC) on October 10, 1949. This news should not have been a surprise because Jiang Jieshi's (Chiang Kai-shek's) nationalist forces had suffered grievous defeats over a three-year span before fleeing to the offshore island of Formosa in 1949. Nevertheless, Truman's congressional critics had long assailed his China policy and blamed the Democrats for the "loss of China" while ignoring the corrupt regime of Jiang, which had fought an ineffective civil war. Due largely to American missionary efforts in China, the U.S. public had developed a strong sympathy for the Chinese people. Although the U.S. State Department (1949) published a detailed *White Paper* on China to explain Jiang's responsibility, this lengthy volume could not compete in the public domain with the China Lobby and the pro-Jiang *Time-Life* publications of Henry Luce, whose influence is described in Robert Herzstein's (1994) study.

Russia's acquisition of atomic weapons and the Chinese communist victory set the stage for the era of extreme anticommunism in America, which began in February 1950 just before North Korea's invasion of South Korea. Although Senator Joseph McCarthy's unverified attacks on Democratic disloyalty were not fully embraced by Taft and Russell, McCarthyism stimulated widespread public opinion against Truman to support congressional critics who attacked the president's domestic program and ended bipartisan backing for Truman's foreign policy, which the illness and death of Senator Vandenberg in 1950–1951 had weakened in Congress.

Consequently, after the Korean War began, Truman could not rely on the Democratic majority or on a bipartisan bloc in Congress to back his domestic or foreign policies. Although Congress usually supported the president's budget requests to support U.S. forces in Korea, Truman's Korean War decisions and the Fair Deal program were under constant attack. In order to get southern Democrat votes for his foreign policies, Truman had to sacrifice his socioeconomic legislation.

Because the national security aspects of the Korean War and the 1953 truce are discussed in other chapters of this book, this chapter deals with the domestic political context of congressional activity, including foreign policy. The political context includes relations between Congress and the president, congressional actions on domestic and economic issues, research and literature on important congressional leaders, and the elections of 1950 and 1952.

Congressional Foreign Policy Activity

Although Congress generally applauded President Truman's decision to save South Korea in June 1950, the few who dissented were immediately joined by others who opposed the president's conduct of the war or other aspects of his foreign policy. Especially after Chinese forces intervened in November 1950, Congress became a focal point for expressing antagonism to Democratic policy since World War II, claiming that the president assumed too much power without the consent of Congress and that Truman was "weak" toward communism. In January 1951, a "great debate" on Truman's foreign policy focused on sending more troops to augment NATO forces. Then in April, after Truman recalled General MacArthur from duty as UN commander, many members of Congress lauded MacArthur's desire for total victory, leading to further attacks on Truman's policies.

Most literature agrees with Robert Donovan (1982), whose biography blames Truman for not requesting a congressional declaration of war against North Korea in late June 1950 when few members of Congress or the public disagreed with the decision to help South Korea. According to accounts by Glenn Paige (1968), Senator Tom Connally (1954), Dean Acheson (1969), and George M. Elsey's papers at the Truman Library, the widespread support expressed during Truman's meeting with members of Congress on June 27, plus an ensuing ten-day congressional recess for the Fourth of July, persuaded Truman to base his action on the United Nations Treaty. As Edwin C. Hoyt (1961) indicates, on June 27 Truman also ordered the U.S. Navy to protect Formosa from Chinese communist forces, an action that had no basis in the UN Treaty but that Truman's critics accepted without question.

Nevertheless, some members of Congress soon complained about "Truman's war," especially connecting the complaint to Truman's calling the war a "police action." Actually, as the sources cited above show, a journalist first used the term "police action" during a presidential press conference, but Truman's critics used it to ridicule the president, especially after the conflict lengthened into years and U.S. casualties multiplied. Just as the 1949 foreign aid dispute caused Senator Vandenberg to criticize the president for acquiring too much authority, Truman's failure to obtain a declaration of war encouraged fears of an "imperial president" who bypassed Congress in conducting policy. Both James Sundquist (1981) and Louis Fisher (1985) believe that Truman's clash with Congress began the presidential conflict with Congress leading to the War Powers Act of 1973.

Although there was no declaration of war, Congress approved Truman's requests to support the military effort. During the summer of 1950, Congress extended the Selective Service Act for another year and approved deficiency appropriation acts to assist South Korea and augment the defense budget. Congress also enacted the Defense Production Act, which gave the president power to ensure priority for the production of military equipment, to requisition scarce commodities required for the war, and to combat inflation.

In addition to obtaining no war declaration, Truman made two other controversial decisions in 1950: extending the war into North Korea and agreeing with NATO to augment U.S. forces stationed in Europe. Although Truman's decision to invade North Korea by having UN forces cross the 38th parallel was made over several weeks in August and September, the Truman administration apparently did not consult any bipartisan allies in Congress, perhaps because Senator Vandenberg was gravely ill and later died in 1951. Rosemary Foot (1985) and Walter LaFeber (1974) indicate that Truman hoped to counteract congressional conservatives by creating a "democratic" Korea, and James Matray (1979) emphasizes Truman's goal of permitting elections in North Korea without interference from South Korea. Yet without bipartisan discussion and despite indications that China would intervene if UN forces advanced toward the Yalu River, Truman authorized MacArthur to attack North Korea. Significantly, Truman did not fully discuss this with members of the United Nations. As Jong-yil Ra (1984) explains, the British knew about Truman's decision and took the initiative of obtaining the UN General Assembly's approval in a resolution of October 7, 1950, a week after South Korean forces crossed the 38th parallel. Unfortunately, Truman, General MacArthur, and their advisers underestimated China's desire to prevent enemy forces from reaching its border. As UN armies approached the Yalu, the Chinese attacked—first in a small raid late in October, later in large numbers on November 26. MacArthur's armies suffered a disastrous rout, and the communists regained Seoul on January 4, 1951.

The crisis caused by China's massive intervention corresponded with the convening of a NATO meeting in Brussels during which the Truman administration agreed to dispatch more U.S. troops to Europe. Since August, the United States had urged NATO members to speed up the formation of an integrated defense force and had nominated Dwight D. Eisenhower for supreme commander of NATO forces. As explained in works by Walter LaFeber (1989) and Lawrence Kaplan (1984), the U.S. requests to NATO were finalized on December 19, 1950, when Truman's opponents began to attack the decision. Just three days earlier, President Truman's issuance of a declaration of national emergency also alarmed conservative groups because it enlarged the president's wartime authority by simplifying Truman's right to expand the U.S. armed forces and to order wartime economic controls, such as wage-price restrictions.

Even before the Eighty-second Congress convened in January 1951, conservative critics launched an attack on Truman's recent actions. Former president Herbert Hoover and former ambassador to Great Britain Joseph P. Kennedy announced their opposition to the NATO agreement and the president's assumption of wartime authority without a declaration of war. These antecedents to the "Great Debate of 1951" in Congress are examined in essays by Ted Galen Carpenter (1986) and Donald Mrozek (1976).

When Congress met in January, Senators Taft and Kenneth Wherry led six months of extensive debates, congressional hearings, and proposed resolutions based on criticism of Truman's national security policies. These congressional efforts tried to restrict presidential decisions, keep U.S. forces from being "permanently" stationed in Europe, and support General MacArthur's call for a "total victory" to liberate North Korea and other peoples "enslaved by the communists." These conservative forces were vociferous and persuasive to many Americans, but they did not have a majority in Congress. Republicans such as John Foster Dulles, Thomas Dewey, and Senator Henry Cabot Lodge, Jr., as well as most of Richard Russell's southern Democrats, supported Truman's basic decisions on NATO, framing a compromise congressional resolution that did not effectively limit the president's NATO authority. This combination of moderate Republicans and Democrats also rejected MacArthur's concept of "total victory" and accepted the idea of a limited UN war in Korea to restore the 38th parallel without threatening China's borders. David Kepley's (1982) article provides details about the 1951 congressional debate.

In addition to the NATO dispute, congressional conservatives obstructed the U.S. ratification of two UN agreements, one that condemned genocide and a second that promoted human rights. These dissenters also tried to alter U.S. foreign policy by restricting future "secret" presidential agreements through a constitutional amendment to protect U.S. sovereignty. The failure of Congress to act on the UN's human rights and genocide conventions did not gain the public attention given to Senator John Bricker's proposal of the Bricker Amendment to restrict presidential power in foreign relations. Because of apparent Senate opposition to the human rights and genocide conventions, Truman did not push their ratification. Bricker, however, persistently introduced his amendment in Congress between 1951 and 1953. Finally, the Eisenhower administration gained bipartisan backing for an amendment that weakened Bricker's proposal by adopting language that nullified restrictions on the president's foreign policy action. Information about these congressional activities is found in Gary Reichard's (1975) and Duane Tananbaum's (1985, 1988) works on the Bricker Amendment; in Natalie Kaufman's (1990) study about Senate opposition to human rights treaties; and in Lawrence Le-Blanc's (1991) volume on the genocide convention, which was finally ratified in 1987.

More serious in 1951 were congressional attacks on the Truman administration for being weak and vacillating in foreign policy while appeasing the communists. As Athan Theoharis (1970) describes in *The Yalta Myths*, these attacks on Democratic foreign policy increased in 1949, focusing on Roosevelt's and Truman's agreements with Stalin at the Tehran, Yalta, and Potsdam conferences between 1943 and 1945, while usually ignoring that Great Britain's prime minister, Winston Churchill, also agreed with these measures. Claiming these agreements allowed the Soviet Union to enslave people in Eastern Europe (especially Poland) and China, Truman's critics offered congressional resolutions that would repudiate or invalidate the Roosevelt-Truman agreements because they were not approved by Congress or the people. Although Congressman Robert Hale introduced the first such resolution in the House of Representatives on March 28, 1950, between January and August 1951, one Senate and four House resolutions tried in some fashion to condemn the wartime agreements and to instruct the Truman administration to adopt policies that would triumph over the communists by liberating the captive nations. In 1952, the Republican National Convention's platform adopted a statement condemning the Yalta agreements and urging "victory" over communism. Moderate Republicans such as Lodge and Dulles rejected these extremist views about Yalta, and in February 1953, Eisenhower backed a much weakened resolution (House Joint Resolution 200), which essentially abrogated the 1952 Republican platform statement by emphasizing that the Soviet Union's violations of the conference agreements caused the cold war problems.

The Yalta dispute also included critics who condemned Truman's containment policies and the UN's limited-war objectives in Korea following the Chinese intervention of November 1950. Conservatives who were strong anticommunists wanted the United States to liberate nations under Soviet control, a concept that depicted General MacArthur as a "hero" because he publicly expressed the desire to defeat communist China. After Truman removed him as the UN commander in April 1951, MacArthur returned to America, where he addressed a joint session of Congress. Soon after, Congress held extensive hearings on U.S. policy in East Asia (see Chapter 16 in this book). John Spanier's (1959) study of the Truman-MacArthur controversy gives special attention to the role of Congress in this dispute.

In addition to congressional criticism of Truman's policies, other congressional activity in foreign affairs between 1950 and 1953 involved the Senate's approval of the Japanese peace treaty and alliance, the move to accept Spain's fascist regime, and an attempt to gain a peace agreement with Russia. The most important of these actions were the Japanese agreements, which the U.S. Senate approved in March 1952. As part of his bipartisan policy in 1950, Truman appointed John Foster Dulles as the chief negotiator of the treaties with Japan, which were finalized in 1951. In Congress, opponents of the Yalta agreements disliked the peace treaty because they did not want to confirm the Soviet Union's occupation of South Sakhalin and the Kuril Islands in 1945. To calm the conservative opposition, the Senate Foreign Relations Committee recommended a reservation that specified that the peace treaty did not confirm the Yalta agreement on the Japanese islands. In this form, the Senate approved the treaty by a vote of 66–10. (Literature regarding these treaties is described in Chapter 8 in this book.)

Unlike the Japanese treaty, which Truman initiated, the proposal to give U.S. aid to Spain originated with Senator Patrick McCarran, a Democrat from Nevada who had also irritated Truman by pushing the Internal Security Act of 1950. In 1946, Spain had been rejected for membership in the United Nations, and the Truman administration usually ignored Spain's fascist government. After 1947, however, both the State and Defense departments considered Spain's future status as a European military base, a situation made more critical by the decision to strengthen NATO after the outbreak of war in Korean.

Although as Louis W. Koenig (1962) indicates, the U.S. Joint Chiefs of Staff may have urged him on, McCarran initiated action for economic aid to Spain in August 1950 by attaching a rider to an appropriations bill. When finalized by Congress, this bill earmarked $62.5 million as a loan to Spain under the Export-Import Bank. President Truman disliked General Ferdinand Franco, Spain's leader, but in November 1950, he authorized the loan and sent U.S. military officers to begin the discussions that led to the building of U.S. air and naval bases in Spain. Data about these activities may be found in Theodore Lowi (1963). Arthur Whitaker (1961) gives most attention to the long-term base negotiations. The role of the United States and Spain in these actions has not been fully analyzed by historians, but some data on the Spanish perspective are in three works by James Cortada (1977, 1978, 1980).

Even more overlooked by historians than the Spanish agreements are the attempts of Senator Brien McMahon, Democrat from Connecticut, to persuade the Truman administration to search for peace, disarmament, and an early end to the Korean War. Alonzo Hamby (1973) has a brief summary of McMahon's activity, but no one has researched these efforts, perhaps because they were quixotic. McMahon did get a congressional resolution passed, which Truman dutifully transmitted to the Soviet Union's president, N. M. Shvernik. Although Shvernik published the message in his country and called for a four-power conference to include the PRC, Truman dismissed Shvernik's reply as "no change" in Soviet policy.

Notable for scholars, Hamby's account relied on contemporary articles, such as Harold Ickes (1951) in the *New Republic*.

In summary, as David Keply (1988) indicates, Truman's relations with Congress over foreign relations lost almost all semblance of bipartisanship after June 1950. Congress approved measures to support the war, and moderate Republicans helped Truman keep U.S. relations with NATO intact and gain approval for the Japanese treaty in March 1952. Otherwise congressional dissent against President Truman's policies became a central issue during 1951 and in the 1952 presidential campaign, including the Republicans' nomination process discussed later in this chapter.

Congressional Relations with the President

When Harry Truman became president in April 1945, the Congress he dealt with in domestic affairs had given Franklin Roosevelt headaches since 1938. As Alonzo Hamby indicates in Michael Lacey's volume (1989), the makeup of Congress was to the right of center and had a minority of members who were determined to use the filibuster, the power of the House Rules Committee, and seniority rights to block certain political, economic, and social reforms that they opposed.

James Patterson (1967) explains that a congressional coalition of southern Democrats and conservative Republicans had stymied Roosevelt's attempts to further New Deal reforms, a situation that Truman could not change during the next seven years. The Republicans gained control of Congress in the 1946 elections and, led by Robert Taft and southern Democrat Richard Russell, opposed Truman's liberal reform proposals even after the Democrats' 1948 victory. The bipartisan cooperation with moderate Republicans and southern Democrats in international programs from 1947 to 1949 did not carry over to domestic affairs, and the outbreak of the Korean War in June 1950 halted any possibility that Truman's 1949 Fair Deal proposals would get through Congress.

The acquisition of global leadership by the United States between 1941 and 1950 raised questions about the president's authority to be the principal director of the nation's foreign and domestic policies. During World War II, President Roosevelt attained vast power over both military and industrial resources in making America the arsenal of democracy to defeat Germany, Italy, and Japan. After the war ended in 1945, some Republicans and some Democrats expressed concern because Roosevelt's wartime authority extended the centralization of the federal government's role, which earlier New Deal legislation had provided in domestic affairs. Following Truman's victory in 1948, when Democrats regained control of Congress, the liberals hoped to advance the Fair Deal program of reforms, which the president proclaimed in his 1949 inaugural address. However, these hopes were dashed because the Taft-Russell alliance prevented the liberals from altering the Senate's cloture rules to end a filibuster. Later, after the Korean War broke out in 1950, these opponents of Truman's policies forced the president either to compromise his legislation or to forget legislation that could not be passed.

In evaluating President Truman's relations with Congress, Alonzo Hamby, in Richard Kirkendall's (1974) volume, indicates that studies favorable to Truman's domestic achievements tend to accept Richard Neustadt's (1960) description of the complex interaction between Congress and the chief executive that leaders must adapt to particular situations. To the contrary, literature critical of Truman follows James MacGregor Burns' (1963, 1965) analysis, which asserts that great presidential leadership means the president obtains party loyalty and maneuvers to obtain the desired legislation. Eventually Neustadt's 1954 essay became the basis for traditional interpretations that concluded that Truman not only transformed the nation's international policies but also obtained a consolidation of New Deal measures to make them permanent and advanced the liberal vision for future Democratic leaders. In contrast, revisionists such as Harvard Sitkoff in the Kirkendall (1974) volume used Burns' analysis to criticize Truman for not using every available executive power to enact the Fair Deal.

From another perspective of Congress-president relations, Burns' *The Deadlock of Democracy* (1963) describes the problems Truman had in dealing with Congress from 1949 to 1953 because there were moderates and conservatives in both major parties, a realistic four-party Congress. David Mayhew's *Divided We Govern* (1991) and *Party Loyalty* (1966) emphasize that Truman could not deal with Congress in terms of the two-party structure that Americans often praise. Truman faced not only Republican opponents but many Democrats in Congress who disagreed with the Fair Deal program. As the 1948 Dixiecrats' revolt against Truman demonstrated, the southern Democrats of the once-solid Democratic South became Truman's most significant problem. Southern Democrats held key leadership positions in Congress because of seniority policies, but Truman wanted party unity and refused to punish the defections of disloyal southern Democrats. Details of the southern Democratic situation are described in a variety of literature, including works by Nunan V. Bartley (1970), Jack Bass and Walter DeVries (1976), Robert Garson (1974), V. O. Key (1949), Herbert Parmet (1976), and Robert Sherrill (1968). Ira Katznelson and coworkers (1993) indicate that the southern opposition was not simply racist but also reflected southern rural opposition to labor and urban issues before Congress.

While Senator Russell led southern forces, Senator Taft's conservative bloc reflected Frederick Hayek's (1944) claim that the New Deal inaugurated "creeping socialism." Taft's 1948 article in the *Saturday Evening Post* stated his group's deep ideological opposition to Truman's program.

Taft and other conservative Republicans' role in Congress are described in the studies by David Reinhard (1983), George Mayer (1964), and Robert Caridi (1968).

To counteract the Taft-Russell conservative coalition in Congress, a center group was formed by moderate Democrats and Republicans who favored the internationalist program of Roosevelt and Truman as well as the basic middle-class welfare reforms of the New Deal. Described by Arthur Schlesinger, Jr., as the "vital center" (1949), this "liberal" bloc is described in books and articles by Alonzo Hamby (1970, 1972, 1973). Anticommunist and pro–New Deal liberals also formed the Americans for Democratic Action (ADA), which generally supported Truman's policies from 1948 to 1953. The ADA's activity is described by Steven M. Gillon (1987) and Clifton Brock (1962). A noteworthy study on the liberals is Gerald Marwell's (1967) article, which concludes that the Korean War influenced the decline of the northern liberal bloc in Congress that favored passage of New Deal–Fair Deal programs. For the perspective of moderate Republicans' promoting Dwight Eisenhower's nomination in 1952, see Arthur Larson's *A Republican Looks at His Party* (1956).

An often overlooked area of presidential-congressional relations are Congress' investigations of the executive branch's activities. Between 1949 and 1952, Congress not only investigated the charges of spies and disloyalty in the executive offices but also allegations of bribes, favoritism, and other corruptions of office-holders. (The role of the House Un-American Activities Committee and Senator Joseph McCarthy's is covered in Chapter 20.) Other investigations were made by committees under the chairmanship of Democratic senators Estes Kefauver (Tennessee), Clyde R. Hoey (North Carolina), and J. William Fulbright (Arkansas).

Kefauver's Special Committee to Investigate Organized Crime tried to prove that there was an organized crime syndicate in America. This committee's hearings were held from May 10, 1950, to May 1, 1951, in a variety of large cities. Although its findings were inconclusive, the hearings disclosed close connections between criminals and some big-city Democratic political machines, the most prominent being that between New York's mayor William O'Dwyer and the mobster Frank Costello. Although the evidence was not sufficient to take criminal proceedings against the mayor, the hearings hurt Truman because they recalled his early career connections with Kansas City's Pendergast machine.

Materials on Senator Kefauver are listed under individual congressmen below. In addition, Kefauver published an account of the hearings, *Crime in America* (1951), which Gordon Hawkins (1969) examined critically. William H. Moore (1974) gives a detailed account of the Kefauver Committee's work and also has an article (1982) that examines charges that Kefauver was blackmailed by a Chicago labor lawyer.

Kefauver's hearings embarrassed Truman's Democratic party, but investigations led by other Democratic congressmen directed attention to Truman's friends and political appointees. During 1949, the Senate Committee on Expenditures in the Executive Department chaired by Senator Hoey looked into charges against Truman's military aide, Harry Vaughan, and other administration officials for granting favors to friends seeking government contracts. Hardly had Hoey's committee finished before Senator J. William Fulbright's Subcommittee on the Reconstruction Finance Corporation (RFC) held hearings from February 8 until April 13, 1950, about other political appointees who allegedly took bribes or granted favors. In 1951 and early 1952, Hoey's committee searched further into the RFC scandals at the same time that Democratic congressman from California Cecil King's Subcommittee on Internal Revenue Service investigated charges against the IRS and the Tax Division of the Justice Department.

Although these hearings resulted in many indictments, only one perjury conviction resulted. Nevertheless, Truman's handling of the cases under investigation made matters worse. Because the president loyally backed his appointees, he appeared to condone unethical or questionable conduct. Furthermore, his efforts to reorganize agencies brought more problems, most notably to the Justice Department, where his appointment of J. Howard McGrath as attorney general led to another conflict that caused Truman to fire McGrath. Each case of these alleged scandals had complex aspects, and they were difficult for the public to follow. The general impression, however, became one of widespread corruption, which carried into the presidential campaign of 1952.

Robert Donovan's (1982) biography of Truman has a general account of these scandals. More details are given in work by Jules Abels (1956), who bases his study on the various committee hearings, summarized in issues of the *Congressional Quarterly Almanac* for 1949 through 1953. For historical perpective, Michael Fullington (1979) examines why scandals have plagued Truman and other recent presidencies.

Several special studies about Congress and the president are worth considering. Charles O. Jones (1994) describes the president's difficulties in operating within the limitations of the congressional system. An article and a book by Jon Bond and Richard Fleisher (1984, 1990) conclude that the ideological makeup of Congress, not presidential popularity, is the principal factor in the success of the president's relations with Congress. J. Richard Piper (1991) examines how conservatives shifted from criticisms of a strong president under Truman to general acceptance of a powerful executive after 1970. Michael L. Mezey (1989) emphasizes the weakness inherent in the shared power of the executive and legislature, while Robert J. Spitzer (1993) argues that the executive-centered government is stronger because the president must be wary of congressional prerogatives, a position similar to that of Mark Peterson (1990).

Finally, in 1966, Alan Wildavsky proposed the concept of "two presidencies," indicating that a study of roll-call votes showed more congressional support on a president's foreign policy (about 70 percent) than on domestic policy (about 40 percent). Lee Sigelman (1979) was more critical of Wildavsky because his data included many insignificant roll-call votes, whereas voting on critical issues of foreign policy showed a lower percentage of congressional support. An article by Bond and Fleisher (1988) contends that the "two presidents" concept applies only to Republican presidents.

Congress' Rejection of the Fair Deal

Although there is no dispute that the major parts of Truman's Fair Deal program failed to be enacted, historians have diverged into traditional and revisionist explanations regarding Truman's domestic agenda. Traditional interpretations emphasize that Truman obtained the best domestic legislation possible at that time because his congressional opponents and the people they represented wanted to preserve but not extend the New Deal reforms that benefited the middle class. In contrast, revisionists, who may be classified as either radical liberals or Marxian, contend that Truman could have obtained additional social and economic legislative reforms if he had been more cooperative with the Soviet Union in foreign affairs or if he had exerted greater political skills as president in manipulating Congress to do his bidding.

As Alonzo Hamby indicates in Kirkendall (1974), the traditional liberal evaluation of Congress under the Truman administration uses Richard Neustadt's 1954 estimate of Truman's achievements as the basis for interpretation. Neustadt asserts the constitutional powers of Congress frustrated the enactment of Truman's program for items such as national health insurance, the Brannan agriculture plan, and civil rights legislation because the elected representatives followed voters' opinions in rejecting these measures. Truman did achieve much, however, because he prevented conservatives from turning back the New Deal's reform legislation and made some advancements by consolidating minimum wage and social security legislation as a permanent feature of American life.

Neustadt's account of the realities of the congressional conservative bloc in limiting Truman's reform program was confirmed by other studies. V. O. Key's (1966) account of southern Democratic voting, David R. Mayhew's (1966) description of the decline of party loyalty, and David Truman's (1959) description of Congress's roll-call votes in 1949 and 1950 each appears to confirm that Truman could not possibly have obtained his Fair Deal legislation. To be sure, Hamby acknowledges that the studies of David Truman and others are not definitive regarding all aspects of the period from 1949 to 1950, largely because no historian has studied the

Eighty-first and Eighty-second Congresses as thoroughly as Susan Hartmann (1971) analyzed the Eightieth Congress. However, Samuel Lubell's *Future of American Politics* (1952) has perceptive comments about the Eighty-first and Eighty-second Congresses.

Hamby is the foremost defender of the traditional perspective regarding Truman and Congress. His essays in Kirkendall (1974) and Lacey (1989), as well as two articles (1970, 1972) and a book (1973), give substance to his criticism of the revisionists' accounts described later. To support his interpretation of what the electorate and Congress wanted, Hamby cites public opinion studies such as those of Warren E. Miller (1953) and Eugene P. Linn (1949), as well as the statistical work of Angus Campbell and associates (1954, 1956), which is based on the initial collection of national voting data at the University of Michigan's Survey Research Center.

Five other important historical accounts also reflect traditional perspectives regarding congressional activity during the Truman era. Eric Goldman's (1956) survey, *The Crucial Decade,* is favorable to Truman, as is Richard Kirkendall's (1971) essay on Truman as one of the ten greatest presidents. Allan Harper (1969) describes Truman's strengths and weaknesses but indicates that weak congressional leaders handicapped Truman's legislative record. Donald McCoy and Richard Ruetten (1973) agree with Neustadt that Truman did the best that was possible in working with Congress at that time. Finally, Arthur Altmeyer (1968) explains the importance of Truman's preventing cuts in social security, as the Republican-dominated Eightieth Congress first tried to do.

Revisionist versions of congressional relations with Truman appeared during the mid-1960s and seriously challenged the traditional accounts in almost every area except the president's civil rights actions. Generally in civil rights, the revisionists recognize that Truman's difficulties with southern Democrats stymied the civil rights laws, and they praise Truman's executive actions (see Chapter 22 in this book.) For a traditional account of Truman's civil rights, see the study by McCoy and Ruetten (1973); for revisionist versions, see William Berman (1970) and Barton Bernstein (1971). The traditionalist-revisionist pespective about civil rights is also found in the essays by Alonzo Hamby and Havard Sitkoff in Richard Kirkendall's (1974) volume. (On the closely related loyalty security issue and McCarthyism, see Chapter 20 in this book.)

In other major areas of Truman's Fair Deal program, revisionists contend that Truman could have done a better job in working with Congress to gain effective legislation. Although more detailed study is needed on congressional dealings with Truman's Fair Deal proposals, revisionists have raised fascinating questions about many of these actions. While Hamby and other traditionalists argue that the Housing Act of 1949 was one important triumph for the president, Harvard Sitkoff's essay in Kirkendall (1974) emphasizes that Richard O. Davies' (1966) so-called traditional view actually has data supporting the revisionists. Davies calls the Housing Act a "hollow victory," which corresponds to Barton J. Bernstein's (1967b) and Mark I. Gelfand's (1975) revisionist interpretation that the act required delays in the public housing provisions that enabled business and real estate lobbies to gain the most benefits from the mortgage insurance provisions. Also, the legislation provided for local controls that preserved most public funds for private housing groups.

The action of the real estate lobby is part of the revisionists' contention that after 1945 there was a rapid increase in lobbying by business and special interest groups. After President Truman criticized lobbies during his 1948 campaign, Congress established the Select Committee on Lobbying Activity in 1949, headed by Democratic congressman Frank Buchanan (Pennsylvania). The Buchanan committee report was published in 1950, following hearings that began on March 27, 1950. Both the Buchanan report and the Republicans' minority report are summarized in the *Congressional Quarterly Almanac for 1950* (1951). This almanac also has an article titled "Lobby Spending Breaking Records," which indicates the biggest spenders were the conservative Committee for Constitutional Government, the American Medical Association, and the American Farm Bureau. A study of the lobbyists was written by Karl Schriftgiesser (1951).

Two of the top lobby groups, the American Medical Association and the American Farm Bureau, played a role in preventing Congress from enacting two of Truman's major Fair Deal proposals. Truman's proposal for national medical insurance stirred the fears of the American Medical Association, which sought to prevent such legislation. Monte M. Poen (1977) describes the profession's criticism of Truman's idea. Paul Starr (1982) fits the issue into the broader development of the AMA, and Stanley Kelley's (1966) study includes data on the AMA's campaign against medical insurance. Although health insurance was opposed, Poen indicates that the medical profession was pleased to accept government funds for hospital construction and medical research since this "aid" was not seen as the "socialist" use of tax money.

Similarly, the Farm Bureau's lobby helped prevent Congress from adopting Secretary of Agriculture Charles F. Brannan's proposals to direct agricultural benefits to low-income farmers and to restrict maximum payments to $27,500 of production, a limit opposed by the wealthy commercial farmers, who profited most from these subsidies. As accounts by Alan Matusow (1970) and Reo Christenson (1959) indicate, Brannan's proposal was not strongly pushed by President Truman. Consequently, Congress rejected Brannan's plan while approving higher price supports for agriculture with no payment maximums. Moreover, as Peter Kirstein (1978) and Richard Craig (1971) have shown, Congress refused to aid the poor migratory workers who provided cheap labor for commercial farms.

For the revisionists, the conservative obstacles to medical and farm reforms were consistent with the increased business mergers of the postwar era. Robert Griffith's essay in Lacey (1989) provides details regarding the methods by which business groups avoided prosecution under the anti-trust acts despite the fact that Truman's Federal Trade Commission (FTC) officials wanted to restrict monopolistic practices. Although Congress passed the Cellar-Kefauver bill of 1951 to strengthen the Clayton Act of 1913 by preventing one corporation from obtaining the assets of another corporation, the business lobbyists persuaded Congress to cut the FTC funds needed to enforce the antitrust laws. Business lobbies also campaigned to prevent antitrust action against the A&P food store industry and the oil industry's cartels operated by American, British, and Dutch oil companies to maximize their profits.

Although no scholar has focused on the antitrust aspects of Truman's administration, Griffith cites several general studies with which future historians can begin. Reports of symposia of the American Economic Association are given in Dexter Keezer and associates (1949) and John Kenneth Galbraith and associates (1954); while both Edward Mason (1957) and Walter Adams and Horace Gray (1955) describe the issue from the perspective of the 1950s. In addition, G. Warren Nutter and Henry A. Einhorn (1968) conclude that between 1899 and 1958, antitrust legislation had little influence in reducing the percentage of businesses with virtual monopolies. Two important works that consider the relation between corporate power and the status of competition are by Abraham D. H. Kaplan (1964) and Andrew Shonfield (1965). Historians should note that Keezer's (1949) report demonstrates the difficulties economists have in defining a "broadly competitive system." Finally, the Federal Trade Commission issued reports on monopolies in 1951 and 1965 showing that businessmen continued to follow John D. Rockefeller's adage that competition is fine, but combination is better.

In the area of conservation, Truman succeeded in stalling legislation to permit states to regulate submerged oil resources in the tidelands by twice vetoing congressional legislation. He was less successful in dealing with the National Association of Electric Companies, which blocked Fair Deal acts designed to build new transmission lines for public power plants. The electric companies made their greatest profits in the transmission and sale of electricity. The power utilities also prevented Truman's attempts to get congressional approval for the Columbia River project and other "small Tennessee Valley Authorities." Elmo Richardson (1973), John M. Blair (1976), Gerald Nash (1968), Burton Kaufman (1978), and Robert Engler (1961, 1977) have important works on oil, natural gas, and public power issues during this period.

Neither the revisionists nor the traditionalist historians have devoted special attention to Truman's failure to obtain federal aid to education. Although many public schools were in bad shape because the Great De-

pression of 1929 lowered local school districts' property tax rates, the
disparity between the few wealthy school districts and the numerous poor
school districts faltered principally over the issue of government aid to
Roman Catholic schools and the separation of church and state. Subsequently, although federal aid bills for public schools were offered in Congress in 1949, these bills were virtually dead on arrival. New York's Roman
Catholic cardinal, Francis Spellman, denounced the legislation, and after
Eleanor Roosevelt responded with sharp criticisms of Spellman, Truman's
congressional leaders ducked the issue so that the bills never got to the
floor of Congress. Not until John F. Kennedy's election as the first Catholic president in 1960 could the education question again be considered.

The aid to education issue has principally been studied by educators,
although it was of political concern to Democratic party candidates in
large cities. Articles on the question include Philip Gleason's (1977) discussion of three court cases between 1947 and 1952; Philip A. Grant's
(1979a) examination of the Spellman-Roosevelt dispute; Seymour Lachman's (1965) description of the 1949 bills and the problems they caused;
and George A. Kizer's (1970) review of the aid to education question from
1945 to 1963.

While the Fair Deal's fate is the major topic of traditionalist-revisionist
literature, the role of Congress in economic fiscal policies was also a critical matter during the Korean War. Both the militarization of U.S. national security policy and government actions to counteract wartime
economic problems challenged Truman and Congress between 1950 and
1953.

Congress, the President, and the Economy

Although President Truman and Congress debated issues about Fair
Deal reforms and the status of New Deal economic measures, they had to
act on current economic affairs, especially after the outbreak of the Korean War altered the government's previous economic expectations. The
war not only required additional military expenditures, which stimulated
business-government cooperation (corporatism), but also raised fiscal
problems about inflation, wage-price controls, taxes, and the allocation of
the nation's resources.

The Korean War's stimulation of military expenses occurred at the very
moment that the National Security Council's NSC-68 urged the militarization of the nation's cold war effort. As Lester H. Brune's (1989) article
explains, from 1945 to 1950, Truman and Congress kept taxes low and
cut military costs in accordance with classical economic theory that military costs damaged domestic needs. In 1949, however, Edwin Nourse, the
conservative chairman of the President's Council of Economic Advisers
(CEA), was replaced by Leon Keyserling, who advocated expansionary ec-

onomic policies, which, he told the authors of NSC-68, would enable the nation to afford both "guns and butter." The National Security Council had proposed NSC-68 as an urgent call for the United States to finance a large military build up against the Soviet Union. Nevertheless, Truman was reluctant to accept Keyserling's concepts and did not approve NSC-68's large-scale military budget increases until the Korean War began.

Once Truman decided to defend South Korea, NSC-68's plans for defense budget increases became a reality. Beginning with a supplemental defense budget in July 1950, Congress readily increased defense expenditures from the original $13 billion requested for 1950 to more than $55 billion for fiscal year 1953. In July, Truman requested only partial mobilization of U.S. forces, but the Chinese intervention in Korea stirred widespread fears of another world war, leading the president to declare a national emergency on December 15, 1950. At the same time, the United States increased its contribution to NATO defense forces. Although the opening of the Korean truce talks during the fall of 1951 reduced cold war tensions, the uncertainty of future "communist aggression" enabled the U.S. armed services to obtain greater military expenditures until President Eisenhower stabilized these costs at about $40 billion after 1953. Further data on the 1950 rearmament decision are contained in essays by Warner R. Schilling and others in *Strategy, Politics and Defense Budgets* (1962) and in an essay by Fred Block (1980). The long-term consequences of the defense buildup are examined by Fred Cook (1962), Charles J. Hitch and Roland N. McKean (1960), and Seymour Melman (1986).

Scholars who examine the close ties between government and business that developed after World War II find that Keyserling's expansionist economic concepts and the 1950 to 1953 militarization of the cold war contributed significantly to the corporatist state and American global hegemony as described by the world systems analysis of Thomas McCormick (1989) and Michael Hogan (1986). Robert Pollard's book (1985) and his essay in Lacey (1989) describe the economic security aspects of corporatist developments between government and business, while Robert Collins (1981) indicates that many businessmen adopted the basic economic principles of John Maynard Keynes as the means to save capitalism from both fascism and communism. These economic developments are also examined by Kim McQuaid (1982) and the essays by David W. Folts, Donald K. Pickens, and Geoffrey T. Miles in the volume edited by William Levantrosser (1986).

In addition to inaugurating a new policy for large defense expenditures thoughout the cold war, the Korean War years raised fiscal controversies, which have extended into the 1990s. The most important of these cold war economic issues concerned taxes, wage-price controls, and monetary practices of federal agencies. With respect to taxes, Truman proposed a pay-as-you-go policy, which would have increased taxes sufficiently to cover the war's defense expenditures, but Congress rejected the increases, a decision that resulted in deficits that added to the national debt.

In contrast to the tax situation, Congress seemed more willing in July 1950 to adopt wage-price controls than were Truman's advisers. Truman tried voluntary controls until January 1951, when the Chinese intervention led to the adoption of wage-price controls on most commodities despite the reluctance of Leon Keyserling of the CEA.

Finally, there was a dispute over monetary controls between officials of the Treasury Department, the CEA, and the Federal Reserve Board. The dispute among these three agencies regarded interest rates and the money supply. The Treasury and the CEA wanted low interest rates and an increase in money allocations, while the Federal Reserve preferred to fight inflation by raising interest rates and tightening the supply of money. During the Korean War, Treasury Department officials agreed to recognize the Federal Reserve Board's right to act independent of the president's policies, a decision that was usually followed after 1953, despite frequent disputes because high interest rates restricted business expansion and affected full employment objectives.

Overall, however, the Korean War promoted the prosperity of the United States, which characterized the era from 1945 to 1968. Unemployment fell below 3 percent, personal income increased, industry profited by raising prices to allow for wage increases, and the nation's share of world production ranked between 33 and 50 percent. As Paul Kennedy (1987) later observed, in 1945 the United States had an unprecedented share of global production and consumption, a situation that, perhaps inevitably, deteriorated after the Europeans and Japanese gradually rebuilt their industries that had been destroyed in World War II.

Numerous studies refer to the U.S. economic prosperity before, during, and after the Korean War. Among the important accounts are those of John Kenneth Galbraith (1958), David Potter (1954), and Herbert Stein (1969). Later works with a more critical attitude toward the economy are by Lawrence Wittner (1974), Otis Graham (1976), and Robert Lekachman (1975).

The most optimistic discussions of Truman's policies during the Korean War are by Leon Keyserling, whose views are in essays edited by Francis Heller (1977) and William Levantrosser (1986), and in an essay (1948) describing his expansion concepts. Keyserling's role as CEA chairman is also described by Edward Flash (1965). Details regarding Truman's tactics to combat the fears of inflation, an increased consumer demand, and a wage-price spiral are explained by Bert Hickman in one study on the years 1950 to 1952 (1955) and in another analysis of the period from 1945 to 1958 (1960). Ralph Freeman (1960) edited a volume of essays on post–World War II trends regarding such topics as monetary theory, income inequality, fiscal policy, labor developments, and capital investments. Francis Heller's (1981) volume of essays principally contains memoirs of Truman administration officials. Favorable assessments of Truman's success in maintaining economic stability are made by A. E. Holmans (1964) and by Crawford D. Goodwin and R. Stanley Herren (1975).

Labor unions in the United States were affected by the cold war and Korean War not only because conservatives sought to restrict their power through passage of the 1947 Taft-Hartley Act but also because the anticommunist atmosphere led unions to purge their radical left-wing leaders. The labor situation from 1945 to 1953 is explained in Nelson Lichtenstein's article in the volume edited by Michael Lacey (1989) and in books by Ronald Radosh (1969) and Arthur McClure (1969). For an account by a "liberal" Democrat who approved the union's purge of communists, see Max Kampelman's (1957) study, which had a laudatory introduction by Minnesota's senator Hubert Humphrey. R. Alton Lee (1966) has the best study about the passage of the Taft-Hartley legislation.

One notable problem resulting from wage-price controls occurred because the Wage Stabilization Board tended to favor business over labor. As Jack Steiber (1980) indicates, labor representatives finally walked out of the Wage Board's meetings in 1951 until the board's powers were revised to give it more authority, including the handling of wage disputes. The wage issue became the vital element in Truman's decision to seize the steel mills in 1952. The president was disturbed in 1952 because steel corporations wanted price increases without comparable wage increases. When the steel unions planned to strike, Truman seized the mills in order to meet the military needs for steel production. After U.S. courts overruled Truman's power to seize the steel mills, which was followed by a fifty-three-day strike, the steel managers agreed on July 14 to accept the wage-price increases offered before Truman had seized the mills in April. The president gained what the unions wanted, but his congressional critics claimed that he sought "dictatorial" powers. The complexities of the steel seizure issue are examined by Frank Schwartz in Levantrosser's (1986) volume and in the book by Maeva Marcus (1977). Also see Daniel Bell's "The Subversion of Collective Bargaining" (1960).

Summary

This survey of the literature regarding Truman and the Congress from 1949 to 1953 indicates that more detailed studies need to be made regarding the congressional role in rejecting Truman's major Fair Deal program. The experience of President Lyndon Johnson's Great Society program, which was eventually rejected by middle-class backlash during the 1970s, may substantiate the traditionalists' conclusions that the first signs of middle-class conservatism were reflected in congressional responses to Truman's attempt to go beyond the New Deal.

LITERATURE ON MEMBERS OF CONGRESS DURING THE WAR

Research on members of Congress during the Korean War is dominated by aspirants to the presidency and prominent members of the Republican party, including Senator Joseph McCarthy of Wisconsin. For the great majority who do not fit these categories, the literature available is principally their published memoirs or unpublished dissertations about their political careers. Furthermore, the Senate is indeed the "upper" house regarding the amount of literature; members of the House of Representatives are usually mentioned only with senators with whom they sponsored a bill or if they became senators. To aid research on Congress, this section begins with a discussion of reference works and general studies on Congress, concluding with available literature on congressional members prominent during the Korean War era.

General Reference Works

Citing lack of historical research on Congress as one reason for publishing *Understanding Congress: Research Perspectives* (1991), Roger H. Davidson and Richard C. Sachs give details of available sources and examine Congress as an institution relative to the other branches of government.

The U.S. Congress' *Congressional Record* is a necessary research source as an official record of Congress' daily activities and a place for members' speeches or statements from articles they deem relevant to present issues. The *Record* gives a member's position on issues he or she is sufficiently concerned about to express their viewpoints.

Several books provide depository information about the personal papers and documents of congressional members. Two valuable works are Katherine Jacob and Elizabeth Ann Hornyak's (1983) guide to senators' collections and Cynthia Pease Miller's (1988) guide for House members' collections. Both list the members alphabetically and give locations of papers, including oral history collections. In contrast, the *National Union Catalog of Manuscript Collections* lists and describes depositories alphabetically, making it difficult to locate papers of individual members. Another important reference work on Congress is the National Archives' two guides to records of the Senate and House in its archives, both published in 1989.

For accounts of congressional activity, the *Congressional Quarterly* publishes an annual almanac (1950–1953) and *Congress and the Nation* (1965). Neil R. Peirce (1967) provides excellent records of Congress' activities from 1945 to 1966, and Garrison Nelson (1993) lists the makeup of committees, including chairs and seniority rankings for each committee. Most recently, Roger Davidson and coworkers have published an *Encyclopedia of the U.S. Congress* (1995). This work's contents include bibliographic materials about each member of Congress.

General Studies on Congress

Most studies regarding Congress during the Korean War are concerned with opposition to the Truman administration, emphasizing Republican views and including Democratic positions principally as rebuttals. Two basic studies examining Republican opposition to Truman's foreign policy are by David R. Kepley (1988) and Athan Theoharis (1970). Kepley studies the reactions of Senate Republicans to major foreign policy initiatives between 1948 and 1952, dividing them into three factions: internationalists, nationalists, and isolationists. He charts the dominance of Taft's nationalists and isolationists to 1951, after which there is a resurgence of the internationalists who sponsored Dwight Eisenhower's Republican candidacy and victory in 1952.

Theoharis describes the isolationists' opposition to the Yalta agreements that Republicans incorporated into their general criticism of Democratic foreign policy. He separates the Republicans into moderates, partisans, and extremists, based on the intensity of their attacks on the Democrats. Notably, he includes data on members of the House of Representatives, a group often overlooked. Theoharis indicates the isolationists used Yalta to verify the Democratic administration's failure to restrain Moscow and to construe Yalta as part of a State Department conspiracy that included Secretary of State Dean Acheson.

Both Kepley and Theoharis believe that two events enabled right-wing critics to increase their influence after 1950: their emphasis on the communists-in-government issue and the illness and death of Senator Arthur Vandenberg, whose moderate bipartisan group had previously helped Truman. The arrest and trials of a few prominent "spies" and allegations against "disloyal" Americans seemed to demonstrate their charges of communists in government, while Vandenberg's absence caused bipartisanship to collapse, leaving Republican moderates without a recognized person to counteract McCarthyism.

Although Kepley and Theoharis portray bipartisanship favorably, Robert Divine (1972), John Rourke (1977), and Arthur J. Schlesinger, Jr. (1973) argue it was detrimental to foreign policy, because meaningful debate might have yielded important changes in Truman's foreign policy. Yet Ronald Caridi (1968) contends that Truman's opponents offered no meaningful alternatives during the Korean War. Focusing on Republican senators and party leaders such as Governor Thomas Dewey, ex-president Herbert Hoover, and National Committee chairman Guy Gabrielson, Caridi describes Republican responses to post-1945 events, concluding they flunked their role as an opposition party because they presented no sincere, consistent alternatives to the president's program but maintained a negative position in denouncing the Democrats.

Caridi's analysis is countered by Thomas Paterson (1971) and David W. Reinhard (1983), who argue that both isolationists and left-wing critics offered alternatives to Truman's policies. Paterson contends the Truman administration ignored the alternatives by calling its left-wing critics "communists" and its right-wing critics "isolationists." Although these critics never obtained their policies, they served as checks on the Truman administration. Reinhard examines the Republican right wing or "Old Guard" whom previous studies had labeled extremists or isolationists. These Republicans supported limited government intervention in the economy, low federal budgets and taxes, a strong defense relying on air and naval power, and a foreign policy allowing the United States to act independent of other nations—in brief, policies of fiscal conservatism and intense, unilateral anticommunism. Reinhard concludes these were real alternatives intended to combat the Democrats' progressive liberalism and cooperative internationalism.

Prominent Senators:

Democrats. Democratic senatorial leaders during the Korean War usually came from two groups: senior southerners and the freshman class of 1948. The former set the rules that governed both party and congressional activities, while the latter supported their elders as a means of becoming future leaders.

Richard B. Russell of Georgia had great influence as the leader of the conservative southern bloc, which formed a coalition with Robert Taft to trade support in stopping civil rights legislation for helping Republicans block Truman's Fair Deal legislation. Following Millard Tydings' defeat in 1950, Harold H. Martin (1951) explains, Russell gained greater voice in the war effort by becoming chairman of the Senate Armed Forces Committee. As Gilbert C. Fite's (1991) biography explains, Russell led the southern Democrats but refused to be majority leader, preferring the independence of working behind the scenes. Russell sought the Democratic presidential nomination in 1952, but as Mark Stern (1991) and David D. Potenziani (1981) show, Russell's segregationist beliefs made him unacceptable.

Other important southern leaders were Harry Bryd of Virginia and Tom Connally of Texas. Notable for his support of Eisenhower in 1952, Byrd was a powerful senator whose control of Virginia's state political machine is described by J. Harvie Wilkinson III (1968). Tom Connally was chairman of the Senate Foreign Relations Committee, and his memoirs (1954) give details of his support of bipartisanship and Truman's policies throughout the war. Nevertheless, Connally's careless statement in the May 1950 *U.S.*

News and World Report that Korea was not "absolutely essential" to U.S. defense strategy enabled critics to cite this in attacking Democratic foreign policy.

The Democrats' class of 1948 included three future vice-presidential candidates, one eventual president, "the uncrowned king of the Senate," and one who became the "Senate's conscience." The six may be subdivided by political alignment into two groups: the liberals were Estes Kefauver of Tennessee, Hubert Humphrey of Minnesota, and Paul Douglas of Illinois; the southwesterners were Lyndon Johnson of Texas, Robert Kerr of Oklahoma, and Clinton Anderson of New Mexico. Although the former group gained the spotlight for their outspokenness, the latter three worked with southern Democratic leaders and became the future holders of party influence in Congress.

Of the 1948 class, Estes Kefauver first gained publicity as chairman of the 1950 Crime Investigating Committee. Theodore Wilson (1975) details the committee's cross-country travels, using television to dramatize its investigation of organized crime. Wilson concludes the committee halted crime indirectly because criminals did not want to attract the committee's attention. Kefauver's *Crime in America* (1951) and his interview for *U.S. News and World Report* (1951) divulge little that was not in the released committee reports. A *Newsweek* article (1951) examines Kefauver's fellow Democrats who disliked the committee for exposing relationships between the Democrat's big-city political machines and crime bosses. Whatever the reaction to the committee, Kefauver emerged as a national figure and made a serious run for the 1952 presidential nomination. Joseph Gorman's (1971) laudatory biography states that Kefauver supported Truman's Korean policy "from the beginning." Charles L. Fontenay (1981) emphasizes his crime and antitrust investigative ventures.

Based on his memoirs (1972), Paul Douglas, an economist, deserved the political title of the "conscience of the Senate." Douglas supported Truman's decision to enter the Korean War but criticized Eisenhower for accepting truce terms for which Democrats would have been persecuted. W. McNeil Lowry (1951) explains Douglas' early importance in the Senate, while Edward L. and Frederick H. Schapsmeier (1974) briefly describe Douglas' life.

Although most literature on Hubert Humphrey concerns his 1960s career as Democratic whip, vice president under Lyndon Johnson, and 1968 presidential candidate, some works discuss his early career. Albert Eisele's (1972) comparative work on Humphrey and Congressman Eugene McCarthy describes Humphrey's civil rights speech at the 1948 Democratic Convention and his confrontation with Byrd's Joint Committee on Reduction of Nonessential Federal Expenditures, an event Humphrey later considered the worst mistake of his career. An outspoken supporter of Truman's Fair Deal, Humphrey's standing with the liberal wing led Lyndon Johnson to court his support for the minority leadership position during 1952, an event that Winthrop Griffith (1965) indicates began a close Humphrey-Johnson relationship.

Lyndon Johnson's actions as Senate minority leader dominate the literature pertaining to his early Senate career. After serving ten years in the House under Speaker Sam Rayburn's guidance, Johnson gained more power as a senator. He received support from Russell while avoiding the southern caucus and creating allies throughout the party, a tactic that led to his election as Senate minority leader for the Eighty-third Congress. Both Rowland Evans and Robert Novak (1966) and Howard Shuman, in Roger Davidson and Richard Baker (1991), describe Johnson's maneuvers to gain the minority leadership. Evans and Novak also discuss Johnson's work on the War Preparedness Committee, a version of Truman's World War II committee, which had oversight of the nation's mobilization for the Korean effort. Johnson criticized Truman's failure to make a total war commitment to Korea, although his committee cut Truman's war appropriations requests. He also backed Eisenhower's Korean truce. Ralph K. Huitt (1961) includes Johnson in examining Democratic party leadership, and Stern (1991) explains his complex civil rights position.

The final two class of 1948 members, Robert Kerr and Clinton Anderson, have few works devoted to their career. Paul Douglas called Kerr the "uncrowned king of the Senate," and Kerr had wide respect in Russell's southern caucus. Kerr shunned the majority leader position, wanting to act independently. Like Russell, he made an abortive run for the 1952 presidential nomination, which, as Ann Hodges Morgan (1977) describes, was killed by the impression that Kerr was a captive of gas and oil interests. Clinton Anderson also chose cloakroom diplomacy to becoming the majority leader. Anderson wrote his memoirs with Milton Viorst (1970), while Richard Baker (1985) describes his Senate career.

Two maverick Democratic senators must be mentioned: J. William Fulbright of Arkansas and Patrick McCarran of Nevada. Fulbright was a Rhodes scholar who established the Fulbright scholarships and was chairman of the Senate Foreign Relations Committee during the Vietnam War. During the Korean War era, he headed an investigation into the Reconstruction Finance Corporation scandals. Haynes Johnson and Bernard M. Gwertzman (1968) describe issues about which Fulbright was inconsistent regarding Korea. Prior to the 1950 invasion, Fulbright believed Korea was a "waif of a country" and not a target of communist aggression. Once the war began, Fulbright did not respond until China intervened, when he advised withdrawal to prevent a possible world war. Finally, after UN victories and the war's stabilization in 1951, Fulbright softened his withdrawal stance, which the authors see as incongruous. Johnson and Gwertzman argue that Fulbright's inconsistency occurred because domestic concerns were his first priority in the early 1950s. Tristam Coffin (1966) focuses on Fulbright's service during the 1960s but includes information on his dislike of the how Republicans handled Korea by using it to rouse public opinion and to campaign in 1952 to end the war.

Senator McCarran, though a registered Democrat, was often grouped with Old Guard Republicans because of his conservative beliefs. From 1950 to 1952, McCarran cosponsored two major pieces of legislation: the Internal Security Act of 1950, which Congress passed despite Truman's veto, and the McCarran-Walter Immigration Act of 1952. McCarran also sponsored the improvement of relations with Spain, a subject not yet investigated. Richard Donovan and Douglas Cater (1953) examine the primary election loss of Alan Bible, McCarran's candidate, to Tom Mechling in 1952, leading McCarran to back Republican George W. Malone who won. James Edwards (1982) explains McCarran's control of Nevada politics, concluding that he "wrecked the Democratic Party" in Nevada and the "benefits of his career . . . were far less than they should have been." Alfred Steinberg (1950) has a sympathetic character study of McCarran, while William R. Tanner and Robert Griffith (1974) use McCarran's Internal Security Act of 1950 to illustrate that a public fear of disloyal Americans existed before McCarthy's rise in 1950. Gilman Ostrander (1966) examines McCarran's activity as Judiciary Committee chairman in opposing many of Truman's proposals.

Republicans. Congressional Republicans did not suffer the serious divisions that plagued the Democrats after World War II, although in international affairs, moderate Republicans led by Arthur Vandenberg were an important party minority factor against the conservative "nationalist-isolationist" wing led by Senator Taft. The Republican victory in the 1946 off-year elections brought in the class of 1946, which augmented Taft's coalition, while only Henry Cabot Lodge, Jr.'s, election assisted Vandenberg's bipartisan group. Moderate Republican support was stronger outside Congress than inside because of prominent Republicans such as John Foster Dulles and Thomas Dewey, the party's 1948 presidential nominee.

From 1944 until his illness in 1950, Vandenberg was an influential member of the Senate Foreign Relations Committee, where his bipartisanship leadership helped Truman get congressional approval for such vital international legislation as the Truman Doctrine, Marshall Plan, and North Atlantic Treaty Organization (NATO). Vandenberg led moderate Republicans by consulting with Truman and defending the administration's European foreign policies. Beginning his political career as an isolationist, Vandenberg shifted to advocate international cooperation shortly after the bombing of Pearl Harbor. David Thompkins (1970) and James Gazell (1973) have details about Vandenberg's conversion. Arthur Vandenberg, Jr. (1952) edited his father's papers, which defined his bipartisanship beliefs in hope that other Republicans would carry them forward. Dean Acheson and Vandenberg's son (1964) laud Vandenberg for supporting the president's national security measures. In contrast, Richard Rovere (1962) and James Fetzer (1974) criticize his bipartisan influence. Objecting to Acheson's praise of Vandenberg, Rovere calls him a "mediocrity" who broke the "back of Republican isolationism in the Senate" by adopting bipartisanship. Fetzer opposes Truman's foreign policies and blames Vandenberg for accepting a program lacking in vision.

Regarding Korea, however, Vandenberg added to the opposition's case against the administration. Although he supported Truman's initial decision to assist South Korea, Vandenberg soon qualified his approval and denied that Truman's Far Eastern policies had bipartisan backing. Moreover, his fatal illness left moderate Republicans leaderless as they tried to adopt bipartisanship positions to questions raised by the Korean War, a situation that Kepley (1988) explains.

H. Alexander Smith of New Jersey and Henry Cabot Lodge, Jr., were the Republican senators who sought to replace Vandenberg by backing internationalism during the war. Although Kepley (1988) indicates Smith did the most to further Vandenberg's practices, the only literature on his career is William Leary's (1966) dissertation. More has been written about Lodge, who not only sought to moderate Republican attitudes but was a leader of the movement that resulted in Dwight Eisenhower's election in 1952. Lodge's memoirs (1973) and William J. Miller's (1967) biography are basic to the study of Lodge's career.

While Vandenberg influenced policies toward Europe in particular, the most influential Republican senator during the Korean War era was Senator Robert A. Taft of Ohio. Robert M. Merry's essay in Roger Davidson and Richard Baker (1991) calls Taft the "actual Republican leader in the Senate" as chairman of the Republican Steering Committee. Caridi (1968) concludes that Taft and his followers failed to offer consistent alternatives to Truman's policy because, as Taft admitted on January 20, 1952, he was inconsistent on the Korean War. Taft's international ideas are described in a book (1951) and a speech for the National Conference of Christians and Jews reprinted in *Vital Speeches* (June 15, 1953). Taft opposed the stationing of U.S. troops in Europe, advocated the use of air and naval power to protect America, and wanted a smaller army based at home. His 1953 speech urged America to "go it alone" if the UN peace talks failed in Korea.

Taft's ideas drew criticism from Arthur M. Schlesinger, Jr. (1952) who called them a "new isolationism," that is, an old isolationist dealing with the modern world by adopting a form of appeasement without the McCarthyist taint of extreme anticommunism. Similarly, McGeorge Bundy (1951) suggests Taft's was a "yes, but" position that approved Truman's decision to help South Korea but demanded congressional consent and claimed Democrats caused the war due to Acheson's Far Eastern appeasement policy. James Patterson (1972) and Richard Kepley (1988) examine

Taft's conflicting positions that resulted because his hostility toward overseas involvement contradicted his militancy toward communism in Asia, and partisan opposition to Truman. For example, in February 1951 Taft advocated withdrawal from Korea to save American lives and improve the U.S. economy, but in April he adopted General MacArthur's plan for total victory over the Chinese without explaining the lives and money to be lost in this effort. Kepley argues that Taft's concepts were based on the exaggerated assumption that airpower plus the "unleashing" of China's nationalist armies could replace U.S. ground forces. After the war stabilized in mid-1951, Taft believed a "stalemate peace at the 38th parallel is better than a stalemate war," but he later supported MacArthur's ideas for winning the war, a view he maintained until his death in July 1953.

Taft's positions on Korea and opposition to most of the Fair Deal have yielded diverse interpretations of his effectiveness. William S. White (1954) praises Taft as a devout but widely misunderstood person. John P. Armstrong (1955) portrays Taft as being poorly informed but forcing Americans to rethink their positions on the war. Henry Berger (1971b) and Ronald Radosh (1975) agree that Taft was not a 1930s-style isolationist, admiring his challenge to Truman's policies. Russell Kirk and James McClellan (1967) emphasize Taft's conservative principles, while Geoffrey Matthews (1982) believes Taft's opposition to Truman was motivated by a desire to restrict presidential power. Vernon Van Dyke and Edward Lane (1952) give a comprehensive study of Taft's Senate career. Both Gary Reichard (1975) and James M. Burns (1963) emphasize Taft's assistance to Eisenhower during his brief stint as Senate majority leader before his death in July 1953.

Taft's foreign policy beliefs were strongly backed by Kenneth Wherry of Nebraska, who was Senate minority leader until his death in 1951. As Richard Cope (1951) indicates, Wherry denounced the president's right to commit troops to Korea, advocated total war against China after November 1950, and criticized the UN's involvement. Marvin Stromer (1969) explains how Wherry attained and used his political influence.

While Wherry, Taft, and Vandenberg represented the Old Guard, the Republican freshman class of 1946 equaled the Democrats' 1948 class in quantity of future leaders. This class also strengthened the party's right wing in Congress. Class members who became party leaders included Senators Joseph McCarthy of Wisconsin, John Bricker of Ohio, William Jenner of Indiana, and both William Knowland and Representative Richard Nixon from California. (The literature about McCarthy is reviewed in Chapter 20 in this book.)

Bricker arrived in the Senate with a national reputation as Ohio's governor and the 1944 Republican vice-presidential candidate. Research on his Senate years is dominated by the Bricker Amendment, which sought to limit presidential power in foreign policy by requiring extensive congressional approval. Terrence Thatcher (1977) indicates the American Bar Association's opposition to several United Nations treaties precipitated the amendment. Frank Holman (1954) compiles public statements, documents, and various versions of the amendment that were proposed, while Duane Tananbaum (1988) evaluates its impact on the political climate of the time. Both Tananbaum (1985) and Gary Reichard (1974) examine Eisenhower's role in preventing passage of the amendment.

There has been little research on Jenner and Knowland. Jenner was McCarthy's main ally and followed the Old Guard in opposing European aid and supporting MacArthur's plans to expand the Korean War, positions that Michael Paul Poder (1976) details. Knowland's detractors called him the "Senator from Formosa" for his support of Jiang Jieshi. Admonishing Truman to prevent Korea from becoming "another Munich," Knowland was an outspoken member of the opposition who, after refusing the job, sponsored Richard Nixon for the 1952 vice presidency. Becoming Senate majority leader after Taft's passing, Knowland gained greater political influence after the war ended. Knowland has no biographer, but his views are found in Ross Koen's *The China Lobby in American Politics* (1974).

Other Republican Old Guard senators deserving mention are New Hampshire's Styles Bridges, Indiana's Homer Capehart, and Illinois' Everett Dirksen. Bridges is overlooked by scholars, although he was the ranking minority member of the Appropriations and Armed Services committees and served as interim minority leader following Wherry's death in 1951. Douglas Cater (1960) explains Bridges' broad political base, concluding that his "field of expertise: manipulating" required his obscurity. Second, Homer Capehart is treated sympathetically by William Pickett (1990) who describes Capehart's nationalism, his role in McCarthy's rise to power, and his reconciliation with Eisenhower in 1952.

Third, Everett Dirksen's early political clout in the Senate was due to sixteen years in the House and an impressive upset over the Democrats' majority leader, Scott Lucas, in 1950. Often criticized for lacking any fixed ideology, Dirksen during the Korean War supported Taft's policies and McCarthy's accusations against Democrats. Dirksen achieved national recognition at the Republicans' 1952 convention for a speech favoring the pro-Taft Georgia delegation during which he shook a finger at Thomas Dewey and exclaimed, "We followed you before, and you took us down the path to defeat!" This sparked an uproar of boos directed at both Dirksen and Dewey, as well as a few brawls. Like Capehart, Dirksen later reconciled with Eisenhower. Neil MacNeil (1970) has a forgiving account of Dirksen's career, while Edward L. Schapsmeier and Frederick H. Schapsmeier have a book (1985) and article (1983) that give a documented biography of his career. Louella Dirksen (1972) offers insight into her husband's private life.

In contrast to the Old Guard, there were two Republican mavericks in the Senate: Wayne Morse of Oregon and William Langer of North Dakota. Because he disagreed with Republican policy, Morse left the party in 1952, but after an Ohio Democrat replaced Taft in 1953, he declared he would vote Republican to keep a Republican majority in the Eighty-third Congress. Ralph K. Huitt (1957) examines Morse's bolt from the party, and both A. Robert Smith (1962) and Lee Wilkins (1985) describe his independent stance on issues.

Langer was an "old progressive" who took unorthodox positions on most issues. He persistently criticized Knowland as the "senator from Formosa" (for supporting Jiang Jieshi), but he also admonished Truman that Korea should not become "another Munich." Langer criticized Truman's policies but blamed Republicans for supporting Acheson's appointment as secretary of state. Yet Langer was one of the few Republicans who steadily defied McCarthyism and opposed the 1950 Internal Security Act on free speech grounds. During debate on that act, Langer filibustered until collapsing in exhaustion on the Senate floor, when Senator Morse replaced him in their futile attempt to kill the bill. Robert P. Wilkins (1974) has an excellent study of Langer's ideas, and Robert Griffith (1979) includes him in a study of the old progressives and the cold war.

The House of Representatives

There is a significant lack of research on House members during the Korean War era. Nevertheless, six representatives played interesting roles during the period: Democrats Sam Rayburn of Texas and Carl Vinson of Georgia; Republicans Joe Martin of Massachusetts, Walter Judd of Minnesota, and Charles Halleck of Indiana; and American Labor party member Vito Marcantonio.

Rayburn had been House Speaker longer than anyone else to that time. Alfred Steinberg's (1975) sympathetic account describes Rayburn's support of Truman's decisions to enter Korea and to fire MacArthur, as well as his relationship with Lyndon Johnson. D. B. Hardeman and Donald C. Bacon (1987) view Rayburn as the "vital cement" of bipartisanship under Eisenhower but also examine his dissatisfaction with the 1953 truce because Truman and Acheson could have obtained "this kind of truce eighteen months ago." Anthony Champagne (1988) summarizes Rayburn's career and has an excellent bibliography, while Deward C. Brown (1972) describes his papers at a private library in Bonham, Texas.

Carl Vinson, the chairman of the House Armed Services Committee, had worked tirelessly on behalf of the U.S. Navy's strength since the 1930s. Beverly Smith (1951) discusses Vinson's role during the Korean War in fighting against budget cuts and for a speedier buildup during the war. Vinson's special help to the navy is described by Louis Stockstill (1961).

Representative Joe Martin was a powerful House personality for many years but has been neglected by scholars of American politics. As House minority leader, Martin cooperated in passing many of Truman's policies and fully supported Eisenhower. During the Korean War, Martin corresponded with General MacArthur and released the MacArthur letter that criticized Truman's handling of the war and became the catalyst for Truman's decision to remove MacArthur as Supreme Allied Commander, although Truman cited other instances of the general's insubordination. In his memoirs, Martin (1960) details this event and his other policy positions. William Albert Hasenfus (1986) examines Martin's leadership in Congress.

Reader's Digest (1950) called Walter Judd "one of Washington's outstanding authorities on the Far East," when it reprinted Judd's speech about the causes of the Korean conflict, a topic Judd's (1980) article also covers. Floyd Russell Goodno (1970) emphasizes Judd's Far Eastern views, while Lee Edwards (1990) and Barbara Stuhler (1973) examine Judd's career.

Charles Halleck became important as the House majority leader who marshaled Republican support for Eisenhower's policies in 1953. Gary W. Reichard (1975) indicates that Halleck unified party support for Eisenhower after Senator Taft's death. Henry Z. Scheele (1966) has a biography on Halleck and an article on Halleck's relationship with Eisenhower (1993) in Shirley Warshaw's book.

Finally, Vito Marcantonio of the American Labor party (ALP) attracted literature as a dissenting voice in Congress. He was the only representative who immediately opposed Truman's June 1950 decision to assist South Korea, a position that led to his defeat in the 1950 election. Elected to Congress in 1934 as a progressive Republican, Marcantonio switched to the newly formed ALP in 1936. Although seen by many as a "communist," he was a pro-labor populist according to Richard Sasuly (1957). Salvatore LaGumina (1969) examines Marcantonio's unorthodox positions and control of the ALP, which Gerald Meyer (1989) describes as a grass-roots organization. Alan Schaffer (1966) sees him as an anomaly of American politics, while Kenneth Walzer (1982) describes the FBI's investigation of the ALP.

THE ELECTION OF 1950

The election of 1950 resulted in the lowest gain for the Republicans in the past three off-year elections. Although the Democrats lost only twenty-eight seats in the House and two in the Senate, the liberal Democratic losses and conservative Republican gains raised questions about whether McCarthyism or Korea was the main factor in the liberals' loss. Francis Thompson (1979), David Kepley (1988), and Ronald Caridi (1968) agree that the liberals' loss was more important than the numbers. The Democrats' Senate majority leader, Scott Lucus, lost to Everett Dirksen in Illinois, majority whip Francis J. Myers lost to moderate Republican James Duff in Pennsylvania, and liberal Democrats lost to Republican conservatives Richard Nixon in California and John Butler in Maryland. Generally liberal Democrats lost to Taft's conservative group, but the literature differs about whether conservative gains were due to McCarthy's charges of disloyalty, the Korean War, or other factors.

The only study devoted solely to the 1950 election is by Richard Fried (1974), who denies that McCarthyism was the significant factor. Fried's research showed that overall, the conservative gains were balanced by the number of moderates who were elected. Fried also explains that the communists-in-government issue had been used in several previous elections and the independent efforts of candidates differed in substance with McCarthy's views. William N. Glazer and William N. McPhee (1962) support this view, concluding that liberals ran better in 1950 than conservatives did and denying McCarthy's importance in the election. Fried cites the studies of Angus Campbell and Homer C. Cooper (1956), Campbell and associates (1960), Alfred De Grazia (1954), Louis Bean (1954), and Samuel A. Stouffer (1955) to support his conclusions.

Although contemporary liberal commentators such as T.R.B. in the *New Republic* (1950) saw McCarthyism as a major issue, the onset of the Korean War during the summer of 1950 pushed McCarthy out of the spotlight. Democrats hoped Korea would terminate accusations that they were "soft on communism" and submerge McCarthy's attacks. By the fall, however the communists-in-government issue was rejuvenated when accused spies such as Moton Sobell and Julius and Ethel Rosenberg were arrested. The public's fears of subversion in government led Congress to override Truman's veto of the Internal Security Act of 1950.

Nevertheless, the Korean War became a factor before the November elections. Although the successful Inchon landing and the UN march into North Korea in October had favored the Democrats, the first Chinese attack on October 27 was only small scale, compared to a later November attack, but it damaged public support for the war. Thus, not only Fried but Athan Theoharis (1970), Gerald Marwell (1967), and Robert Griffith (1970b) conclude that Korea, not McCarthyism, was the overriding issue in 1950.

While Korea and McCarthyism were factors in the 1950 elections, other issues affected particular elections. Joseph G. LaPalombara (1952) and Stanley Kelley, Jr. (1956) indicate the 1950 election saw the medical profession's political influence because of Truman's health insurance proposals. Also, issues of labor, race, civil rights, and economic conservatism influenced local elections.

In Illinois where majority leader Lucas lost, McCarthy campaigned for Dirksen, but the critical factor appears to have been Estes Kefauver's investigation of crime and Chicago's political machine. Although Dirksen and McCarthy berated Lucas for being on the Tydings subcommittee, which "whitewashed" the State Department and the "facts" of communists in government, Lucas noted Dirksen's inconsistent international position, citing his initial support for the Marshall Plan, which Dirksen now said was pouring money down a "rathole." Despite these disputes, the Crime Investigating Committee was significant because Kefauver came to Chicago during the campaign and associated Chicago's Democratic machine with organized crime. Lucas' previous success owed much to the Chicago machine, whose image was damaged just when Lucas needed the Chicago votes. Thus, Neil MacNeil (1970), Edward L. and Frederick H. Schapsmeier (1985), and Richard Fried (1974) find that Kefauver may have hurt Lucas more than McCarthy.

In Pennsylvania, majority whip Myers' loss is largely attributed to Duff's popularity as governor. A moderate Republican, Duff criticized the Democrats for their "socialistic experiments," the Yalta agreements, and the national unpreparedness for Korea, but he avoided McCarthyism. As Fried (1974) and Robert Bendiner (1950) explain, Myers cited his Senate seniority and claimed the Republicans used "communistic tactics and techniques" against opponents, but he did not win with these arguments.

A variety of domestic issues featured the Florida Democratic primary where George Smathers attacked the incumbent, Claude Pepper, for his racial, economic, and foreign policy beliefs. Smathers accused Pepper of being "soft" on communism and published a pamphlet, "The Red Record of Senator Claude Pepper." Although *Time* (1950) saw McCarthyism as the key Florida issue, the studies of Thomas Paterson (1971), Hugh Douglas Price (1955, 1957), Herbert L. Doherty (1952), and Fried (1974) indicate that Pepper's liberal civil rights and economic views cost him the election. Also see Pepper's (1987) memoirs written with Gorey Hays.

In Florida, labor unions supported Pepper, but in Ohio, labor focused on the defeat of its arch-nemesis, Robert Taft. *U.S. News and World Report* (1950b) described Ohio as "organized labor's real showdown of the year." Taft hoped the election would promote his 1952 presidential candidacy, while the Congress of Industrial Organizations' Political Action Committee (CIO-PAC) wanted to end his career. Although the CIO purged its communists, Taft asserted the CIO-PAC "still uses Communist techniques." Taft supporters saw Democrat candidate Homer T. Ferguson as a CIO-PAC puppet, although Ferguson argued that Taft used "communistic tactics in branding labor union leaders and union members as Communists." Both Patterson (1972) and Theoharis (1970) cite the special character of the communist issue in Ohio. Taft won an impressive victory over Ferguson, which Fried (1974) and Fay Calkins (1952) believe was voter resentment of labor and labor's waning power as a political force.

Race played the major role in North Carolina's Democratic primary between incumbent Frank Porter Graham and Willis Smith. Julian Pleasant's and Augusta M. Burns' (1990) study favors Graham's "political liberalism" and "racial enlightenment," although these issues caused his defeat. Despite winning the primary with a 53,000-vote plurality, Graham lacked a majority, and Smith won the runoff election after Smith's supporters published a racist broadside, "White People Wake Up." Both Samuel Lubell (1965) and Taylor McMillan (1959) cite the significance of race in Graham's loss, with Lubell adding middle-class economic conservatism as a factor in some precincts.

McCarthyism had significant effects in the Maryland, California, Utah, and Idaho elections. McCarthy's involvement was most direct in Maryland, where Democratic incumbent Millard Tydings earned McCarthy's hatred as chairman of the special Senate subcommittee whose report denounced as baseless McCarthy's charges of communists in the State Department. McCarthy called the Tydings report a "whitewash" and campaigned for GOP candidate John Marshall Butler with visits, legwork by his Washington staff, and political funds. McCarthy aides published the tabloid "From the Record," which included the campaign's infamous photograph, a "composite photo" showing former U.S. Communist party chairman Earl Browder cheek by jowl with Tydings. Later the Senate Committee on Rules and Administration report (1951) found the picture was in fact a recent photo of Browder spliced with a photo of Tydings listening to 1938 election returns. Despite such attacks, Tydings ignored the reports about McCarthy's effect on the electorate and campaigned on his record of seniority and heavy responsibilities. Thus, McCarthy had a major influence in Maryland even though other factors were present, including the increased Republican activity in Maryland, which Dewey carried in 1948; losses in Korea, blamed on Tydings as chairman of the Armed Services Committee, which "permitted" the nation's "unpreparedness"; African Americans' dislike of Tydings; and the southern Democrats' opposition to civil rights. For works on Maryland politics and the 1950 election, consult John H. Fenton (1957) and Evelyn Wentworth (1959).

In California, McCarthy-style accusations took place in both the Democratic primary and the November election. Democratic representative Helen Gahagan Douglas first faced communist allegations from primary opponent E. Manchester Boddy, who claimed her voting record resembled New York's "communist" representative Vito Marcantonio's. After defeating Boddy, Douglas confronted Republican congressman Richard Nixon. Characterized as a contest between the "Pink Lady" and "Tricky Dick," Nixon denounced Douglas for being pro-communist. In an ugly campaign, Nixon's attacks on Douglas are acknowledged as the reason for his success in accounts by Earl Mazo and Stephen Hess (1968) and by Burton R. Brazil (1951).

Two other elections notable for their anticommunist campaigns were in Utah and Idaho. In the 1950 Utah election, Wallace Bennett attacked Democratic incumbent Elbert Thomas for having "communist" positions on issues and circulated pamphlets that associated Thomas with communist-front organizations. The most effective pamphlet was the *United States Senate News,* which claimed Thomas' foreign policy had Soviet approval and involved Thomas with prominent communist figures. Thomas was also opposed by the Mormon church in a campaign described by Frank H. Jonas (1951, 1957, 1970), the *New Republic* (1950), and Benjamin R. Epstein and Arnold Forster (1970).

The Idaho election was between Democrat D. Worth Clark and Republican Herman Welker after Clark used anticommunist charges to defeat incumbent senator Glen Taylor in the primary. Taylor was susceptible to attacks because he defected from the Democrats in 1948 to become progressive Henry Wallace's vice-presidential candidate. Although similar procommunist charges could not be directed at Clark in the November campaign, Welker's hard-line stance is considered the major factor in his victory. William C. Pratt (1971) describes Taylor's career, while Boyd A. Martin (1951) and Richard Neuberger (1950) describe the Idaho election.

In contrast to its role in four states, McCarthyism was ineffective in Missouri, Connecticut, and West Virginia. In Missouri, Donald J. Kemper (1965), Ernest Kirschten (1950), and Fried (1974) examine the loss by Republican incumbent senator Forrest Donnell to Thomas C. Hennings, Jr. Although McCarthy campaigned for Donnell, a staunch reactionary, Hennings' support of Truman's veto of the McCarran Act and warnings of McCarthyism's danger to American politics assisted Hennings' victory. In the case of Connecticut, Fried (1974) explains that McCarthy visited the state to attack Brien McMahon, who had been a member of the Tydings subcommittee, but McMahon won. In West Virginia, Robert F. Maddox (1981) shows that Democratic senator Harley Kilgore won his third consecutive term despite his opponent's smearing tactics,

To summarize, although Korea and McCarthyism both played a role in the off-year elections of 1950, many issues were at work in various states. As often is the case in congressional elections, the results may depend on local factors in each state.

THE ELECTION OF 1952

The presidential election of 1952 holds a significant place in American history because Dwight Eisenhower's victory affected both major parties. Most important, the Democrats' hold on the Solid South was broken in 1952. In addition, Truman's decision not to run left the Democrats without a clear candidate, and the draft of Adlai Stevenson during the convention may never again be duplicated. For the Republicans, in addition to ending twenty years of Democratic control, Eisenhower's election was a victory for the international wing of the party and modern Republicanism but a setback to the Old Guard's conservatism, which persuaded some members of the right wing to seek other methods to obtain party control, a goal they achieved in 1964. Besides these party shifts, the 1952 election introduced television as a valuable political medium.

Robert Divine's (1974) study of post-1945 elections is an excellent starting point for understanding the Korean War's role in the election. Examining the entire year, Divine concludes that Korea was the major campaign issue. He also indicates that Eisenhower was an able, "instinctive" politician, though not a strategist like twice-Republican candidate Thomas Dewey. John Robert Greene (1985) portrays both Eisenhower and Stevenson as aggressively seeking their nominations, and Hugh A. Bone (1953) surveys state and local elections in twelve western states, finding the West had become as solidly Republican as it was once Democratic. Barton Bernstein (1971c), Eugene H. Roseboom and Alfred Eikes, Jr. (1979), and Robert Blanchard and coworkers (1961) have summary descriptions of the election, with Bernstein's account including both party platforms.

Study about the prenomination activity for each party's 1952 presidential candidates must begin with the five volumes edited by Paul T. David and coworkers (1954), who describes the local primaries and national convention activity, devoting four volumes to each state's primary activity. James W. Davis (1980) has a study of presidential primaries, believing those in 1952 influenced national opinion as well as the party convention. Philip A. Grant (1979b) examines the write-in votes for Eisenhower in Minnesota. Grant also analyzed the New Hampshire (1972) and South Dakota (1977) Republican state primaries and has evaluated Kefauver's Democratic victory in New Hampshire (1972).

Few studies other than Grant's (1972) are devoted to the Democratic primaries, probably because the drafting of Stevenson dominates the scene. Truman met with Stevenson on January 20, 1952, but Stevenson dismissed his candidacy, citing a commitment to be reelected as governor and fearing national exposure could harm his sons. In February, however, Walter Johnson and George Overton organized the Illinois Committee of Stevenson for President whose role Johnson (1955) explains. Despite Stevenson's reluctance, the Illinois Democratic Committee promoted him nationally and gained support of other party leaders. Both Roger Biles (1979) and the Democratic party's (1955) publication describe Stevenson's nomination at the convention and John Sparkman's vice-presidential nomination.

The National Conventions

For both parties, the national conventions became arenas for intraparty ideological conflict. The Democrats struggled to reunite the southern and urban-liberal bloc created by Franklin D. Roosevelt. To obtain unity, the delegates approved a "loyalty pledge" to prevent a Dixiecrat walkout as in 1948, but, following southern protests, the "pledge" was amended to become effective in 1956. Yet the unity Democrats still needed an acceptable candidate.

As the leader in committed convention delegates, Estes Kefauver hoped to be nominated with votes from the liberal majority at the convention, but Averell Harriman also expected the liberal votes. To stop these two candidates, Truman and other organization Democrats joined moderate southerners to draft Stevenson as a consensus nominee who satisfied many liberals and southerners. The organization wheels went to work and obtained a majority of convention votes to "draft" him. Stevenson accepted and further placated the South by naming Senator Sparkman of Alabama as his running mate.

The 1952 Democratic Convention has not been fully studied, but several authors cover some of the convention's events. Everett Collier (1966) details convention chairman Sam Rayburn's possible nomination as a result of the convention's infighting. Richard M. Fried (1970) examines Kefauver's campaign, and Allan P. Spindler (1962) relates the Solid South's decline to the conflicting nominating strategies.

In contrast to the Democrats' sectional battles, the Republican convention was a showdown between two ideological groups: Taft's isolationist, conservative right wing and Eisenhower's internationalist, progressive centrist group. The focus of this conflict became the "fair play" amendment to convention rules proposed by the Eisenhower delegates as a means of delaying the seating of ninety-six contested delegates from Georgia, Louisiana, and Texas. This dispute resulted because these three states sent one group committed to Taft and another group for Eisenhower. In Texas, for example, Eisenhower Republicans and former Democrats who had changed their party membership became the majority at the precinct meetings, where delegates pledged to Eisenhower were selected. The regular Texas organization Republicans objected and held rump sessions to elect Taft delegates. This pro-Taft group expected the Old Guard's Convention Credentials Committee to seat them and reject the pro-Eisenhower delegates.

To counter the Old Guard, moderate Republicans, led by Henry Cabot Lodge, Jr., drew up the fair play amendment to keep the disputed delegates from being seated until the other convention delegates voted to select the credentials of the proper delegations. Aided by the Republican governor's conference endorsement, the convention approved the fair play amendment. Although Taft's members maneuvered to save their candidate, Lodge's ploy worked. Eisenhower's delegates were seated, and on the first roll-call nomination ballot, after Minnesota changed its votes, the former army general won. John Bricker, a Taft delegate, moved to make the vote unanimous.

Eisenhower's role in this nominating process has received divergent interpretations. Although traditional works portray him as secluded in a hotel room surrounded by family and friends while his campaign team maneuvered on the convention floor, other literature casts Eisenhower in an active political role. Henry Cabot Lodge (1973) offers a traditional account of Eisenhower as a reluctant candidate being drafted and the fair play amendment as a "moral" issue. To the contrary, Eisenhower's conservative opponents, such as William P. Hoar (1977) and Medford Evans (1976), see the fair play amendment as anything but fair. Hoar claims Eisenhower "stole" the Republican nomination from Taft through "dirty tricks," and Evans criticizes Eisenhower's nomination for repudiating traditional Republican principles, arguing that Taft's delegates were legitimate. Roger Olien (1973) describes the negative effects the contest had on Republican leaders in Texas, and Leonard Lurie (1971) uses the convention antics to demonstrate that the people are powerless because nominations were decided in backrooms. However, James McGregor Burns (1952) defends the value of backroom deals.

For a summary of both conventions' activities, consult the *Congressional Quarterly*'s (1979) book on party conventions. Emphasizing the southern delegates' role at both conventions, Judith H. Parris (1972) describes the issues and the resulting changes in convention politics. James Davis (1983) describes the historical uniqueness of the Democrats' draft of Stevenson and the fair play amendment's impact on the Republican convention.

One purpose of a national convention is drafting a party platform. Edward F. Cooke (1956) describes each party's platform committee and discusses planks causing conflict at each convention. Kirk H. Porter and Donald Bruce Johnson (1972) reprint the platforms of all major and minor parties having a presidential candidate in all presidential elections. In 1952, these parties were the Democrats, Republicans, Socialist Workers, Socialist Laborites, Socialists, Prohibitionists, and Christian Nationalists.

The Post-convention Campaigns

The presidential campaign was highlighted by Stevenson's rhetoric, which some Republican critics stigmatized by dubbing it "egghead"; by Vice President Richard Nixon's "Checkers" speech to rebuke his accusations of illegal contributions; and by Eisenhower's assertion that he would end the war by going to Korea.

Stevenson's rhetorical skill was especially telling early in the campaign because it contrasted with Eisenhower's hazy, fumbling speeches that led one pro-Eisenhower news editor to complain that "Ike is running like a dry creek." Stevenson also came across well on television, and, as Eric Goldman (1956) noted, TV critic John Crosby wrote that Stevenson was a TV personality "the like of which has never been seen before." Eventually, however, Stevenson's sparkling style was tarnished after pro-Ike columnist Stewart Alsop used the term "egghead" to depict Stevenson's intellectual supporters. Eisenhower's backers turned "egghead" into a sneering word, which conservative novelist Louis Bromfield described as being a pretentious professor who was a "bleeding heart" socialist.

If Stevenson's intelligent rhetoric became a negative factor, Richard Nixon's "Checkers" speech turned charges of unethical practices into sympathetic praise. Seen as one of the most effective uses of television in a political campaign, the "Checkers" speech not only saved Nixon's spot on the Republican ticket but also increased his popularity and political base. Resulting from an inquiry about a fund raised by seventy-five Californian contributors for Nixon's 1950 senatorial election, the disclosure of the fund threatened the Republican ticket with allegations of corruption. On September 23, Nixon defended himself on national television and radio, explaining that the fund was used to cover campaign expenses. Nixon then disclosed all of his income and assets, claiming that the only gift he received was a dog named Checkers, which he refused to take away from his daughters—hence the speech's namesake. After challenging Stevenson and Sparkman to disclose their financial histories, Nixon asked the American people to voice their opinion of whether he should remain on the ticket by contacting the Republican National Committee, an astute maneuver on Nixon's part. By appealing to the national committee, the decision was disassociated from General Eisenhower's having to make a negative decision if the public called for Nixon's removal, while a positive response would increase Nixon's personal political base. As it happened, those who responded overwhelmingly supported Nixon, who remained on the ticket.

Nixon describes the preparations for his television appearance and the surrounding events in *Six Crises* (1962). Stephen Ambrose's (1987) biography discusses the favorable effect that Nixon's speech had on the campaign but also indicates that Nixon cost Eisenhower votes from those Democrats who were repelled by Nixon's attacking style of campaigning. Robert McGuckin (1958) critiques Nixon's speech techniques in convincing voters of his integrity. Nixon's radio speech is printed in *Vital Speeches* (1952).

While Stevenson's rhetoric was stimulating and the Checkers affair interesting, the most crucial campaign event was Eisenhower's dramatic statement that he would seek peace by "going to Korea." Although some advisers had previously suggested a similar statement, Eisenhower selected an October political rally in Detroit to announce how he would end the stalled truce talks in Korea. These negotiations should be speeded up, he told the Detroit crowd, and to do so, "I shall go to Korea" after being elected. The audience cheered wildly, and even Democratic observers said the statement hurt their candidate's chances. Of the three principal Republican campaign slogans—"communism in the government, corruption in the government, and ending the Korean War"—the war appears to have concerned Americans the most.

With these highlights as background, literature evaluating the campaign can be described. Research on Stevenson's campaign usually praises his witty and intelligent speeches, denying the criticism that claimed he spoke over his audiences' heads. But most research is also critical of his campaign's overall management. Stevenson's *Major Campaign Speeches* (1953) and papers edited by Walter Johnson (1973) are primary sources on the campaign. His papers include the essay "Korea in Perspective," which appeared in *Foreign Affairs* (1952). Richard T. Ruetten (1975) reviews the first four volumes of Stevenson's papers, and Alden Whitman (1965) gives impressions of the 1952 campaign environment. James Reston (1952) details Stevenson's campaign travels, while John Bartlow Martin's (1976) biography criticizes many aspects of Stevenson's campaign, such as his spoiling nationwide television appearances by running overtime and spending too much time writing speeches and too little time with voters. Jeff Broadwater (1994) provides an account of Stevenson's political career. Three sympathetic works about Stevenson see Eisenhower's victory as inevitable and defend Stevenson as the needed voice of the liberal conscience: by Kenneth Davis (1967), Porter McKeever (1989), and Edward P. Doyle (1966). Two critical studies of Stevenson and the campaign are by Joseph Epstein (1968) and Rodney Sievers (1973), who both contend Stevenson's beliefs were neither unique nor remarkable.

Postcampaign literature on Eisenhower's candidacy revised the traditional view that Eisenhower was as reluctant to run as Stevenson. In addition to Lodge's (1973) memoirs, there is a traditional account by Joseph M. Dailey (1987). Robert Divine (1981) refutes this view by showing that Eisenhower sought the presidency for some time and exploited the Korean War announcement for political gain. Elmo Richardson (1979) supports Divine, asserting Eisenhower thought of the Korean pledge early in the campaign but waited until other candidates raised the issue. Criticizing the convention's handling of the Texas delegation, Peter Lyon (1974) also depicts Eisenhower as an able politician. Stephen Ambrose (1983–1984) views Eisenhower as a dominating personality during the campaign, and Cabell Phillips (1966) gives a liberal's critique of the campaign. Robert Griffith (1970a) examines Eisenhower's relationship with McCarthy while campaigning in Wisconsin. In addition, works about Eisenhower's campaign advisers include Steve M. Barkin's (1987) on *New York Herald-Tribune* publisher William Robinson who developed Eisenhower's campaign strategy, and Robert Bishop's (1966) on Bruce Barton who was Eisenhower's "stage manager." The public relations director for the Republican National Committee, Richard Guylay (1987), also offers insights on Eisenhower's campaign.

Detailed studies on the 1952 campaign have been based on information at the Survey Research Center of the University of Michigan. Using this database, Angus Campbell and associates (1960) concluded that Eisenhower's personality had the greatest effect on the electorate but the communism-in-government issue was less vital than campaign rhetoric suggests. In *The Voter Decides,* Campbell and associates (1954) attribute the Republican victory to their mobilization of party regulars, previous nonvoters, and former Democrats. In their larger work, Campbell and associates (1966) examine this mobilization more fully, classifying the 1952 election results as a "deviating election" because temporary forces defeated the majority party. James R. Beniger (1976) classifies Kefauver's defeat at the Democratic convention as a "deviating election" because he led in committed delegates when the convention began.

Many political science studies use the 1952 election as a focus of study. Bernard R. Berelson and Paul F. Layersfield (1954) include the 1952 election in studying the electorate's voting behavior. James C. Davies (1954) uses Eisenhower and Stevenson to study charisma's effect on voting behavior. Heinz Eulau (1962) compares the influence of party and class on the 1952 and 1956 elections, concluding each had elements of stabilization, not disruption, in the political system. Donald Stokes and associates (1958) studied voting factors and attributed Eisenhower's victory to his popularity, voter support of Republican foreign policy, and voter disapproval of Democratic management of government.

Because Eisenhower's victories in Florida, Tennessee, Texas, and Virginia indicated increased Republican activity in the South, which ended the Solid South, three important articles analyze the southern change. Philip Grant (1990) and James Sweeney (1978) examine the impact that Senator Harry Byrd's rejection of Stevenson had on the Virginia electorate. Grant concludes that Eisenhower's victory made the Republicans a true political force in Virginia. Sweeney emphasizes that Byrd opposed Stevenson and Truman because they both accepted the ideology of the New Deal that Byrd rejected. Allen Spindler (1962) explains that the Democrats' "loyalty pledge" caused many southern defections and damaged the Democrats in the South. Historians will note that any analysis of southern party developments must consider the influence of the 1954 school desegregation decision of the U.S. Supreme Court.

A unique aspect of the 1952 election was television's arrival into the political arena. With the three major networks broadcasting gavel-to-gavel coverage of both conventions and each candidate utilizing TV in his campaign, television became a primary technology for elections. Each party employed different strategies for this new political medium. The Democrats hired ad man Joseph Katz to orchestrate their television campaign, while the Republicans had three public relations organizations for their campaign: the B.B.D. & O. advertising group for television and radio; the

Kudner advertising firm for print media; and the Ted Bates Company for spot ads. The parties also differed in scheduling television ads. The Democrats bought eighteen half-hour time slots for televised speeches broadcast early in the campaign when rates were cheaper because they wanted to increase voter recognition of Stevenson. In contrast, the Republicans paid the extra costs of preempting top-rated TV shows, hoping the large audiences would stay tuned since few top shows ran at the same time. Both candidates garnered respectable audiences and relied increasingly on television as the campaign progressed, culminating when the final two hours of election eve TV were filled by political programs.

In its fledgling stage, television's effect on the electorate has received frequent study. Ithiel De Sola Pool (1959) demonstrates the 1952 election's uniqueness in distinguishing information available to TV viewers from nonviewers because designated areas of the United States did not yet receive television broadcasts. Comparing these two groups, Pool concludes television helped to "humanize" Eisenhower and acquainted more voters with Stevenson. Pool also notes that Stevenson came across best on radio. Edward W. Chester's (1969) examination of television and radio's effects finds radio remained the more important political medium in 1952.

Eisenhower's television political spot ads were a campaign innovation used in all subsequent presidential elections. Stephen C. Wood (1990) aspires to correct the misperceptions of previous studies about Eisenhower's spot ad campaign, arguing that the spot ad was "vital and successful" to the Republicans' campaign strategy. John Holitz (1982) indicates that Eisenhower's spot ad campaign ensured television's role in future elections, and Stanley Kelley, Jr. (1956) describes Eisenhower's election eve programs. Although television was the new technology of the media, Nathan B. Blumberg (1954) provides an account of press coverage of the election in thirty-five daily newspapers.

For a study of all candidates' expenditures during the campaign, refer to Alexander Heard (1962). Heard explains the intricacies of political funding and the individual expenses of each candidate, comparing them with expenses for the election of 1956. Jasper Shannon (1959) describes the amounts spent in election primaries as part of the political process.

REFERENCES

Abels, Jules. *The Truman Scandals.* Chicago: Regnery, 1956.

Acheson, Dean. *Present at the Creation: My Years in the State Department.* New York: New American Library, 1969.

Acheson, Dean, and Arthur H. Vandenberg, Jr., "From Doubt to Leadership: Senator Arthur Vandenberg." In James D. Barber, comp., *Political Leadership in American Government,* pp. 67–83. Boston: Little, Brown, 1964.

Adams, Walter, and Horace Gray. *Monopoly in America: The Government as Promoter.* New York: Macmillan, 1955.

Altmeyer, Arthur J. *The Formative Years of Social Security.* Madison: University of Wisconsin Press, 1968

Ambrose, Stephen E. *Eisenhower.* 2 vols. New York: Simon and Schuster, 1983–1984.

———. *Nixon: Education of a Politician, 1913–1962.* New York: Simon and Schuster, 1987.

Anderson, Clinton P., with Milton Viorst. *Outsider in the Senate: Senator Clinton Anderson's Memoirs.* New York: World Publishing Co., 1970.

Armstrong, John P. "The Enigma of Senator Taft and American Foreign Policy." *Review of Politics* 17:2 (1955): 206–231.

Baker, Richard A. *Conservation Politics: The Senate Career of Clinton P. Anderson.* Albuquerque: University of New Mexico Press, 1985.

Barber, James D., comp. *Political Leadership in American Government.* Boston: Little, Brown, 1964.

Barkin, Steve M. "Eisenhower's Secret Strategy: Television Planning in the 1952 Campaign." *Journal of Advertising History* 9 (1986): 18–28.

———. "Eisenhower and Robinson: The Candidate and the Publisher in the 1952 Campaign." In Joann P. Krieg, ed., *Dwight D. Eisenhower,* pp. 11–19. Westport, CT: Greenwood, 1987.

Bartley, Numan V. *From Thurmond to Wallace.* Baltimore: Johns Hopkins University Press, 1970.

Bass, Jack, and Walter DeVries. *The Transformation of Southern Politics: Social Change and Political Consequences.* New York: Basic Books, 1976.

Bean, Louis. *Influences in the 1954 Mid-Term Elections: War, Jobs, Parity, McCarthy.* Washington, DC: Public Affairs Institute, 1954.

Bell, Daniel. "The Subversion of Collective Bargaining." *Commentary* 29 (1960): 185–197.

Bendiner, Robert. "Anything Goes in Pennsylvania." *Nation,* October 28, 1950, p. 386.

Beniger, James R. "Winning the Presidential Nomination: National Polls and State Primary Elections, 1937–1962." *Public Opinion* 40 (1976): 22–38.

Berelson, Bernard R., and Paul F. Layersfield. *Voting: A Study of Opinion Formation in a Presidential Campaign.* Chicago: University of Chicago Press, 1954.

Berger, Henry. "A Conservative Critique of Containment: Senator Taft on the Early Cold War Program." In David Horowitz, ed., *Containment and Revolution.* Boston: Beacon, 1971a.

———. "Senator Robert A. Taft Dissents from Military Escalation." In Thomas G. Paterson, ed., *Cold War Critics: Alternatives to American Foreign Policy in the Truman Years.* Chicago: Quadrangle Books, 1971b.

Berman, William. *The Politics of Civil Rights in the Truman Administration.* Columbus, OH: Ohio State University Press, 1970.

Bernstein, Barton J. "The Removal of War Production Controls on Business, 1944–1946." *Business History Review* 39 (Summer 1965): 243–260.

———. "America in War and Peace: The Test of Liberalism." In Barton Bernstein, *Towards a New Past: Dissenting Essays in American History.* New York: Vintage Books, 1967a.

———. "Reluctance and Resistance: Wilson Wyatt and Veterans' Housing in the

Truman Administration." *Register of the Kentucky Historical Society* 65 (January 1967b): 47–66.

———. "Election of 1952." In Arthur M. Schlesinger, Jr., and Fred L. Israel, eds., *History of American Presidential Elections, 1789–1968.* Vol. 4. New York: Chelsea House, 1971c.

Biles, Roger. "Jacob M. Arvey, Kingmaker: The Nomination of Adlai E. Stevenson in 1952." *Chicago History* 8 (1979): 130–143.

Bishop, Robert L. "Bruce Barton—Presidential State Manager." *Journalism Quarterly* 43 (1966): 85–89.

Blair, John M. *The Control of Oil.* New York: Pantheon Books, 1976.

Blanchard, Robert, Richard Meyer, and Blaine Morley. *Presidential Elections, 1948–1960.* Research Monograph 4. Salt Lake City: Institute of Government, University of Utah, 1961.

Block, Fred. "Economic Instability and Military Strength: The Paradox of the 1950 Rearmament Decision." *Politics and Society* 10:1 (1980): 35–58.

Blumberg, Nathan B. *One Party Press? Coverage of the 1952 Presidential Campaign in 35 Daily Newspapers.* Lincoln: University of Nebraska Press, 1954.

Bond, Jon R., and Richard Fleischer. "Are There Two Presidencies? Yes, But Only for Republicans." *Journal of Politics* 50 (1985): 747–767.

———. "Presidential Popularity and Congressional Voting: A Reexamination of Public Opinion as a Source of Influence in Congress." *Western Political Quarterly* 37 (1984): 291–306.

———. *The President in the Legislative Arena.* Chicago: University of Chicago Press, 1990.

Bone, Hugh A. "Western Politics and the 1952 Elections." *Western Political Quarterly* 6 (1953): 93–99.

Brazil, Burton R. "The 1950 Elections in California." *Western Political Quarterly* 4 (March 1951): 67.

Broadwater, Jeff. *Adlai Stevenson and American Politics: The Odyssey of a Cold War Liberal.* New York: Twayne, 1994.

Brock, Clifton. *Americans for Democratic Action: Its Role in National Politics.* Washington, DC: Public Affairs Press, 1962.

Brown, Deward C. "The Sam Rayburn Papers: A Preliminary Investigation." *American Archives* 35 (1972): 331–336.

Brune, Lester H. "Guns and Butter: The Pre-Korean War Dispute over Budget Allocation." *American Journal of Economics and Sociology* 48:3 (July 1989): 357–372.

Bulletin of Atomic Science, ed. "Did the Soviet Bomb Come Sooner Than Expected?" 5 (October 1949): 262–264.

Bundy, McGeorge. "The Private World of Robert Taft." *Reporter,* December 11, 1951, pp. 37–39.

Burns, James MacGregor. "The Case for the Smoke-Filled Room." *New York Times Magazine,* June 15, 1952, p. 144–150.

———. *The Deadlock of Democracy: Four-Party Politics in America.* Englewood Cliffs, NJ: Prentice-Hall, 1963.

———. *Presidential Government: The Crucible of Leadership in America.* Englewood Cliffs, NJ: Prentice-Hall, 1965.

Calkins, Fay. *The CIO and the Democratic Party*. Chicago: University of Chicago Press, 1952.

Campbell, Angus, and Homer C. Cooper. *Group Difference in Attitudes and Votes: A Study of the 1954 Congressional Election*. Ann Arbor, MI: Survey Research Center, Institute for Social Research, University of Michigan, 1956.

Campbell, Angus, Philip E. Converse, Warren E. Miller, and Donald E. Stokes. *The American Voter*. New York: John Wiley & Sons, 1960.

Campbell, Angus, et. al. *Elections and the Political Order*. New York: Wiley, 1966.

Campbell, Angus, Gerald Gurin, and Warren E. Miller. *The Voter Decides*. Evanston, IL: Row, Peterson, 1954.

Caridi, Ronald J. "The G.O.P. and the Korean War." *Pacific Historical Review* 37:4 (1968): 423–443.

———. *The Korean War and American Politics: The Republican Party as a Case Study*. Philadelphia: University of Pennsylvania Press, 1969.

Carpenter, Ted Galen. "United States' NATO Policy at the Crossroads: The 'Great Debate' of 1950–1951." *International History Review* 8:3 (August 1986): 345–516.

Cater, Douglas. "Senator Styles Bridges and His Far-Flung Constituents." In Max Ascoli, ed., *Our Times: The Best from Reporter*, pp. 280–309. New York: Farrar, Strauss and Cudaky, 1960.

Champagne, Anthony. *Sam Rayburn: A Bio-Bibliography*. Westport, CT: Greenwood Press, 1988.

Chester, Edward W. *Radio, Television, and American Politics*. New York: Sheed and Ward, 1969.

Christenson, Reo. *The Brannan Plan*. Ann Arbor: University of Michigan Press, 1959.

Clayton, James L. *The Economic Impact of the Cold War*. New York: Harcourt, Brace and World, 1970.

Cochran, Bert. *Labor and Communism: The Conflict That Shaped American Unions*. Princeton, NJ: Princeton University Press, 1977.

Coffin, Tristram. *Senator Fulbright: Portrait of a Public Philosopher*. New York: Dutton, 1966.

Collier, Everett. "Rayburn for President? A Footnote to the 1952 Elections." *Texas Quarterly* 9 (1966): 102–106.

Collins, Robert. *The Business Response to Keynes, 1929–1964*. New York: Columbia University Press, 1981.

Congressional Quarterly. *Almanac 81st–83rd Congress—1948–1953*. Vols. 7–9. Washington, DC: Congressional Quarterly News Features, 1950–1953.

———. *Congress and the Nation: A Review of Government and Politics in the Postwar Years*. Washington, DC: Congressional Quarterly, 1965.

———. *National Party Conventions, 1831–1976*. Washington, DC: Congressional Quarterly, 1979.

Connally, Tom. *My Name Is Tom Connally*. New York: Crowell, 1954.

Cook, Fred J. *The Warfare State*. New York: Macmillan, 1962.

Cooke, Edward F. "Drafting the 1952 Platforms." *Western Political Quarterly* 9 (September 1956).

Cope, Richard. "Kenneth Wherry, Negativist from Nebraska." *Reporter*, April 17, 1951, pp. 4–10.

Cortada, James W. *A Bibliographic Guide to Spanish Diplomatic History, 1460–1977.* Westport, CT: Greenwood Press, 1977.

————. *Two Nations over Time: Spain and the United States, 1776–1977.* Westport, CT: Greenwood Press, 1978.

————, ed. *Spain in the Twentieth-Century World: Essays on Spanish Diplomacy, 1898–1978.* Westport, CT: Greenwood Press, 1980.

Craig, Richard B. *The Bracero Program: Interest Groups and Foreign Policy.* Austin, TX: University of Texas Press, 1971.

Dailey, Joseph M. "The Reluctant Candidate: Dwight D. Eisenhower in 1951." In Joann P. Krieg, ed., *Dwight D. Eisenhower,* pp. 1–10. Westport, CT: Greenwood Press, 1987.

David, Paul T., Ralph M. Goldman, and Richard C. Bain. *The Politics of National Party Conventions.* 5 vols. Washington, DC: Brookings Institution, 1954.

Davidson, Roger H., Donald Bacon, and Morton Keller. *Encyclopedia of the United States Congress.* 4 vols. New York: Simon and Schuster, 1995.

Davidson, Roger H., and Richard A. Baker, eds. *First among Equals: Outstanding Senate Leaders of the Twentieth Century.* Washington, DC: Congressional Quarterly, 1991.

Davidson, Roger H., and Richard C. Sachs. *Understanding Congress: Research Perspectives.* Washington, DC: U.S. Government Printing Office, 1991.

Davies, James C. "Charisma in the 1952 Campaign." *American Political Science Review* 48 (1954): 1083–1102.

Davies, Richard. *Housing Reforms under the Truman Administration.* Columbia, MD: University of Missouri Press, 1966.

Davis, James W. *Presidential Primaries: Road to the White House.* Westport, CT: Greenwood Press, 1980.

————. *National Conventions in an Age of Party Reform.* Westport, CT: Greenwood Press, 1983.

Davis, Kenneth S. *The Politics of Honor: A Biography of Adlai E. Stevenson.* New York: Putnam, 1967.

De Grazia, Alfred. *The Western Public: 1952 and Beyond.* Stanford, CA: Stanford University Press, 1954.

Democratic Party, National Convention, Chicago, 1952. *Official Report of the Proceedings . . . Chicago, Illinois, July 21 to July 26, Inclusive, 1952, Resulting in the Nomination of Adlai E. Stevenson of Illinois for President and the Nomination of John J. Sparkman of Alabama for Vice-President.* Washington, DC: Democratic National Committee, 1955.

Dirksen, Louella, with Norma Lee Browning. *The Honorable Mr. Marigold: My Life with Everett Dirksen.* Garden City, NY: Doubleday, 1972.

Divine, Robert A. "The Cold War and the Election of 1948." *Journal of American History* 59 (1972): 90–110.

————. *Foreign Policy and U.S. Presidential Elections, 1952–1960.* New York: New Viewpoints, 1974.

————. *Eisenhower and the Cold War.* New York: Oxford University Press, 1981.

Doherty, Herbert L. "Liberal and Conservative Voting Patterns in Florida." *Journal of Politics* 14 (August 1952): 413–414.

Donovan, Richard, and Douglas Cater. "Of Gambling, a Senator, and a *Sun* That Wouldn't Set." *Reporter,* June 9, 1953, pp. 25–30.

Donovan, Robert J. *Tumultuous Years: The Presidency of Harry S. Truman, 1949–1953,* New York: Norton, 1982.

Douglas, Paul H. *In the Fullness of Time: The Memoirs of Paul H. Douglas.* New York: Harcourt Brace Jovanovich, 1972.

Doyle, Edward P. *As We Knew Adlai.* New York: Harper & Row, 1966.

Edwards, James E. *Pat McCarran, Political Boss of Nevada.* Reno, NV: University of Nevada Press, 1982.

Edwards, Lee. *Missionary for Freedom: The Life and Times of Walter Judd.* New York: Paragon House, 1990.

Engler, Robert. *The Politics of Oil: A Study of Private Power and Democratic Direction.* Chicago: University of Chicago Press, 1961.

———. *The Brotherhood of Oil.* Chicago: University of Chicago Press, 1977.

Eisele, Albert. *Almost to the Presidency: A Biography of Two American Politicians.* Blue Earth, MN: Piper, 1972.

Epstein, Benjamin R., and Arnold Forster. *The Trouble-Makers.* Westport, CT: Negro Universities Press, 1970.

Epstein, Joseph. "Adlai Stevenson in Retrospect." *Commentary* 46 (1968): 71–83.

Eulau, Heinz. *Class and Party in the Eisenhower Years: Class Roles and Perspectives in the 1952 and 1956 Elections.* New York: Free Press of Glencoe, 1962.

Evans, Medford. "The 1952 Republican Convention." *American Opinion* 19:9 (October 1976): 23–35.

Evans, Rowland, and Robert Novak. *Lyndon B. Johnson: The Exercise of Power.* New York: New American Library, 1966.

Fenton, John. *Politics in the Border States: A Study of the Patterns of Political Organization, and Political Change, Common to the Border States—Maryland, West Virginia, Kentucky and Missouri.* New Orleans, LA: Hauser, 1957.

Fetzer, James. "Senator Vandenberg and the American Commitment to China, 1945–1950." *Historian* 36 (February 1974): 283–303.

Fisher, Louis. *Constitutional Conflict between Congress and the President.* Princeton, NJ: Princeton University Press, 1985.

Fite, Gilbert C. *Richard B. Russell, Jr.: Senator from Georgia.* Chapel Hill, NC: University of North Carolina Press, 1991.

Flash, Edward S., Jr. *Economic Advice and Presidential Leadership: The Council of Economic Advisers.* New York: Columbia University Press, 1965.

Fontenay, Charles L. *Estes Kefauver: A Biography.* Knoxville, TN: University of Tennessee Press, 1981.

Foot, Rosemary. *The Wrong War.* Ithaca, NY: Cornell University Press, 1985.

Freeman, Ralph, ed. *Postwar Economic Trends in the United States.* New York: Harper, 1960.

Fried, Richard M. "Electoral Politics and McCarthyism: The 1950 Campaign." In Robert Griffith and Athan Theoharis, *The Specter: Original Essays on the Cold War and the Origins of McCarthyism.* New York: New Viewpoints, 1974.

Fried, Richard M., ed. "Fighting Words Never Delivered: Proposed Draft of Senator Kefauver's Acceptance Speech." *Tennessee Historical Quarterly* 29 (1970): 176–183.

Fullington, Michael G. "Presidential Management and Executive Scandals." *Presidential Studies Quarterly* 9 (1979): 192–202.

Galbraith, John Kenneth. *The Affluent Society.* Boston: Houghton, Mifflin, 1958; 2d ed. rev., 1969.

Galbraith, John Kenneth, et al. (symposium). "Fundamental Characteristics of the American Economy: Degrees of Competition, of Monopoly, and of Countervailing Power." *American Economic Review* 44 (May 1954): 1–34.

Garson, Robert A. *The Democratic Party and the Politics of Sectionalism, 1941–1948.* Baton Rouge, LA: Louisiana State University Press, 1974.

Gazell, James A. "Arthur Vandenberg, Internationalism, and the United Nations." *Political Science Quarterly* 88 (1973): 375–394.

Gelfand, Mark I. *A Nation of Cities: The Federal Government and Urban America, 1933–1965.* New York: Oxford University Press, 1975.

Gillon, Steven M. *Politics and Vision: The ADA and American Liberalism, 1947–1985.* New York: Oxford University Press, 1987.

Glazer, William A., and William N. McPhee, eds. *Public Opinion and Congressional Elections.* New York: Free Press of Glencoe, 1962.

Gleason, Philip. "Blurring the Line of Separation: Education, Civil Rights, and Teaching about Religion." *Journal of Church and State* 19 (1977): 517–538.

Goldman, Eric F. *The Crucial Decade: America 1945–55.* New York: Knopf, 1956.

Goodno, Floyd R. "Walter H. Judd: Spokesman for China in the United States House of Representatives." Ed.D. dissertation, Oklahoma State University, 1970.

Goodwin, Craufurd D., and R. Stanley Herren. *Exhortation and Controls: The Search for a Wage-Price Policy.* Washington, DC: Brookings Institution, 1975.

Gorman, Joseph Bruce. *Kefauver: A Political Biography.* New York: Oxford University Press, 1971.

Graham, Otis. *Toward a Planned Society: From Roosevelt to Nixon.* New York: Oxford University Press, 1976.

Grant, Philip A. "Kefauver and the New Hampshire Presidential Primary." *Tennessee Historical Quarterly* 31 (1972a): 372–380.

———. "The 1952 New Hampshire Presidential Primary: A Press Reaction." *Historical New Hampshire* 27 (1972b): 210–233.

———. "Editorial Reaction to the 1952 Presidential Candidacy of Richard B. Russell." *Georgia Historical Quarterly* 57 (1973): 167–178.

———. "The 1952 Republican Presidential Primary." *South Dakota History* 8 (1977): 46–58.

———. "Catholic Congressmen, Cardinal Spellman, Eleanor Roosevelt, and the 1949–1950 Federal Aid to Education Controversy." *Records of the American Catholic Historical Society of Philadelphia* 90 (1979a): 3–14.

———. "The 1952 Minnesota Republican Primary and the Eisenhower Candidacy." *Presidential Studies Quarterly* 9 (1979b): 311–315.

———. "Eisenhower and the 1952 Invasion of the South: The Case of Virginia." *Presidential Studies Quarterly* 20 (1990): 285–293.

Greene, John Robert. *The Crusade: The Presidential Election of 1952.* Lanham, MD: University Press of America, 1985.

Griffith, Robert. "The General and the Senator: Republican Politics and the 1952 Campaign in Wisconsin." *Wisconsin Magazine of History* 54 (1970a): 23–29.

———. *The Politics of Fear: Joseph R. McCarthy and the Senate.* Lexington, KY: University of Kentucky, 1970b.

————. "Old Progressives and the Cold War." *Journal of American History* 66:2 (September 1979): 334–347.

Griffith, Winthrop. *Humphrey, A Candid Biography.* New York: Morrow, 1965.

Guylay, L. Richard. "Eisenhower's Two Presidential Campaigns, 1952 and 1956." In Joann P. Krieg, ed., *Dwight D. Eisenhower,* pp. 21–30. Westport, CT: Greenwood Press, 1987.

Hamby, Alonzo L. "The Liberals, Truman, and FDR as Symbol and Myth." *Journal of American History* 56 (1970): 859–867.

————. "The Vital Center, the Fair Deal, and the Quest for a Liberal Political Economy." *American Historical Review* 77 (June 1972): 653–678.

————. *Beyond the New Deal: Harry S. Truman and American Liberalism.* New York: Columbia University Press, 1973.

————, ed. *Harry S. Truman and the Fair Deal.* Lexington, MA: D. C. Heath, 1974.

Hardeman, D. B., and Donald C. Bacon. *Rayburn: A Biography.* Austin, TX: Texas Monthly Press, 1987.

Harper, Alan D. *The Politics of Loyalty: The White House and the Communist Issue, 1946–1952.* Westwood, CT: Greenwood Press, 1969.

Hartmann, Susan M. *Truman and the 80th Congress.* Columbia, MO: University of Missouri Press, 1971.

Hasenfus, William A. "Managing Partner: Joseph W. Martin, Jr., Republican Leader of the United States House of Representatives, 1939–1959." Ph.D. dissertation, Boston College, 1986.

Hawkins, Gordon. "God and the Mafia." *Public Interest* (1969): 24–51.

Hayek, Freidrich. *Road to Serfdom.* Chicago: University of Chicago Press, 1944.

Heard, Alexander. *The Cost of Democracy: Financing American Political Campaigns.* Garden City, NY: Doubleday, 1962.

Heller, Francis H., ed. *The Korean War: A 25-Year Perspective.* Lawrence, KS: Regents Press of Kansas, 1977.

————, ed. *Economics and the Truman Administration.* Lawrence, KS: Regents Press of Kansas, 1981.

Herken, Gregg. *The Winning Weapon: The Atomic Bomb in the Cold War.* New York: Knopf, 1981.

Herzstein, Robert E. *Henry R. Luce: A Political Portrait of the Man Who Created the American Century.* New York: Charles Scribner's Sons, 1994.

Hickman, Bert. *The Korean War and United States Economic Activity, 1950–1952.* New York: National Bureau of Economic Research, 1955.

————. *Growth and Stability of the Postwar Economy.* Washington, D.C.: Brookings Institution, 1960.

Hitch, Charles, and Roland N. McKean. *The Economics of Defense in the Nuclear Age.* Cambridge, MA: Harvard University Press, 1960.

Hoar, William P. "Presidential Atrocities." *American Opinion* 20 (September 1977): 11–16.

Hogan, Michael J. "Corporatism: A Positive Appraisal." *Diplomatic History* 10 (Fall 1986): 363–372.

Holitz, John E. "Eisenhower and the Admen: The Television 'Spot' Campaign of 1952." *Wisconsin Magazine of History* 66 (1982): 25–39.

Holman, Frank E. *Story of the "Bricker" Amendment.* New York: Committee for Constitutional Government, 1954.

Holmans, A. E. *United States Fiscal Policy, 1945–1959.* New York: Oxford University Press, 1964.

Hoyt, Edwin C. "The United States Reaction to the Korean Attack: A Study of the Principles of the UN Charter as a Factor in American Policy-Making." *American Journal of International Law* 55:1 (January 1961): 45–76.

Huitt, Ralpk K. "The Morse Committee Assignment Controversy: A Study of Senate Norms." *American Political Science Review* 51 (1957): 313–329.

———. "Democratic Party Leadership in the Senate." *American Political Science Review* 55 (June 1961): 331–344.

Ickes, Harold. "Diplomacy with an Ax." *New Republic,* December 3, 1951, p. 17.

Jacob, Kathryn, and Elizabeth Ann Hornyak. *Guide to Research Collections of Former United States Senators, 1789–1982.* Washington, DC: Historical Office, United States Senate, 1983.

Johnson, Haynes B., and Bernard M. Gwertzman. *Fulbright: The Dissenter.* Garden City, NY: Doubleday, 1968.

Johnson, Walter. *How We Drafted Adlai Stevenson: Story of the Democratic Presidential Convention of 1952.* New York: Knopf, 1955.

———, ed. *The Papers of Adlai Stevenson.* Vol 3: *Governor of Illinois, 1949–1953.* Boston: Little, Brown, 1973.

Jonas, Frank H. "The 1950 Elections in Utah." *Western Political Quarterly* 4 (March 1951): 83, 88–90.

———. "The Art of Political Dynamiting." *Western Political Quarterly* 10 (June 1957): 374–378.

———. "Setting the Stage for the Political Dynamiter." In Frank H. Jonas, ed., *Political Dynamiting.* Salt Lake City, UT: University of Utah Press, 1970.

Jones, Charles O. *The Presidency in a Separated System.* Washington, DC: Brookings Institution, 1994.

Judd, Walter H., "The Mistakes That Led to Korea." *Reader's Digest* 57:343 (November 1950): 51.

Judd, Walter H., with Edward J. Rozek, ed. *Walter H. Judd: Chronicles of a Statesman.* Denver: Grier and Co., 1980.

Kampelman, Max. *The Communist Party vs. the C.I.O.: A Study in Power Politics.* New York: Praeger, 1957.

Kaplan, A. D. H. *Big Enterprise in a Competitive System.* Rev. ed. Washington, DC: Brookings Institution, 1964.

Kaplan, Lawrence. *The United States and NATO: The Formative Years.* Lexington, KY: University of Kentucky Press, 1984.

Katznelson, Ira, Kim Geiger, and Daniel Kryder. "Limiting Liberalism: The Southern Veto in Congress, 1933–1950." *Political Science Quarterly* 108 (Summer 1993): 283–306.

Kaufman, Burton I. "Oil and Antitrust: The Oil Cartel Case and the Cold War." *Business History Review* 51 (1977): 35–56.

———. *The Oil Cartel Case: A Documentary Study of Antitrust Activity in the Cold War.* Westport, CT: Greenwood Press, 1978.

Kaufman, Natalie H. *Human Rights Treaties and the Senate: A History of Opposition.* Chapel Hill, NC: University of North Carolina, 1990.

Keezer, Dexter Merriman, et al. "The Effectiveness of the Federal Antitrust Laws." *American Economic Review* 39 (June 1949): 689–724.

Kefauver, Estes. *Crime in America.* Garden City, NY: Doubleday, 1951.

Kelley, Stanley. *Professional Public Relations and Political Power.* Baltimore, MD: Johns Hopkins Press, 1966; 1st ed., 1956.

Kemper, Donald J., S.J. *Decade of Fear: Senator Hennings and Civil Liberties.* Columbia, MO: University of Missouri Press, 1965.

Kennedy, Paul M. *The Rise and Fall of the Great Powers.* New York: Random House, 1987.

Kepley, David R. "The Senate and the Great Debate of 1951." *Prologue* 14 (Winter 1982): 213–226.

————. *The Collapse of the Middle Way: Senate Republicans and the Bipartisan Foreign Policy, 1948–52.* Westport, CT: Greenwood Press, 1988.

Key, Vladimer O., Jr. *Southern Politics in State and Nation.* New York: Knopf, 1949.

————. *The Responsible Electorate: Rationality in Presidential Voting, 1936–1960.* New York: Vintage Books, 1966.

Keyserling, Leon. "Deficiencies of Past Programs and the Nature of New Needs." In Seymour Harris, ed., *Saving American Capitalism.* New York: Alfred Knopf, 1948.

Kirk, Russell, and James McClellan. *The Political Principles of Robert A. Taft.* New York: Fleet Press, 1967.

Kirkendall, Richard S. "Harry S. Truman." In Morton Borden, ed., *America's Eleven Greatest Presidents,* pp. 255–288 Chicago: Rand McNally, 1971.

————, ed. *The Truman Period as a Research Field: A Reappraisal, 1972.* Columbia, MO: University of Missouri 1974.

Kirschten, Ernest. "Donnell Luck and Missouri Scandal." *Nation,* October 14, 1950, pp. 332–333.

Kirstein, Peter N. "Agribusiness, Labor, and the Wetbacks: Truman's Commission on Migratory Labor." *Historian* 40 (August 1978): 650–667.

Kizer, George A. "Federal Aid to Education, 1945–1963." *History of Education Quarterly* 10 (1970): 84–102.

Koen, Ross Y. *The China Lobby in American Politics.* New York: Octagon Books, 1974.

Koenig, Louis W. "Foreign Aid to Spain and Yugoslavia: Harry Truman Does His Duty." In Alan F. Westin, ed., *The Uses of Power,* pp. 73–116. New York: Harcourt, Brace and World, 1962.

Kogan, Herman. "Illinois: A Sorry Choice." *Nation,* October 21, 1950, p. 363.

Lacey, Michael, ed. *The Truman Presidency.* New York: Cambridge University Press, 1989.

Lachman, Seymour P. "The Cardinal, the Congressman, and the First Lady." *Journal of Church and State* 7 (1965): 35–66.

LaFeber, Walter. "Crossing the 38th: The Cold War in Microcosm." In Lynn H. Miller and Ronald W. Pruessen, eds., *Reflections on the Cold War.* Philadelphia, PA: Temple University Press, 1974.

————. "NATO and the Korean War: A Context." *Diplomatic History* 13:4 (Fall 1989): 461–478.

LaGumina, Salvatore J. *Vito Marcantonio: The People's Politician.* Dubuque, IA: Kendall/Hunt, 1969.

LaPalombara, Joseph G. "Pressure, Propaganda, and Political Action in the Elections of 1950." *Journal of Politics* 14 (May 1952): 308–309.

Larson, Arthur. *A Republican Looks at His Party.* New York: Harper, 1956.

Leary, William Matthew, Jr. "Smith of New Jersey: A Biography of H. Alexander Smith, United States Senator from New Jersey, 1949–1959." Ph.D. dissertation, Princeton University, 1966.

LeBlanc, Lawrence J. *The United States and the Genocide Convention.* Durham, NC: Duke University Press, 1991.

Lee, R. Alton. "The Army 'Mutiny' of 1946." *Journal of American History* 53 (December 1966): 555–571.

———. *Truman and Taft-Hartley: A Question of Mandate.* Lexington, KY: University of Kentucky Press, 1966; reprint, Westport, CT: Greenwood Press, 1980.

Lekachman, Robert. *The Age of Keynes.* New York: McGraw-Hill, 1975.

Levantrosser, William F., ed. *Harry S. Truman: The Man from Independence.* Westport, CT: Greenwood Press, 1986.

Linn, Erwin R. "The Influence of Liberalism and Conservatism on Voting Behavior." *Public Opinion Quarterly* 13 (Summer 1949): 299–309.

Lodge, Henry Cabot. *The Storm Has Many Eyes: A Personal Narrative.* New York: Norton, 1973.

Lowi, Theodore J. "Bases in Spain." In Harold Stein, ed., *American Civil-Military Decisions,* pp. 666–702. University, AL: University of Alabama Press, 1963.

Lowry, W. McNeil. "Douglas of Illinois, Liberal with a Difference." *Reporter,* April 17, 1951, pp. 4–10.

Lubell, Samuel. *The Future of American Politics.* New York: Harper Colophon, 1965.

Lurie, Leonard. *The King Makers.* New York: Coward, McCann & Geoghegan, 1971.

Lyon, Peter. *Eisenhower: Portrait of the Hero.* Boston: Little, Brown, 1974.

McAuliffe, Mary S. *Crisis on the Left: Cold War Politics and American Liberals, 1947–1954.* Amherst, MA: University of Massachusetts Press, 1978.

McClure, Arthur F. *The Truman Administration and the Problems of Postwar Labor, 1945–1948.* Rutherford, NJ: Fairleigh Dickinson University Press, 1969.

McCormick, Thomas J. *America's Half Century.* Baltimore, MD: Johns Hopkins University Press, 1989.

McCoy, Donald R., and Richard T. Ruetten. *Quest and Response: Minority Rights and the Truman Administration,* Lawrence, KS: University of Kansas, 1973.

McGuckin, Robert. "A Value Analysis of Richard Nixon's 1952 Campaign Fund Speech." *Southern Speech Journal* 33 (1958): 259–269.

McKeever, Porter. *Adlai Stevenson: His Life and Legacy.* New York: Morrow, 1989.

McMillan, Taylor. "Who Beat Frank Graham?" Unpublished ms. University of North Carolina Political Studies Program, Research Report 1, May 20, 1959.

MacNeil, Neil. *Dirksen: Portrait of a Public Man.* New York: World Publishing Co., 1970.

McQuaid, Kim. *Big Business and Presidential Power: From FDR to Reagan.* New York, Morrow, 1982.

Maddox, Robert F. *The Senatorial Career of Harley Martin Kilgore.* New York: Garland Publishing, 1981.

Marcus, Maeva. *Truman and the Steel Seizure Case: The Limits of Presidential Power.* New York: Columbia University Press, 1977.

Martin, Boyd A. "The 1950 Elections in Idaho." *Western Political Quarterly* 4 (March 1951): 76–79.

Martin, Harold H. "The Man behind the Brass." *Saturday Evening Post*, 223:49 (1951): 22–23, 42, 45–48.

Martin, Joe. *My First Fifty Years in Politics*. New York: McGraw-Hill, 1960.

Martin, John Bartlow. *Adlai Stevenson of Illinois*. Garden City, NY: Doubleday, 1976.

Marwell, Gerald. "Party, Region, and the Dimensions of Conflict in the House of Representatives, 1949–1954." *American Political Science Review* 61:2 (June 1967): 380–399.

Mason, Edward S. *Economic Concentration and the Monopoly Problem*. Cambridge, MA: Harvard University Press, 1957.

Matray, James I. "Truman's Plan for Victory: National Self-Determination and the Thirty-Eighth Parallel Decision in Korea." *Journal of American History* 66 (September 1979): 314–333.

Matthews, Geoffrey. "Robert A. Taft, the Constitution and American Foreign Policy, 1939–1953." *Journal of Contemporary History* [Great Britain] 17 (1982): 507–522.

Matusow, Allen. *Farm Policies and Politics in the Truman Years*. New York: Atheneum, 1970.

Mayhew, David. *Party Loyalty among Congressmen: The Difference between Democrats and Republicans, 1947–1962*. Cambridge: Harvard University Press, 1966.

———. *Divided We Govern: Party Control, Lawmaking, and Investigations, 1946–1990*. New Haven, CT: Yale University Press, 1991.

Mazo, Earl, and Stephen Hess. *Nixon: A Political Portrait*. New York: Harper & Row, 1968.

Mayer, George. *The Republican Party, 1854–1959*. New York: Oxford University Press, 1964.

Melman, Seymour. "Limits of Military Power: Economic and Other." *International Security* 11 (Summer 1986): 72–87.

Meyer, Gerald. *Vito Marcantonio: Radical Politician, 1902–1954*. Albany, NY: State University of New York Press, 1989.

Mezey, Michael L. *Congress, the President, and Public Policy*. Boulder, CO: Westview Press, 1989.

Miller, Cynthia Pease. *Guide to Research Collections of Former Members of the United States House of Representatives, 1789–1987*. Washington, DC: Office of the Bicentennial of the House of Representatives, 1988.

Miller, Warren E. "Party Preference and Attitudes on Political Issues: 1948–1951." *American Political Science Review* 47 (March 1953): 45–60.

Miller, William J. *Henry Cabot Lodge: A Biography*. New York: Heineman, 1967.

Moore, William H. *The Kefauver Committee and the Politics of Crime, 1950–1952*. Columbus, MO: University of Missouri Press, 1974.

———. "Was Estes Kefauver 'Blackmailed' during the Chicago Crime Hearings? A Historian's Perspective." *Public Historian* 4 (1982): 4–28.

Morgan, Ann Hodges. *Robert S. Kerr*. Norman: University of Oklahoma Press, 1977.

Mrozek, Donald J. "Progressive Dissenter: Herbert Hoover's Opposition to Truman's Overseas Military Policy." *Annals of Iowa* 43 (1976): 275–291.

Nash, Gerald D. *United States Oil Policy, 1890–1964: Business and Government in Twentieth Century America*. Pittsburgh: University of Pittsburgh Press, 1968.

Nelson, Garrison. *Committees in the U.S. Congress, 1947–1992.* Washington, DC: Congressional Quarterly, 1993.

Neuberger, Richard. "Stand-off in the Northwest." *Nation,* October 30, 1950, p. 334.

Neustadt, Richard E. "Congress and the Fair Deal: A Legislative Balance Sheet." *Public Policy* 5 (1954): 349–381.

———. *Presidential Power: The Politics of Leadership.* New York: John Wiley, 1960.

New Republic. "Douglas Defeated" and "After the Deluge." November 20, 1950, pp. 6–10.

Newsweek. "Keeping Kefauver." April 15, 1951, p. 18.

Nixon, Richard M. "My Side of the Story: Truth the Best Answer to a Smear." *Vital Speeches,* October 15, 1952, pp. 11–15.

———. *Six Crises.* Garden City, NY: Doubleday, 1962.

Nutter, G. Warren, and Henry Adler Einhorn. *Enterprise Monopoly in the United States, 1899–1958.* New York: Columbia University Press, 1968.

Olien, Roger M. "The Republican Party of Texas." Ph.D. dissertation. Brown University, 1973.

Ostrander, Gilman M. *Nevada: The Great Rotten Borough, 1859–1964.* New York: Knopf, 1966.

Paige, Glenn. *The Korean Decision: June 24–30, 1950.* New York: Free Press, 1968.

Parmet, Herbert S. *The Democrats: The Years after FDR.* New York: Macmillan, 1976.

Parris, Judith H. *The Convention Problem: Issues in Reform of Presidential Nominating Procedures.* Washington, DC: Bookings Institution, 1972.

Paterson, Thomas G. "The Dissent of Senator Claude Pepper." In Thomas G. Paterson, ed., *Cold War Critics: Alternatives to American Foreign Policy in the Truman Years.* Chicago: Quadrangle Books, 1971.

Patterson, James. *Congressional Conservatism and the New Deal: The Growth of the Conservative Coalition in Congress, 1933–1939.* Lexington, KY: University of Kentucky Press, 1967.

———. *Mr. Republican: A Biography of Robert A. Taft.* Boston: Houghton Mifflin, 1972.

Peirce, Neal R. *Politics in America, 1945–1966.* Washington, DC: Congressional Quarterly Service, 1967.

Pepper, Claude, with Hays Gorey. *Pepper, Eyewitness to a Century.* San Diego, CA: Harcourt Brace Jovanovich, 1987.

Peterson, Mark. *Legislating Together: The White House and Capitol Hill from Eisenhower to Reagan.* Cambridge: Harvard University Press, 1990.

Phillips, Cabell. *The Truman Presidency.* New York: Macmillan, 1966.

Pickett, William B. *Homer E. Capehart: A Senator's Life, 1897–1979.* Indianapolis: Indiana Historical Society, 1990.

Piper, J. Richard. "Presidential-Congressional Power Prescriptions in Conservative Political Thought since 1933." *Presidential Studies Quarterly* 21 (Winter 1991): 35–54.

Pleasants, Julian, and Augustus M. Burns. *Frank Porter Graham and the 1950 Senate Race in North Carolina.* Chapel Hill: University of North Carolina Press, 1990.

Poder, Michael P. "The Senatorial Career of William E. Jenner." Ph.D. dissertation, University of Notre Dame, 1976.

Poen, Monte. *Harry S. Truman Versus the Medical Lobby: The Genesis of Medicare.*
    Columbia, MO: University of Missouri Press, 1977.
Pollard, Robert A. *Economic Security and the Origins of the Cold War.* New York: Co-
    lumbia University Press, 1985.
Pool, Ithiel Da Sola. "TV: A New Dimension in Politics." In Eugene Burdick and
    Arthur J. Brodbeck, *American Voting Behavior.* Glencoe, IL: Free Press, 1959.
Porter, Kirk H., and Donald Bruce Johnson, eds. *National Party Platforms, 1840–
    1968.* Urbana: University of Illinois Press, 1972.
Potter, David. *People of Plenty: Economic Abundance and the American Character.* Chi-
    cago: University of Chicago, 1954.
Potenziani, David D. "Striking Back: Richard B. Russell and Racial Relocation."
    Georgia History 65 (1981): 263–277.
Pratt, William C. "Senator Glenn Taylor: Questioning American Unilateralism."
    In Thomas G. Paterson, ed., *Cold War Critics: Alternatives to American Foreign
    Policy in the Truman Years.* Chicago: Quadrangle Books, 1971.
Price, Hugh Douglas. "The Negro and Florida Politics, 1944–1954." *Journal of
    Politics* 17 (May 1955): 216–217.
———. *The Negro and Southern Politics: A Chapter of Florida History.* New York: New
    York University Press, 1957.
Ra, Jong-yil. "Special Relationship at War: The Anglo-American Relationship dur-
    ing the Korean War." *Journal of Strategic Studies* 7 (September 1984): 301–
    317.
Rabinowitch, Eugene. "Five Years After." *Bulletin of Atomic Scientists* 7 (January
    1951): 3–5, 12.
Radosh, Ronald. *American Labor and United States Foreign Policy.* New York: Random
    House, 1969.
———. *Prophets on the Right: Profiles of Conservative Critics of American Globalism.* New
    York: Free Life Editions, 1975.
Reichard, Gary W. *The Reaffirmation of Republicanism: Eisenhower and the Eighty-third
    Congress.* Knoxville: University of Tennessee Press, 1975.
———. "The Domestic Politics of National Security." In Norman A. Graebner,
    ed., *The National Security: Its Theory and Practices, 1945–1960.* New York: Ox-
    ford University Press, 1986.
Reinhard, David W. *The Republican Right since 1945.* Lexington: University Press of
    Kentucky, 1983.
Republican Party. National Convention. *Official Report of the Proceedings, Resulting in
    the Nomination of Dwight D. Eisenhower, of New York, for President and the Nom-
    ination of Richard M. Nixon, of California, for Vice-President.* Reported by
    George L. Hart, official reporter. Washington, DC: Republican National
    Committee, 1952.
Reston, James B. "Our Campaign Techniques Examined." *New York Times Maga-
    zine,* November 9, 1952, pp. 8ff.
Richardson, Elmo. *Dams, Parks and Politics: Resource Development and Preservation in
    the Truman-Eisenhower Era.* Lexington, KY: University Press of Kentucky,
    1973.
———. *The Presidency of Dwight D. Eisenhower.* Lawrence, KS: Regents Press of Kan-
    sas, 1979; rev. ed., with Charles J. Pach, 1991.

Roseboom, Eugene H., and Alfred E. Eckes, Jr. *A History of Presidential Elections from George Washington to Jimmy Carter.* New York: Macmillan, 1979.

Rourke, John. "Congress and the Cold War." *World Affairs* 139 (Spring 1977).

Rovere, Richard H. "Annals of Politics: New Man in the Pantheon." *New Yorker,* March 24, 1962, pp. 151–166.

Ruetten, Richard T. "Adlai Stevenson and the Rhetoric of Moderate Liberalism." *Reviews in American History* 3 (1975): 389–393.

Sasuly, Richard. "Vito Marcantonio: The People's Politician." In Harvey Goldberg, *American Radicals.* New York: Monthly Review, 1957; Modern Reader ed. 1969.

Schaffer, Alan. *Vito Marcantonio, Radical in Congress.* Syracuse, NY: University of Syracuse Press, 1966.

Schapsmeier, Edward L., and Frederick H. Schapsmeier. "Paul H. Douglas: From Pacifist to Soldier-Statesman." *Journal of the Illinois State Historical Society* 67 (1974): 307–323.

———. "Everett M. Dirksen of Pekin: Politician Par Excellence." *Journal of Illinois State Historical Society* 76:1 (1983): 2–16.

———. *Dirksen of Illinois: Senatorial Statesman.* Urbana: University of Illinois Press, 1985.

Scheele, Henry Z. *Charlie Halleck: A Political Biography.* New York: Exposition Press, 1966.

———. "Executive-Legislative Relations: Eisenhower and Halleck." In Shirley Anne Warshaw, ed., *Reexamining the Eisenhower Presidency.* Westport, CT: Greenwood Press, 1993.

Schilling, Warner R., Paul Y. Hammond, and Glenn H. Synder, eds. *Strategy, Politics and Defense Budgets.* New York: Columbia University Press, 1962.

Schlesinger, Arthur M., Jr. "The New Isolationism." *Atlantic* 189:5 (May 1952): 34–38.

———. *The Vital Center: The Politics of Freedom.* Boston: Houghton Mifflin, 1949.

———. *The Imperial Presidency.* Boston: Houghton Mifflin, 1973.

Schriftgiesser, Karl. *The Lobbyists: The Art and Business of Influencing Lawmakers.* Boston: Little, Brown, 1951.

Shannon, Jasper Berry. *Money and Politics.* New York: Random House, 1959.

Sherrill, Robert. *Gothic Politics in the Deep South: Star of the New Confederacy.* New York: Grossman, 1968.

Shonfield, Andrew. *Modern Capitalism: The Changing Balance of Public and Private Power.* New York: Oxford University Press, 1965.

Sievers, Rodney M. "Adlai E. Stevenson and the Crisis of Liberalism." *Midwestern Quarterly* 14 (1973): 135–149.

Sigelman, Lee. "A Reassessment of the Two Presidencies Thesis." *Journal of Politics* 41 (1979): 1195–1205.

Smith, A. Robert. *Tiger in the Senate: The Biography of Wayne Morse.* Garden City, NY: Doubleday, 1962.

Smith, Beverly. "He Makes the Generals Listen." *Saturday Evening Post* 223:37 (1951): 20–21, 134–138.

Spanier, John W. *The Truman-MacArthur Controversy.* Cambridge: Belknap Press of Harvard University Press, 1959.

Spindler, Allan P. "The Unsolid South: A Challenge to the Democratic National

Party." In Alan F. Westin, *The Uses of Power: Seven Cases in American Politics.* New York: Harcourt, Brace, and World, 1962.

Spitzer, Robert J. *President and Congress: Executive Hegemony at the Crossroads of American Government.* Philadelphia: Temple University Press, 1993.

Starr, Paul. *The Social Transformation of American Medicine: The Rise of a Sovereign Profession and the Making of a Vast Industry.* New York: Basic Books, 1982.

Stein, Herbert. *The Fiscal Revolution in America.* Chicago: University of Chicago Press, 1969.

Steiber, Jack. "Labor's Walkout from the Korean War Stabilization Board." *Labor History* 21:2 (1980): 239–269.

Steinberg, Alfred. "McCarran: Lone Wolf of the Senate." *Harper's* 201 (November 1950): 89–95.

———. *Sam Rayburn: A Biography.* New York: Hawthorne Books, 1975.

Stern, Mark. "Lyndon Johnson and Richard Russell: Institutions, Ambitions and Civil Rights." *Presidential Studies Quarterly* 21 (Fall 1991): 687–704.

Stevenson, Adlai. "Korea in Perspective." *Foreign Affairs* 30 (April 1952): 349–360.

———. *Major Campaign Speeches of Adlai Stevenson, 1952.* New York: Random House, 1953.

Stockstill, Louis R. "Uncle Carl Vinson: Backstage Boss of the Pentagon." *Army, Navy, Air Force Journal,* February 18, 1961, pp. 22–28.

Stokes, Donald E., Angus Campbell, and Warren E. Miller. "Components of Electoral Decision." *American Political Science Review* 52 (June 1958): 367–387.

Stouffer, Samuel A. *Communism, Conformity, and Civil Liberties: A Cross-section of the Nation Speaks Its Mind.* Garden City, NY: Doubleday, 1955.

Stromer, Marvin E. *The Making of a Political Leader: Kenneth B. Wherry and the United States Senate.* Lincoln: University of Nebraska Press, 1969.

Stuhler, Barbara. *Ten Men of Minnesota and American Foreign Policy, 1898–1968.* St. Paul, MN: Minnesota Historical Society, 1973.

Sundquist, James L. *The Decline and Resurgence of Congress.* Washington, DC: Brookings Institution, 1981.

Sweeney, James R. "Revolt in Virginia: Harry Byrd and the 1952 Presidential Election." *Virginia Magazine of History and Biography* 86 (1978): 180–195.

Taft, Robert A. *A Foreign Policy for Americans.* Garden City, NY: Doubleday, 1951.

———. "United States Foreign Policy: Forget United Nations in Korea and Far East." *Vital Speeches,* June 15, 1953, pp. 529–531.

Tananbaum, Duane. "The Bricker Amendment Controversy: Its Origins and Eisenhower's Role." *Diplomatic History* 9 (1985): 73–93.

———. *The Bricker Amendment Controversy: A Test of Eisenhower's Political Leadership.* Ithaca, NY: Cornell University Press, 1988.

Tanner, William R., and Robert Griffith. "Legislative Politics and 'McCarthyism': The Internal Security Act of 1950." In Robert Griffith and Athan Theoharis, eds., *The Specter: Original Essays on the Cold War and the Origins of McCarthyism.* New York: New Viewpoints, 1974.

Thatcher, Terrence L. "The Bricker Amendment: 1952–54." *Northwest Ohio Quarterly* 49 (1977): 107–120.

Theoharis, Athan G. *The Yalta Myths: An Issue in U.S. Politics, 1945–1955.* Columbia, MO: University of Missouri Press, 1970.

Thompkins, C. David. *Senator Arthur H. Vandenberg: The Evolution of a Modern Republican, 1884–1945.* Lansing, MI: Michigan State University Press, 1970.

Thompson, Francis H. *The Frustration of Politics: Truman, Congress, and the Loyalty Issue, 1945–1953.* Rutherford, NJ: Farleigh Dickinson University Press, 1979.

Time. "Hitting the Road." April 3, 1950a, p. 23.

———. "Anything Goes." April 17, 1950b, p. 28.

———. "Next in Line." May 15, 1950c, p. 25.

T.R.B. "Washington Wire." *New Republic,* November 20, 1950, pp. 3–4.

Truman, David. *The Congressional Party: A Case Study.* New York: Wiley, 1959.

United States Congress. *Congressional Record: Proceedings and Debates of the Congress.* Washington, DC: GPO, 1873–.

———. House of Representatives. House Select Committee on Lobbying Activities (Buchanan Committee). *Hearings.* Washington, DC: GPO, 1950.

———. House of Representatives. Joint Committee on Atomic Energy. *Soviet Atomic Energy.* 82d Cong. 1st sess, 1951.

U.S. Federal Trade Commission. *Report of the Federal Trade Commission on Interlocking Directorates.* Washington, DC: GPO, 1951.

———. *Interlocks in Corporate Management.* Washington, DC: GPO, 1965.

U.S. Senate, Committee on Rules and Administration. *Maryland Senatorial Election of 1950.* 82d Cong. 1st sess., 1951.

———. Special Committee on Small Business. Subcommittee on Monopoly. *The International Petroleum Cartel.* Staff Report of the Federal Trade Commission. 82d Cong., 2d sess., 1952.

U.S. State Department. *United States Relations with China.* (China White Paper.) Washington, DC: GPO, 1949.

U.S. National Archives and Records Administration. *Guide to the Records of the United States Senate at the National Archives: 1789–1989.* Bicentennial ed. Washington, DC: GPO, 1989.

———. *Guide to the Records of the United States House of Representatives at the National Archives: 1789–1989.* Bicentennial ed. Washington, DC: GPO, 1989.

U.S. News and World Report. "World Policy and Bipartisanship: An Interview with Senator Tom Connally." May 5, 1950a, pp. 28–31.

———. "Unions Drive to Beat Taft." October 20, 1950b, pp. 11–12.

———. "Elections Issues Grow Hot: Crime, Communism, Deals Stirs Voters." October 27, 1950c, p. 19.

Vandenberg, Arthur, Jr., ed. *The Private Papers of Senator Vandenberg.* Boston: Houghton Mifflin, 1952.

Van Dyke, Vernon, and Edward Lane. "Senator Taft and American Security." *Journal of Politics* 14 (1952): 177–202.

Walzer, Kenneth. "The FBI, Congressman Vito Marcantonio and the American Labor Party." In Athan Theoharis, ed., *Beyond the Hiss Case: The FBI, Congress, and the Cold War.* Philadelphia: Temple University Press, 1982.

Warshaw, Shirley. *Reexamining the Eisenhower Administration.* Westport, CT: Greenwood Press, 1993.

Welch, Robert H. W. *The Politician.* Belmont, MA: Belmont Publishing Co., 1964.

Wentworth, Evelyn L. *Election Statistics in Maryland, 1934–1958.* College Park, MD: Bureau of Governmental Research, College of Business and Public Administration, University of Maryland, 1959.

Whitaker, Arthur. *Spain and Defense of the West: Ally and Liability.* New York: Harper, 1961.

White, William S. *The Taft Story.* New York: Harper, 1954.

Whitman, Alden, and the *New York Times. Portrait: Adlai E. Stevenson: Politician, Diplomat, Friend.* New York: Harper & Row, 1965.

Wildavsky, Alan. "The Two Presidencies." *Trans-Action* 4 (1966): 7–14.

Wilkins, Lee. *Wayne Morse: A Bio-Bibliography.* Westport, CT: Greenwood Press, 1985.

Wilkins, Robert P. "Senator William Langer and National Priorities: An Agrarian Radical's View of American Foreign Policy, 1945–1952." *North Dakota Quarterly* 42 (1974): 42–59.

Wilkinson, J. Harvie. *Harry Byrd and the Changing Face of Virginia Politics, 1945–1966.* Charlottesville, VA: University Press of Virginia, 1968.

Wilson, Theodore. "The Kefauver Committee, 1950." In Arthur M. Schlesinger, Jr., and Roger Bruns, eds., *Congress Investigates: A Documented History, 1792–1974.* Vol. 5. New York: Chelsea House Publishers, 1975.

Wittner, Lawrence S. *Cold War America: From Hiroshima to Watergate.* New York: Praeger, 1974.

Wood, Stephen C. "Television's First Political Spot-Ad Campaign: Eisenhower Answers America." *Presidential Studies Quarterly* 20 (1990): 265–283.

20   Disloyalty Charges and McCarthyism

Lester H. Brune

One of President Truman's most vexing problems was the activity of the House Un-American Activities Committee (HUAC) and Senator Joseph McCarthy in levying charges of disloyalty in places of influence on American society and the government. The HUAC's investigative hearings had begun in 1938 when it searched for "disloyal" persons who favored the German Nazis and Soviet communists, and just before the end of World War II the House of Representatives gave it permanent status. By 1947, the HUAC had delved into the lives and activities of many individuals, including Hollywood figures such as actress Rita Hayworth and movie director Elia Kazan, causing many to be arrested, fired, or blacklisted, often for using their Fifth Amendment right not to testify or for refusing to name friends and acquaintances with possible left-wing affiliations.

Senator Joseph R. McCarthy stole center stage from the HUAC by gaining the attention of the U.S. media in February 1950 with charges that over 250 "known communists" held office in the U.S. government. Although a Senate investigating committee under Senator Millard Tydings reported during the summer of 1950 that McCarthy's charges were baseless, the Chinese intervention in the Korean War in the fall of 1950 and China's initial success in driving UN forces out of North Korea revived popular communist fears. Reviving disloyalty charges, McCarthy and his followers claimed that communist successes could have resulted only because there were spies and disloyal U.S. government officials, who had to be ferreted out and punished.

During the next four years, McCarthyism spread like a plague into U.S. society, reaching not only into the State and Defense departments but into many state governments, universities and schools, the entertainment business, and the intellectual community. McCarthy ultimately lost face in

November 1954 when the U.S. Senate censured his activity, but the paranoia he brought to U.S. society lived on. As a permanent committee, however, the HUAC continued its work and again gained prominence during the dissenting activities of the Vietnam War years.

GENERAL STUDIES OF LOYALTY AND SECURITY

The literature on the loyalty and security issue during the period 1945–1953 is so large that this chapter must be supplemented with bibliographic materials. For a list of books, articles, and pamphlets published at that time, the 1955 work edited by Charles Corker is valuable. Charles Seidman (1969) has a bibliography on communism in the United States, and both David Caute's (1978) and Ellen W. Schrecker's (1986) studies have excellent bibliographies. Perhaps the best annotated list of works on almost all aspects of the internal security question is in Richard Dean Burns' (1984) bibliography on the Truman years.

The division between traditional and revisionist studies of the Truman presidency definitely exists regarding the security issue especially concerning Truman's relation to McCarthyism. The traditionalists' view, expressed most recently in Alonzo Hamby's (1989) essay, contends that Truman tried to divert public attention from the HUAC, and later McCarthy, by instituting the Loyalty Security Board in 1947 and by using anticommunist rhetoric not only to justify such items as the Marshall Plan and the North Atlantic Treaty Organization but to convince others that he was an ardent anticommunist.

In contrast, revisionist historians such as Athan Theoharis (1971) blamed Truman for raising the level of anticommunistic rhetoric so high between 1947 and 1950 that both the HUAC and McCarthy appeared to be justified in their search for domestic supporters of Moscow, especially after 1949, when the Soviet Union successfully performed atomic bomb tests and Chinese communists gained control of mainland China. In other studies, Theoharis (1979) examines a variety of repressive measures that various government agencies adopted so that the "national security state" could fight the cold war. In particular, he finds that the Federal Bureau of Investigation (FBI) under J. Edgar Hoover overstepped constitutional limits on civil rights (1981) and worked with the HUAC in violating civil liberties (1982).

The earliest general accounts of the investigative charges of disloyalty are by Earl Latham (1966), who surveys these activities from 1938 to 1952, and Fred Cook (1971), who discusses the 1950s. Stanley Kutler (1982) examines a variety of repressive cases during this period, indicating that Senator Patrick McCarran, who fought for passage of the 1950 Internal Security Act, also caused many repressive practices. Michel Belknap (1978) examines the question of justice during the cold war with special reference to the 1940 Smith Act, which made it illegal to join any organization that taught, advocated, or encouraged the overthrow of the government by force.

THE HOUSE COMMITTEE ON UN-AMERICAN ACTIVITIES

The hearings of the House Committee on Un-American Activities influenced the American culture over thirty years, from the 1930s through the 1960s. Two general studies of the HUAC are Robert K. Carr's (1979) work on the period from 1945 to 1950 and Walter Goodman's (1964) account, which carries into the 1950s as well. Kenneth O'Reilley (1983) discusses the relationship between the HUAC and the FBI, while another Theoharis (1991) volume contains edited material from J. Edgar Hoover's secret files, which adds to Theoharis' 1981 and 1982 studies of this topic.

The Un-American Activities Committee encouraged individuals secretly or publicly to divulge names of alleged communists or those who may have "aided" communists. This method, which particularly disrupted the theater and movie business, gained widespread attention for the committee. Victor Navsky's *Naming Names* (1980, 1991) examines the complex moral questions this tactic had for both the victim and the person who cooperated with the HUAC by giving names of "friends." In his 1991 Afterword, Navsky updates his information, citing, among other items, that Ronald Reagan, as chairman of the Screen Actors Guild, cooperated so often in giving names to the FBI that he had a special FBI identity code name.

One result of HUAC hearings was the blacklisting of persons who had been accused of disloyalty with the recommendation that they should be fired from their positions or not be employed. The American Business Consultants' *Red Channels* (1950) became the official blacklist publication, although its apologists contended the volume was only a "credit-rating" list such as Dun and Bradstreet issued for the stock market. Such semantics were deceptive in trying to hide the life-destroying effects the blacklist had on many lives, a deception explained in John Cogley's *Report on the Blacklist* (1956) and in later studies by Navsky (1980) and Schrecker (1986).

Other literature on the informers and their victims includes Frank Donner's *The UnAmericans* (1961) and an essay (1973); Erving Goffman's *Stigma* (1972); Stefan Kanfer's *A Journal of the Plague Years* (1978); and *The Inquisition in Hollywood* by Larry Ceplair and Steven Englund (1980).

For a sample of theater that led the State Department to deny playwright Arthur Miller a passport in 1954, read Miller's 1953 play *The Crucible*, based on the Salem witchcraft trials in New England during the seventeenth century. Miller dramatically depicts how false, unsubstantiated accusations can generate evil effects on an entire community, the cultural symptom experienced in the United States during the McCarthy-HUAC years.

For an illustration of how Truman's Loyalty Security Board affected individuals during this period, see O. Edmund Clubb's (1974) memoir. After twenty-two years in the foreign service, where he was an expert on China, Clubb became the State Department's director for the Office of Chinese Affairs in July 1950. Then his troubles began. In 1951, the Loyalty Board raised questions about his activity in 1932 because "repentant communist" Whittaker Chambers, better known as the accuser of Alger Hiss, reported that Clubb in 1932 had delivered a "sealed envelope" to the office of a left-wing magazine, *New Masses*. Clubb was suspended from duty and interrogated constantly, until he finally retired in February 1952. Clubb concludes that the board fired eleven State Department employees as "security risks" but never found a single case of disloyalty and indicates the situation became worse under Eisenhower. Clubb also has an article (1969) describing how subsequent presidential administrations suffered because they lacked expert advice from Asian specialists who deserted Washington due to the experiences of the early 1950s.

McCARTHYISM

Because of the publicity following Senator McCarthy's trail of allegations and the fears generated by Chinese victories in Korea during November 1950, McCarthy's charges against disloyal government officials mushroomed to make "McCarthyism" a household word in the United States even after McCarthy was condemned by the U.S. Senate in late 1954. Throughout 1951 and 1952, McCarthy leveled charges against many alleged communists and especially proclaimed that Truman and Secretary of State Dean Acheson (the "Red Dean") conspired with communists. In 1952, McCarthy even issued a lengthy diatribe against General George C. Marshall, whom he claimed would "follow Stalin and oppose Churchill" during World War II. McCarthy's list of fellow travelers and communists was large. Among the books he wanted banned were those by such authors as Sherwood Anderson, W. H. Auden, John Dewey, and Edna Ferber. He said the U.S. Information Office in Germany had 30,000 to 40,000 books by communists and fellow travelers that should be removed.

Eisenhower's election as president in 1952 and the Republican takeover of Congress gave McCarthy a new base of power as the chairman of the Senate Committee on Government Operations. In this post and as chairman of the Subcommittee on Investigations, he dominated committee hearings, inquiries, and public hearings, which usually became a forum for anticommunist accusations.

Although President Eisenhower disliked McCarthy, he refused to "get down in the gutter with him," which also meant he refused to attack him publicly throughout 1952 and 1953. Within Eisenhower's administration, Vice President Nixon successfully defended McCarthy until the spring of 1954, when McCarthy attacked army brigadier general Ralph Zwicker and other army officials. He made claims with so little foundation that eventually twenty-three Republicans in the Senate joined forty-four Democrats to approve a December 1954 Senate resolution censuring McCarthy, although officially Vice President Nixon softened McCarthy's blow by replacing the word *censure* with *condemned* in the title. The vote against McCarthy was 67 to 22. Moreover, the Democrats regained control of the Senate in the 1954 elections, and McCarthy lost his chairmanship of Senate committees.

The demise of McCarthy finally came, although, in retrospect, the speeches of McCarthy reprinted in 1953 and his condemnation of General George C. Marshall (1952) leave the impression he had overstepped the bounds of reason much earlier. The nation's dissatisfaction with the drawn-out Korean negotiations and the fears of Soviet nuclear superiority made it difficult to quell the emotions the senator aroused and the media attention exacerbated.

Some historians believe that a large part of McCarthyism resulted because elite intellectuals refused to speak strongly against McCarthy's tactics. Although in essays edited in 1955 by Daniel Bell, a group of these intellectuals defended themselves by attributing McCarthyism to a populist surge they could not control, Michael Paul Rogin's *McCarthy and the Intellectuals* (1967) refutes the ideas in Bell's collection and lays much blame for McCarthy's influence at the feet of the anticommunist intellectuals, a position also accepted by Ellen Schrecker in *No Ivory Tower* (1986).

Although traditional historians agree that Truman tried to stem the exaggerated disloyalty charges of the HUAC and McCarthyism, revisionist writers argue that Truman was especially to blame for McCarthyism because of his anticommunist rhetoric and the formation of the Loyalty Board in 1947. Thus, the traditionalist Alan Harper (1969) finds that Truman's best intentions could not dampen the anticommunist fears that antedated World War II and were aroused by Stalin's actions after 1945. In addition, it was the Republicans and other conservatives who nourished the criticism of the Democratic policies that enabled the HUAC and McCarthy to flourish.

The revisionists' complaints against Truman are found in the essays edited by Robert Griffith and Athan Theoharis (1974), in Griffith's (1970) book about McCarthy's rise to influence, in Richard Freeland's (1976) study of Truman's role from 1947 to 1950, and in Lewis M. Purifoy's (1976) research on the connection between McCarthyism and allegations that Truman had "lost China" to the communists.

On McCarthy's career, both Jack Anderson (1952) and Richard H. Rovere (1959) provide contemporary biographic accounts of McCarthy. The articles edited by Allen Matusow (1970) depict various aspects of the senator's life. David Caute (1978) gives a fairly complete account of McCarthyism and anticommunism as the "great fear," while David Oshinsky (1976, 1983) has studied McCarthy's effects on labor unions, which had previously sought to purge their communists, and has a general study of McCarthy's entire career. Edwin R. Bayley (1981) describes newsmen's relations with McCarthy, a relationship benefiting the senator. Finally, Ellen W. Schrecker (1986, 1994) describes McCarthy's effect on universities, where many faculty members lost their academic freedom, and also writes a brief history of McCarthyism that introduces selected documents on this phenomenon.

REFERENCES

American Business Consultants. *Red Channels: The Report of Communist Influence in Radio and Television.* New York: American Business Consultants, 1950.

Anderson, Jack. *McCarthy: The Man, the Senator, the "Ism."* Boston: Beacon Press, 1952.

Bayley, Edwin R. *Joe McCarthy and the Press.* Madison, WI: University of Wisconsin Press, 1981.

Belknap, Michael R. *Cold War Political Justice.* Westport, CT: Greenwood Press, 1978.

Bell, Daniel, ed. *The New American Right.* New York: Criterion, 1955.

Bernstein, Barton J. "The Ambigious Legacy: The Truman Administration and Civil Rights." In Barton J. Bernstein, ed., *Politics and Policies of the Truman Administration.* Chicago: Quadrangle, 1970.

Burns, Richard Dean, ed. *Harry S. Truman: A Bibliography of His Times and Presidency.* Wilmington, DE: Scholarly Resources, 1984.

Carr, Robert Kenneth. *The House Committee on Un-American Activities.* New York: Octagon Books, 1979.

Caute, David. *The Great Fear: The Anti-Communist Purge under Truman and Eisenhower.* New York: Simon and Schuster, 1978.

Ceplair, Larry, and Steven Englund. *The Inquisition in Hollywood.* New York: Anchor Press, 1980.

Clubb, O. Edmund. "McCarthyism and Our Asian Policy." *Bulletin of Concerned Asian Scholars,* no. 4 (May 1969): 23–26.

———. *The Witness and I.* New York: Columbia University Press, 1974.

Cogley, John. *Report on Blacklisting.* 2 vols. New York: Fund for the Republic, 1956.

Cook, Fred. *The Nightmare Decade: The Life and Times of Joe McCarthy.* New York: Random House, 1971.

Corker, Charles B. *Bibliography on the Communist Problem in the United States.* New York: Fund for the Republic, 1955.

Donner, Frank. *The Un-Americans.* New York: Ballantine, 1961.

———. "Political Informers." In Pat Walters and Stephen Gillers, *Investigating the FBI.* Garden City, NY: Doubleday, 1973.

Freeland, Richard M. *The Truman Doctrine and the Origins of McCarthyism: Foreign Policy, Domestic Politics, and Internal Security, 1946–1948.* New York: Knopf, 1976.

Fried, Richard R. *Men against McCarthy.* New York: Columbia University Press, 1976.
———. *Nightmare in Red: The McCarthy Era in Perspective.* New York: Oxford University Press, 1991.
Goffman, Erving. *Stigma.* Englewood Cliffs, NJ: Pantheon, 1972.
Goodman, Walter. *The Committee.* New York: Farrar, Straus and Giroux, 1964.
Griffith, Robert. *The Politics of Fear: Joseph R. McCarthy and the Senate.* Lexington, KY: University Press of Kentucky, 1970.
Griffith, Robert, and Athan Theoharis, eds. *The Specter: Original Essays on the Cold War and the Origins of McCarthyism.* New York: New Viewpoints, 1974.
Hamby, Alonzo L. "The Mind and Character of Harry S. Truman." In Michael Lacey, *The Truman Presidency.* New York: Cambridge University Press, 1989.
Harper, Alan. *The Politics of Loyalty: The White House and the Communist Issue, 1946–1952.* Westport, CT: Greenwood Press, 1966.
Kanfer, Stefan. *A Journal of the Plague Years.* New York: Atheneum, 1978.
Kutler, Stanley. *The American Inquisition: Justice and Injustice in the Cold War.* New York: Hill and Wang, 1982.
Latham, Earl. *The Communist Conspiracy in Washington: From the New Deal to McCarthy.* Cambridge: Harvard University Press, 1966.
McCarthy, Joseph. *America's Retreat from Victory: The Story of George Catlett Marshall.* New York: Devin-Adair, 1952.
———. *Major Speeches and Debates of Senator Joe McCarthy Delivered in the United States Senate, 1950–1951.* Washington: Government Printing Office, 1953.
McCoy, Donald R., and Richard T. Ruetten. *Quest and Response: Minority Rights and the Truman Administration.* Lawrence, KS: University of Kansas Press, 1973.
Matusow, Allen J., ed. *Joseph R. McCarthy.* Englewood Cliffs, NJ: Prentice-Hall, 1970.
Miller, Arthur. "The Crucible." In Arthur Miller, *Arthur Miller's Collected Plays.* New York: Viking, 1957.
Navsky, Victor S. *Naming Names.* New York: Viking Press, 1980; with a new Afterword in Penguin Books, 1991.
O'Reilly, Kenneth. *Hoover and the UnAmericans: The FBI, HUAC and the Red Menace.* Philadelphia: Temple University Press, 1983.
Oshinsky, David M. *Senator Joseph McCarthy and the American Labor Movement.* Columbia, MO: University of Missouri Press, 1976.
———. *A Conspiracy So Immense: The World of Joe McCarthy.* New York: Free Press, 1983.
Purifoy, Lewis. *Harry Truman's China Policy: McCarthyism and the Diplomacy of Hysteria, 1947–1951.* New York: New Viewpoints, 1976.
Rogin, Michael Paul. *McCarthy and the Intellectuals.* Cambridge, MA: MIT Press, 1967.
Rovere, Richard H. *Senator Joe McCarthy.* New York: Harcourt, Brace and Co., 1959.
Schrecker, Ellen W. *No Ivory Tower: McCarthyism and the University.* New York: Oxford University Press, 1986.
———. *The Age of McCarthyism: A Brief History with Documents.* New York: Bedford Books/St. Martin's Press, 1994.
Seidman, Joel, ed. *Communism in the United States: A Bibliography.* Ithaca, NY: Cornell University Press, 1969.
Theoharis, Athan. *Seeds of Repression: Harry S. Truman and the Origins of McCarthyism.* Chicago: Quadrangle Books, 1971.

———. "The Truman Administration and the Decline of Civil Liberty: The FBI's Success in Securing Authorization for a Preventive Detention Program," *Journal of American History* 64 (1978): 1010–1030.

———. ed. *The Truman Presidency: The Origins of the Imperial Presidency and the National Security State.* New York: E. M. Coleman, 1979.

———. "FBI Surveillance during the Cold War Years: A Constitutional Crisis." *Public Historian* 3 (1981): 4–14.

———, ed. *From the Secret Files of J. Edgar Hoover.* Chicago: I. R. Dee, 1991.

Theoharis, Athan G., ed. *Beyond the Hiss Case: The FBI, Congress and the Cold War.* Philadelphia: Temple University Press, 1982.

Thompson, Francis H. *Frustration of Politics: Truman, Congress and the Loyalty Issue: 1945–1953.* Rutherford, NJ: Fairleigh Dickinson University Press, 1979.

21 Public Opinion and the Korean War

Gary L. Huey

By every measure used in public opinion polls, the Korean War was one of the most unpopular wars ever fought by the United States. It had an enormous impact on the country's foreign policy and on its people. During the three years of fighting, this war that cost in excess of $100 billion claimed approximately 54,000 American lives, with another 150,000 wounded. The loss of Koreans and Chinese must be counted in the millions. As George Donelson Moss notes in his book, *Moving On* (1994), the Korean War turned the cold war into a shooting war. No longer merely an ideological struggle, the cold war became deadly for Americans, as well as others. This change and the sacrifices might have been acceptable if the war had been won, but the long negotiations ended in a draw at best. Anger and frustration over the results of this "limited war" characterized the typical American attitude toward involvement in Korea. In August 1953, according to data collected in Hazel Erskine's article, "The Polls: Is War a Mistake?" (1970), 62 percent said that the war in Korea had not been worth fighting. When did opposition to the war arise? Who was against this war, and why? What were the effects of this opposition on President Harry S. Truman and the United States?

INITIAL ACCEPTANCE OF THE WAR

When North Korea invaded South Korea in June 1950, President Harry Truman responded quickly. With China having fallen to the communists in 1949, Truman did not want the Republicans to have another issue in the upcoming off-year elections. Bypassing Congress for fear that a protracted debate might allow Kim Il-sung's forces to take control of the entire country, the president went to the United Nations for approval to send troops to help the beleaguered forces of South Korea. The UN complied because the Soviet Union was boycotting the Security Council. As noted in Allan Millett and Peter Maslowski's *For the Common Defense* (1994), the UN aimed to restore the 38th parallel as the border between North and South Korea, which would fulfill the idea of containment of communism.

Truman eventually asked for and got congressional approval for supplemental defense funds, draft extensions, and wartime powers for himself. Congress and the American people supported the president's goal of halting communist aggression. The Gallup poll in July 1950 showed 66 percent approved the decision to send American troops to stop the North Koreans. John Mueller's *War, Presidents and Public Opinion* (1973) and his articles, especially "Trends in Popular Support for the Wars in Korea and Vietnam" (1971), demonstrate that Truman rode the wave of overwhelming popular support into the fall of that year. With UN troops pushing the communist forces north to the border of China, many Americans saw an opportunity to unite all of Korea under "democratic" leadership. Despite a few Chinese border incursions in late October, General Douglas MacArthur's mid-November promise to have the troops home by Christmas strengthened Truman's hand. According to Mueller, as long as the public believes a war will be successful but short, public support remains high.

OPPOSITION ARISES

At the end of November 1950, MacArthur proved to be wrong; China entered the war with large numbers of troops, sent thousands of UN soldiers back across the 38th parallel into South Korea, and recaptured Seoul. The UN armies, made up primarily of Americans, had to make a rapid retreat. As they were pushed south of Seoul, a UN and U.S. defeat seemed a real possibility. These events led Truman's conservative Republican opponents to react in dismay, and support for the war and President Truman dropped considerably. By December 1950, support for the war fell from 66 to 39 percent, with 49 percent now opposed to it. Both Elmo Roper's *You and Your Leaders* (1957) and George Gallup's *The Gallup Poll* (1972) chart this fall. Also instructive on this changing course of public opinion are Larry Elozitz and John W. Spanier's "Korea and Vietnam" (1974); William Caspary's "Public Reactions to International Events" (1968); Philip Caine's "The United States in Korea and Vietnam" (1968); and Matthew Mantell's "Opposition to the Korean War" (1973).

From late 1950 on, support of the war remained rather steady, at about 40 percent. Despite rising casualties, the on again–off again peace talks, the Truman-MacArthur controversy, the protracted nature of the conflict, and the 1952 elections, the basic core of support remained intact, although it was less than a majority. According to Gallup, during the next two and a half years, between 36 percent and 47 percent stayed the course with the president.

John Mueller (1971) suggests that for many of those who no longer backed the president after December 1950, their support was always tenuous at best. The Chinese intervention had scared them into joining the opponents of the war who previously had believed it was a mistake to have gotten involved in Korea. Together they formed nearly 60 percent of the population, and their numbers remained constant for the duration of the conflict. For all but four months of the three years of fighting, this was a most unpopular war. Who were the people opposing the war, and why did they do so?

KOREAN WAR OPPONENTS

While overwhelmingly conservative in their politics, Truman's opposition criticized him from different directions. Some argued that the United States should neither have committed troops to this cause nor crossed the 38th parallel, turning the fight into a liberation war. Eventually, however, more of Truman's opponents denounced him for not expanding the war to attack and liberate China as well as North Korea. Given this divided opposition and the war's proponents who accepted the limited war fought after January 1951, the president would have had difficulty in winning over even a sizable minority of his 60 percent of adversaries.

Isolationist Critics

As discussed by Selig Adler in *The Isolationist Impulse* (1957) and by James T. Patterson in *America since 1941* (1994), isolationists argued that Truman, and especially Secretary of State Dean Acheson, had practically invited the North Koreans to attack the South. American occupation troops had been removed, and by not giving the Republic of Korea sufficient military aid, Truman had left Syngman Rhee's government practically defenseless. Most of all, they blamed Secretary of State Acheson, who in a January 1950 speech had outlined America's defense perimeter in the Pacific as excluding South Korea. Acheson stated that countries that were not in the U.S. strategic interest to protect would have to seek assistance from the United Nations. If this speech did not invite an attack, according to these critics, it surely came close. Adler also notes that the isolationists' most dangerous argument was aimed at U.S. allies. They questioned the whole idea of collective security represented by the United Nations and the newly formed North Atlantic Treaty Organization. Many people were persuaded that U.S. allies were more than willing "to fight to the last American." Of the sixty nations in the UN, only sixteen sent troops. Thus, the United States was bearing the brunt of the fighting and dying despite all of the foreign aid previously dispensed to allies. This was a difficult argument to accept even for those who were not isolationists. Herbert Hoover, who had returned to prominence in 1947 after Truman appointed him to head a government reorganization commission, became a leading opponent of Truman in December 1950. Among other comments, Hoover stated that unless the UN and U.S. allies got rid of the communists in the UN, the United States should give up collective security and guard only areas of the world important to it.

This new type of isolationism did not demand neutrality as it had before World War II. As noted by the journalist Samuel Lubell in "Is America Going Isolationist Again?" (1952), the American public wanted to build a common front against Soviet aggression, but conservatives, such as Senator Robert Taft, hoped to rely more on airpower and seapower than on large numbers of U.S. foot soldiers. The nation should defend itself, and the other free nations should be willing to do similarly. These objections and proposals formed the heart of the isolationist case.

Asia First Critics

When the war bogged down after the Chinese intervention, Asia First critics, who had contended previously that Truman had "lost China" in 1949, now complained that President Truman was not doing enough to win in Korea. Led by General Douglas MacArthur, they demanded greater U.S. action, not only to win in Korea but to liberate China from the communists. Americans, they argued, were only tired of not fighting to win a total victory. The United States, they said, had the power to end this conflict, but after the Chinese debacle, Truman was holding back. Books such as those by David Rees, *Korea* (1964), Callum MacDonald, *Korea* (1986), Burton I. Kaufman, *The Korean War* (1986), John Spainer, *The Truman-MacArthur Controversy and the Korean War* (1959), and Joseph Goulden, *Korea* (1982) offer detailed explanations of these opposition arguments.

After having erred in November 1950 with the promise to end the war by Christmas, MacArthur called for blocking mainland China, unleashing Jiang Jieshi's (Chiang Kai-shek's) troops for raids against North Korea and China, and staging air-sea attacks on enemy supply depots in Manchuria. In advocating such a plan, MacArthur argued that the main communist thrust was in Asia, and here was where communism must be stopped. Unlike Truman's military and diplomatic advisers in Washington and the European allied leaders, MacArthur believed that if the United States succeeded in the East, Europe would be saved as well. Stalin would have neither the nerve nor the nuclear weapons to challenge the United States. This Asia First position would be adopted by many of Truman's opponents after December 1950.

In contrast to MacArthur, Truman and his advisers believed war with

China could mean a world war with the Soviet Union in both Asia and Europe, a war that Truman did not desire to risk because NATO military defense had just begun to develop in December 1950, when Dwight Eisenhower was named NATO's supreme commander. A global conflict would threaten Western Europe as well as Japan, with disastrous results. Europe, not Asia, had been the critical area during World War II, and it remained the critical area, a perspective that MacArthur and his conservative Republican backers rejected in both 1949 and 1951.

Unwilling or unable to restrict his proposals to consult with the Joint Chiefs of Staff and Truman, his superior officers, MacArthur openly publicized his ideas after his superiors told him to be quiet. Shortly after, in April 1951, President Truman relieved him of his command.

The public outcry of Truman's opponents was swift. As Callum MacDonald (1986) notes, MacArthur was portrayed by his admirers as a martyr to Truman's appeasement of Asian communism. The uproar over his firing also reflected a general dissatisfaction with what many regarded as the half-measures being taken to fight the war, for the concept of limited war was not familiar given the unconditional surrender terms followed during World War II. Many Americans much preferred MacArthur's stirring calls for victory and his plea to achieve it without the European allies if necessary. To these individuals, neither limited war nor the containment of communism was acceptable. Only total victory would do.

At this point, as Selig Adler (1957) explains, an unusual and seemingly illogical melding of ideas occurred when the isolationists rallied to support MacArthur's call for a more active intervention abroad. These ardent nationalists who wanted unilateral U.S. interests to be followed had longed for a hero, and MacArthur, who had been fired by the hated internationalist Truman, was embraced as the champion who opposed collective security. In some ways, MacArthur's ideas had never strayed too far from the isolationists. The general thought interventions might be necessary, but they should not be done simply to appease European allies nor should the United States waste its resources on these allies. MacArthur advocated unilateral U.S. decisions that, Adler contends, were the modern expression of the old isolationist belief in American self-sufficiency. Reinhold Niebuhr offers another explanation why the seemingly different groups of isolationists and Asia Firsters would ally to oppose the way Truman handled the Korean War. Niebuhr believes the isolationists had concluded that if the United States was to be active in world politics, it must be in charge of everything. For them, Asia seemed to be the place the nation could easily achieve this goal. Niebuhr elaborates this idea in *The Irony of American History* (1952) and *Christianity and Power Politics* (1946).

After the two groups opposed to the war had united, no significant increase in opposition to the war and no significant increase in support of the war could be reflected in the opinion polls. After MacArthur's relief and return home to some celebrations, Gallup recorded 42 percent in favor and 41 percent opposed to the war in early June 1951.

Truman's dismissal of MacArthur politicized the war. As John Mueller observes in "Presidential Popularity from Truman to Johnson" (1970), Republicans took the general's side in arguing that President Truman refused to allow the military to win. Former isolationist Senator Taft contended that Truman had never obtained a declaration of war from Congress and had not fully consulted with Congress before seeking UN support. The Republican attacks against Truman heated up considerably, although moderate Republicans usually backed the president. Thus, popular discontent toward the war remained fairly constant, with those polled as undecided often preventing a majority either way.

The discontent may have been more reflected in President Truman's approval rating; his personal popularity dropped eleven to twelve percentage points each year. There seems little doubt that the war was the major factor in Truman's not seeking reelection in 1952, although other difficulties certainly contributed to his loss of support after 1948. Higher wartime taxes, a large national debt, inflation, labor strife, the fall of China, and detonation of the first Soviet nuclear bomb all contributed to his woes, but by 1952 the war must remain the chief reason. Discussions of this can be found in David McCullough's *Truman* (1992), Robert J. Donovan's *Tumultuous Years* (1982), and Richard Neustadt's *Presidential Power* (1960).

Leftist Critics of the War

Opposing the war from a far different perspective were pacifists and radical leftists. Their numbers were relatively small compared to the other opponents of the war, and for the most part they were ineffective. Charles DeBenedetti discusses these dissenters in *The Peace Reform in American History* (1980), as do Alonzo Hamby (1978), Mueller (1973), and Mantell (1973). Because the left and pacifist groups had little influence during this period, the most effective opposition to the Korean War centered on the demand of those adopting MacArthur's position that the war in Asia should be escalated, not for protesters advocating a U.S. withdrawal or immediate peace.

SUPPORTERS OF THE WAR

Who made up the solid group between 36 and 47 percent of the population that backed the Korean War after it became a limited conflict? Here there are some surprises. John Mueller (1973) discovered that supporters of the war were disproportionately among the affluent, the better educated, and the young. These people, Mueller finds, are more likely to favor the president's policies than the poor, the less educated, and the old. Because of their advantages, these groups appear to have closer ties to their country and president. They supported the current policy but refused to accept any drastic change, such as escalation or withdrawal. For information on these considerations see Matthew E. Mantell's "Opposition to the Korean War" (1973), Hugh G. Wood's "American Reaction to Limited War in Asia" (1974), and Andre Modigliani's "Hawks and Doves, Isolationism and Political Distrust" (1972).

Another group that favored Truman's policies was the intellectual left, which advocated domestic reforms but also was anticommunist after 1947. Alonzo Hamby's "Public Opinion" (1978) discusses the political climate of the early 1950s when the cold war became a hot war in Korea. The radical left had been declining due to the nation's fear of nuclear war, Stalinist expansionism, the Berlin blockade, the fall of China, and the spread of McCarthyism. The old radical left had failed to develop convincing arguments to oppose Truman's policy, while the moderate left stayed with Truman in 1948 when Henry Wallace seemed sympathetic to Stalin. Under such circumstances, many liberals believed that Korea was an unpleasant but necessary war. Hans J. Morgenthau, the realists' apostle who later opposed the Vietnam War from the beginning, argued that the Korean containment of communism was essential. The appeasement experiences of the years before World War II and its consequences were much on the liberals' minds. Thus, as Hamby (1978) indicates, in the "vital center," many moderate liberals joined moderate Republicans, leaving the radical left with a declining base of influence.

Another consideration involves the liberal academicians. This important element of the left had very real economic problems because, as Mueller notes, the academic marketplace was a buyers' market. To oppose the war loudly from a radical leftist perspective might result in being labeled a communist, which could cause the faculty member to be fired. McCarthyism certainly had life in academia, as Ellen W. Schrecker documents in *No Ivory Tower* (1986). Job insecurity may have prompted many to remain quiet; those who spoke out suffered dire consequences.

CONCLUSION

Unpopularity for a war cannot be judged solely by public opinion pools, the number of petitions issued, or protest demonstrations, which were few during the Korean conflict. While many people believe that the Vietnam War was more unpopular than the Korean War, public opinion of both wars had similarities, as Mueller shows (1971). Opposition to the Vietnam involvement became more obvious than for Korea, not only because the Vietnam conflict lasted much longer but also because Vietnam protests became tangled up with civil rights protests, feminist protests, the drafting of young recruits while military reserves and the National Guard stayed home, and because others protested for greater attention to the Great Society goals of Lyndon Johnson.

REFERENCES

Adler, Selig. *The Isolationist Impulse: Its Twentieth Century Reaction.* New York: Abelard, 1957.

Aronson, James. *The Press and the Cold War.* Boston: Beacon Press, 1970.

Berger, Carl. *The Korea Knot: A Military and Political History.* Philadelphia: University of Pennsylvania Press, 1957.

Buckley, Gary S. "American Public Opinion and the Origins of the Cold War: A Speculative Reassessment." *Mid-America* 60 (January 1978): 35–42.

Caine, Philip D. "The United States in Korea and Vietnam: A Study in Public Opinion." *Air University Quarterly Review* 20:1 (1968): 49–58.

Caspary, William R. "Public Reactions to International Events," Ph.D. dissertation. Northwestern University, 1968.

DeBenedetti, Charles. *The Peace Reform in American History.* Bloomington: Indiana University Press, 1980.

Donovan, Robert J. *Tumultuous Years: The Presidency of Harry S Truman, 1949–1953.* New York: W. W. Norton and Company, 1982.

Elowitz, Larry, and John W. Spanier. "Korea and Vietnam: Limited War and the American Political System." *Orbis* 18:2 (1974): 510–534.

Epstein, Laurence B. "The American Philosophy of War, 1945–1967." Ph.D. dissertation, University of Southern California, 1967.

Erskine, Hazel. "The Polls: Is War a Mistake?" *Public Opinion Quarterly* 34:1 (1970): 134–150.

Gallup, George. *The Gallup Poll: Public Opinion, 1935–1971.* Vol. 2. New York: Random House, 1972.

Gietschier, Steven P. "Limited War and the Home Front: Ohio during the Korean War." Ph.D. dissertation, Ohio State University, 1977.

Goulden, Joseph. *Korea: The Untold Story of the War.* New York: New York Times Books, 1982.

Halberstam, David. *The Fifties.* New York: Villard Books, 1993.

Hallin, Daniel C. *The Uncensored War: The Media and Vietnam.* Berkeley: University of California Press, 1986.

Hamby, Alonzo L. "Public Opinion: Korea and Vietnam." *Wilson Quarterly* 2:3 (1978): 137–141.

Herzon, Frederick D. et al. "Personality and Public Opinion: The Case of Authoritarianism, Prejudice and Support for the Korean and Vietnam Wars." *Polity* 11:1 (1978): 92–113.

Hodgson, Godfrey. *America in Our Time: From World War II to Nixon, What Happened and Why.* New York: Vintage Books, 1976.

Kaufman, Burton I. *The Korean War: Challenges in Crisis, Credibility, and Command.* New York: Alfred Knopf, 1986.

Knightly, Phillip. *The First Casualty.* New York: Harcourt Brace Jovanovich, 1975.

Lian, B., and J. R. Oneal. "Presidents, the Use of Military Force, and Public Opinion." *Journal of Conflict Resolution* 37:2 (June 1993) 277–300.

Lubell, Samuel. "Is America Going Isolationist Again?" *Saturday Evening Post,* June 7, 1952, pp. 19–21, 48, 51–54.

McCullough, David. *Truman.* New York: Simon and Schuster, 1992.

MacDonald, Callum A. *Korea: The War before Vietnam.* New York: Free Press, 1986.

Mantell, Matthew E. "Opposition to the Korean War: A Study in American Dissent." Ph.D. dissertation, New York University, 1973.

Millett, Allan, and Peter Maslowski. *For the Common Defense: A Military History of the United States.* New York: Free Press, 1984; 2d ed., 1994.

Modigliani, Andre. "Hawks and Doves, Isolationism and Political Distrust: An Analysis of Public Opinions on Military Policy." *American Political Science Review* 66:3 (1972): 960–978.

Moss, George D. "News or Nemesis: Did Television Lose the Vietnam War?" In George D. Moss, ed., *A Vietnam Reader: Sources and Essays.* pp. 245–300. Englewood Cliffs, NJ: Prentice-Hall, 1991.

———. *Moving On: The American People since 1945.* Englewood Cliffs, NJ: Prentice-Hall, 1994.

Mueller, John E. "Presidential Popularity from Truman to Johnson." *American Political Science Review* 64:1 (1970): 18–34.

———. "Trends in Popular Support for the Wars in Korea and Vietnam." *American Political Science Review* 65:2 (1971): 358–375.

———. *War, Presidents, and Public Opinion.* New York: John Wiley and Sons, 1973.

Niebuhr, Reinhold. *Christianity and Power Politics.* New York: Charles Scribner's Sons, 1946.

———. *The Irony of American History.* New York: Charles Scribner's Sons, 1962.

Neustadt, Richard. *Presidential Power: The Politics of Leadership.* New York: John Wiley and Sons, 1960.

Patterson, James T. *America since 1941: A History.* New York: Harcourt Brace College Publishers, 1994.

Rees, David. *Korea: The Limited War.* New York: St. Martin's Press, 1964.

Roeder, George H. *The Censored War: American Visual Experience during World War Two.* New Haven: Yale University Press, 1993.

Roper, Elmo. *You and Your Leaders: Their Actions and Your Reactions.* New York: Morrow, 1957.

Schrecker, Ellen. *No Ivory Tower: McCarthyism and the Universities.* New York: Oxford University Press, 1986.

Spanier, John. *The Truman-MacArthur Controversy and the Korean War.* Cambridge: Belknap Press of Harvard University Press, 1959.

Thomas, James A. "Collapse of the Defensive War Argument." *Military Review* 53: 5 (1973): 35–38.

Toner, James H. "American Society and the American Way of War: Korea and Beyond." *Parameters* 11:1 (1981): 79–90.

Turner, Kathleen J. *Lyndon Johnson's Dual War: Vietnam and the Press.* Chicago: University of Chicago Press, 1985.

Wiltz, John E. "The Korean War and American Society." In Francis H. Heller, ed., *The Korean War: A 25-Year Perspective,* pp. 112–158. Lawrence, KS: Regents Press of Kansas, 1977.

Wood, Hugh G. "American Reaction to Limited War in Asia: Korea and Vietnam, 1950–1968." Ph.D. dissertation, University of Colorado, 1974.

22   The Status of Women
and Minorities

Lester H. Brune

Although women have been a majority or near majority of the population throughout American history, at the mid-twentieth century they were often confined to subordinate roles in society just as were African Americans and other minorities. As William Chafe (1989) indicates, both women and African Americans had made significant gains in status during World War II, but after 1945 they were again relegated to their prewar roles of housewife and male helpmate, and African Americans were again discriminated against and in 1946 even lynched as white southerners reasserted their authority. Although President Harry Truman spelled out a civil rights agenda during his 1948 election campaign and issued executive orders to end discrimination in federal employment and the armed forces, many women accepted their pre-1941 status, leaving a group of feminist activists to nurture the concept that both genders should be able to fulfill their talents in life, whatever they chose to do. At the same time, the conservative southern Democrat-Republican coalition in Congress prevented the passage of Truman's Fair Deal. Thus, women and African Americans experienced few gains during the era from 1945 to 1953, although their efforts created a momentum for future advances.

WOMEN DURING THE KOREAN WAR ERA

There is little literature dealing specifically with the role of women during the Korean War. However, most of the general studies about women during the 1945–1960 period indicate some relationship between the cold war becoming a hot war in Korea and the postwar expectations of women and family members during the 1950s. Insofar as such phenomena as McCarthyism and conservative attacks on civil rights also heightened tensions in the United States, the movement for women's rights was directly influenced. As many of the general studies on these issues conclude, the women's issues that became more prominent during the 1960s were usually based on developments that had taken place in the 1950s. In specific areas, such as women's service in the military and the factory workplace, the Korean War was chronologically in the exact middle between World War II's utilization of women in new economic roles and the 1960s, when a major feminist effort was undertaken to achieve equal rights for women.

Except for Peter A. Soderbergh's (1994) account of women in the U.S. Marines during the Korean War, the literature about women in the armed forces is confined to a part of studies spanning many years. Thus, Mary V. Stremlow (1986) has the Korean War as part of a study of women in the Marines Corps from 1946 to 1977. Similarly, the works by Charlotte Palmer Seeley (1992) on women in the armed forces, Marie Bennet Alsmeyer (1981) and Jean Ebbert (1993) on women in the U.S. Navy, and Deborah G. Douglas (1990) on women in aviation each cover broad periods in which the Korean War is a segment.

Feminist activity outside the military during the 1950s has been the subject of many studies that consider the Korean War's effect, with varying degrees of attention. The nation's large military production needs during World War II had given more women employment on manufacturing production lines, which paid better wages than did the traditional clerical, nursing, teaching, and secretarial jobs that women held before 1941. After the war, however, women whose work had been symbolized as the wartime's ''Rosie the Riveter'' were expected to return to their previous roles and to abandon their expectations for better wages and careers outside the home. Popular books such as *Modern Women: The Lost Sex* by Ferdinand Lundberg and Marynia Fornham (1946) proclaimed that only ''masculinized women'' sought careers outside the home and urged women to find their ''true selves'' as mothers and homemakers.

For many women, however, the times had changed, and they provided a larger number of individuals whom women's rights advocates could attract by offering new possibilities for their future. Immediately after World War II, however, returning war veterans received special government aid in returning to their old jobs while congressional conservatives restricted the New Deal–Fair Deal liberal proposals and caused new difficulties for women seeking recognition and equality of rights.

General information surveying women's issue throughout U.S. history is contained in Mary Ellen Huls' (1993) two-volume bibliography identifying U.S. government documents regarding social and labor issues of women from 1800 to 1990. Esther Peter (1974) has data about working women's employment, salaries, and occupations from 1940 to 1962, and Midge Decter (1961) has similar data, plus a discussion of the relation of labor unions to these women workers. More particularly, Marijean Suelzle

(1970) finds that women continued to receive low pay compared to men on the same job, and Nancy Gabin (1980) describes how United Auto Workers union leaders opposed giving women seniority rights or permitting married women to work.

Several studies demonstrate that the much-publicized feminist movement of the 1960s was based on efforts by women activists between 1945 and 1960. Leila Rupp and Varta Taylor (1987) study the efforts of the National Women's party to promote women's rights during the 1950s. Susan Lynn (1992) has a similar theme but uses the work of women in the Young Women's Christian Association and the American Friends Service Committee who tried to counteract conservative attitudes of this period. Harriet Hyman Alonso (1993) describes women in the peace movement, including their divisions after 1945, which led some members to make charges of other members' disloyalty to such groups as the House Un-American Activities Committee. Kate Weigand (1992) shows how Ohio's Un-American Commission equated domesticity with "patriotism" when they investigated women activists.

The two books by Elaine Tyler May (1988, 1994) examine the tendency of many women to return to their domestic roles after 1945 and the women activists who pushed the limits of what could be achieved in the face of the conservative attitudes of the period before 1960. Emily Rosenberg (1994) explores two movies of the period as cultural influences in the early cold war years that promoted the role of women as homemakers and as guides who should help their husbands accept family responsibilities despite their overseas extramarital affairs during or after World War II. Rosenberg also indicates these films denoted the shift from the 1948 beliefs in isolationism to the 1956 acceptance of internationalism. From an important perspective that uncovers the myths of American family life, Stephanie Coontz (1992) concludes that the reality of U.S. families' problems during the 1950s is overlooked by those in the 1980s and 1990s who extol traditional family values.

Finally regarding individual women with prominent roles in society at this time, an article by Lenore Bradley (1994) offers an excellent summation of women whom Truman appointed to government positions. Among the twelve women Bradley mentions were Eugenie Anderson, the first American woman to become an ambassador; Anna Rosenberg, who was named assistant secretary of defense in 1950; and, most prominent, Eleanor Roosevelt, who became the U.S. representative to the United Nations. Eleanor Roosevelt's post-1945 activities are also described by Joseph Lash (1972) and Lois Scharf (1987).

Other women with active careers during this period include Marguerite Higgins (1951), a news correspondent whose book describes activity in the early part of the Korean War, and Representative Frances P. Bolton. David Loth (1957) describes Bolton's conservative views on all issues ex-

cept woman's rights, which she strongly defended. In William F. Levantrosser's (1986) volume, Maurine Beasley has an article on Bess Truman,
and Cynthia E. Harrison explains the stalemate on federal legislation for
women during the Truman years.

AFRICAN AMERICANS' CIVIL RIGHTS

Among the U.S. minorities during World War II, Japanese Americans
had experienced abominable treatment by being sent to concentration
camps, a situation that was not recognized and rectified until the 1980s.
Similarly, the rights of Native Americans and Spanish-speaking Americans
did not gain attention until the mid-1960s, although both had made some
previous attempts to gain recognition. In contrast to the experience of
these groups, African Americans had been struggling for their equal rights
since the end of the Civil War in 1865 and presumed that their World
War II service in the nation's armed forces and in national defense production would improve their status after 1945, a future President Franklin
D. Roosevelt had mentioned when he revived his New Deal objectives
during the 1944 presidential campaign. As it happened, however, Roosevelt's death in April 1945 and the election of a Republican-dominated
Congress in 1946 effectively limited African-American leaders' expectations of an immediate resolution of their past grievances.

Although President Truman used the executive office to promote some
aspects of minority rights, the powerful positions of white southern Democrats and Republican conservatives in Congress and past Supreme Court
rulings recognizing separation blocked a quick solution to discriminatory
practices against African Americans regardless of Truman's executive decisions and his 1949 Fair Deal agenda.

Most literature focuses on the African-American movement to gain
equal rights, but information about the southern opposition to these civil
rights may be found in studies such as V. O. Key's (1949) on southern
politics, Numan V. Bartley and Hugh Graham's (1975) on the massive
southern resistance to desegregation, and Alberta Lachicotte's (1966) biography of the 1948 Dixiecrat presidential candidate Strom Thurmond.

As examined in more detail in Chapter 19 in this book, civil rights is
the one area of Truman's presidency about which traditionalists and revisionists generally agree. The essays in Richard Kirkendall (1974) by the
traditionalist Alonzo Hamby and the revisionist Harvard Sitkoff both
praise Truman's overall advancement of civil rights, although the revisionists contend that Truman did not properly handle the civil rights legislation and was not fully committed to do as much to assist this program
as his rhetoric proclaimed. Thus, Sitkoff and other revisionists believe
Truman may have encouraged civil rights only to obtain African-American
votes in 1948 or because it was an essential cold war tactic to prove that

civil rights achievements in the United States could outdo those rights in the Soviet Union.

One particular area of Truman's civil rights activity that traditionalists and revisionists both approve is the executive orders in 1948 requiring an end to segregation in federal government employment and the armed forces. The standard work on the armed forces decision is by Richard M. Dalfiume (1969). Details about the individual services are found in the general accounts by Bernard Nalty (1986) and Jack D. Foner (1974). More information can be found in the book by Morris J. MacGregor, Jr. (1981), and the thirteen volumes of documents edited by MacGregor and Nalty (1977). Lenwood O. Davis and George Hill (1985) have a bibliography, *Blacks in the American Armed Forces, 1776–1983,* and University Publications of America (1989) has microforms of the papers of the National Association for the Advancement of Colored People (NAACP) on the armed forces' discriminatory practices between 1918 and 1955.

A variety of other studies deal with aspects of the civil rights movement during this period. Roy Wilkins (1982), the director of the NAACP, has an autobiography favorable to Truman's activity on civil rights. Steven Lawson's (1976, 1990) books are about voting rights in the South from 1944 to 1949 and the civil rights movement after 1941. Jack Greenberg, a lawyer who was Thurgood Marshall's assistant counsel during the years leading to the 1954 Supreme Court decision to desegregate schools, has one 1950s study (1959) of the civil rights crusade and a recent update (1994) of the people involved in that effort. Donald Kemper (1965) writes about Senator Thomas C. Hennings, a Democrat from Missouri who was an ardent advocate of civil rights and one of the few members of Congress to speak against McCarthyism in 1950 and later. From a programmatic view of Truman's civil rights advocacy, Gary W. Richard (1986) writes about Democratic election strategies and civil rights, and Mary Dudziak (1988) explains how the improvement of U.S. civil rights was essential to demonstrate the nation's superiority over communism.

Because the Korean War era overlapped with the first years of Dwight D. Eisenhower's presidency, three works on his policies are important. Herbert Brownell (1991), Eisenhower's attorney general, assesses this president's position on civil rights. Mark Stern (1989) indicates that Eisenhower generally supported the federal government's recognition of African-American civil rights from 1952 to 1954. And Robert Frederick Burt (1984) has a critical assessment of Eisenhower's civil rights policies, arguing the president was not forthright in promoting civil rights.

REFERENCES

Alonso, Harriet Hyman. *Peace as a Women's Issue: A History of the U.S. Movement for World Peace and Women's Rights.* Syracuse, NY: Syracuse University Press, 1993.

Alsmeyer, Marie Bennett. *The Way of the Waves: Women in the Navy.* Conway, AK: Hamba Books, 1981.

Bartley, Numan V., and Hugh B. Graham, *Southern Politics and the Second Reconstruction.* Baltimore: John Hopkins University Press, 1975.

Bradley, Lenore. "The Uphill Climb: Women in the Truman Administration." *Whistle Stop, Harry S. Truman Library Institute Newsletter* 23:2 (Summer 1994): 1–5.

Brownell, Herbert. "Eisenhower's Civil Rights Program: A Personal Assessment." *Presidential Studies Quarterly* 21:2 (Spring 1991): 235–242.

Burt, Robert Frederick. *The Eisenhower Administration and Black Civil Rights.* Knoxville, TN: University of Tennessee Press, 1984.

Byars, Jackie. *All That Hollywood Allows: Re-Reading Gender in the 1950s Melodrama.* Chapel Hill, NC: University of North Carolina Press, 1991.

Campbell, D'Ann. *Women at War with America: Private Lives in a Patriotic Era.* Cambridge: Harvard University Press, 1984.

Chafe, William H. "Postwar American Society: Dissent and Social Reform." In Michael J. Lacey, ed., *The Truman Presidency.* New York: Cambridge University Press, 1989.

Cook, Blanche W. *Eleanor Roosevelt.* New York: Viking, 1992.

Coontz, Stephanie. *The Way We Never Were: American Families and the Nostalgia Trap.* New York: Basic Books, 1992.

Dalfiume, Richard M. *Desegregation of the Armed Forces: Fighting on Two Fronts, 1939–1953.* Columbia: University of Missouri Press, 1969.

Davis, Lenwood O., and George Hill, comps. *Blacks in the American Armed Forces, 1776–1983: A Bibliography.* Westport, CT: Greenwood Press, 1985.

Decter, Midge. "Women at Work." *Commentary* 31 (1961): 243–250.

Douglas, Deborah G. *United States Women in Aviation: 1940–1985.* Washington, DC: Smithsonian Institute Press, 1990.

Dudziak, Mary. "Desegregation as a Cold War Imperative." *Stanford Law Review* 41 (November 1988): 61–120.

Ebbert, Jean. *Crossed Currents: Navy Women from WWI to Tailhook.* Washington, DC: Brassey's, 1993.

Foner, Jack D. *Blacks and the Military in American History.* New York: Praeger Publishers, 1974.

Gabin, Nancy. "Women Workers and the UAW in the Post–World War II Period, 1945–54." *Labor History* 21 (1980): 5–30.

Greenberg, Jack. *Race Relations and American Law.* New York: Columbia University Press, 1959.

———. *Crusaders in the Courts: How a Dedicated Band of Lawyers Fought for the Civil Rights Revolution.* New York: Basic Books, 1994.

Higgins, Marguerite. *War in Korea: The Report of a Woman Combat Correspondent.* Garden City, NY: Doubleday, 1951.

Huls, Mary Ellen. *United States Government Documents on Women, 1800–1990: A Comprehensive Bibliography.* Vols. 1 and 2. Westport, CT: Greenwood Press, 1993.

Katz, Donald. *Home Fires: An Intimate Portrait of One Middle-Class Family in Postwar America.* New York: Aaron Asher Books, 1992.

Kemper, Donald J. *Decade of Fear: Senator Hennings and Civil Liberties.* Columbia, MO: University of Missouri Press, 1965.

Key, Vladimer O., Jr. *Southern Politics in State and Nation.* New York: Knopf, 1949.

Kirkendall, Richard, ed. *The Truman Period as a Research Field: A Reappraisal, 1972.* Columbia, MO: University of Missouri Press, 1974.

Lachicotte, Alberta. *Rebel Senator: Strom Thurmond of South Carolina.* New York: Devin-Adair, 1966.

Lash, Joseph P. *Eleanor: The Years Alone.* New York: W. W. Norton, 1972.

Lawson, Steven F. *Black Ballots: Voting Rights in the South, 1944–1969.* New York: Columbia University Press, 1976.

———. *Running for Freedom: Civil Rights and Black Politics in America since 1941.* New York: McGraw-Hill, 1990.

Levantrosser, William F., ed. *Harry S. Truman: The Man from Independence.* Westport, CT: Greenwood Press, 1986.

Loth, David. *A Long Way Forward: The Biography of Congresswoman Frances P. Bolton.* New York: Longmans, Green, 1957.

Lundberg, Ferdinand, and Marynia Farnham. *Modern Women: The Lost Sex.* New York: Grosset and Dunlap, 1946.

Lynn, Susan. *Progressive Women in Conservative Times: Racial Justice, Peace, and Feminism, 1945 to the 1960s.* New Brunswick, NJ: Rutgers University Press, 1992.

MacGregor, Morris J., Jr. *Integration of the Armed Forces, 1940–1965.* Washington, DC: Center of Military History, 1981.

MacGregor, Morris, and Bernard Nalty, eds. *Blacks in the United States Armed Forces: Basic Documents.* 13 vols. Wilmington, DE: Scholarly Resources, 1977.

May, Elaine Tyler. *Homeward Bound: American Families in the Cold War Era.* New York: Basic Books, 1988.

———. *Pushing the Limits: American Women, 1940–1961.* New York: Oxford University Press, 1994.

Nalty, Bernard D. *Strength for the Fight: A History of Black Americans in the Military.* New York: Free Press, 1986.

Peter, Esther. ''Working Women.'' *Daedalus* 93 (1974): 671–699.

Richard, Gary W. ''Democrats, Civil Rights, and Electoral Strategies in the 1950s.'' *Congress and the Presidency* 13 (Spring 1986): 59–82.

Rosenberg, Emily, et al. ''Foreign Affairs after World War II: Connecting Sexual and International Politics'' and ''Comments.'' *Diplomatic History* 18:1 (Winter 1994): 59–124.

Rupp, Leila, and Varta Taylor. *Survival in the Doldrums: The American Women's Rights Movement: 1945 to the 1960s.* New York: Oxford University Press, 1987.

Scharf, Lois. *Eleanor Roosevelt: First Lady of American Liberalism.* Boston: Twayne Publishers, 1987.

Seeley, Charlotte Palmer, comp. Revised by Virginia C. Purdy and Robert Gruber. *American Women in the U.S. Armed Forces: A Guide to the Records of Military Agencies in the National Archives Relating to American Women.* Washington, DC: National Archives, 1992.

Sochen, June. *Movers and Shakers: American Women—Thinkers and Activists, 1990–1970.* New York: Quadrangle, 1973.

Soderbergh, Peter A. *Women Marines in the Korean War Era.* Westport, CT: Greenwood Press, 1994.

Stern, Mark. ''Presidential Strategies and Civil Rights: Eisenhower, the Early Years, 1952–1954.'' *Presidential Studies Quarterly* 19:4 (Fall 1989): 769–795.

Stremlow, Mary V. *A History of the Women Marines, 1946–1977.* Washington, DC: U.S. Marines History and Museums Division, 1986.

Suelzle, Marijean. ''Women in Labor.'' *Transaction* 8 (1970): 50–58.

University Publications of America. *Papers of the NAACP, Part Nine, Discrimination in the U.S. Armed Forces, 1918–1955.* Frederick, MD: University Publications of America, 1989.

Weigand, Kate. ''The Red Menace, the Feminine Mystique, and the Ohio Un-American Activities Commission: Gender and Anti-Communism in Ohio, 1951–1954.'' *Journal of Women's History* 3 (Winter 1992): 70–94.

Wilkins, Roy. *Standing Fast: The Autobiography of Roy Wilkins.* New York: Viking Press, 1982.

23   Cinema and Television in the Early 1950s

Lester H. Brune

The literature about movies related to the Korean War is contained only in larger works. Korean War–based movies of the early 1950s are part of reference works such as Arthur F. McClure's *Research Guide to Film History* (1983), Larry Langman and Edgar Borg's *Encyclopedia of War Films* (1994), and Lawrence H. Suid's *Guts and Glory* (1978). Suid and David Culbert (1991) also have a study of the use of films to influence opinion after 1945. Paul Virilio (1989), a Spanish-American author, has interesting comments about war movies that are useful for studies of this genre.

Other works with some data on the Korean War examine the movie industry's readiness to use films to promote the cold war policies of the U.S. government, a frequent criticism of many films. Political propaganda in films is the theme of Richard A. Maynard's (1975) review of films made in America before and during World War II and in the early cold war years. Maynard defines propaganda as the "persuasive dissemination of a particular set of attitudes and ideas to a large mass of people," and he indicates this use has been "general in history." This political aspect of cinema's relationship to the cold war is also examined by Daniel J. Leab and John H. Lenihan in Robert Brent Toplin's (1993) volume.

Richard Slotkin's *Gunfighter Nation* (1992) relates the popularity of western films about the nineteenth century to U.S. cultural attitudes during the cold war, which held that in America's heroic past, individual gunfighters had to resort to violence to bring law, order, and democracy to the wild frontier, just as the nation's foreign interventions during the cold war would spread democracy.

Closely related to the movie industry's willingness to create myths of America's past were the accusations that entertainers who questioned the nobility of the U.S. past were "pinko comm-symps" or outright communists. Particularly, investigations of Hollywood personalities by the House

Un-American Activities Committee resulted in threats and blacklists that greatly affected the movie business. This issue is examined in Chapter 20 in this book.

From a different perspective, Ed Sikov (1994) concludes that comedy films of the 1950s did not conform to the fixed pattern of family values that has previously been assumed. Rather, directors of comic films developed innovative approaches for the history of film comedies.

Also notable is that two of the best movies on the Korean War were based on novels written before the war ended: James Michener's (1953) novel about aircraft carrier pilots' planning and carrying out the bombing of a communist bridge and Pat Frank's (1952) story of U.S. Marines' facing the Chinese armies during the Chosin Reservoir retreat in November– December 1950. Both the books and the films emphasized the heroic character of U.S. involvement in Korea. In addition, Richard Hooker's (1968) book on the U.S. Army's mobile surgical units in Korea became both a movie and a television series.

Although the movie business had not yet felt the full effects of television, more households than previously owned television sets during the early 1950s. Lynn Spigel (1992) describes television's rapid expansion between 1945 and 1955 and examines the contemporary controversies about whether television was having a positive or negative influence on society, especially on family life.

Nancy E. Bernhard's essay in William S. Solomon and Robert Mc-Chesney's (1993) book discusses the relationship developing between television network news and the federal government. Thomas Rosteck (1994) uses Edward R. Murrow's "See It Now" television program on McCarthyism to examine the role of politically oriented documentaries. (Chapter 19 in this book describes the first significant use of television during a presidential race.)

REFERENCES

Barnouw, Erik. *Tube of Plenty: The Evolution of American Television.* New York: Oxford University Press, 1990.

Biskind, Peter. *Seeing Is Believing: Film and Politics in the 1950s.* New York: Pantheon Books, 1983.

Frank, Pat. *Hold Back the Night.* Philadelphia: Lippincott, 1952.

Hooker, Richard. *MASH.* New York: Morrow, 1968.

Langman, Larry, and Edgar Borg. *Encyclopedia of War Films.* New York: Garland, 1994.

McClure, Arthur F. *Research Guide to Film History.* Saratoga, CA: R&E Publishers, 1983.

Maynard, Richard A. *Propaganda on Film: A Nation at War.* Rochelle Park, NJ: Hayden Book Company, 1975.

Michener, James R. *The Bridges of Toko-ri.* New York: Random House, 1953.

Rosteck, Thomas. *See It Now Confronts McCarthy: Television Documentaries and the Politics of Representation.* Tuscaloosa, AL: University of Alabama Press, 1994.

Sikov, Ed. *Laughlin Hysterically: American Screen Comedy of the 1950s.* New York: Columbia University Press, 1994.

Slotkin, Richard. *Gunfighter Nation: The Myth of the Frontier in Twentieth Century America.* New York: Atheneum, 1992.

Solomon, William S., and Robert W. McChesney, eds. *Ruthless Criticism: New Perspectives in U.S. Communications History.* Minneapolis: University of Minnesota Press, 1993.

Spigel, Lynn. *Make Room for TV: Television and the Family Ideal in Postwar America.* Chicago: University of Chicago Press, 1992.

Suid, Larry. *Guts and Glory: Great American War Movies.* Reading, MA: Addison-Wesley, 1978.

Suid, Lawrence H., and David Culbert. *Film and Propaganda in America: A Documentary History.* Vol. 4: *1945 and After.* Westport, CT: Greenwood Press, 1991.

Toplin, Robert Brent, ed. *Hollywood as Mirror: Changing Views of "Outsiders" and "Enemies" in American Movies.* Westport, CT: Greenwood Press, 1993.

Virilio, Paul. *War and Cinema.* Trans. Patrick Camiller. London: Verso, 1989.

Author Index

Taylor, Varta, 420, 424
Teiwes, Frederick C., 178, 187
Terzibaschitsch, Stefan, 277, 282
Teschner, Charles G., 264
Textor, Robert, 53, 79
Thach, John S., 270, 282
Thatcher, Terrence L., 370, 398
Theoharis, Athan, 23, 33, 41, 79, 348, 363, 373–74, 398, 405, 407–8
Thomas, James A., 417
Thomas, Peter, 109, 116
Thompkins, C. David, 367, 399
Thompson, Annis G., 253, 264
Thompson, Anthony, 183, 187
Thompson, Francis H., 372, 399
Thompson, Reginald, 104, 116
Thorne, Christopher, 40, 79
Thornton, John W., 238, 249
Thurston, Anne, 185
Thurston, Robert W., 181, 187
Thyng, Harrison R., 264
Tillema, Herbert K., 5, 13
Tillman, Barrett, 270, 282
Time, 182, 187, 374, 399
Time-Life, 338, 344
Tinker, Hugh, 40, 79
Tohata, Shiro, 143, 155
Toland, John, 201, 205
Tomedi, Rudy, 241, 249
Toner, James H., 417
Toplin, Robert Brent, 426, 428
Tormoen, George E., 264
Trachtenburg, Marc, 290, 305
Traeger, Frank N., 40, 41
Trancy, Glenn, 204
Truman, Harry S., 9, 13, 19, 33, 58, 79, 295, 305
Tsien, Tsuen-Hsuin, 36, 79
Tsou, Mingde, 36, 79
Tsurumi, E. Patricia, 57, 79
Tsutsui, William M., 140, 155
Tuchman, Barbara W., 40, 46
Tucker, Nancy B., 50, 51
Tucker, Robert C., 28, 33, 180, 187
Tunstall, Julian, 109, 116
Turner, Kathleen J., 417
Tyrrell, John V., 264

U.S. Air Force, 13
U.S. Army, 13, 232
U.S. Bureau of Naval Personnel, 276, 282
U.S. Congress, House, 48, 79, 344, 399
U.S. Department of State, 7, 13, 48, 79, 135, 155, 311–12, 314, 332, 344, 399
U.S. Deputy Chief of Naval Operations and Air Warfare, 282
U.S. Federal Trade Commission, 399
U.S. Joint Chiefs of Staff, 282
U.S. Marine Corps, 269
U.S. Navy Department, 275–76
U.S. News and World Report, 238, 249
U.S. Senate, 7, 13
U.S. Senate, Committee on Rules and Administration, 375, 399
U.S. Senate, Special Committee of the Subcommittee on Small Business, 399
Ulam, Adam, 48, 51, 206, 209
Unger, Irwin, 17, 33
United Nations, 8, 13
United States National Archives and Records Administration, 399
University Publications of America, 422, 425
Utley, Freda, 46, 79
Uyehara, Cecil H., 130, 155

Van Dyke, Vernon, 369, 399
Van Ness, Peter, 177, 187
Vandenberg, Arthur H. Jr., 19, 33, 366, 367, 383, 399
Veaudry, Wallace F., 263
Villasanta, Juan F., 90, 92
Vinacke, Harold, 79
Virilio, Paul, 426, 428
Volkogonov, Dimitri, 28, 33, 180, 187, 214, 219

Walker, J. Samuel, 17, 33
Wall, Irwin M., 43, 80
Wallace, Henry A., 20, 33
Wallerstein, Immanuel, 26, 34
Walton, Richard J., 34
Walzer, Kenneth, 372, 399

Subject Index

Great Asian Conspiracy, alleged, 41
Great Debate of 1951, U.S. Congress, 345–47
Great Proletarian Cultural Revolution, China, 192
Greece, 16, 18, 21–22, 27, 90
Grew, Joseph, 34, 129
Guam, 41–42, 299

Hale, Robert, 348
Halleck, Charles, 371–72
Hammarskjold, Dag, 8
Harriman, W. Averell, 377–78
Hawaii, 41–42
Hennings, Thomas, 376
Hirohito, Emperor, 137–38
Hiss, Alger, 340, 404
Hitler, Adolf, 99, 101–3
Hodes, Henry I., Gen., 343
Hodge, John R., Lt. Gen., 61
Hoe, Clyde R., 352–53
Holland, Sidney, 121
Hollywood blacklist, 401, 403, 427
Homefront, U.S., 335–39. *See also* Britain, homefront
Hook, battle of, 109, 125, 235
Hoover, Herbert, 8, 347, 363–64, 412
Hoover, J. Edgar, 402
House Un-American Activities Committee (HUAC), 403–4, 427, 420
Huang, Hua, 50
Humphrey, Hubert, 361, 365–66
Hungary, 208–9
Hurley, Patrick J., 46–48
Hwachon Dam, bombing of, 270, 289

Ienaga, Soburo, 145–46
Imjin River, battle of, 109
Inchon Landing (Operation Chromite), 132, 197–98, 224–25, 240, 244, 269, 271, 290
India, 86, 88, 98, 101, 139–40, 289, 293
Indonesia, 236
Institute for Policy Studies, 26
Internal Security Act of 1950, 367, 403
International Atomic Energy Agency (IAEA), 325–26

International Research and Exchange Board (IREX), 18, 181–82
Interservice disputes (U.S. armed forces), 269–70
Iran, 21–22, 27
Iraq, 3
Isolationism, U.S., 22–24, 90, 363–64, 368–69, 403, 405

Japan, 5–6, 15, 26–28, 42; Constitution, 137–40, 207; cultural, 143–47; demilitarization and rearming, 137–39; economy, 113, 140–44; education, 144–45; and Korea, 135, 147, 158–59, 273–74, 309, 311; labor unions, 136–37; land reform, 143–44; mass media, 137, 145–46; purges, 136–37; reference sources, 129–31; religion, 146–47; and U.S. policy toward, 35–37, 42, 50, 52–58, 99, 120, 128–47; U.S. "reverse course" policy, 54–56, 128–29; U.S. treaties with, 40, 42, 53, 138–40, 348–50
Japan Lobby, 56
Jebb, Sir H. M. Gladwyn, 99
Jenner, William, 369–70
Jessup, Philip C., 89
Jiang Jieshi (Chiang Kai-shek): and Britain, 210–11; and People's Republic of China, 135, 176, 210–11, 294–95; and U.S., 23–24, 44–48, 50–52; and U.S. domestic politics, 344, 412
John Birch Society, 23
Johnson, Louis A., 211, 266, 274
Johnson, Lyndon B., 42, 287, 365–66, 416
Joy, C. Turner, Vice-Adm., 268, 296
Judd, Walter, 371–72

Kang Sok-ju, 326–27
Kapyong, battle of, 122–23
Kefauver, Estes, 352, 364–65, 377
Kennan, George F., 18, 21
Kennedy, John F., 17, 41, 287
Kerr, Robert, 365–66
Keynes, John Maynard, 359

About the Editor and Contributors

LESTER H. BRUNE is the John and Augusta Oglesby Professor of American Heritage at Bradley University. Previous publications include the three volume *Chronological History of United States Foreign Relations, 1776 to 1989; America and the Iraqi Crisis, 1990–1992; The Missile Crisis of October 1962;* and chapters on defense policy and diplomacy for Robin Higham and Donald J. Mrozek's *A Guide to the Sources of U.S. Military History, Supplements II and III.*

CHEN JIAN is Associate Professor of History at the Southern Illinois University at Carbondale and the editor of *Chinese Historians.* In addition to articles and translations, he has published articles on China and the Korean War and a book, *China's Road to the Korean War: The Making of Sino-American Confrontation* (1994).

JACK J. GIFFORD was Professor and Chairman of the History Department at Westminister College before joining the Faculty of the U.S. Army's Command and General Staff College at Fort Leavenworth, Kansas. He served with the 24th Division during the Korean War and was a prisoner-of-war in China for 21 months. He has also worked for the Army's Security Agency and wrote its history of the Korean War period.

JEFFREY GREY is Senior Lecturer at University College, the University of New South Wales, Australian Defense Force Academy. He is author of *The Commonwealth Armies and the Korean War: An Alliance Study,* and *A Military History of Australia,* as well as a contributor to James Matray's *Historical Dictionary of the Korean War.*

GARY L. HUEY is an Associate Professor of History at Ferris State University in Big Rapids, Michigan. He is the author of *Rebel with a Cause: P.D. East, Southern Liberalism and the Civil Rights Movement, 1953–1971.*

IN K. HWANG is Professor of International Studies and Director of the International Studies Institute at Bradley University. In addition to many articles, his book publications include *The Korean Reform Movement of the 1880s; The Neutralized Unification of Korea in Perspective;* and *The Peaceful Management of Korean Unification.*

EDWARD C. KEEFER is a Historian at the Department of State in Washington, D.C. and an editor of the *Foreign Relations of the United States* series. He was the editor of *Foreign Relation, 1952–1954, XV Korea,* a co-editor or editor for volumes on Vietnam, Laos, Cambodia, and Korea for 1955–1963, and has contributed to James Matray's *Historical Dictionary of the Korean War.* Please note that the opinions expressed in his article are his own and not those of the Department of State.

KIM CHULL BAUM is Associate Professor of International Politics at the Korean National Defence University, Seoul, Korea. He has published *The United States and the Korean War,* and has edited several volumes of essays on the Korean War, including *Perspectives on the Korean War, The Truth About the Korean War,* and *Korea and the Cold War* (1993) with James I. Matray.

MARK LEACH graduated from Bradley University in May 1995. Since his freshman year he has worked with Professor Brune under a special Bradley Research-Mentor Scholarship designed for students with creative talent. He plans to attend graduate school after graduation. He co-authored the chapter on "Congress and the Korean War," assisted by a grant Professor Brune received from the Everett Dirksen Congressional Research Center and the Caterpillar Foundation.

CALLUM MacDONALD is Professor of Modern History at the University of Warwick, Coventry, England. His publications include *The United States, Britain and Appeasement, 1936–1939; Britain and the Korean War;* and *Korea: The War Before Vietnam.*

WARREN A. TREST is Senior Historian with the USAF Historical Research Agency, Maxwell AFB, Alabama. A Korean War veteran, he later joined the Air Force's historical program, serving in two major command history programs of the Air Training Command and the U.S. Air Forces in Europe. He has authored or co-authored fifty special studies on air power in Southeast Asia.